AF592990

ILLUSTRATOR'S REFERENCE MANUAL
SPORT

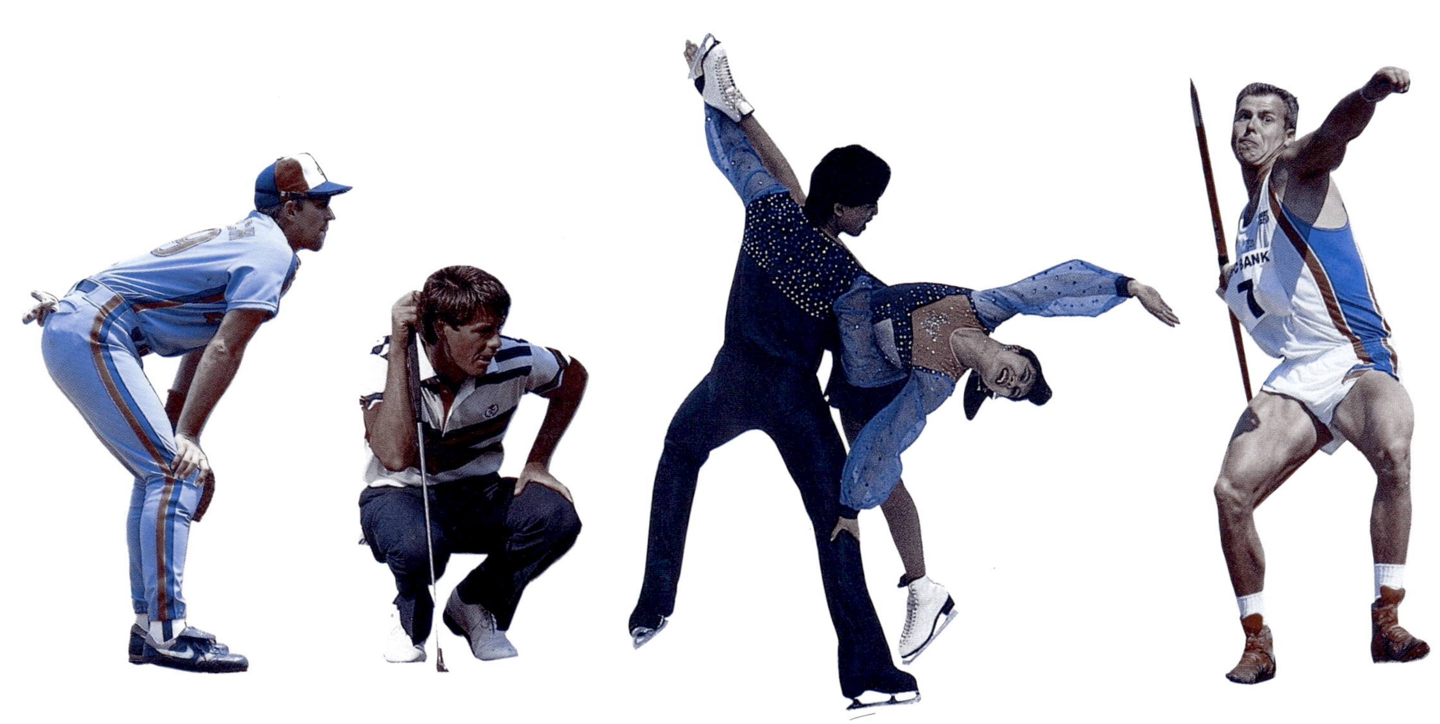

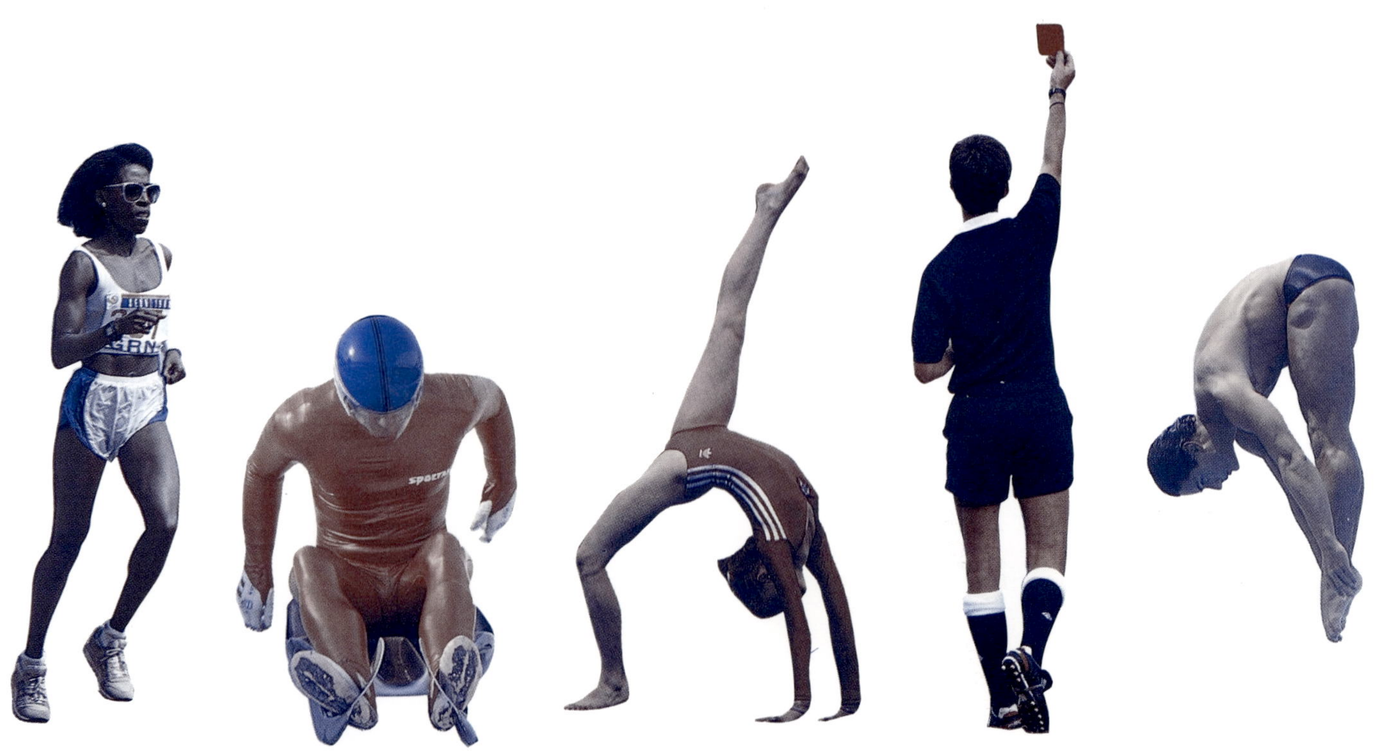

ILLUSTRATOR'S REFERENCE MANUAL
SPORT

CHARTWELL BOOKS, INC.

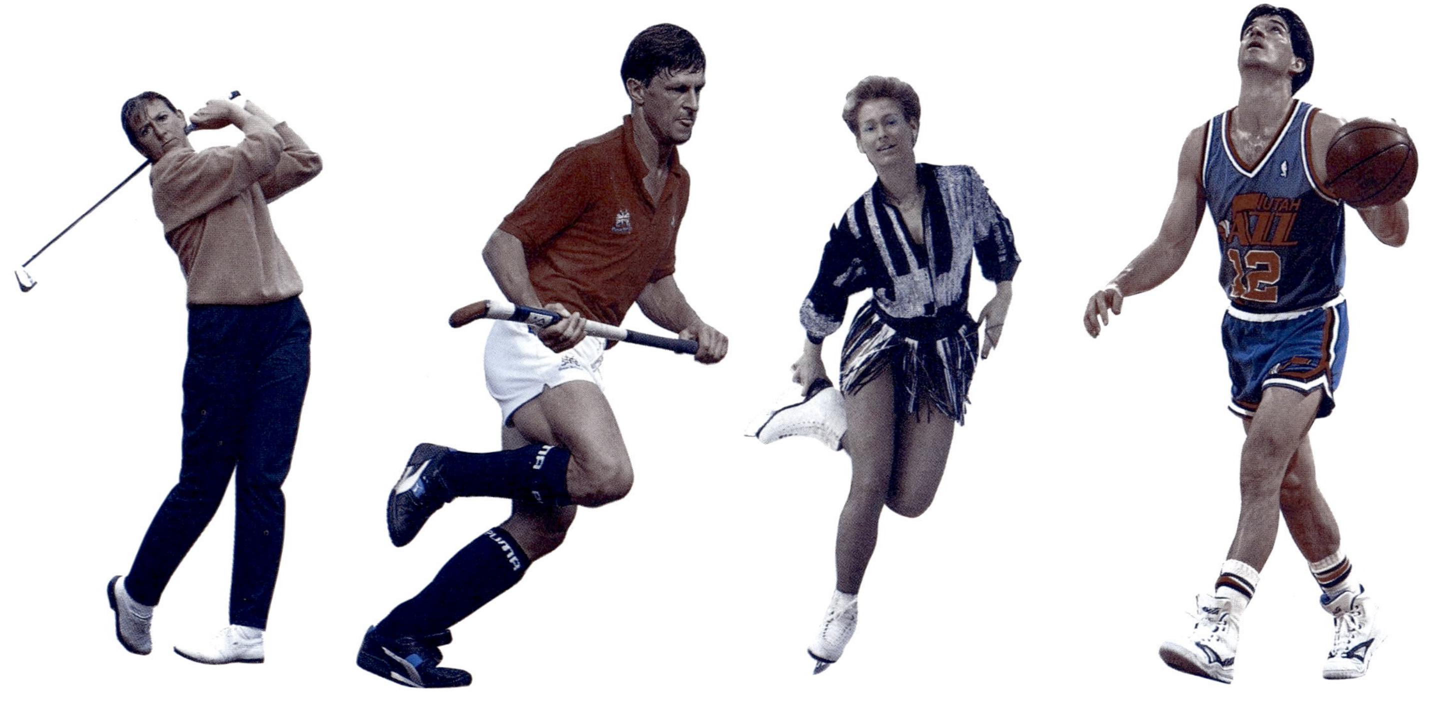

A QUARTO BOOK

Published by Chartwell Books
A Division of Book Sales, Inc.
110 Enterprise Avenue
Secaucus, New Jersey 07094

This edition produced for sale in the U.S.A.,
its territories and dependencies only.

ISBN 1-55521-791-5

This book was designed and produced by
Quarto Publishing plc,
The Old Brewery, 6 Blundell Street,
London N7 9BH

Senior Editor: Honor Head
Art Editor: Penny Dawes
Design: Elly King

Art Director: Moira Clinch
Publishing Director: Janet Slingsby

Typeset by QV Typesetting, London

Manufactured in Hong Kong by Regent Publishing Services Limited
Printed by Lee Fung Asco Printers Limited

All pictures supplied by Sporting Pictures, UK Ltd. Special thanks to Steve Brown for his help in the selection of the pictures used.

Contents

Ball sports

Athletics: male

Athletics: female

Gymnastics: male

Gymnastics: female

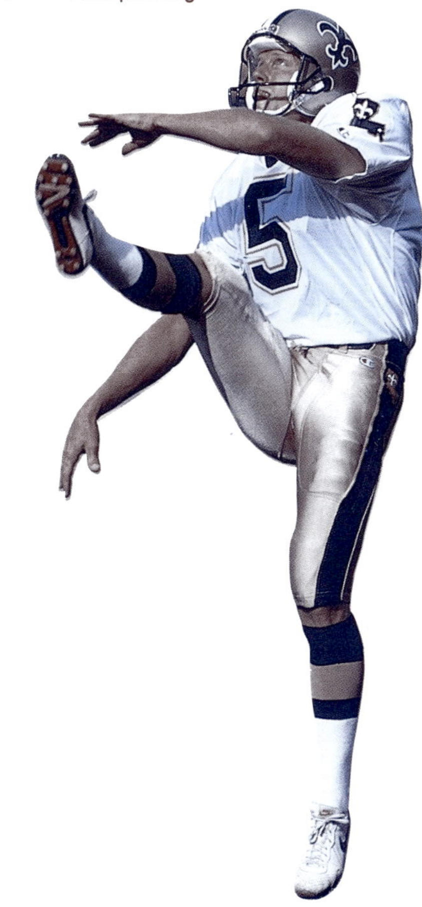

Combat sports

Weightlifting

Target sports

Water sports

Winter sports

Adventure sports

Cycle sports

Horse sports

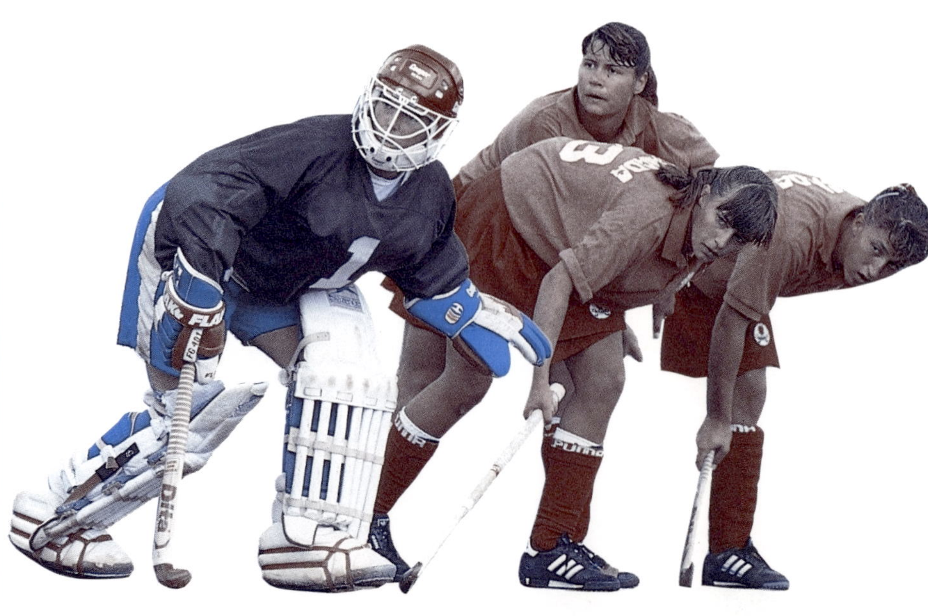

Using the sport manual

The ILLUSTRATOR'S REFERENCE MANUAL: SPORT comprises over 80 sports divided into the following categories — Ball Sports, Athletics, Gymnastics, Combat Sports, Weightlifting, Target Sports, Water Sports, Winter Sports, Adventure Sports, Cycle Sports and Horse Sports. Each category is numbered and within these categories each individual sport has its own sub-number for ease of reference.

Within each individual sport, design permitting and as appropriate, the main poses are divided as follows: singles/solo then doubles/group shots; male then female shots are followed by mixed where applicable. Where possible, poses of the same nature, ie bowling, goal scoring, serving, have been grouped together, but look through all the pictures given for a sport before making a final choice.

Single figures from a number of different sports or the same sport can be grouped together to form a composite picture or, in many instances, a single figure can be extracted from a group shot. The pictures have been chosen to ensure maximum scope and flexibility for the artist.

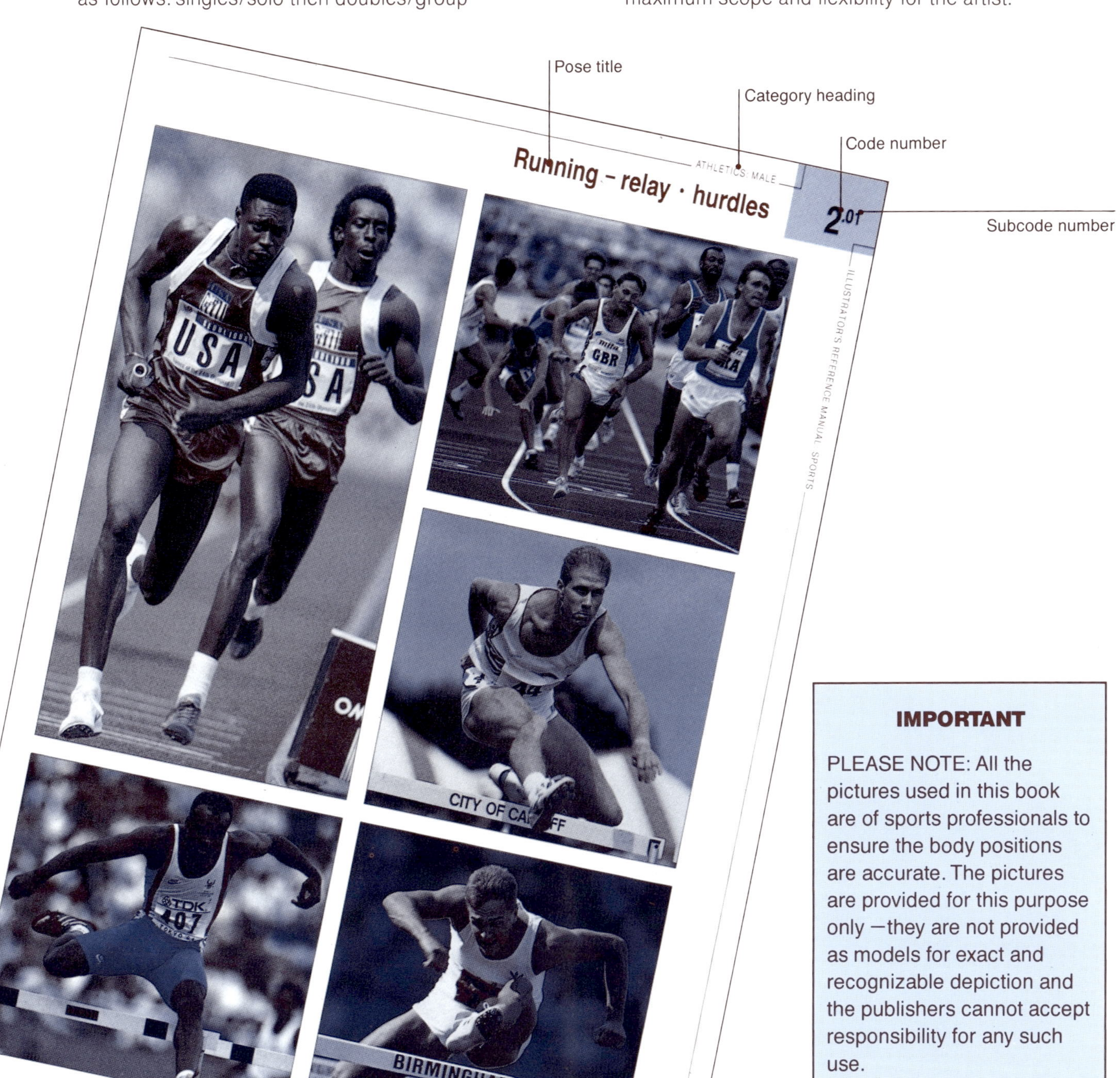

IMPORTANT

PLEASE NOTE: All the pictures used in this book are of sports professionals to ensure the body positions are accurate. The pictures are provided for this purpose only —they are not provided as models for exact and recognizable depiction and the publishers cannot accept responsibility for any such use.

Tennis – male singles

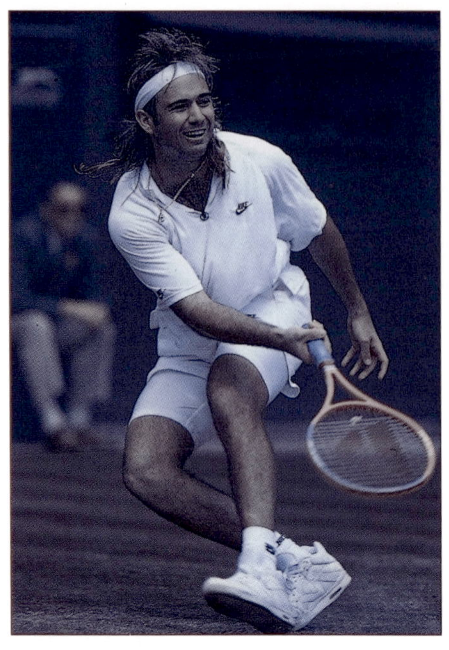
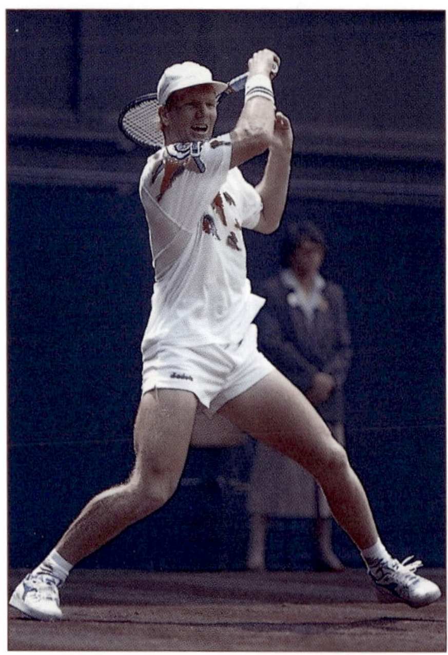
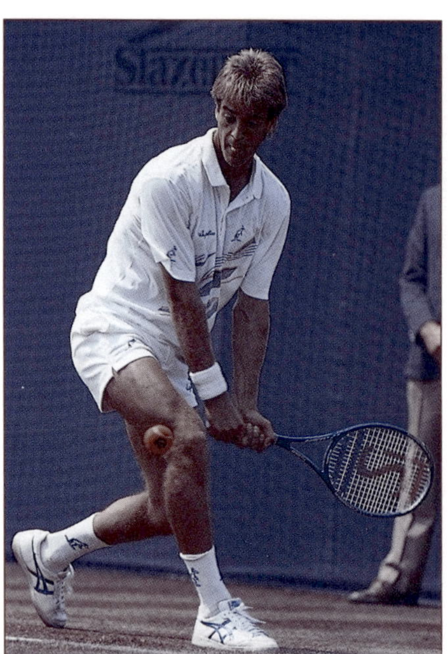
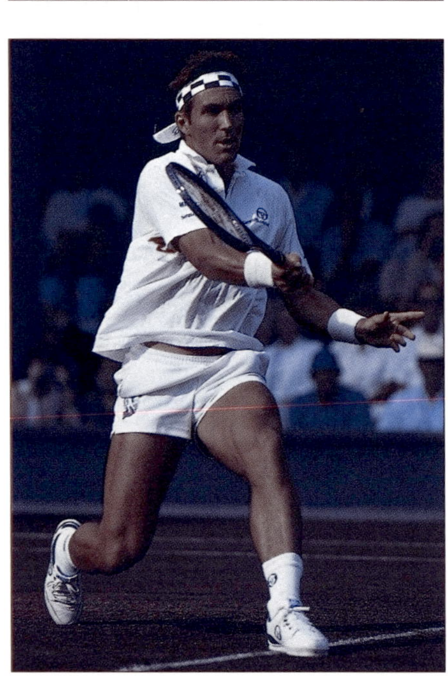
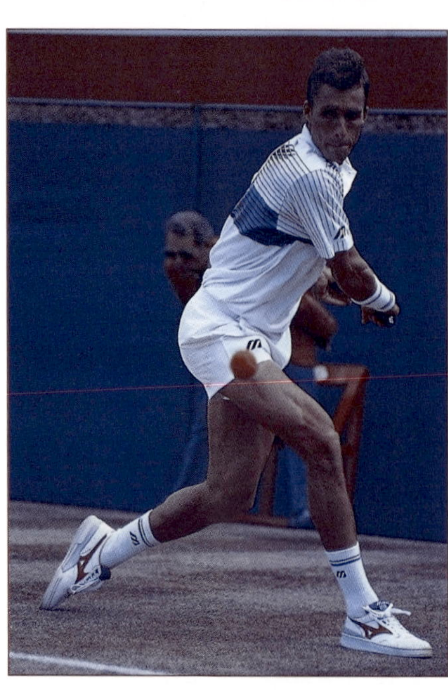
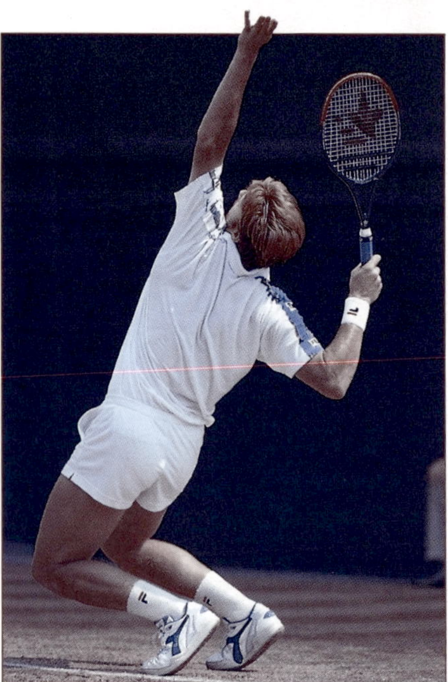
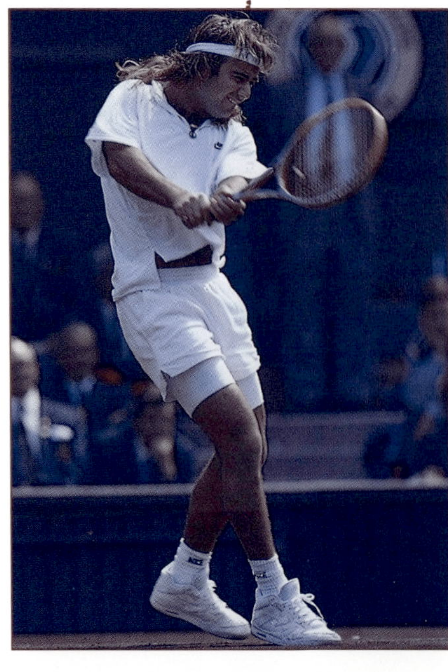
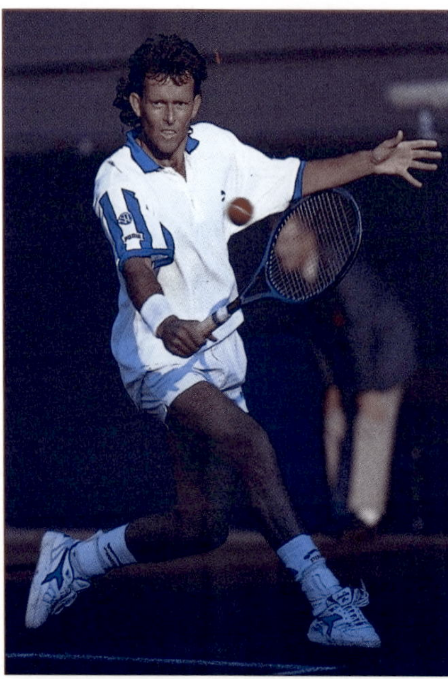
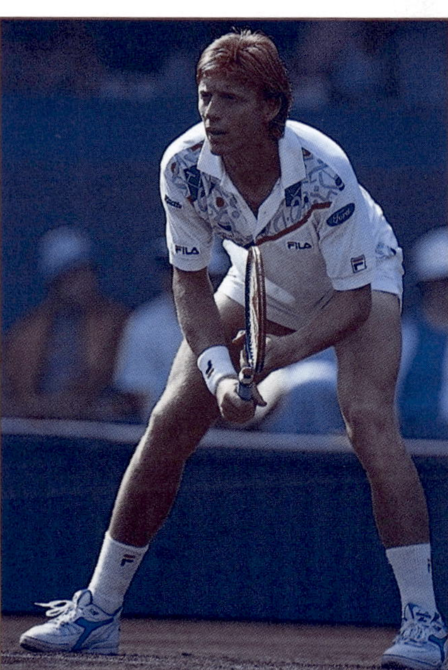

Tennis – male singles

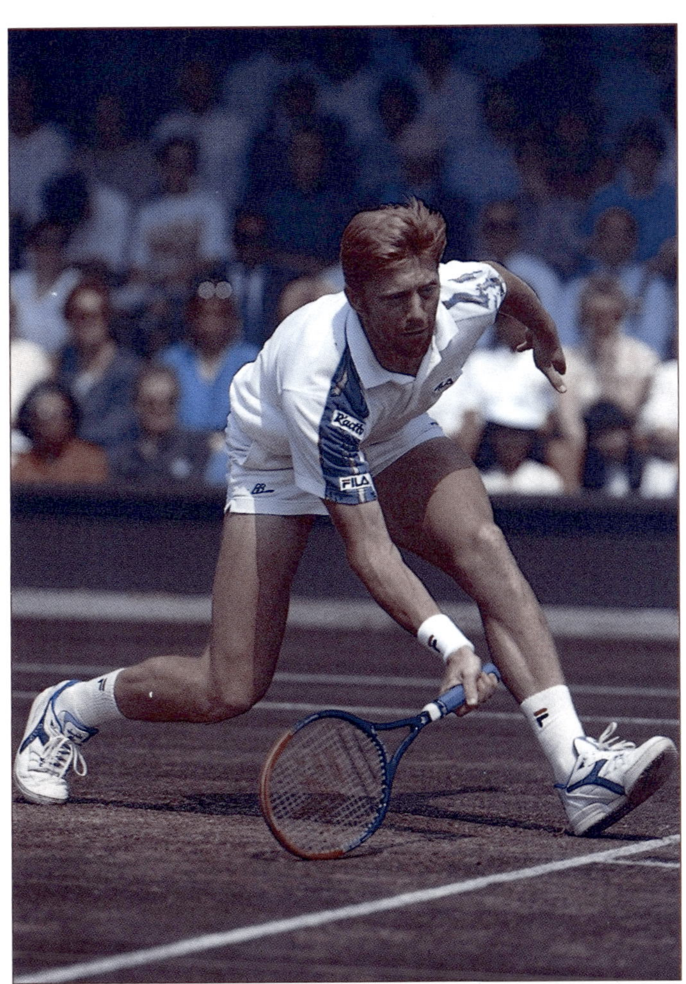

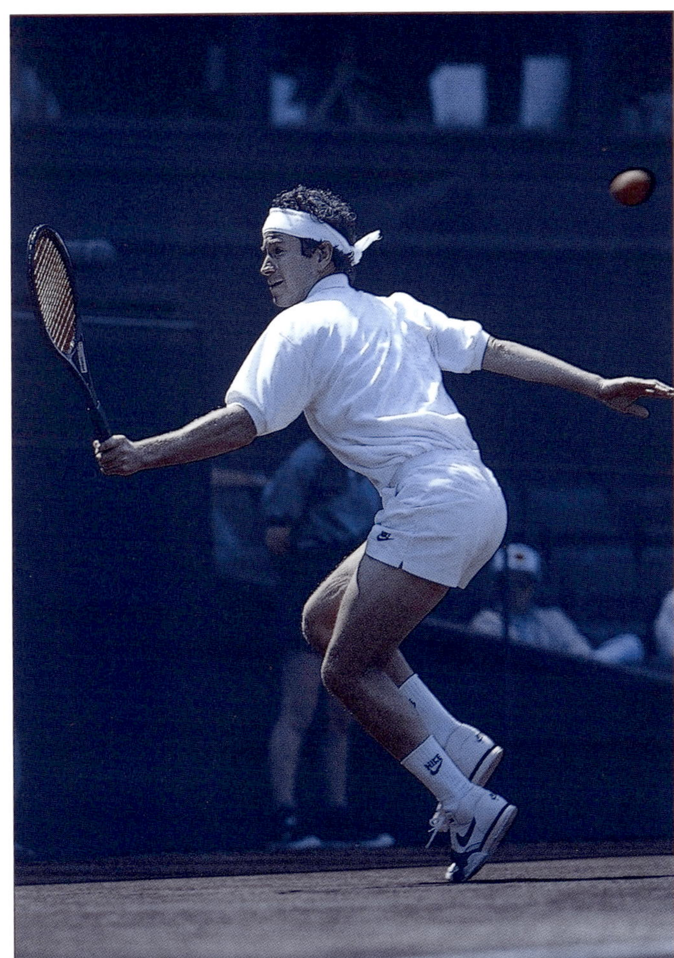

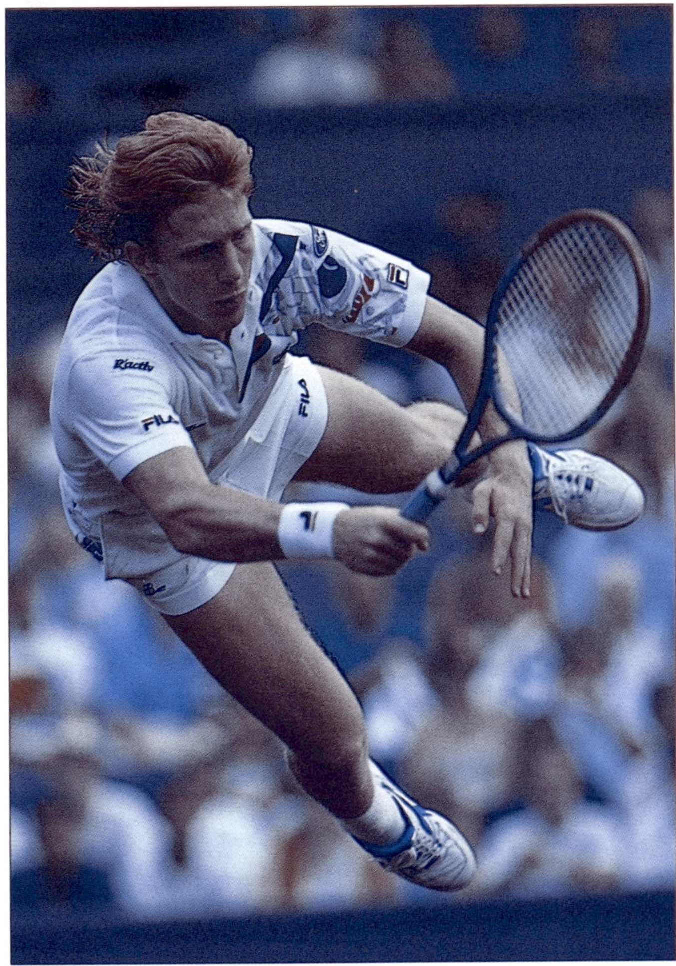

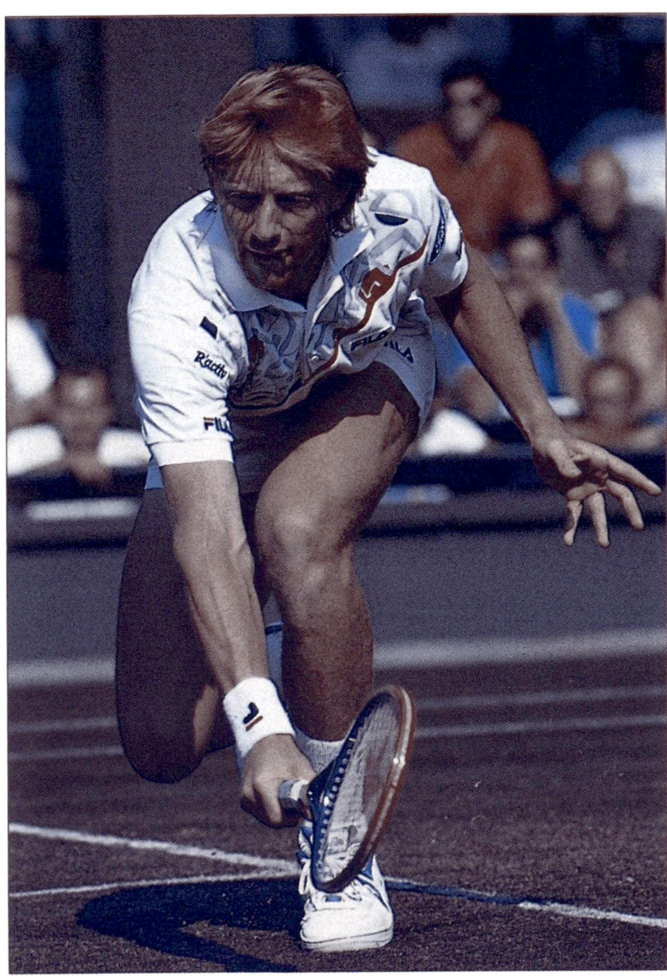

Tennis – male singles

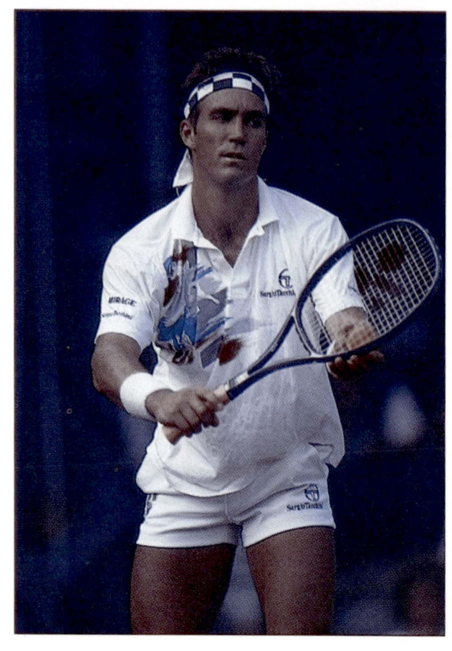
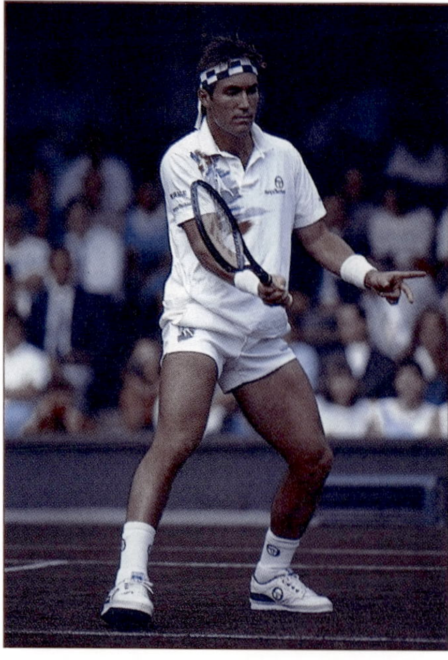
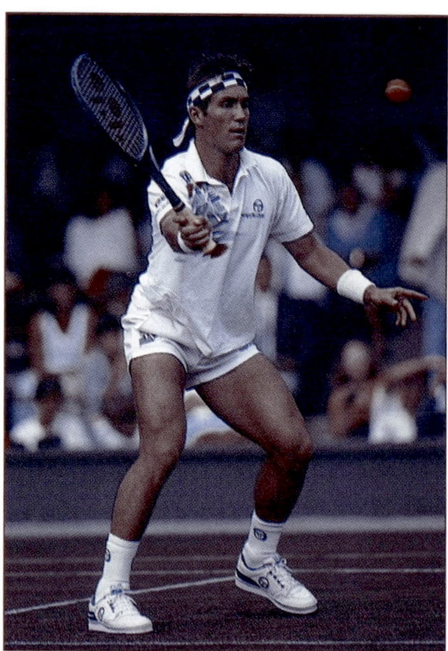
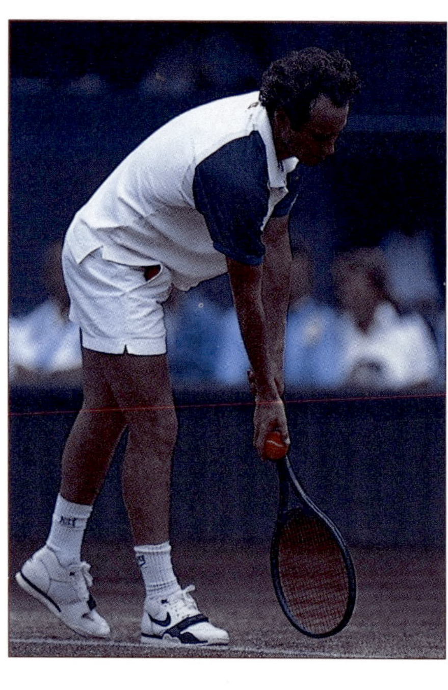
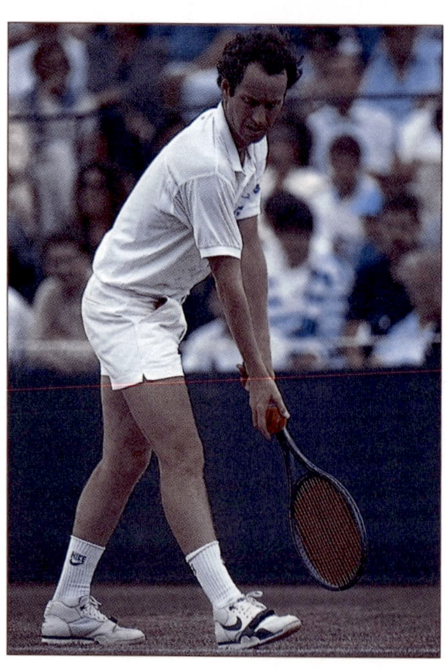
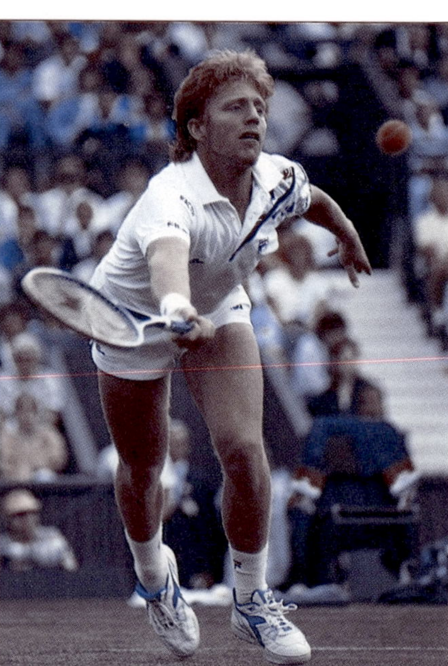
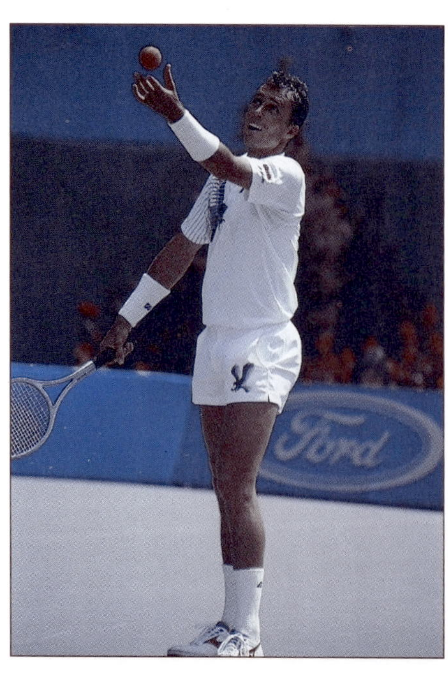

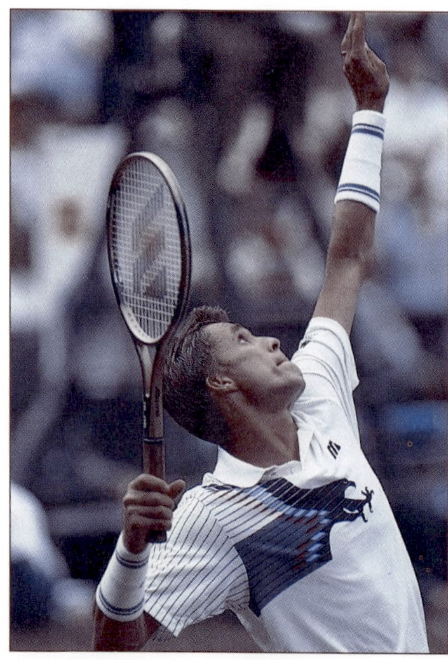
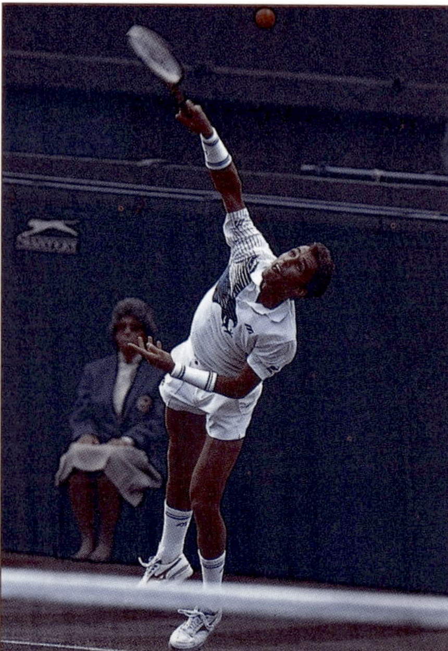

Tennis – male singles

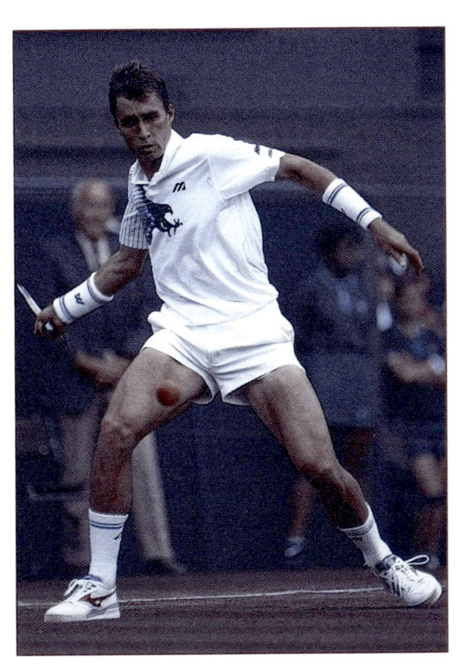

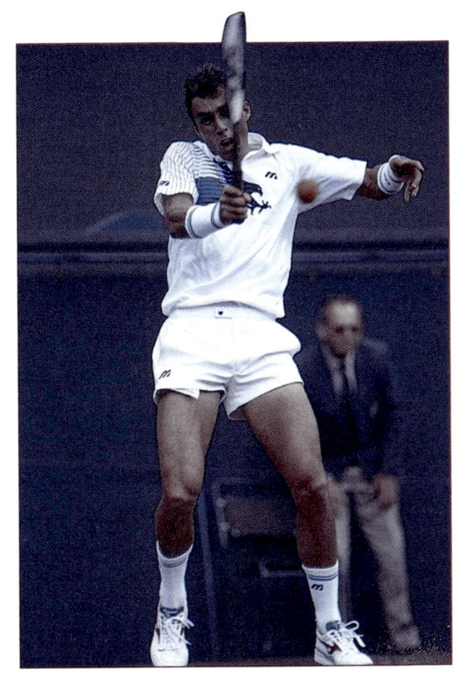

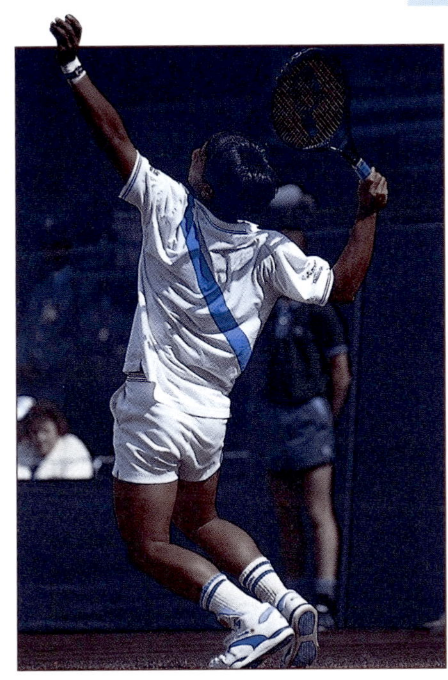

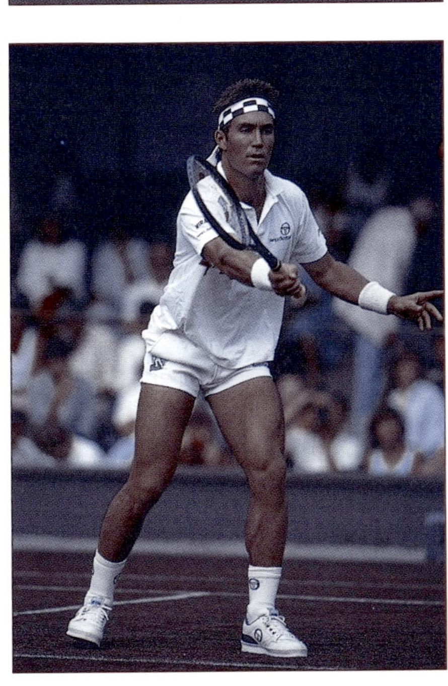

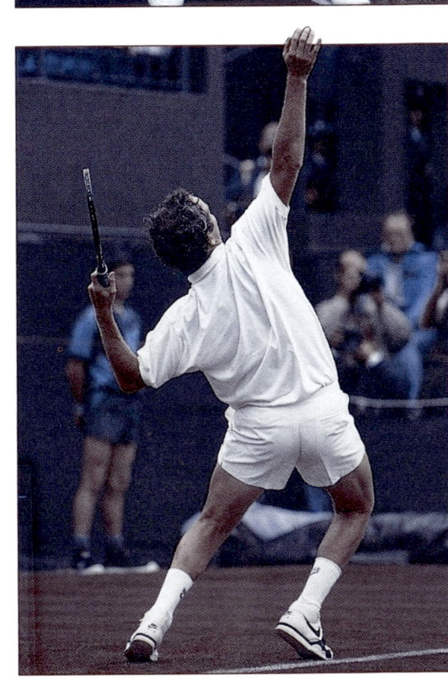

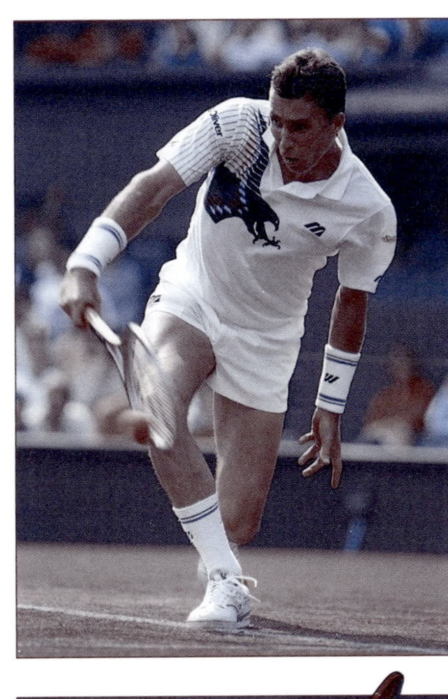

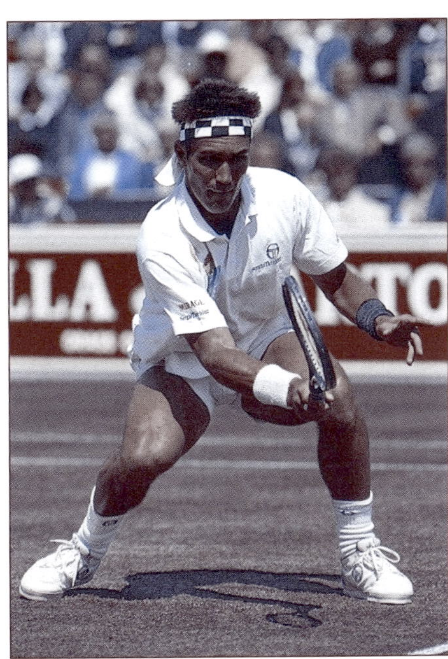

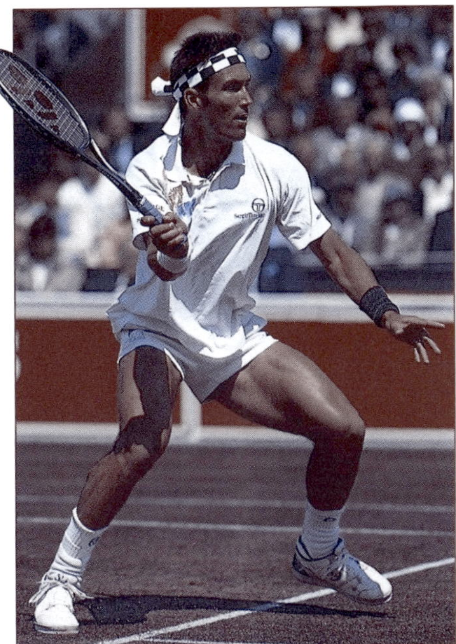

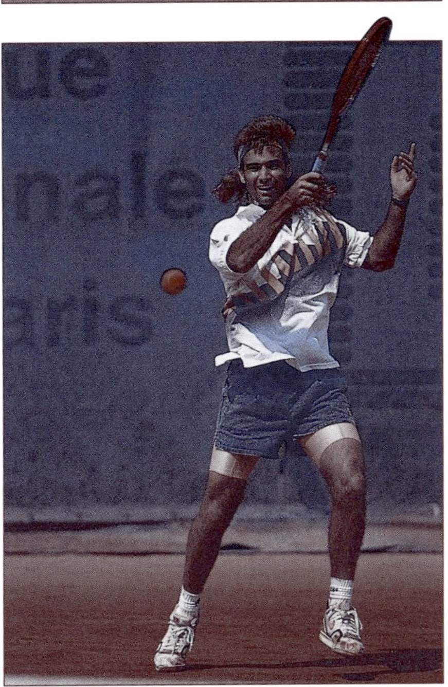

Tennis – male singles

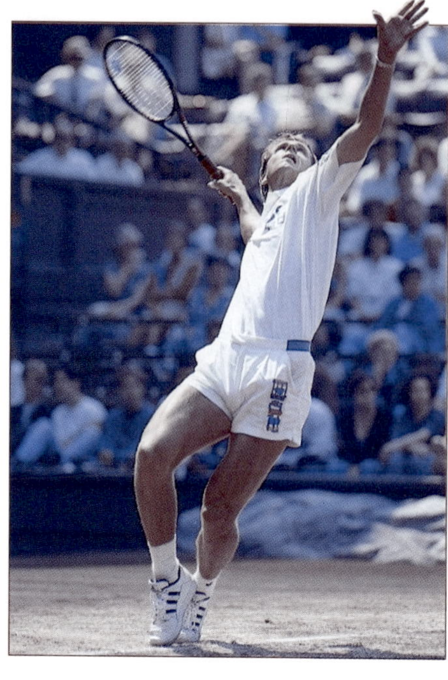

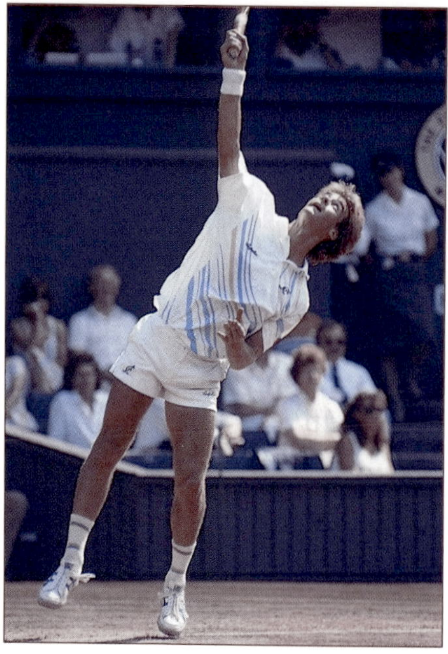

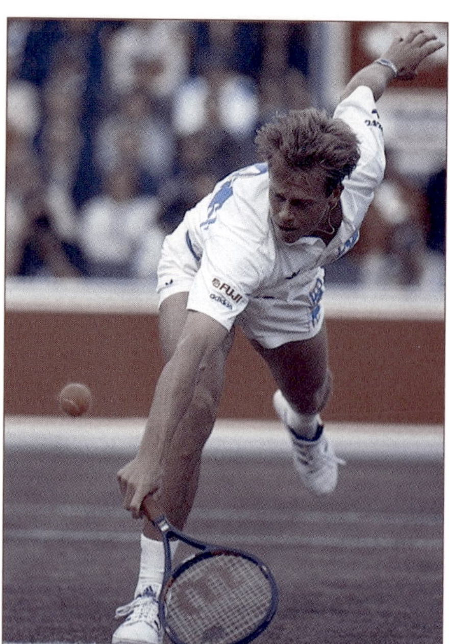

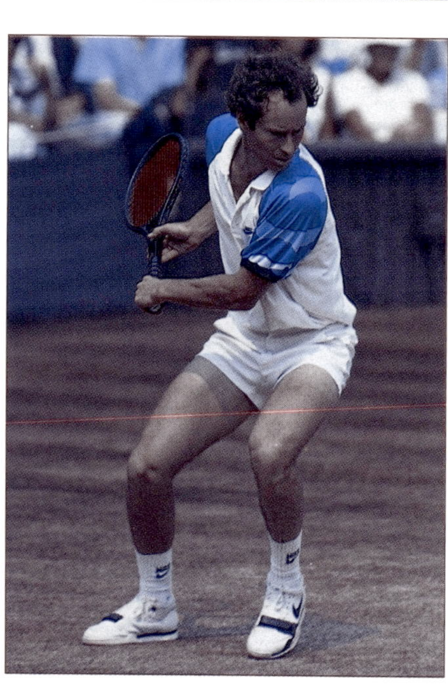

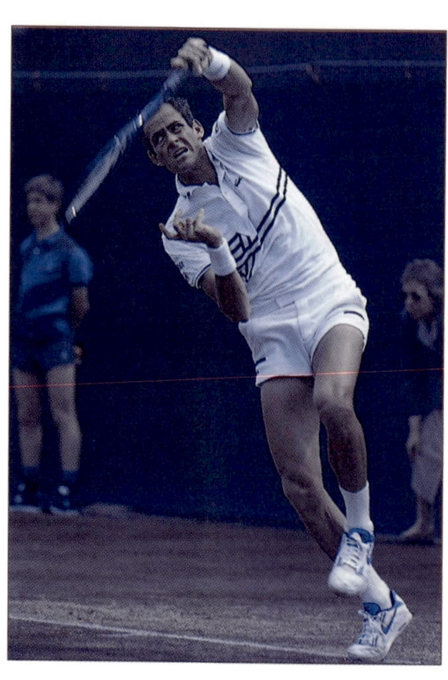

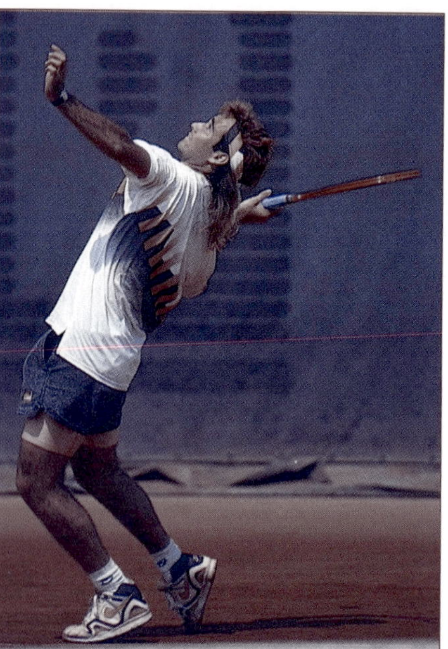

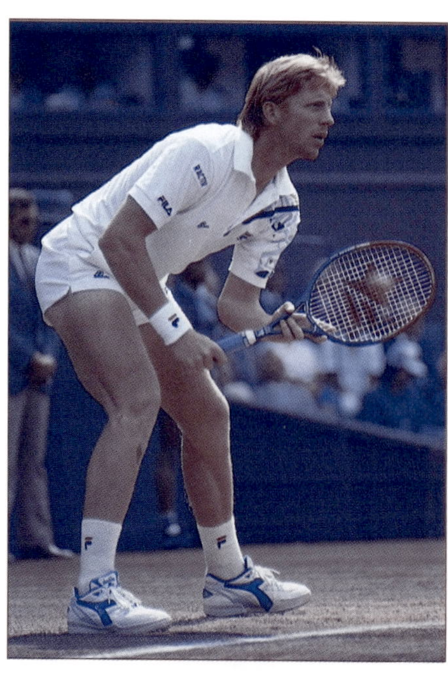

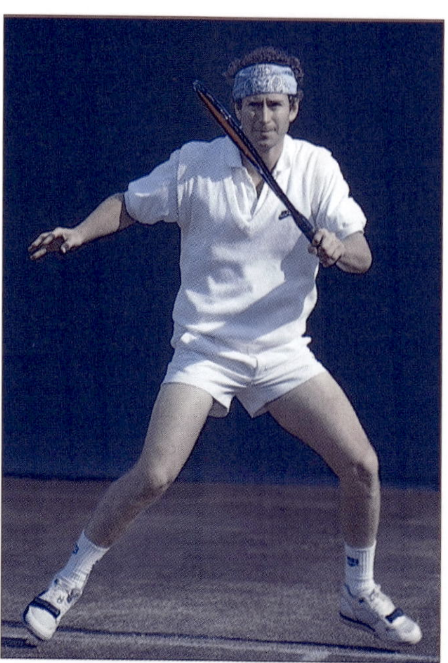

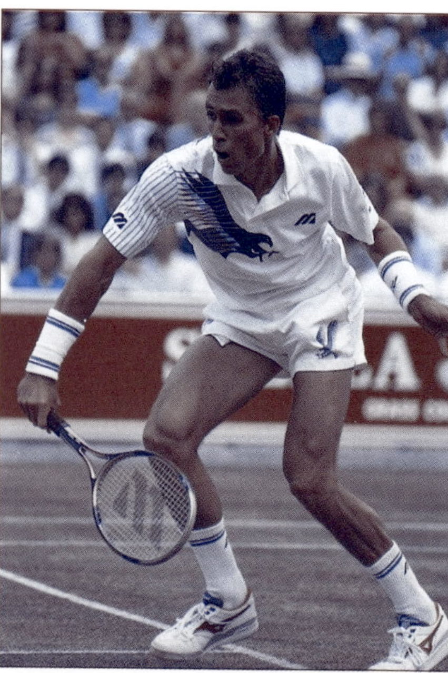

Tennis – female singles

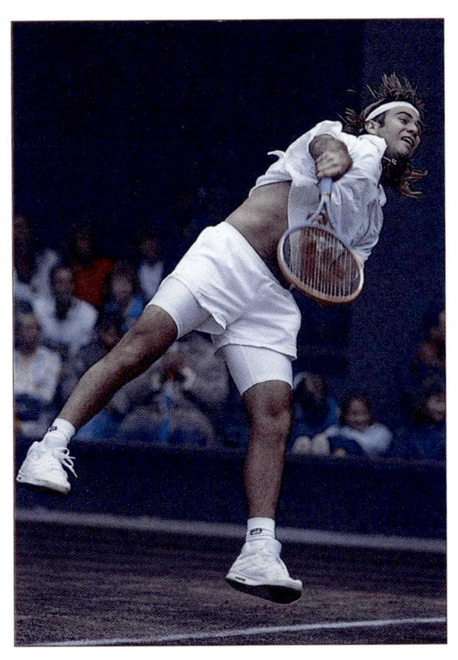
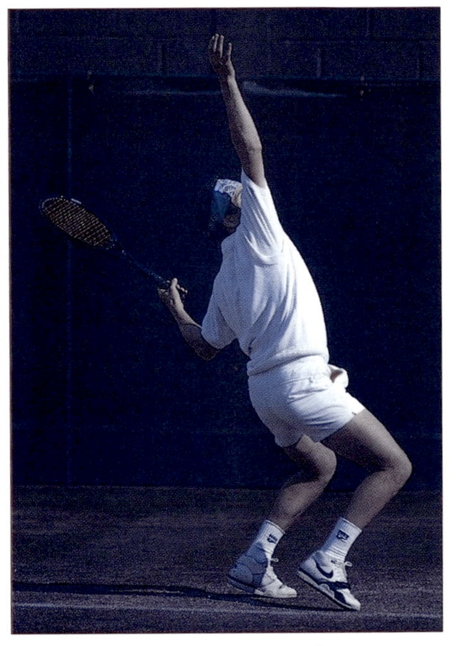
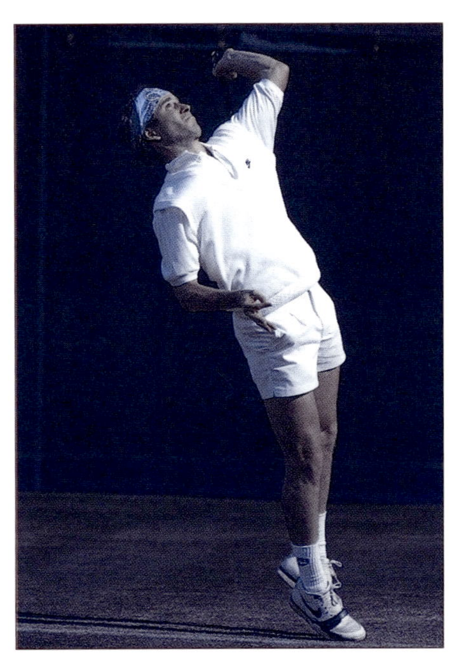
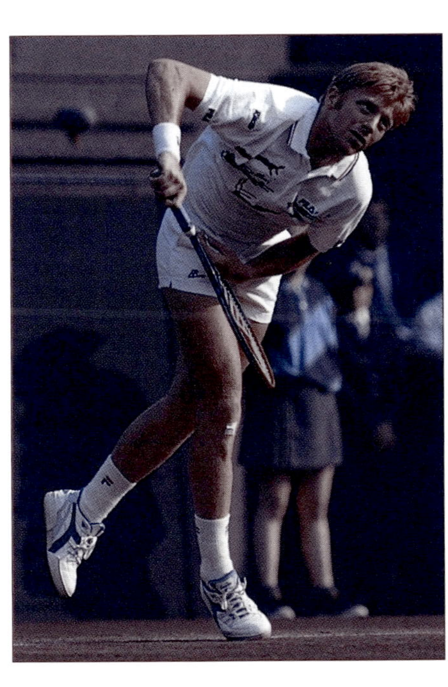
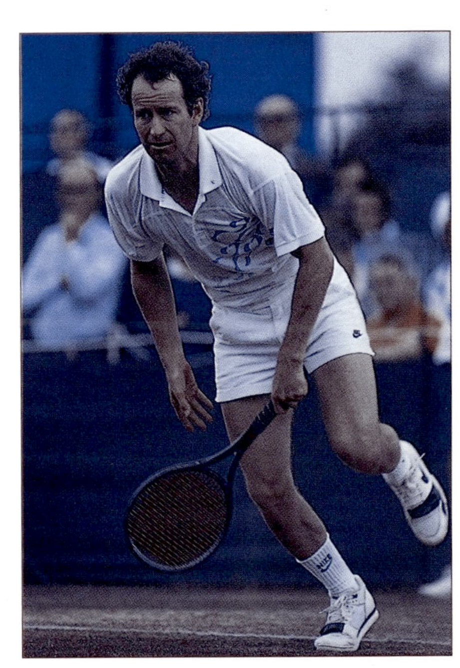
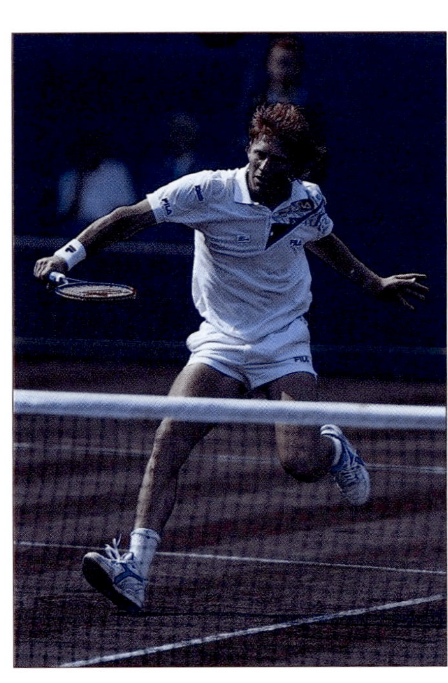
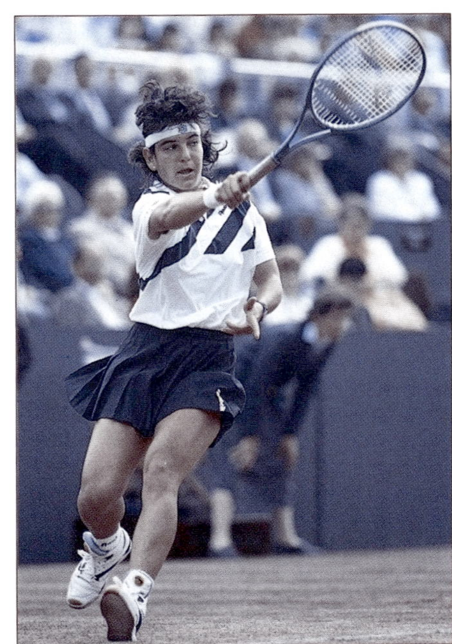
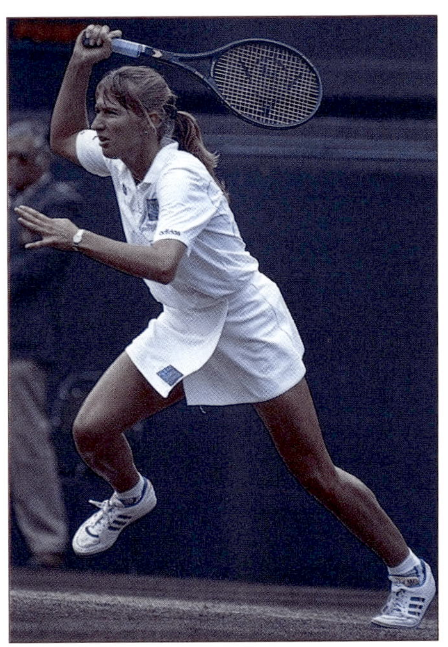
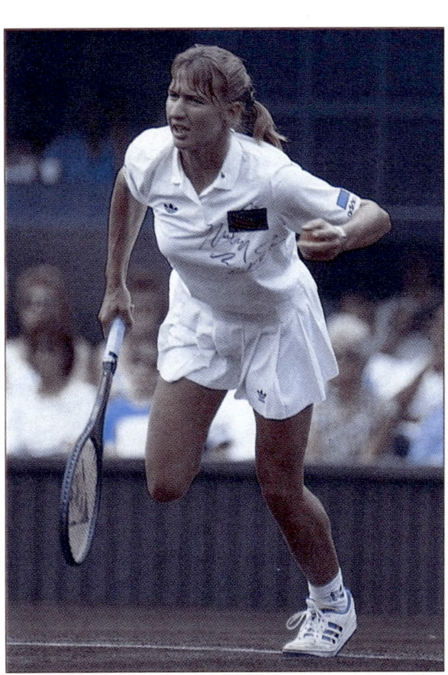

Tennis – female singles

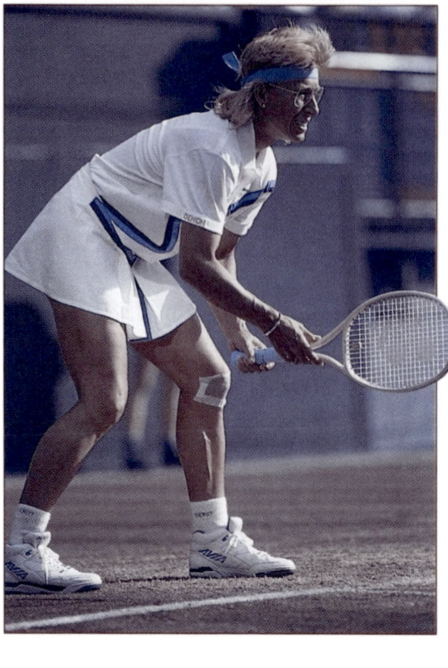
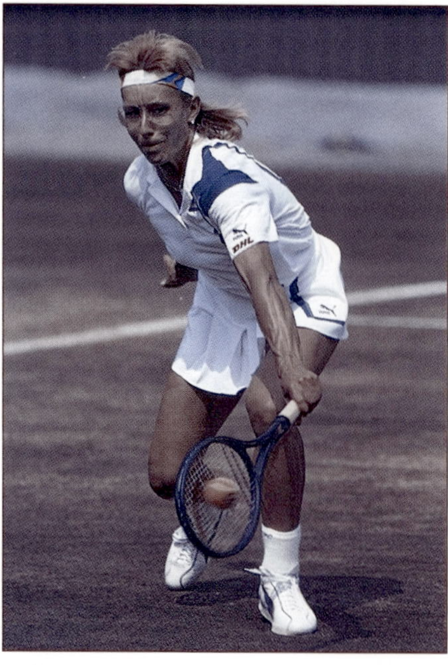
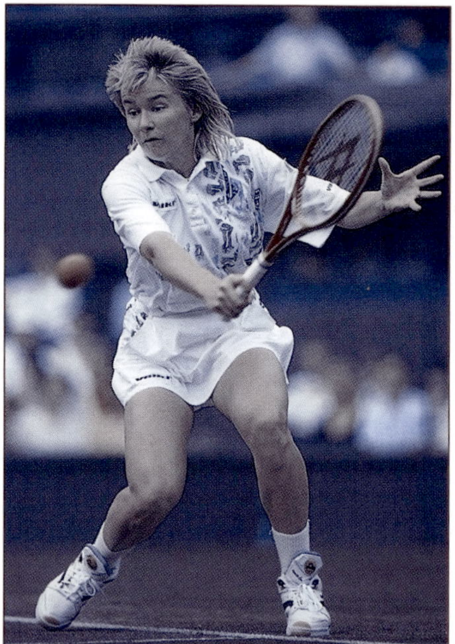
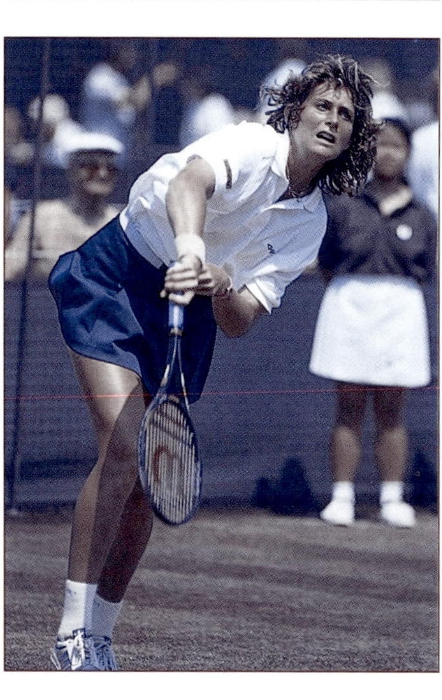
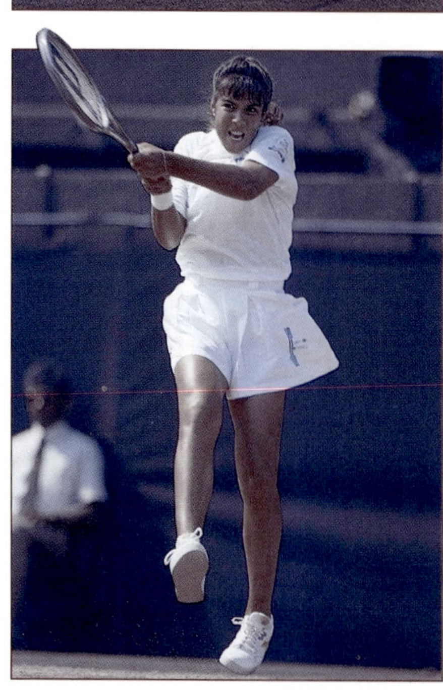
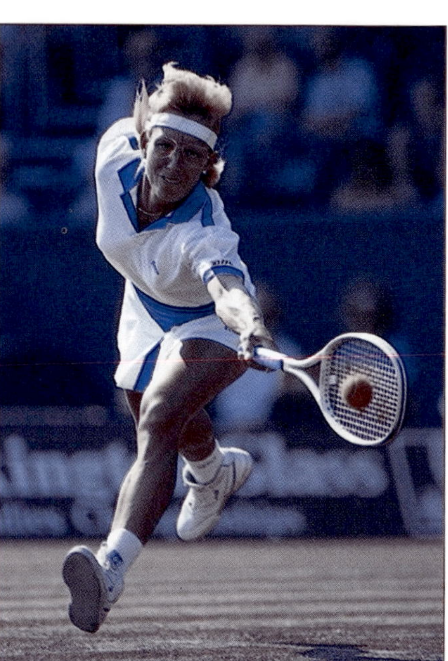
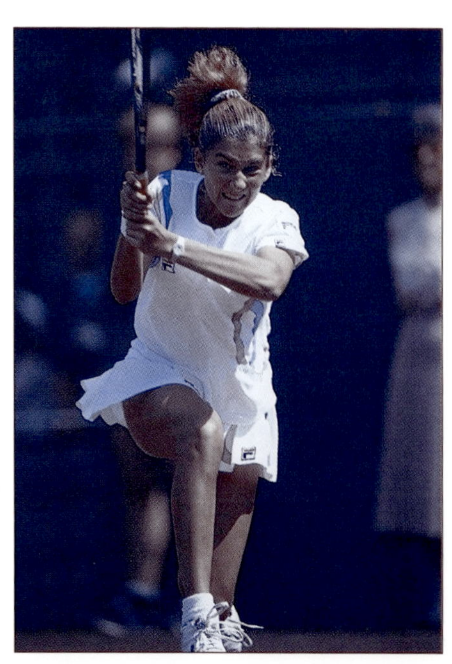
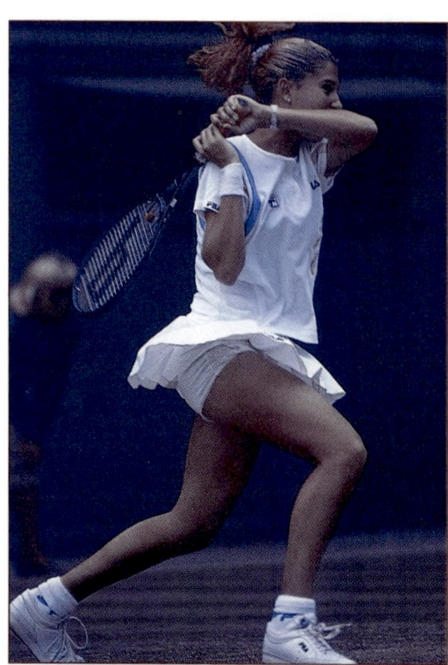
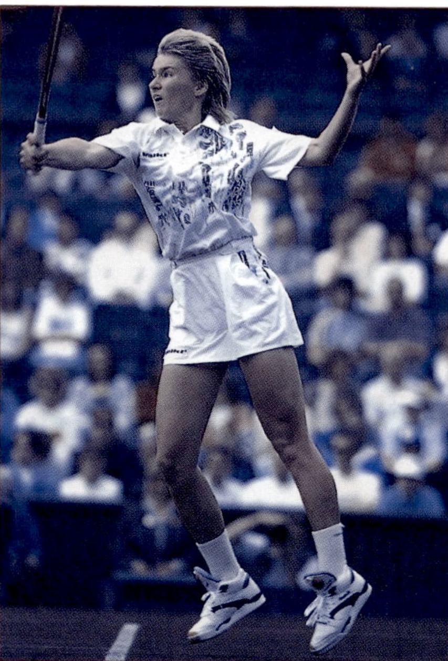

Tennis – female singles

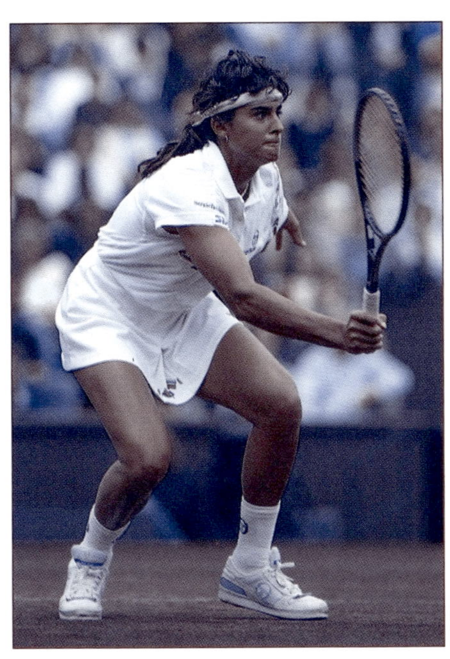

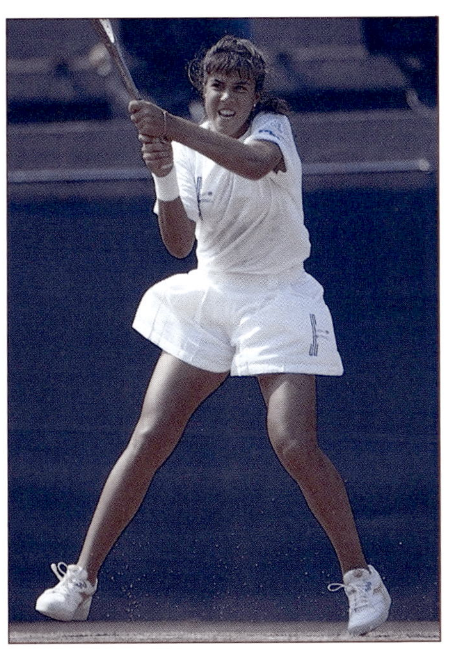

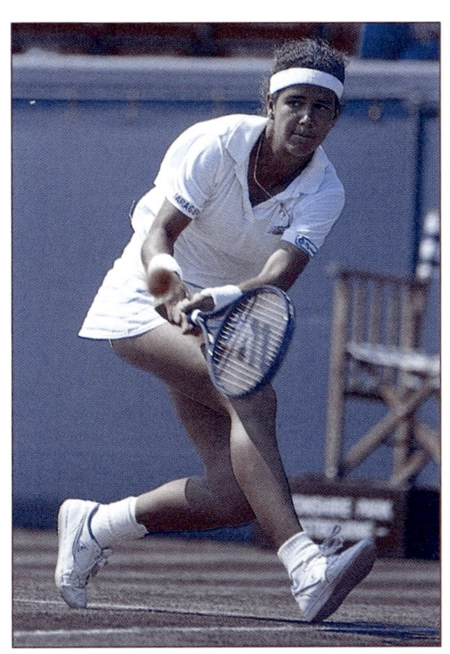

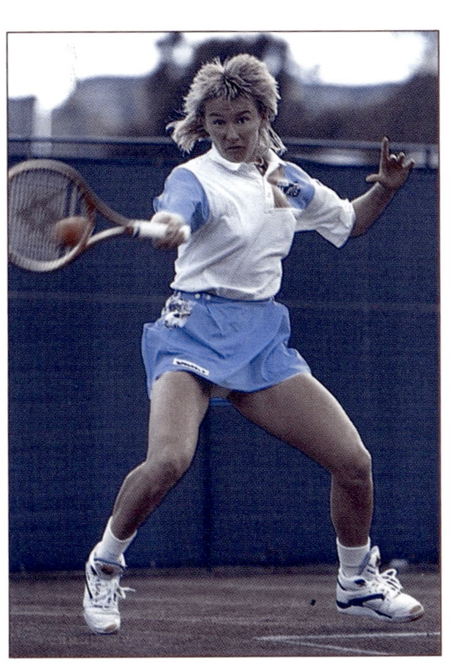

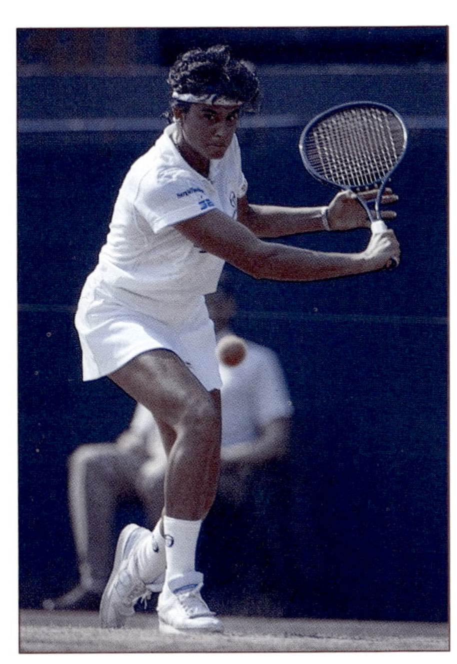

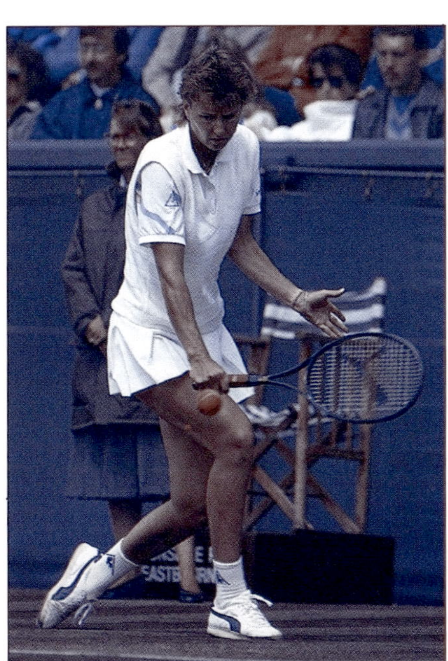

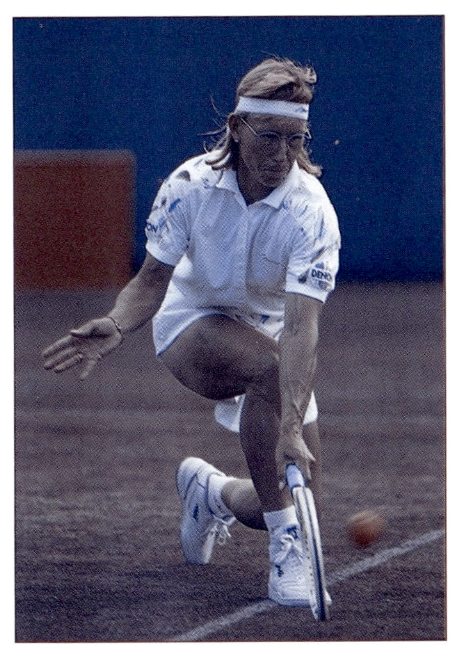

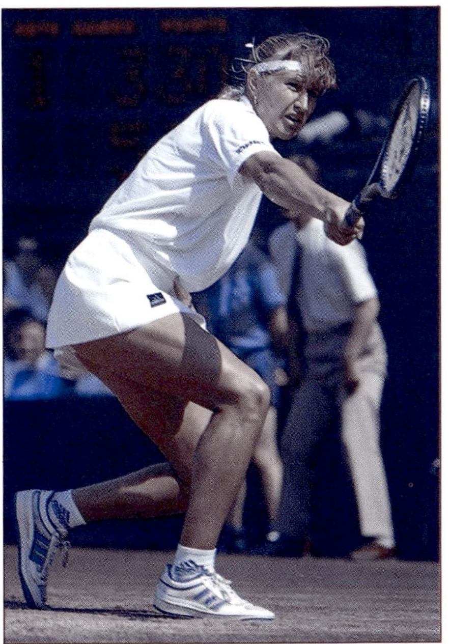

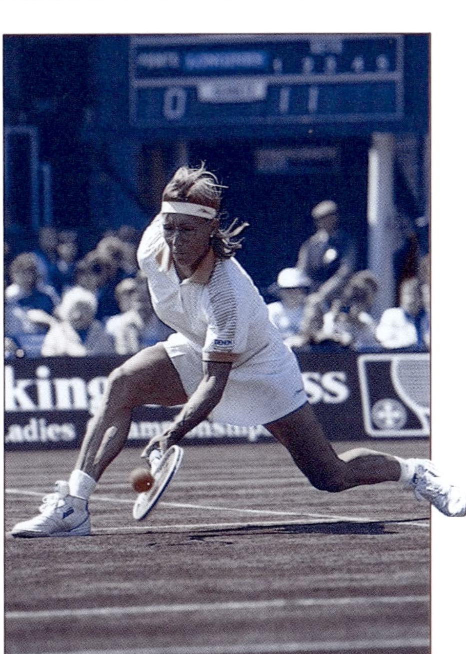

Tennis – female singles

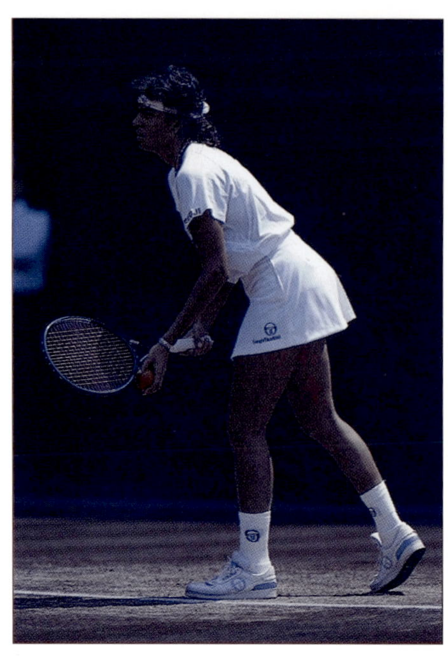

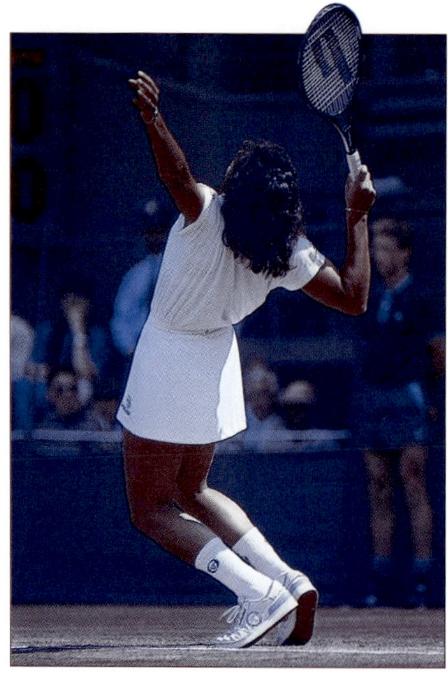

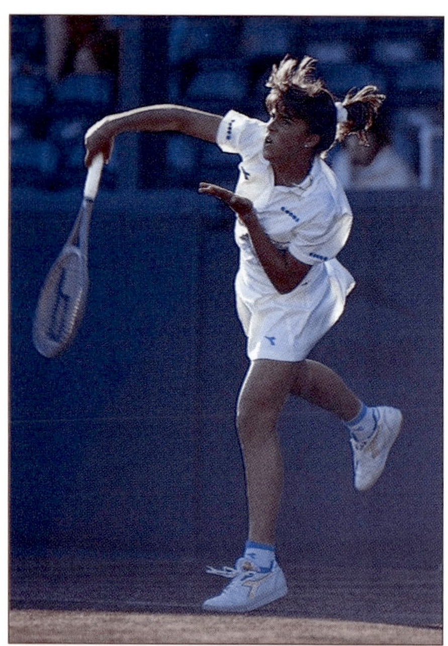

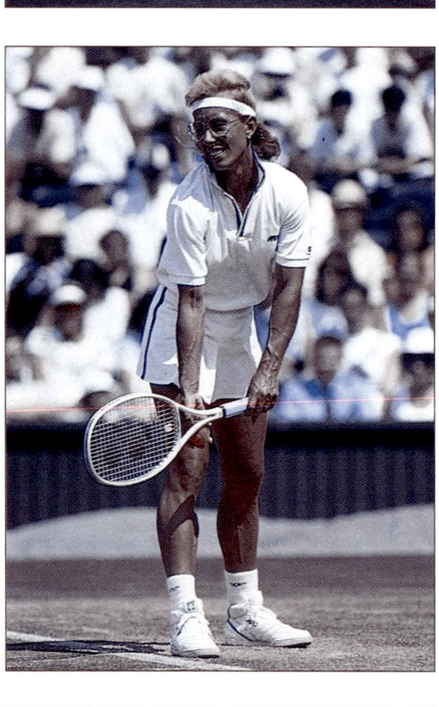

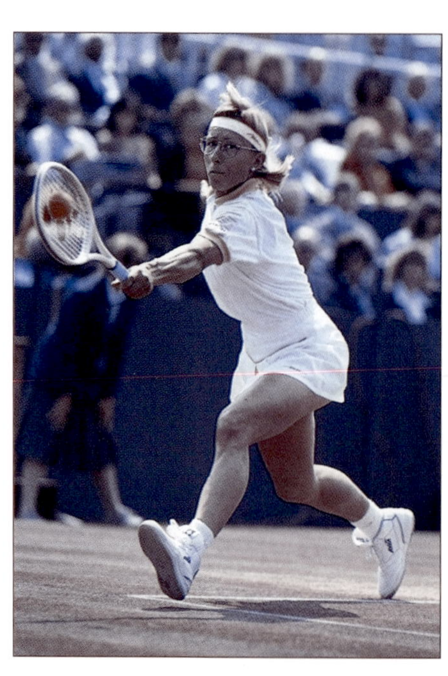

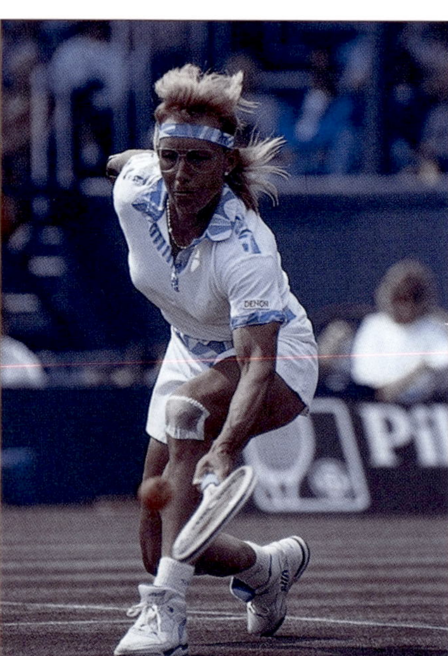

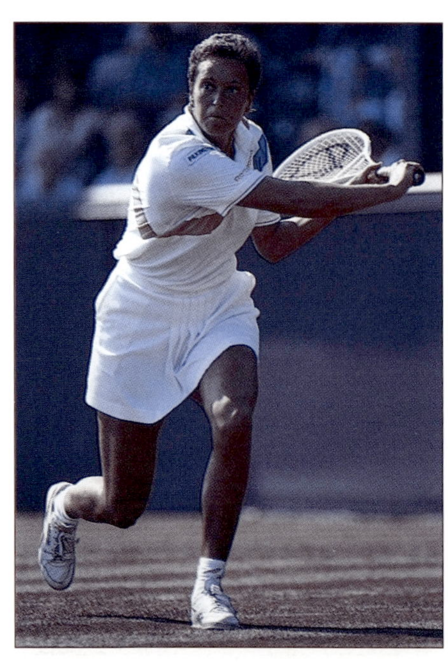

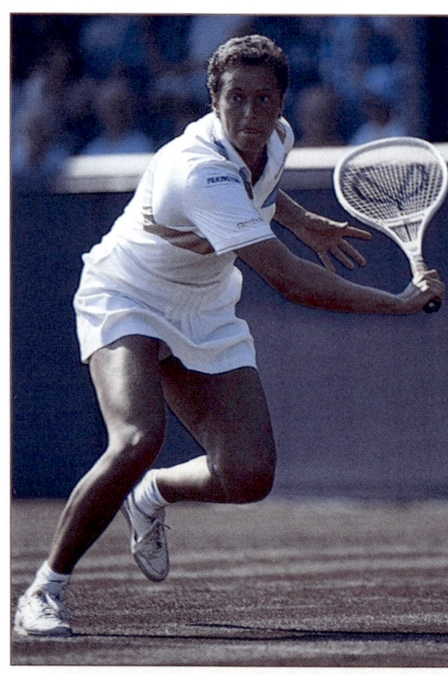

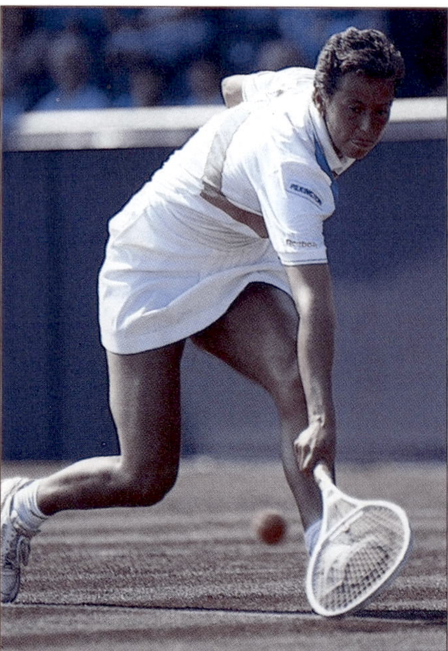

Tennis – female singles

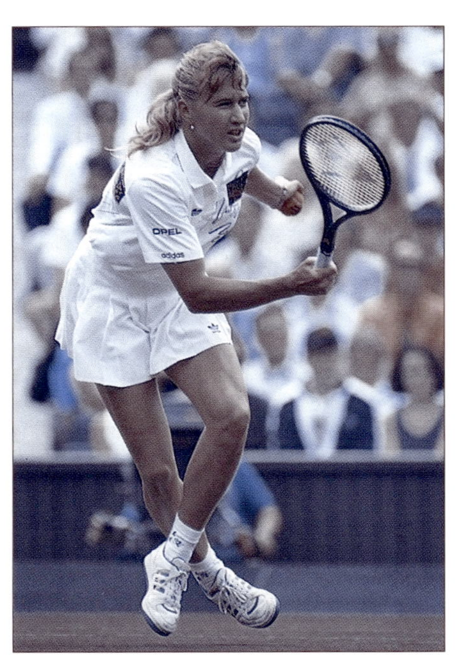

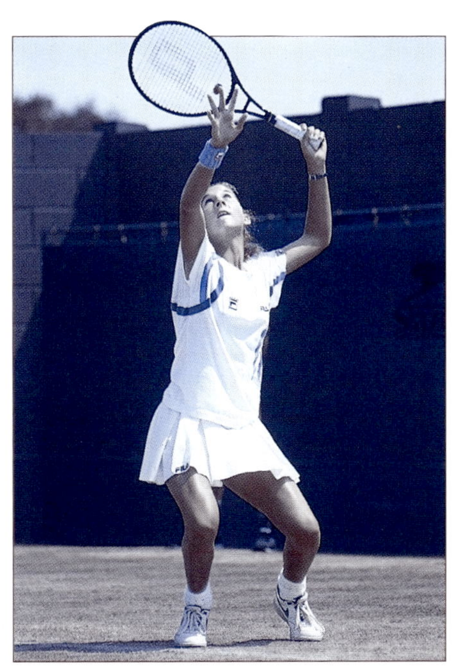

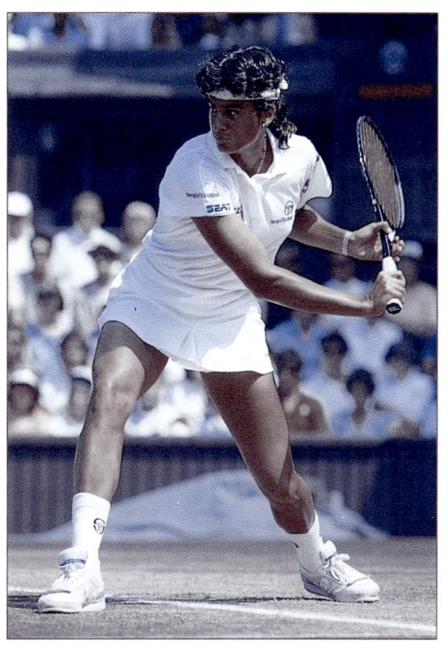

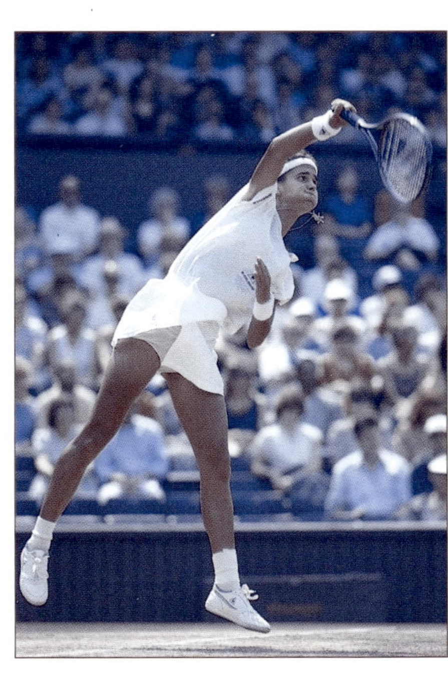

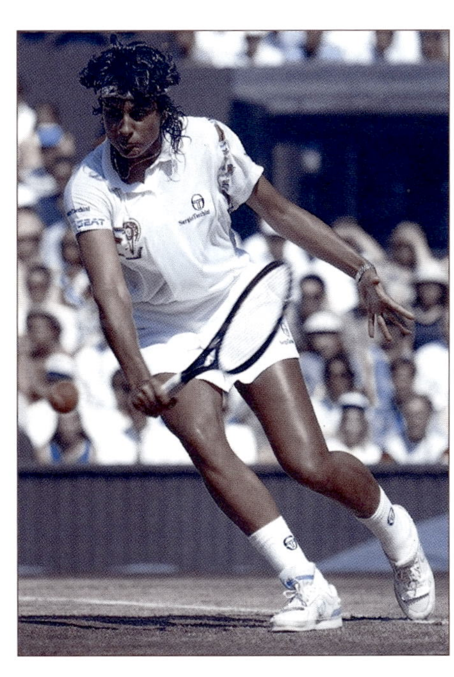

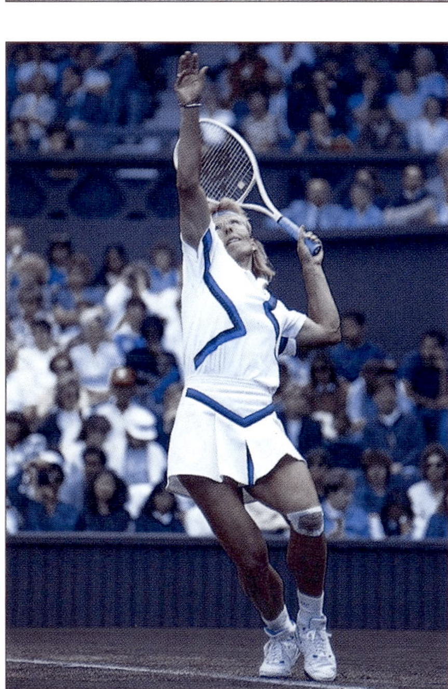

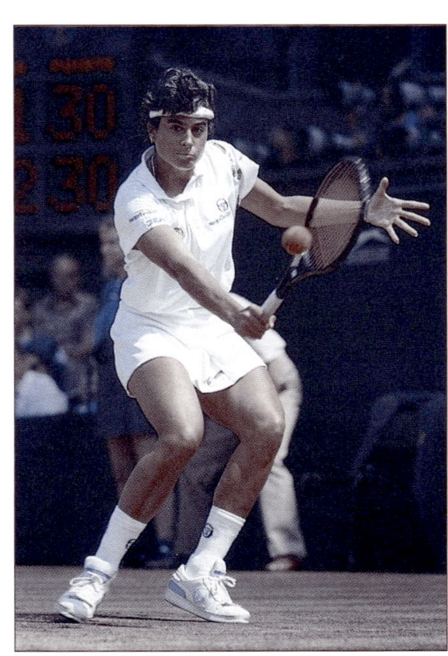

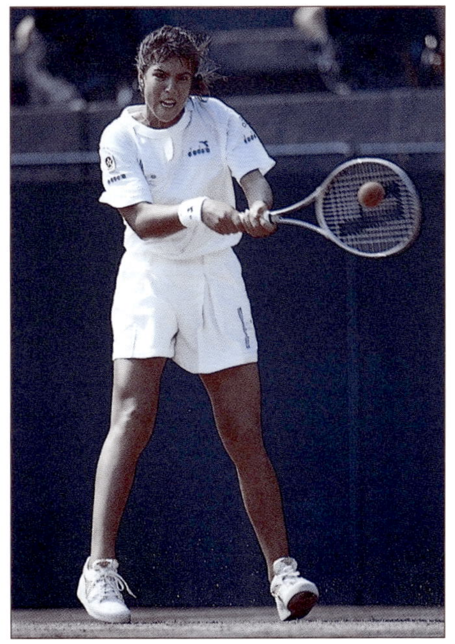

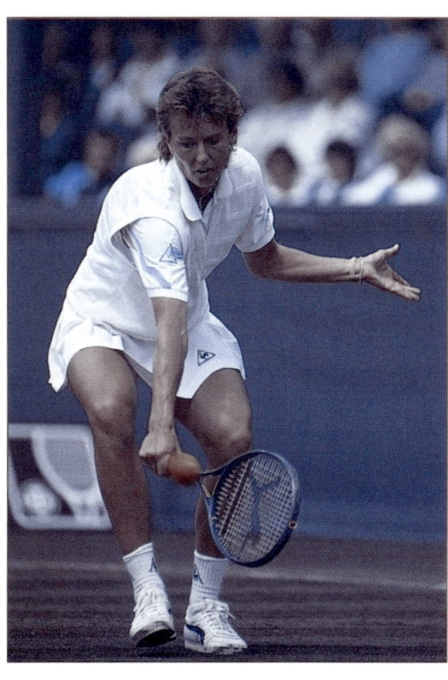

Tennis – doubles

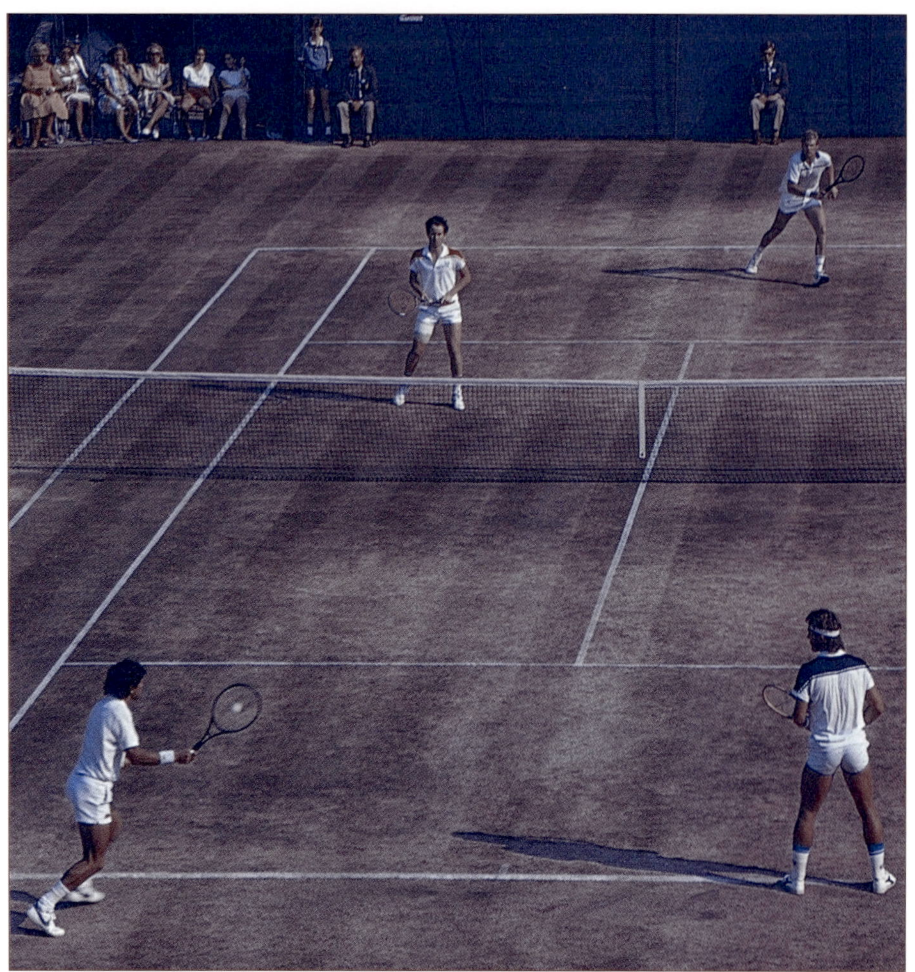

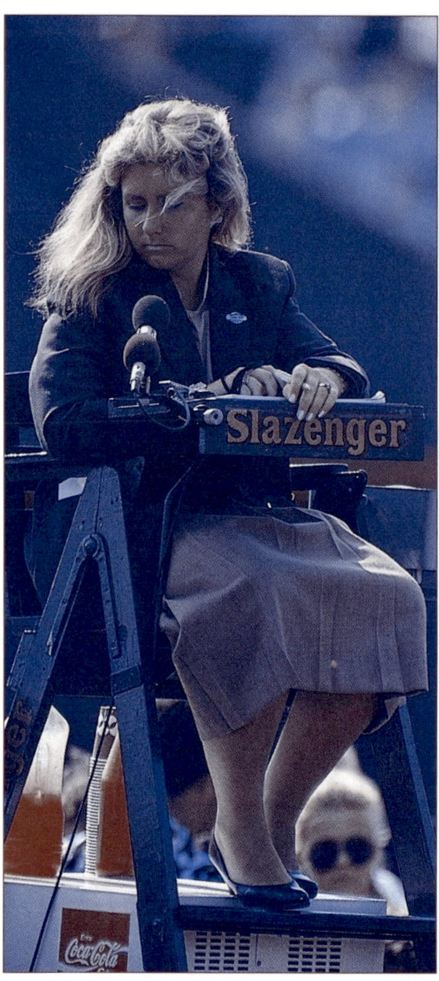

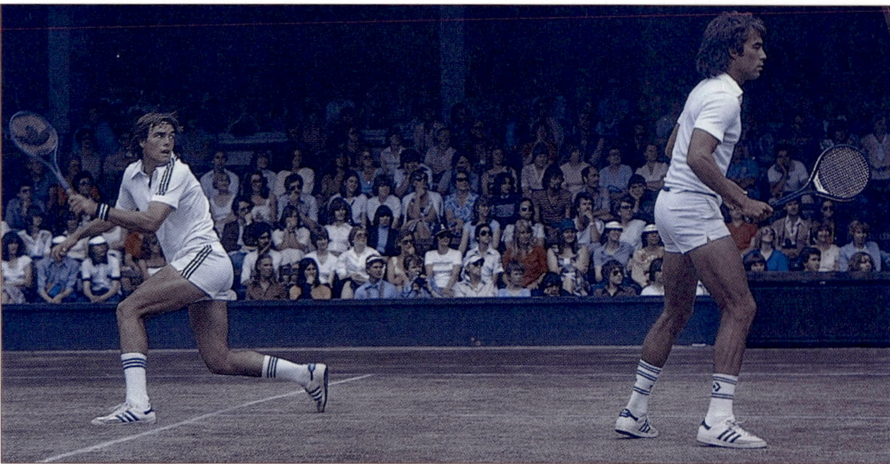

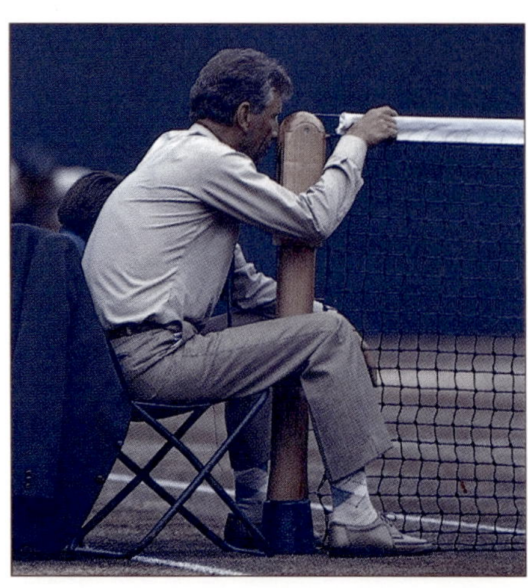

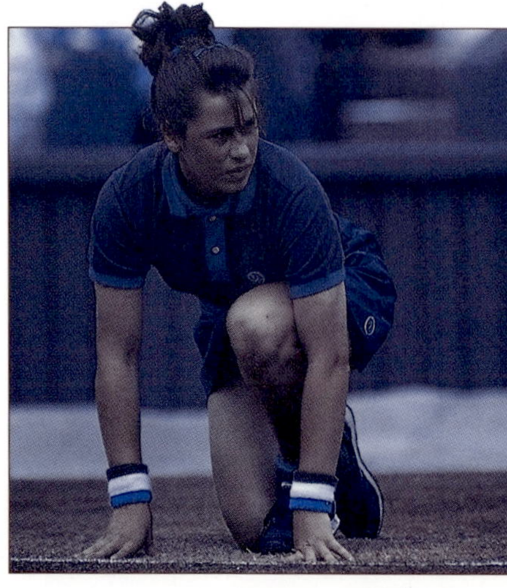

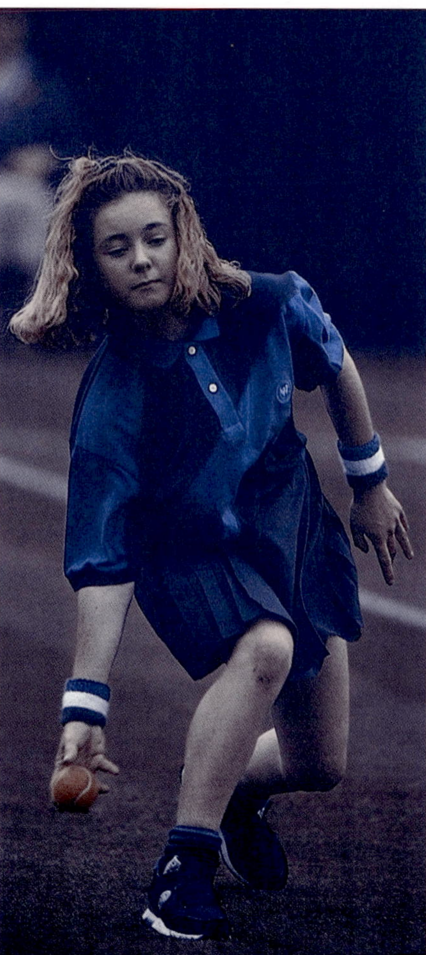

Tennis – ball girls and boys · court officials

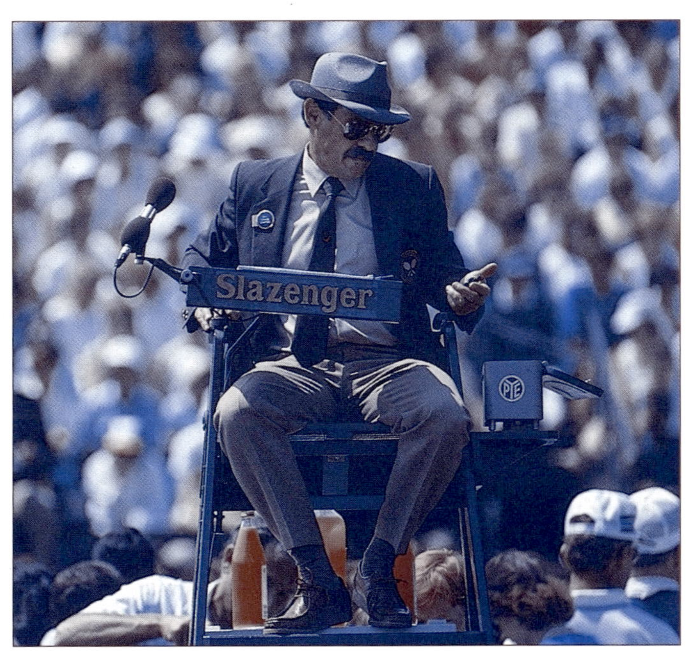

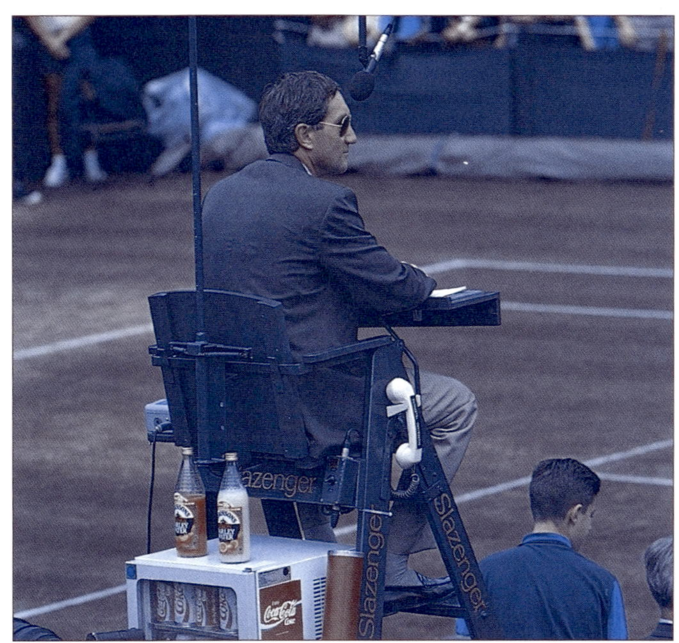

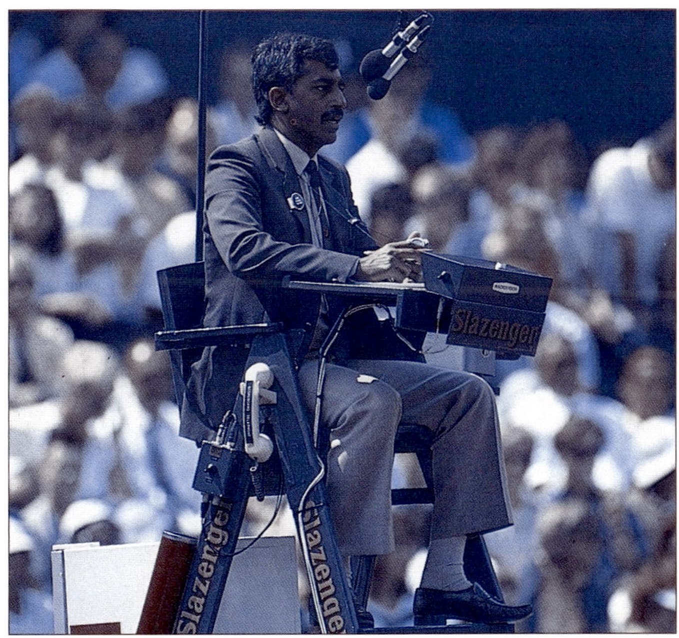

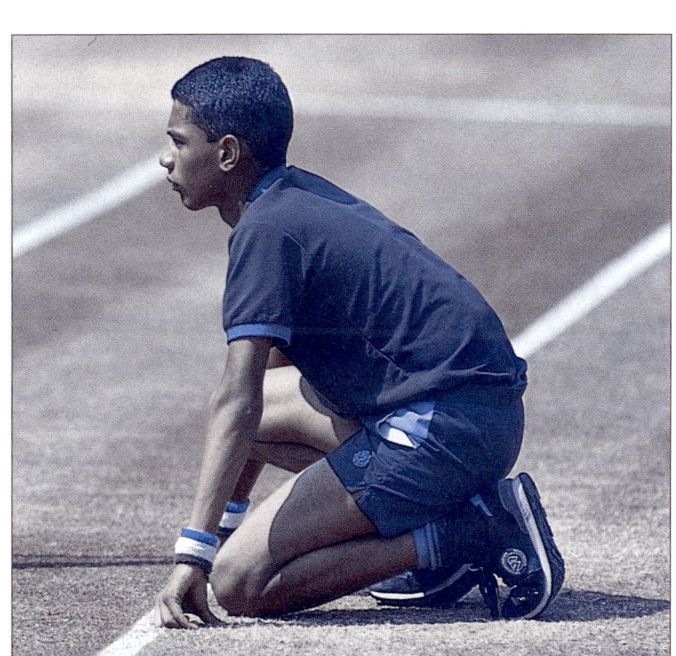

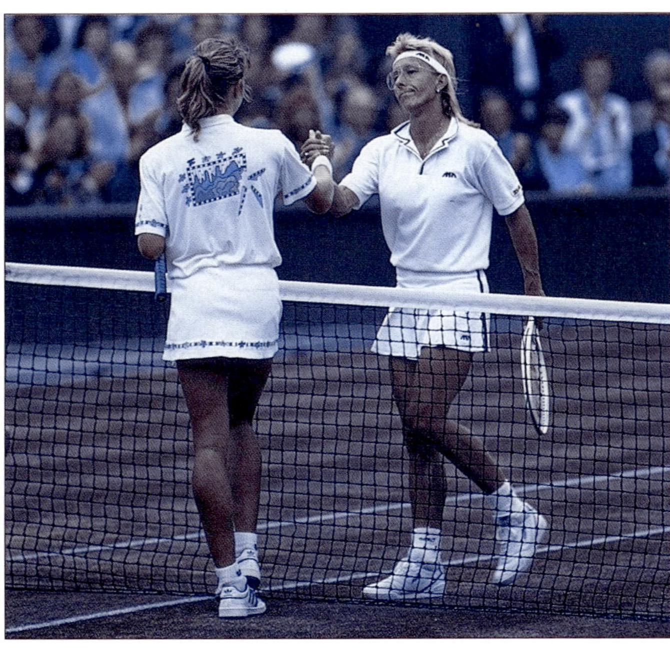

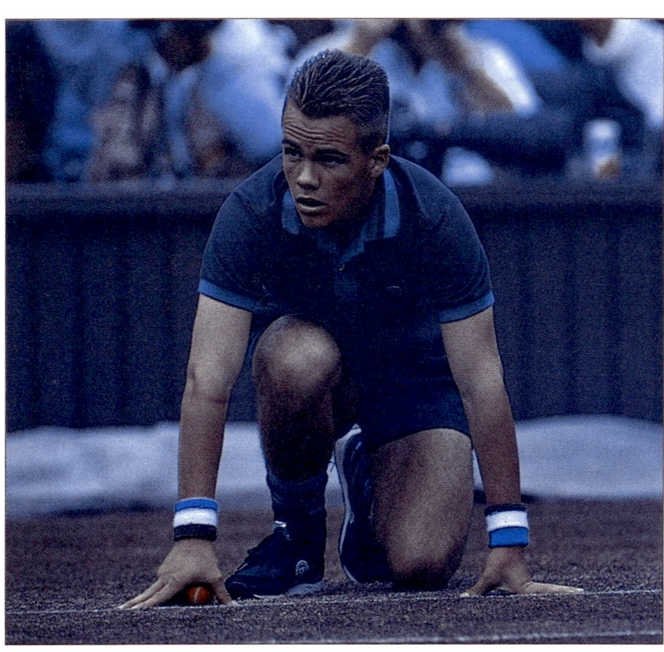

Table tennis – male

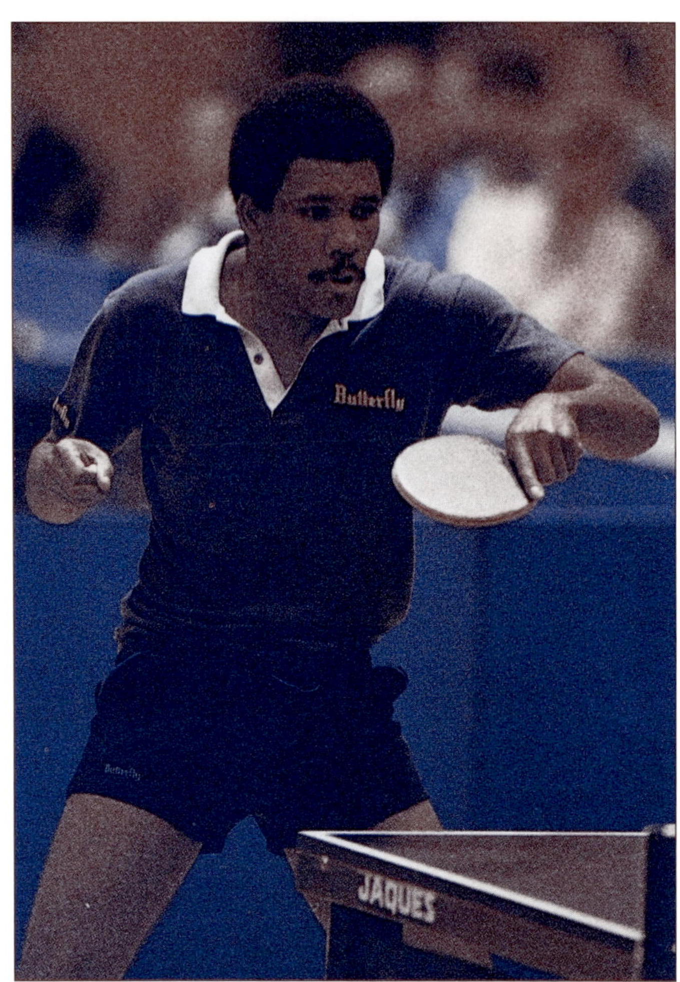

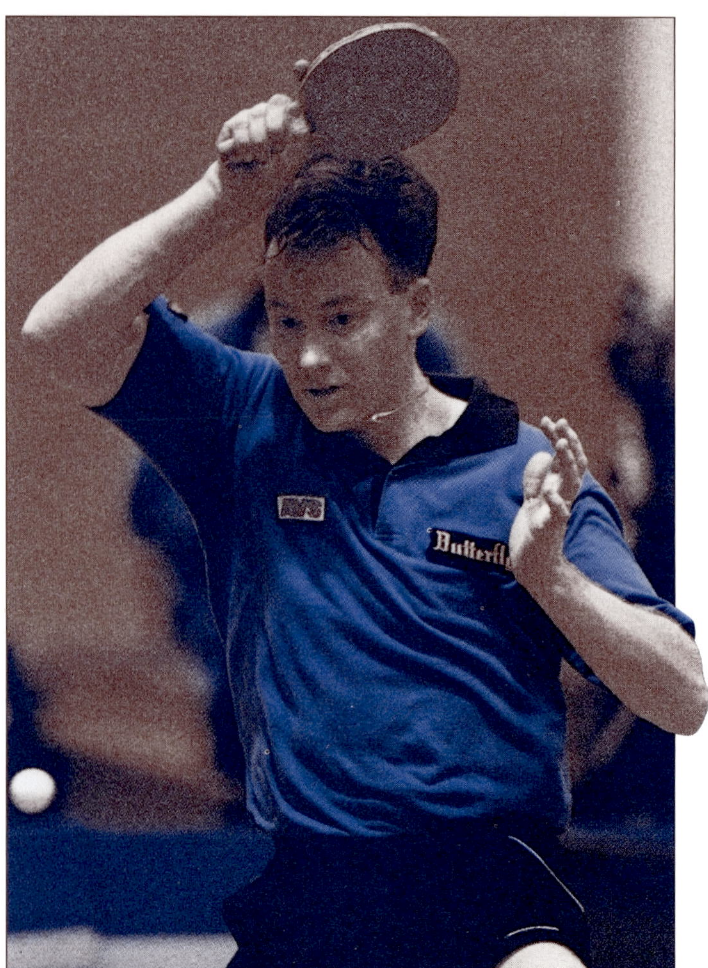

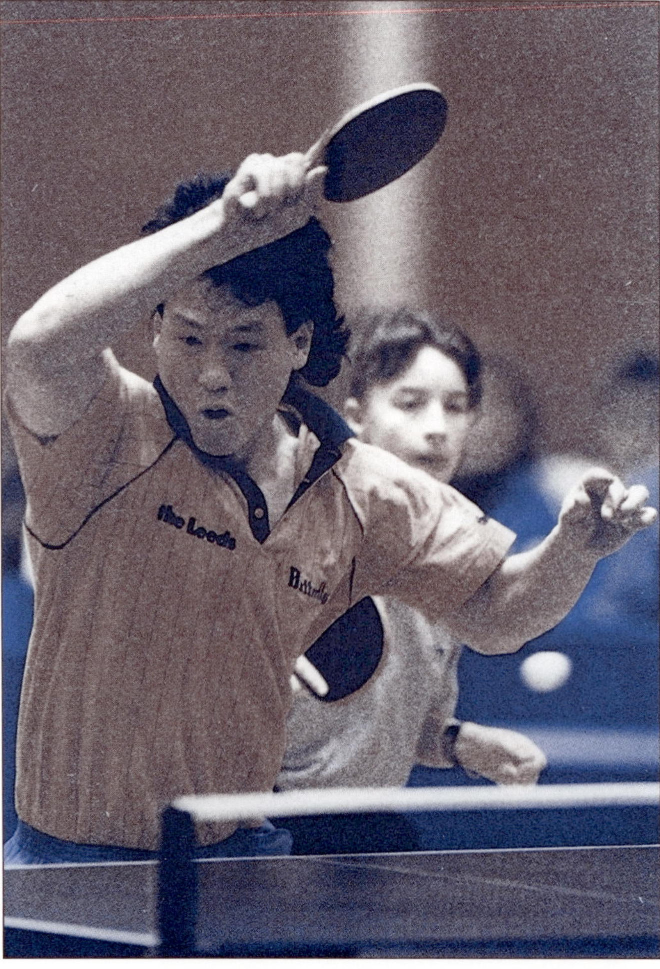

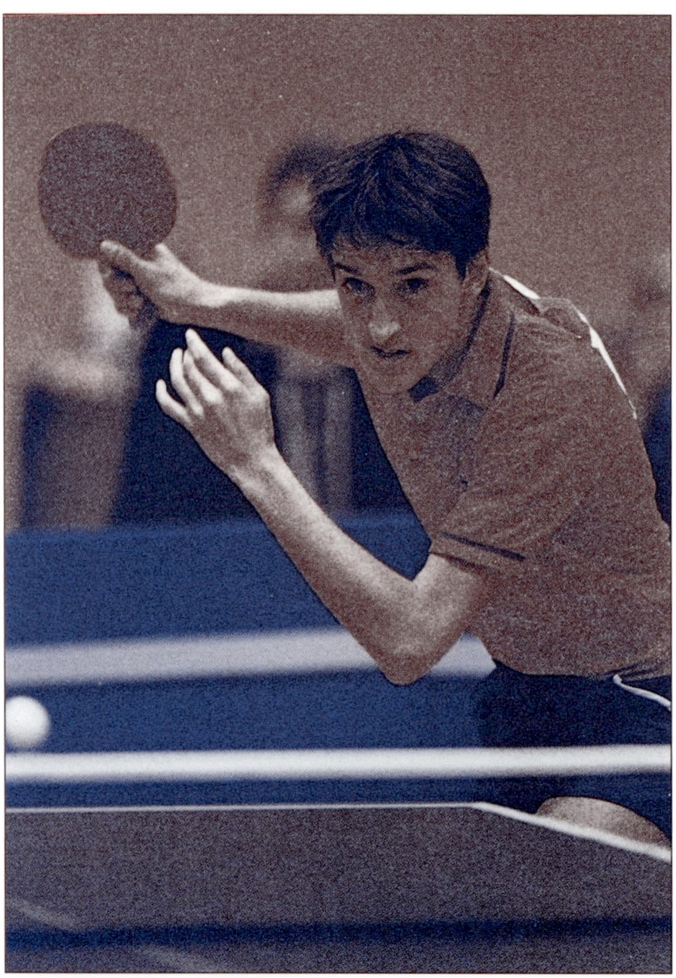

Table tennis – male/female

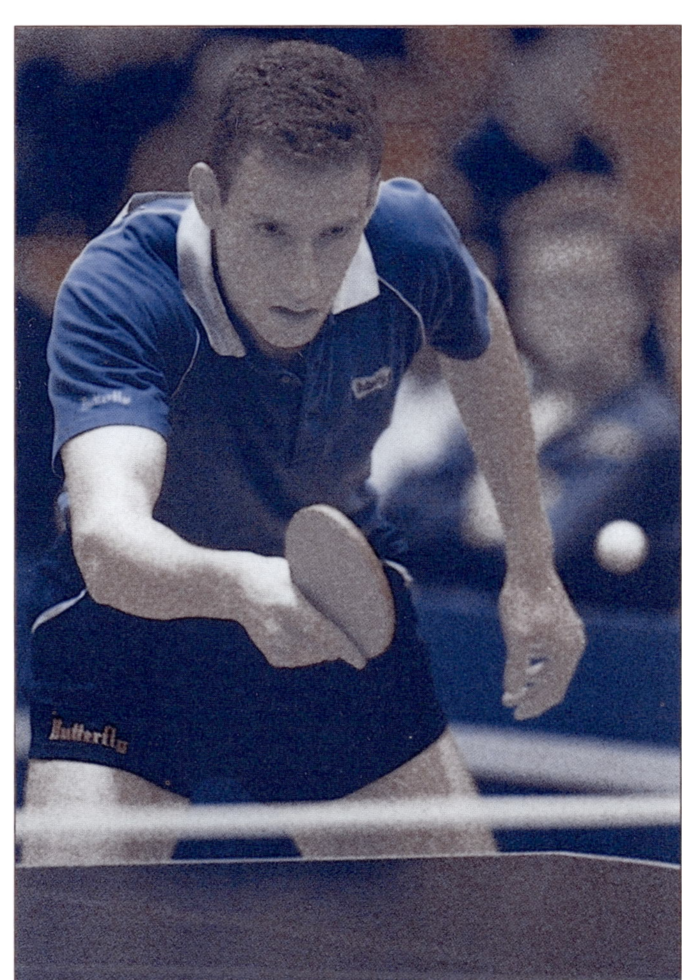

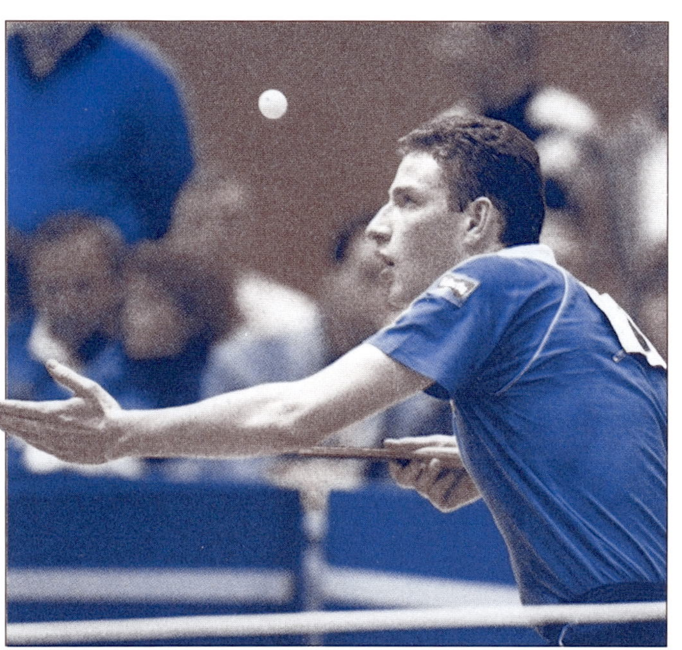

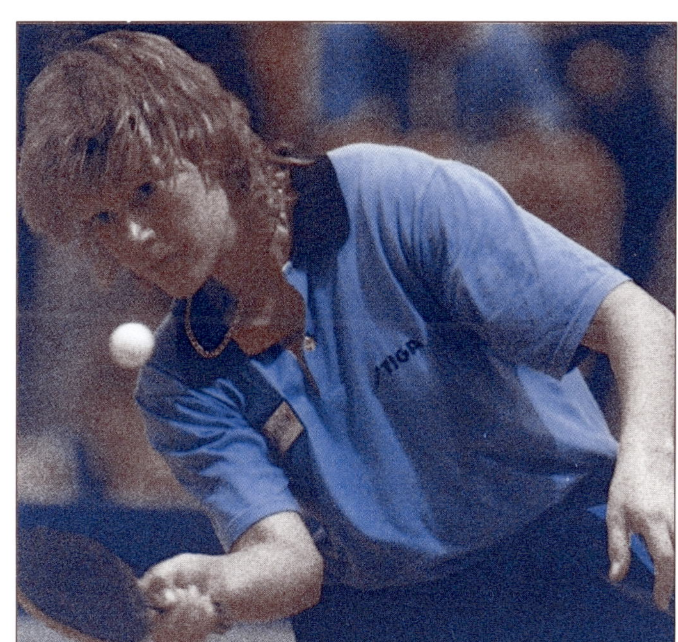

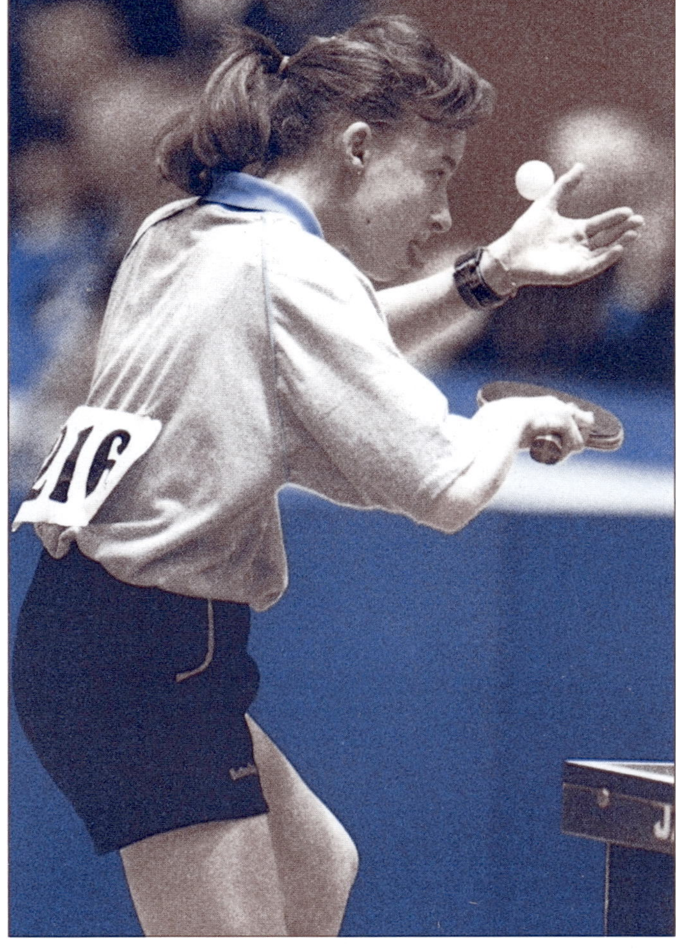

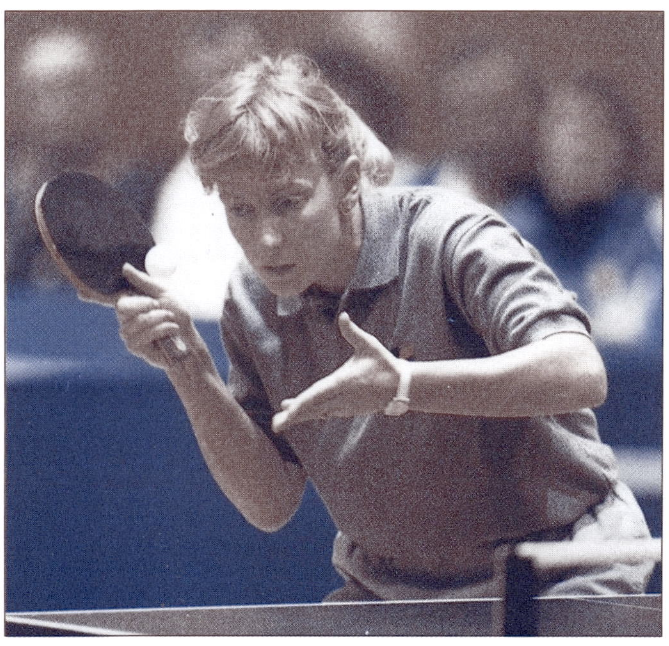

Squash

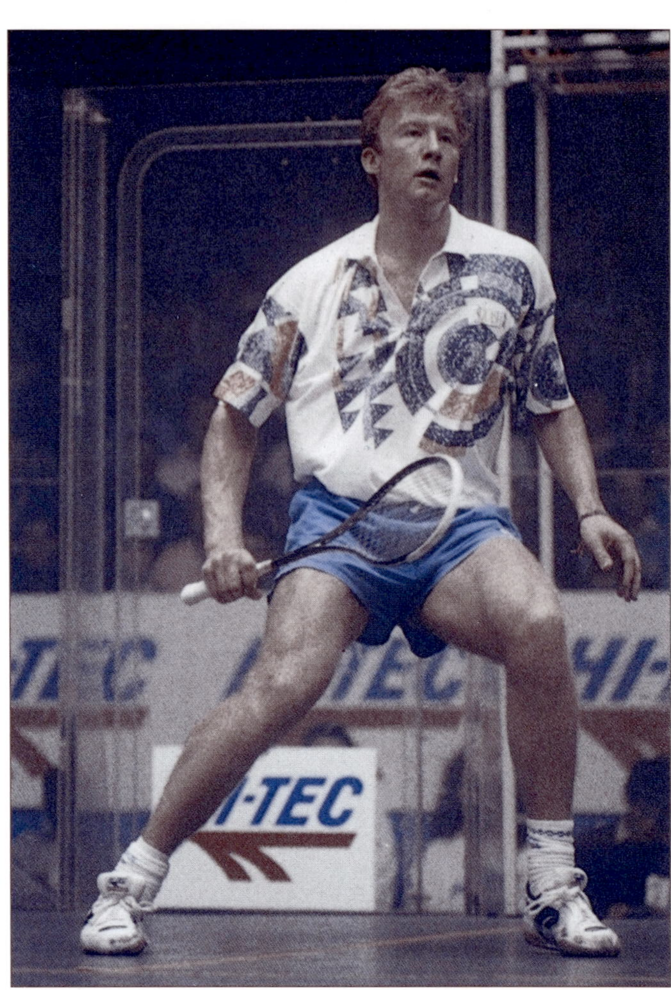

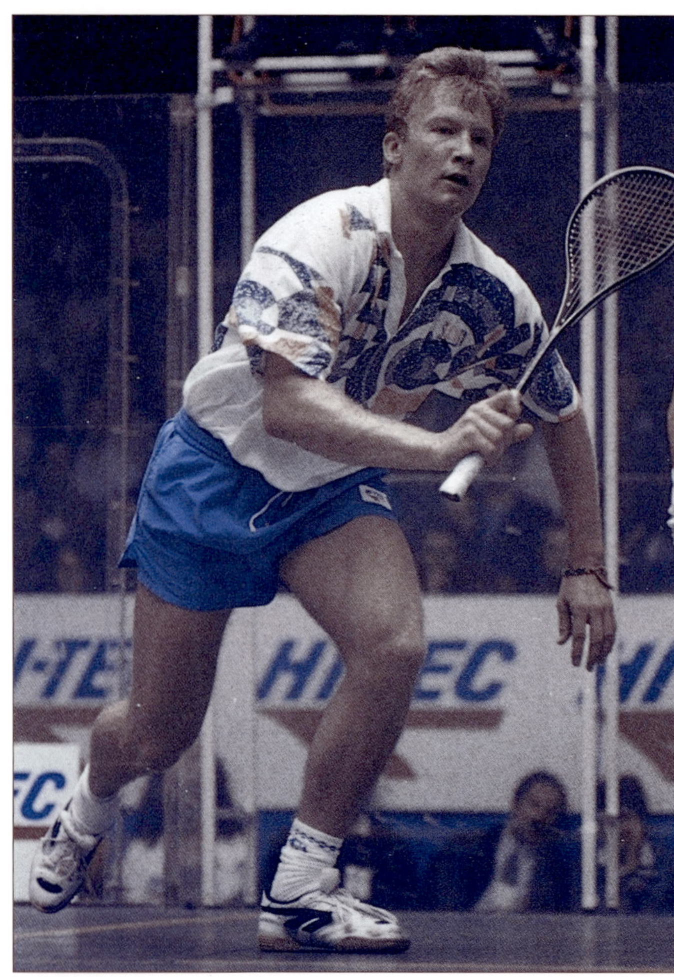

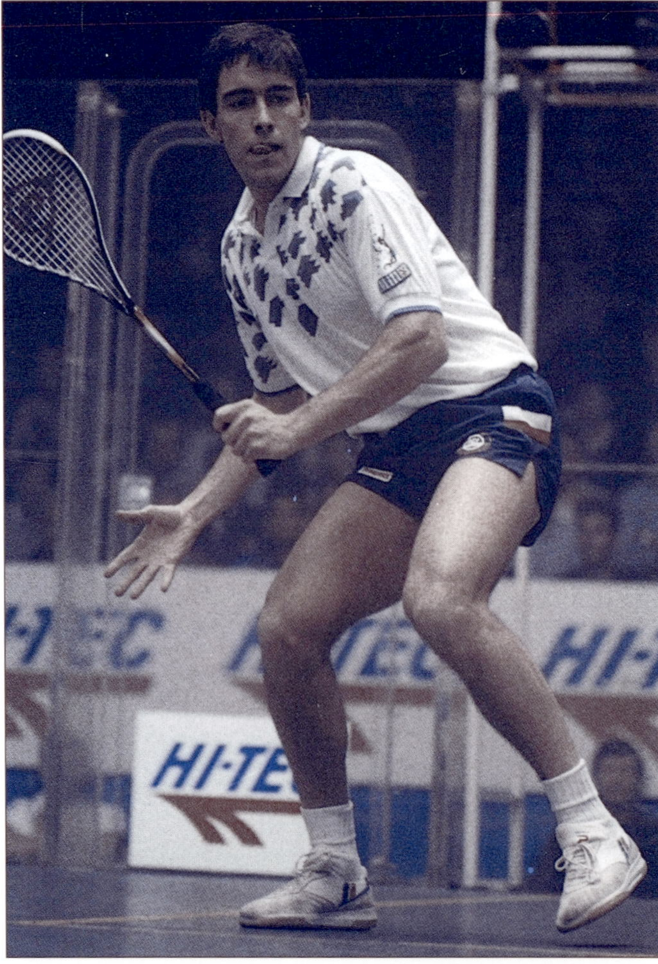

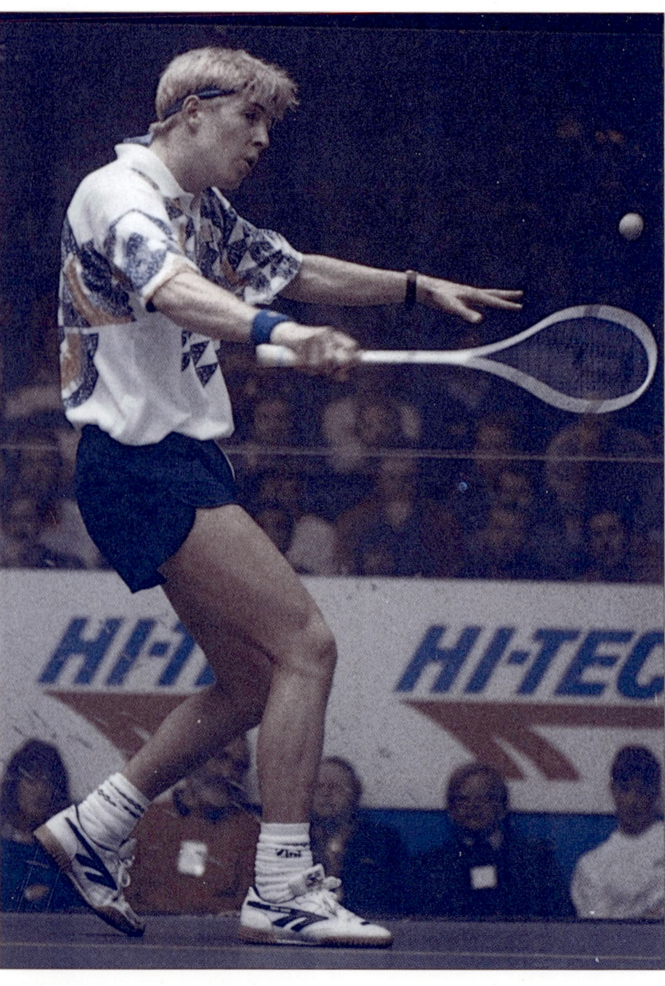

Squash

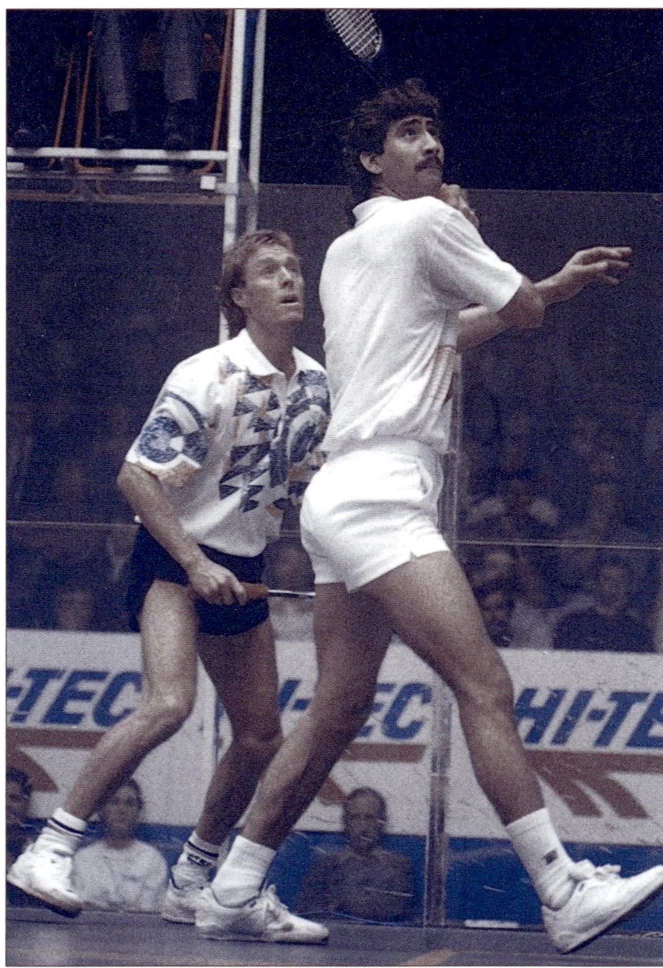

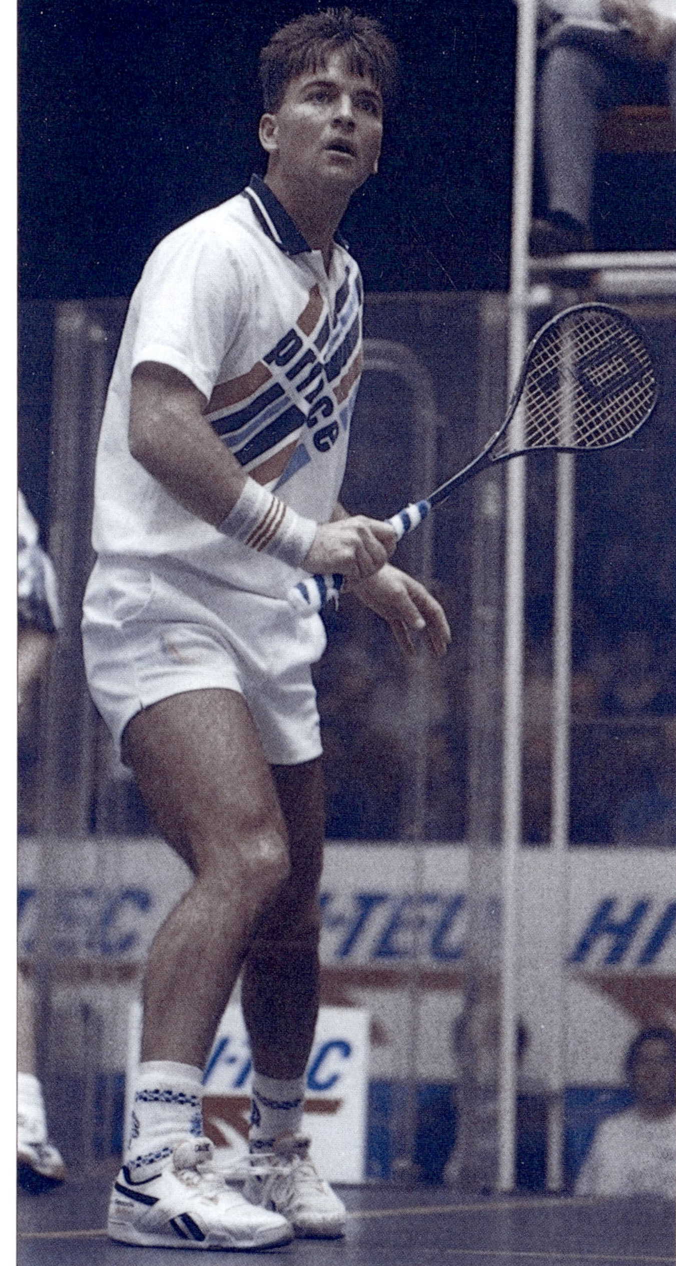

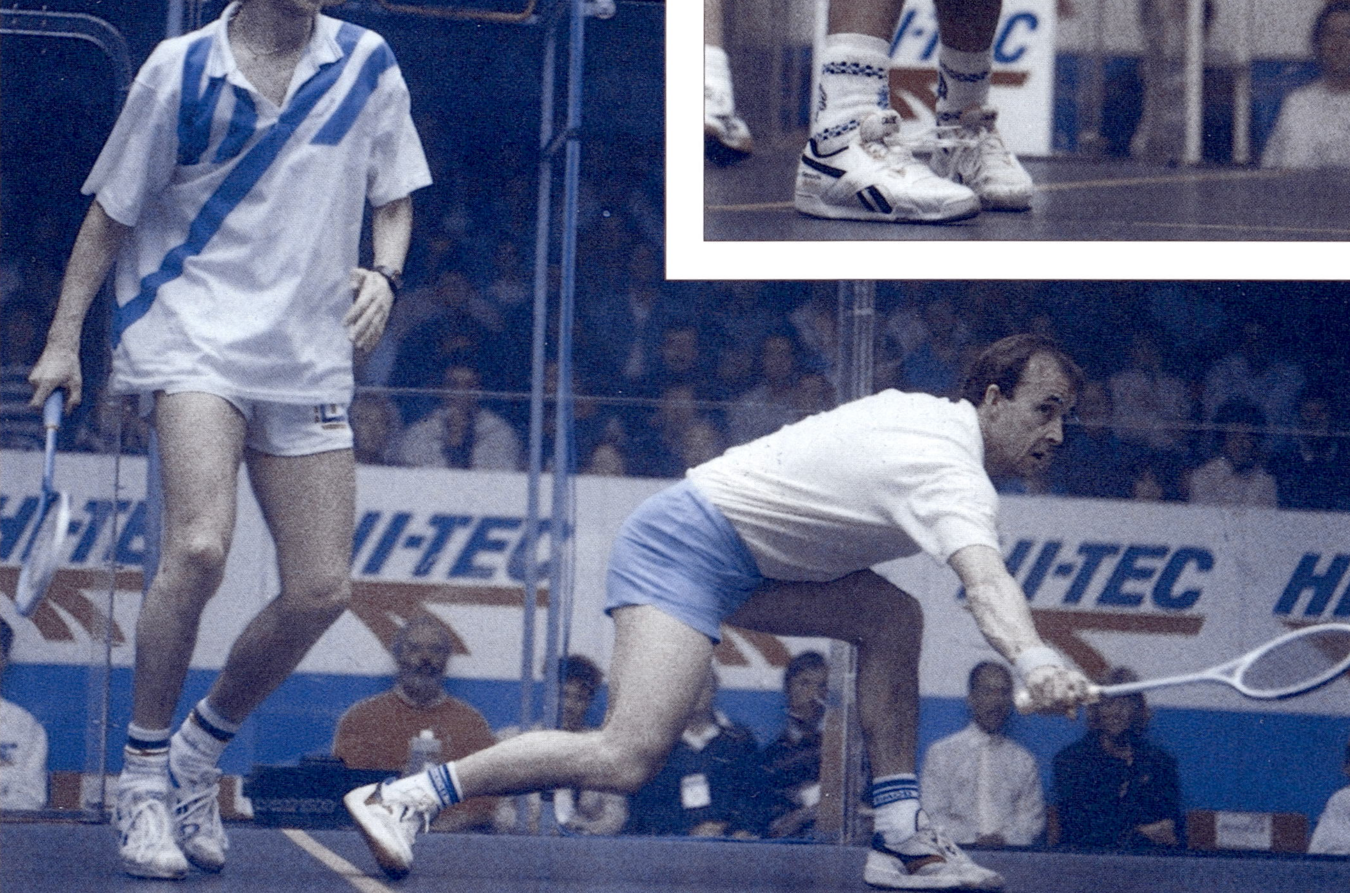

Badminton – male singles

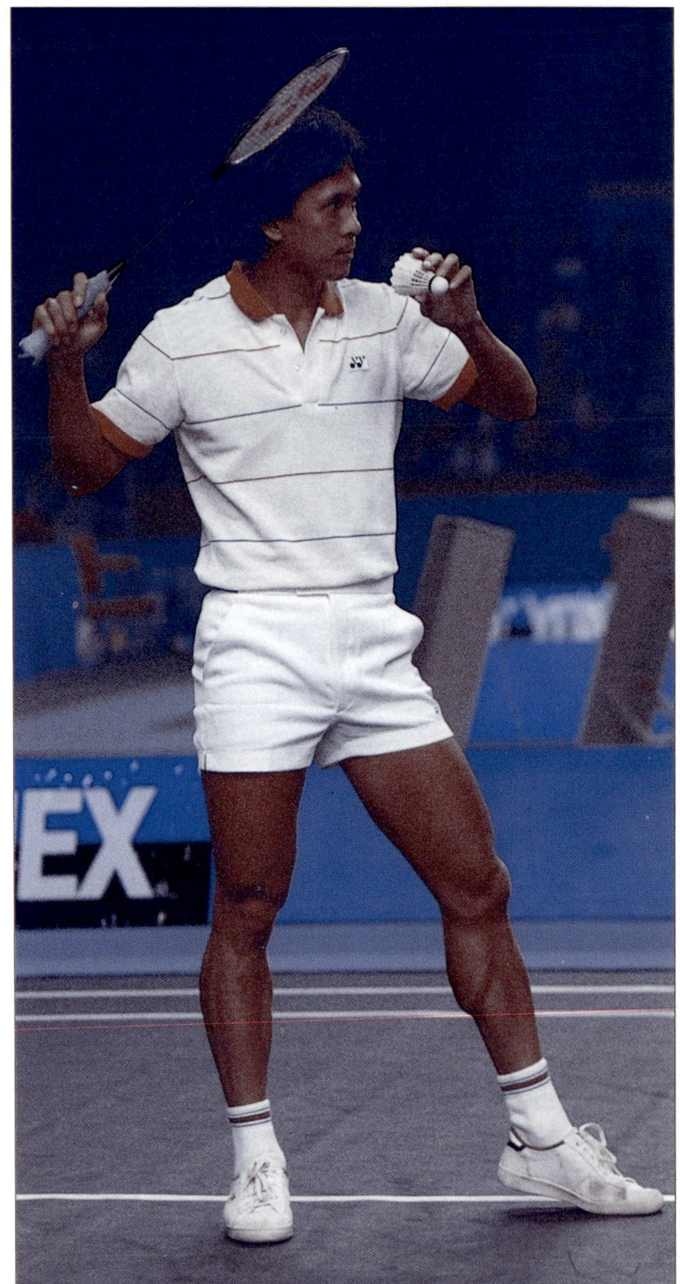

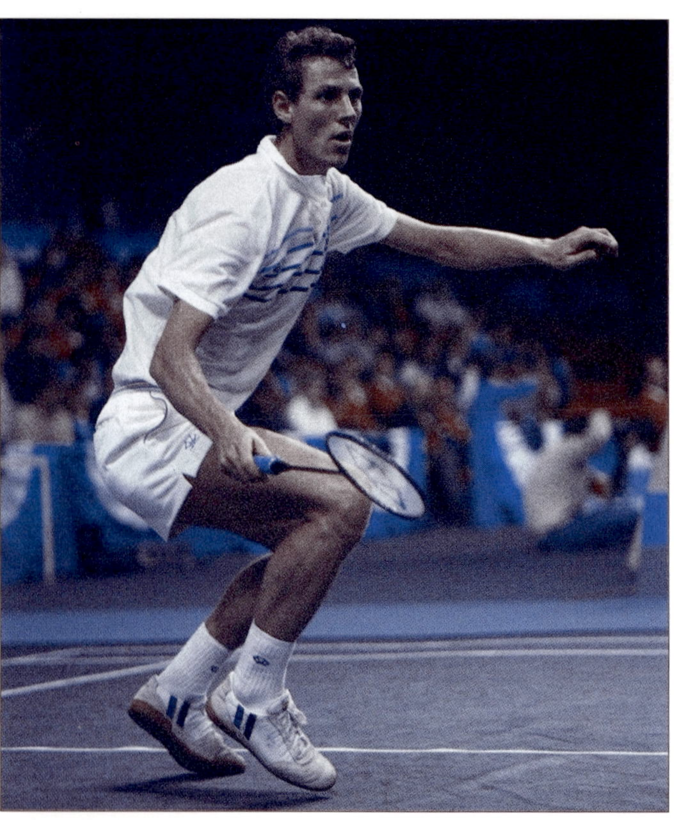

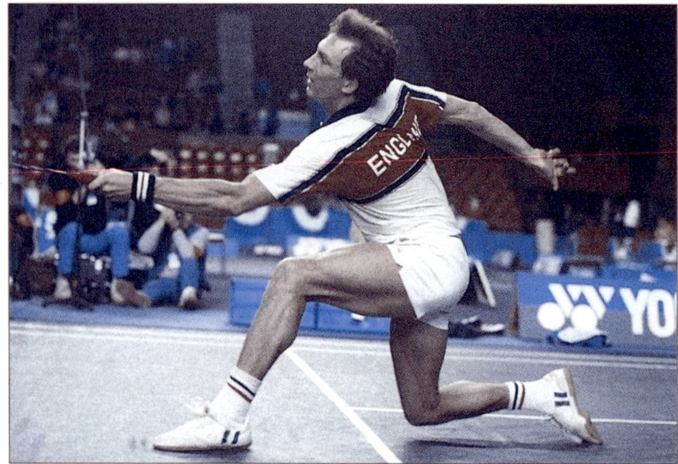

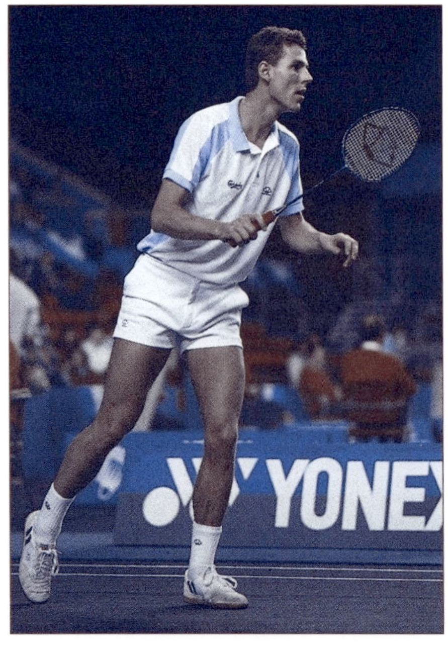

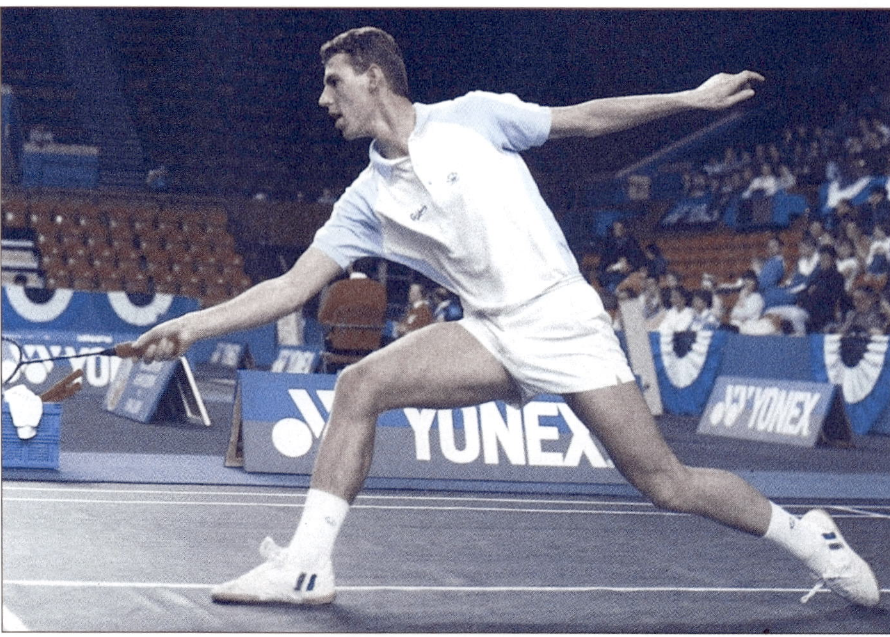

Badminton – female singles · doubles

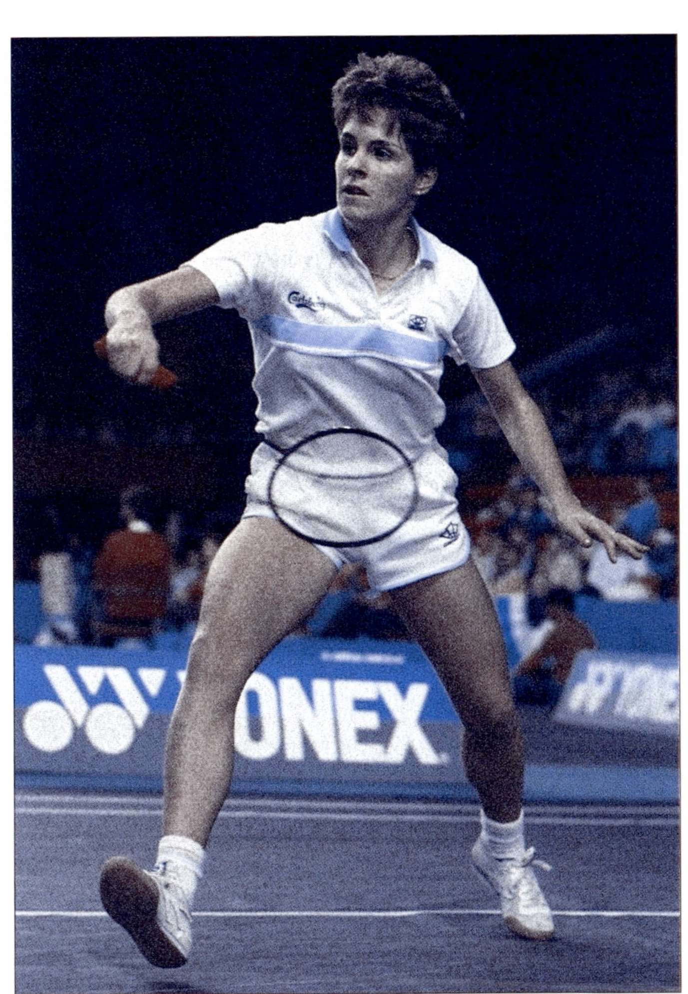

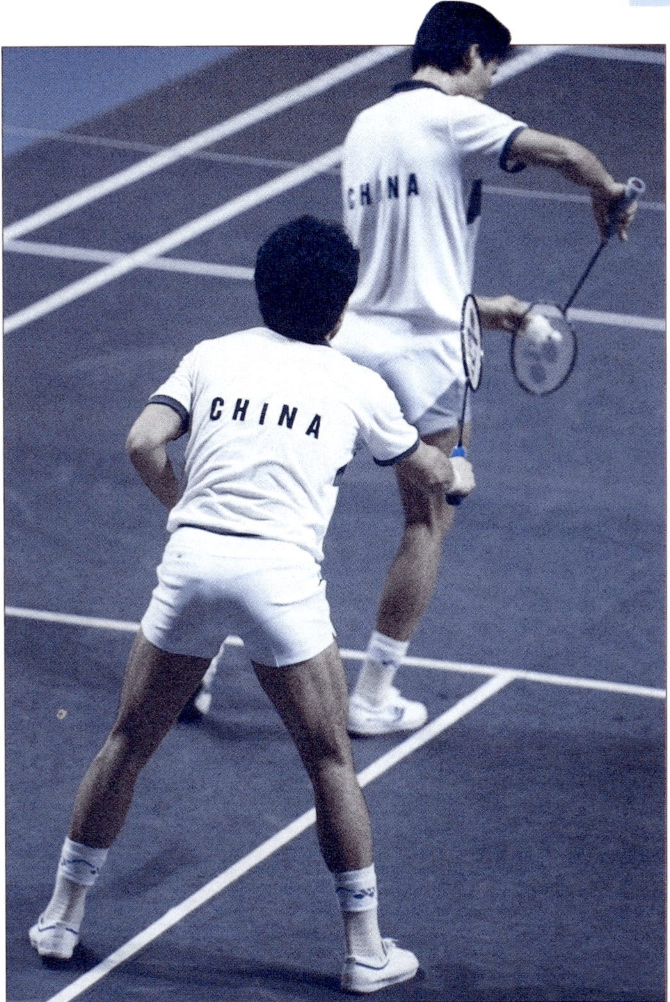

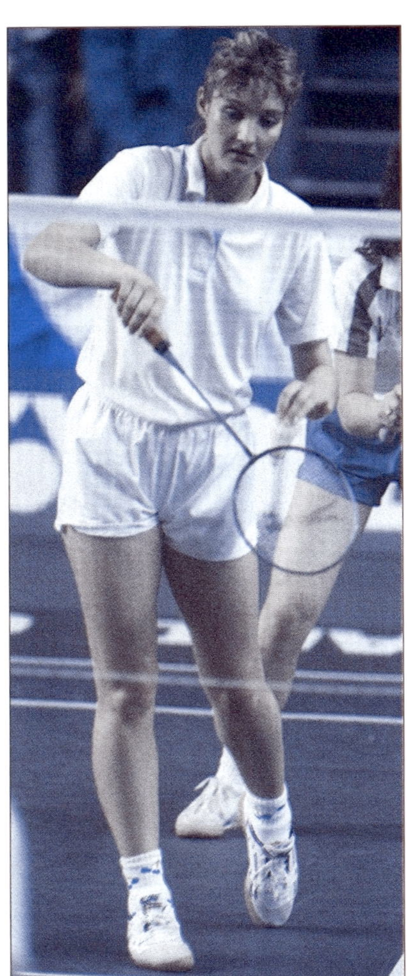

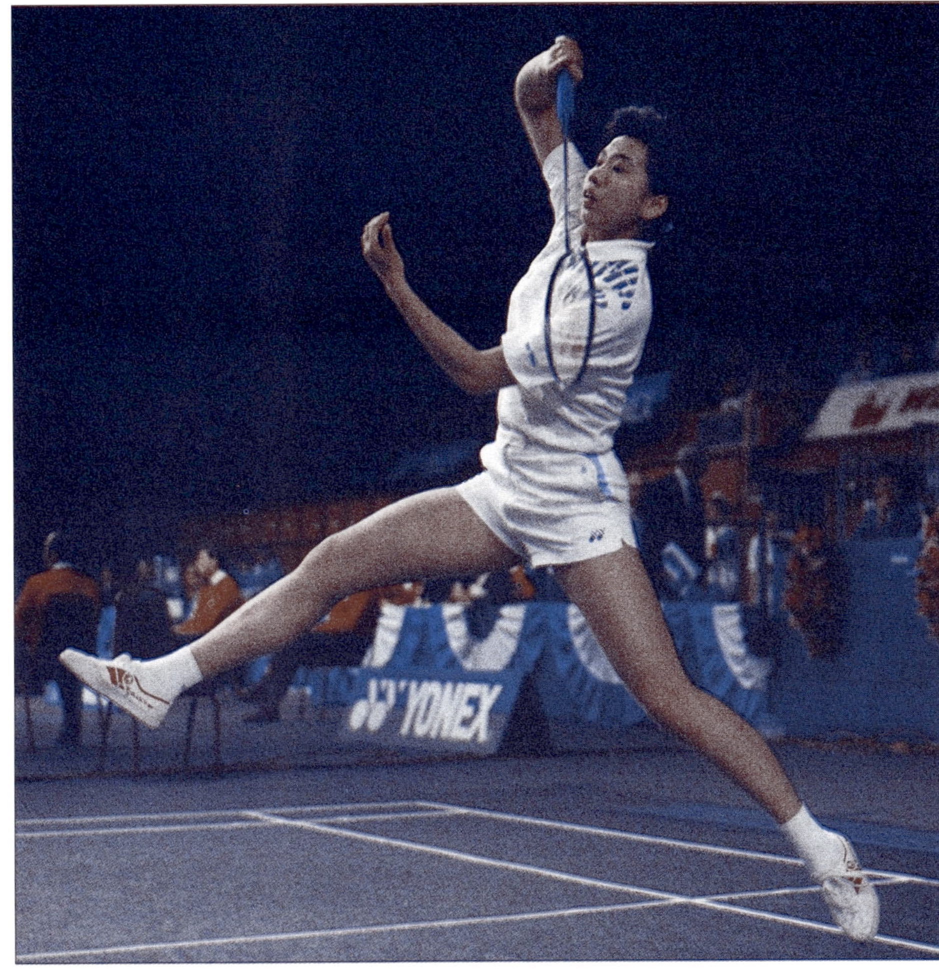

Baseball

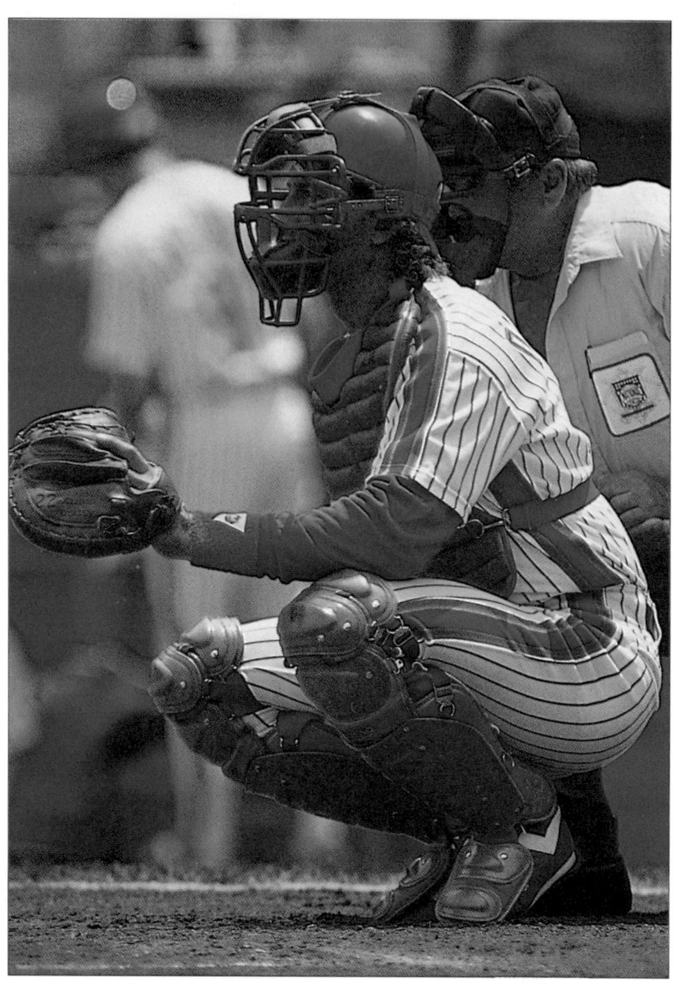

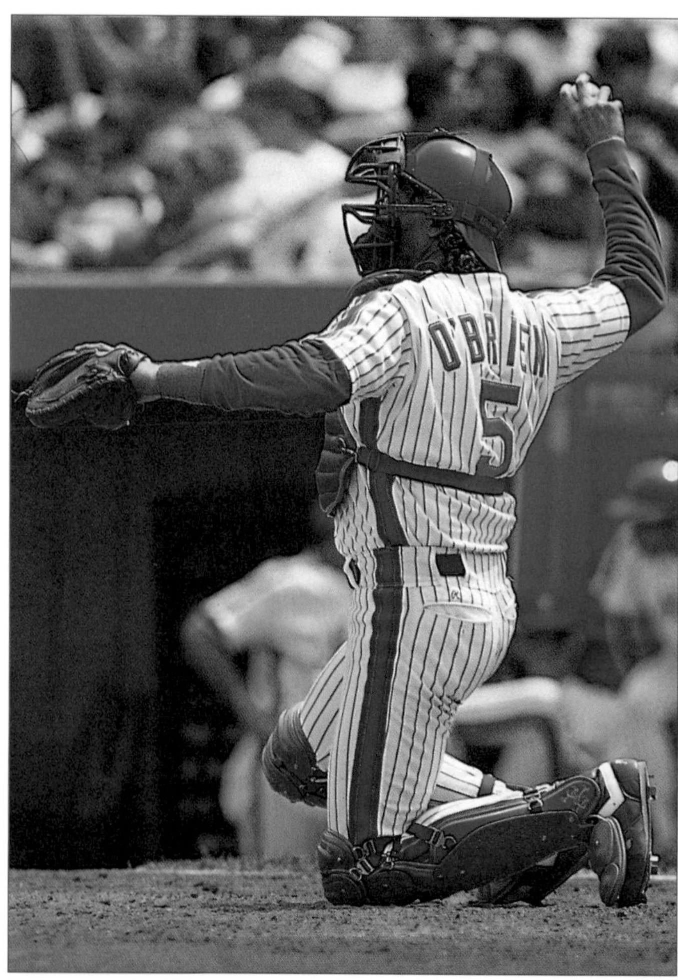

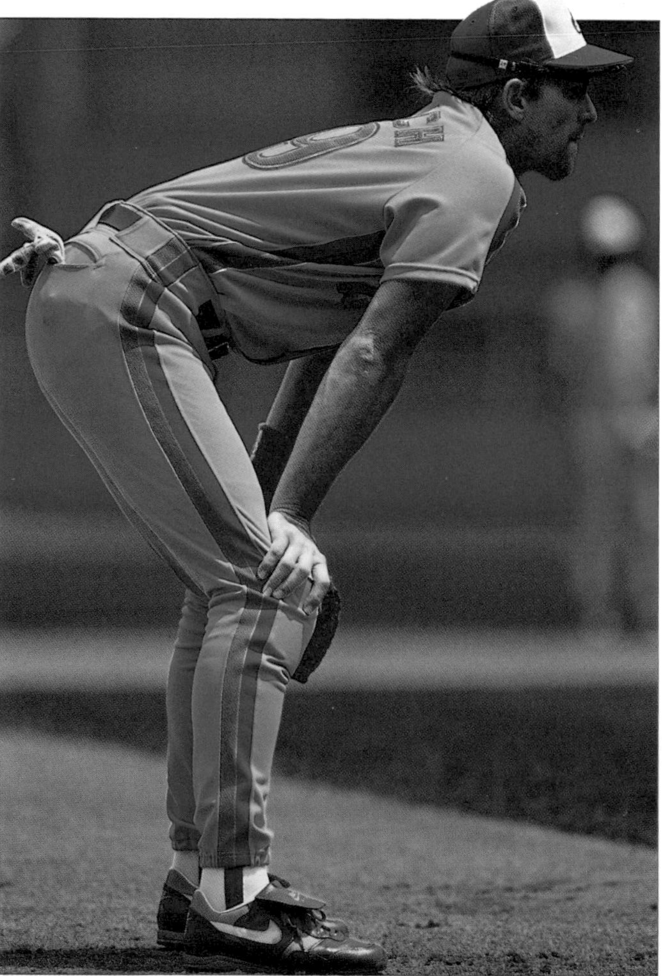

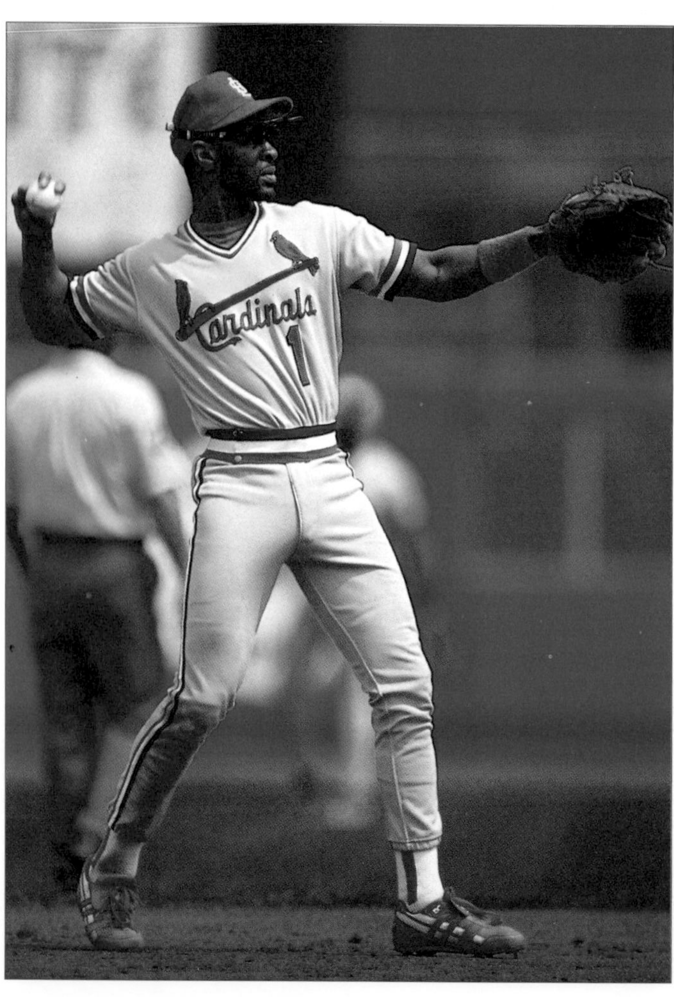

Baseball

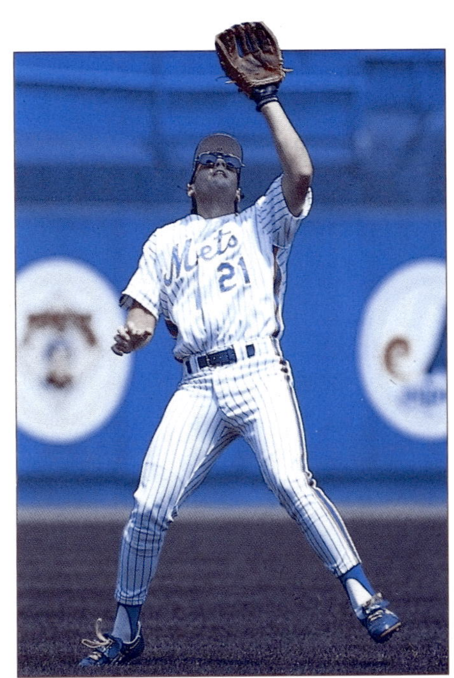

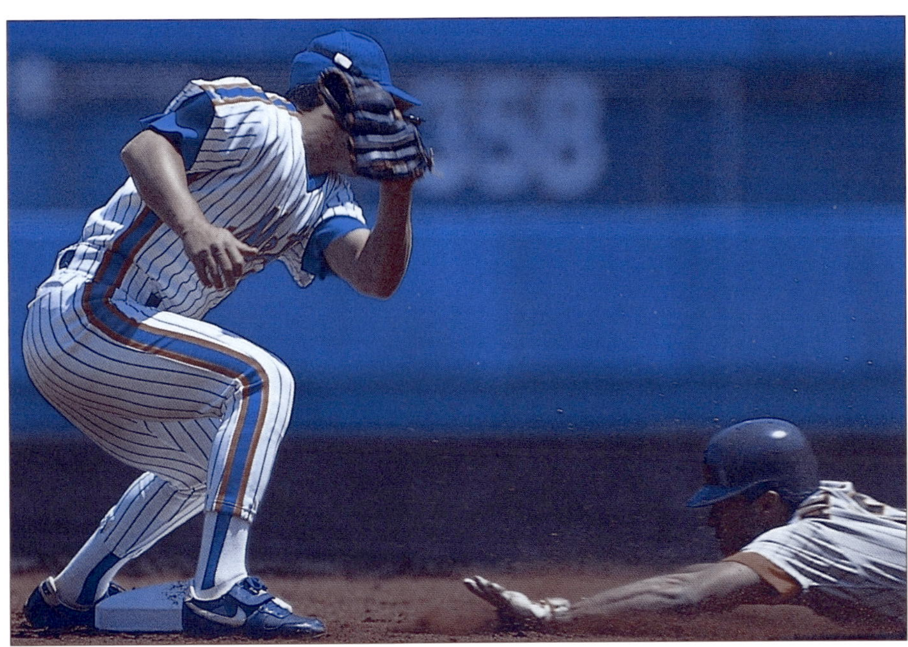

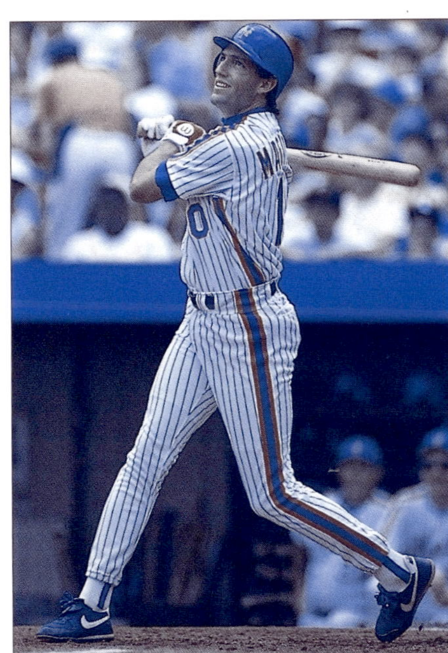

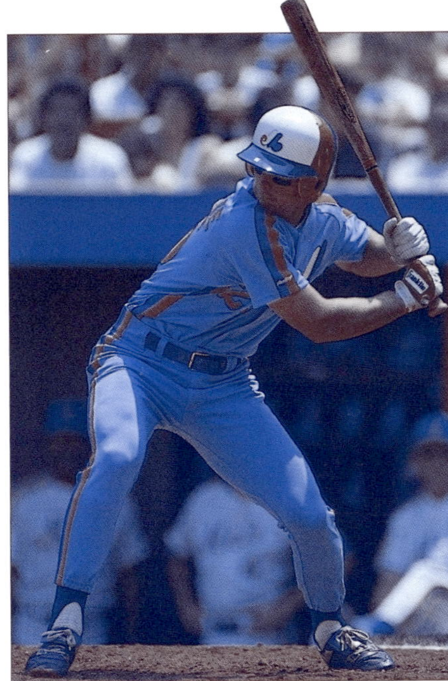

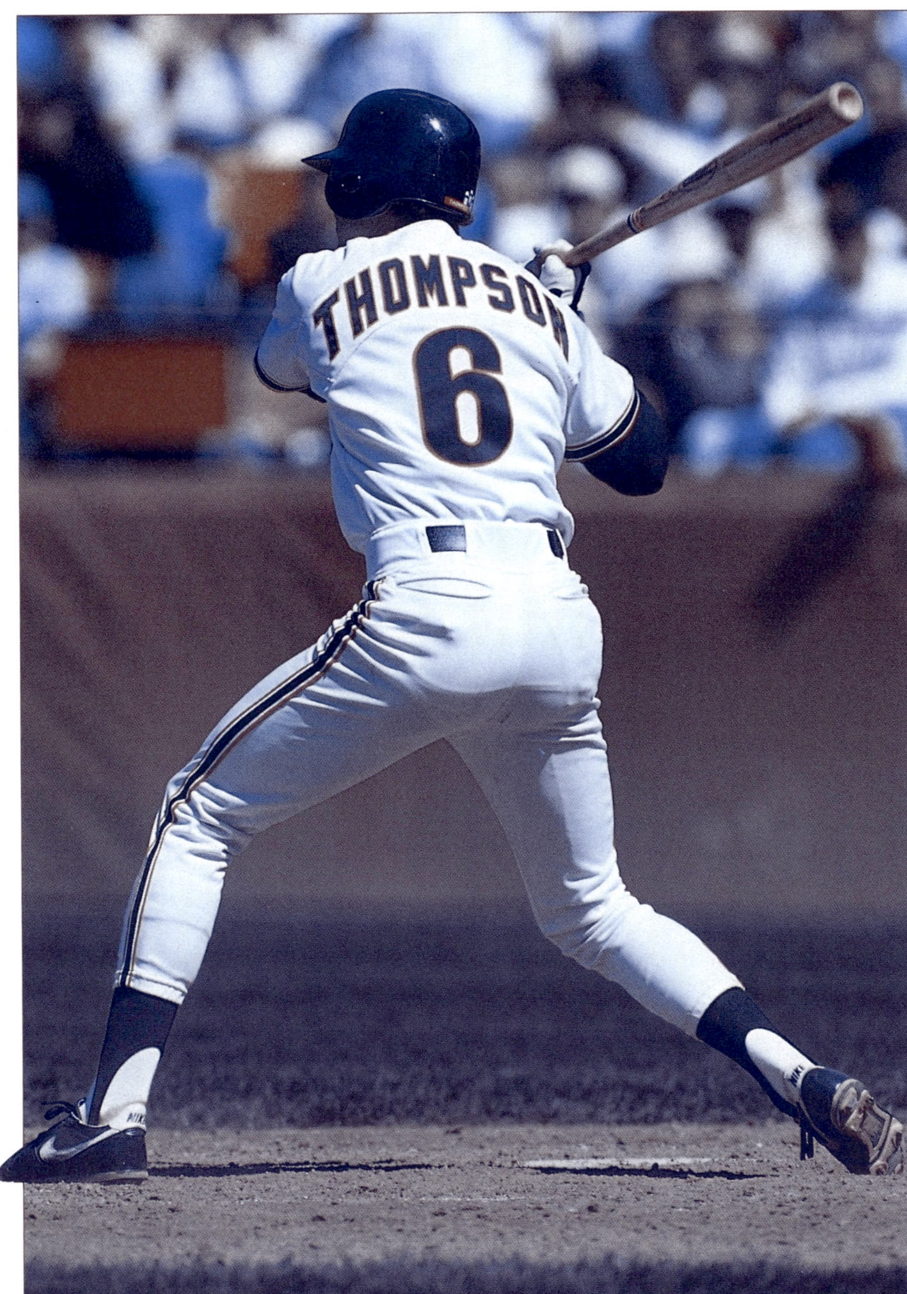

Baseball

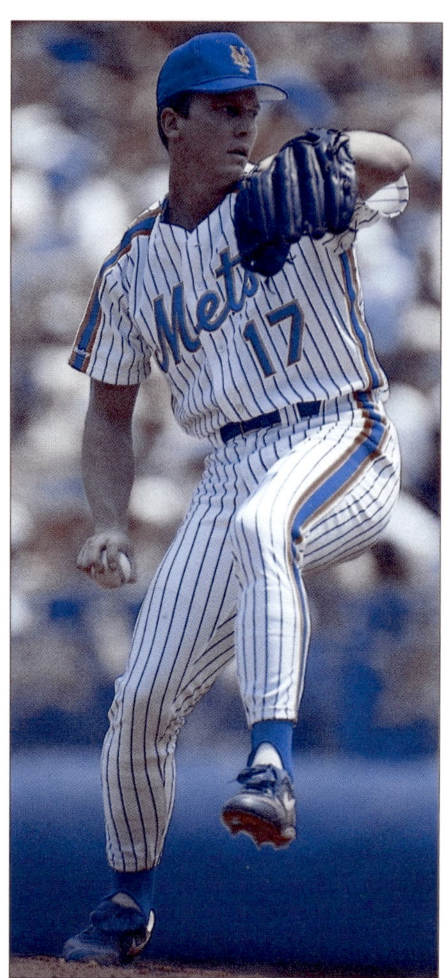

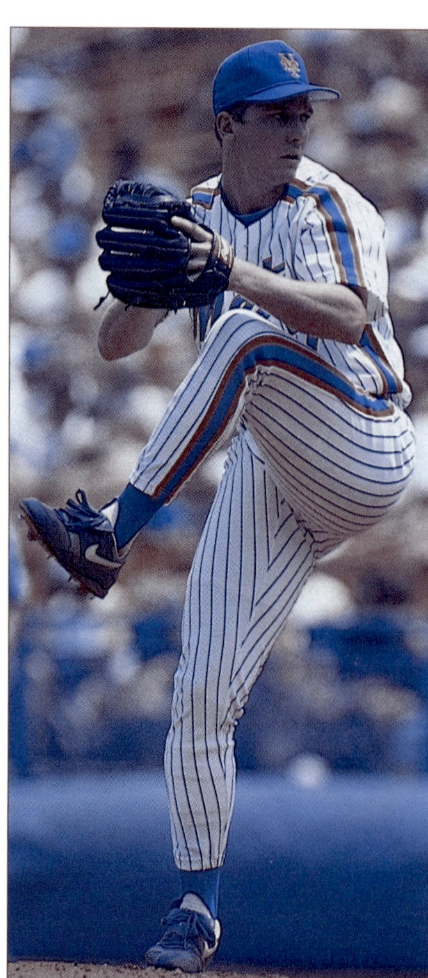

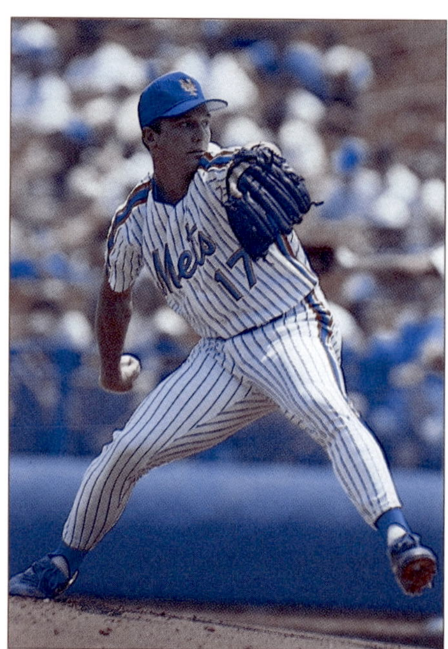

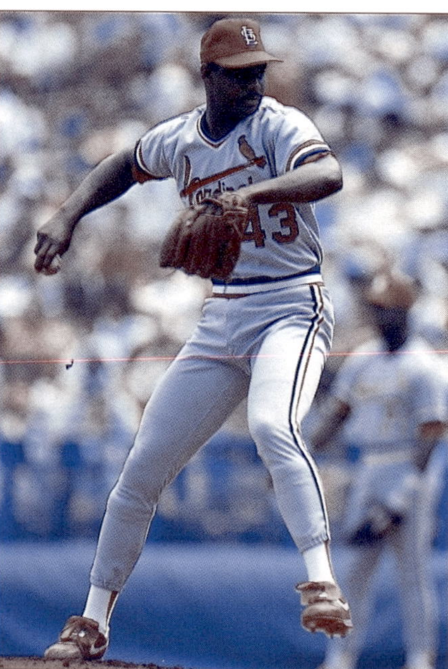

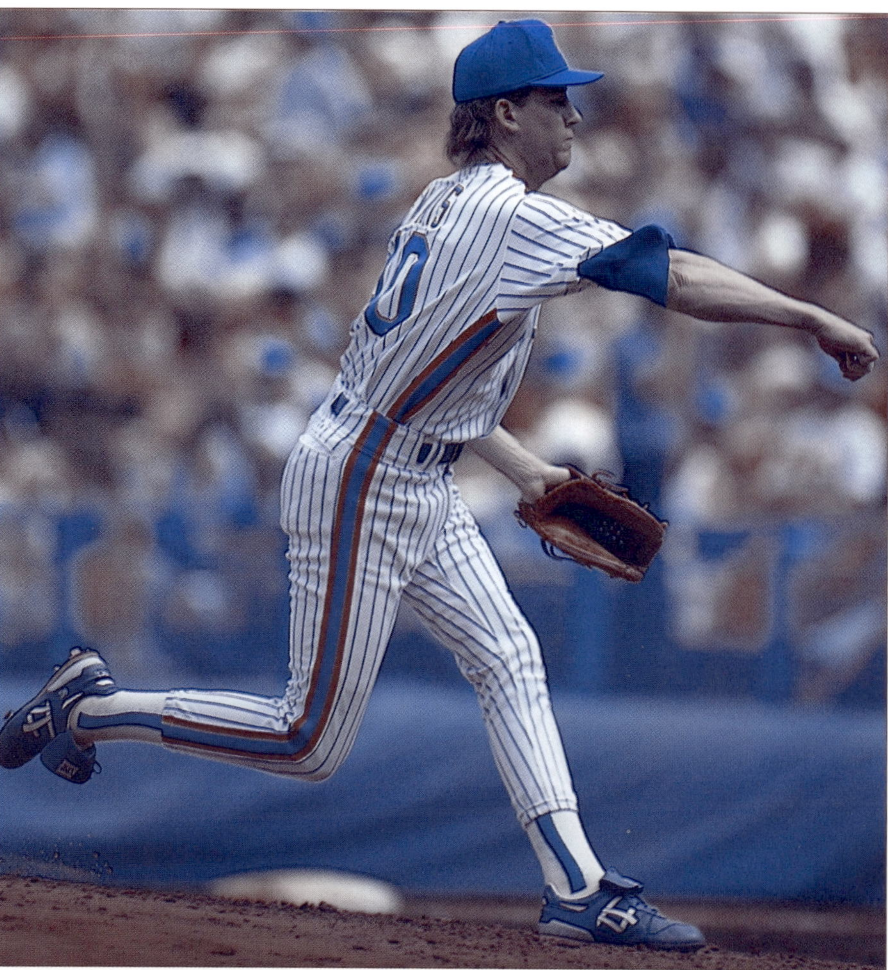

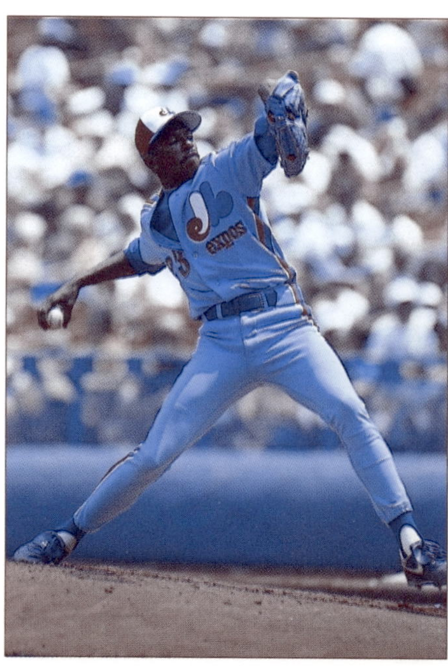

Softball

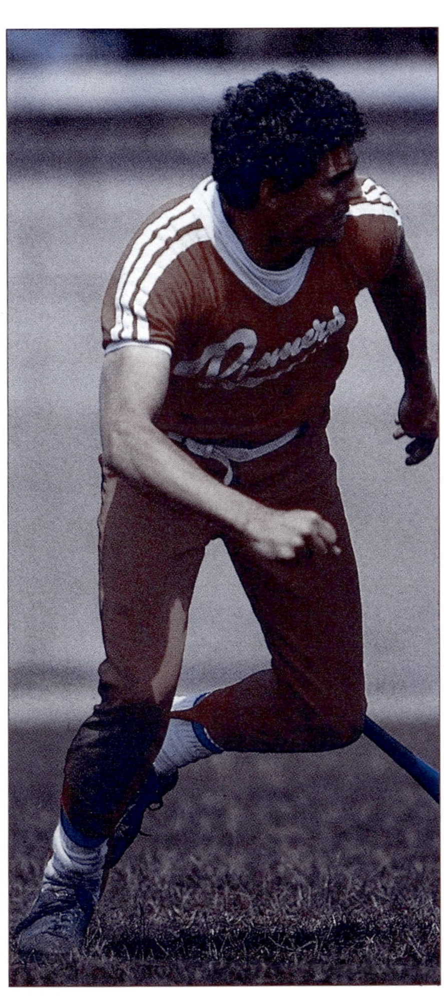

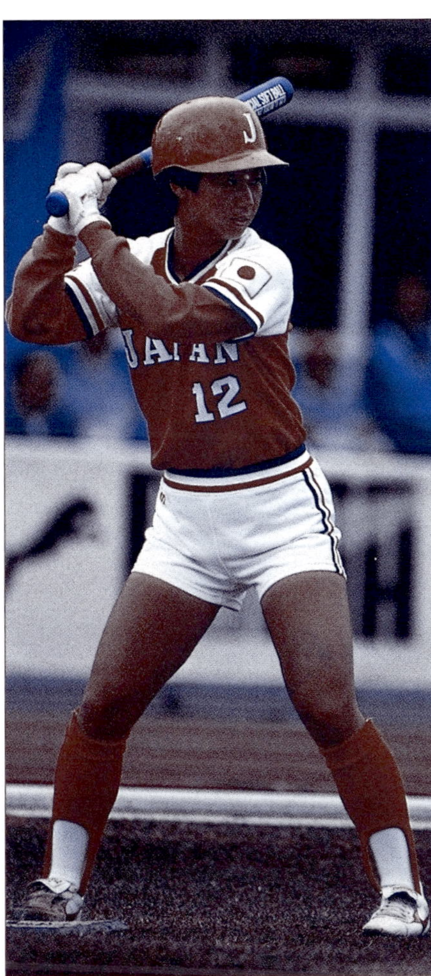

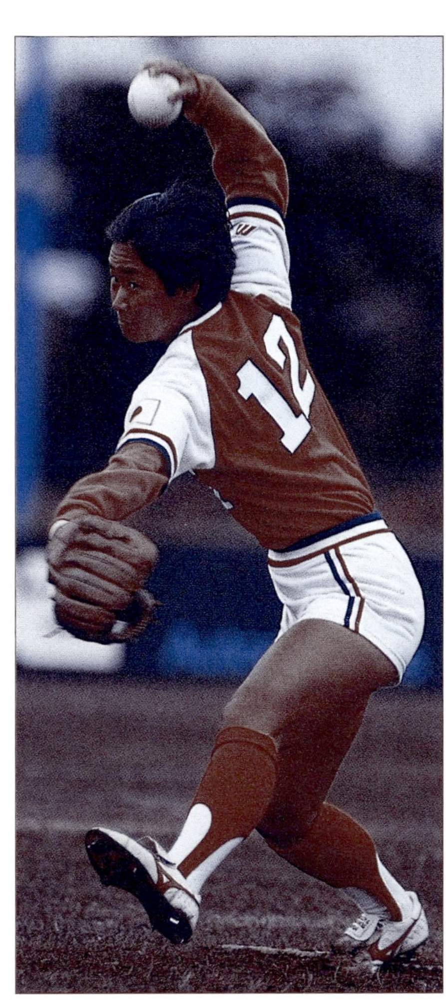

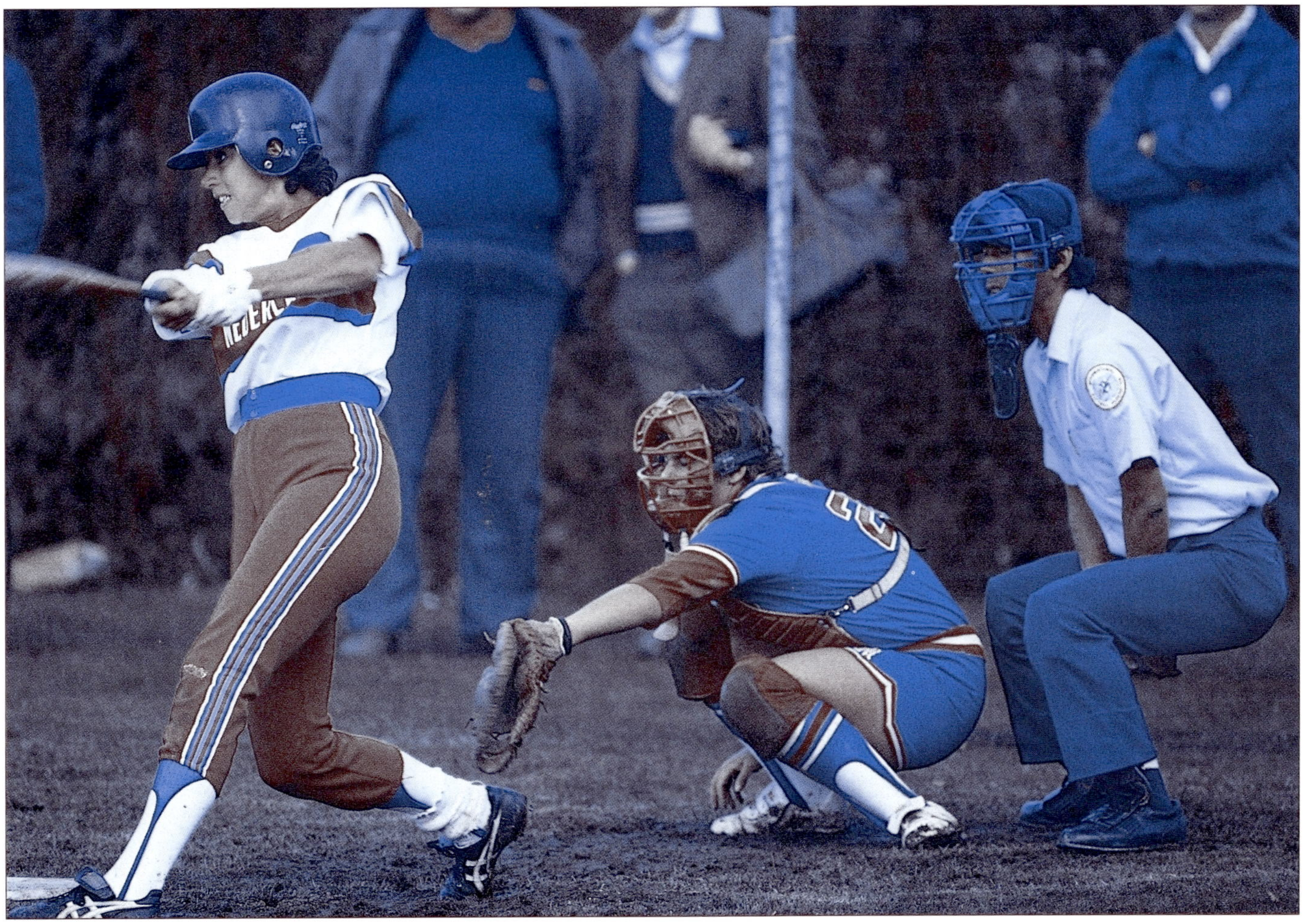

Croquet

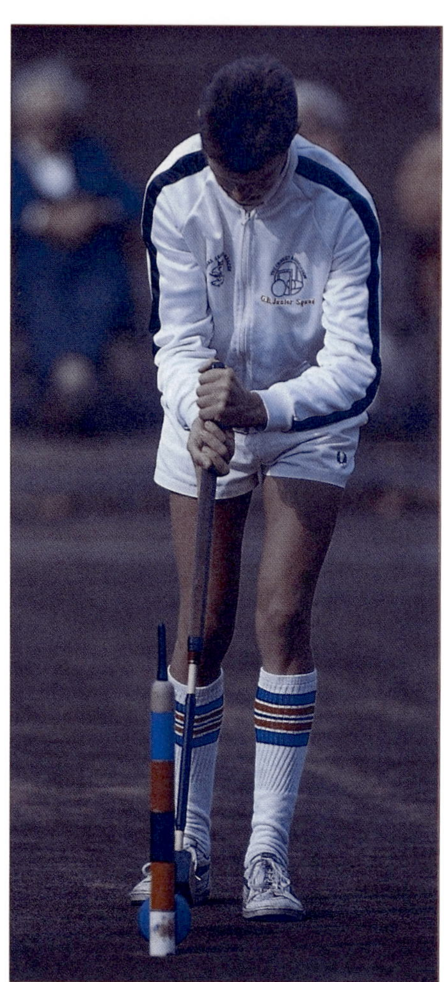

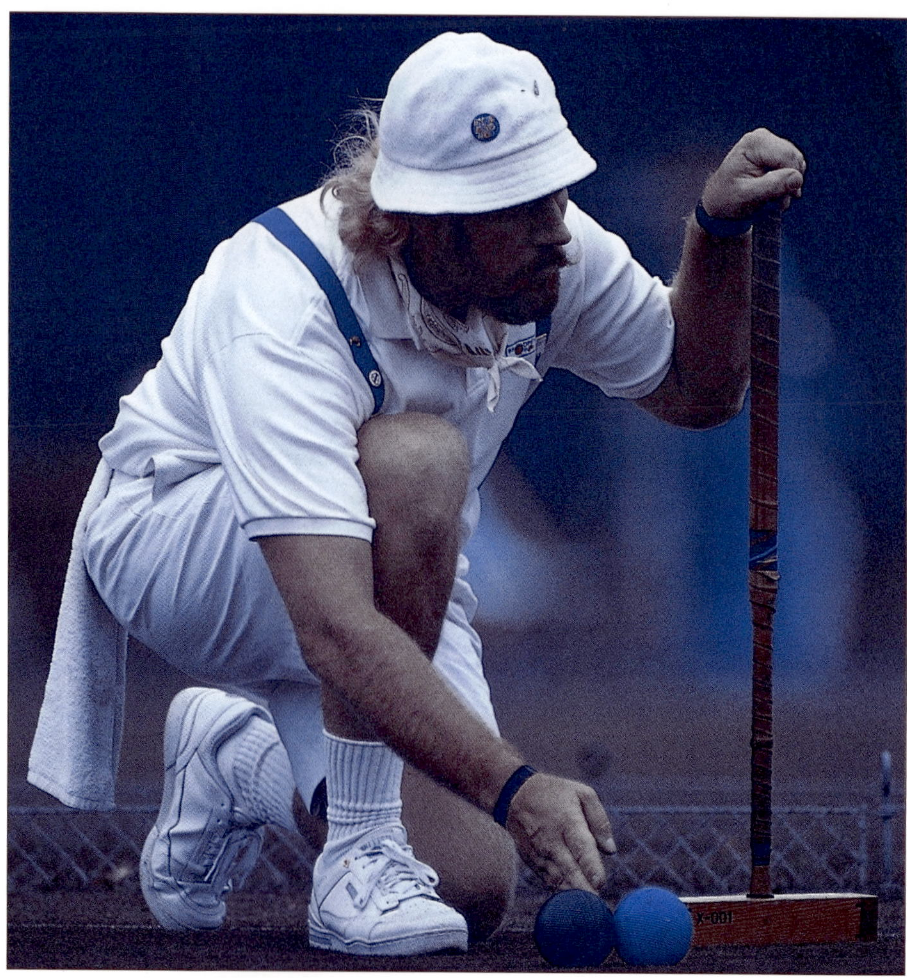

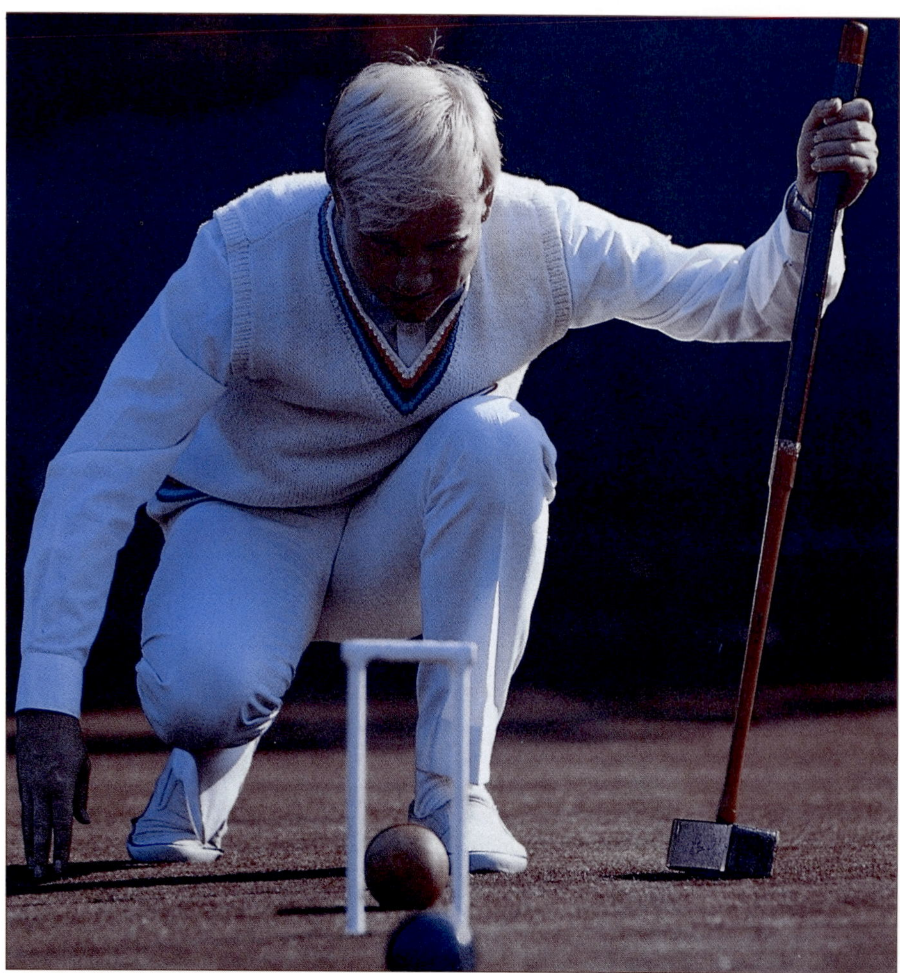

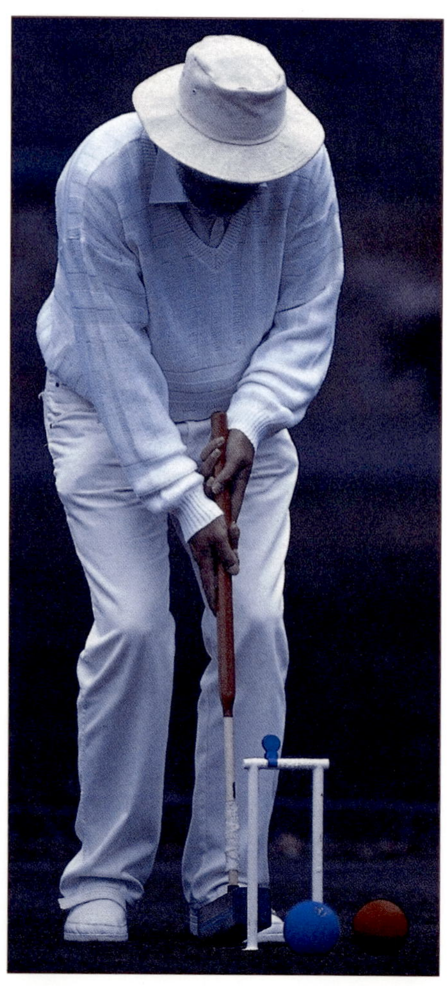

Croquet

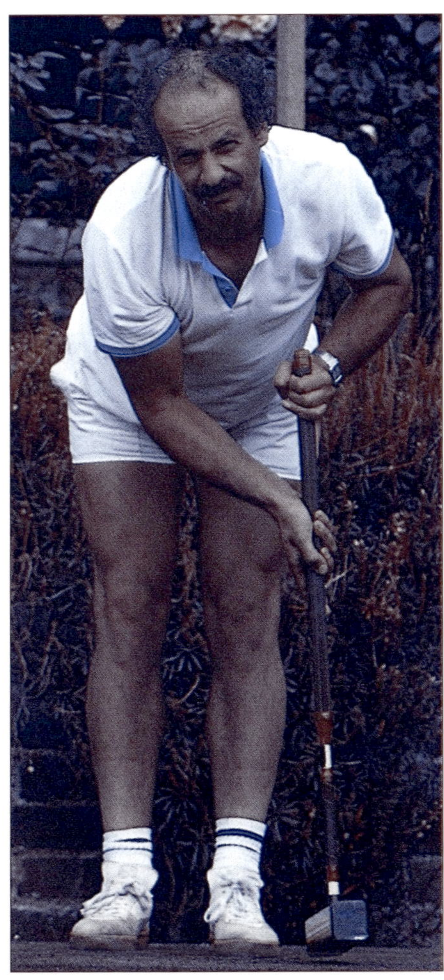

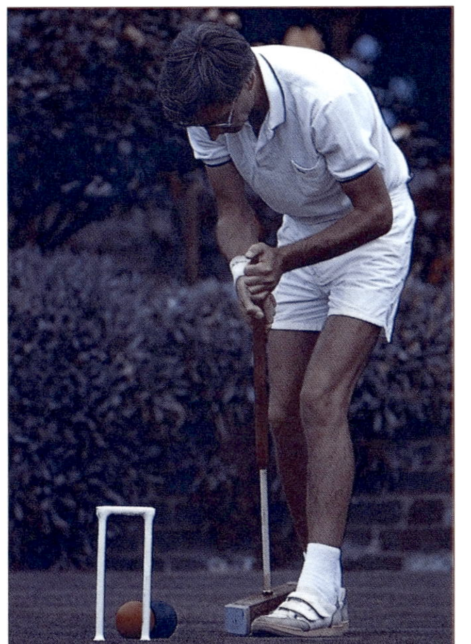

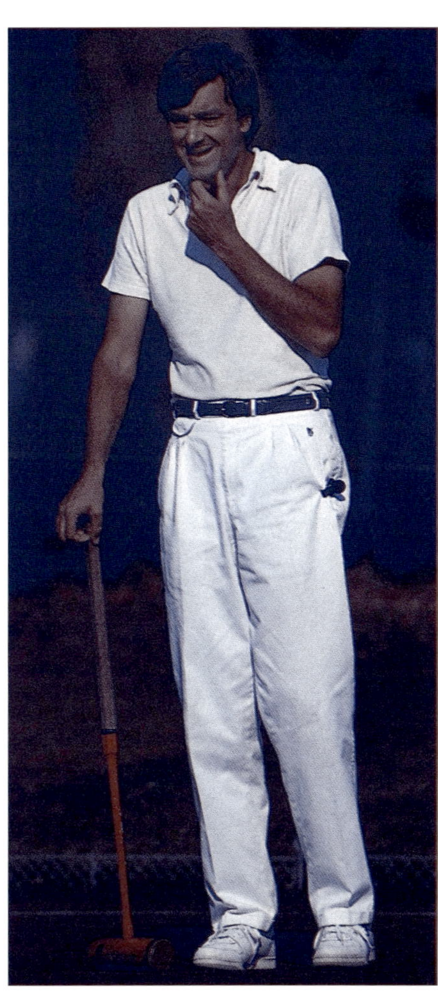

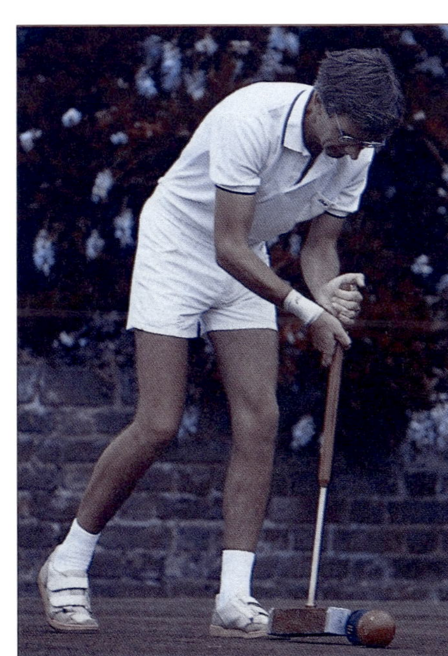

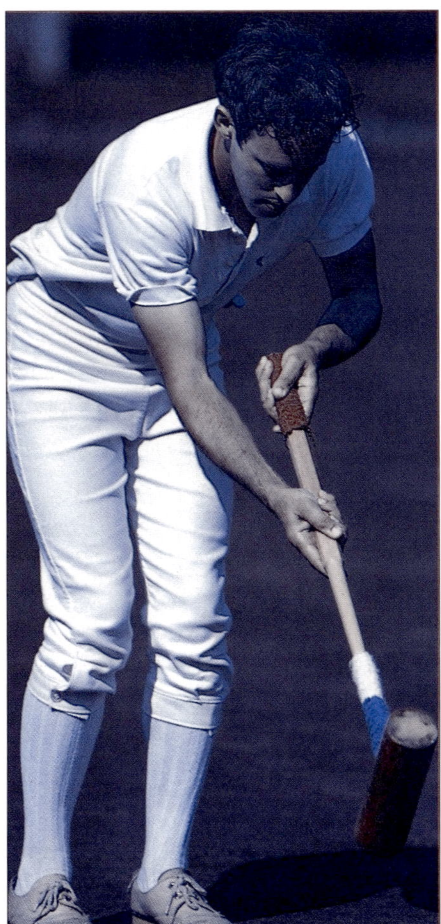

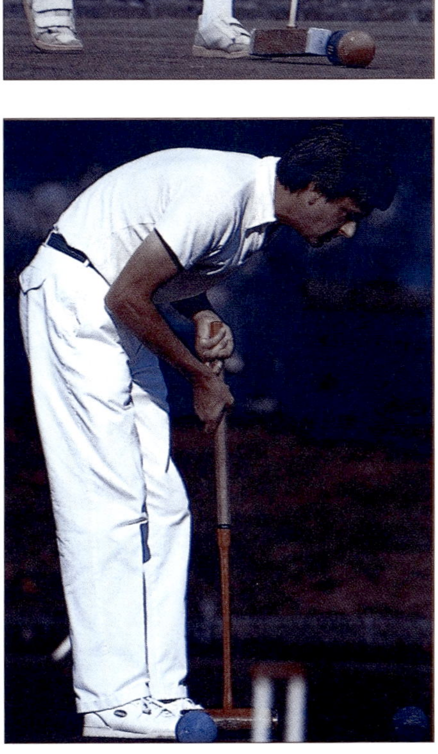

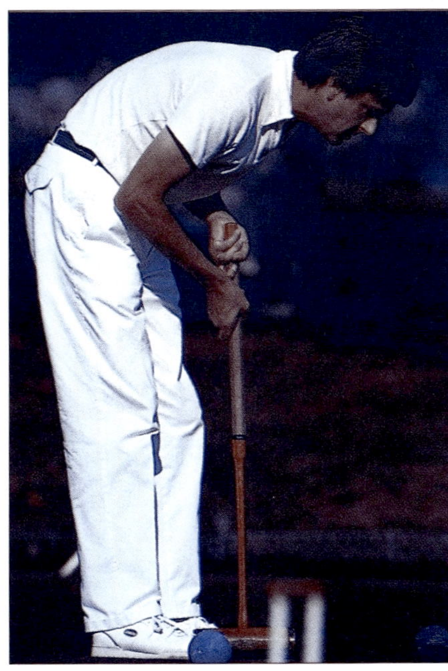

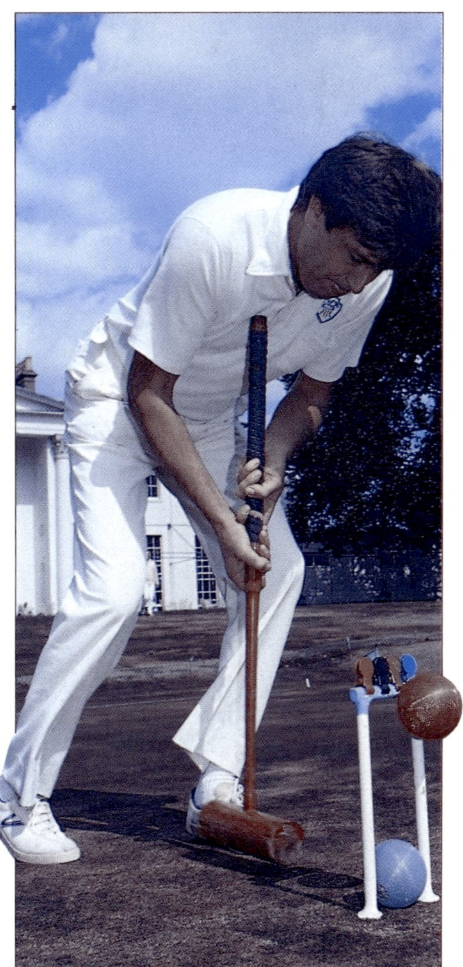

Lacrosse

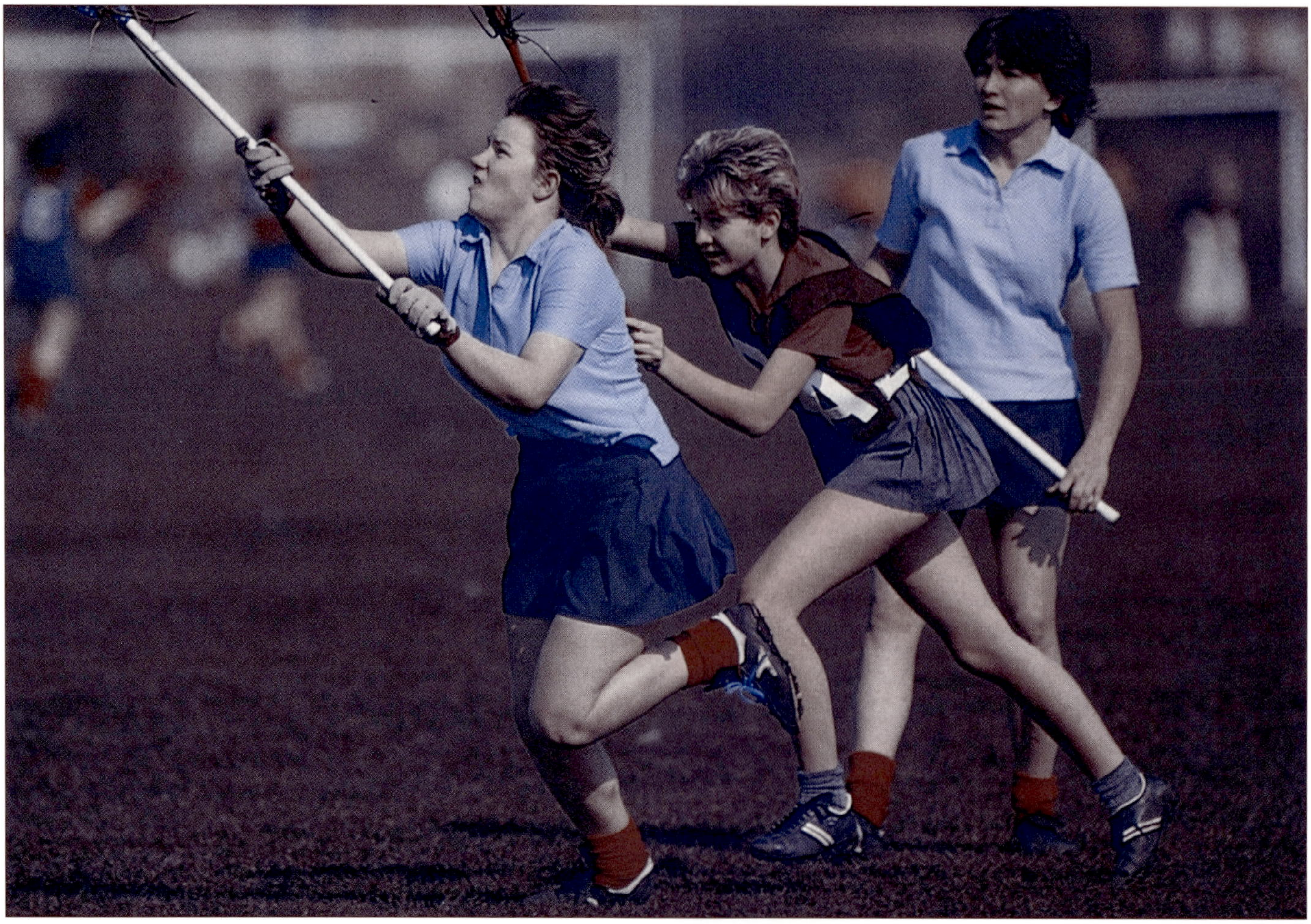

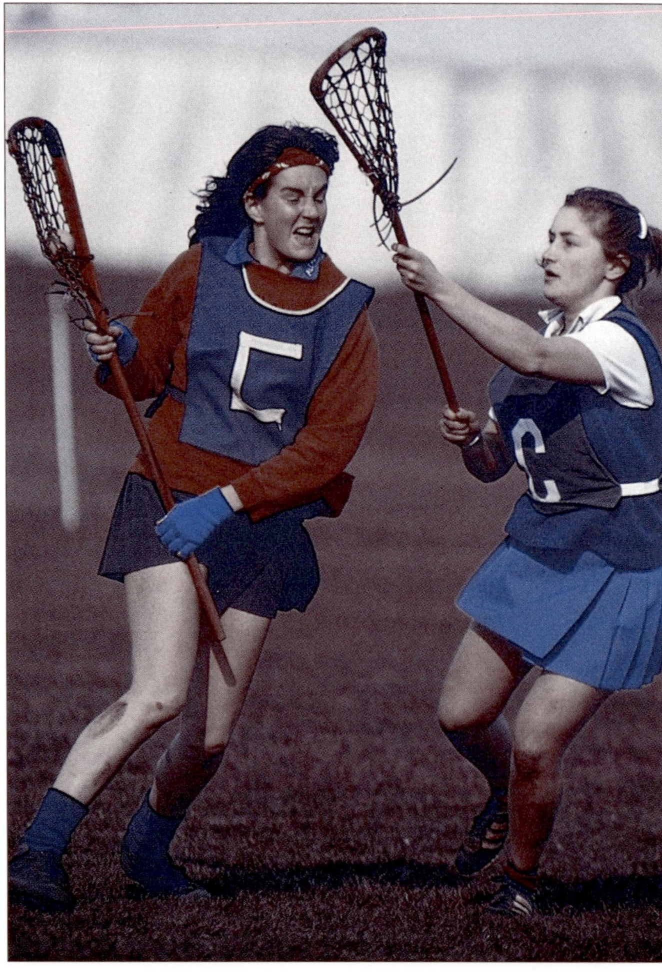

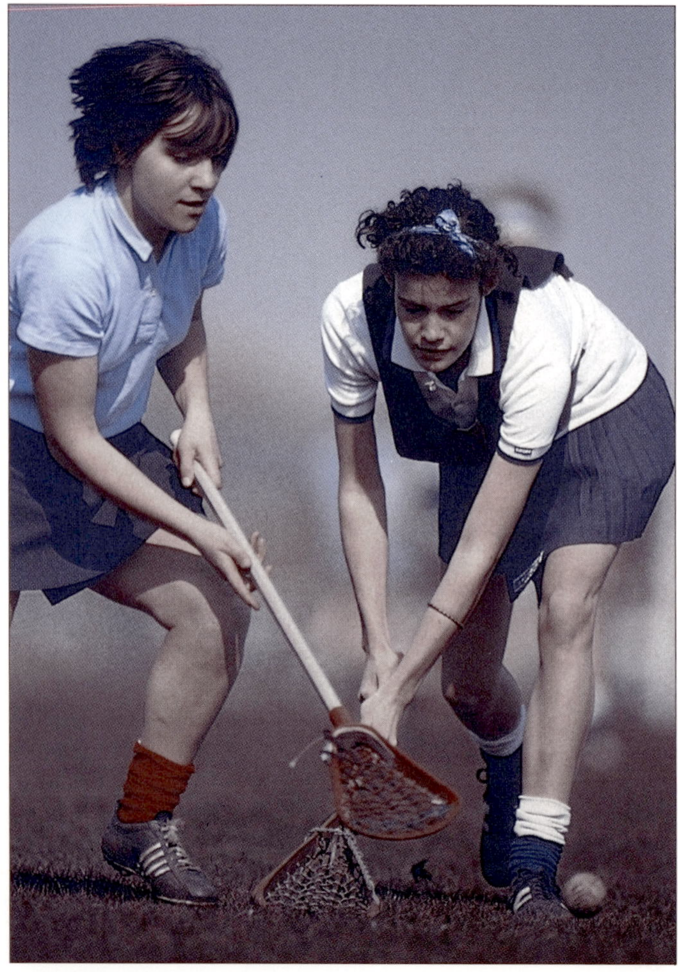

Lacrosse

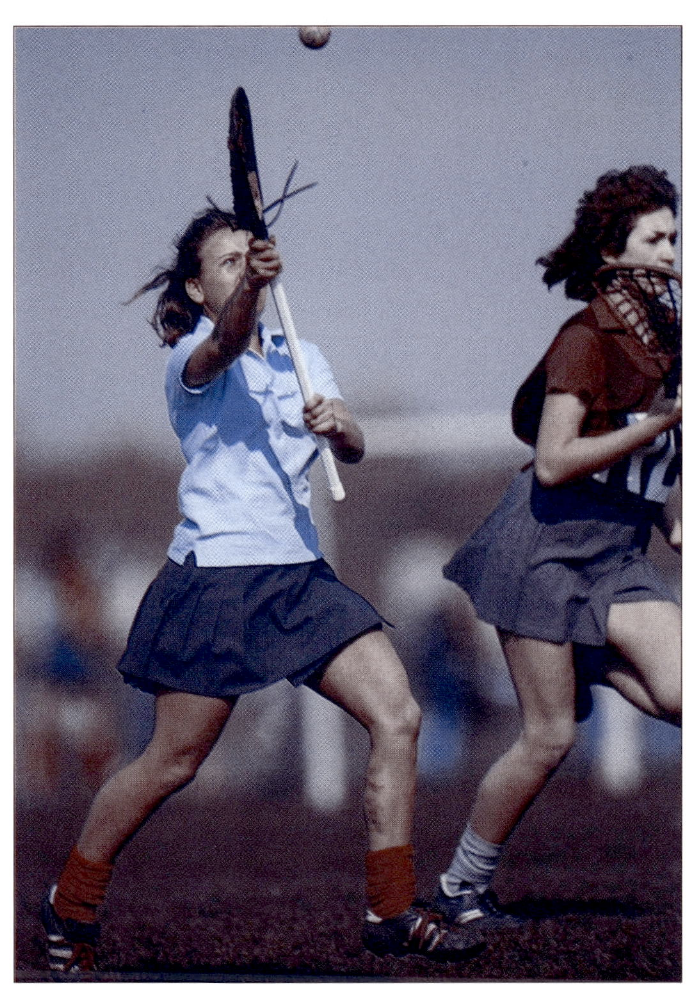

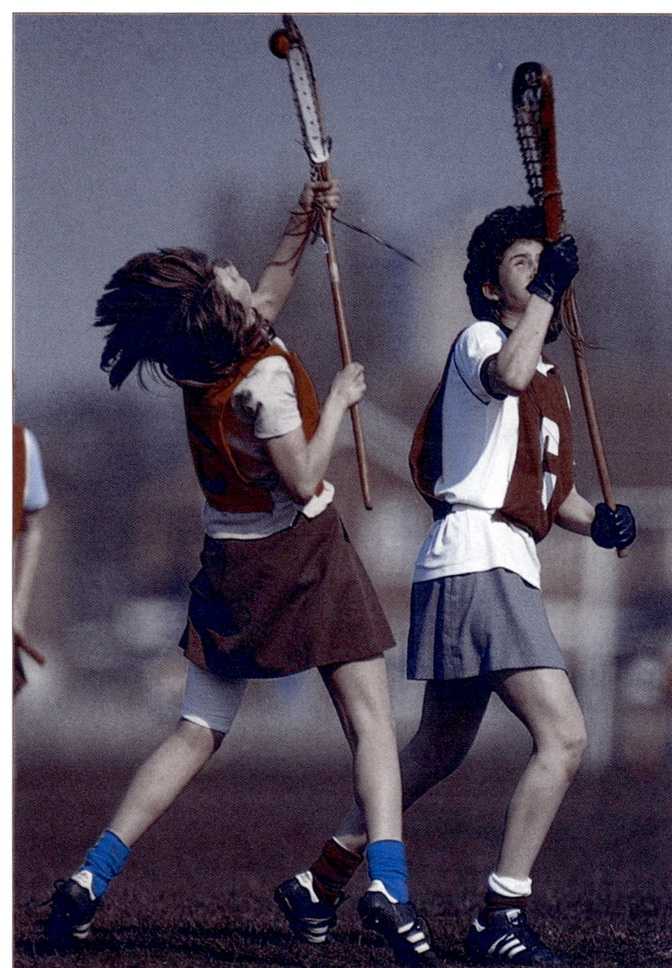

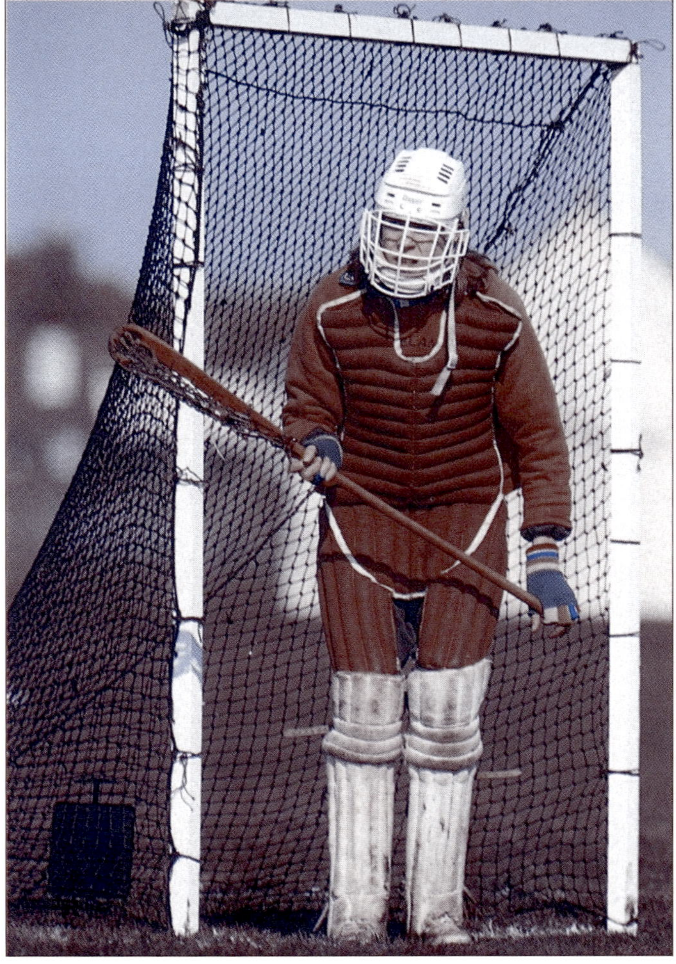

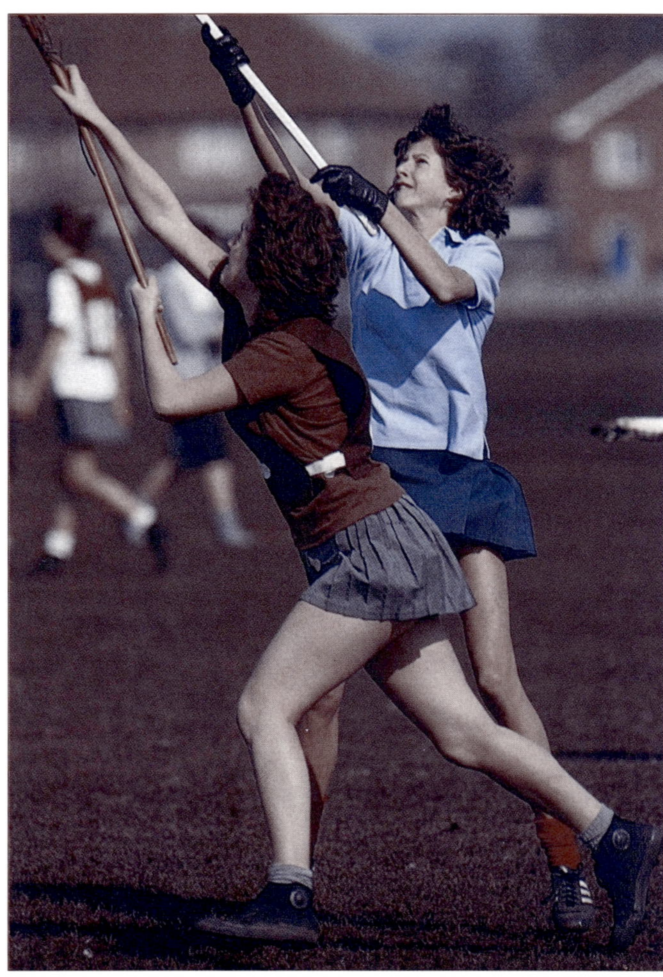

Cricket – male

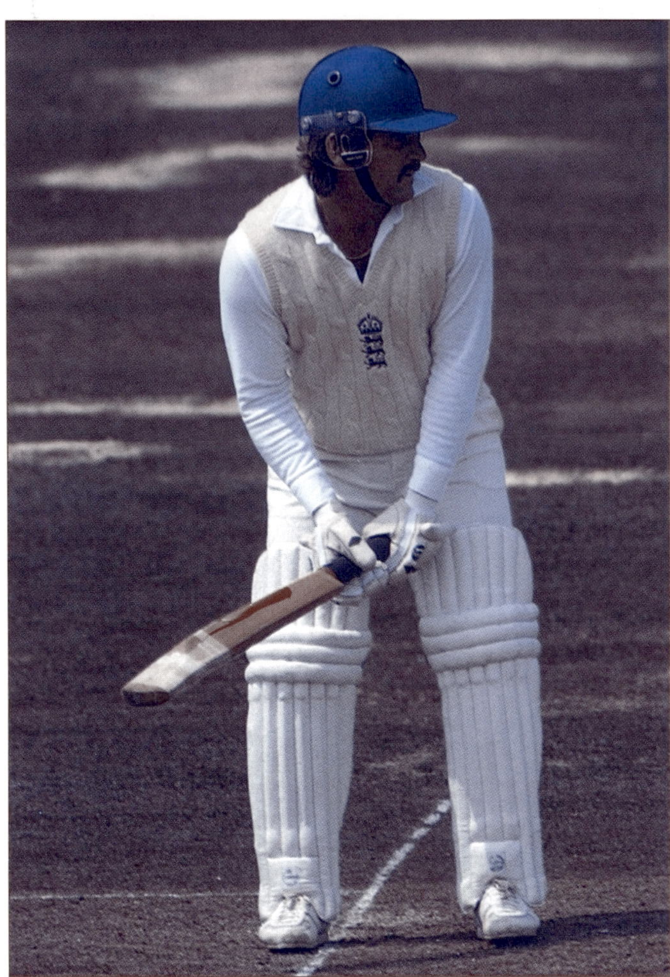

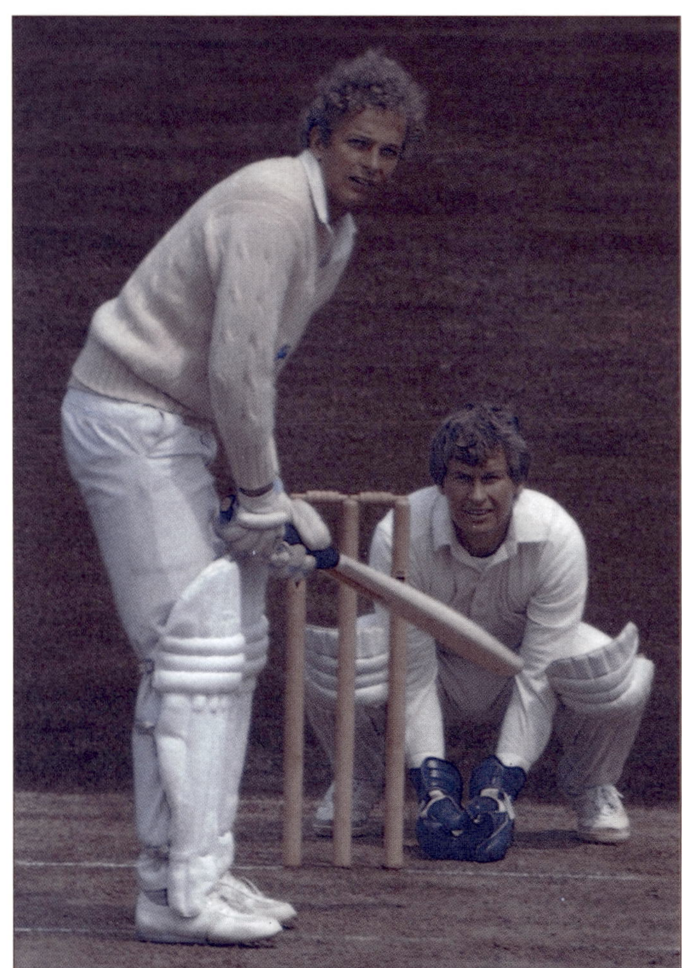

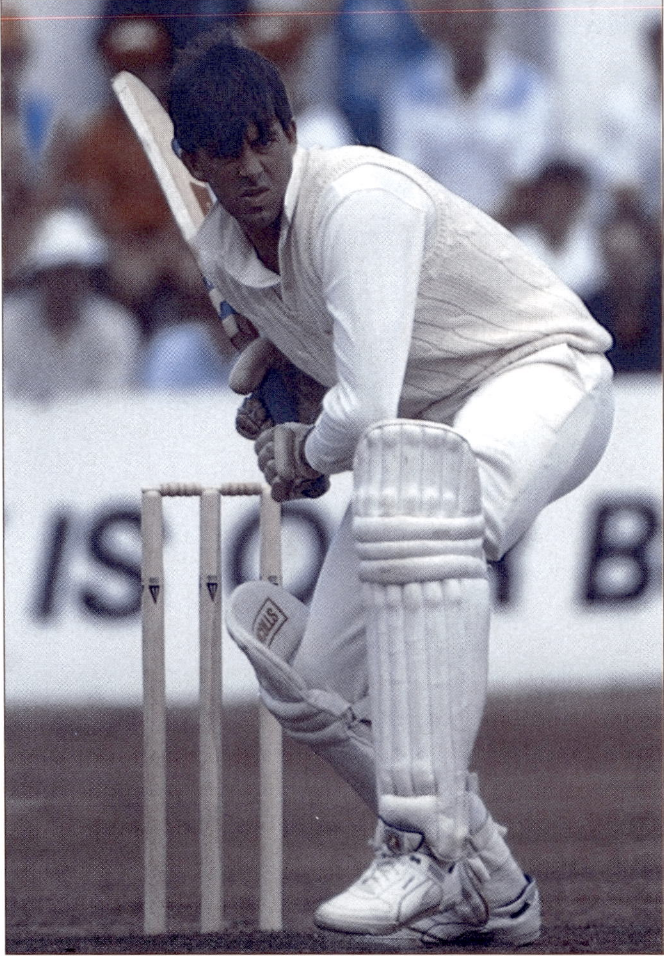

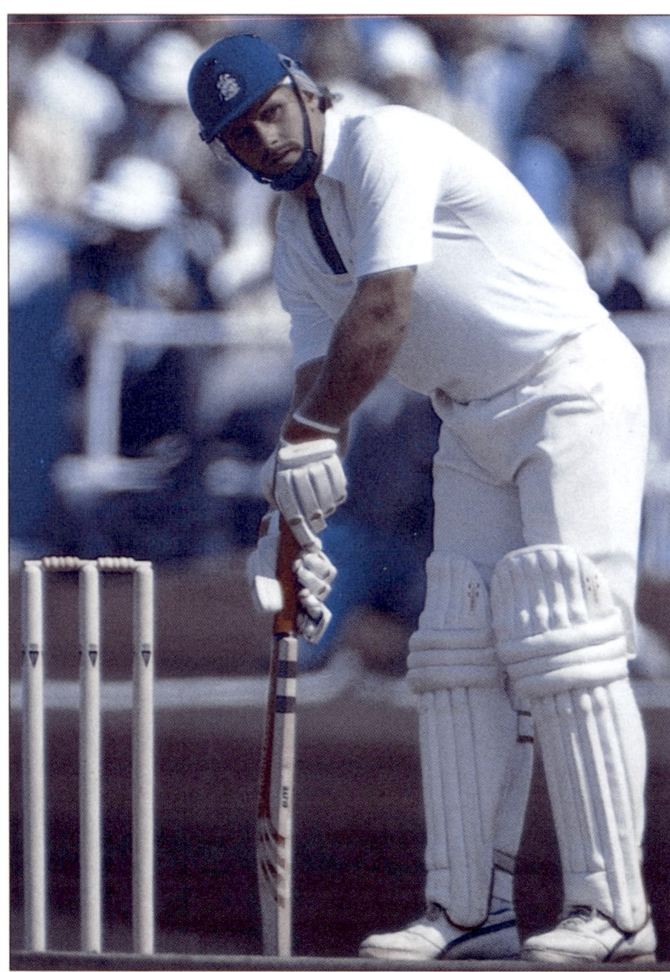

Cricket – male

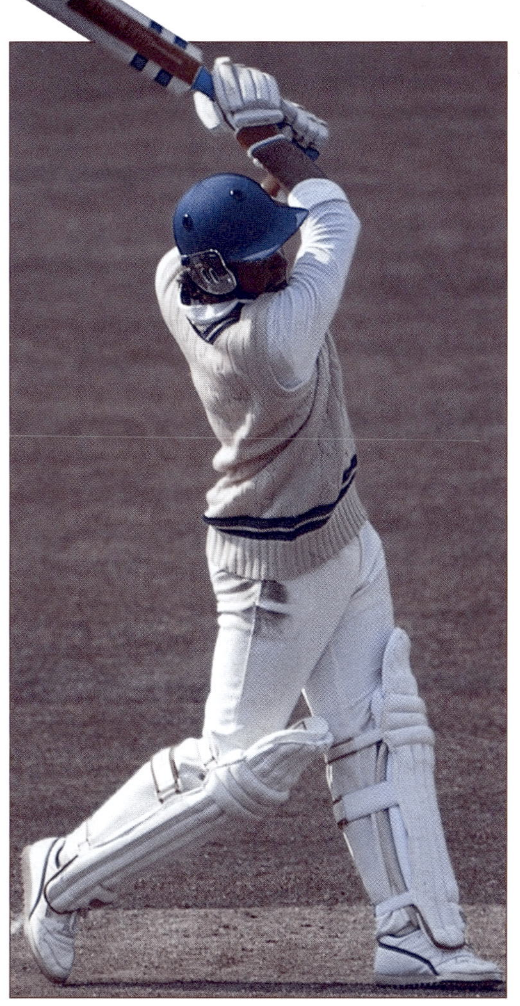

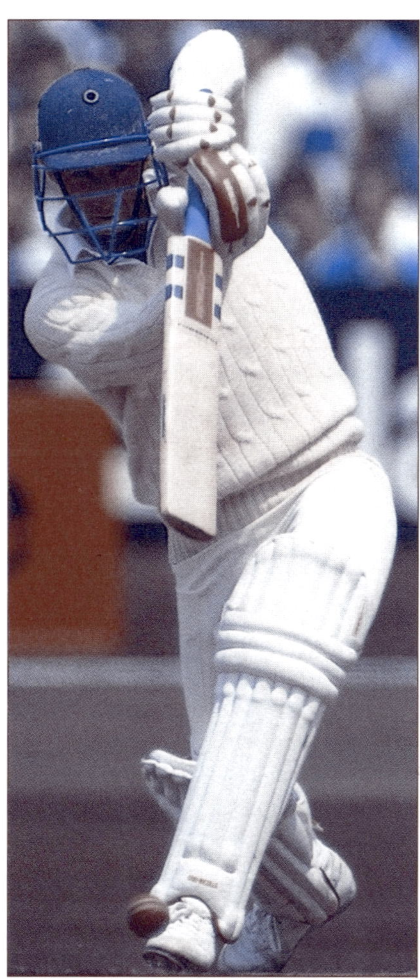

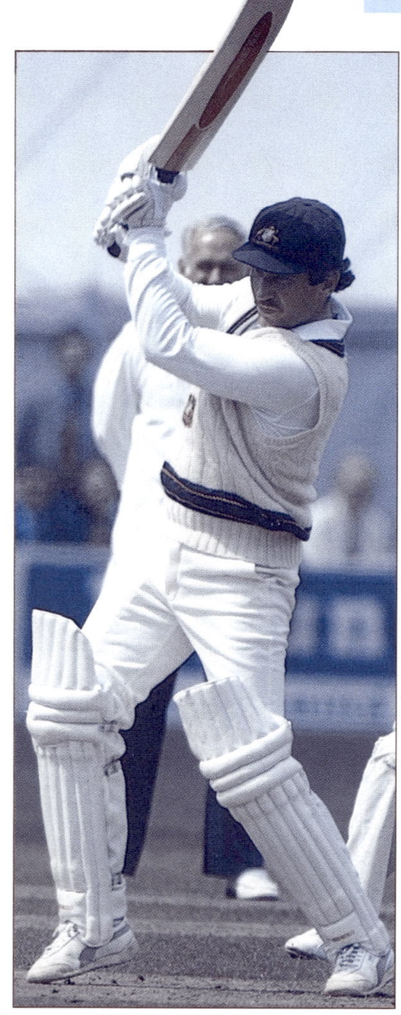

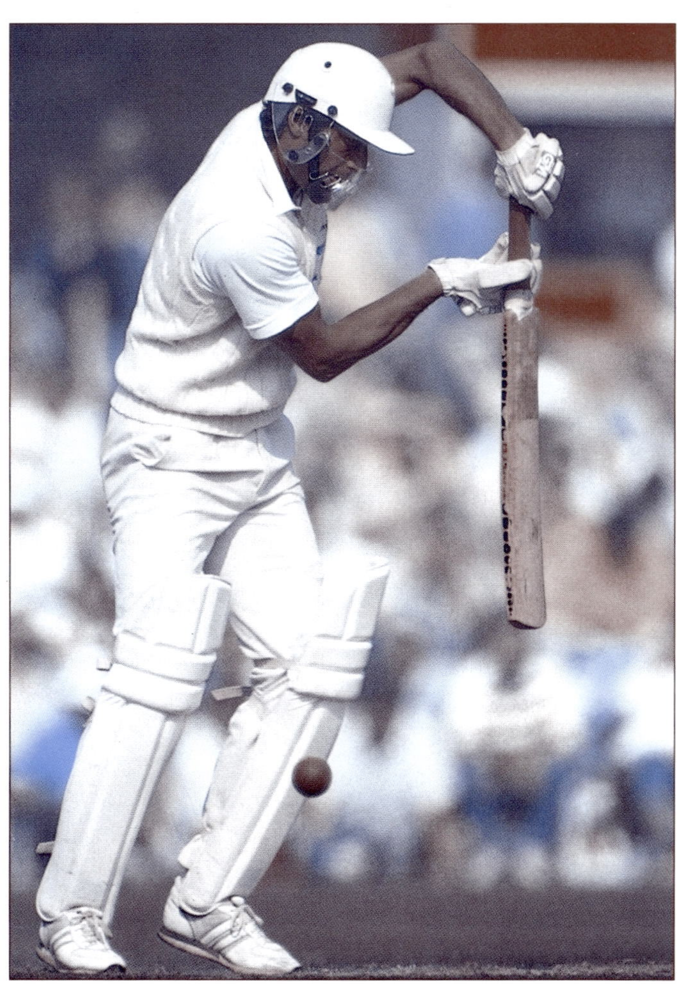

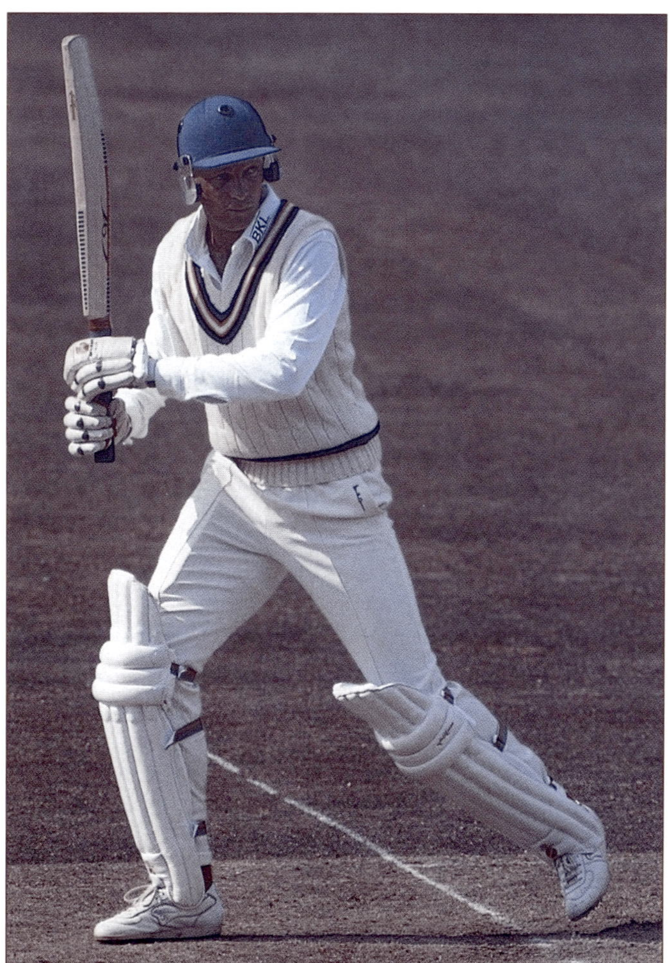

Cricket – male

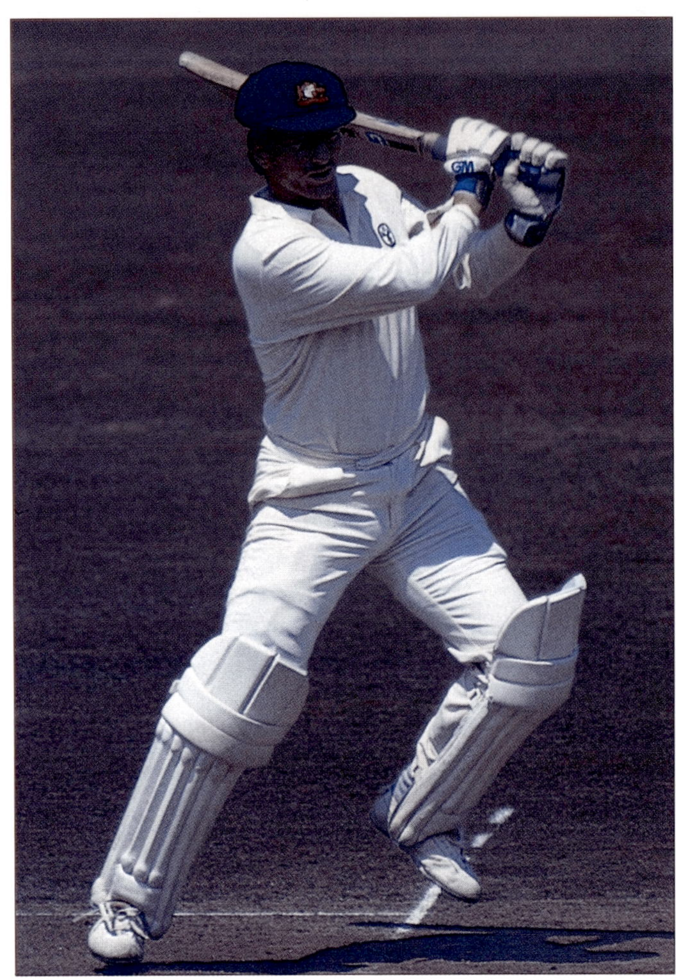

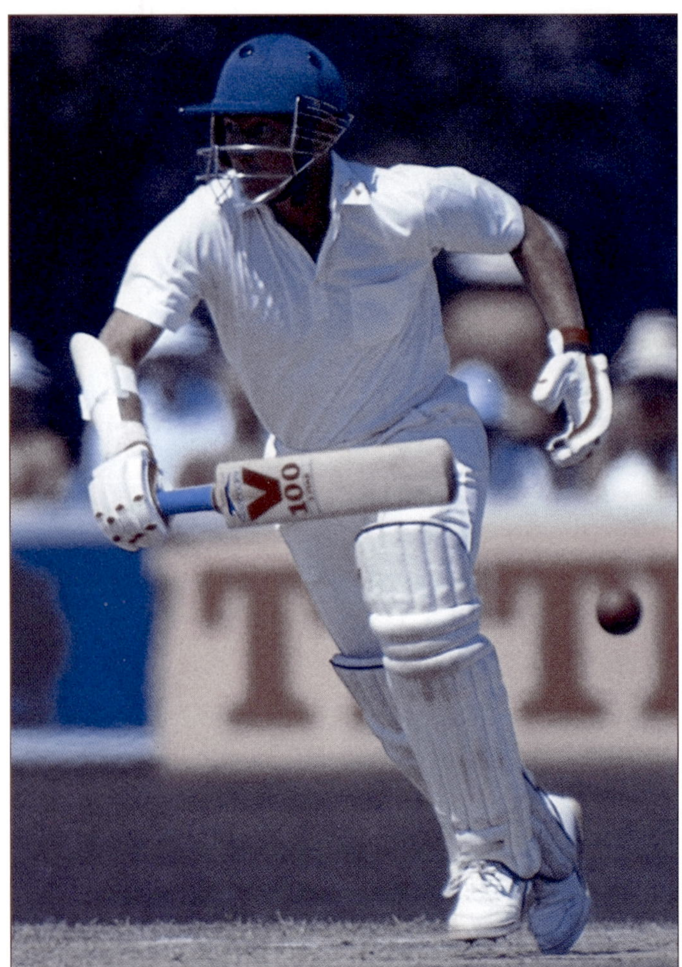

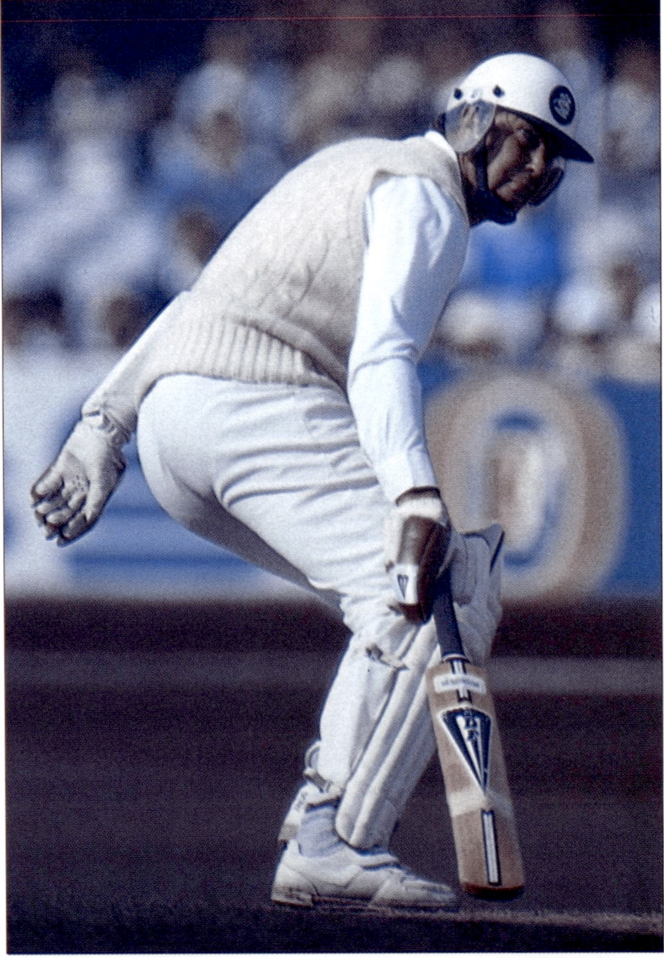

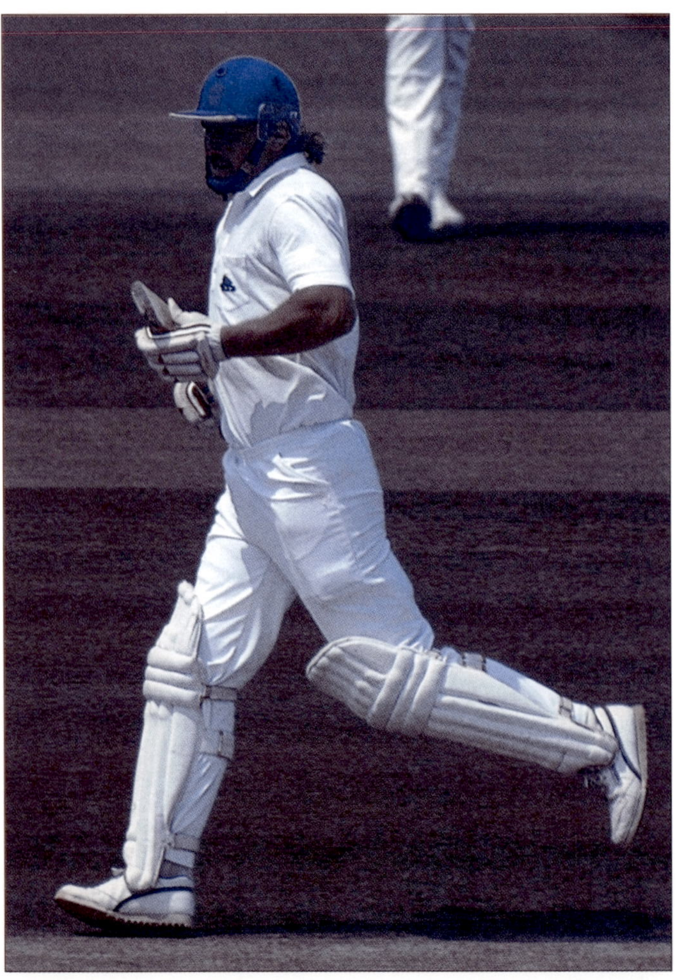

Cricket – male

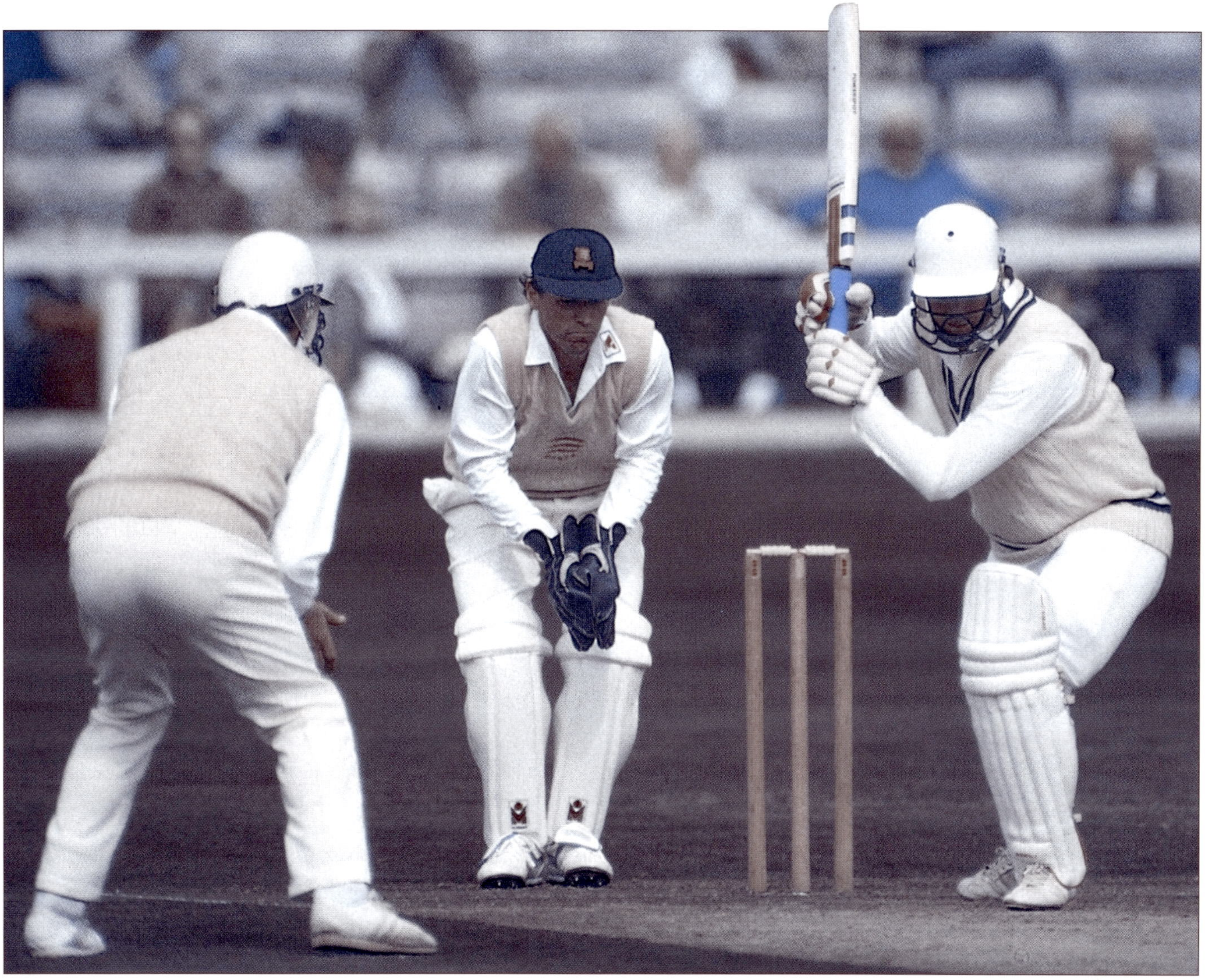

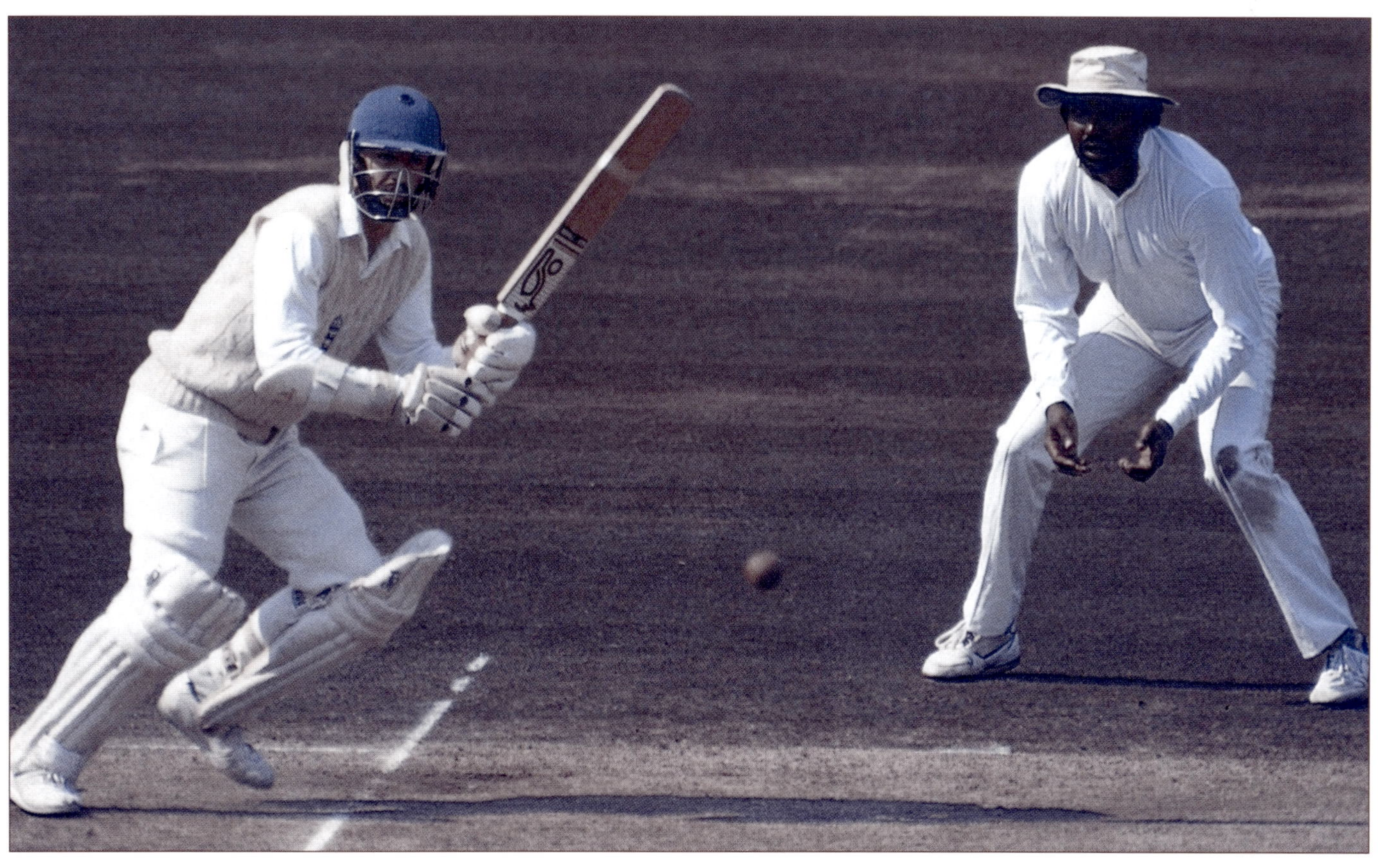

Cricket – male

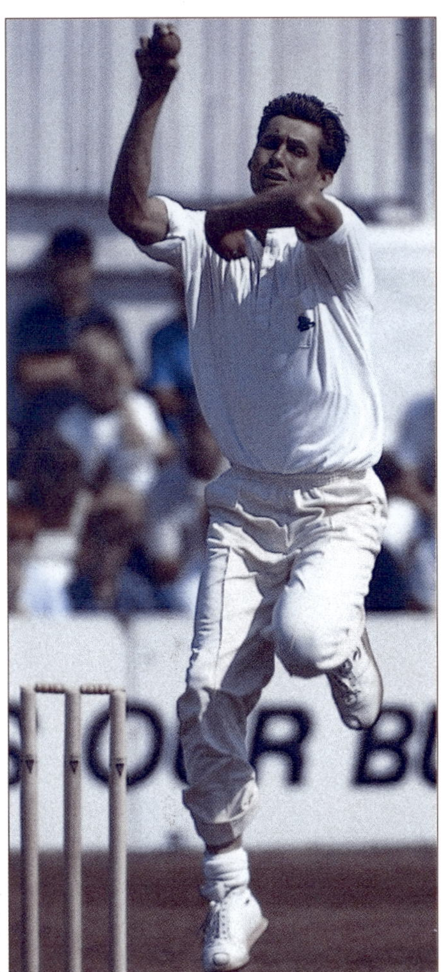

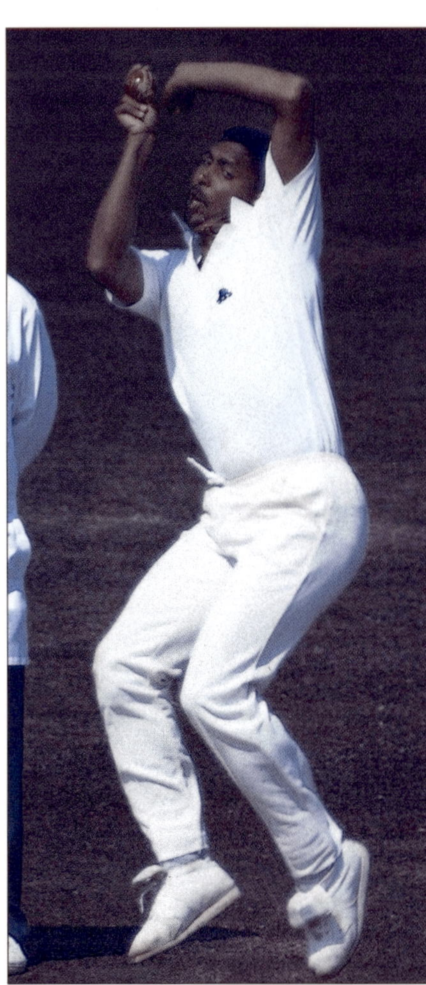

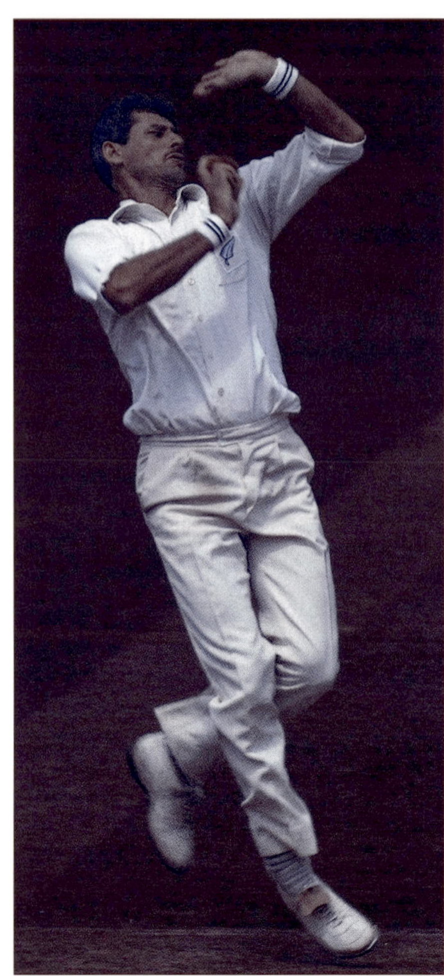

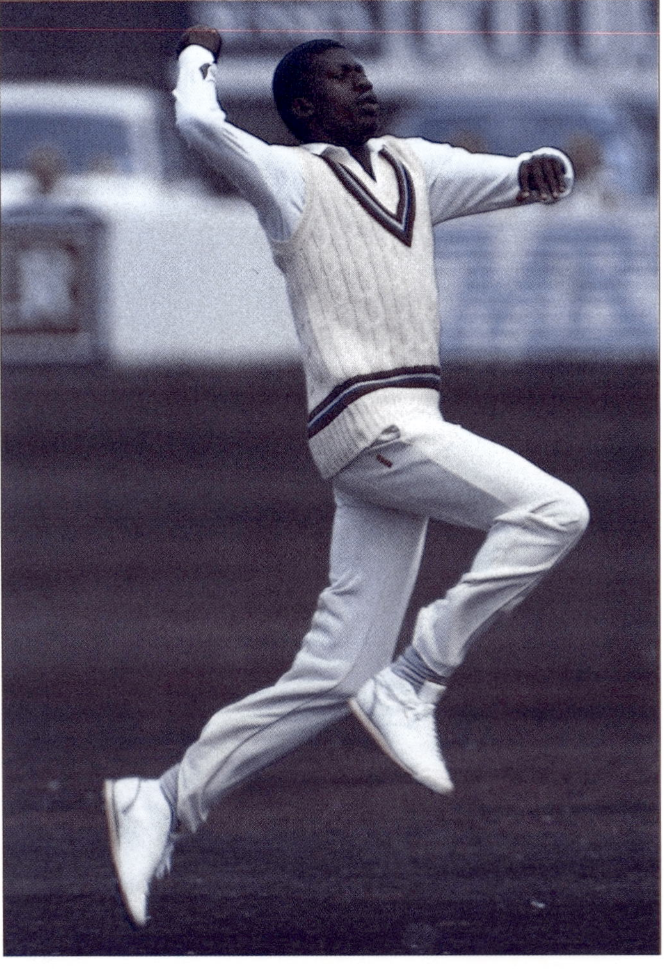

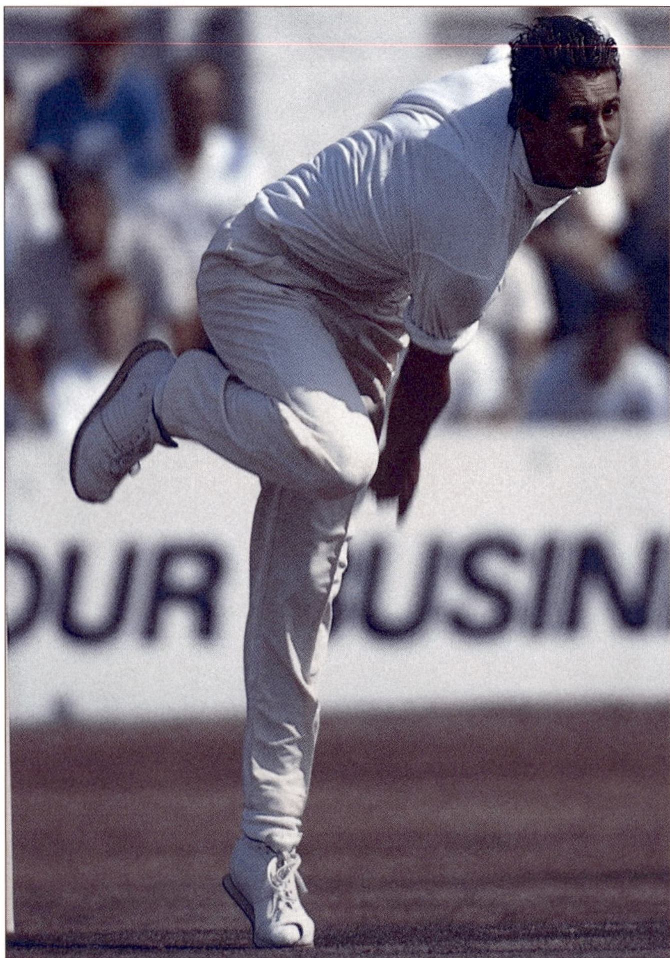

Cricket – male

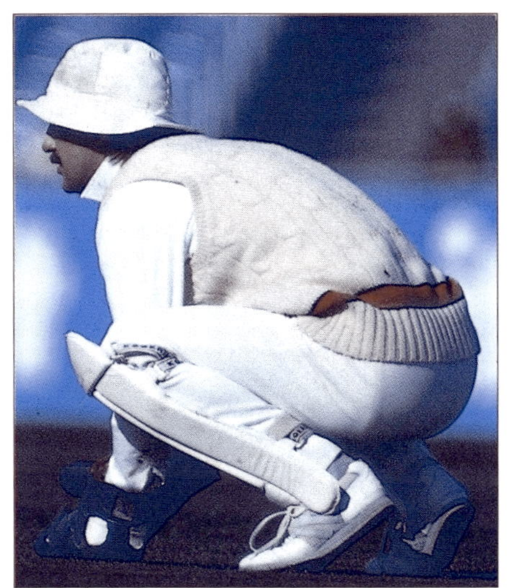

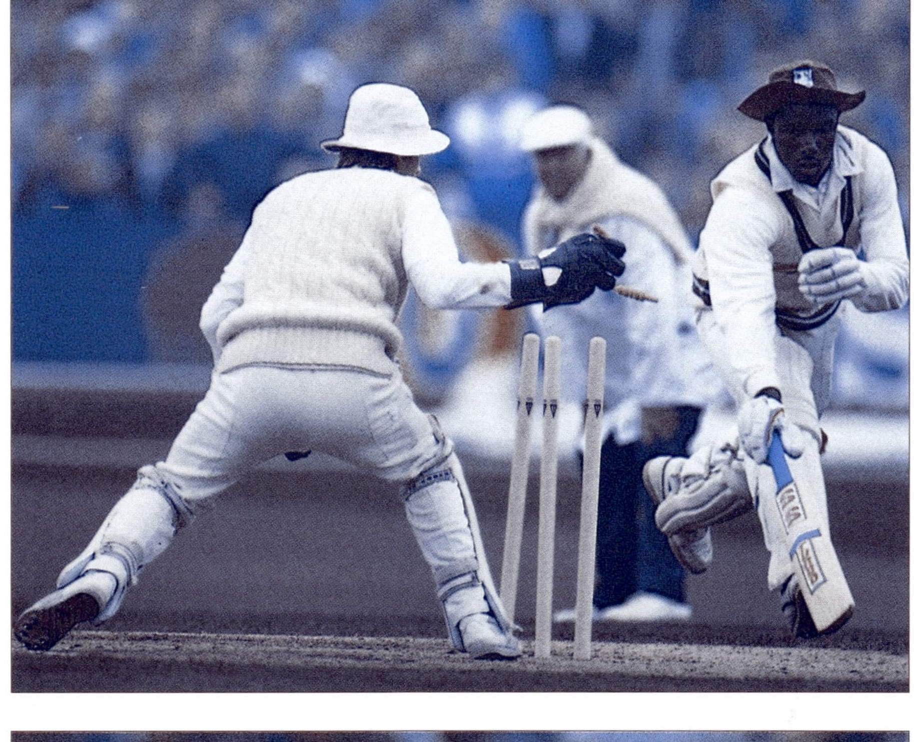

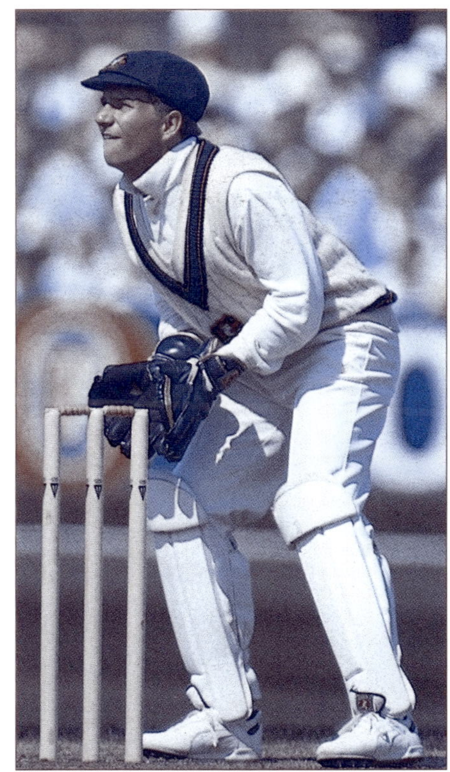

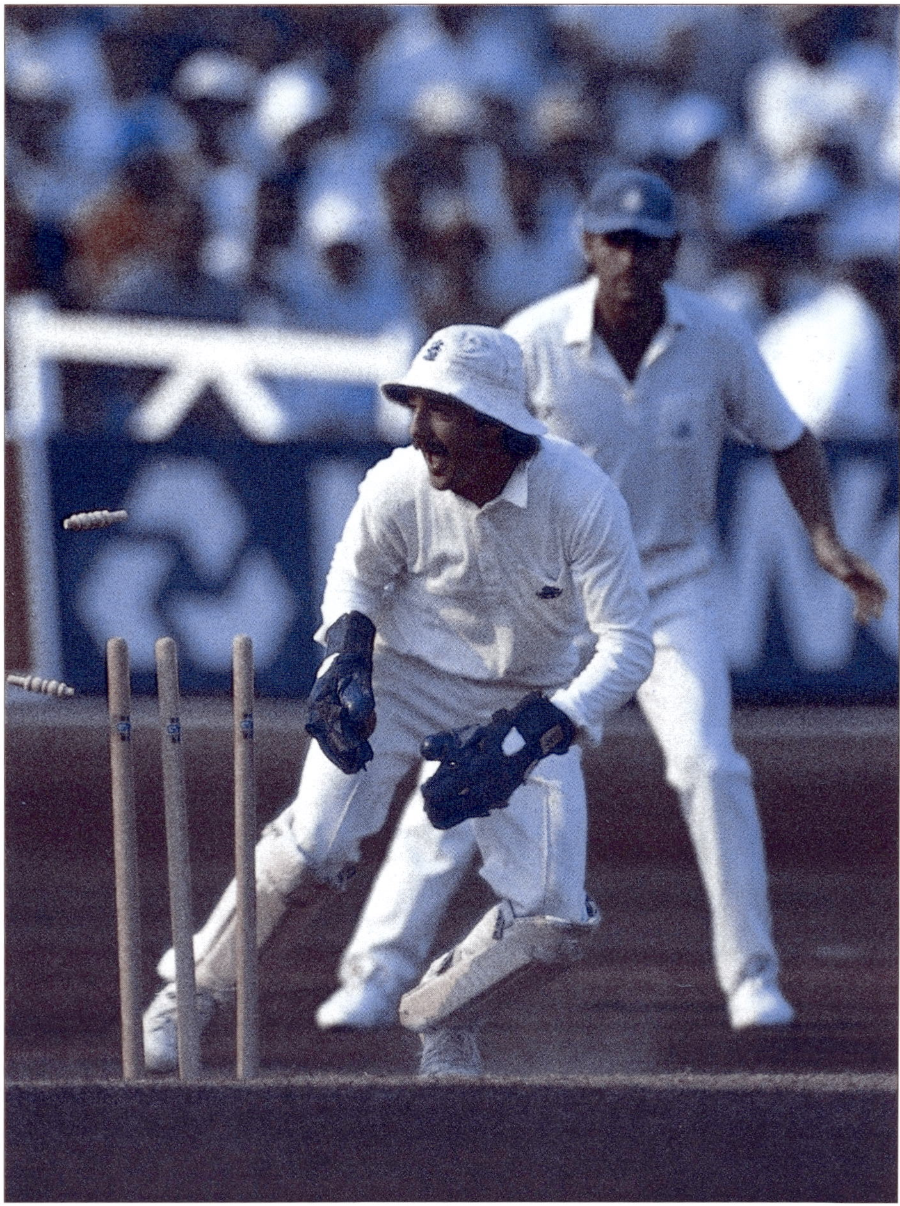

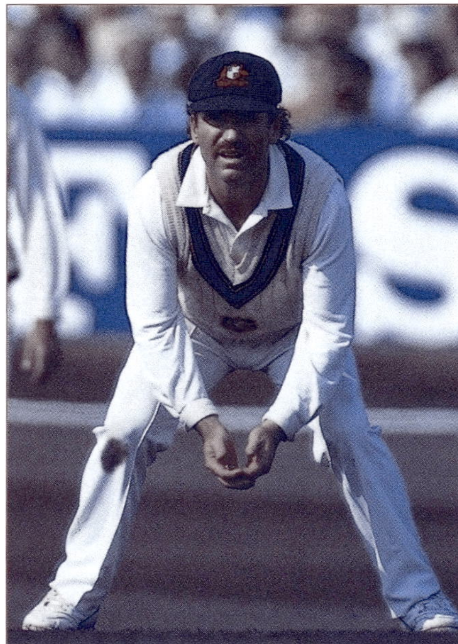

Cricket – male

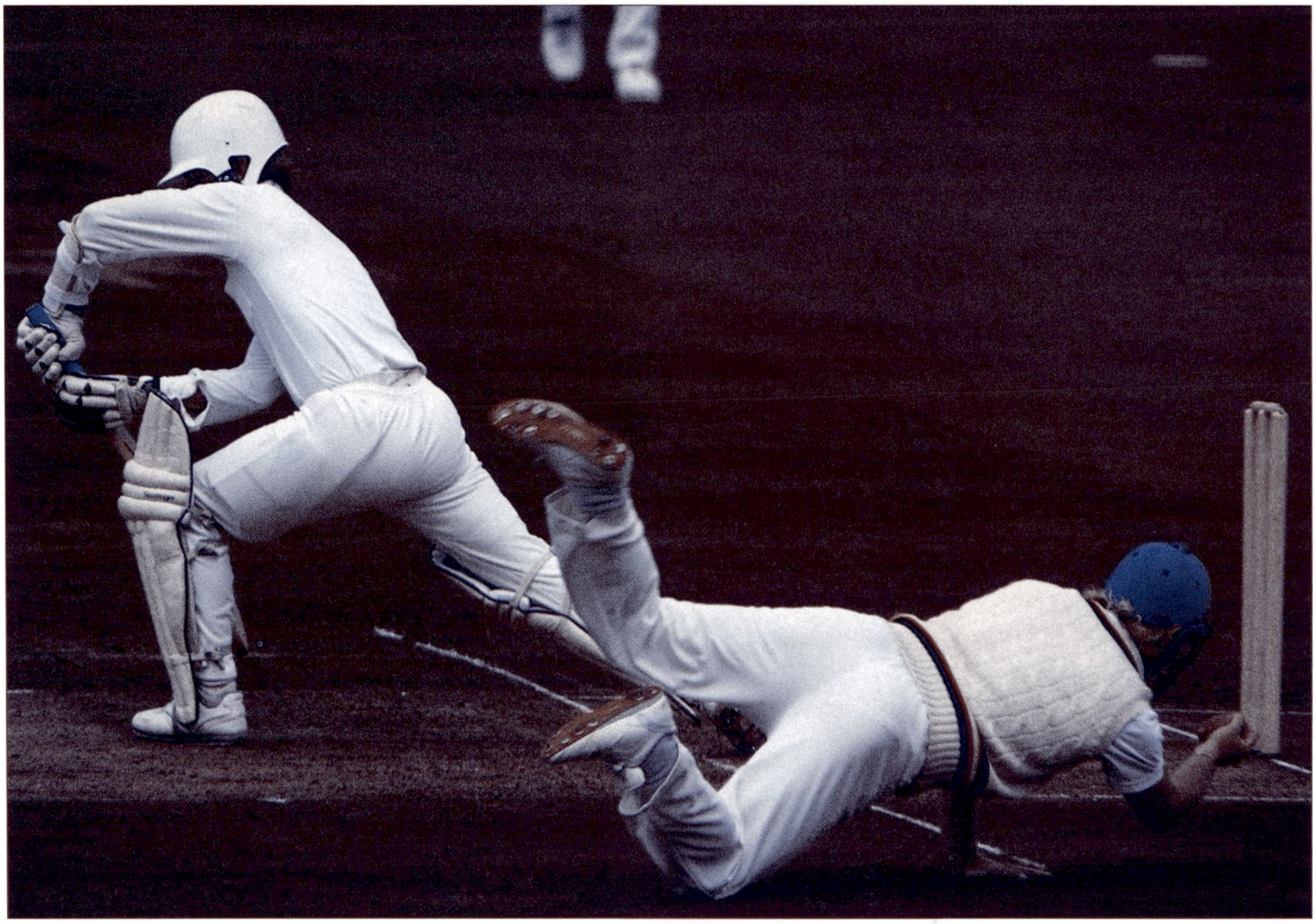

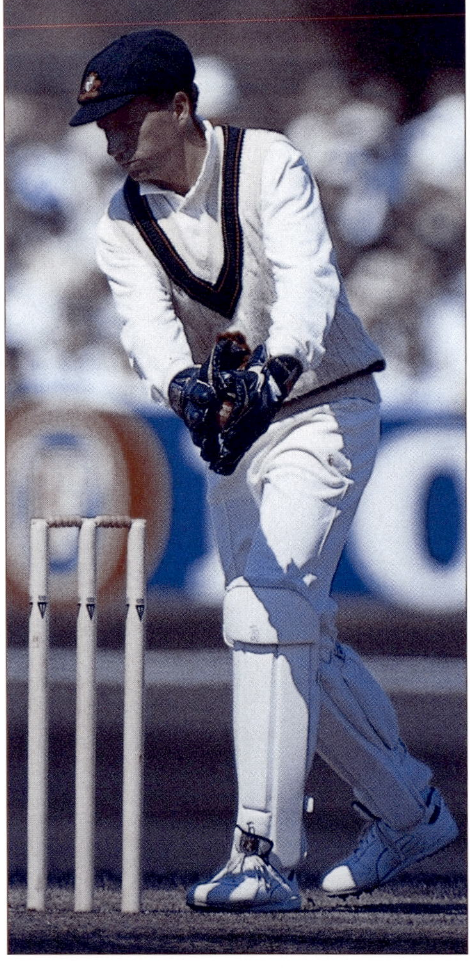

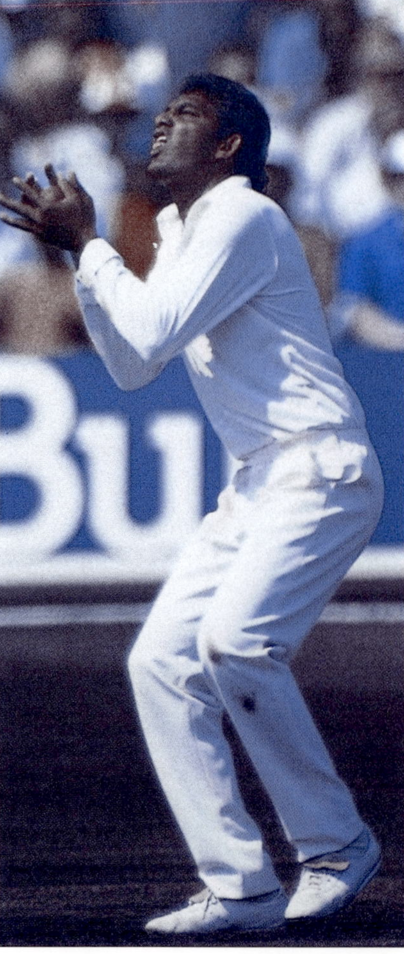

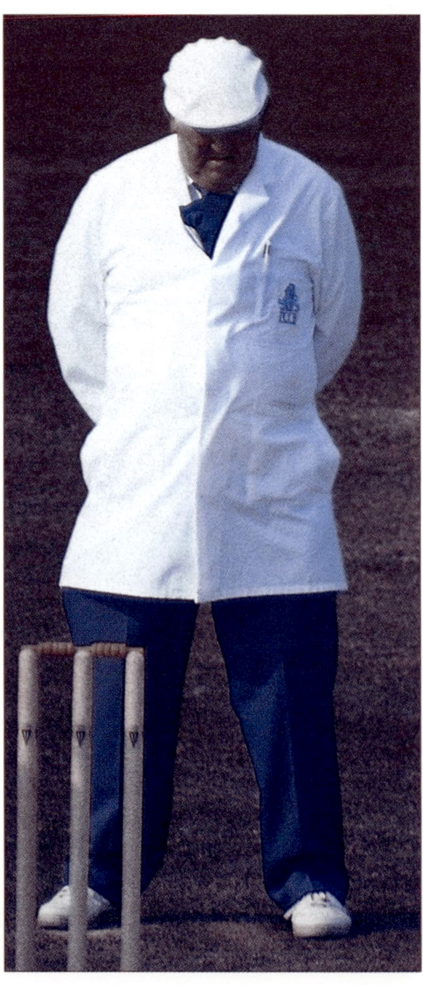

Cricket – female

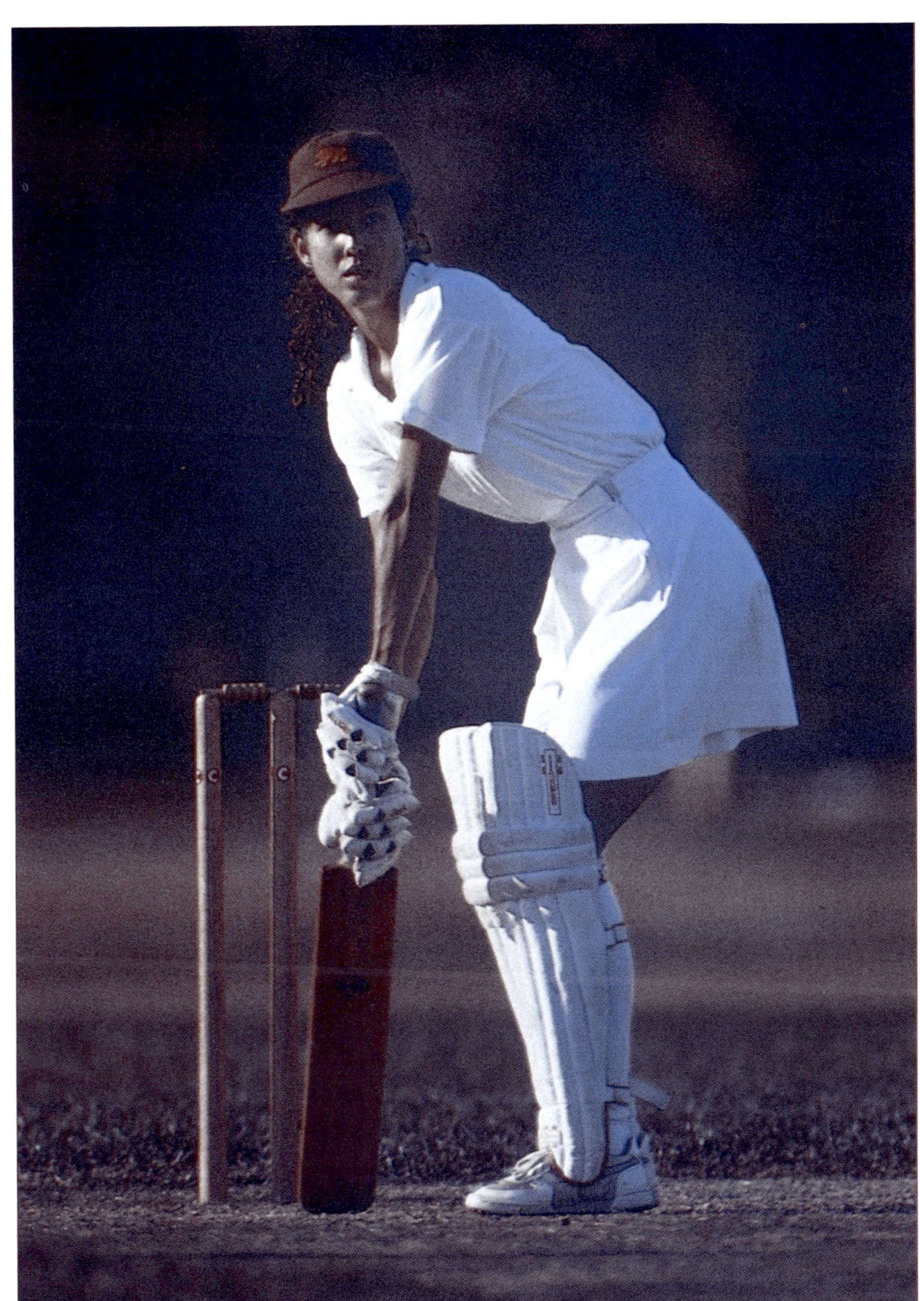

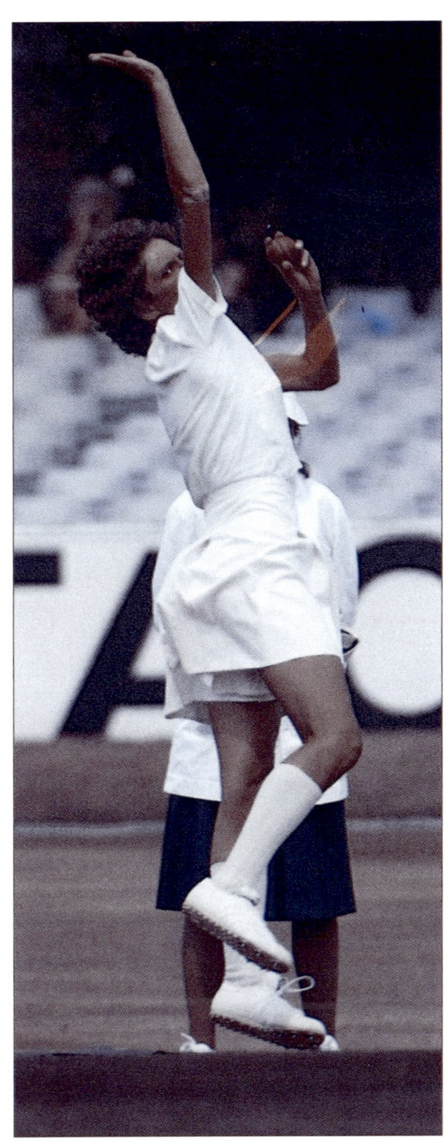

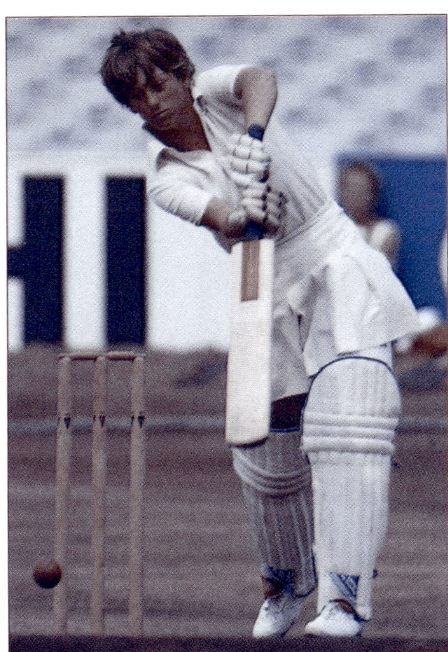

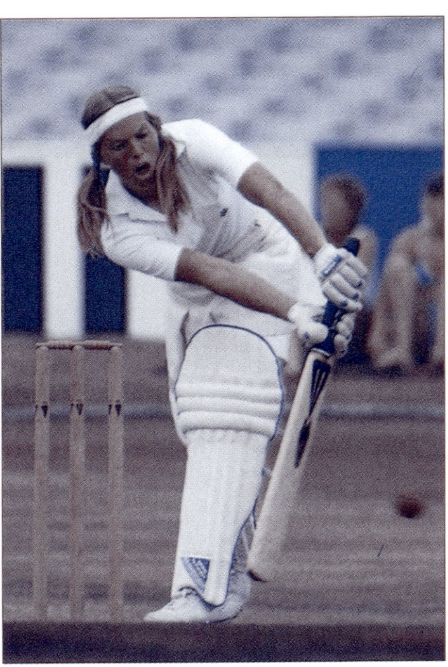

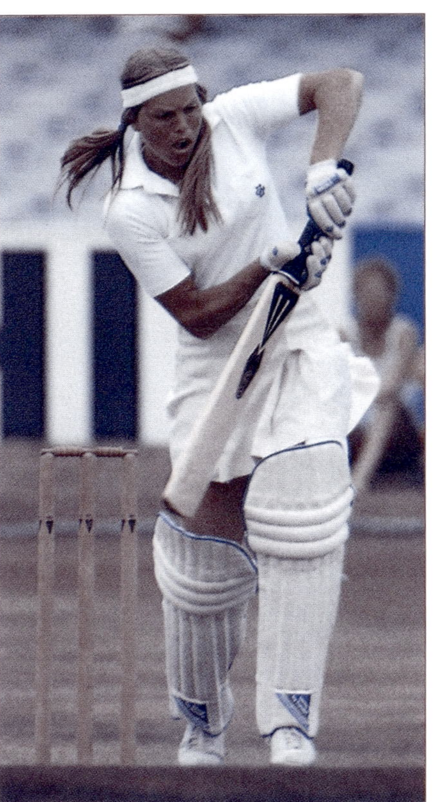

Golf – male

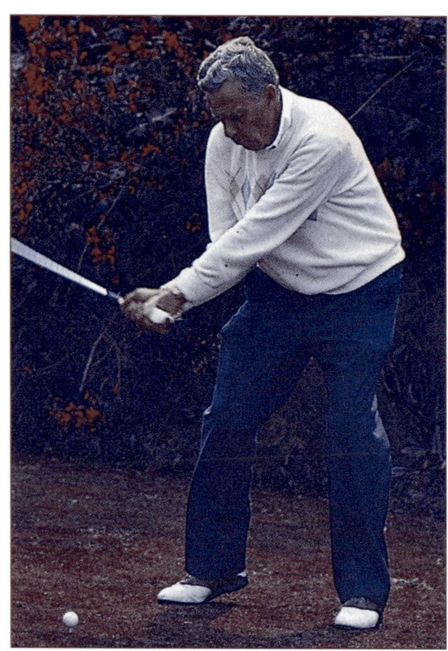

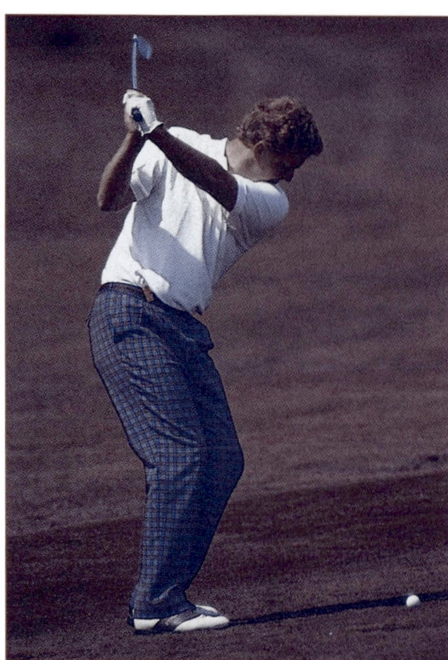

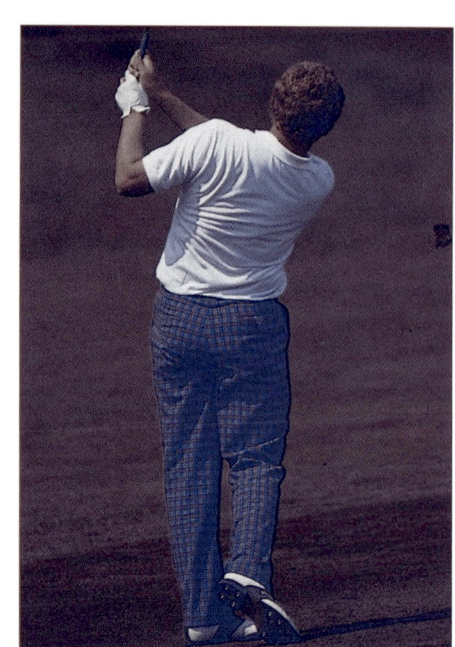

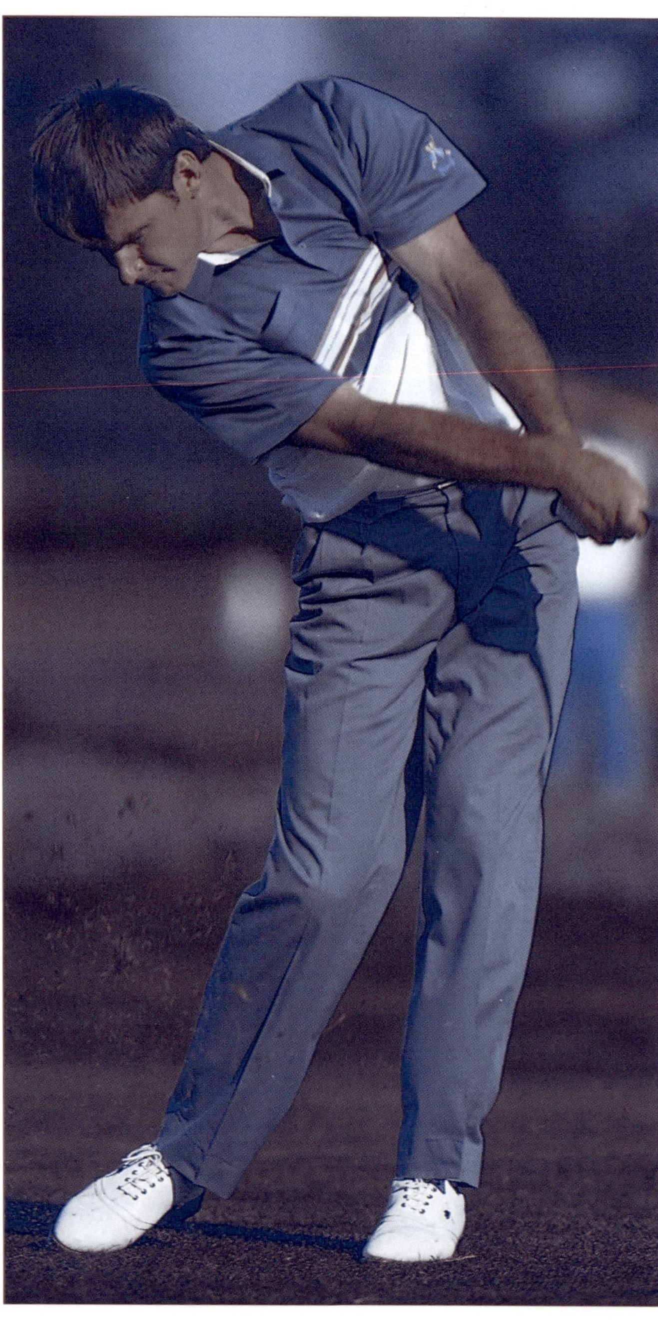

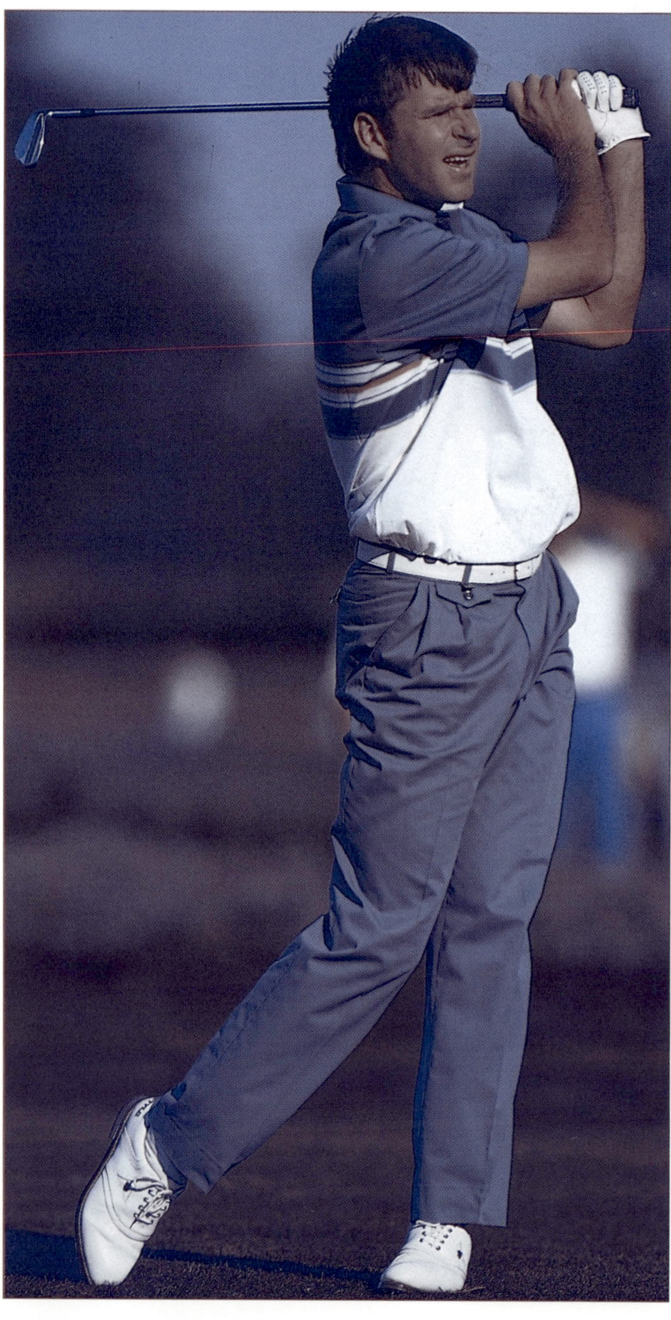

Golf – male

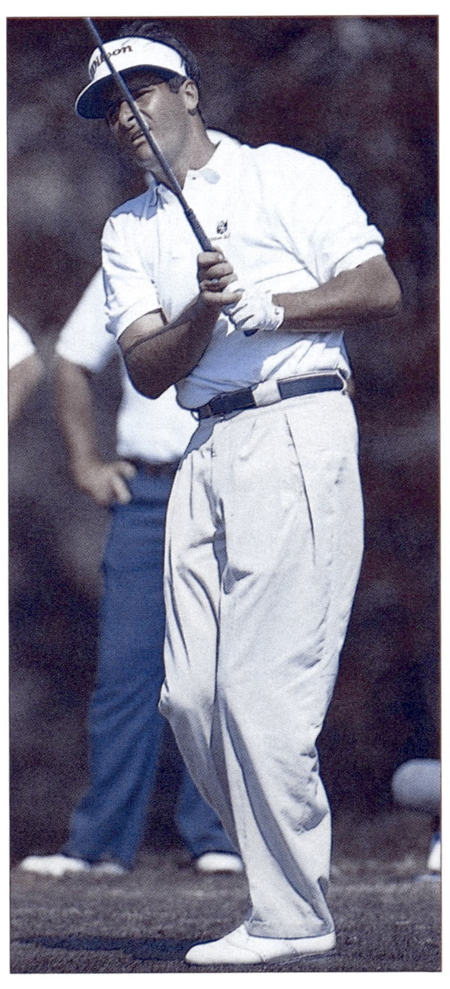

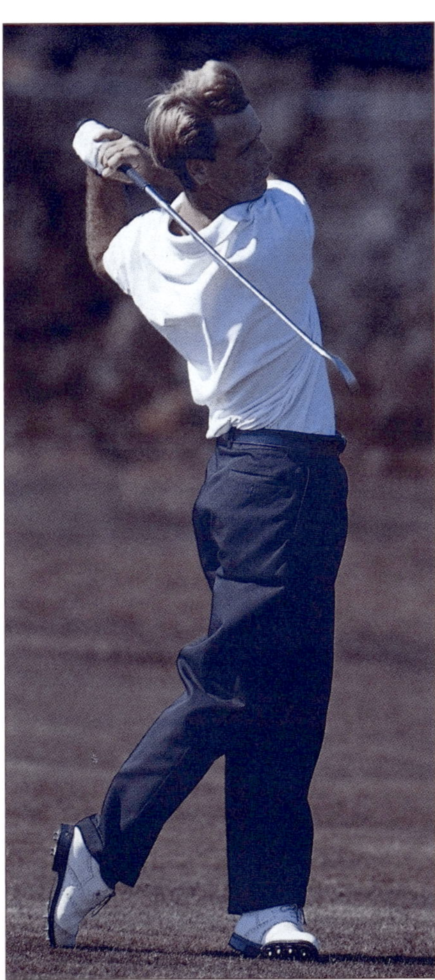

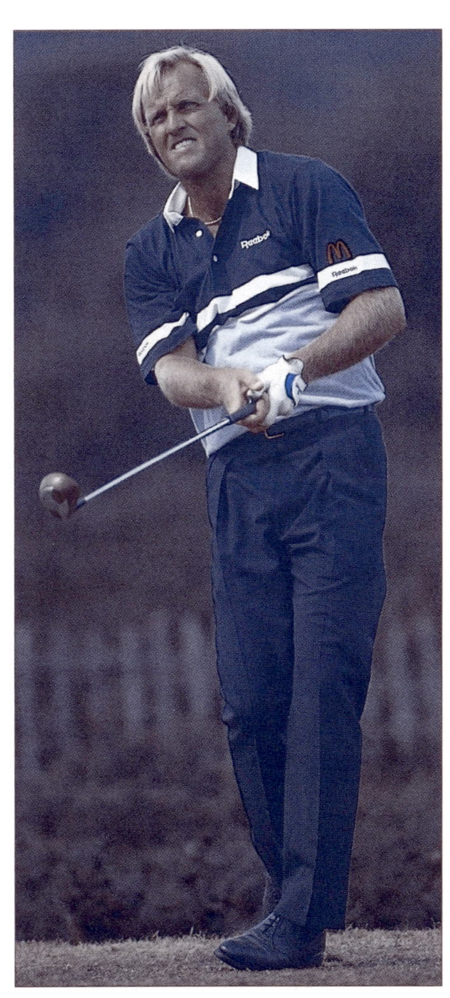

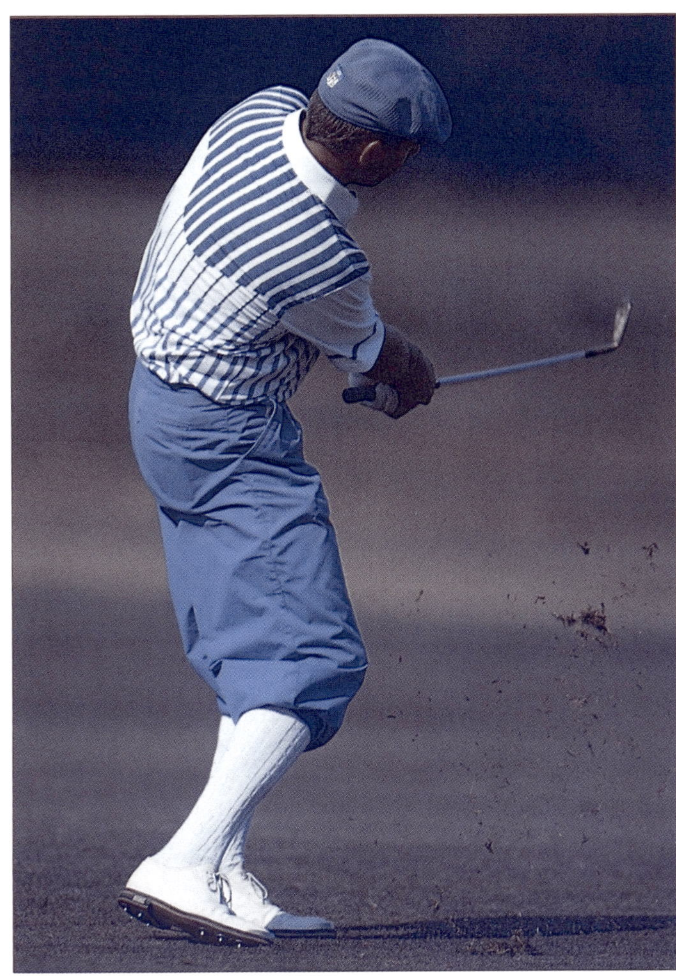

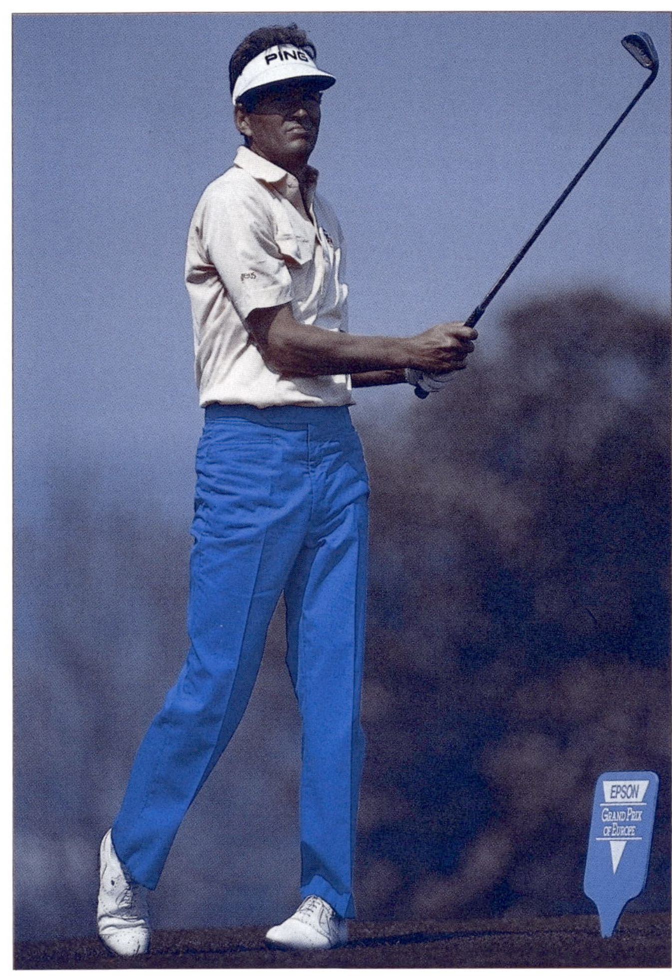

Golf – male

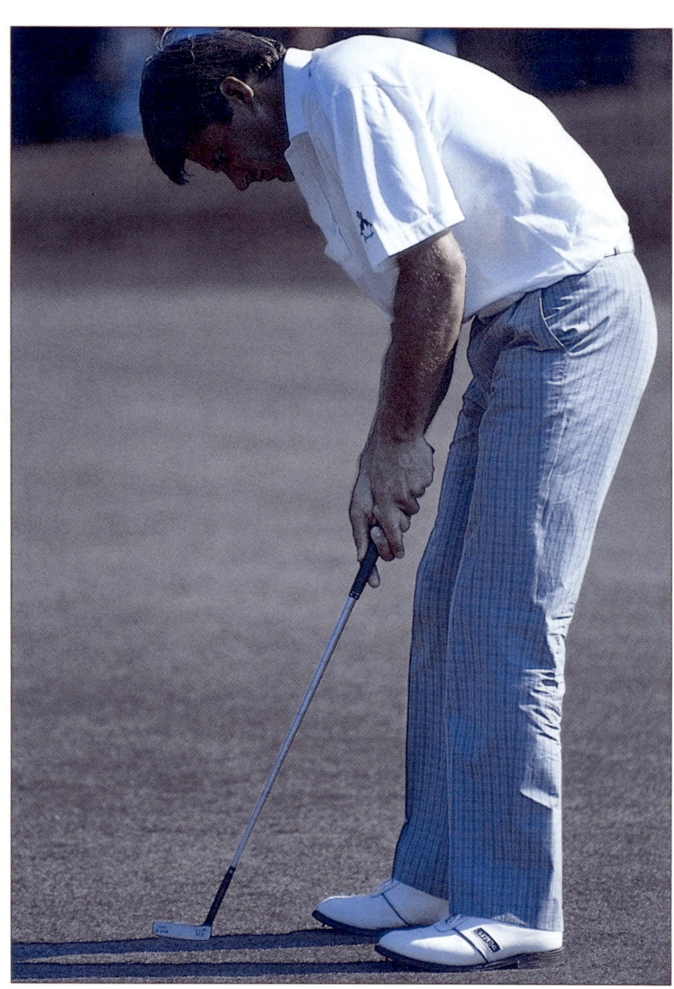

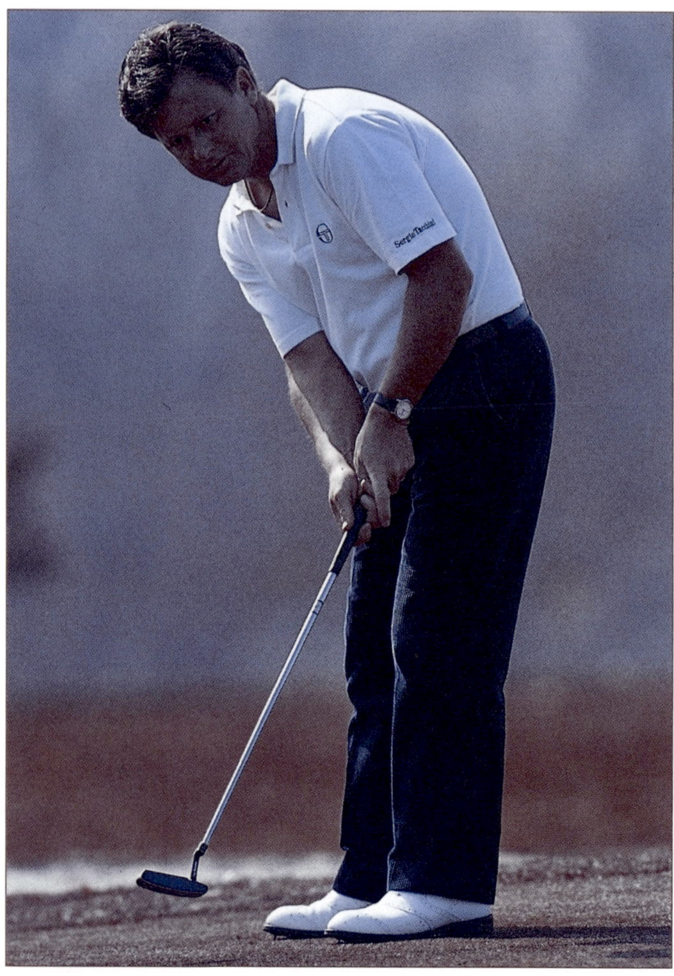

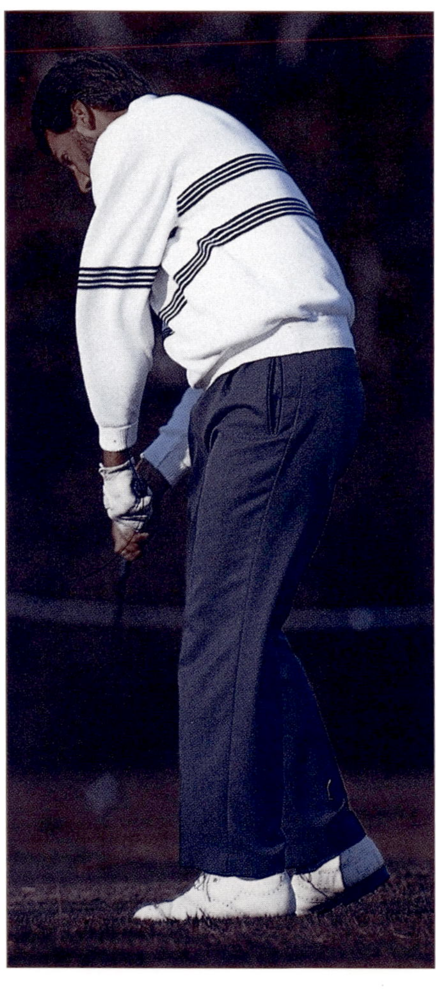

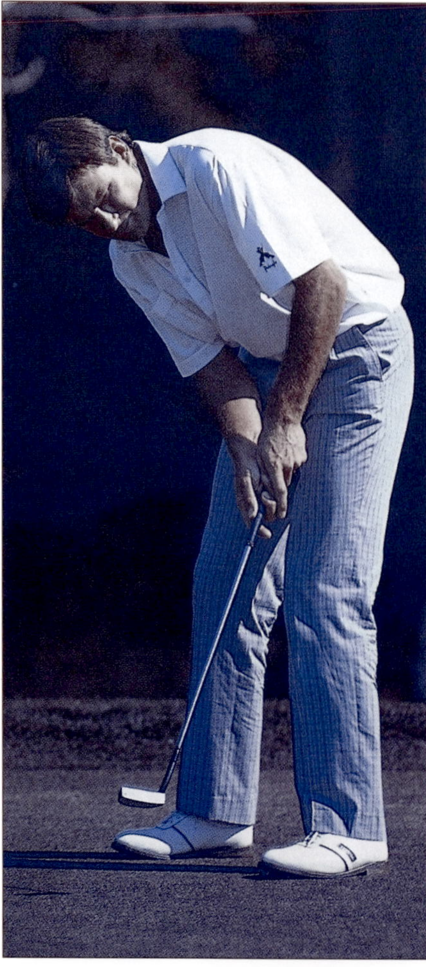

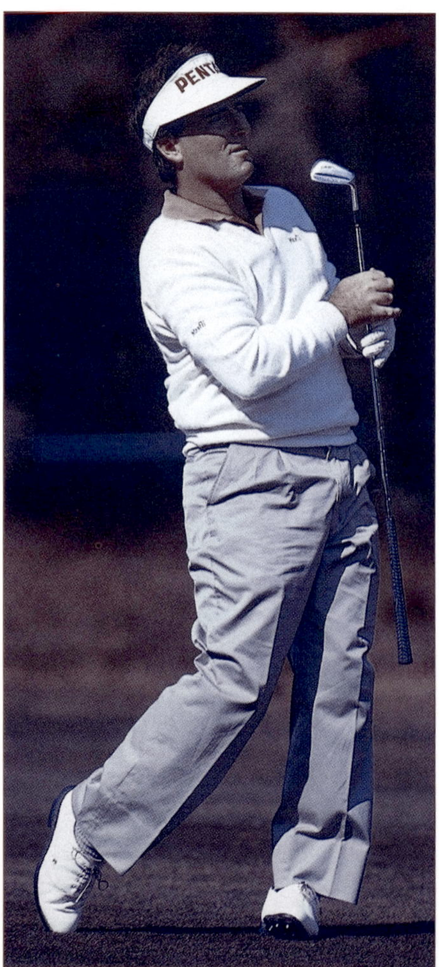

Golf – male

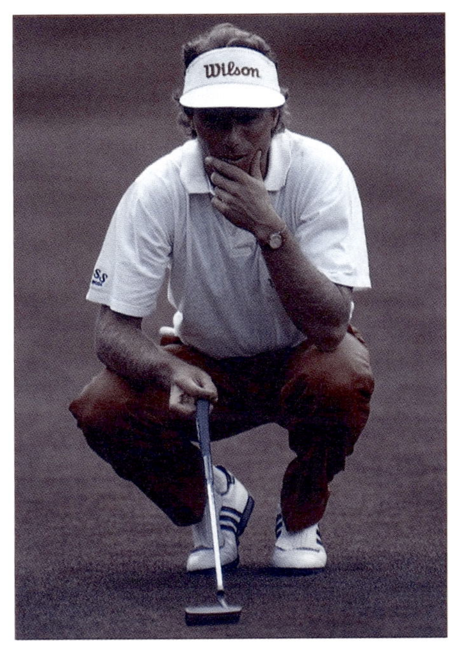

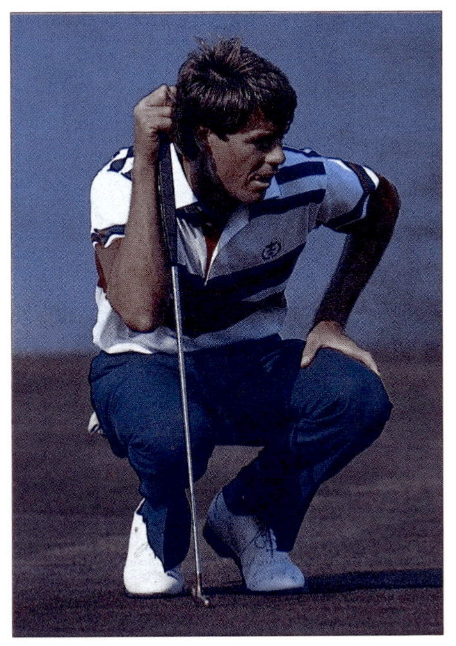

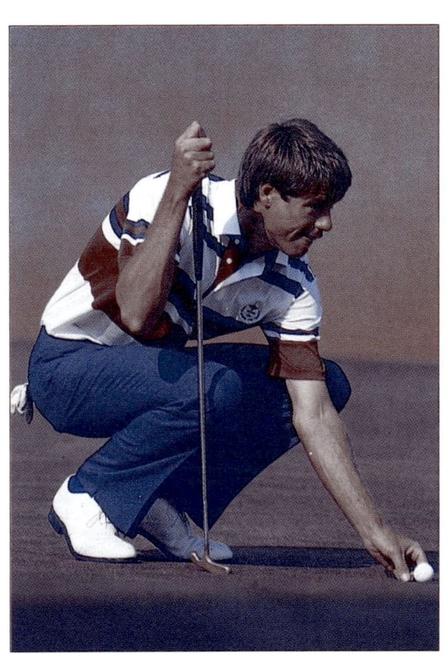

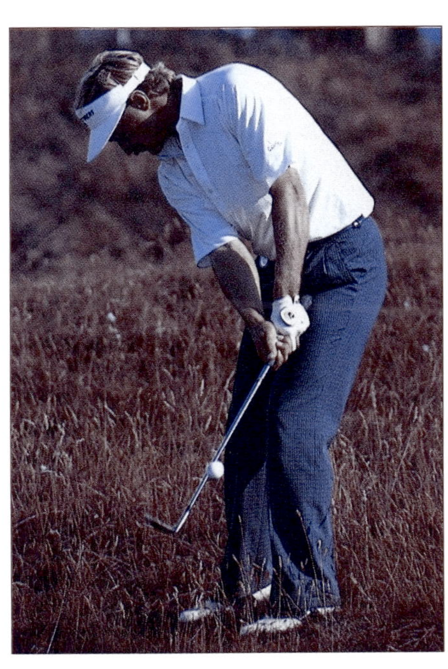

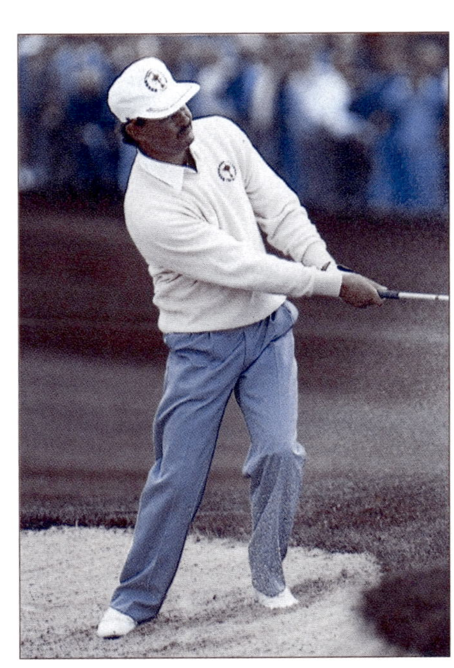

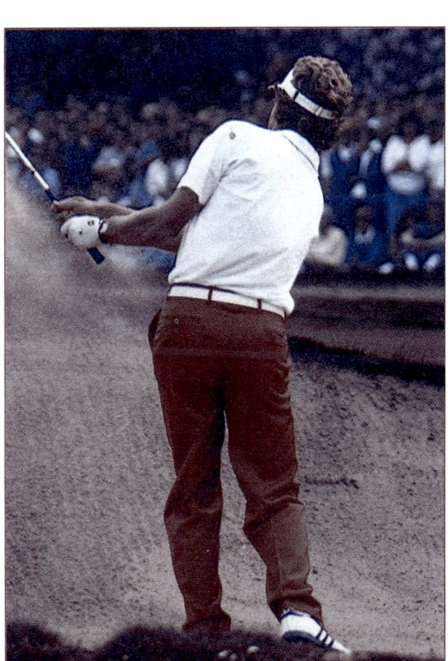

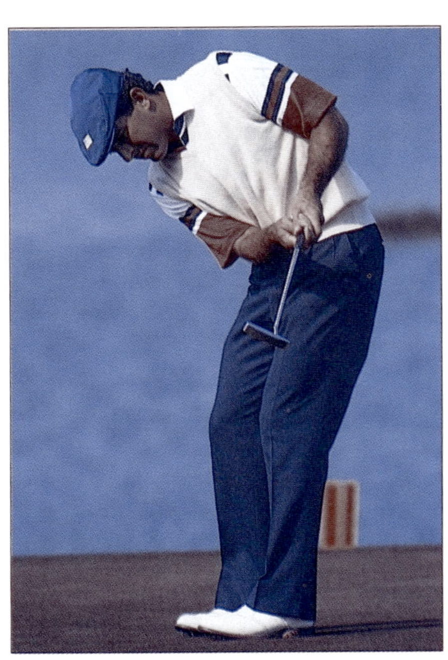

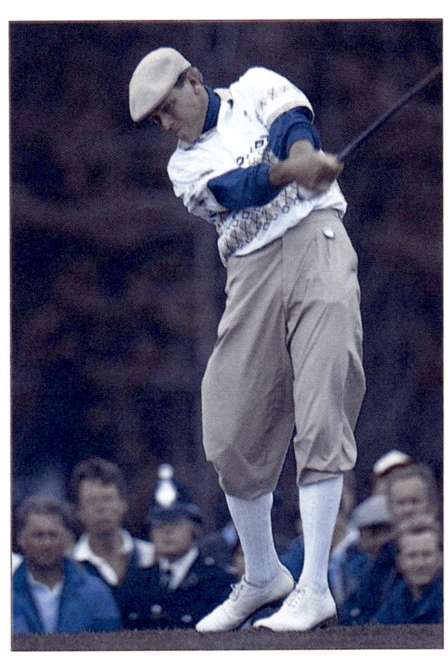

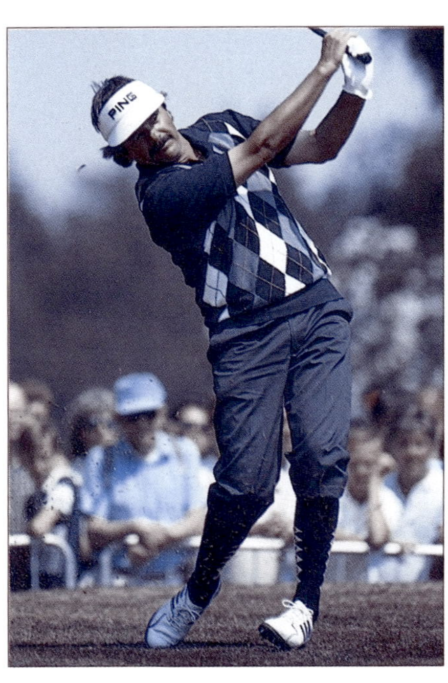

Golf – female

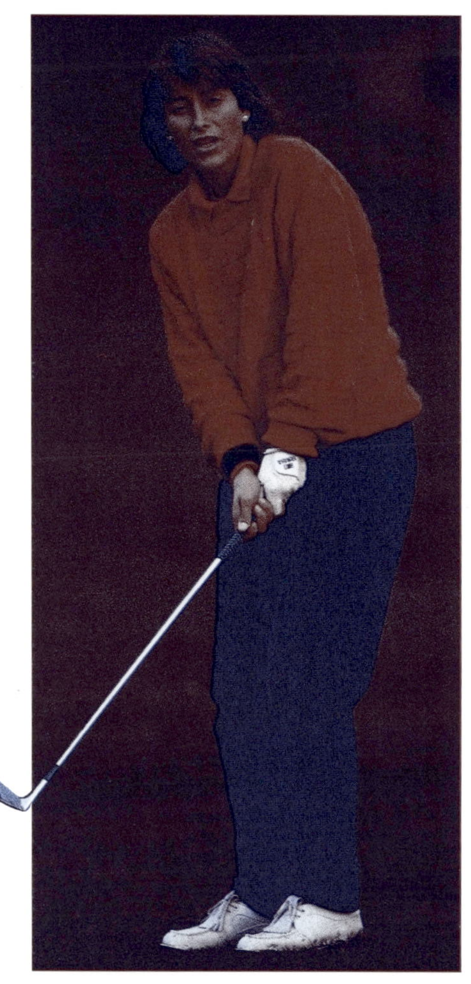

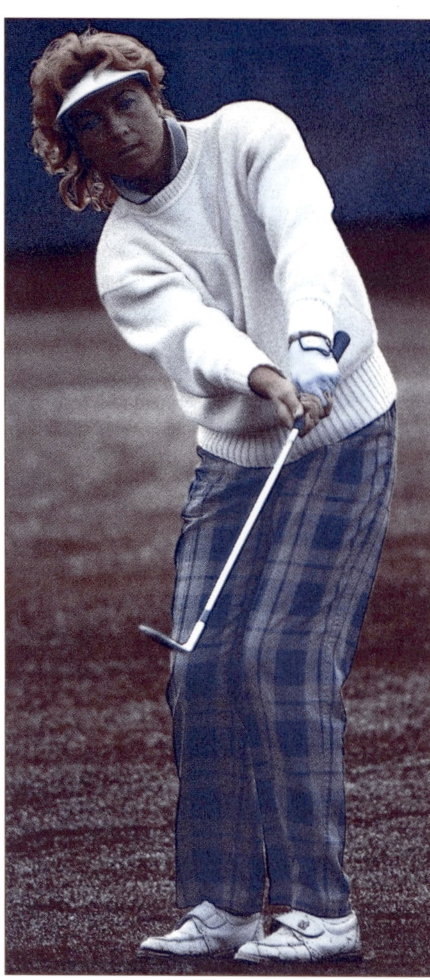

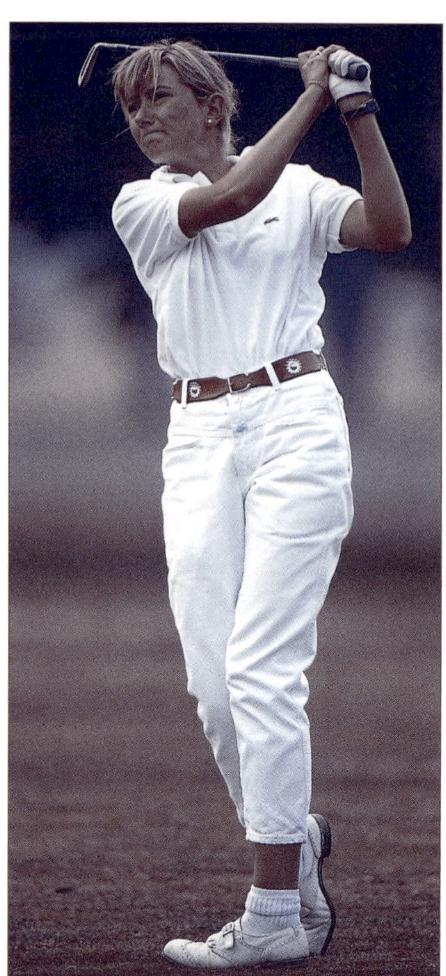

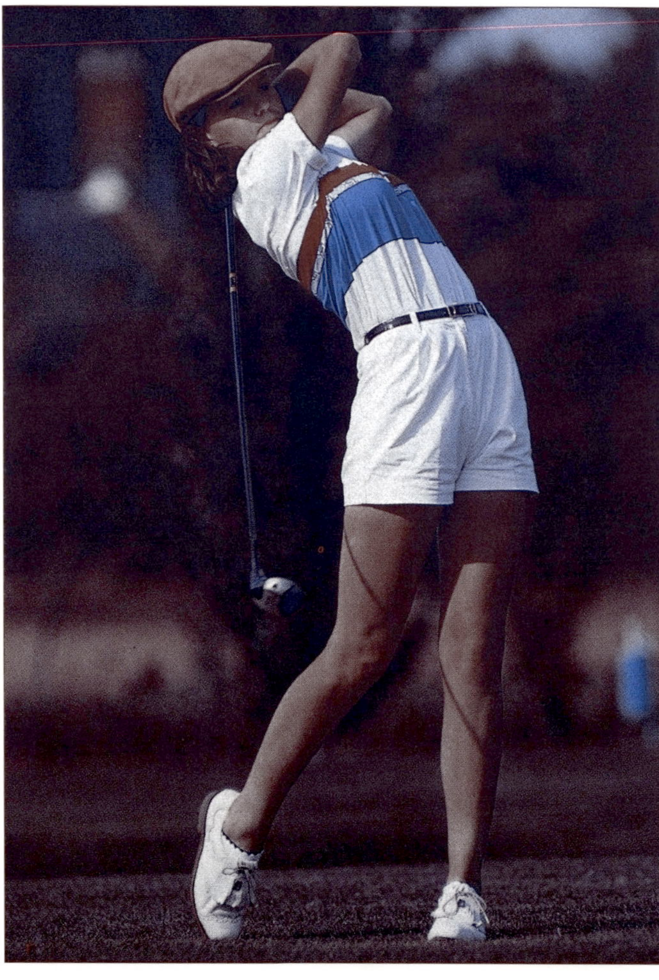

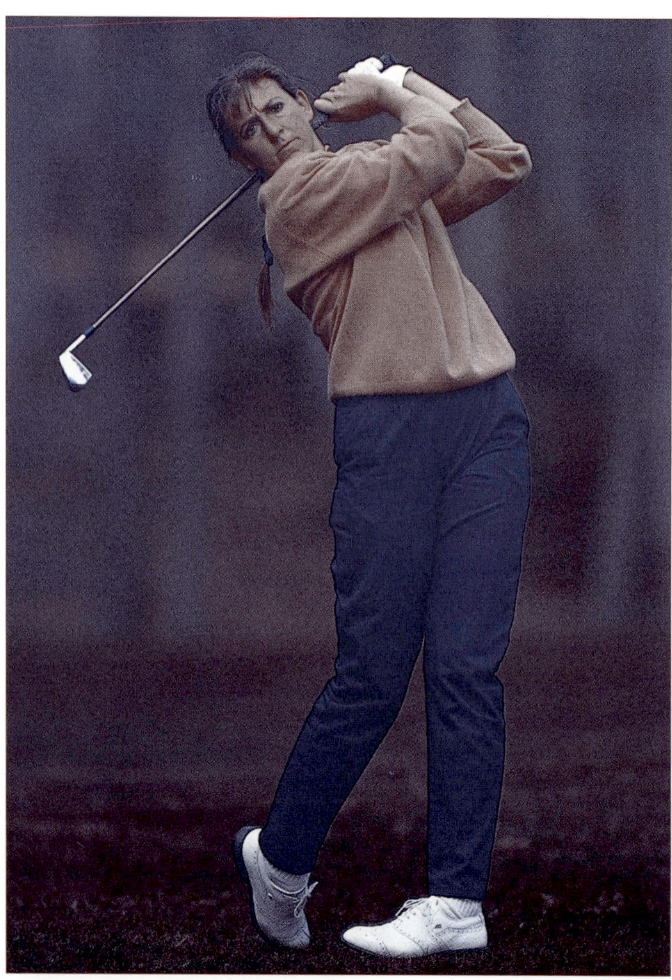

Golf – female · caddy

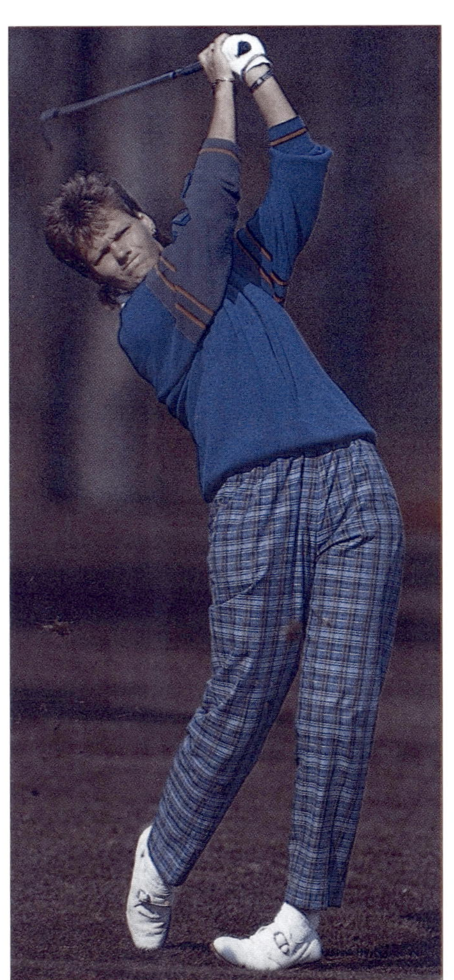

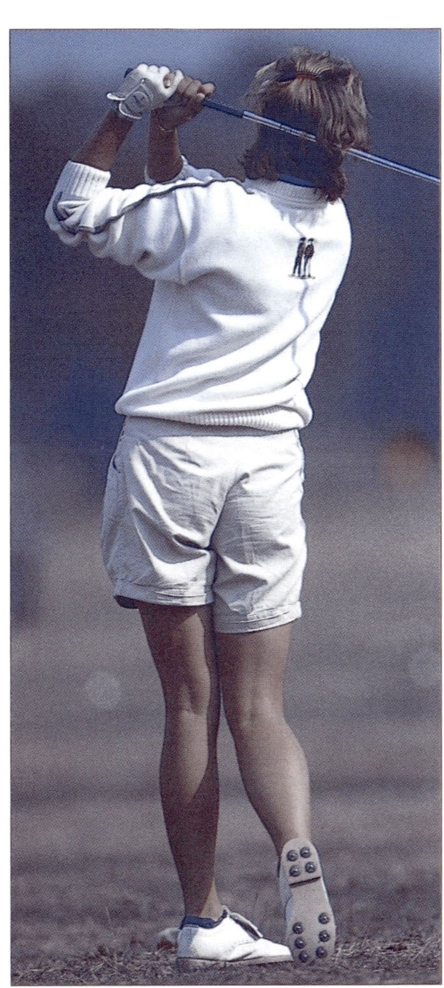

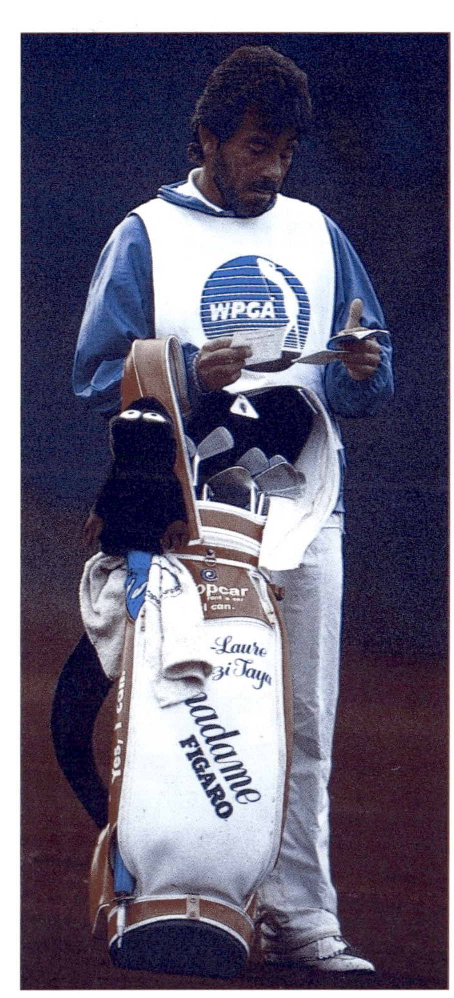

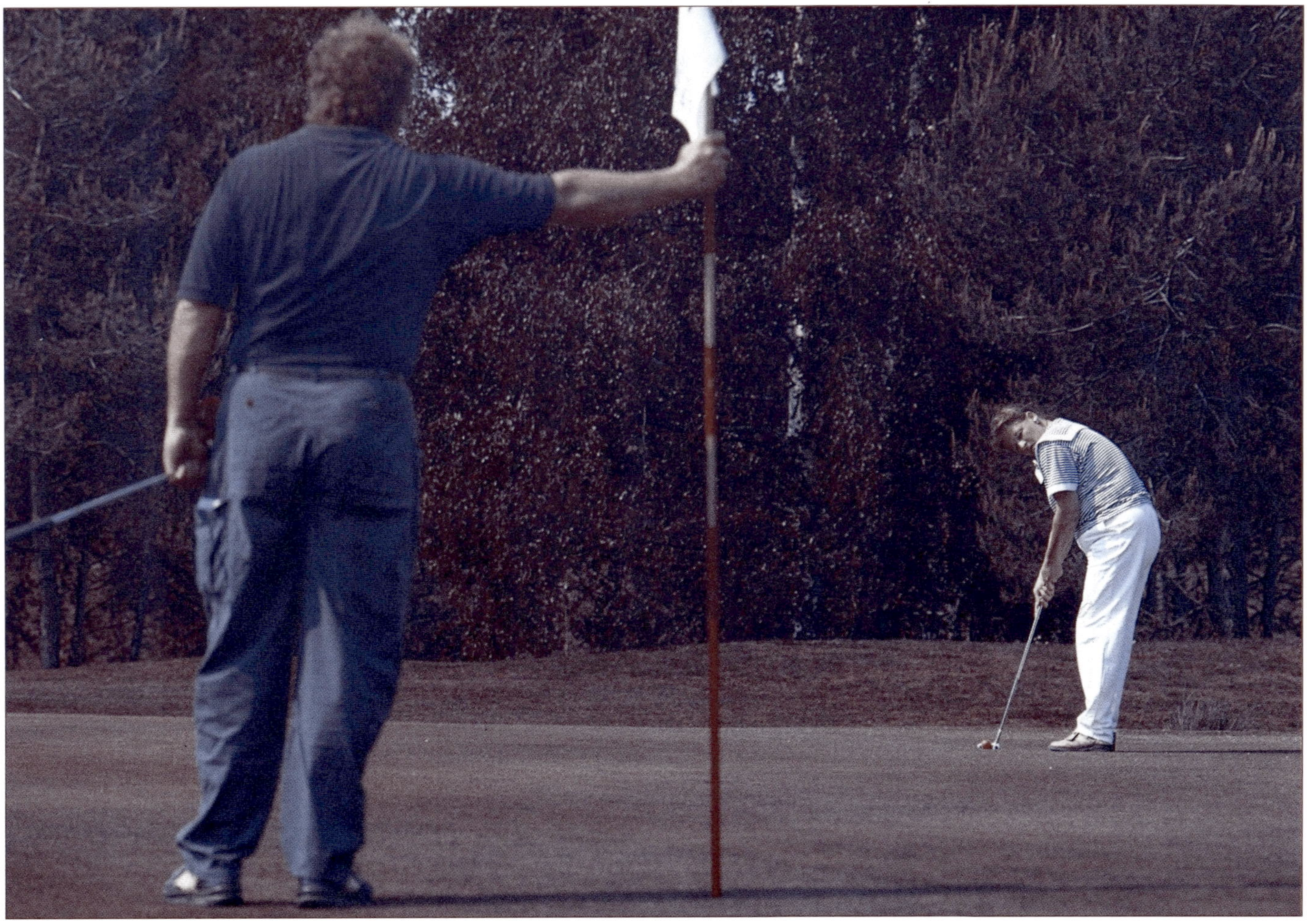

Field Hockey – male

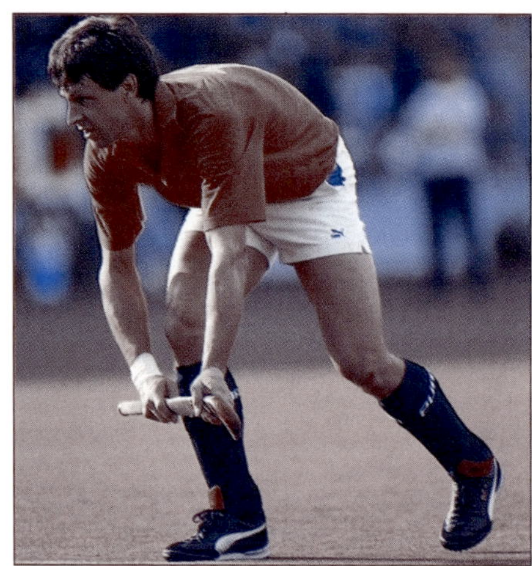

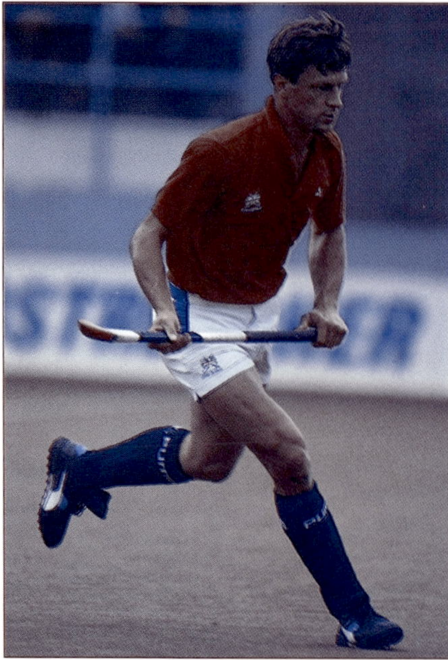

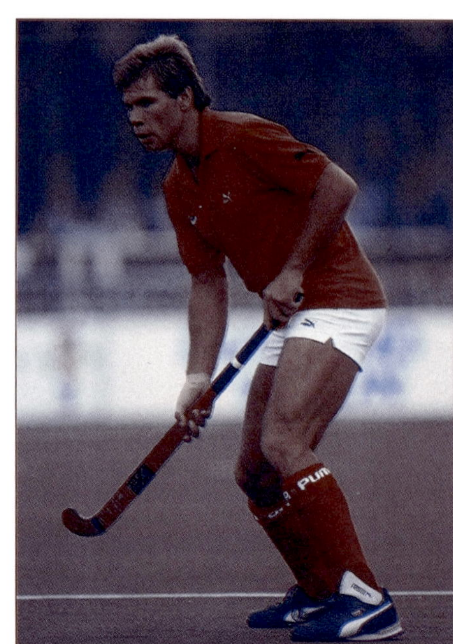

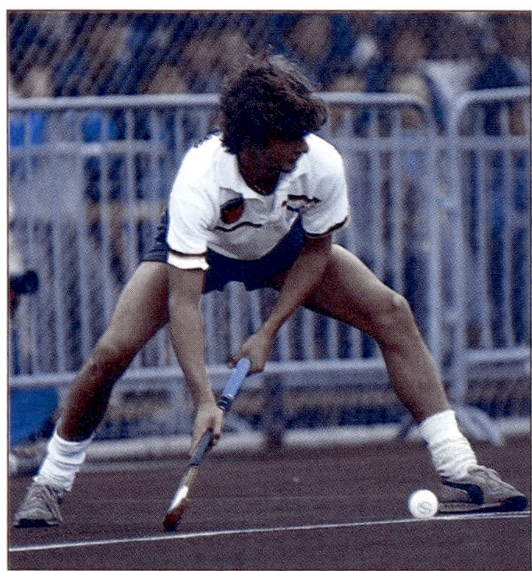

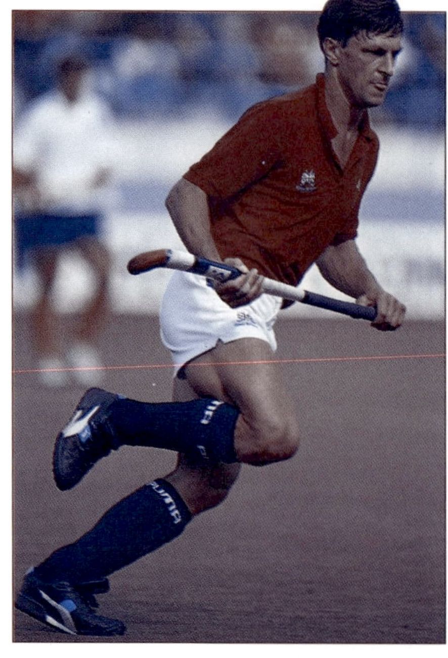

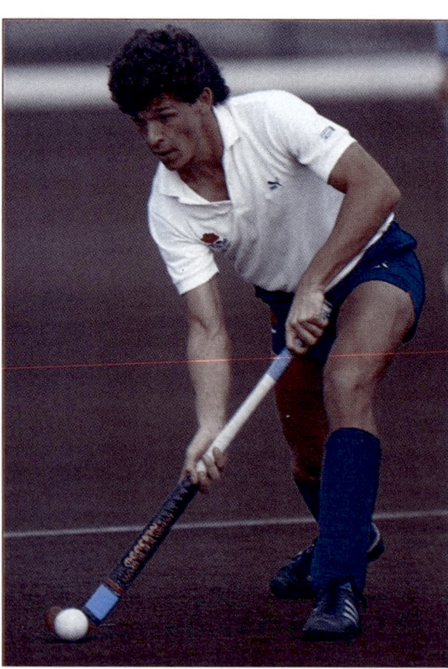

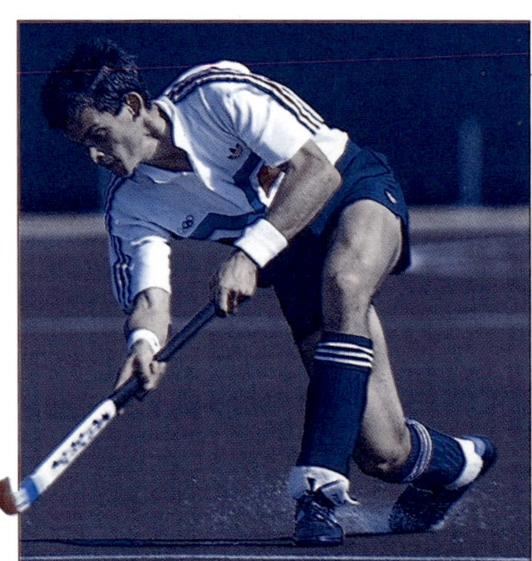

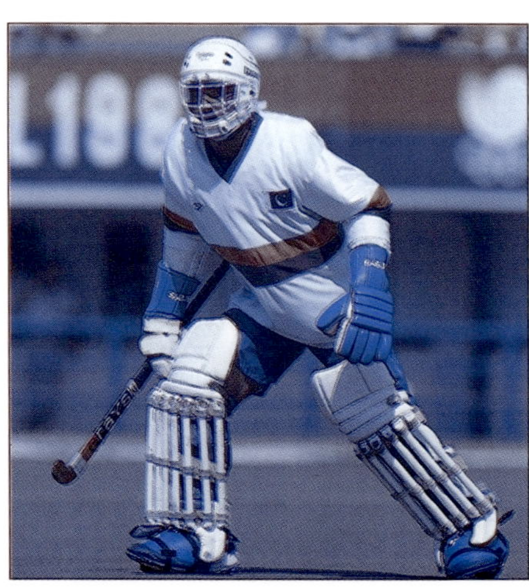

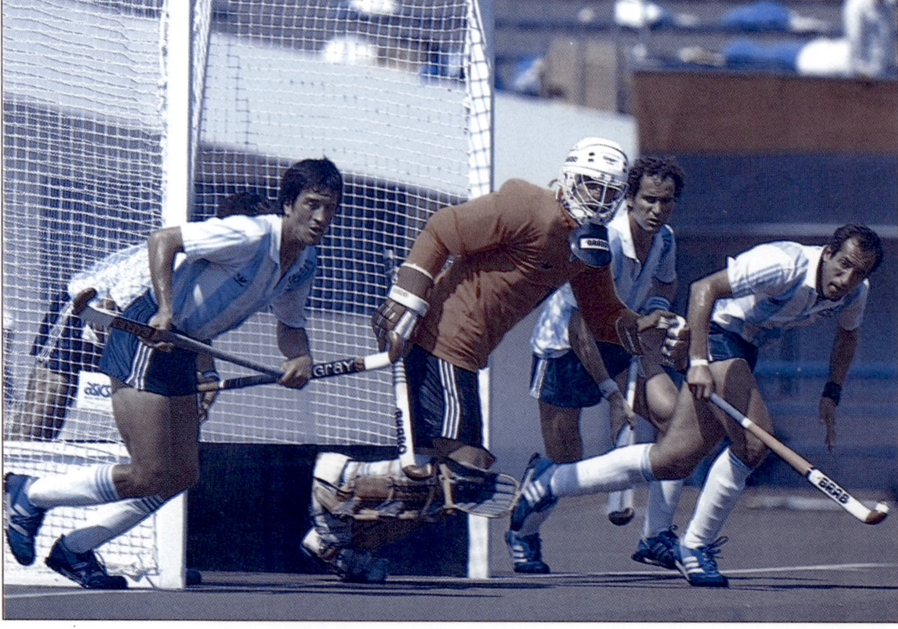

Field Hockey – female

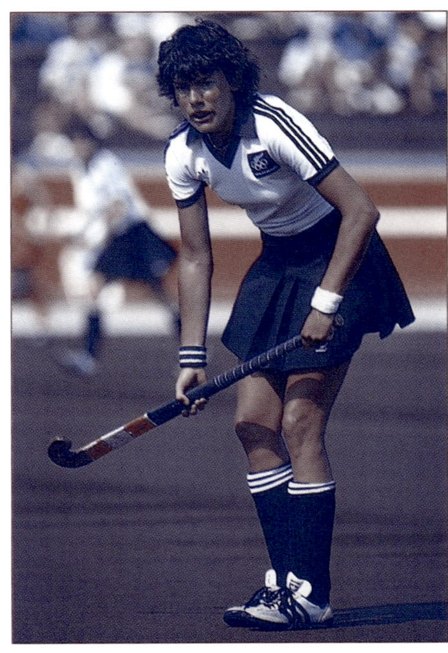

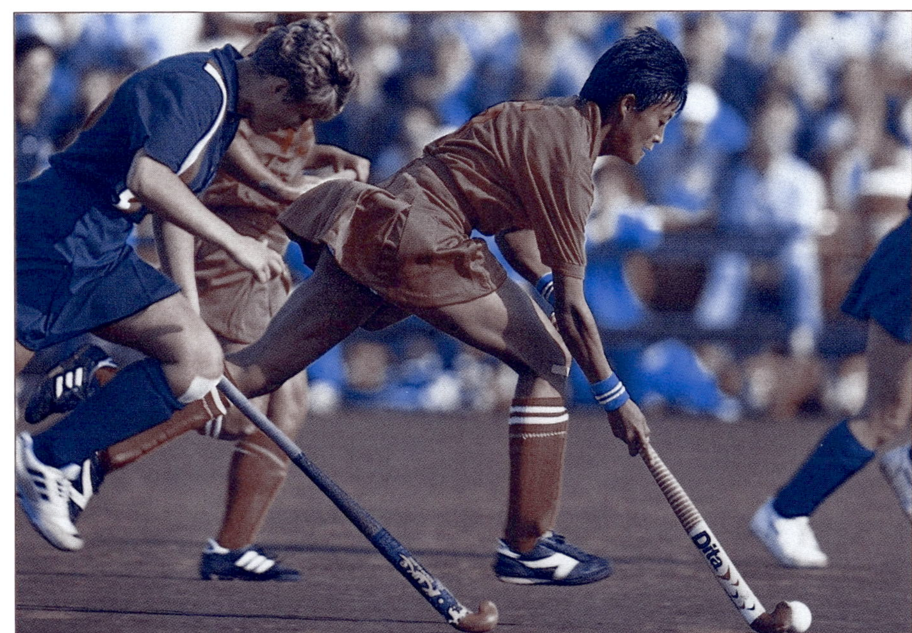

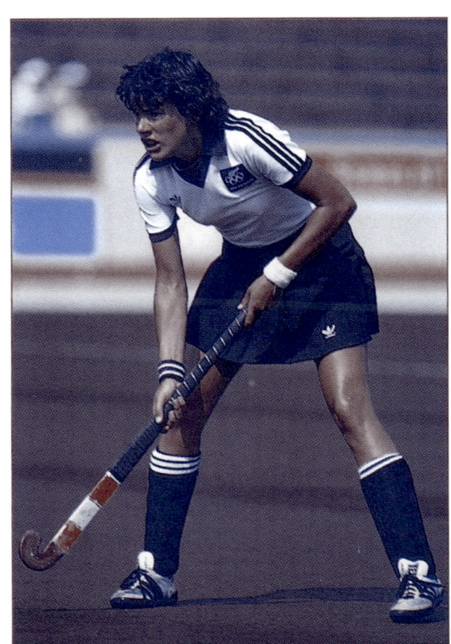

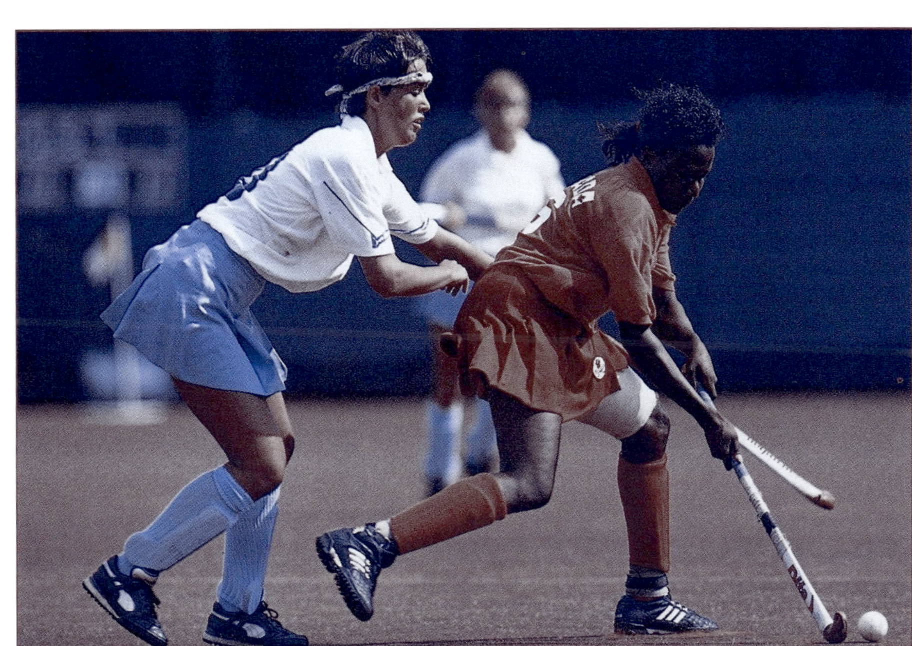

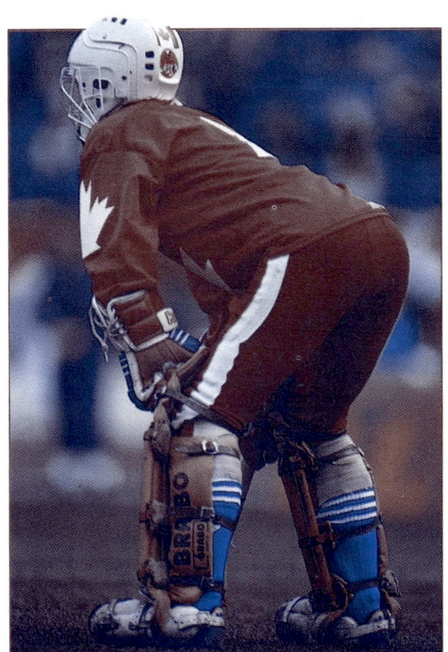

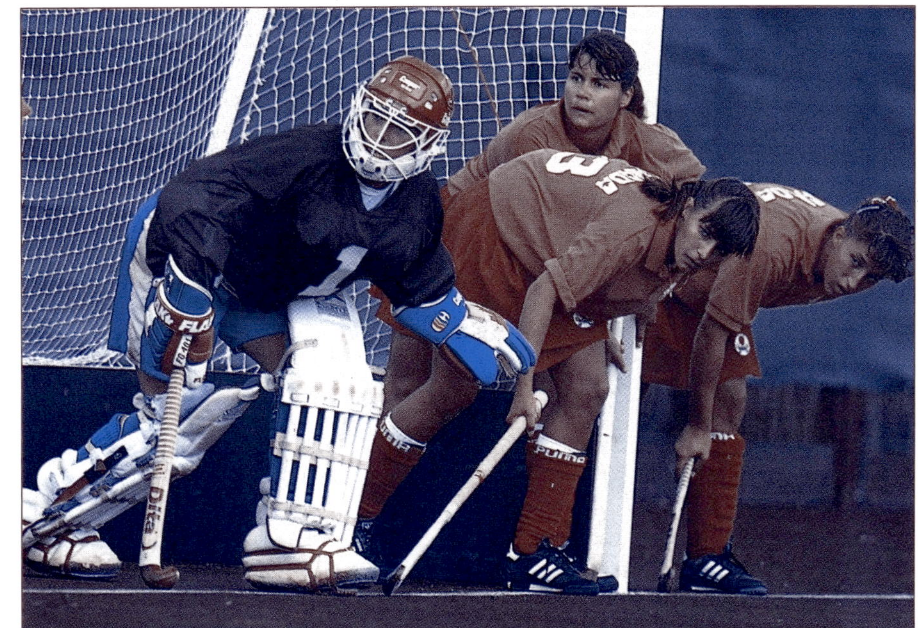

Basketball

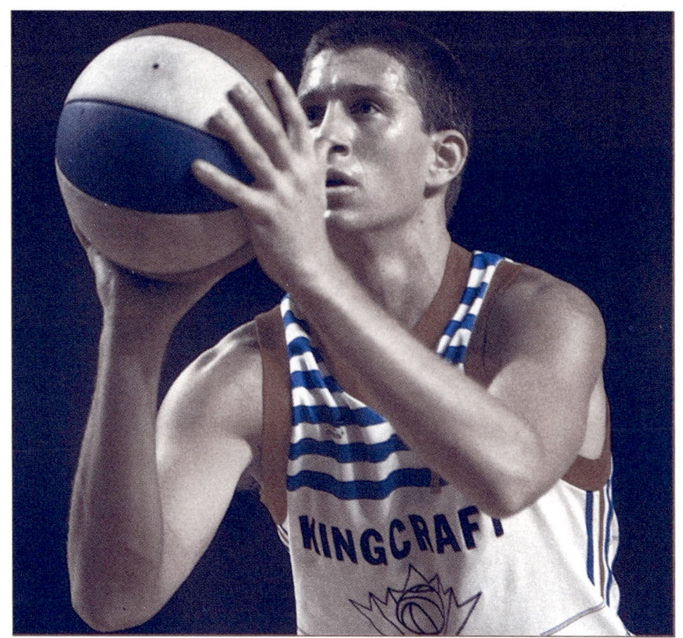

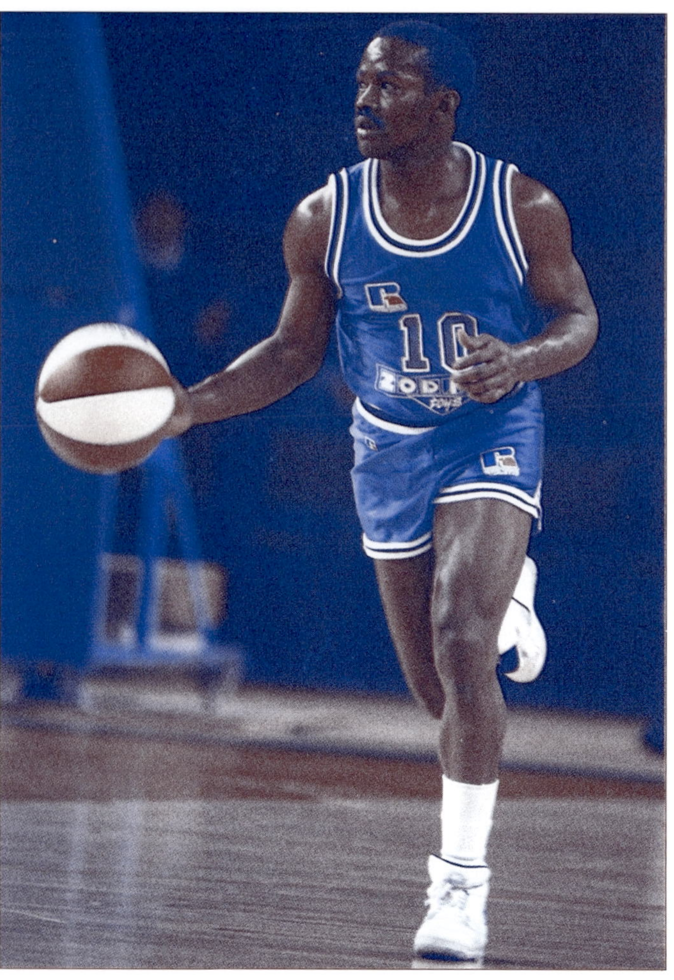

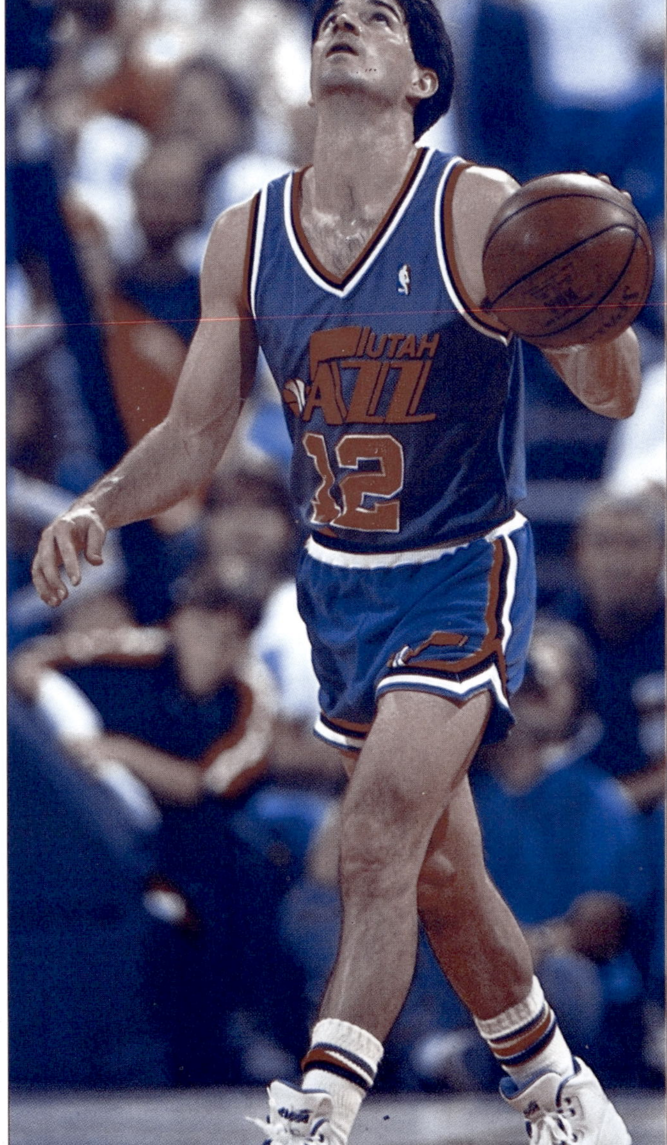

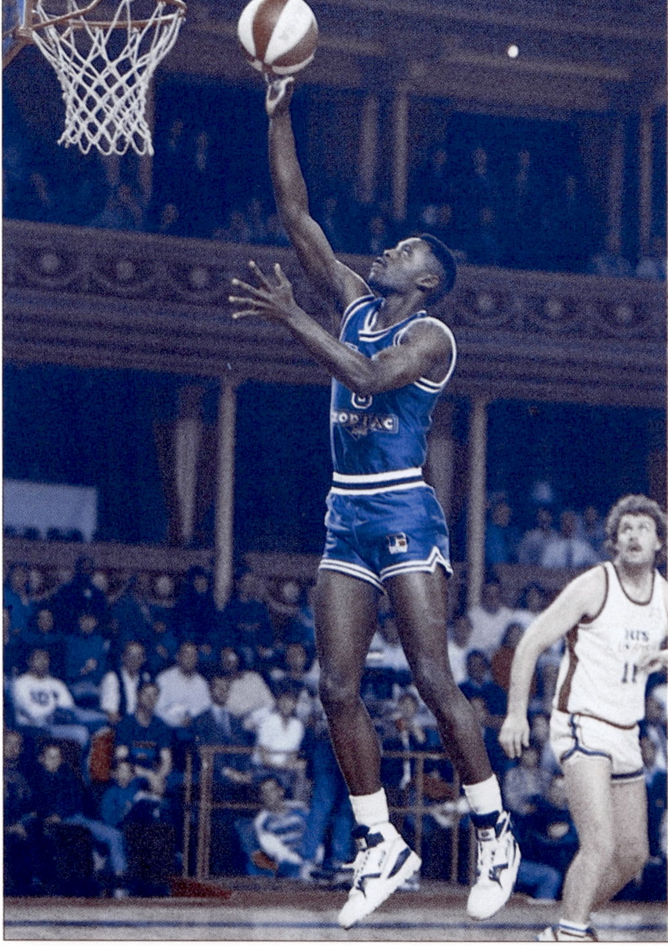

Basketball

SONICS
22
SONICS

SIXERS
34
HEAT

DeYurre !
HEAT
21
55
CUMMINGS
42

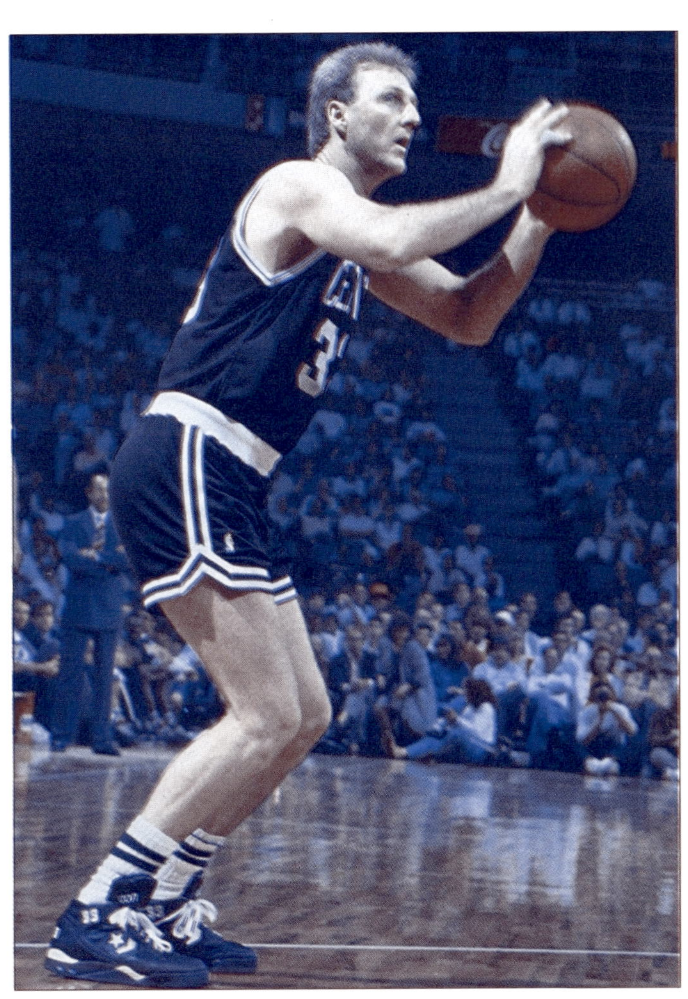

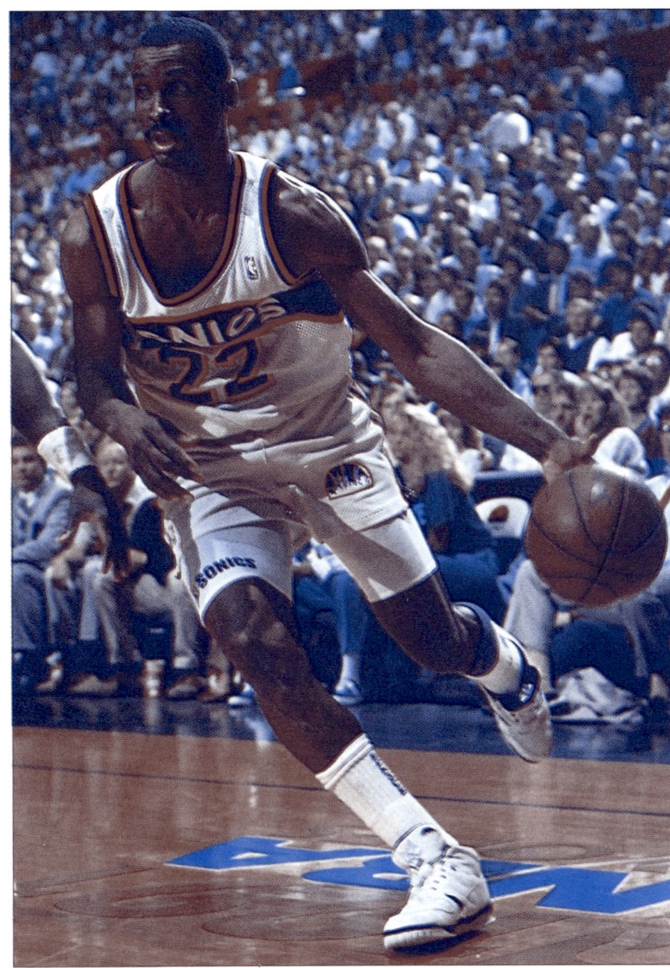

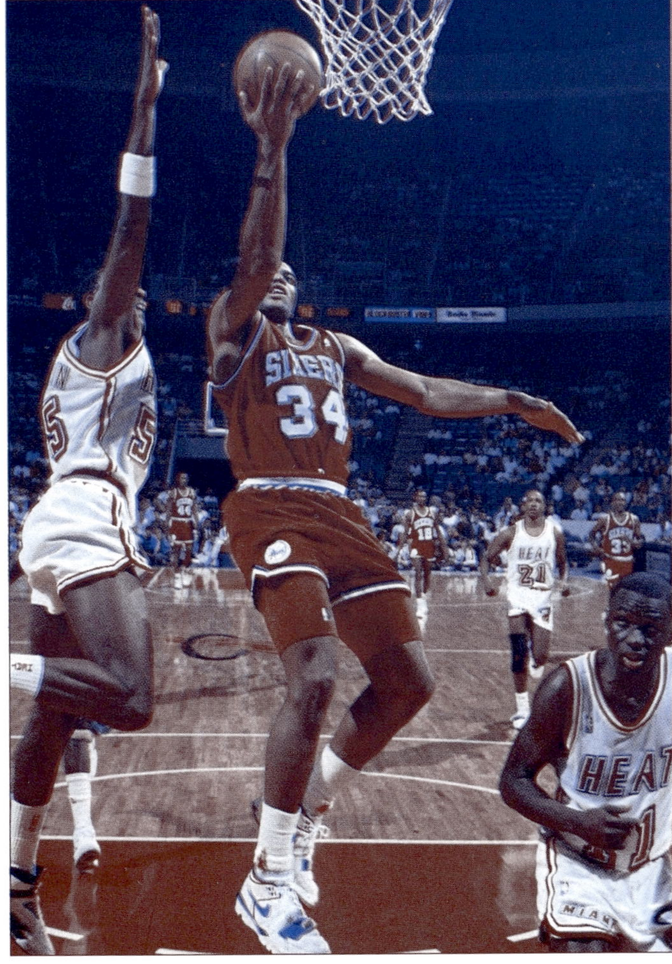

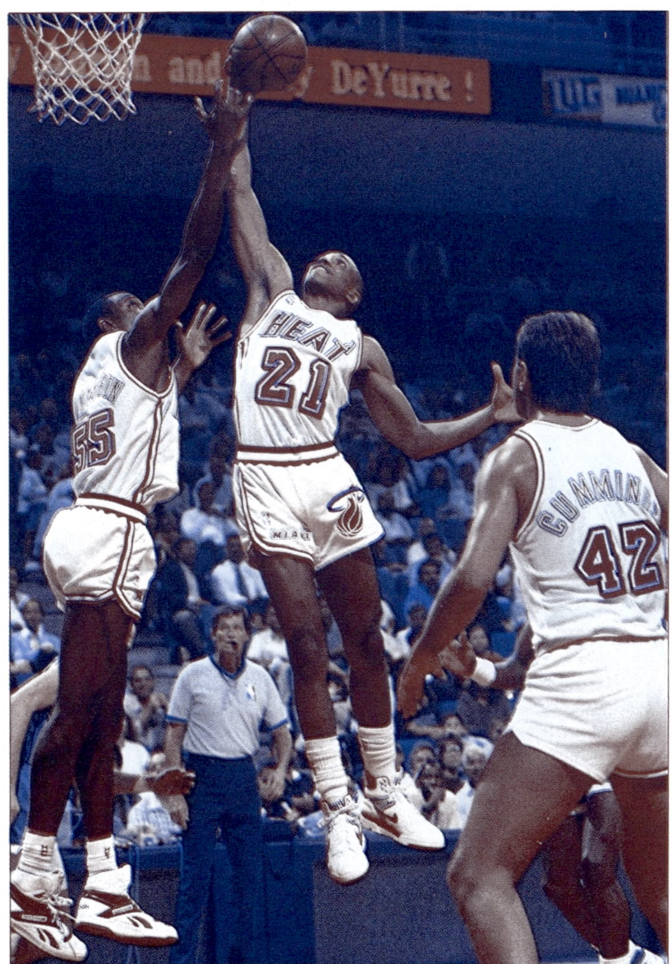

Volleyball – male

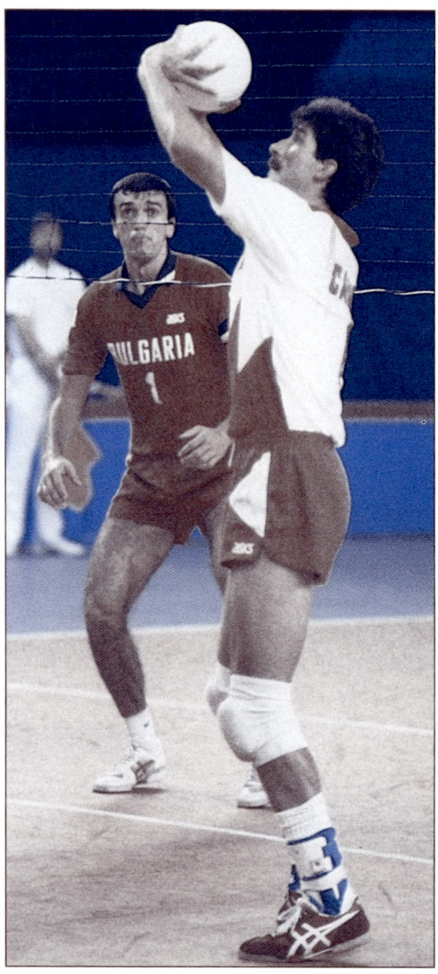

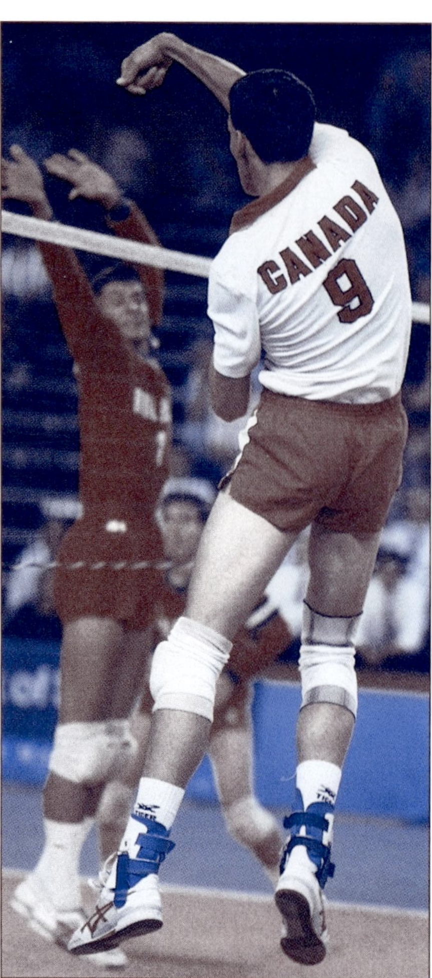

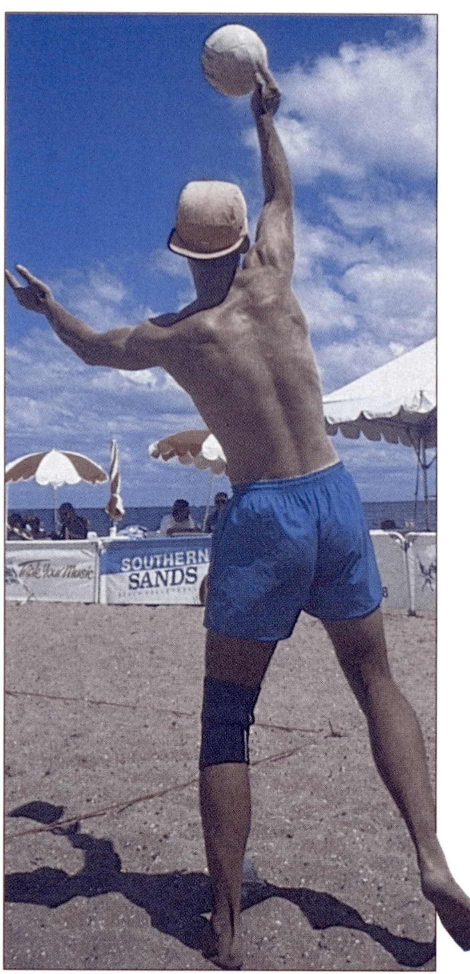

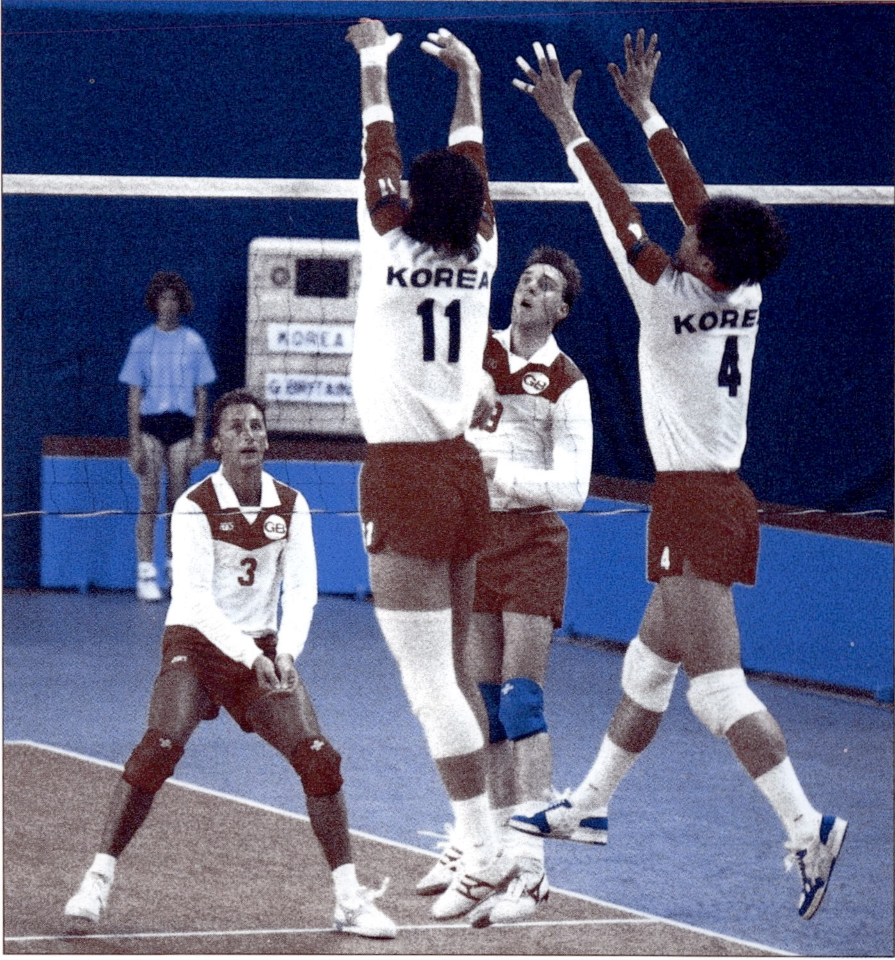

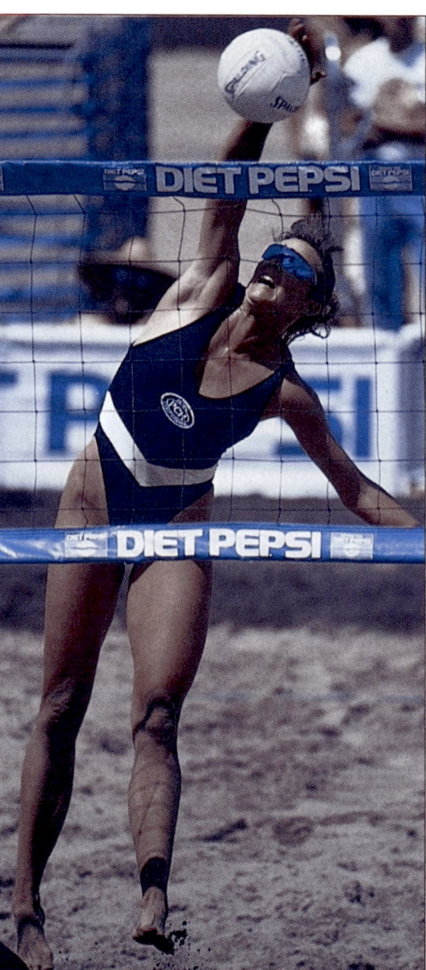

Volleyball – female

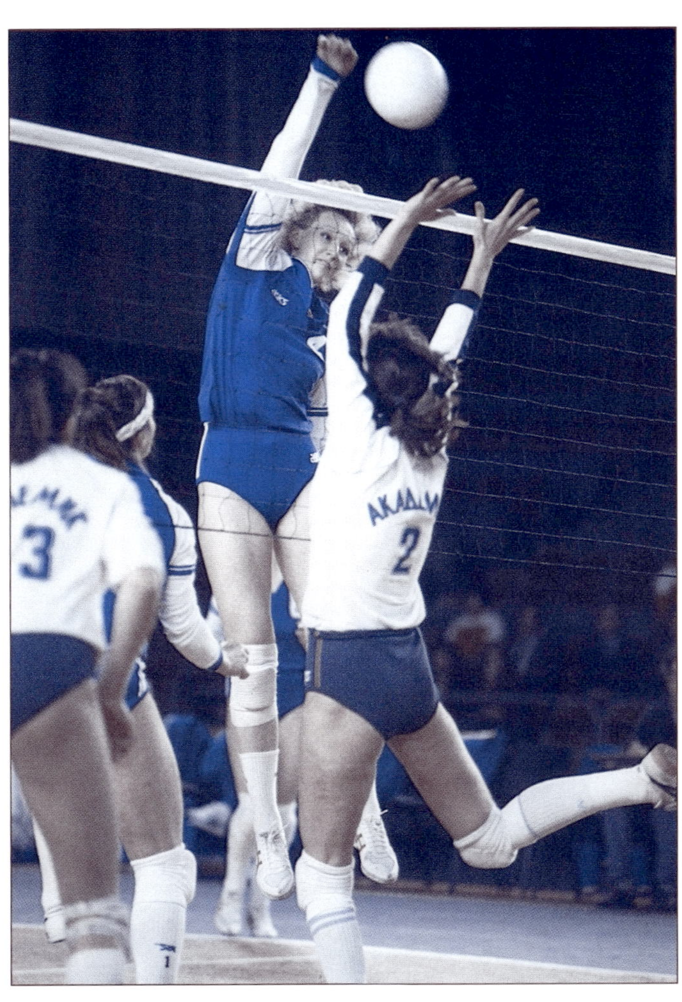

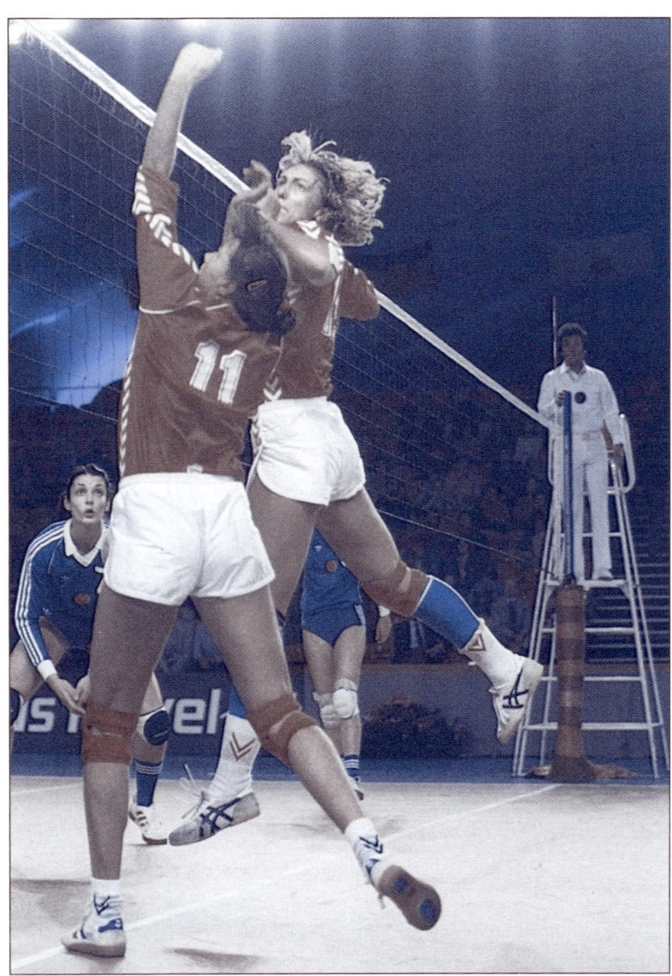

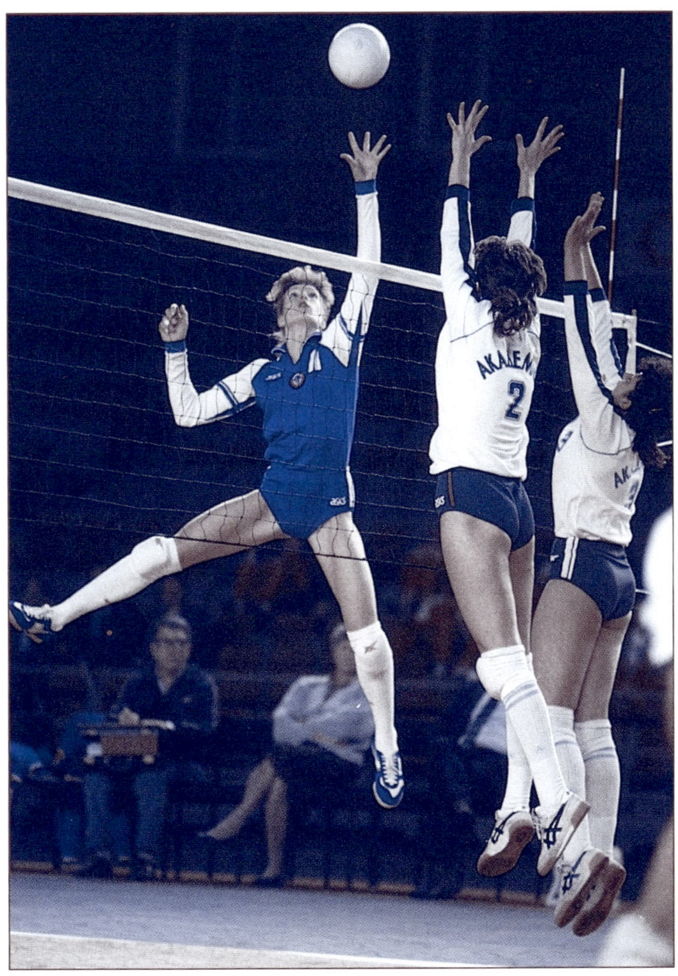

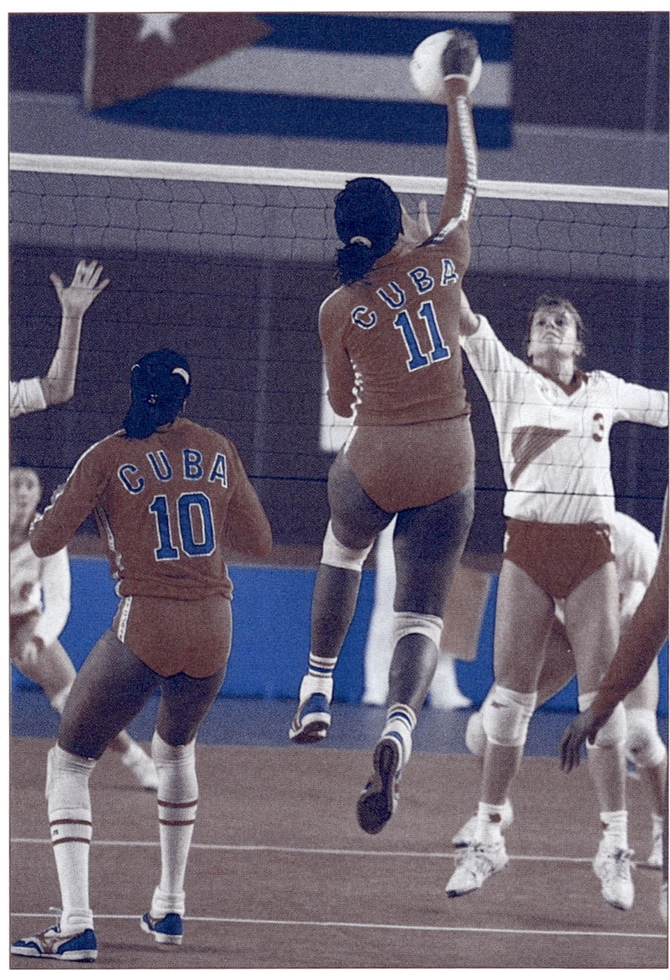

Soccer

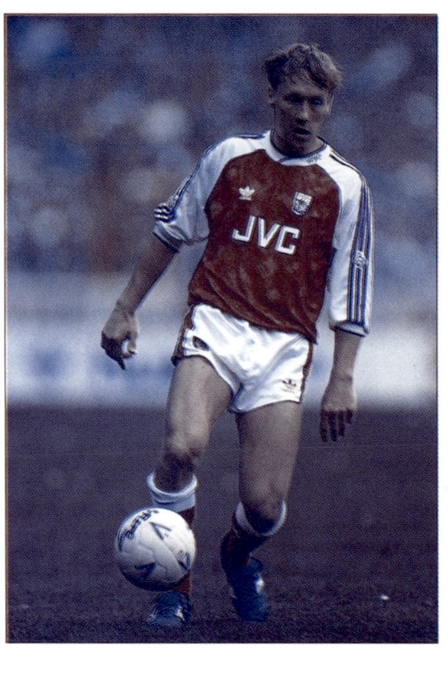

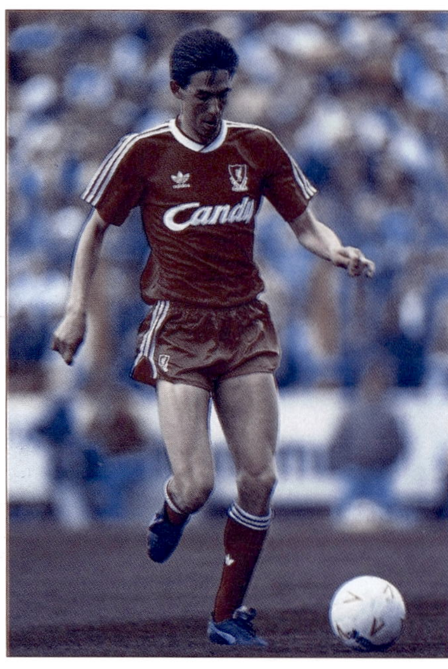

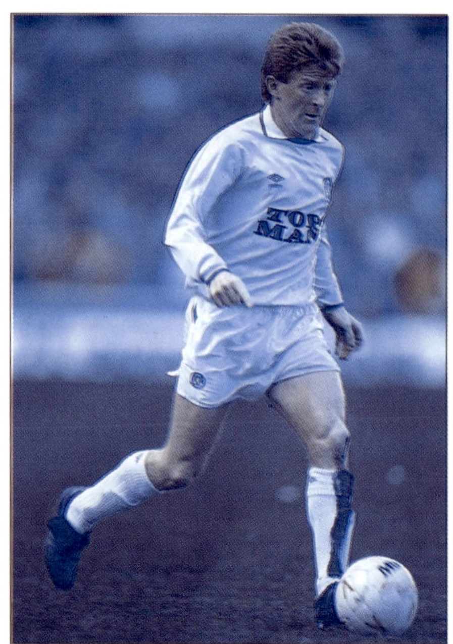

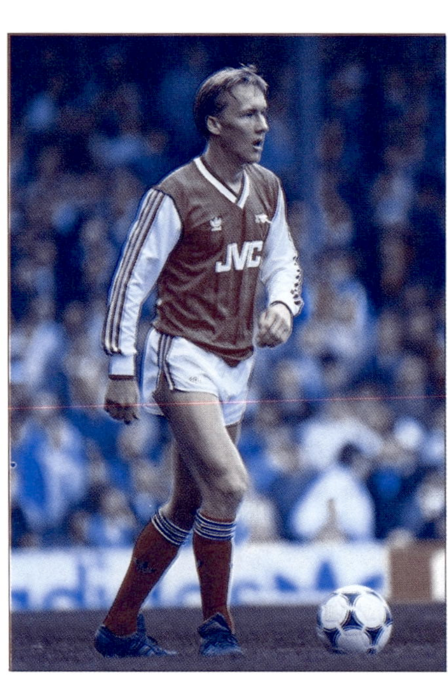

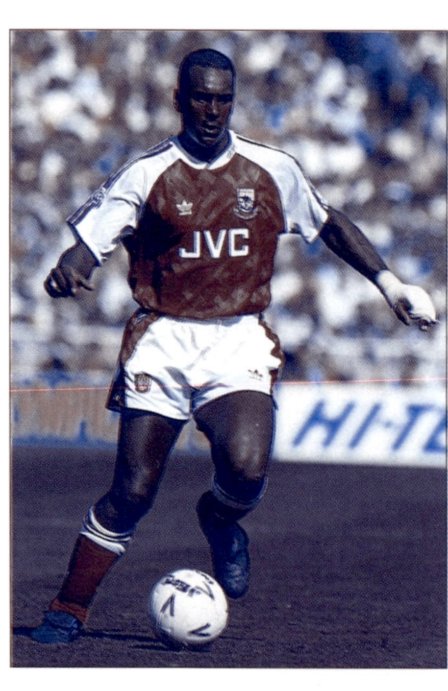

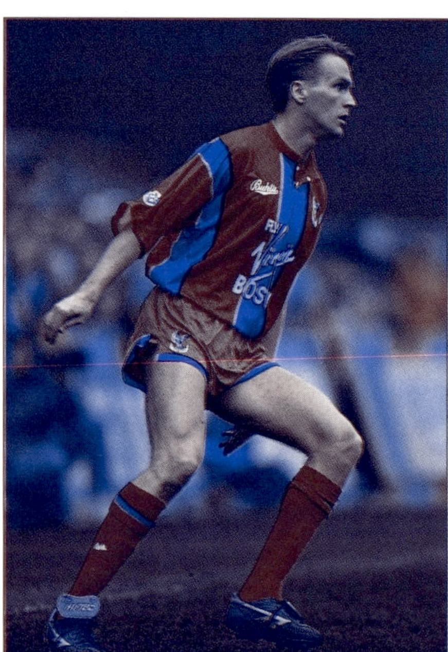

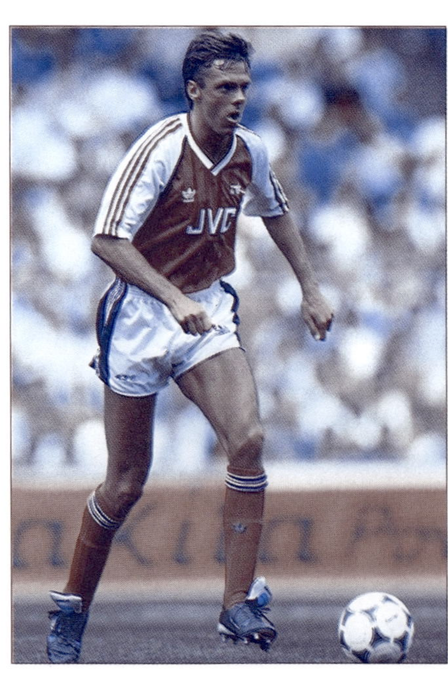

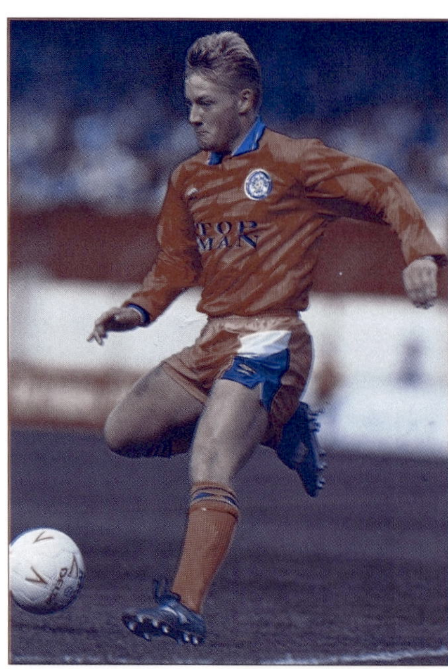

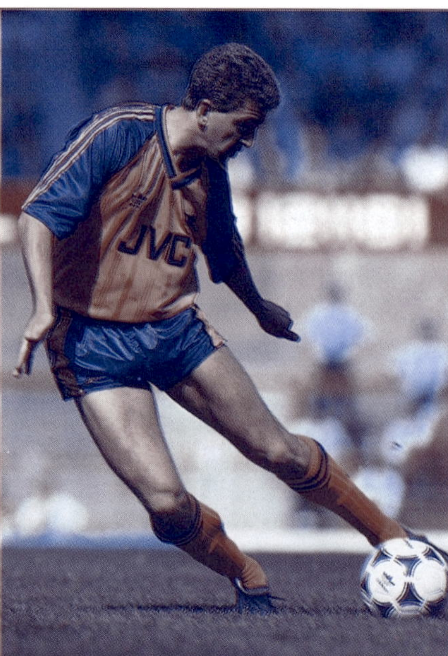

Soccer

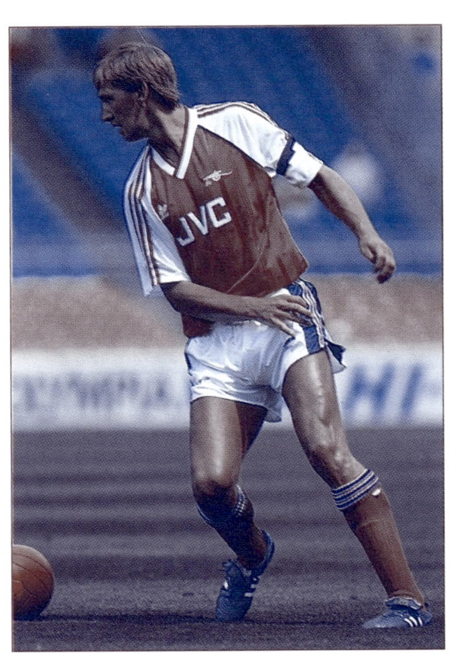

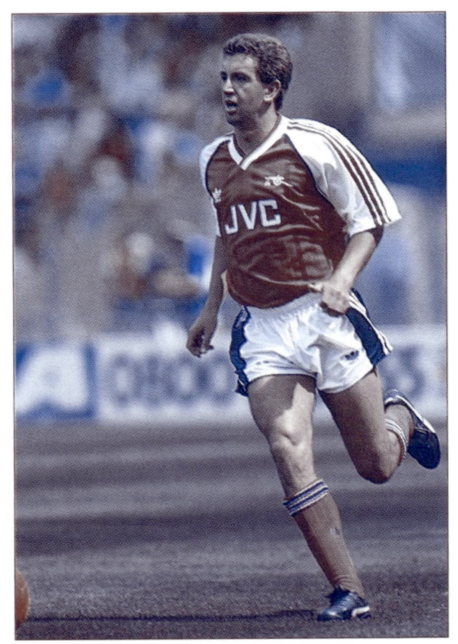

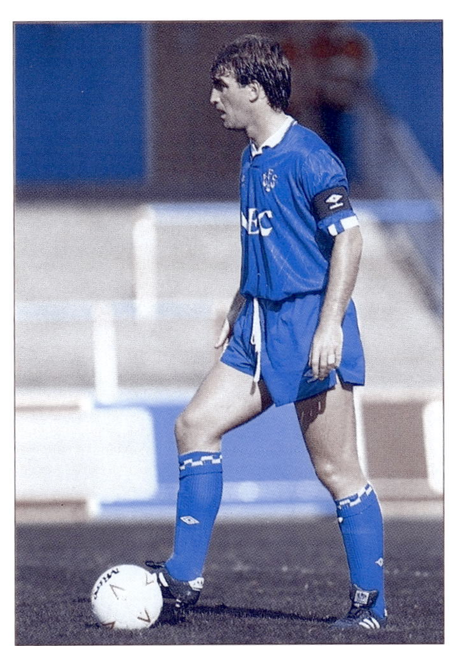

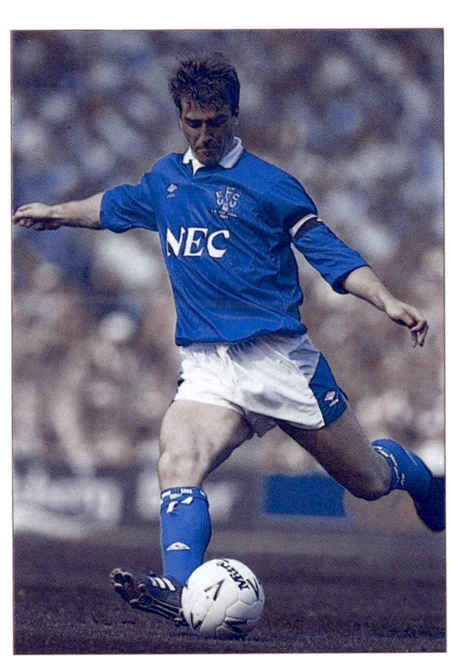

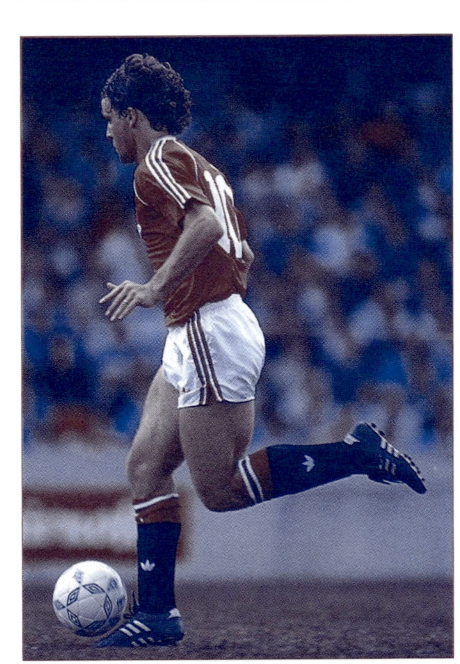

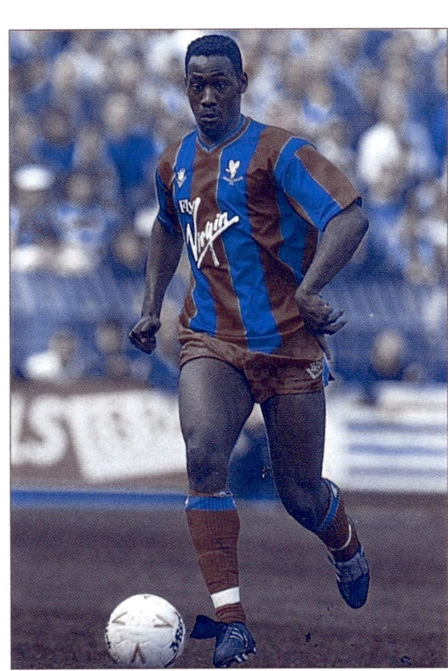

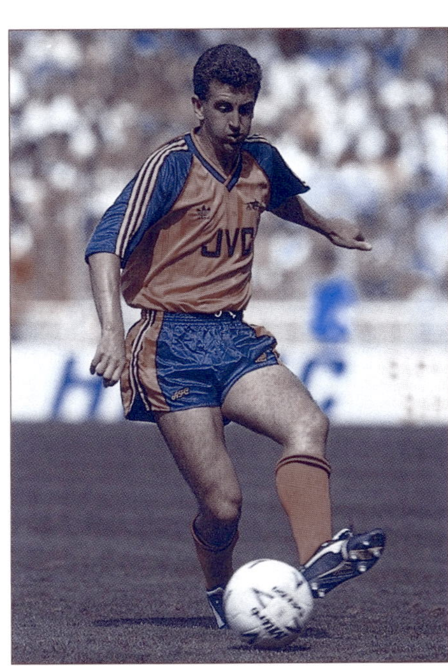

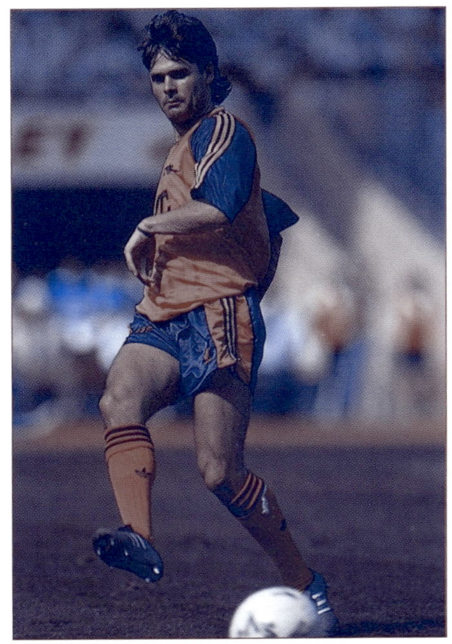

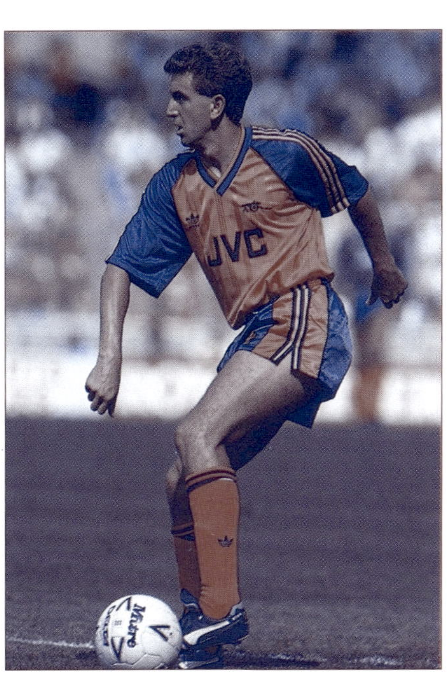

Soccer

JVC
HOLSTEN
HOLSTEN
HOLSTEN
HOLSTEN
HOLSTEN

Candy

JVC

JVC

THE WOOLWICH

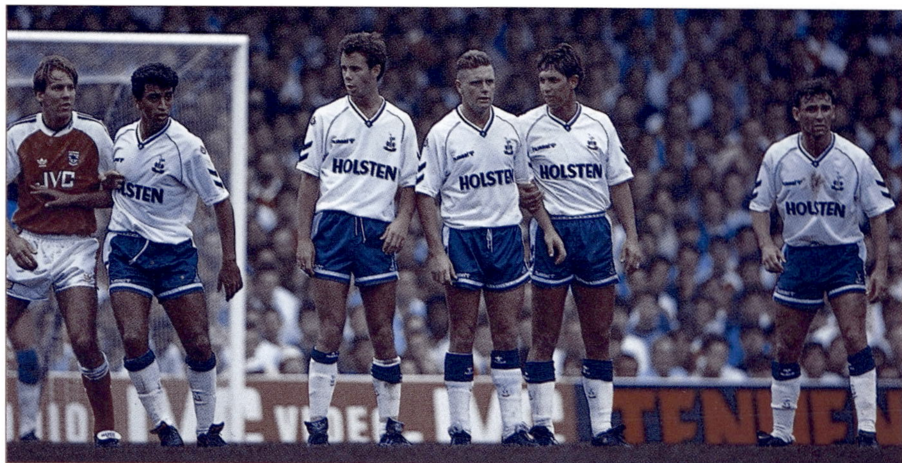

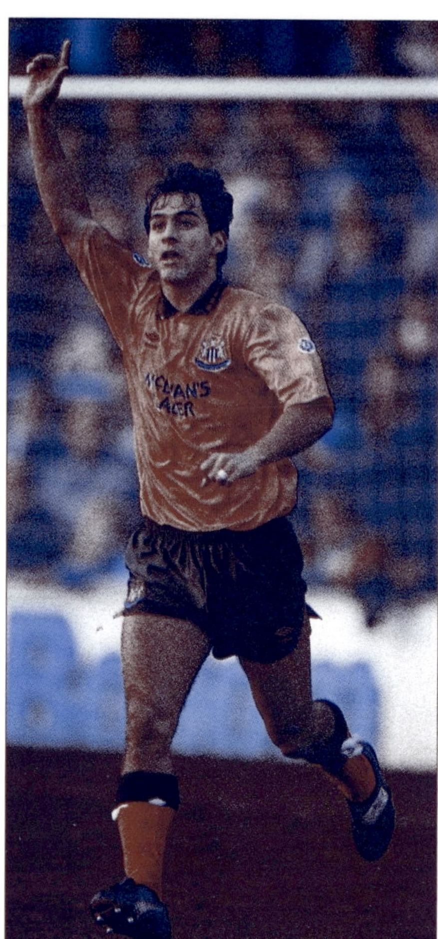

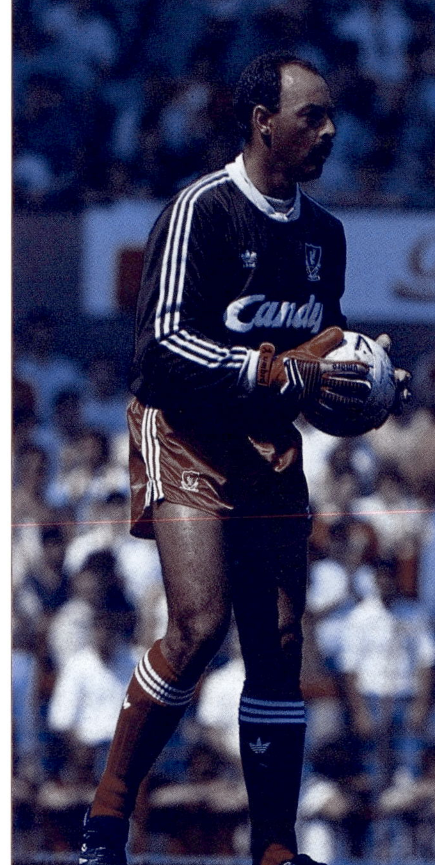

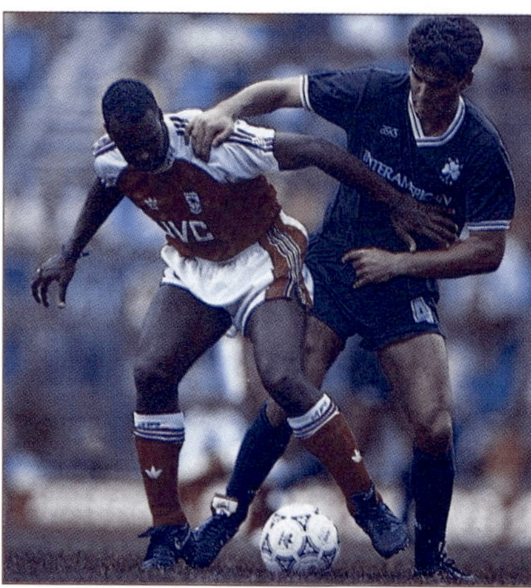

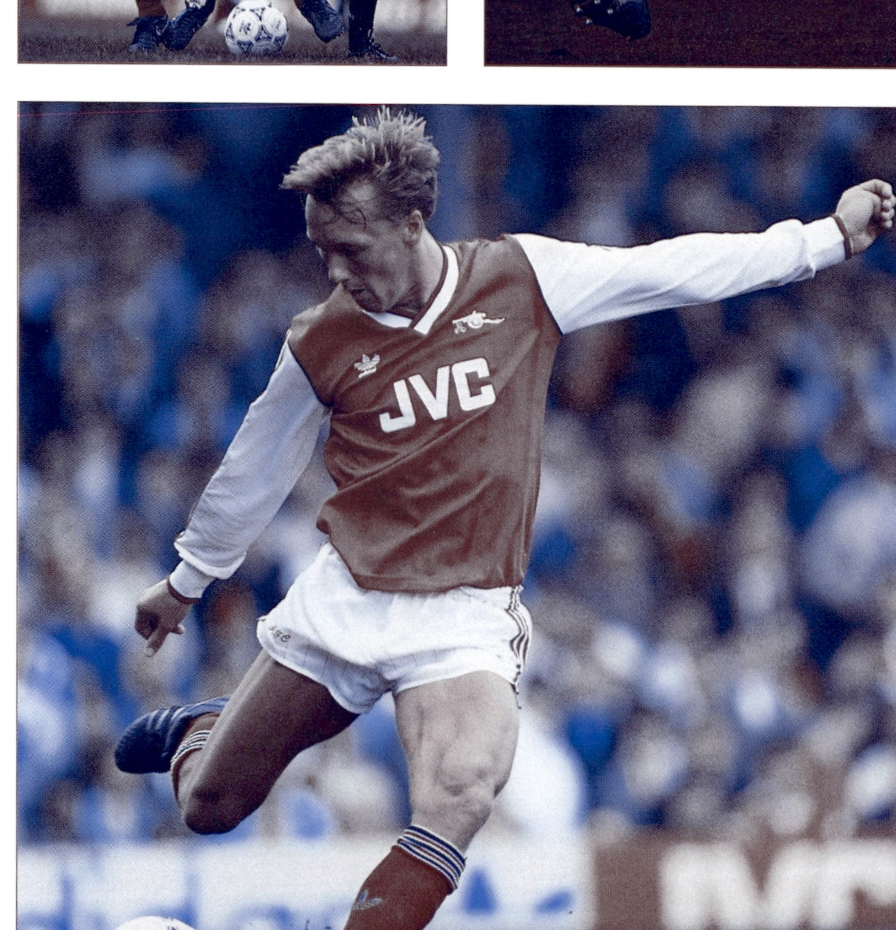

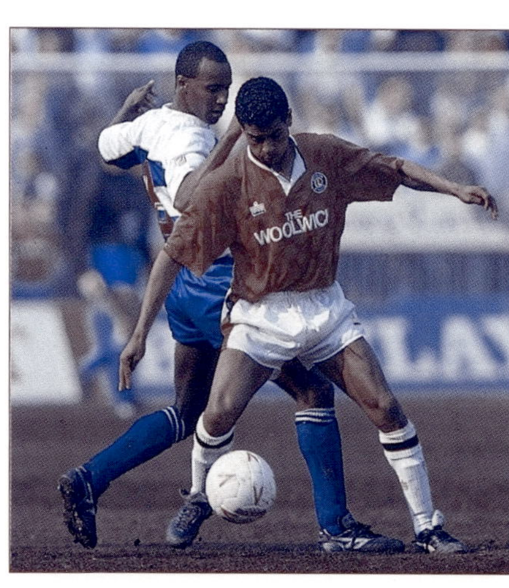

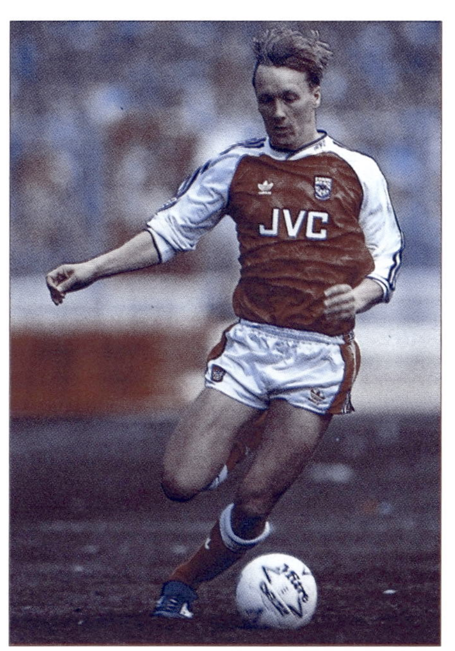
JVC

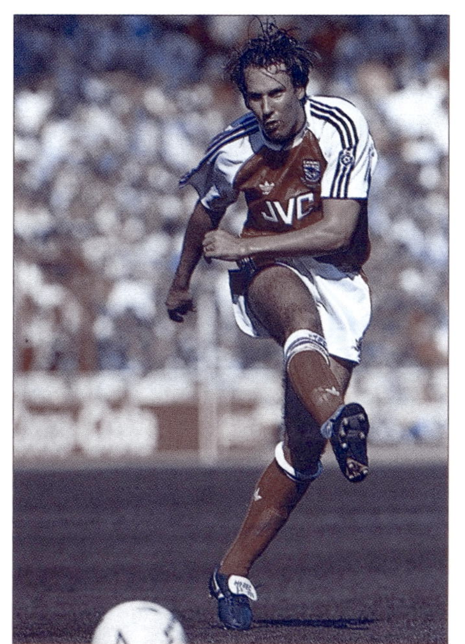
JVC

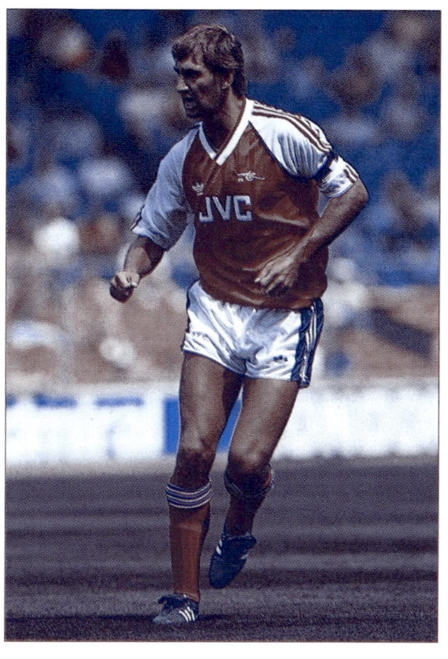
JVC

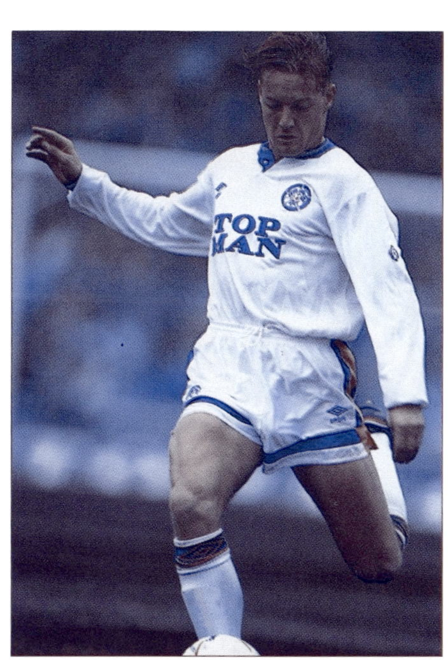
TOP MAN

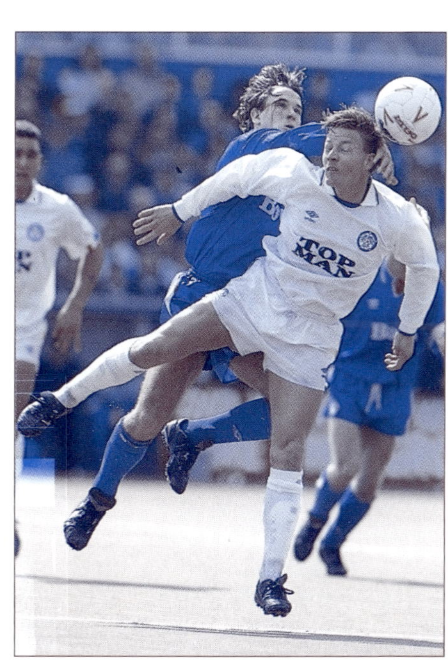
TOP MAN

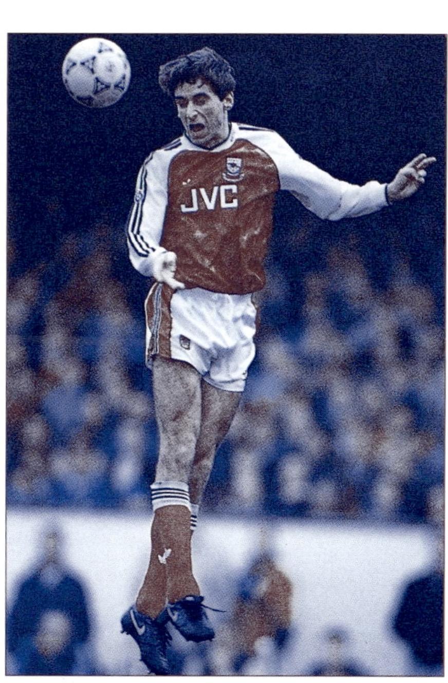
JVC

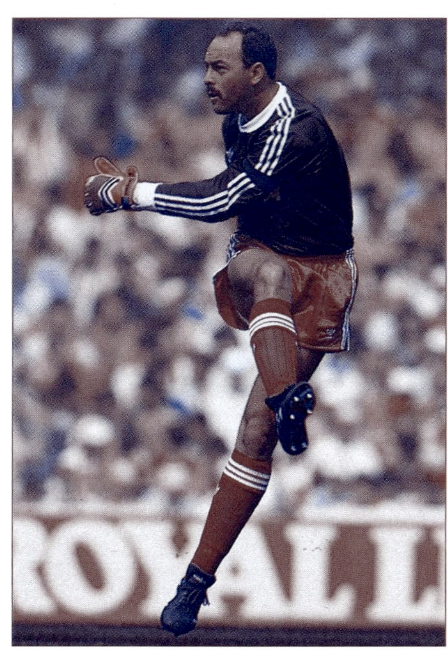
ROYAL L

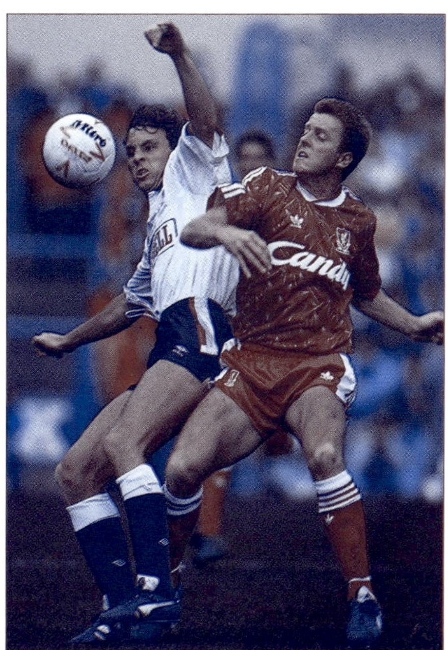
Mitre
Candy

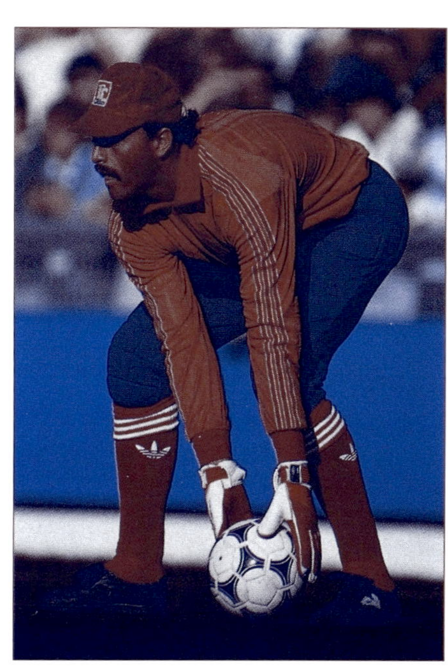

Soccer

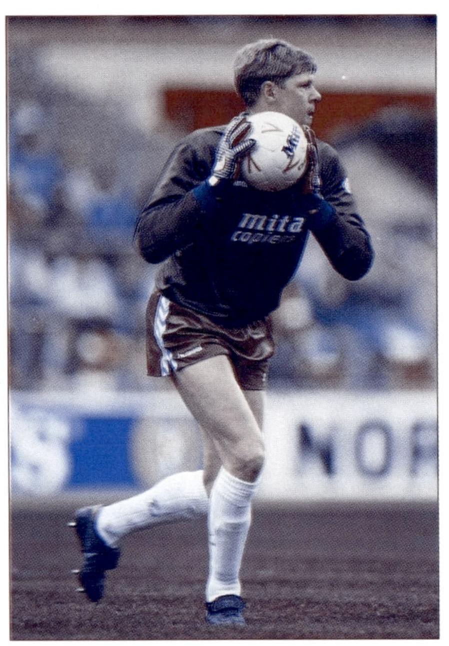

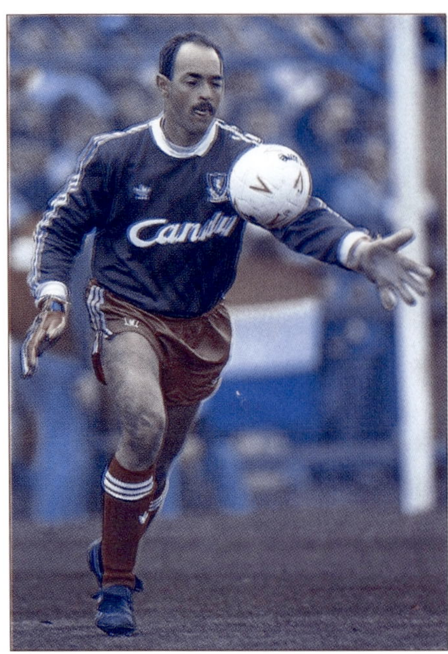

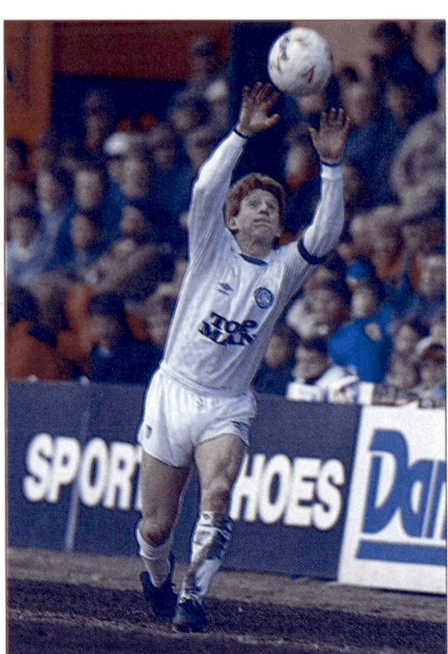

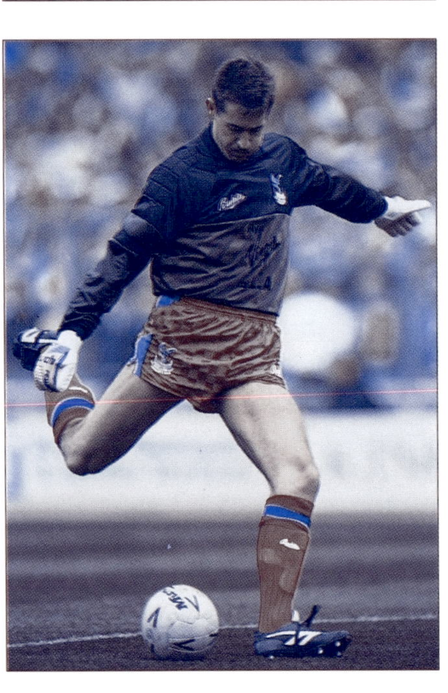

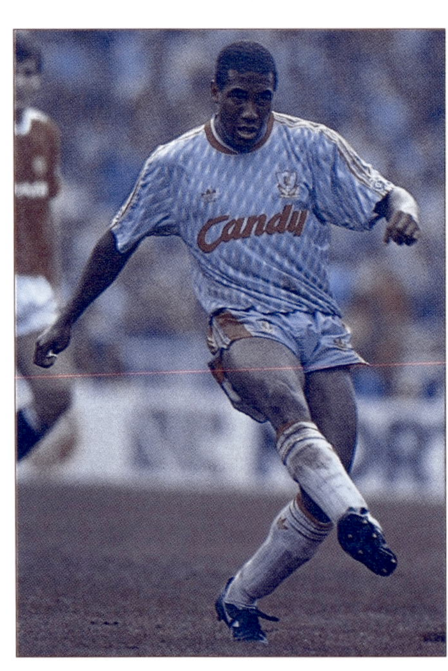

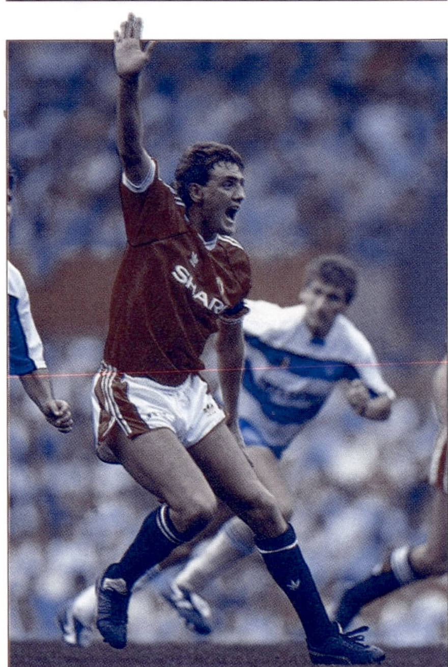

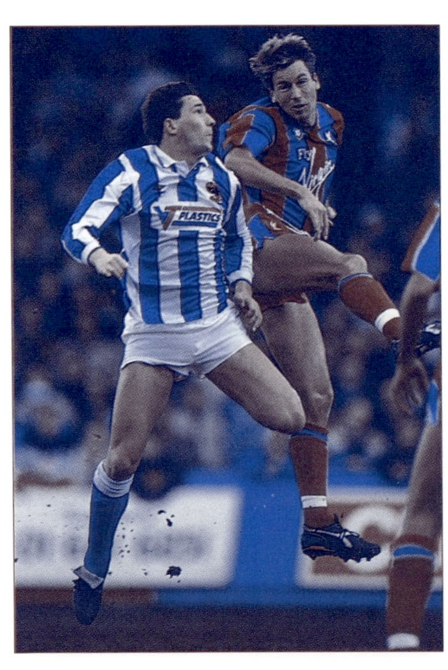

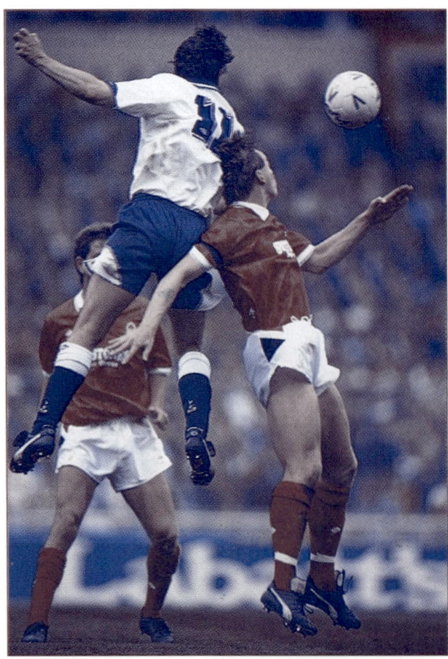

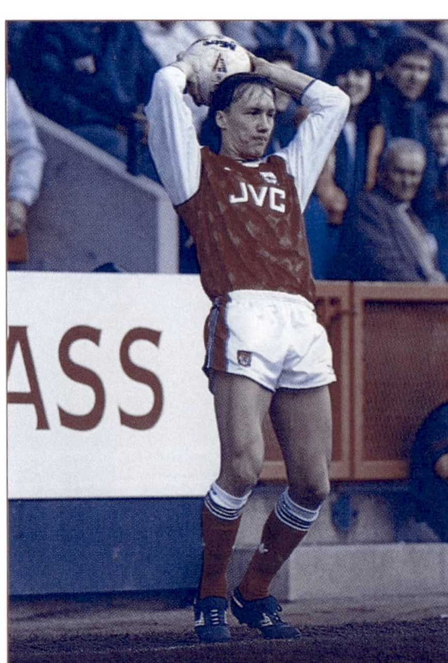

Soccer

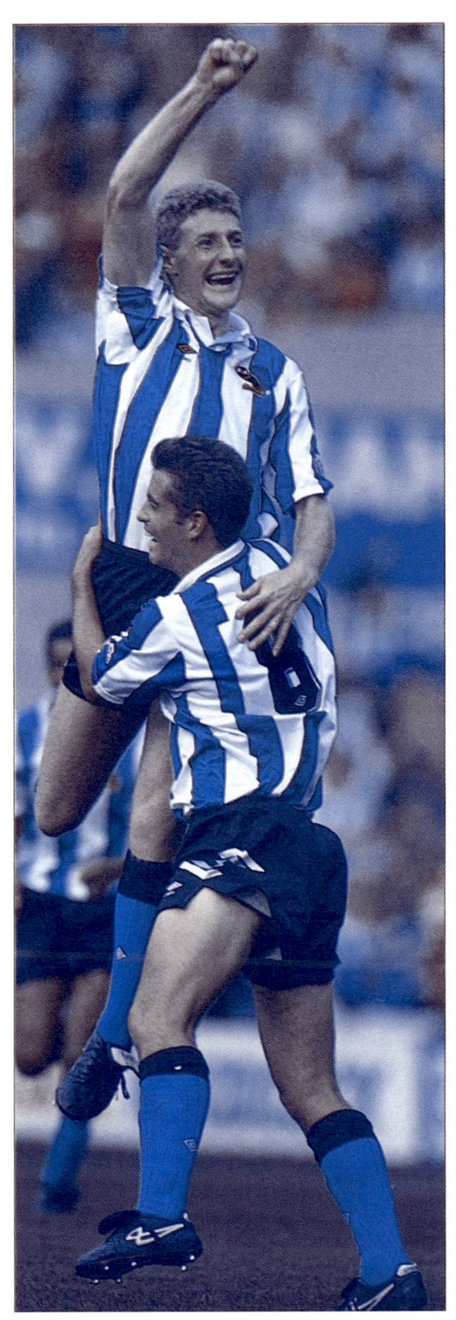

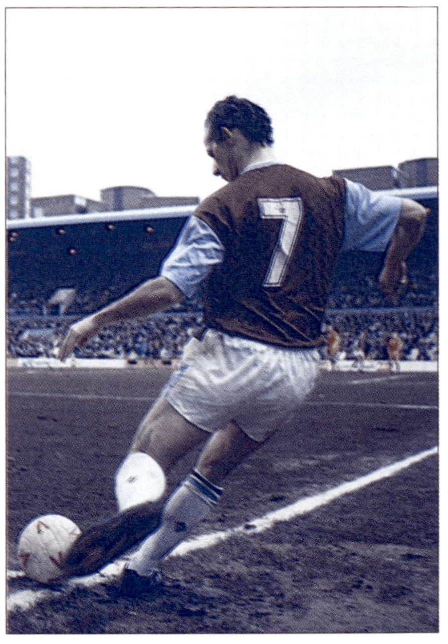

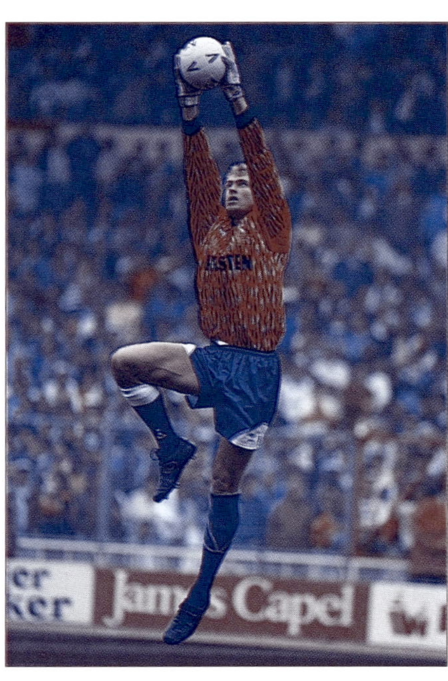

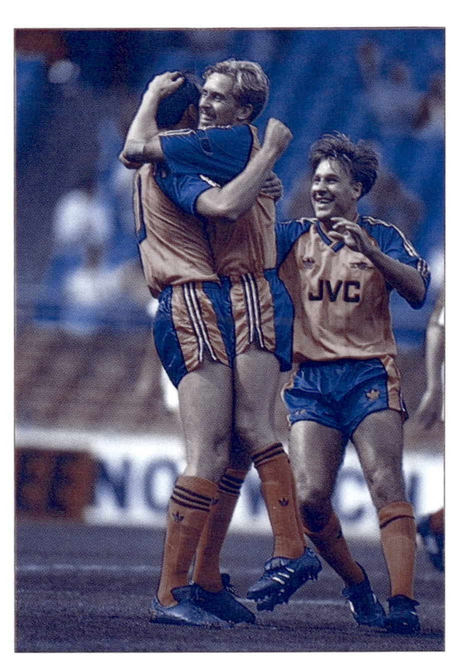

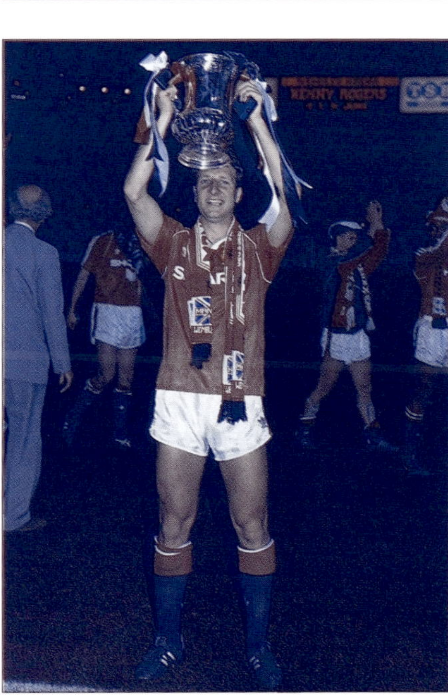

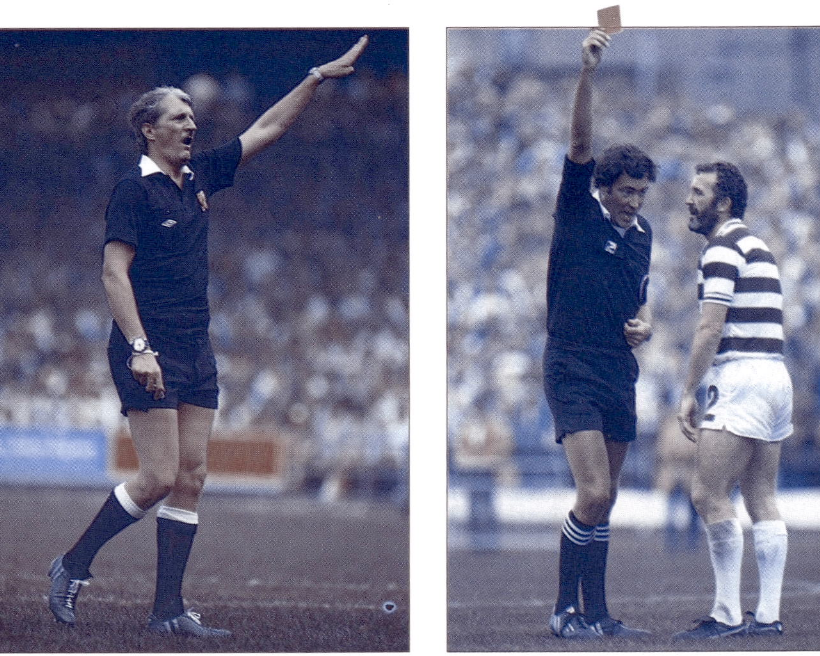

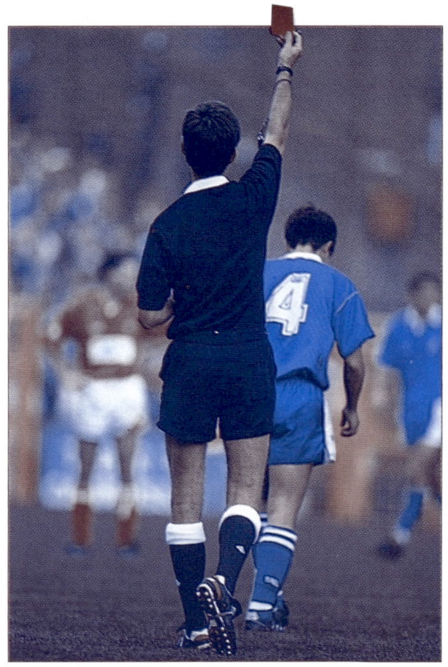

Football

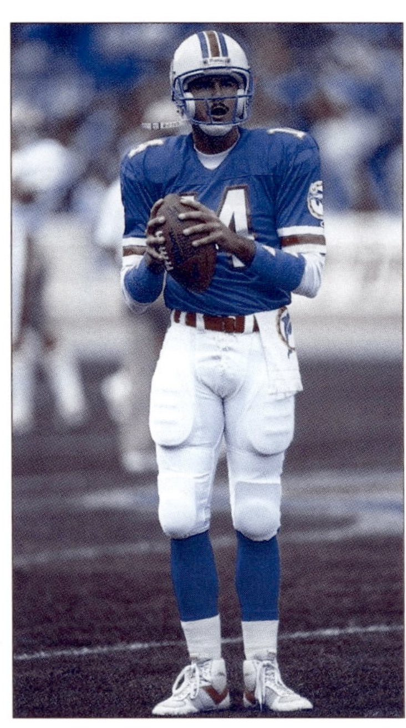

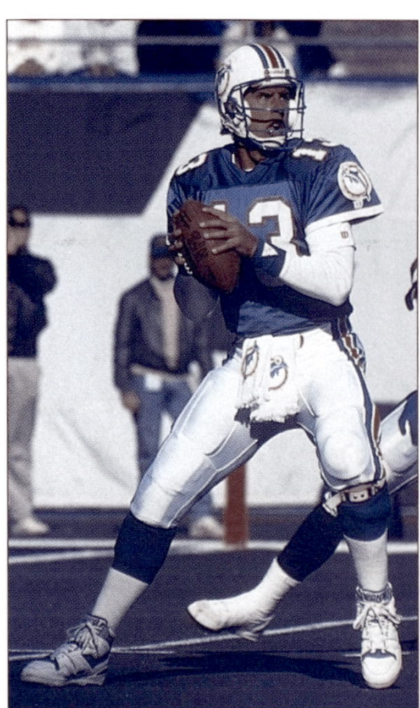

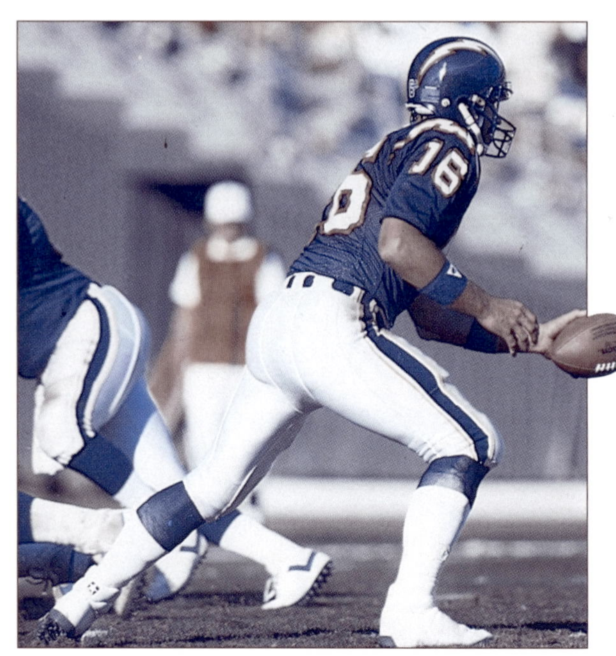

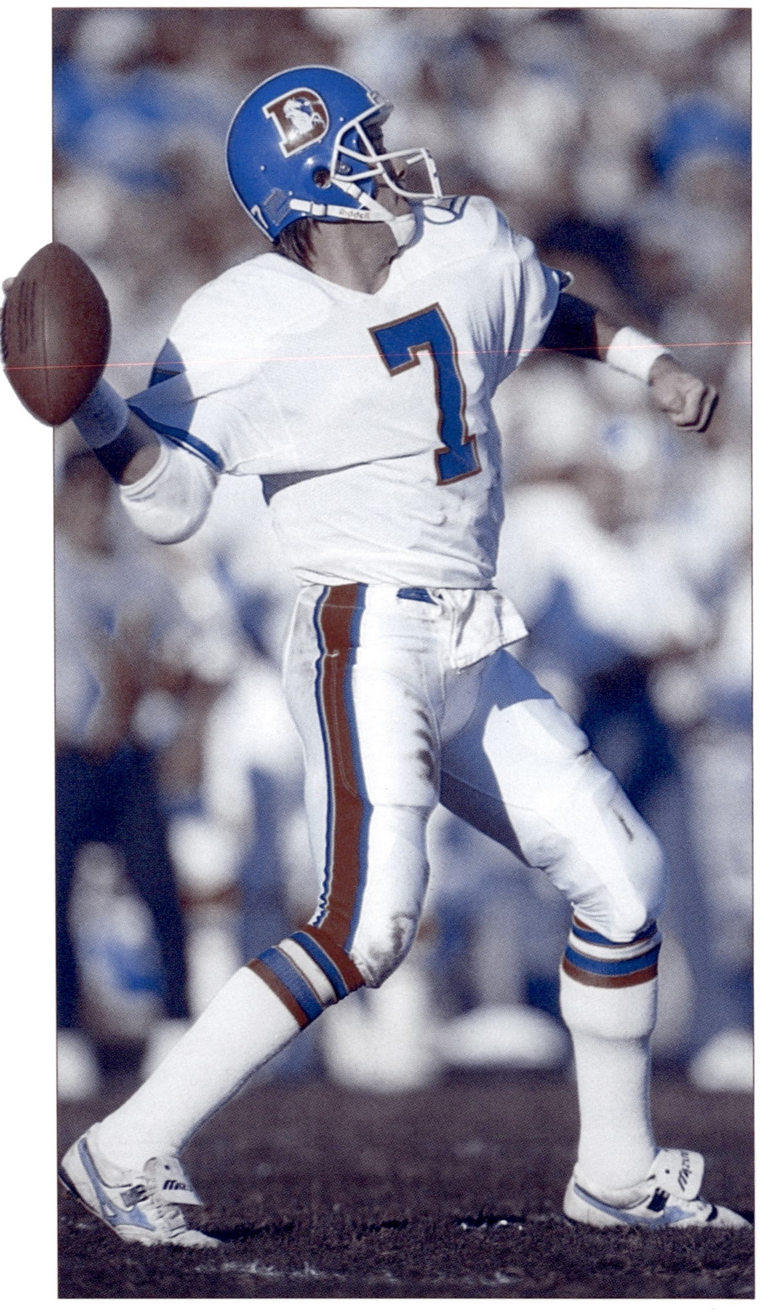

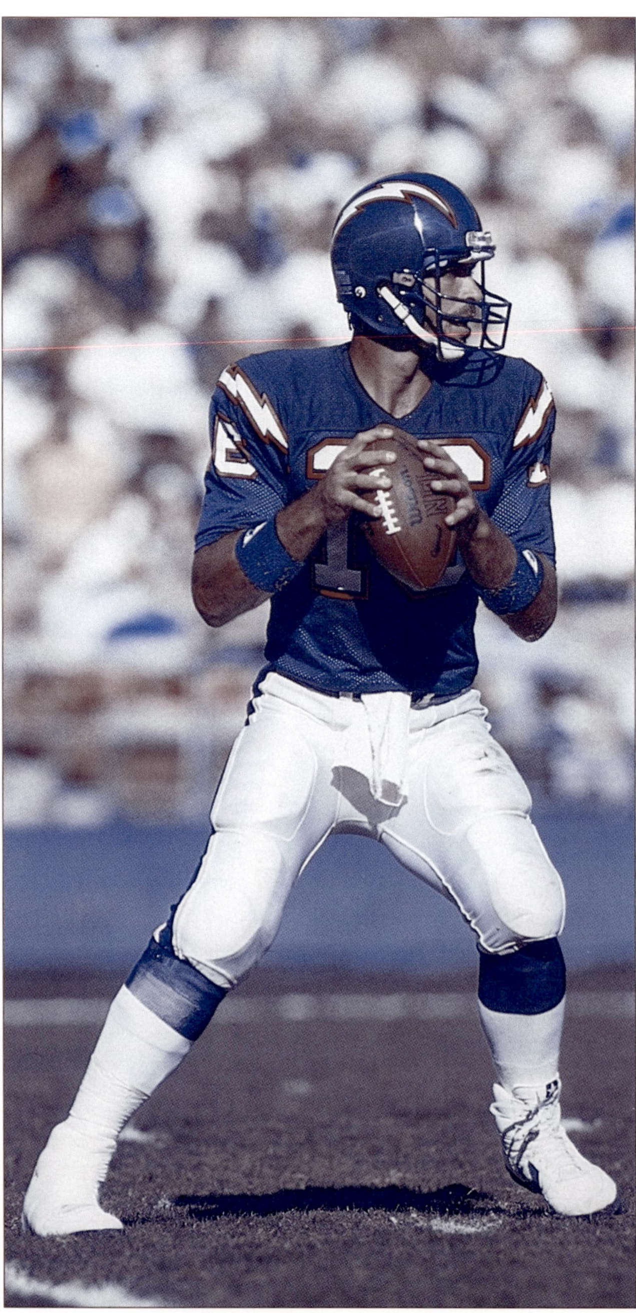

Football

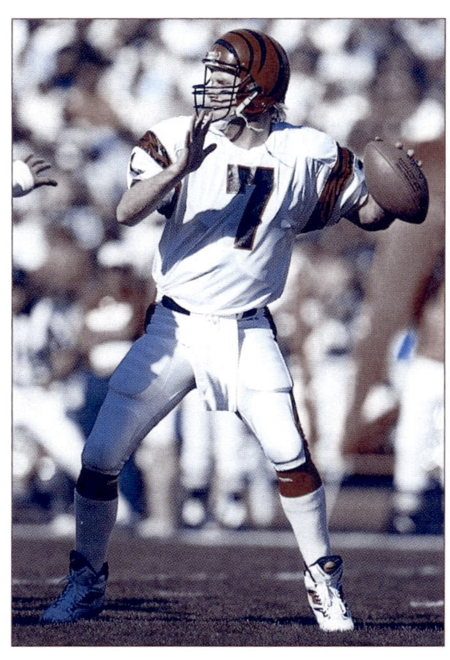

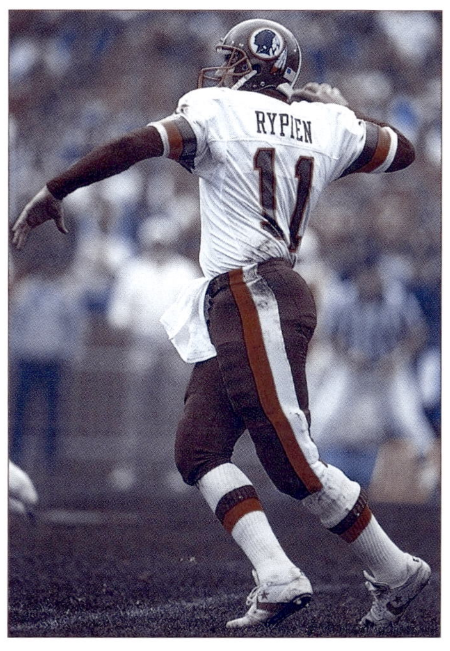

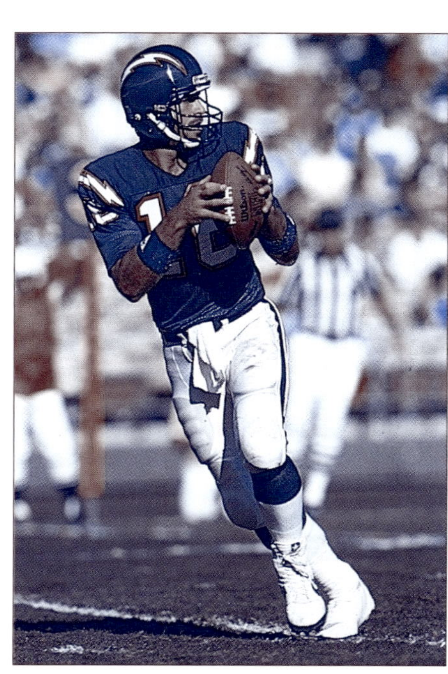

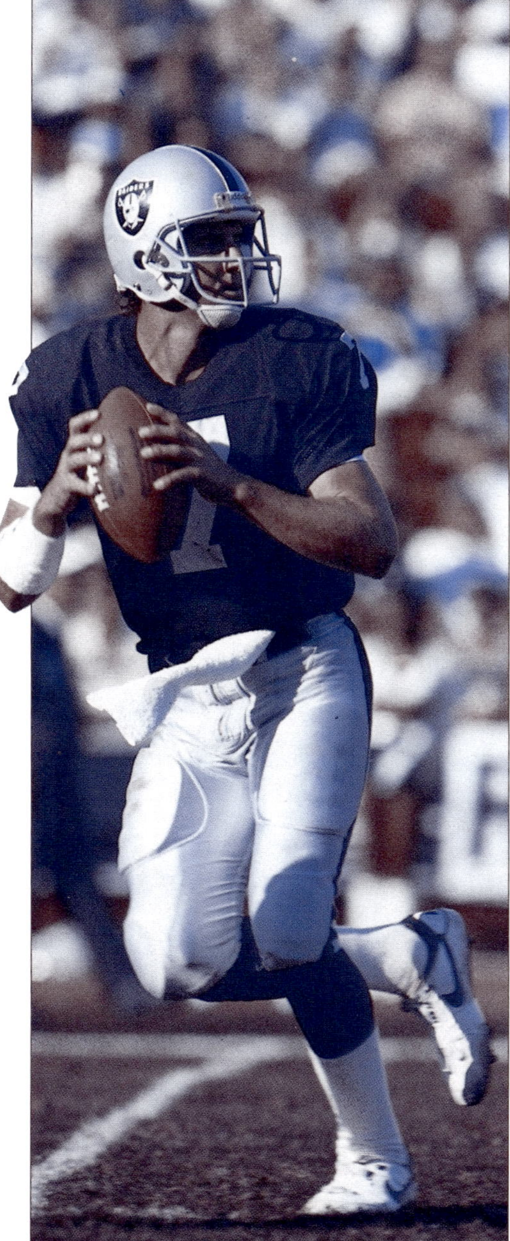

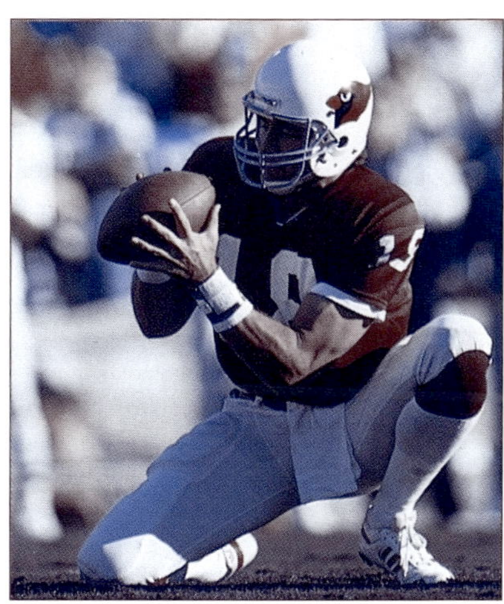

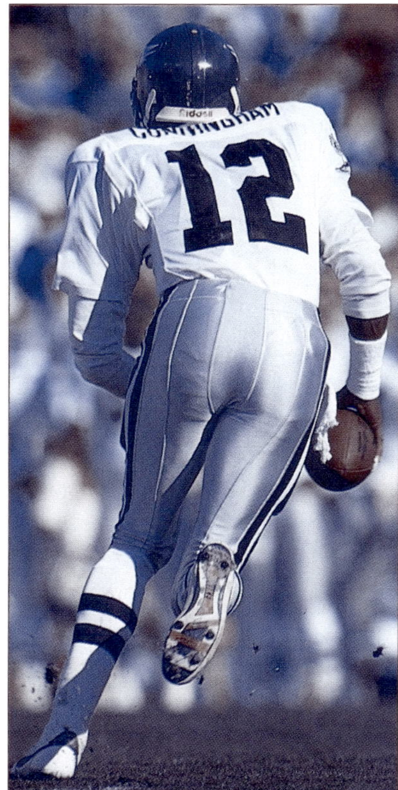

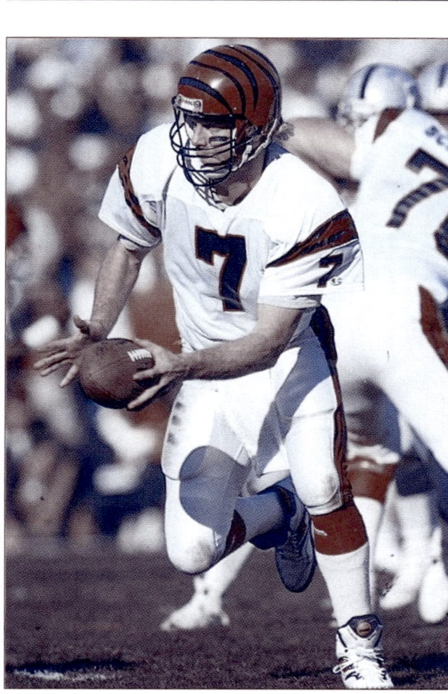

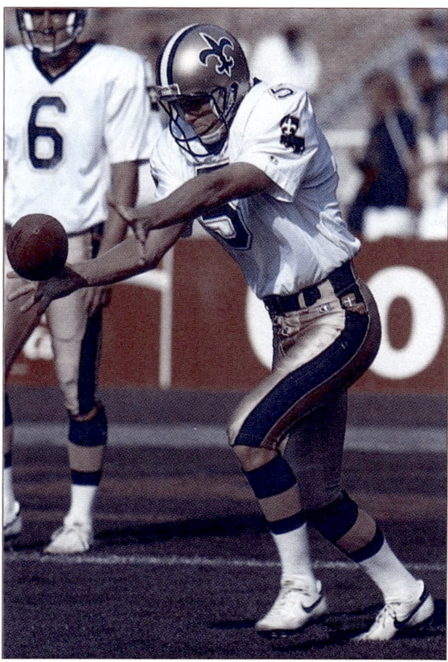

Football

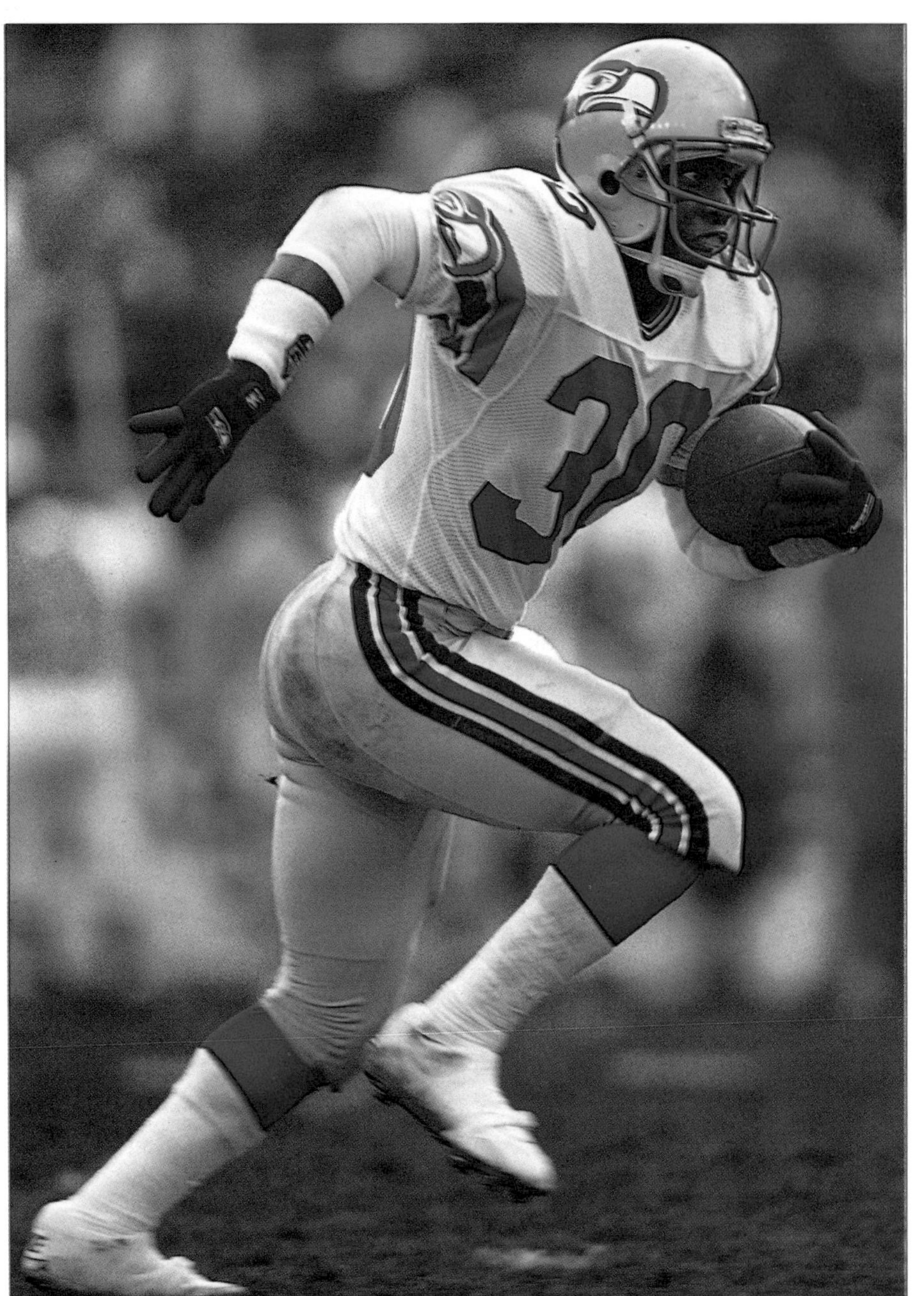
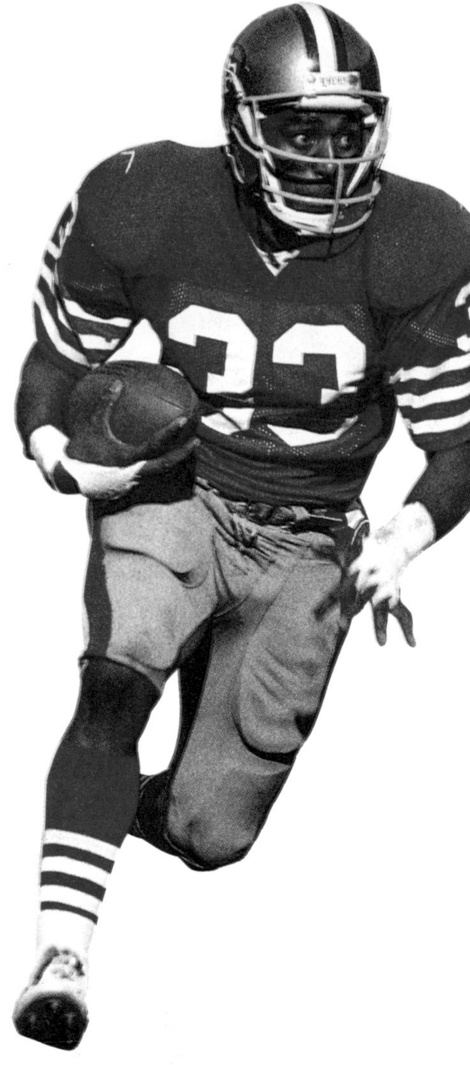
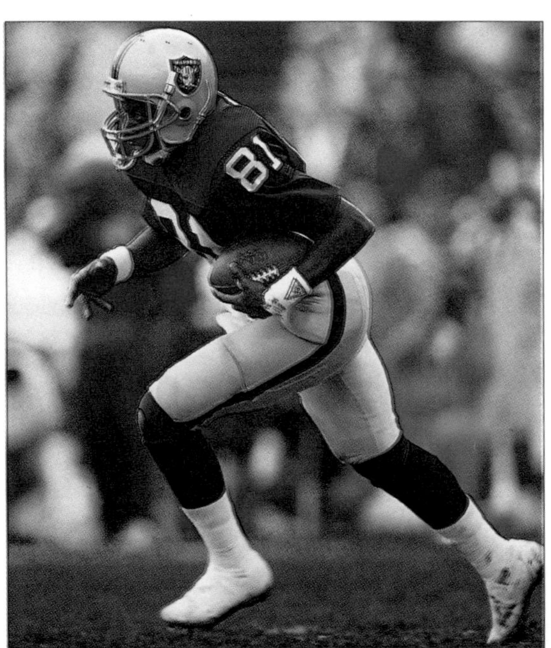
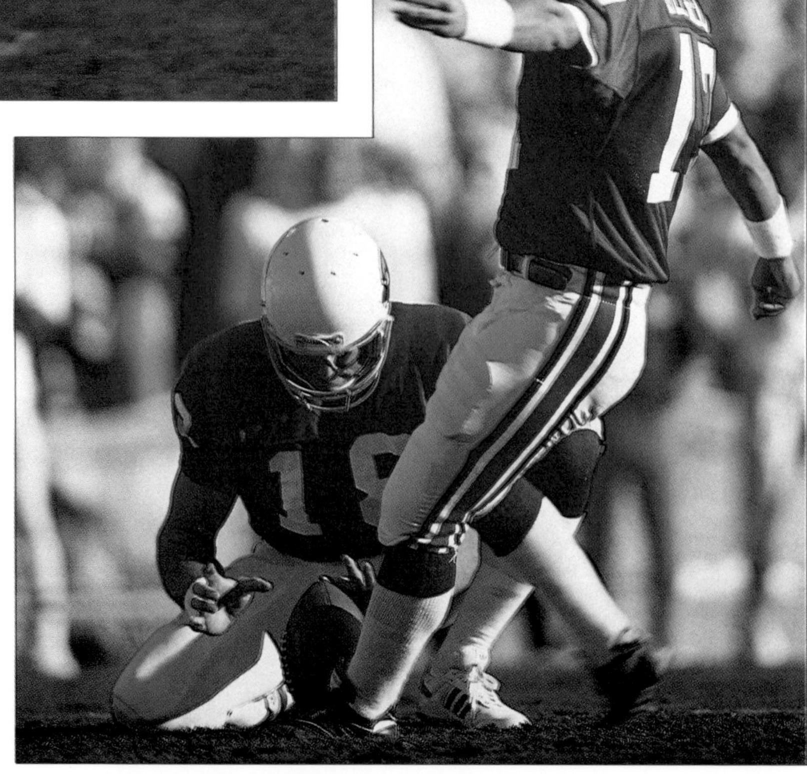

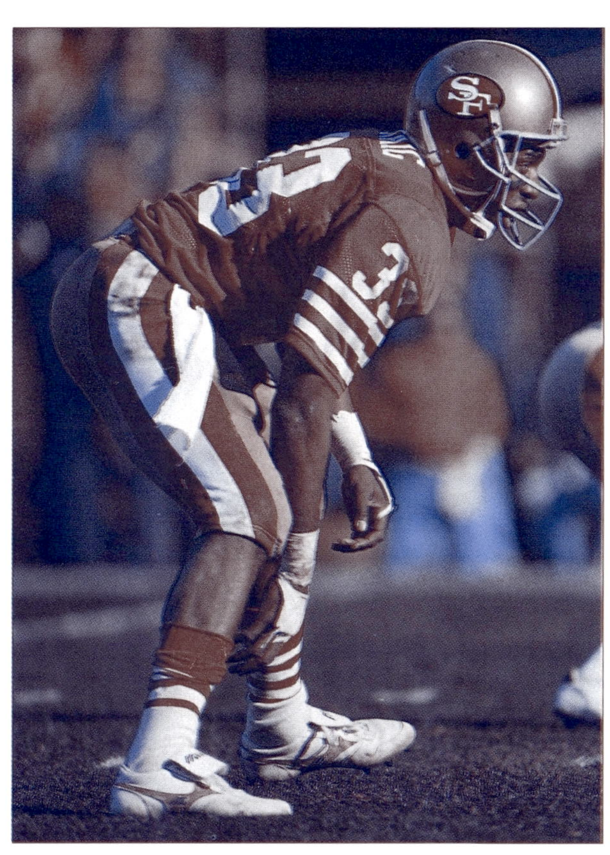

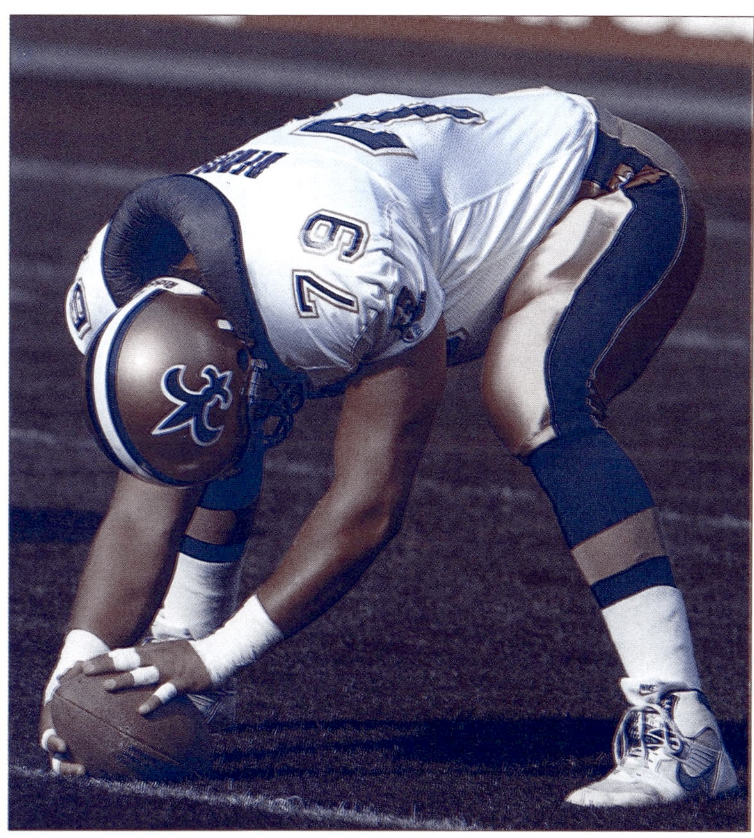

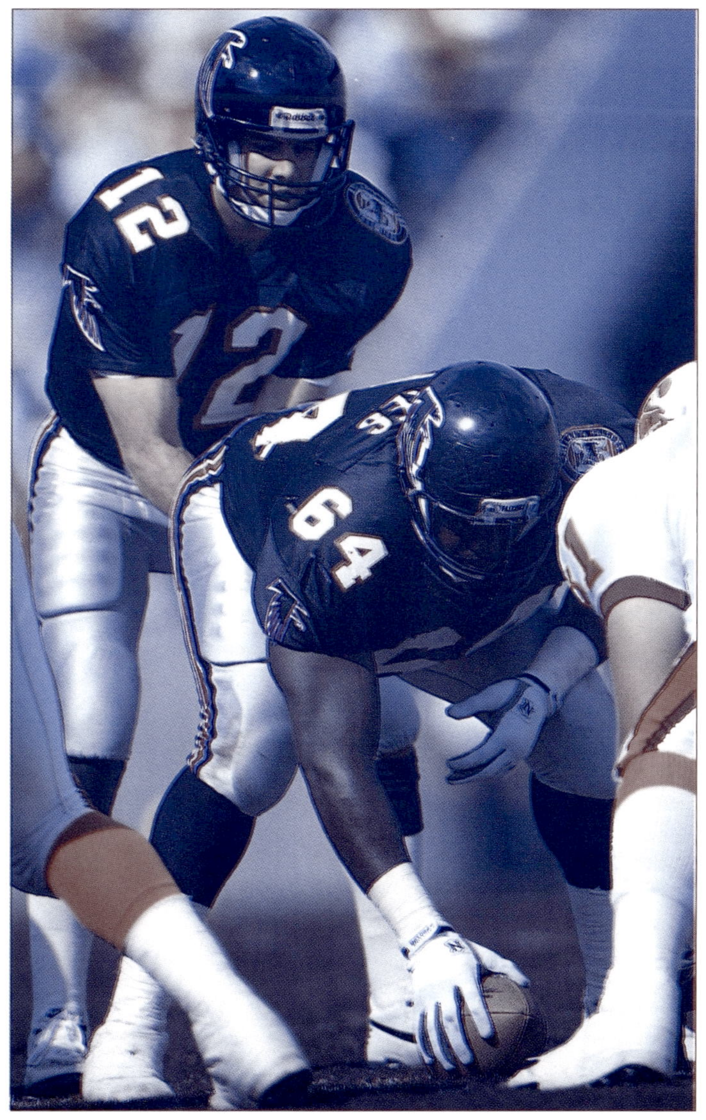

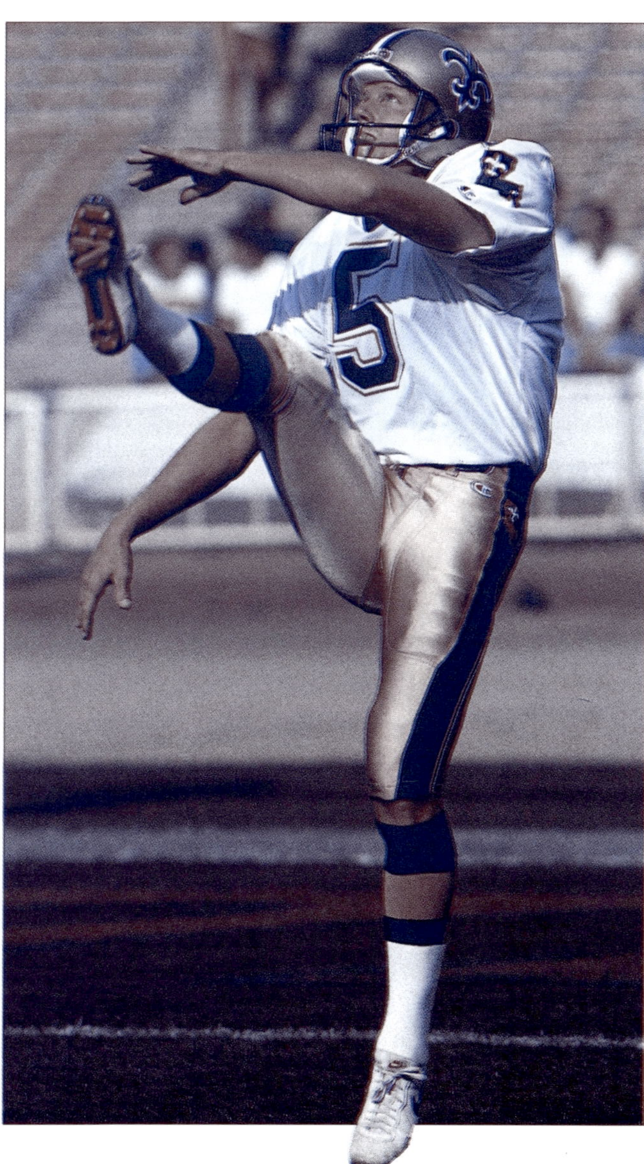

Football

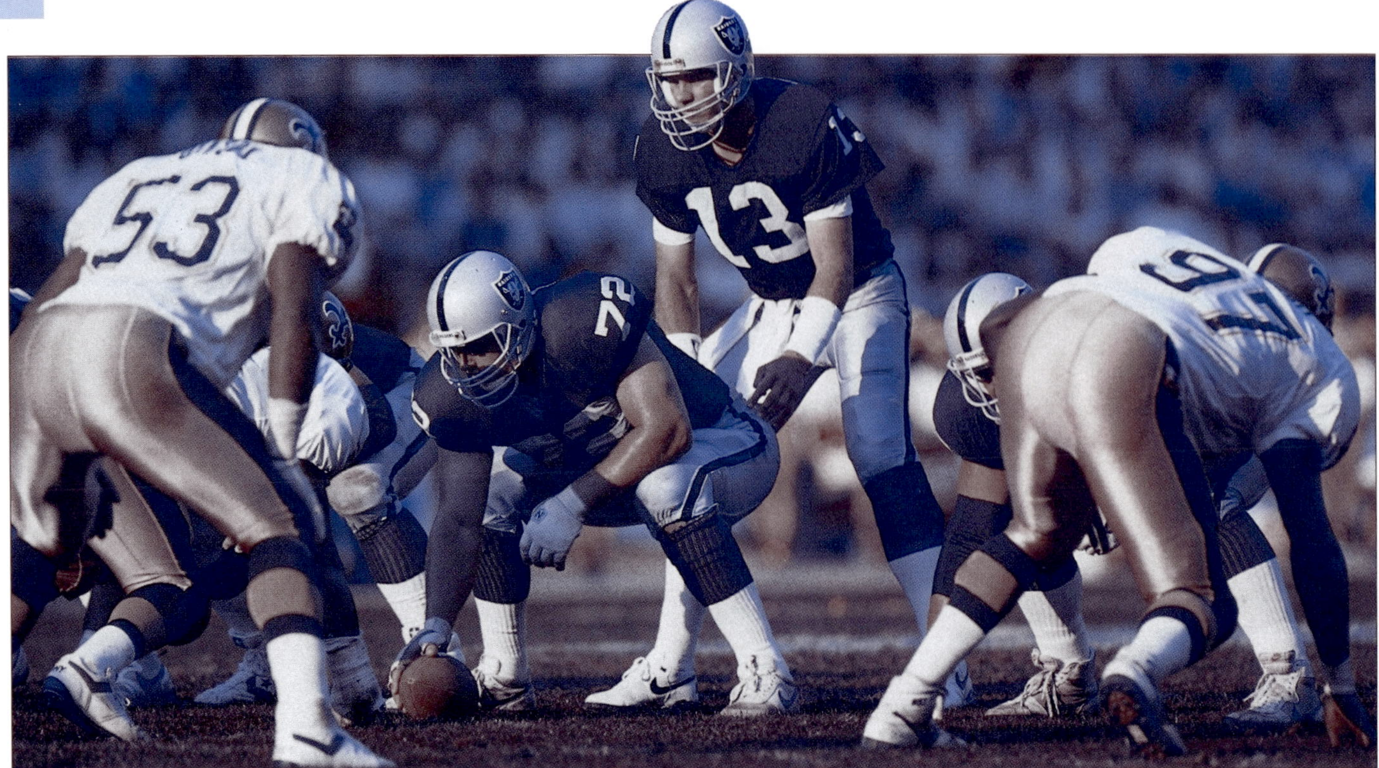

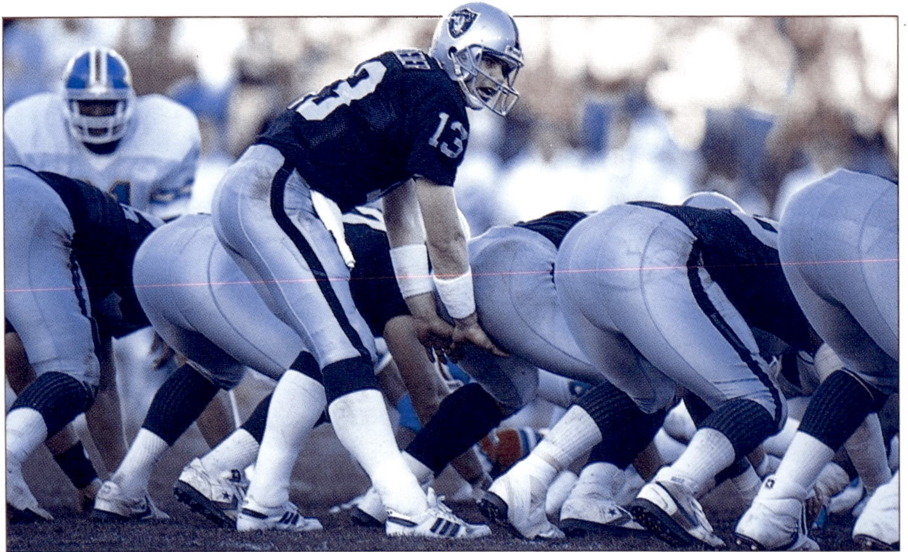

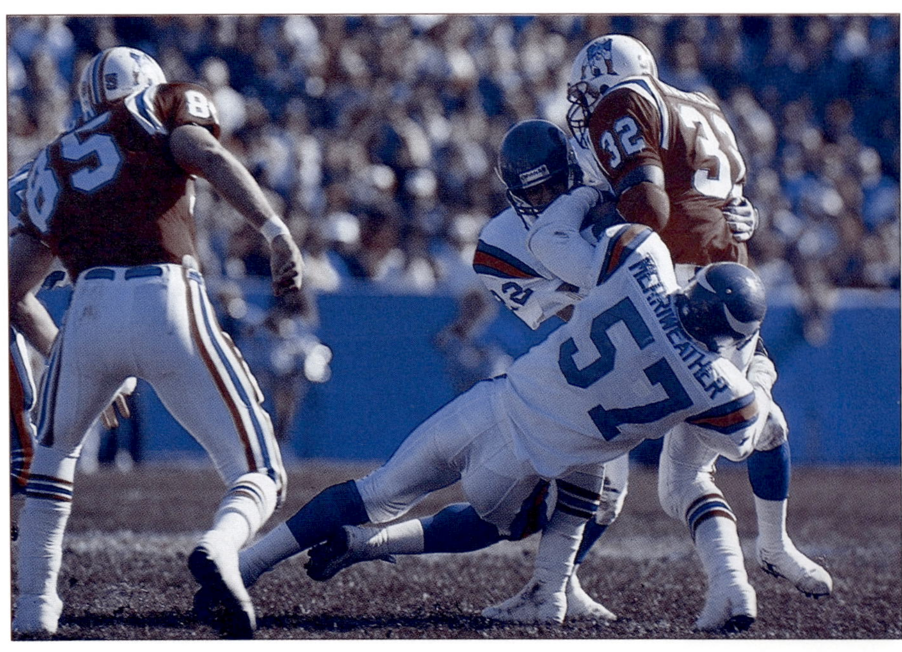

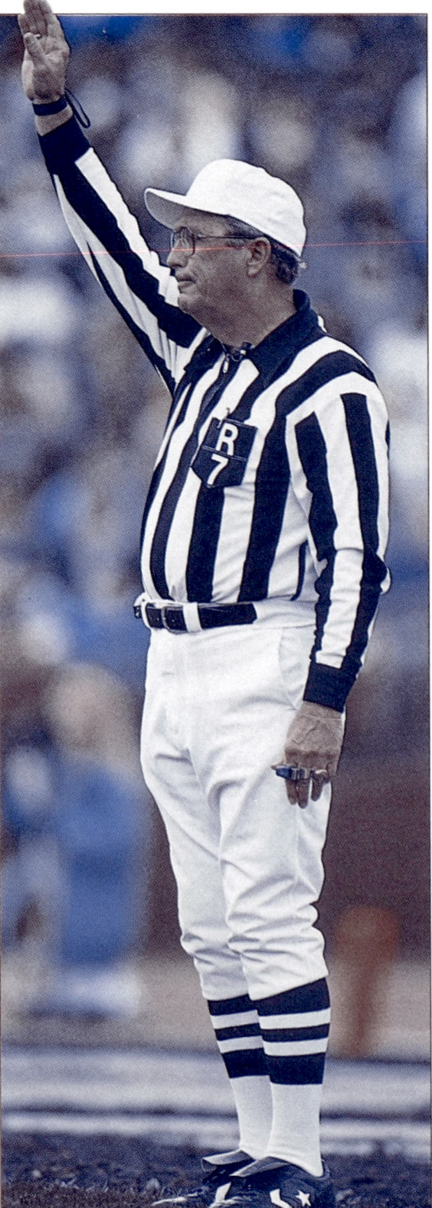

Cheerleaders

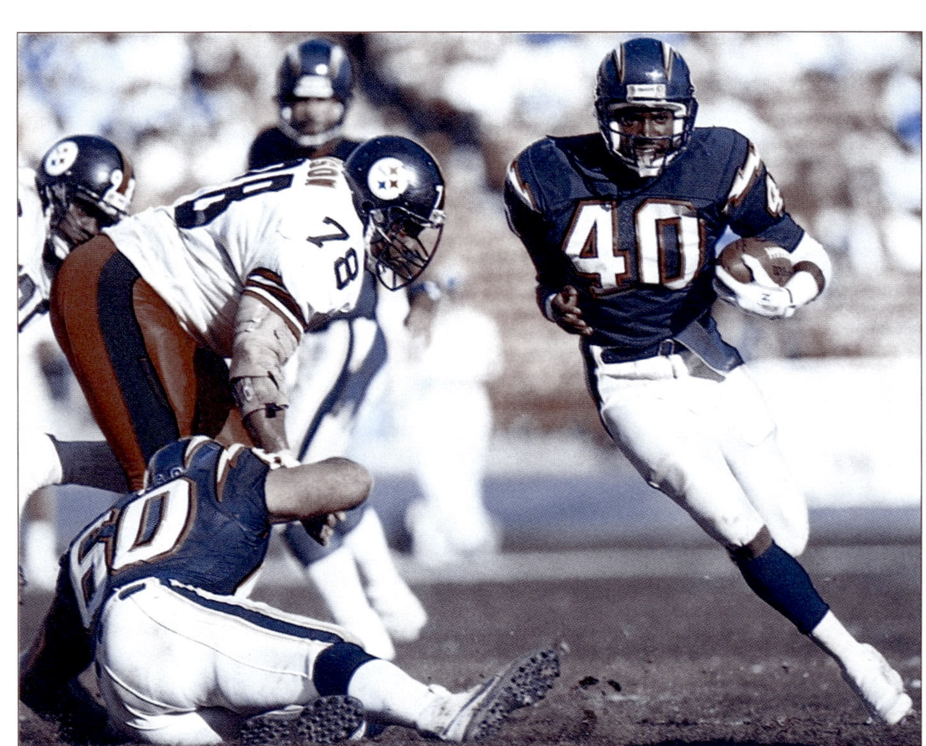

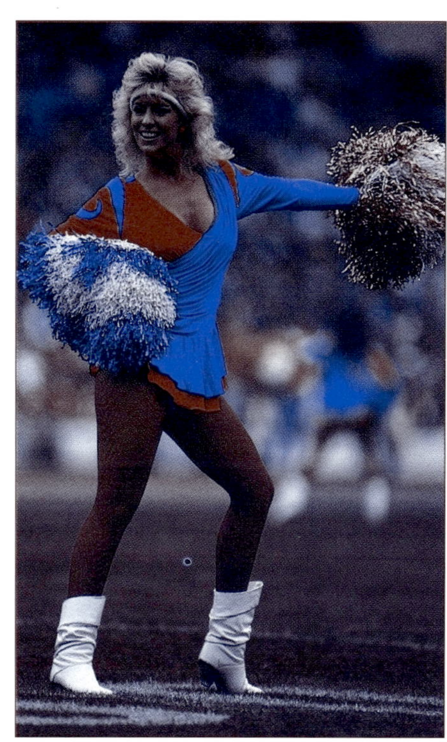

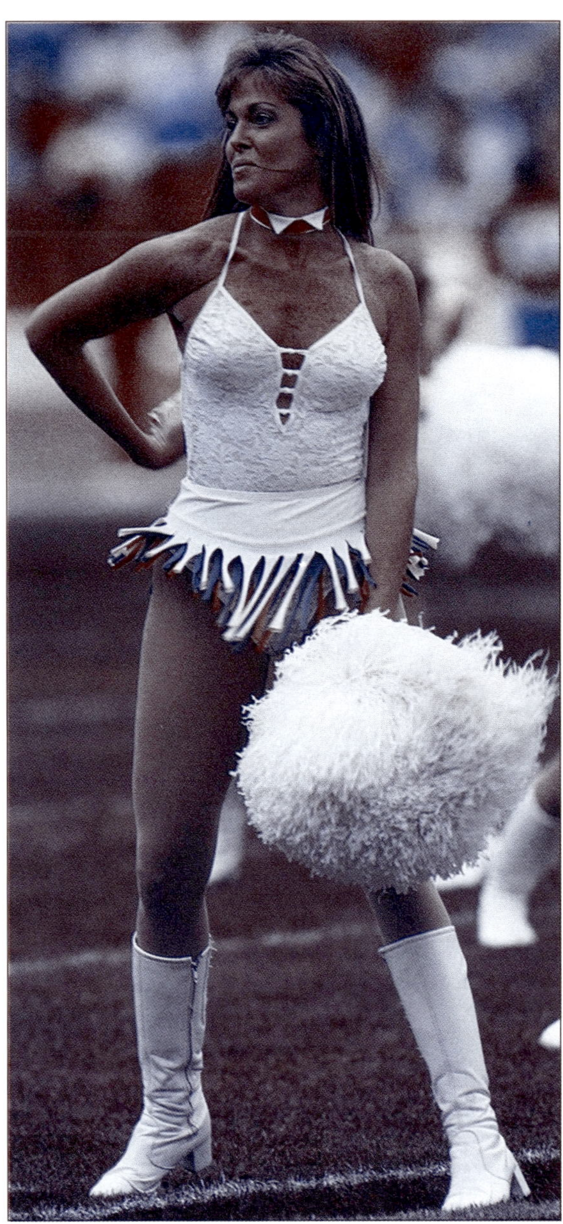

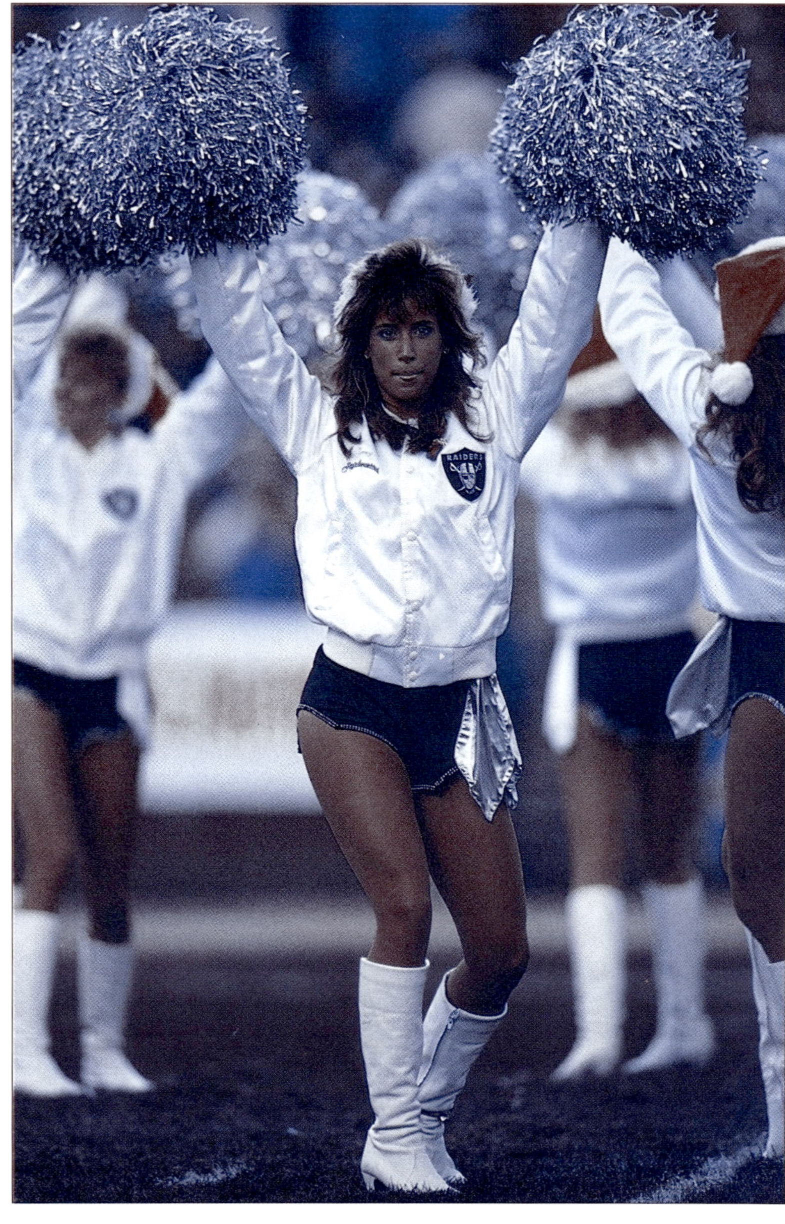

Rugby Union

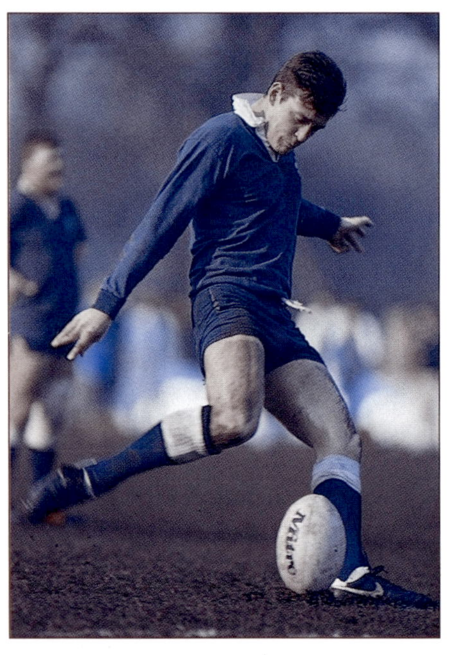

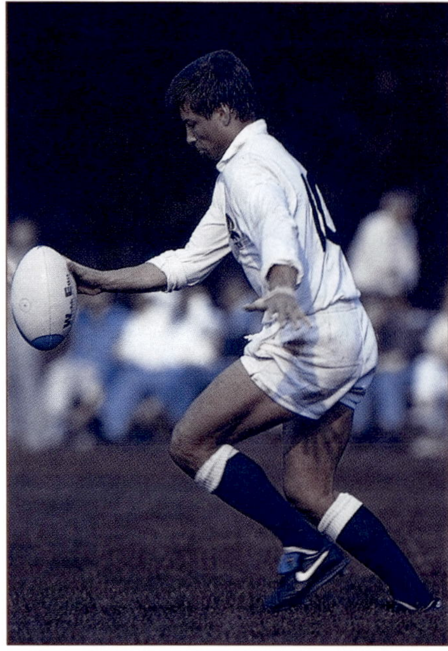

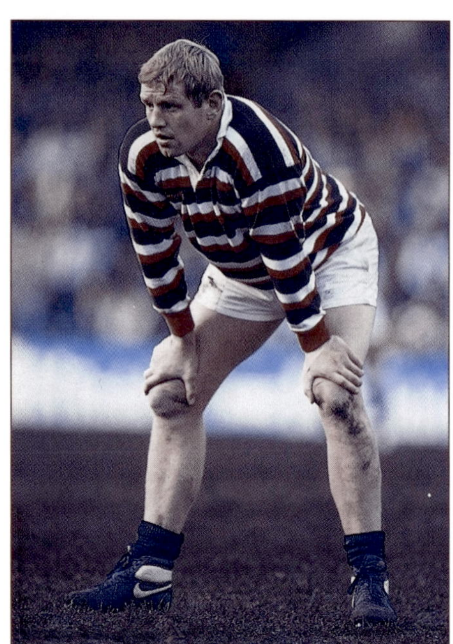

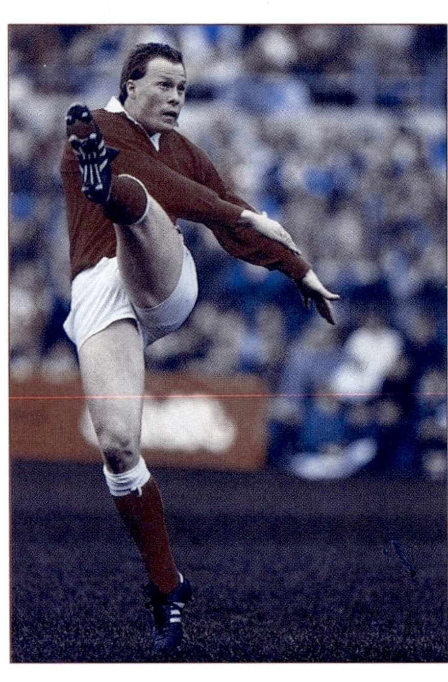

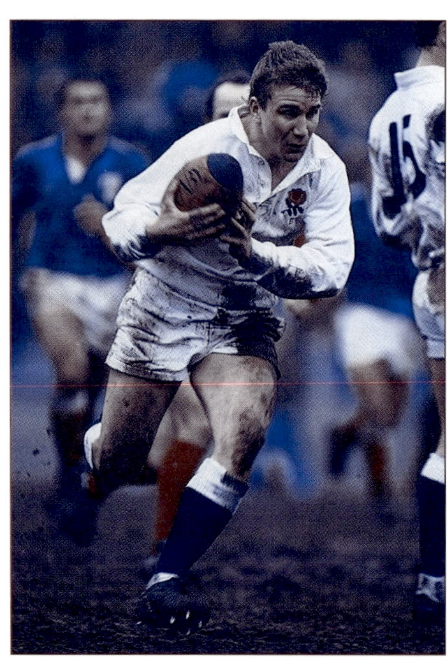

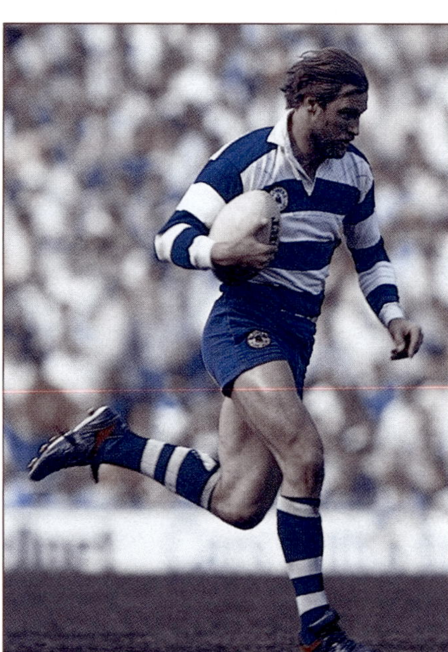

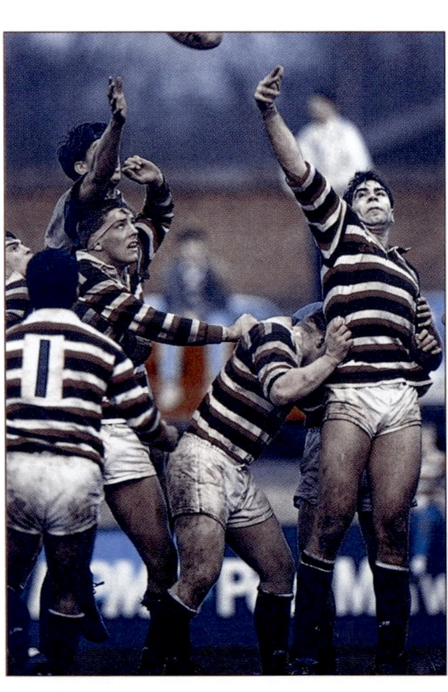

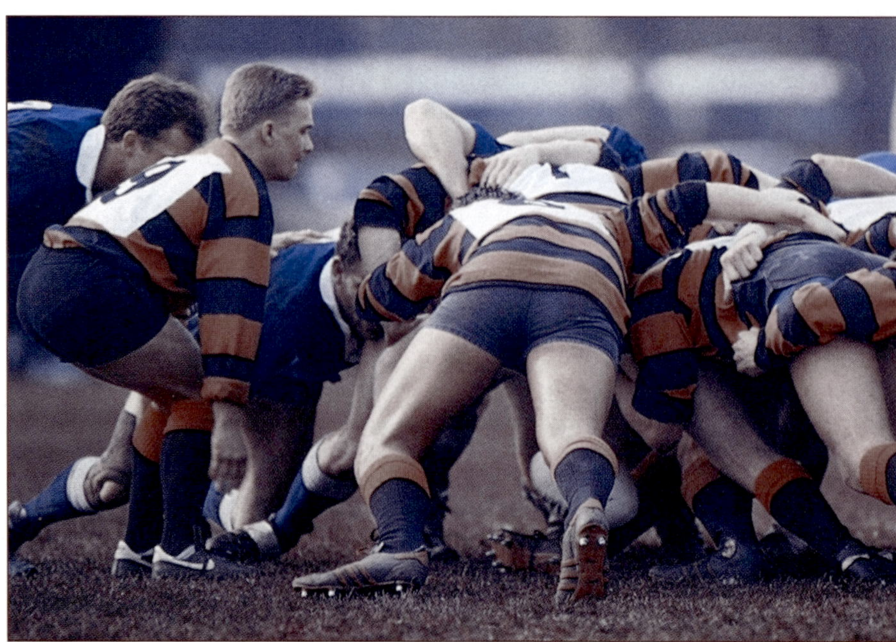

Rugby Union

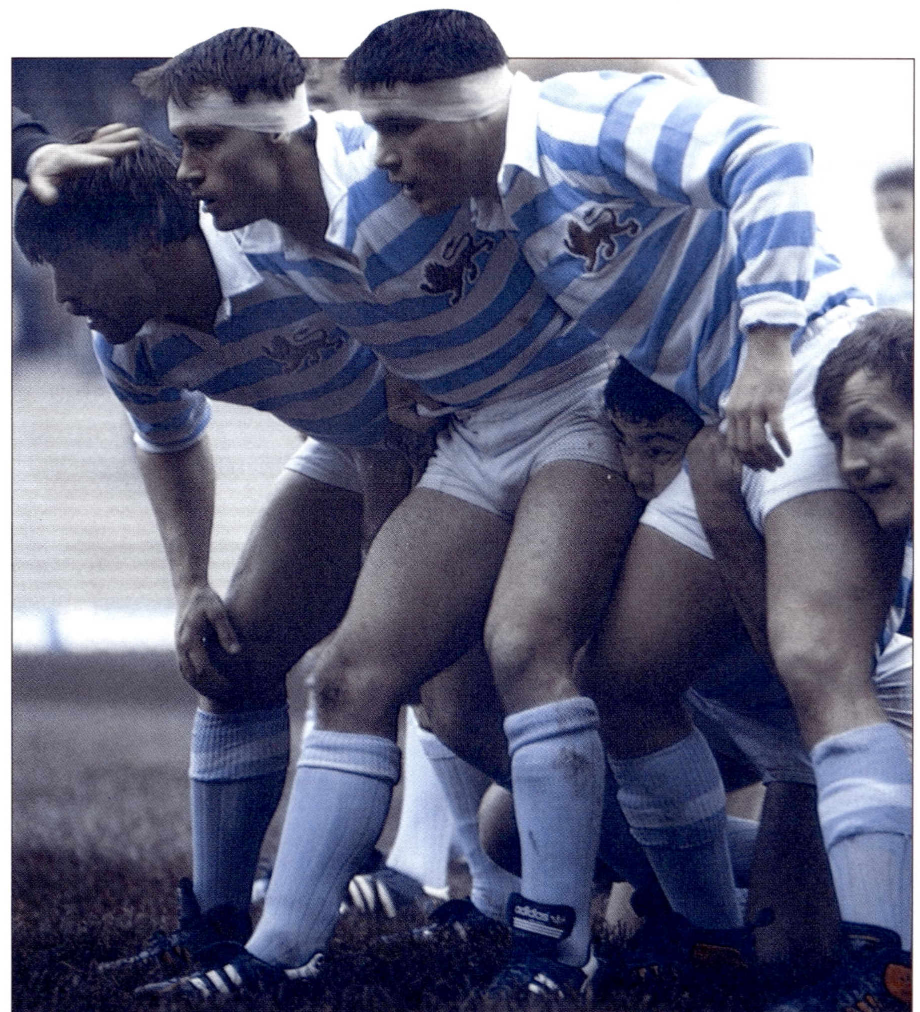

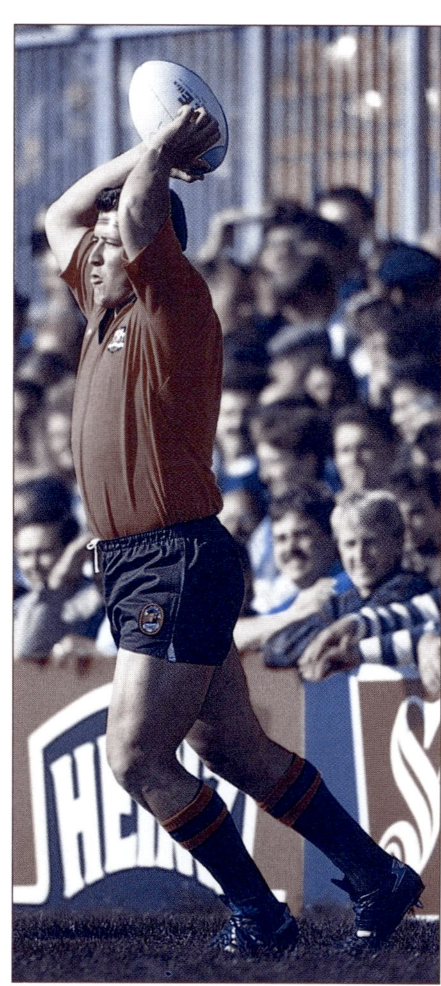

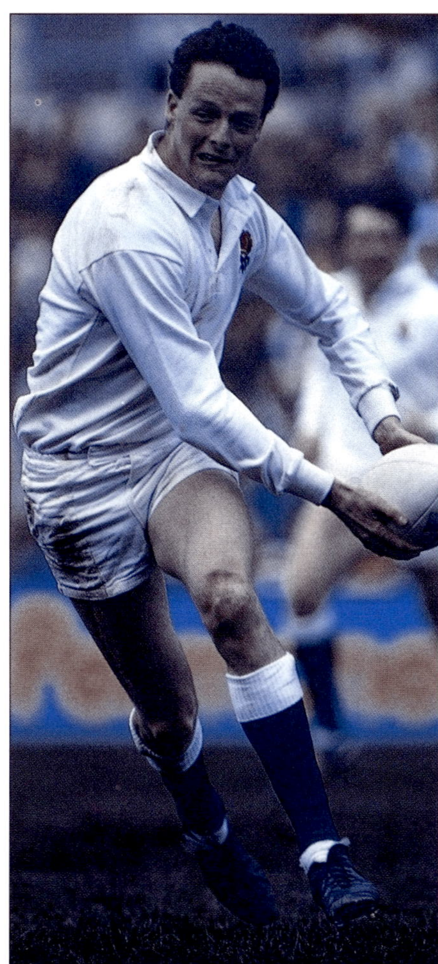

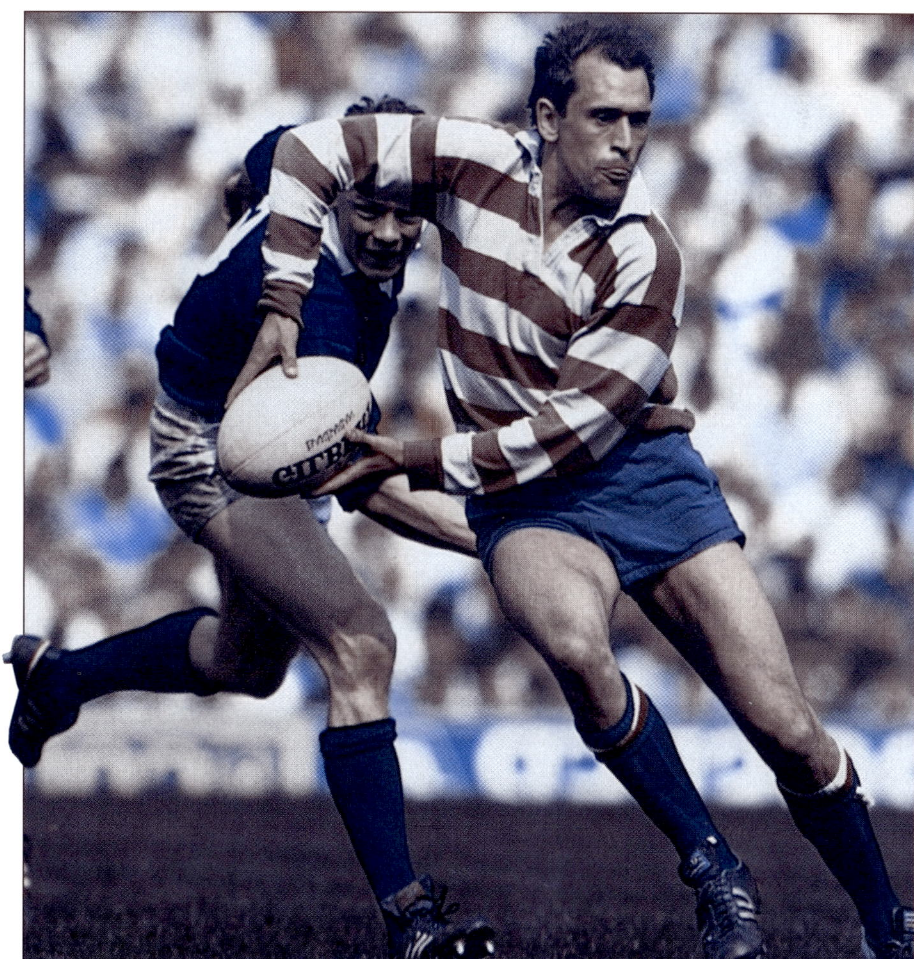

Rugby Union

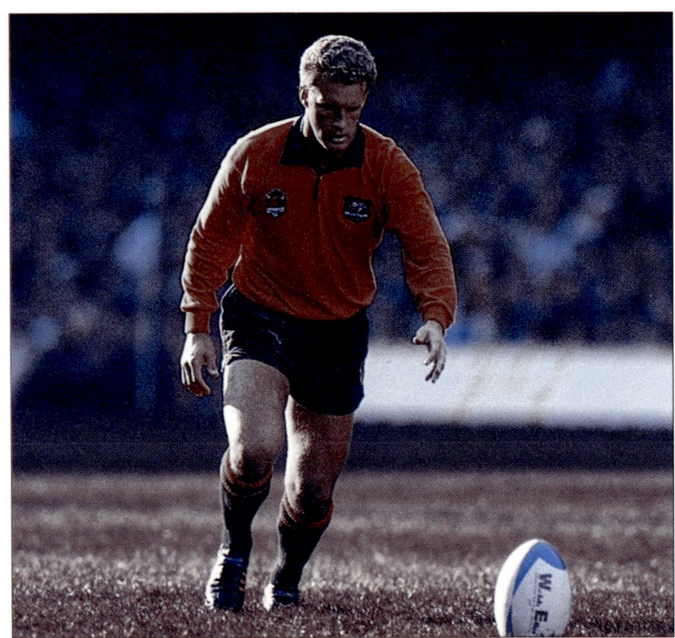

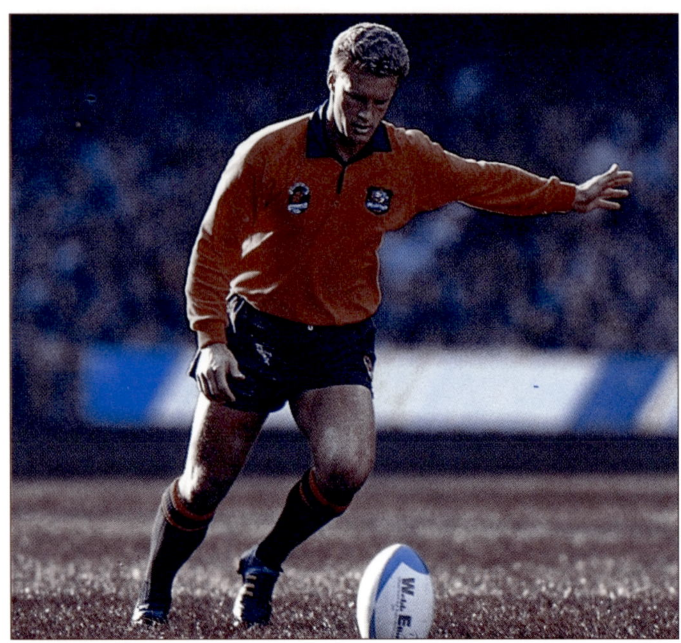

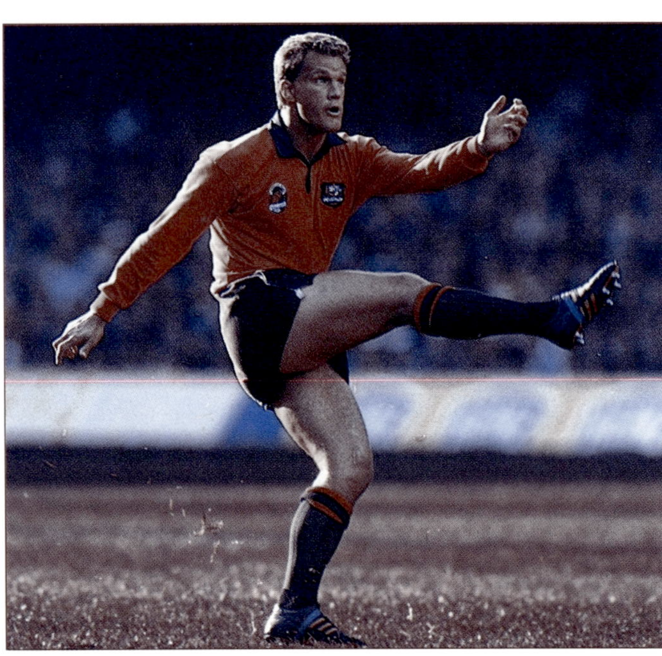

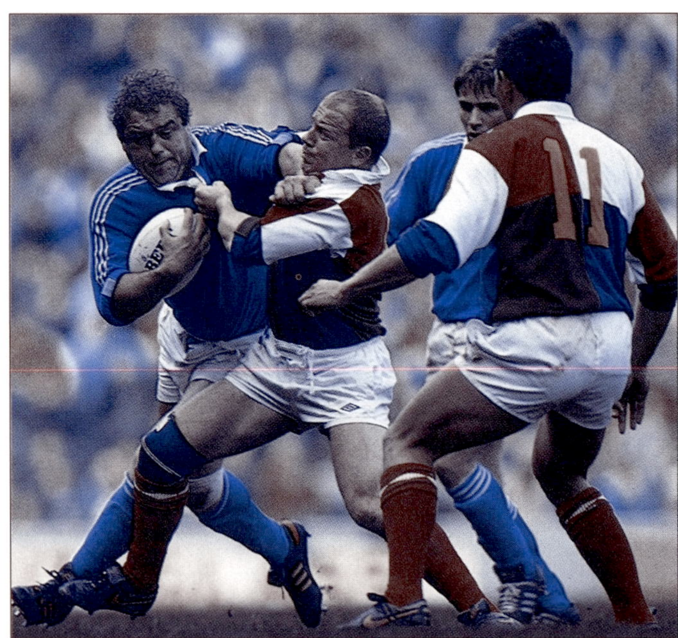

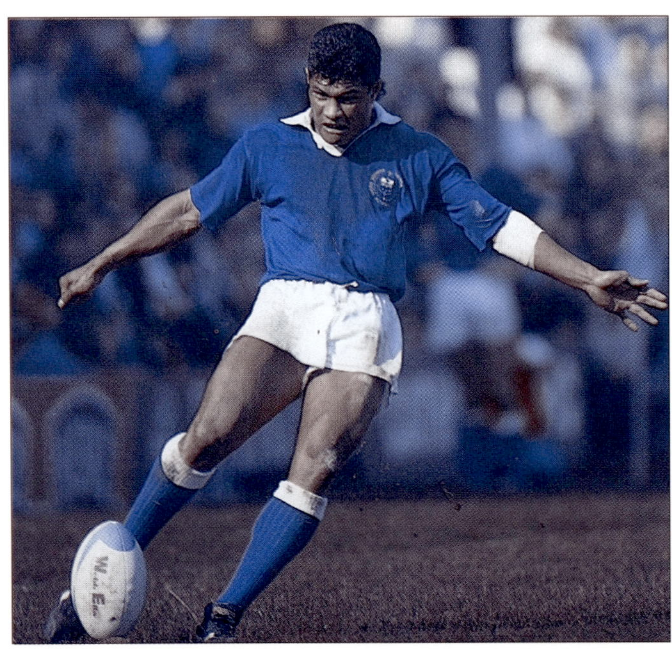

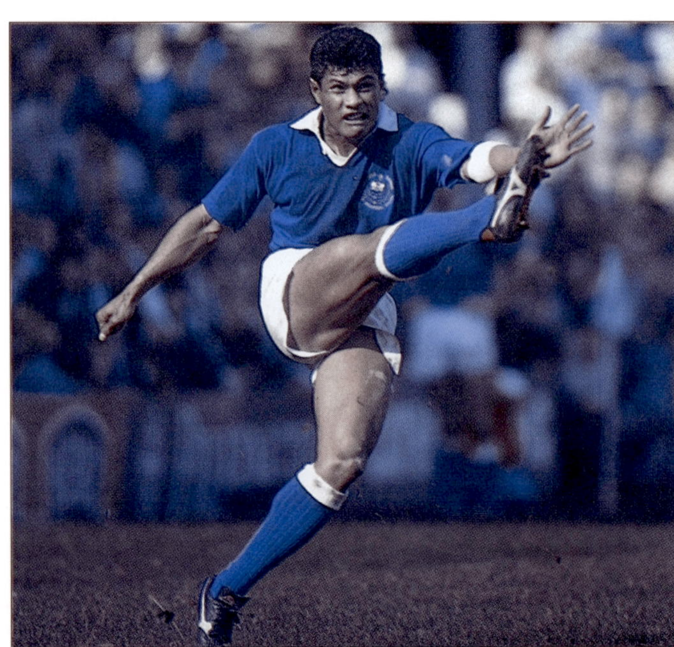

Rugby Union

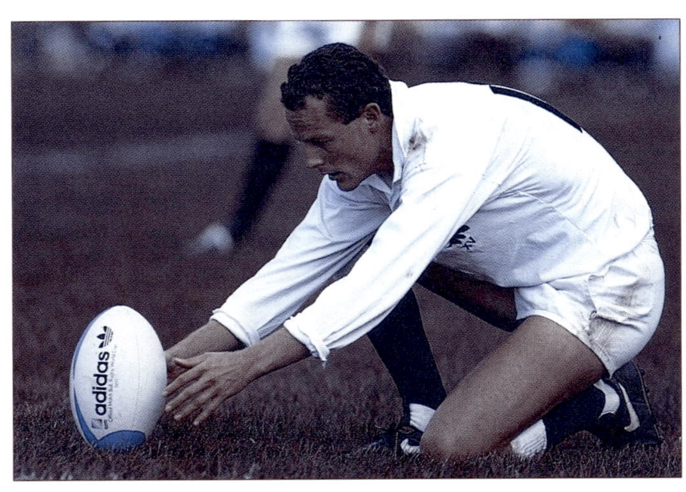

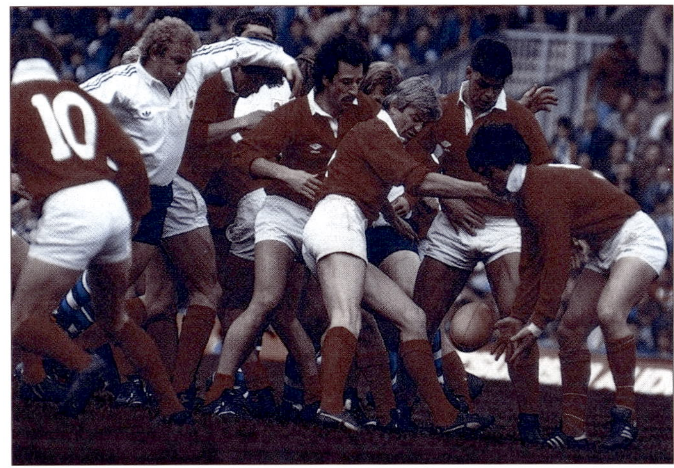

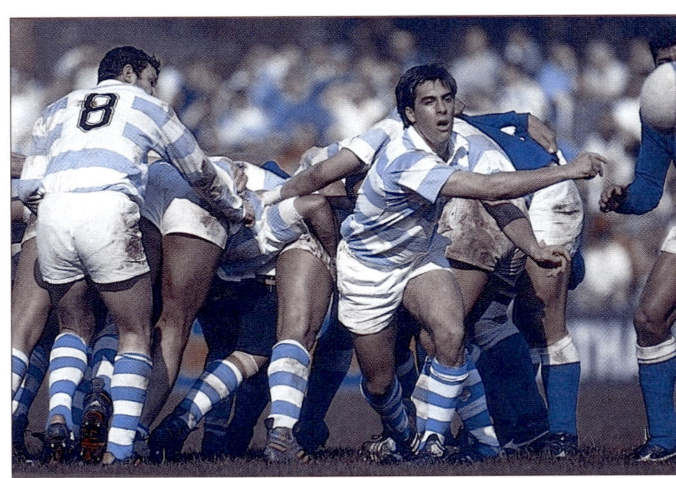

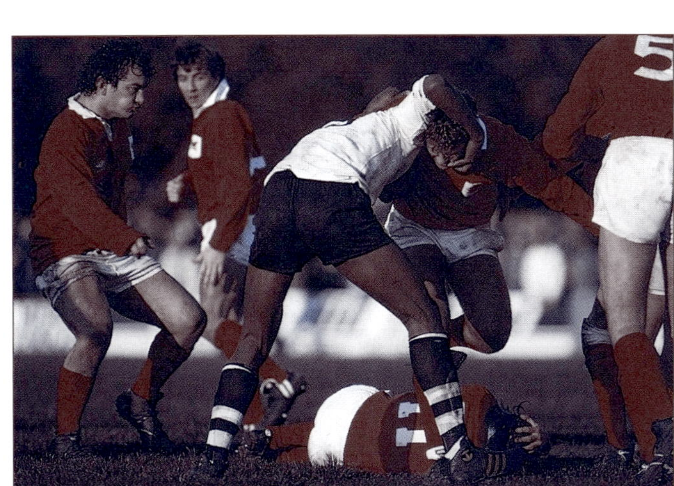

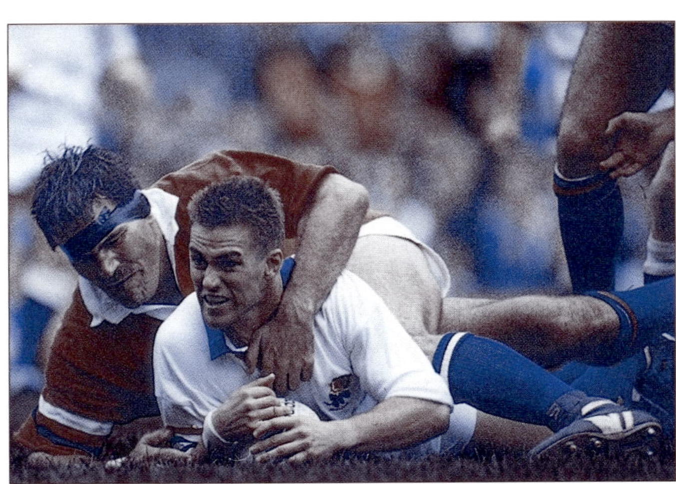

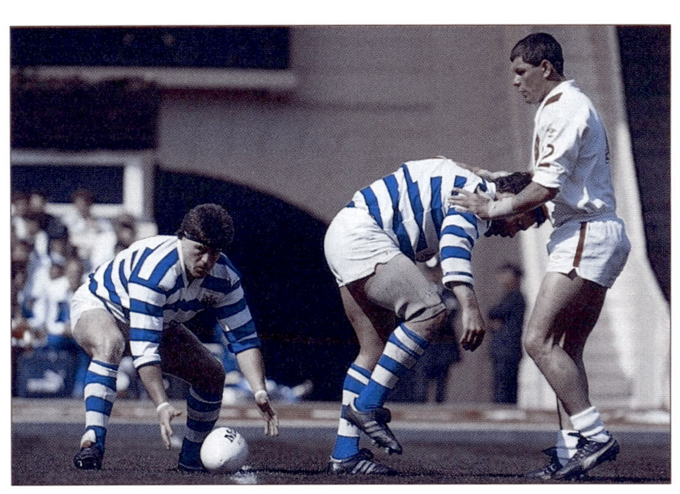

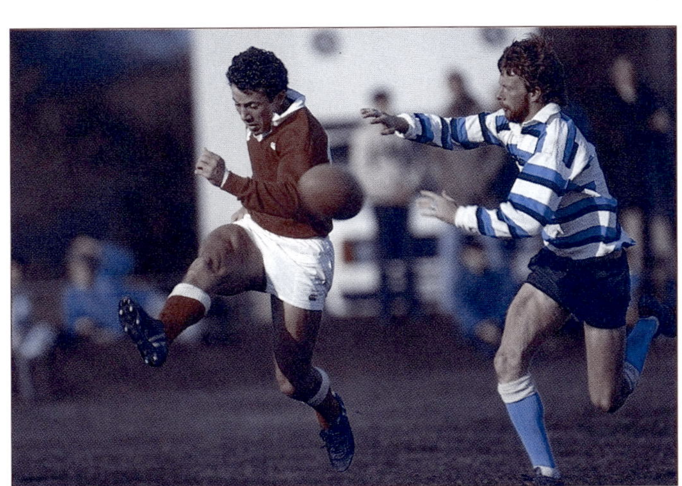

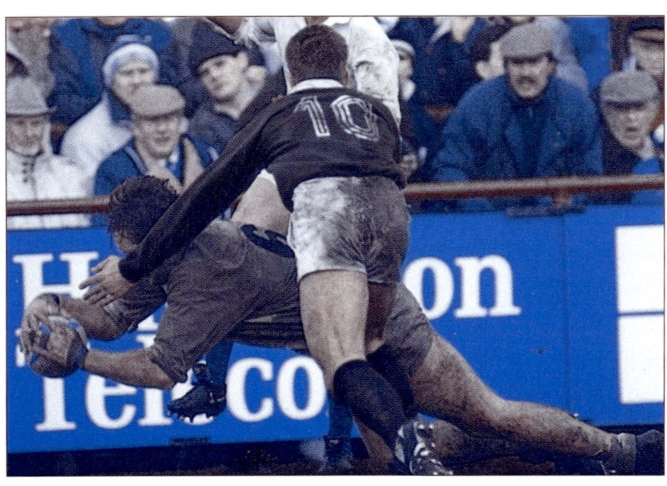

Rugby League

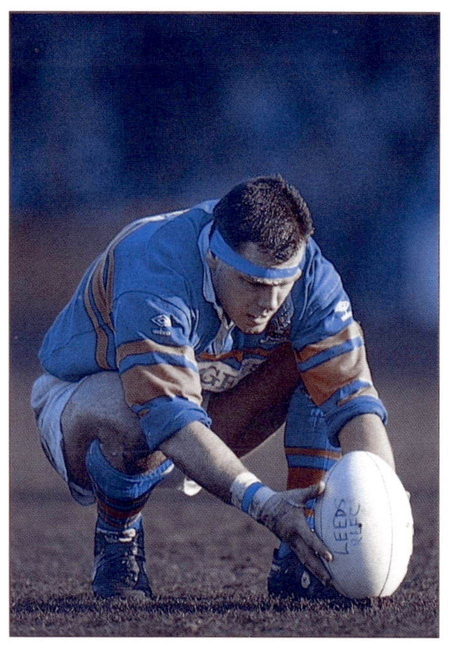
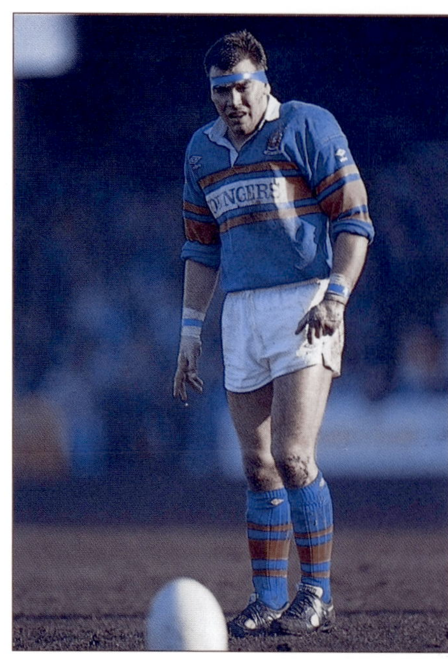
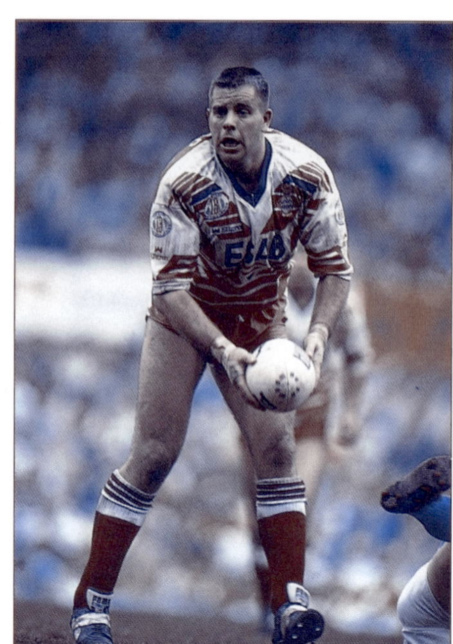
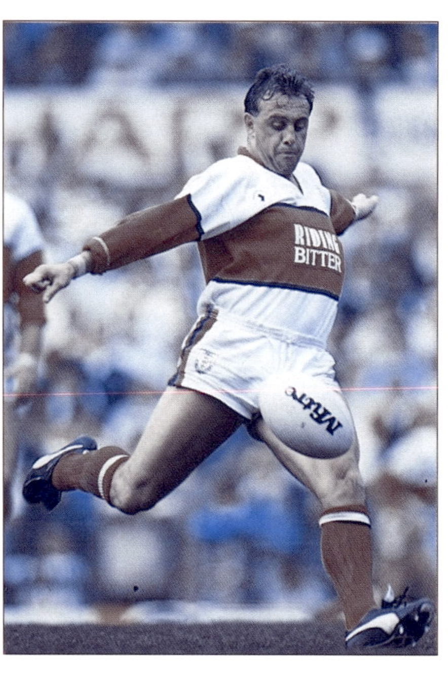

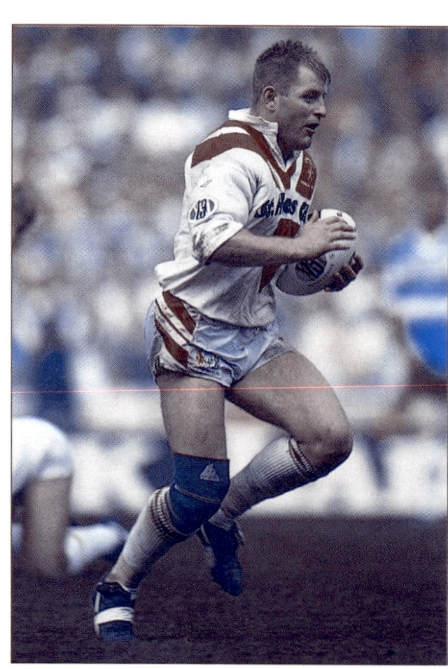
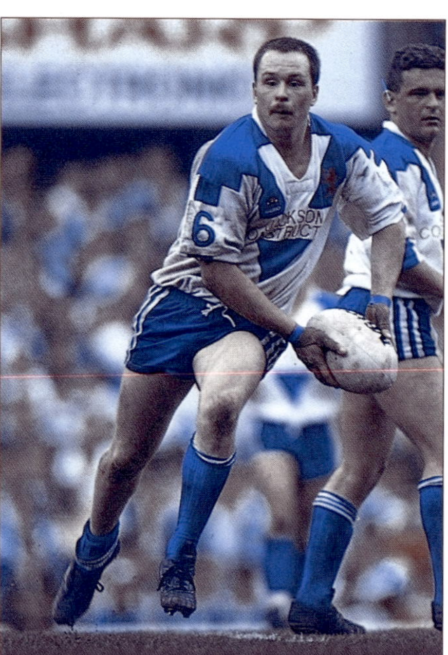
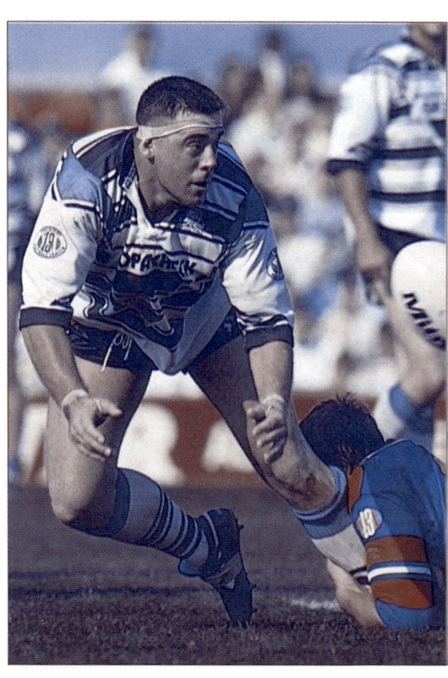
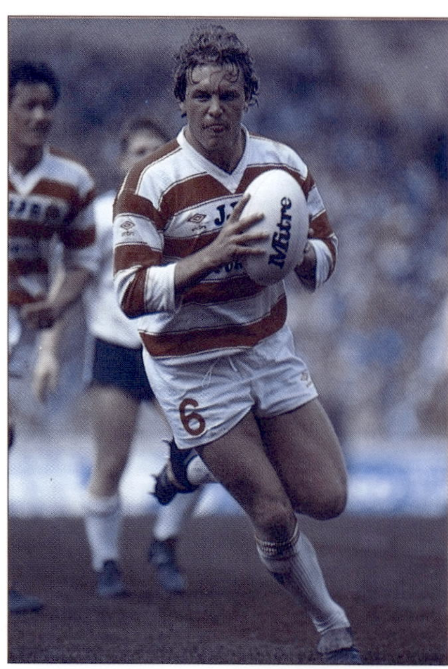

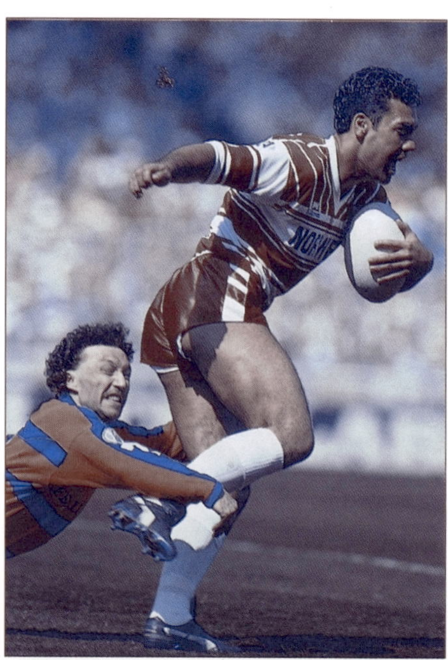

Rugby League

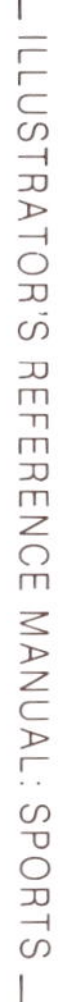

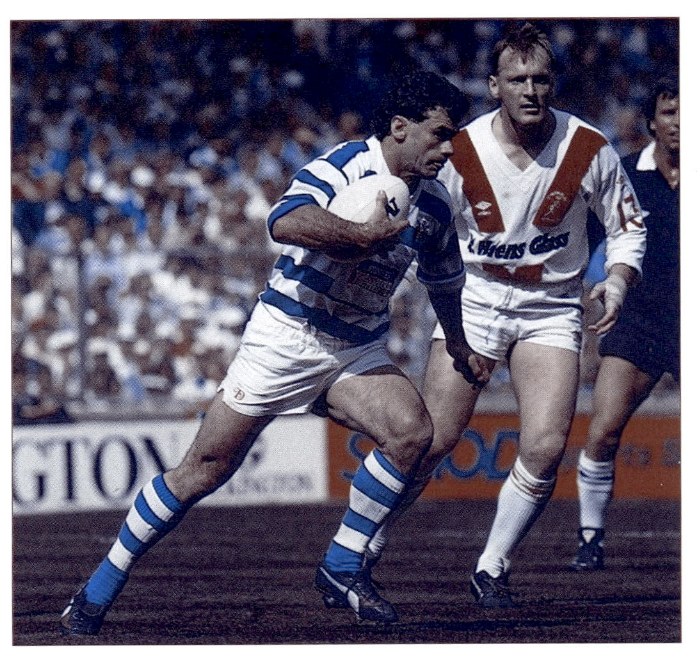

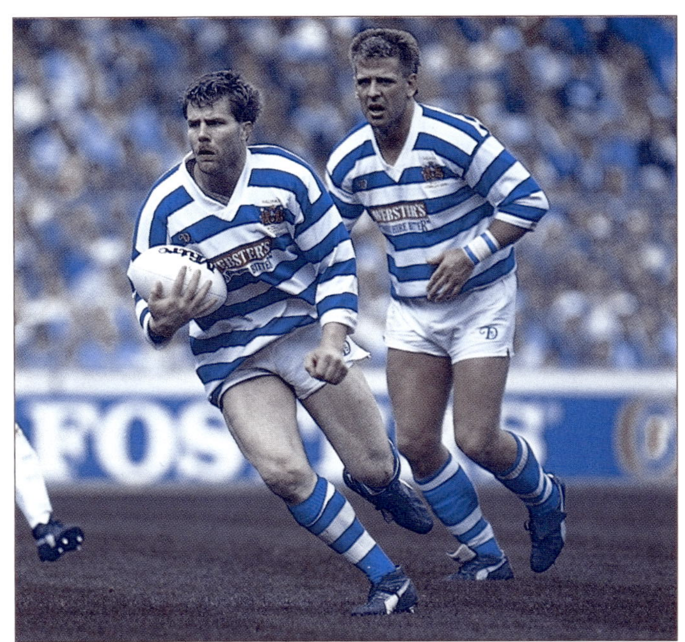

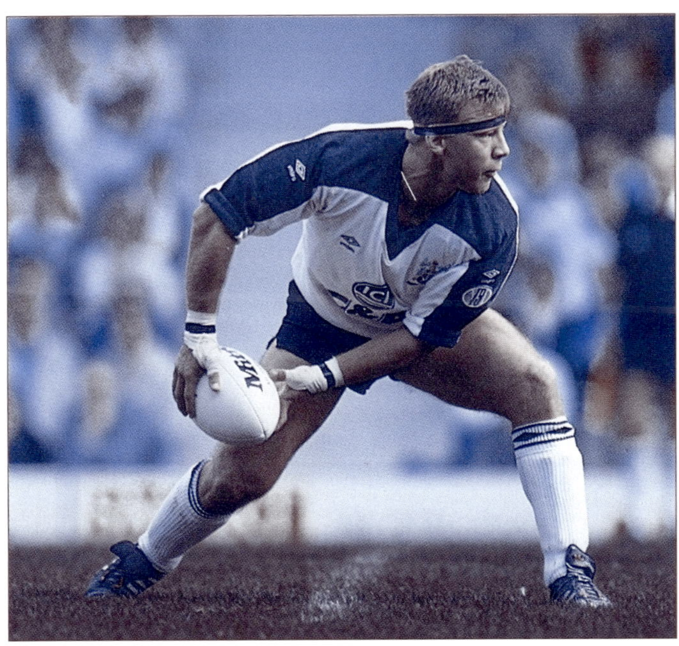

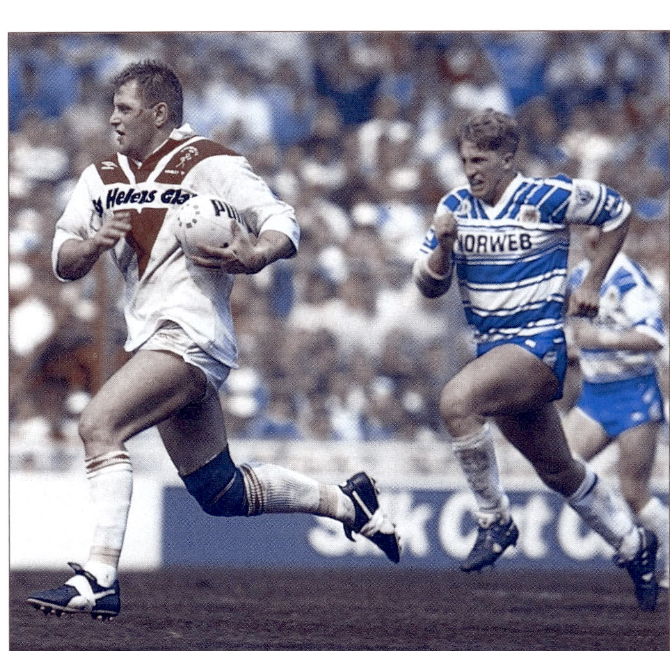

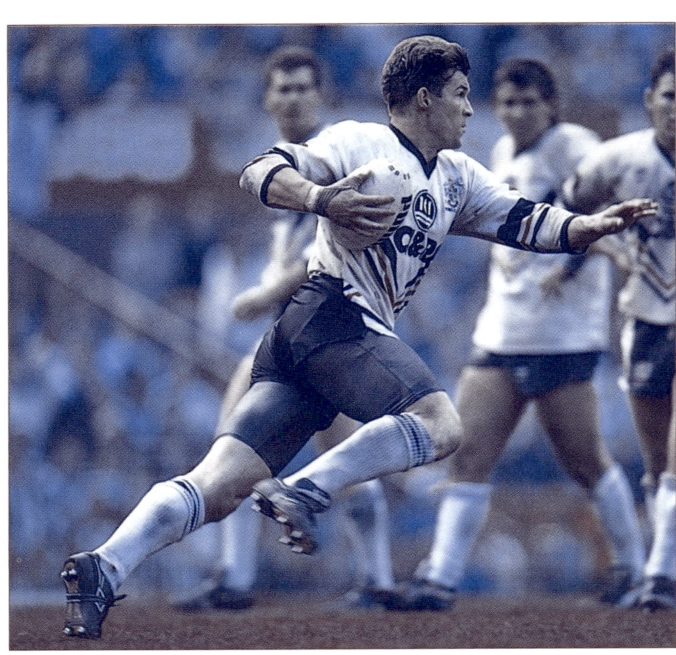

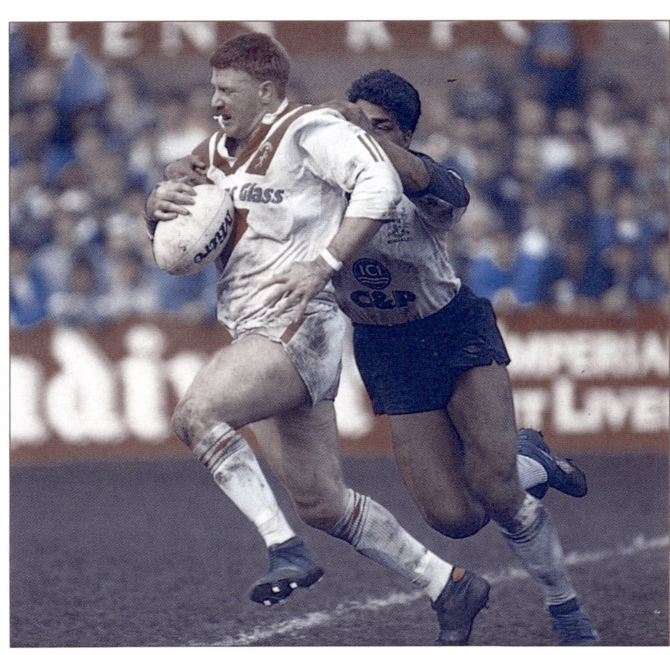

Bowls

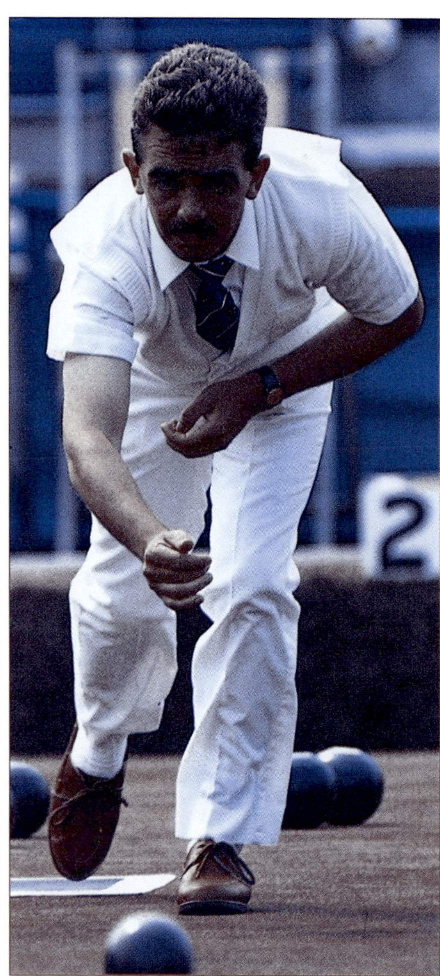

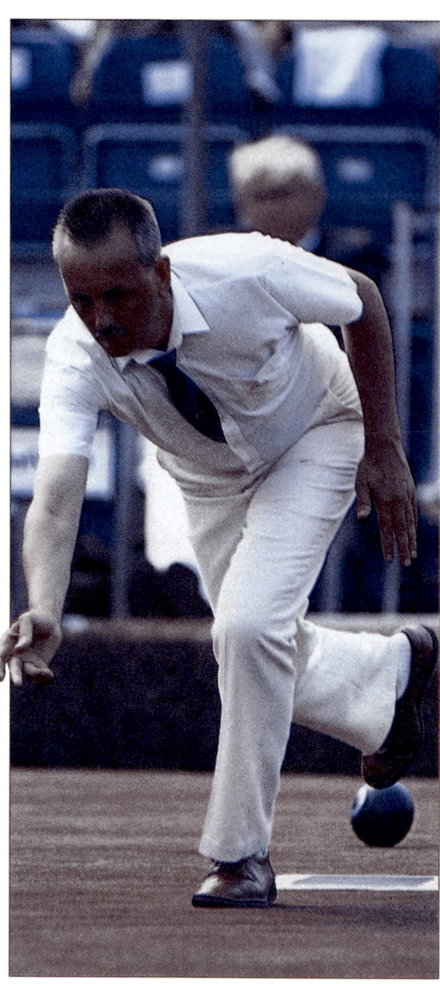

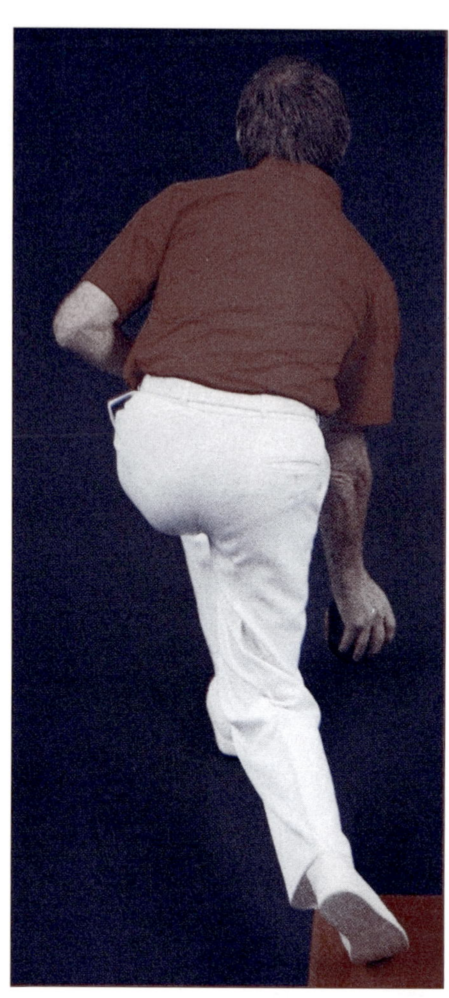

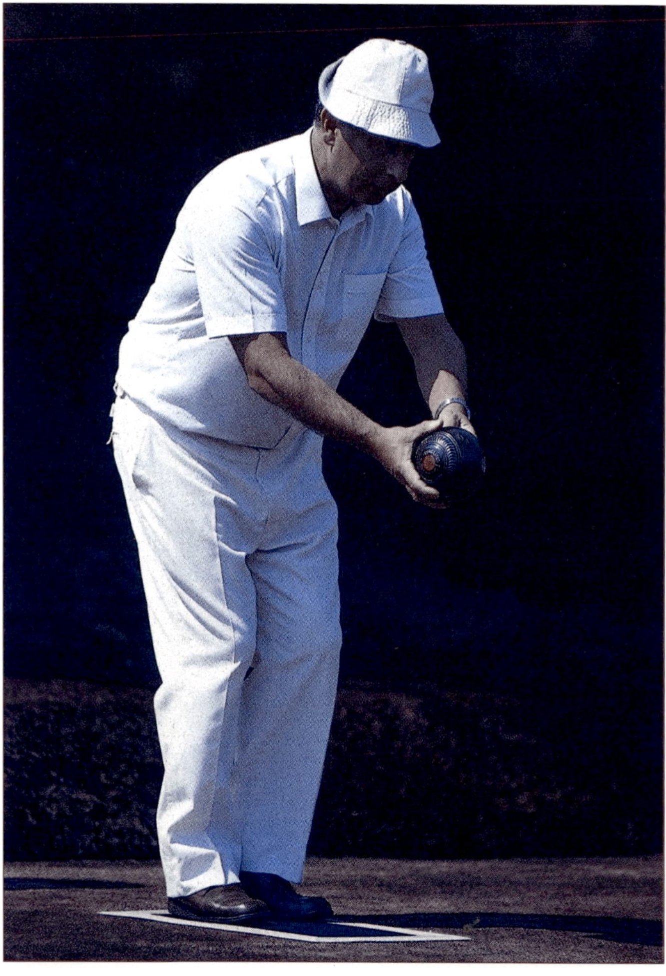

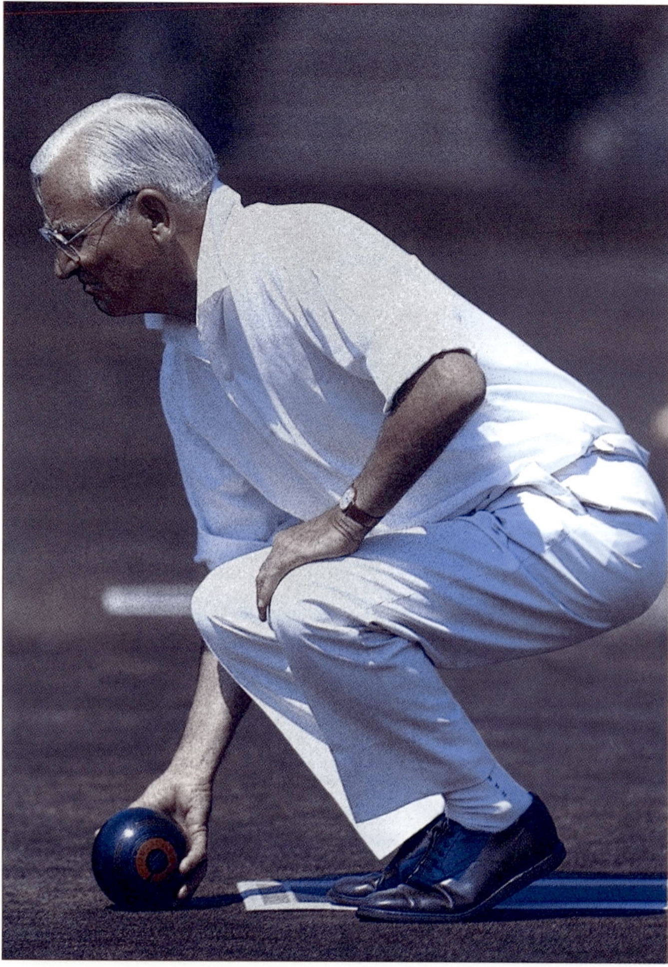

Tenpin bowling

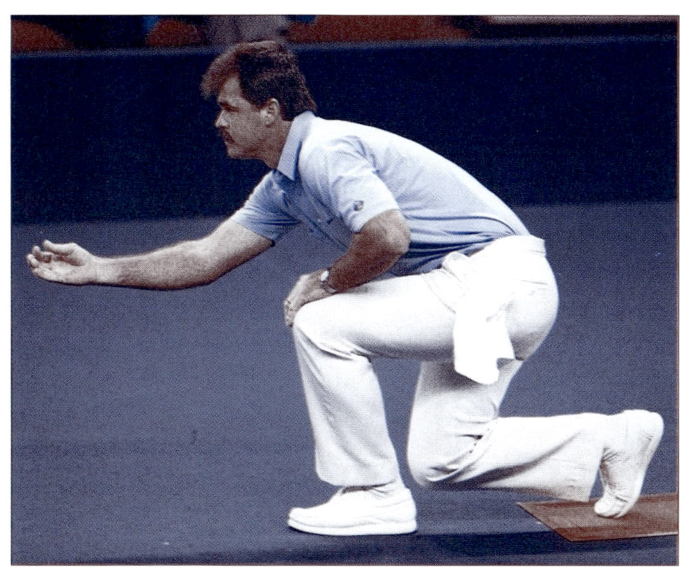

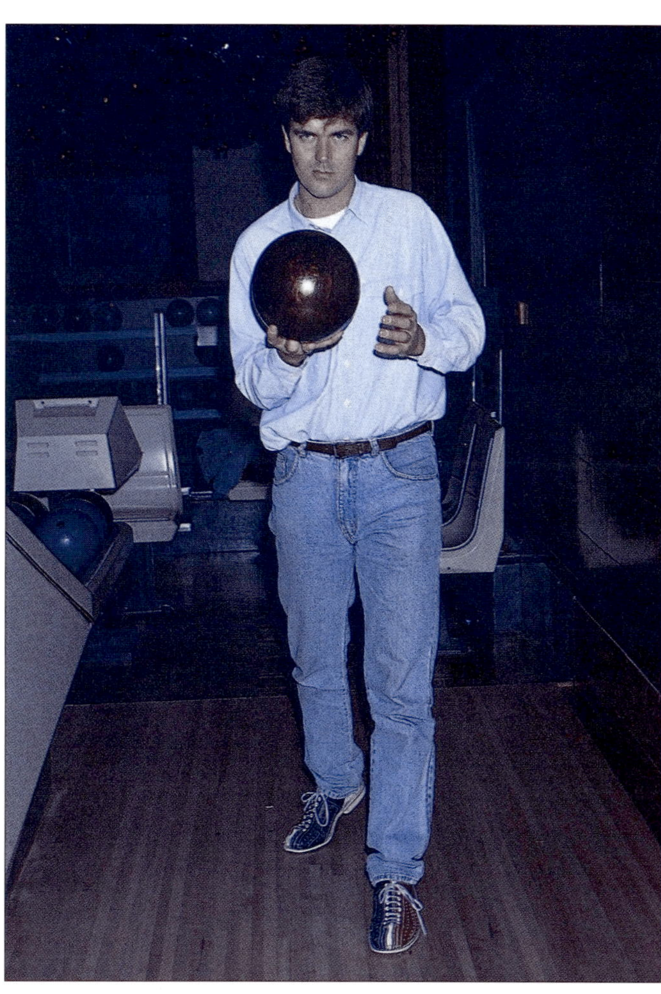

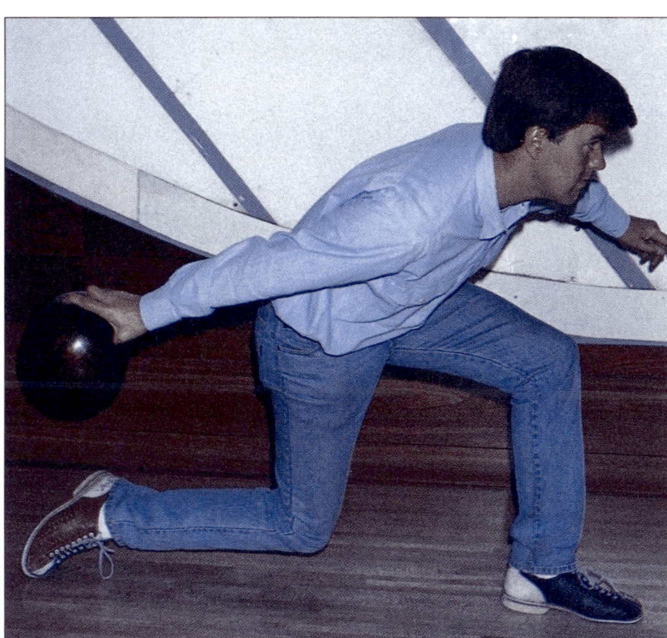

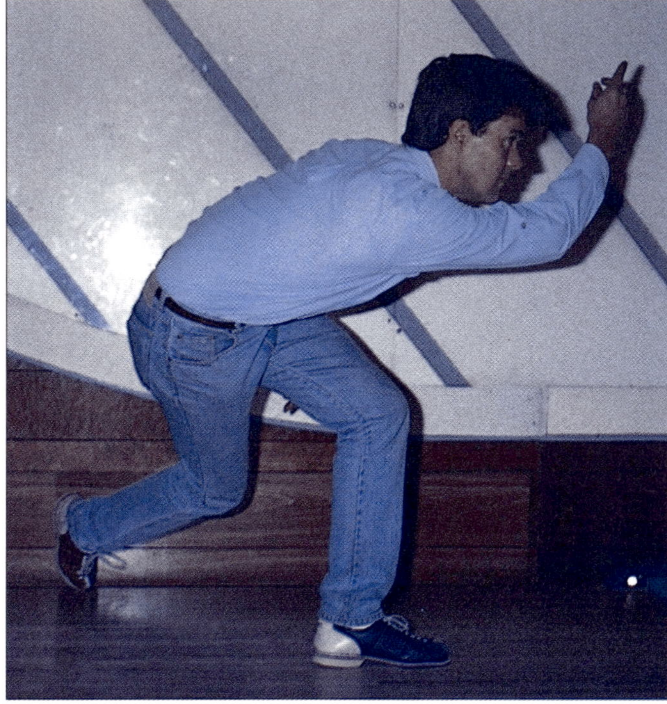

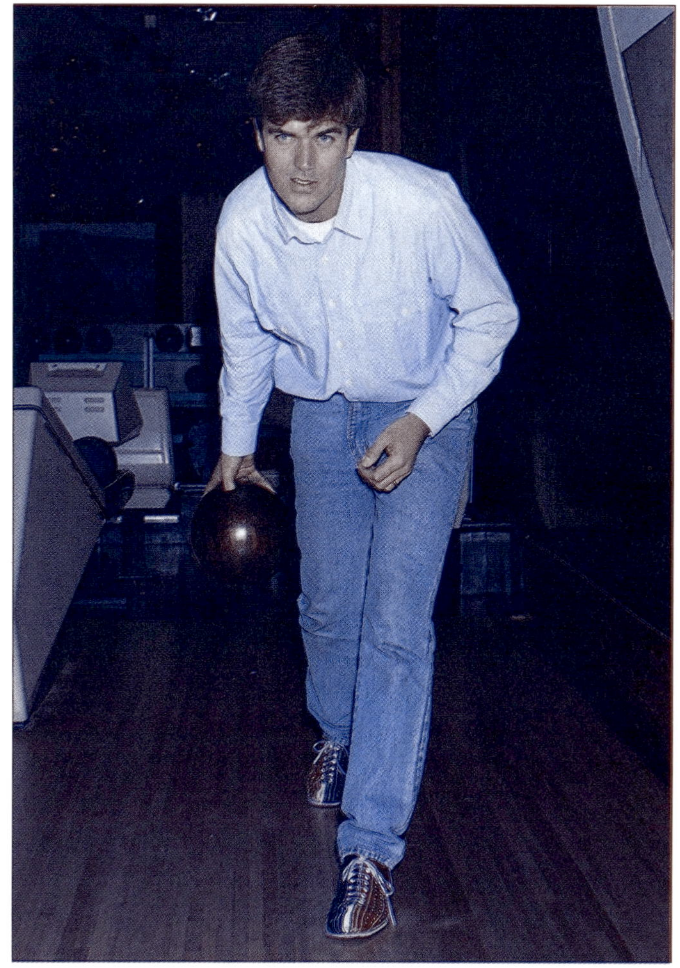

Snooker – male

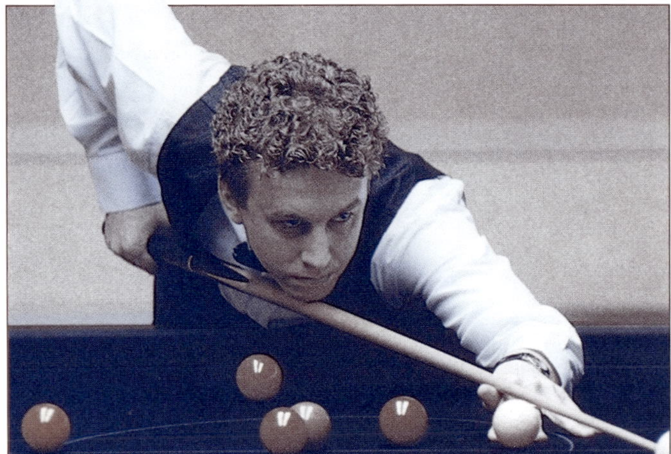

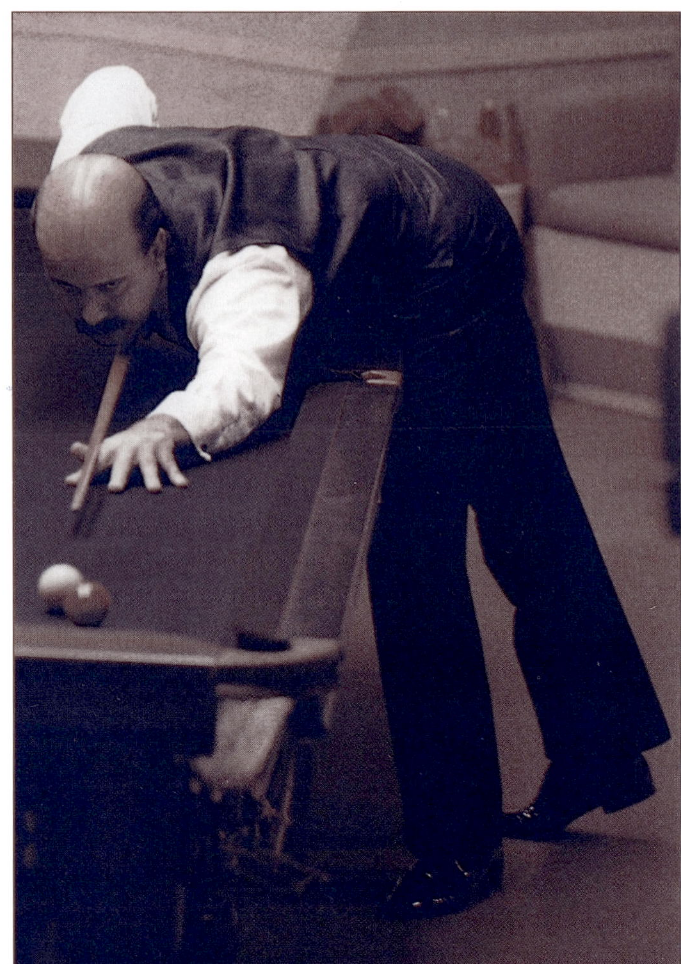

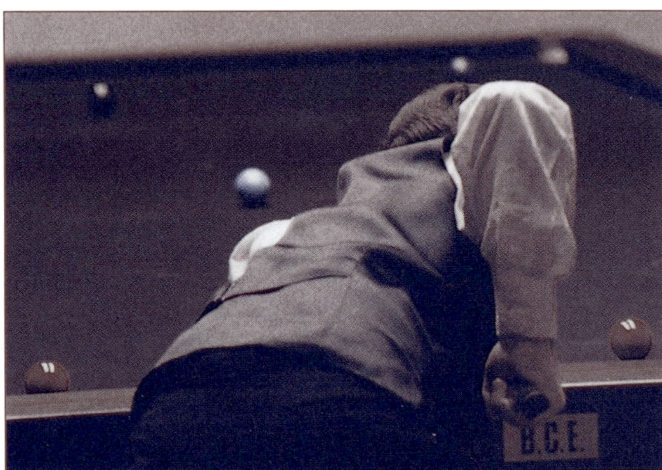

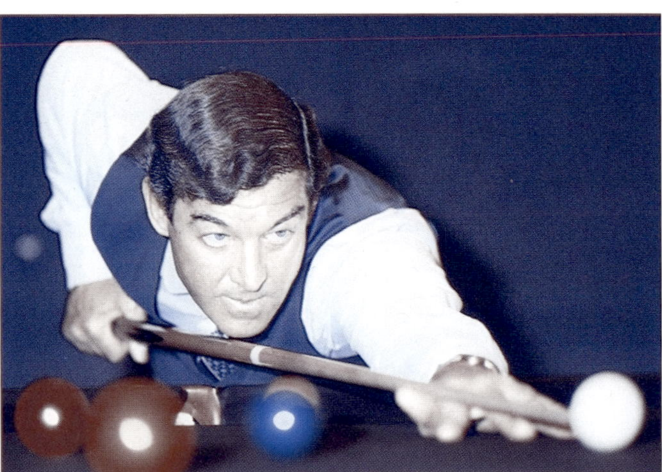

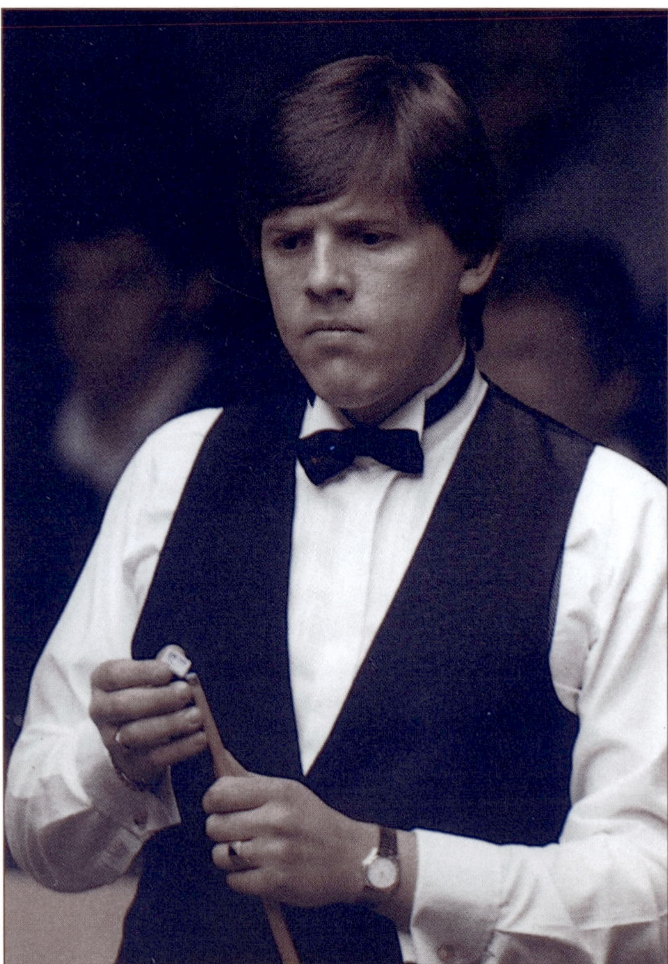

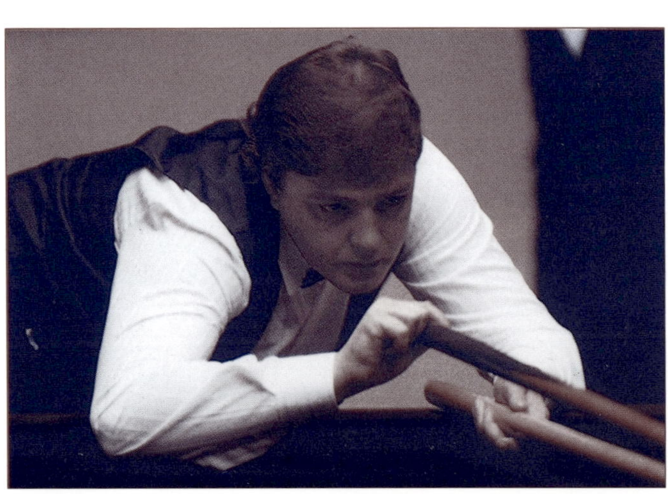

Snooker – female

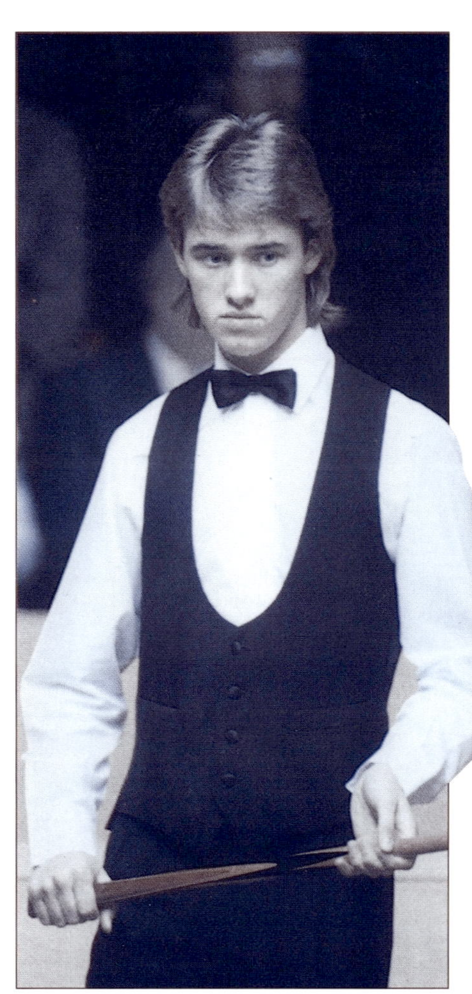

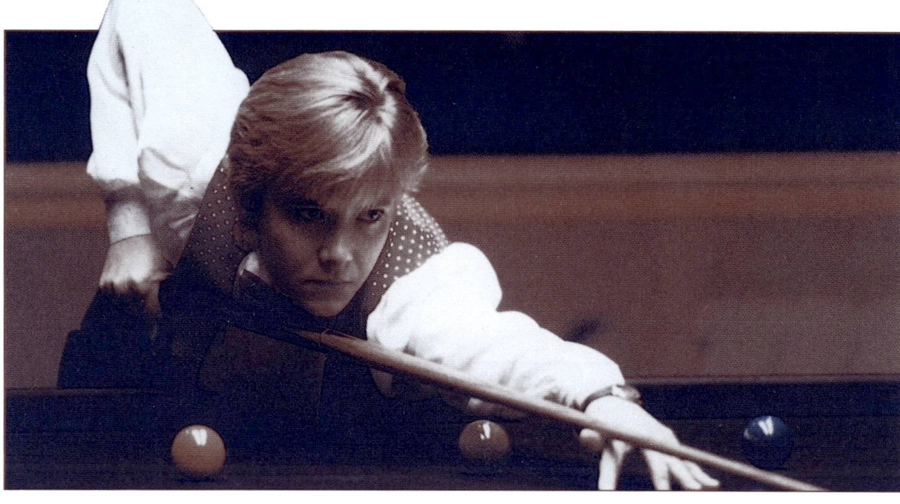

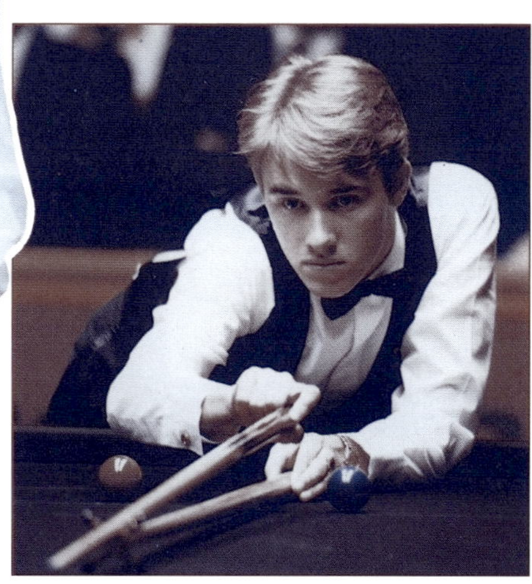

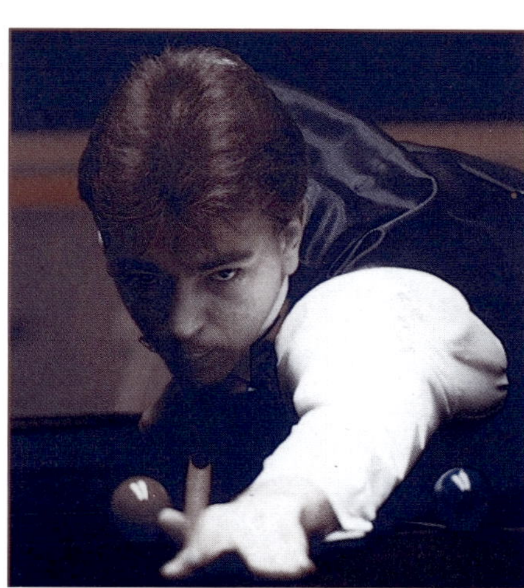

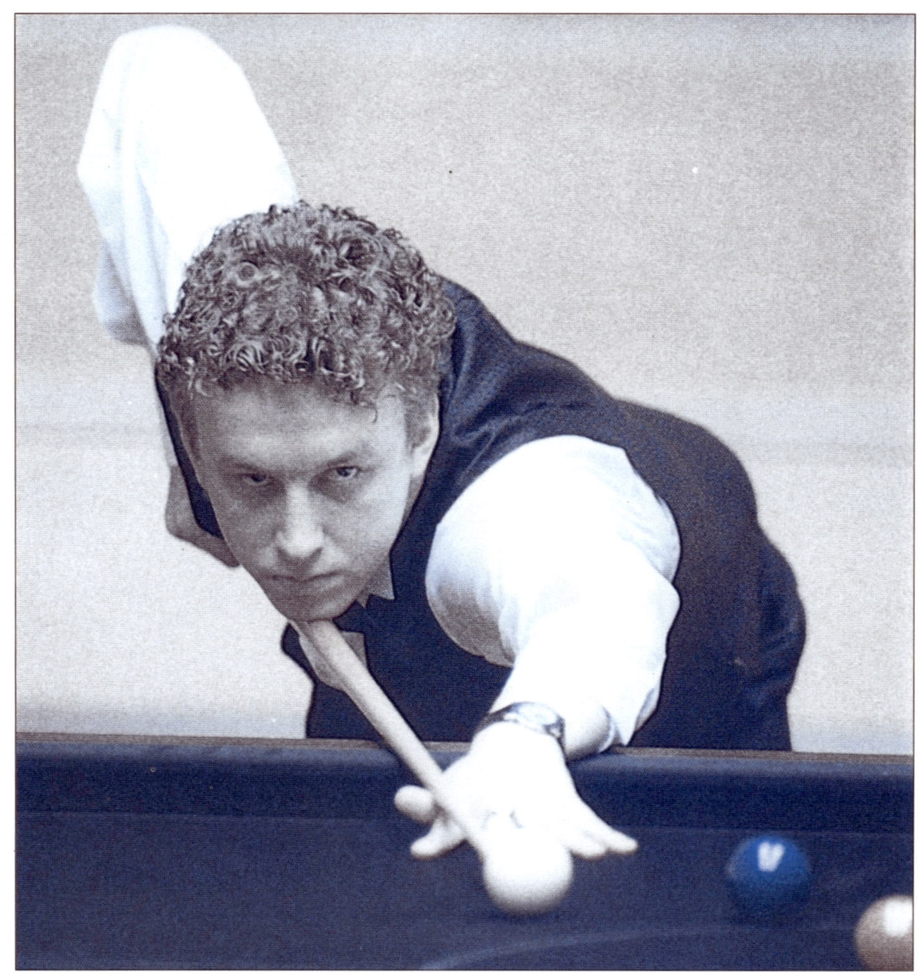

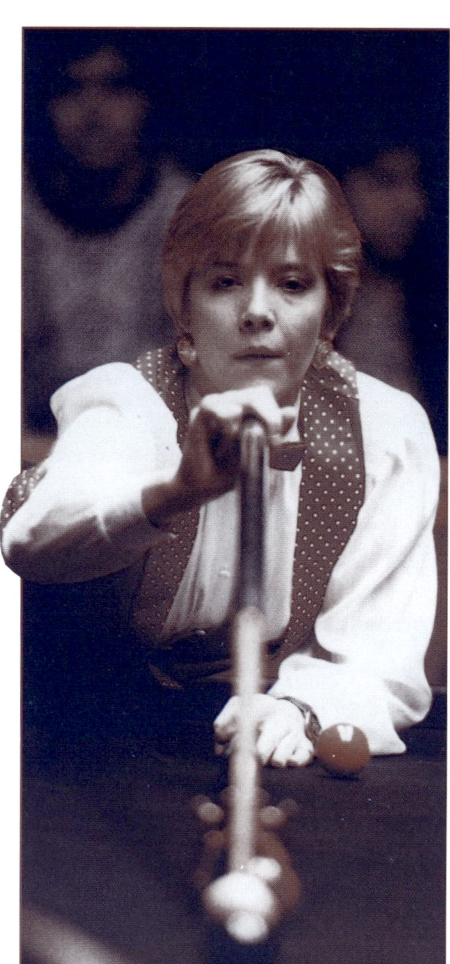

Running – starting

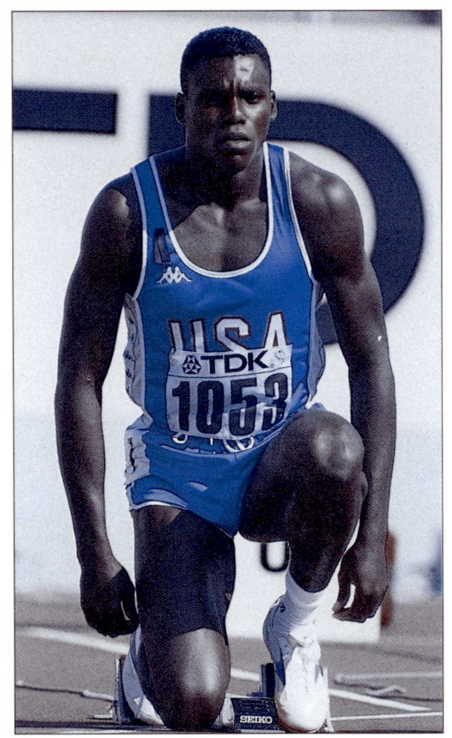

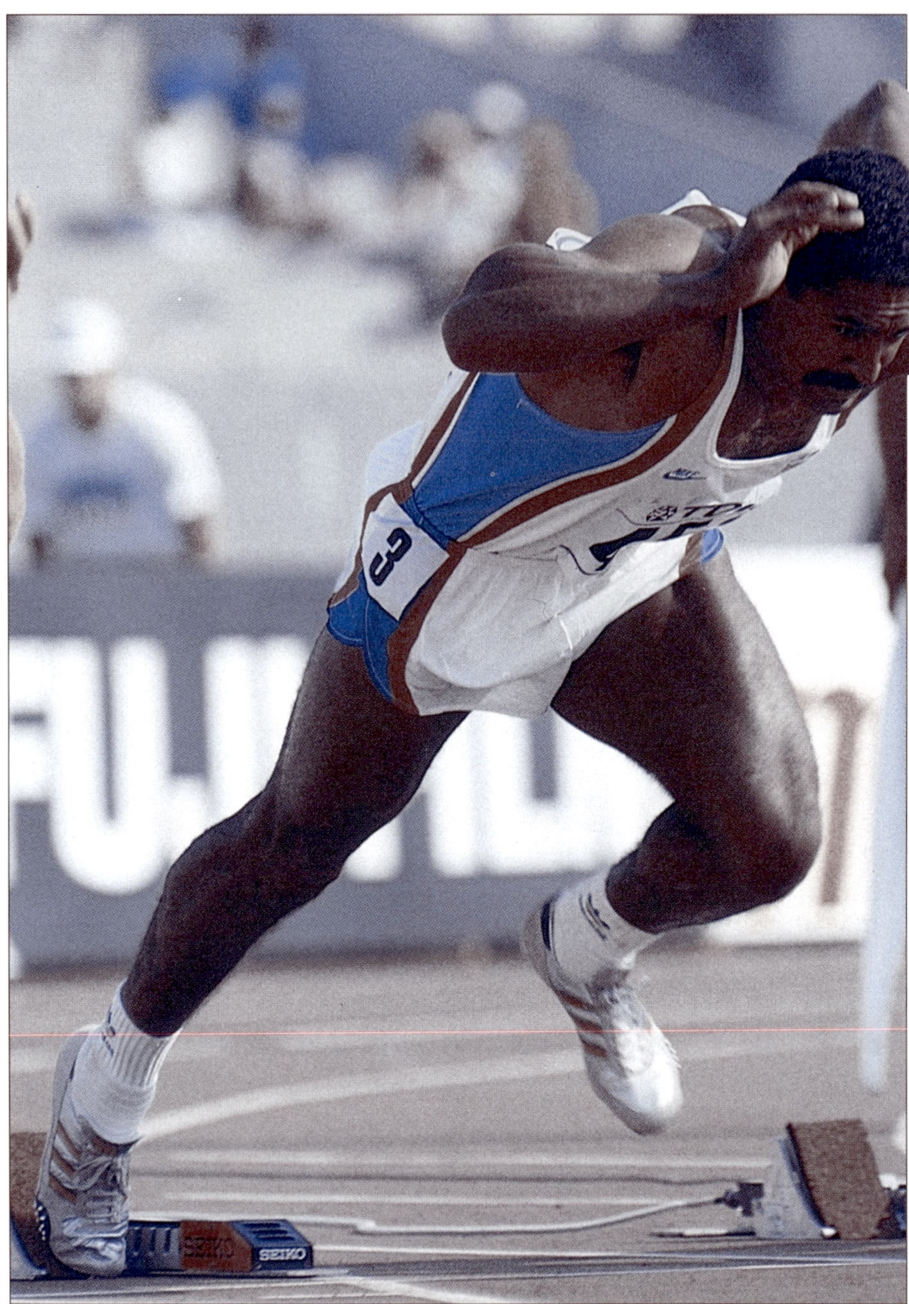

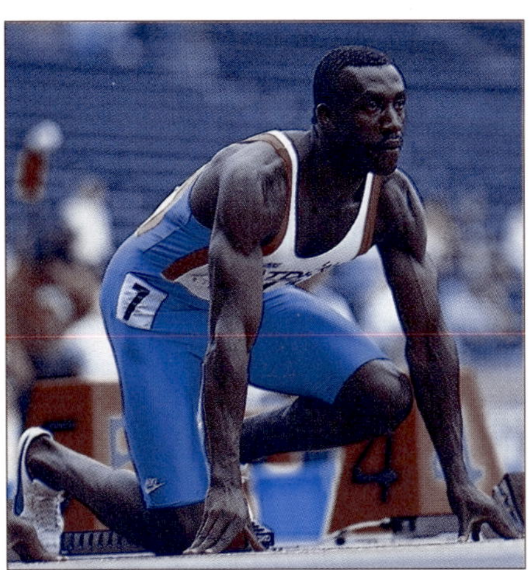

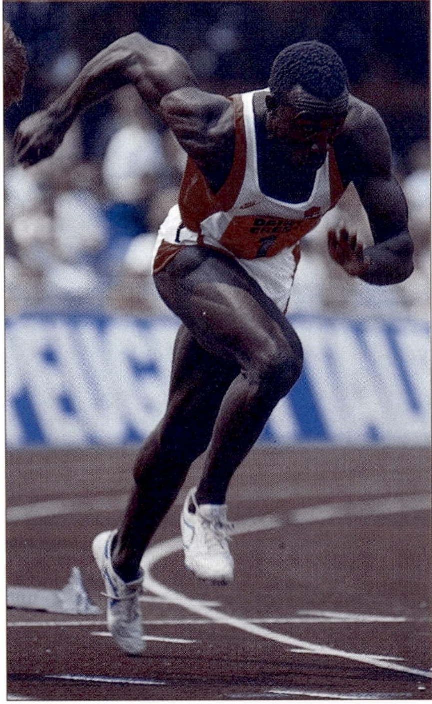

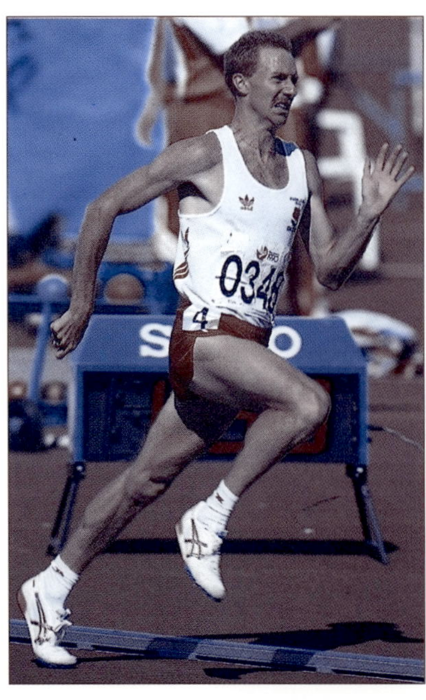

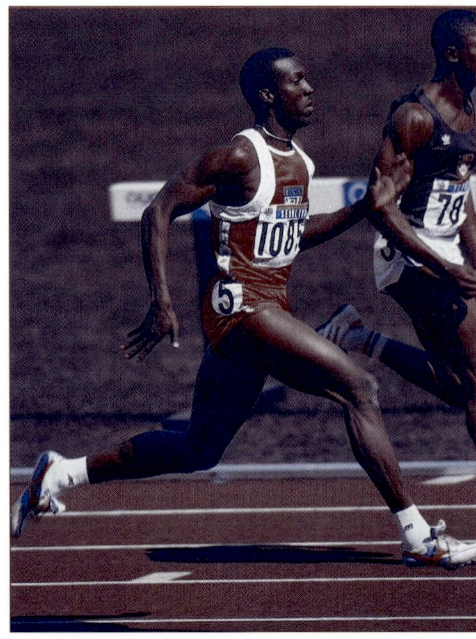

Running

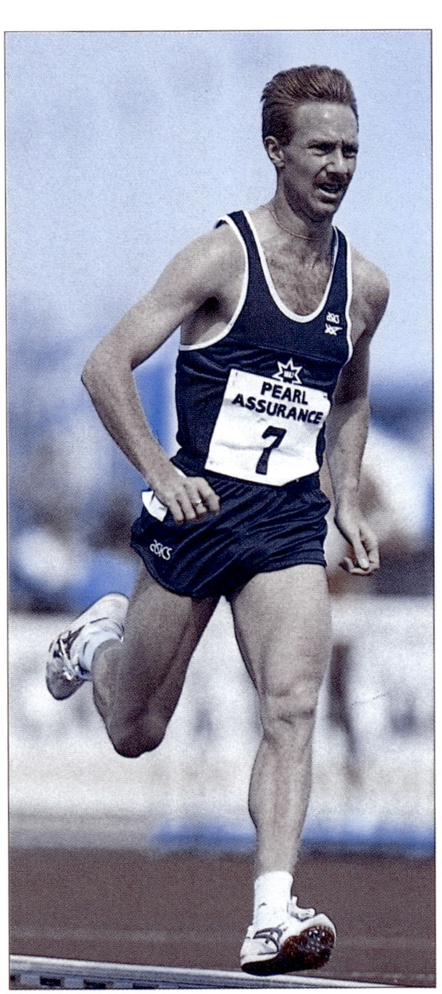

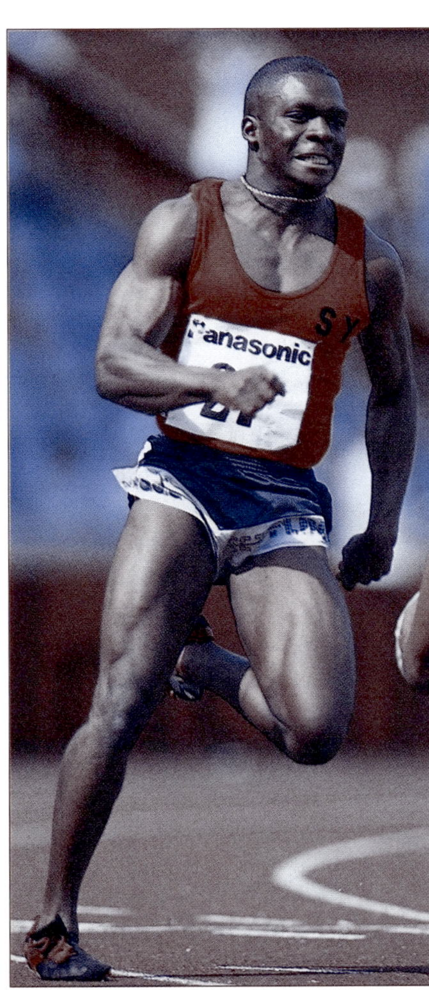

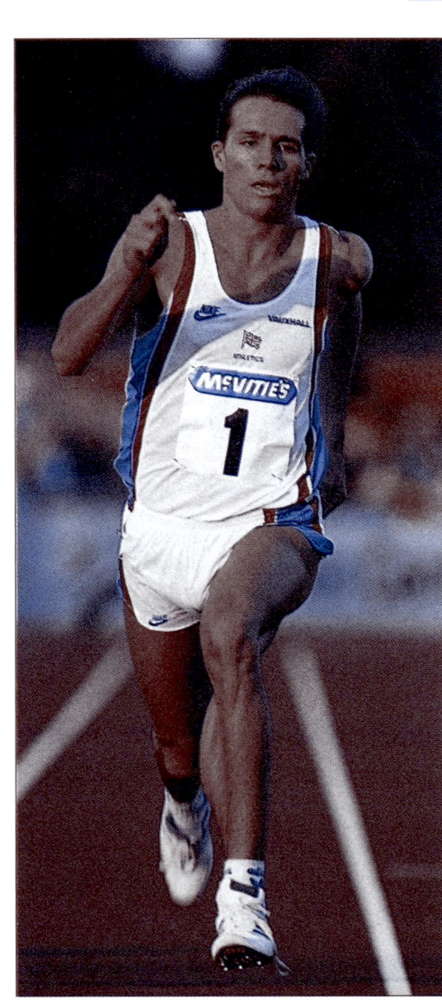

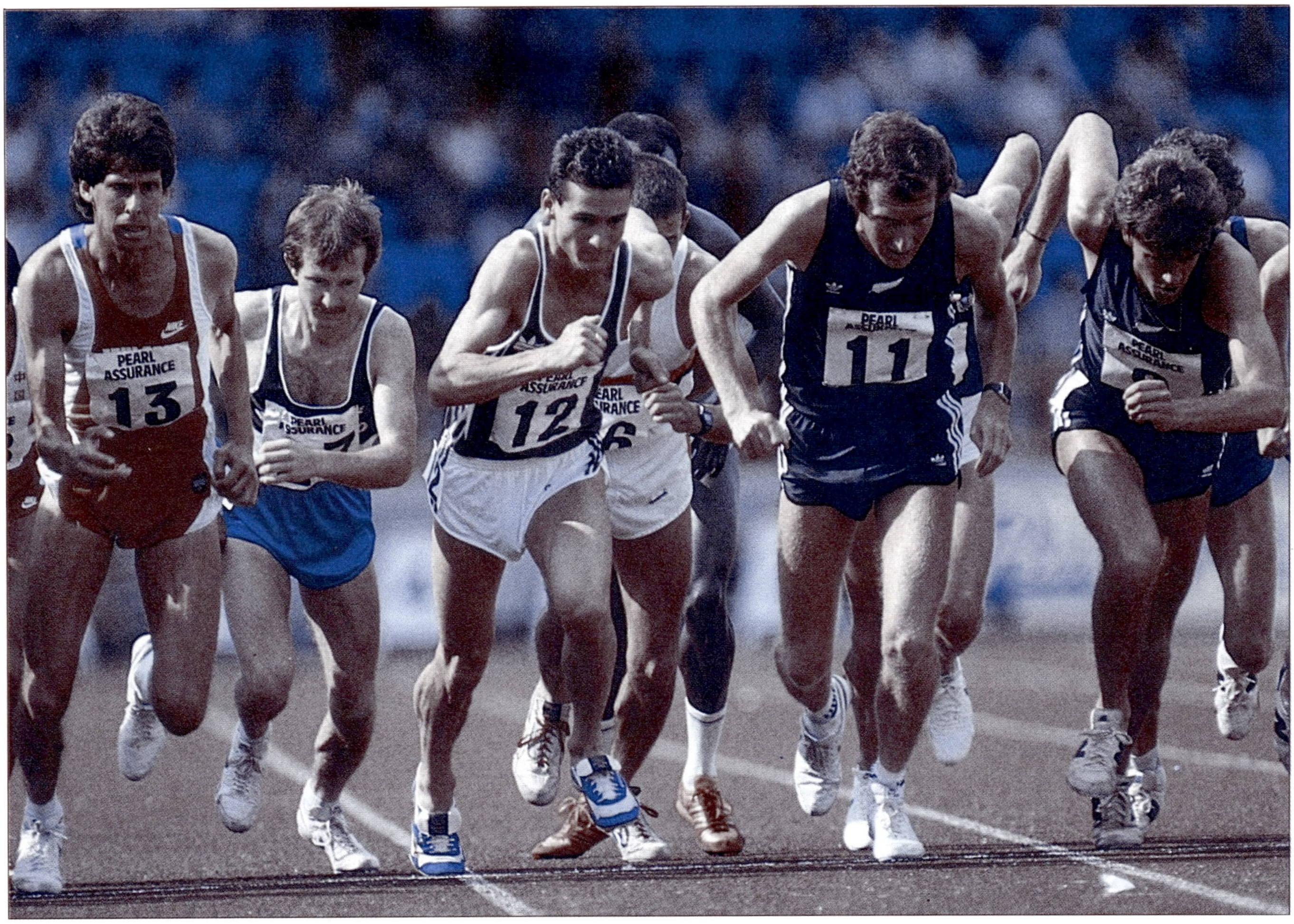

Running

TDK
717
TOKYO 91

NIKE
DAIRY CREST
PEARL ASSURANCE
2
PEARL ASSURANCE
1

Ford
HFC BANK
35
23

ITA
URS

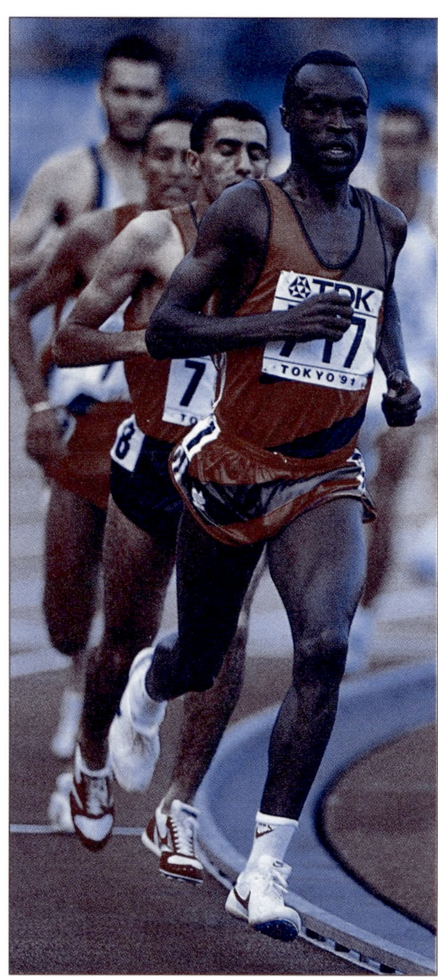

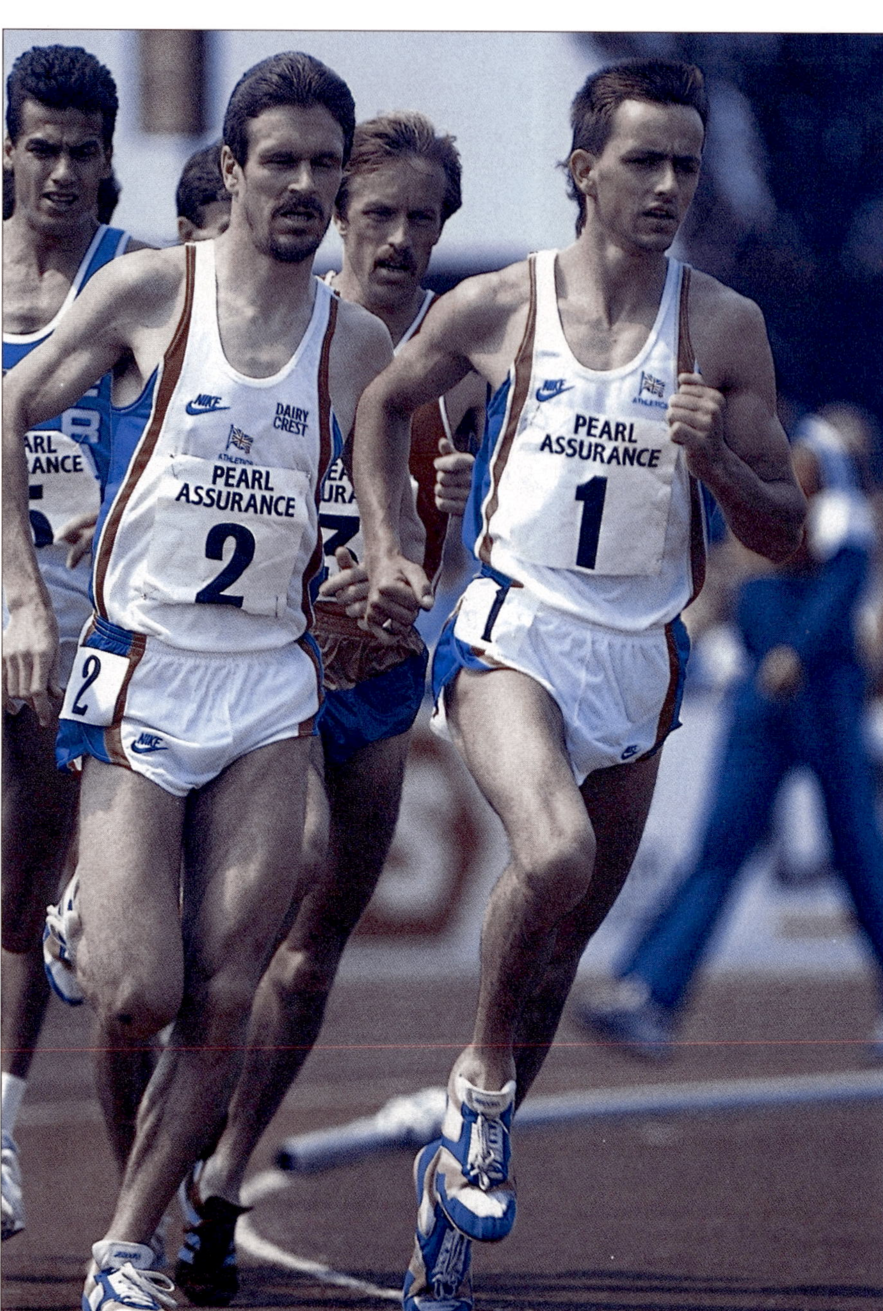

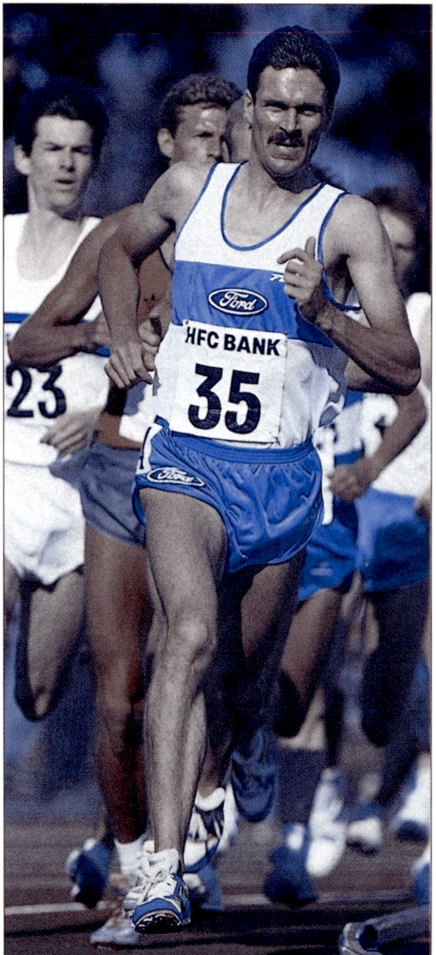

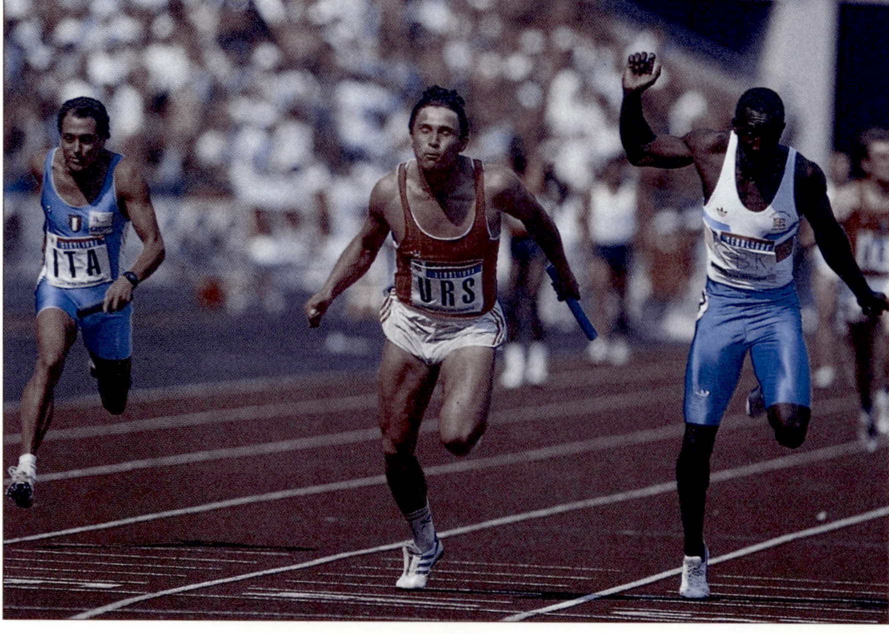

Running – relay · hurdles

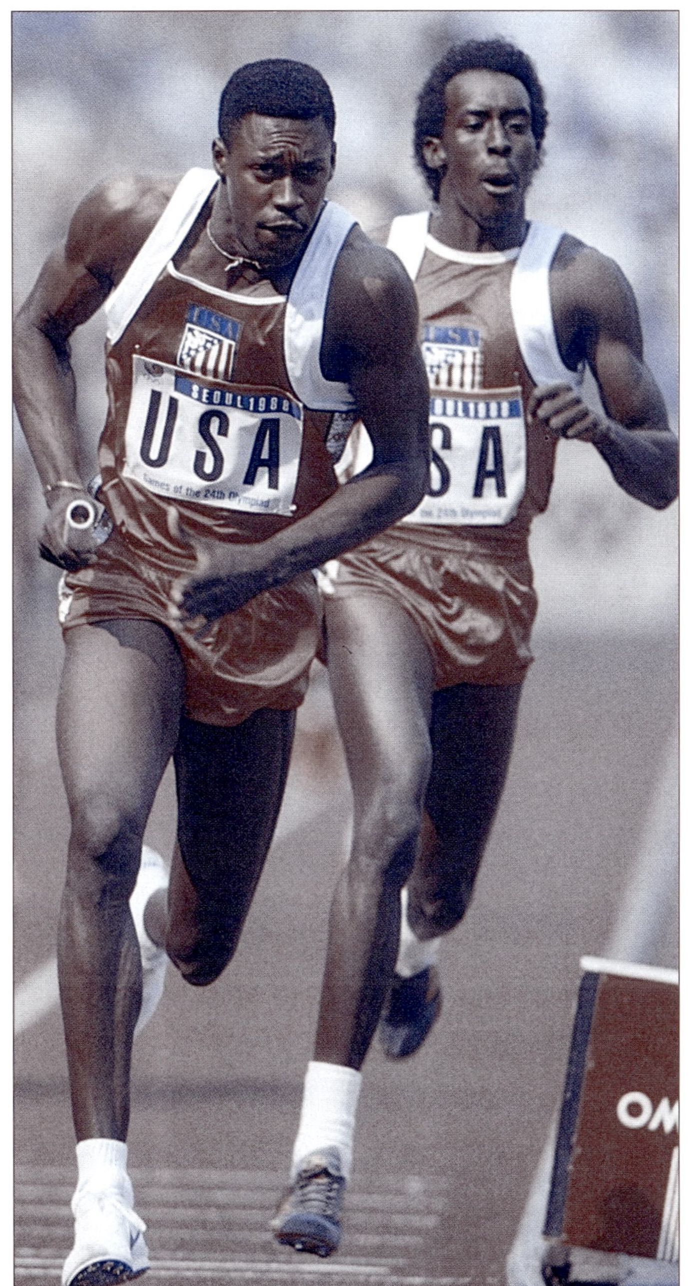

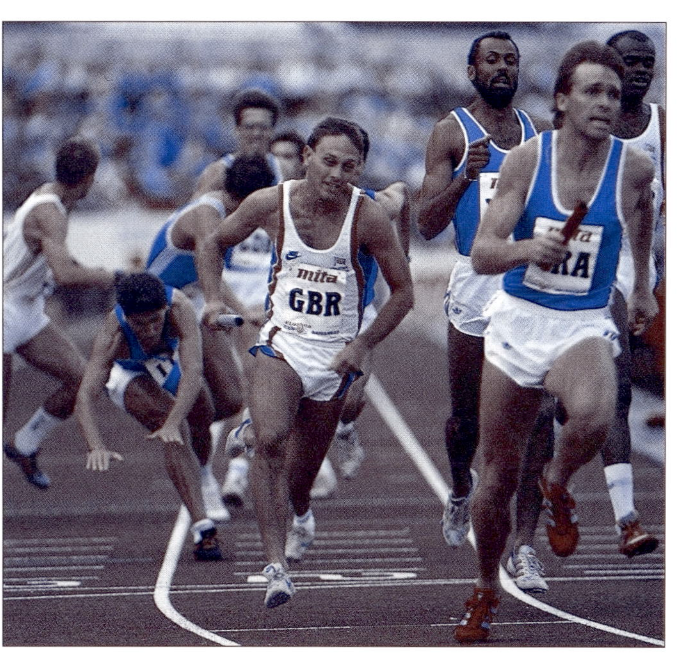

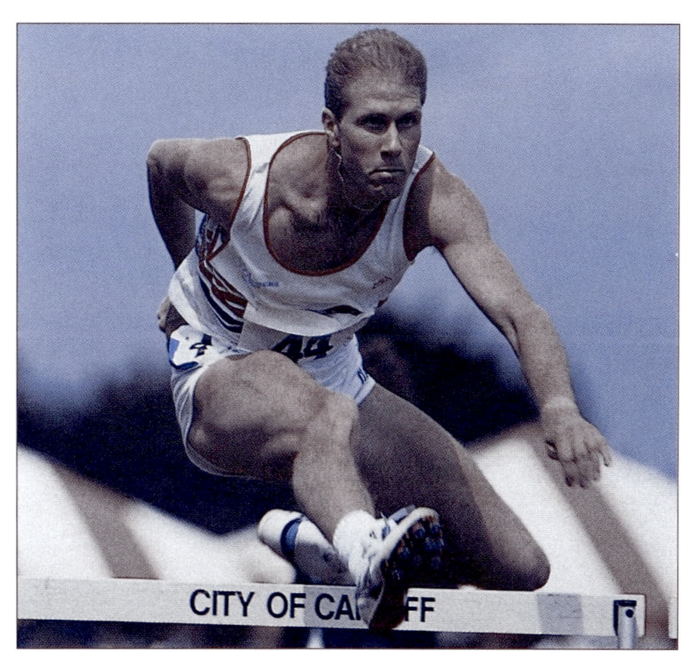

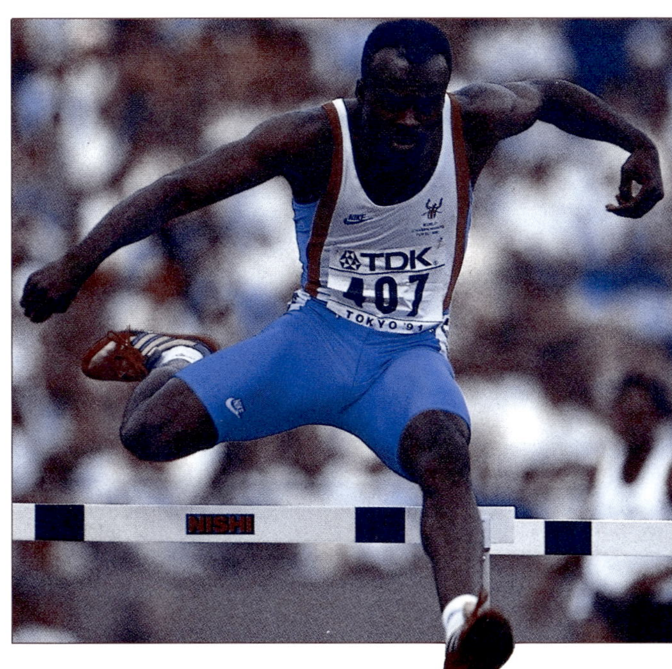

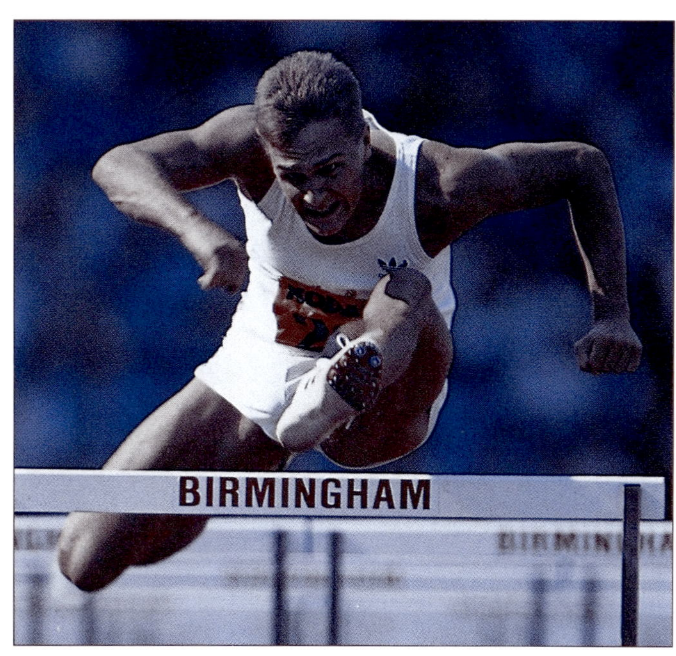

Running – hurdles · steeplechase

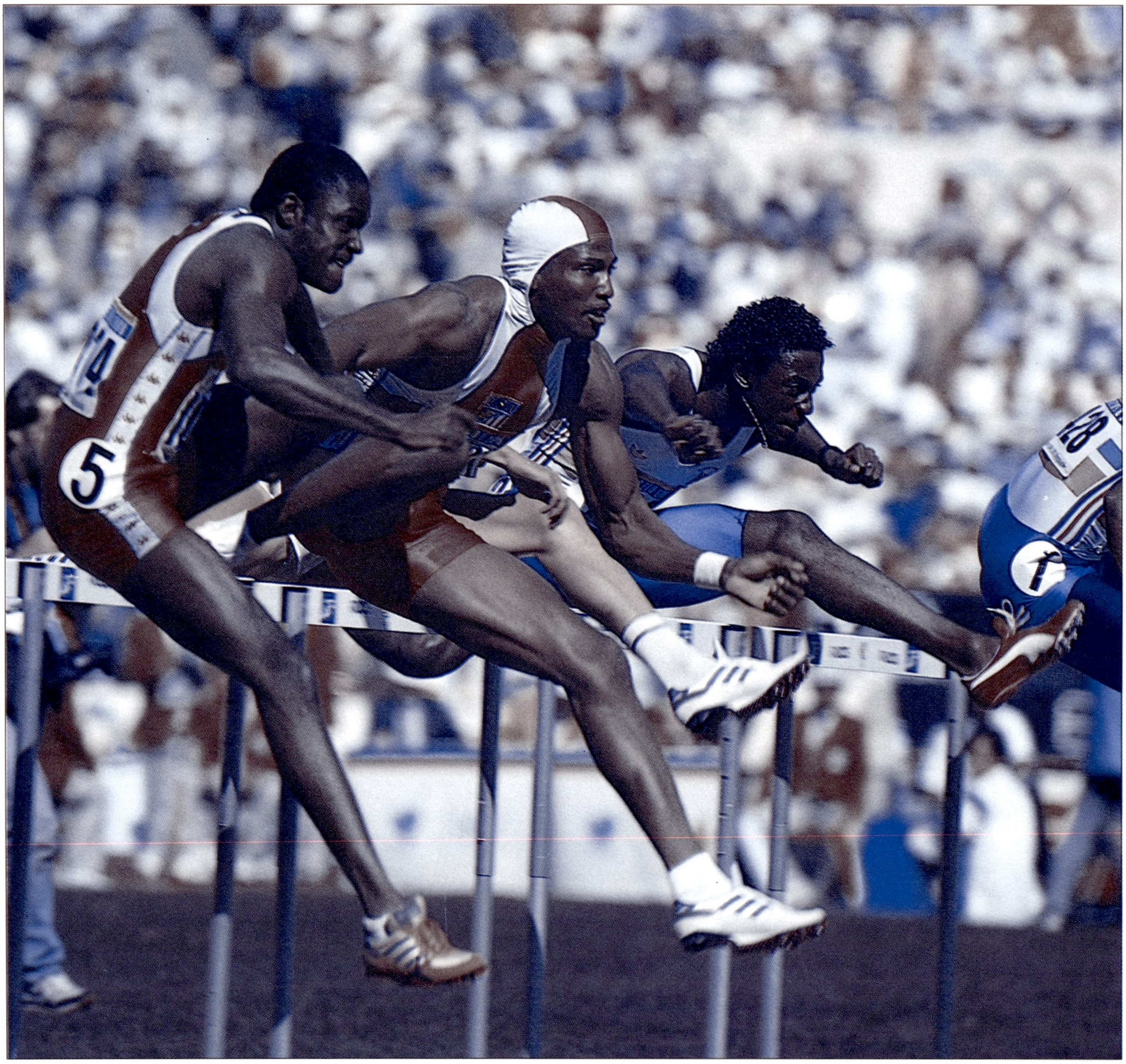

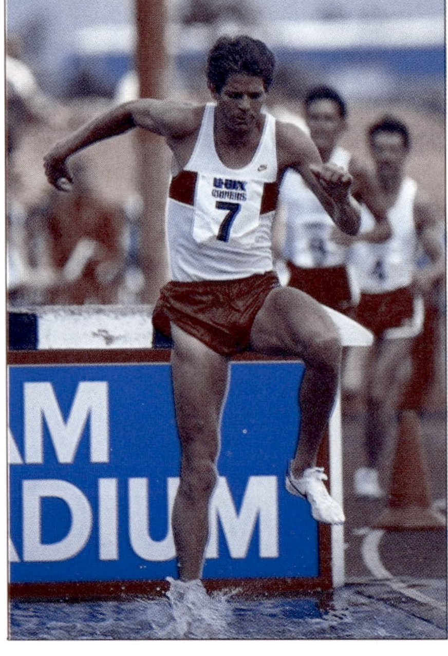

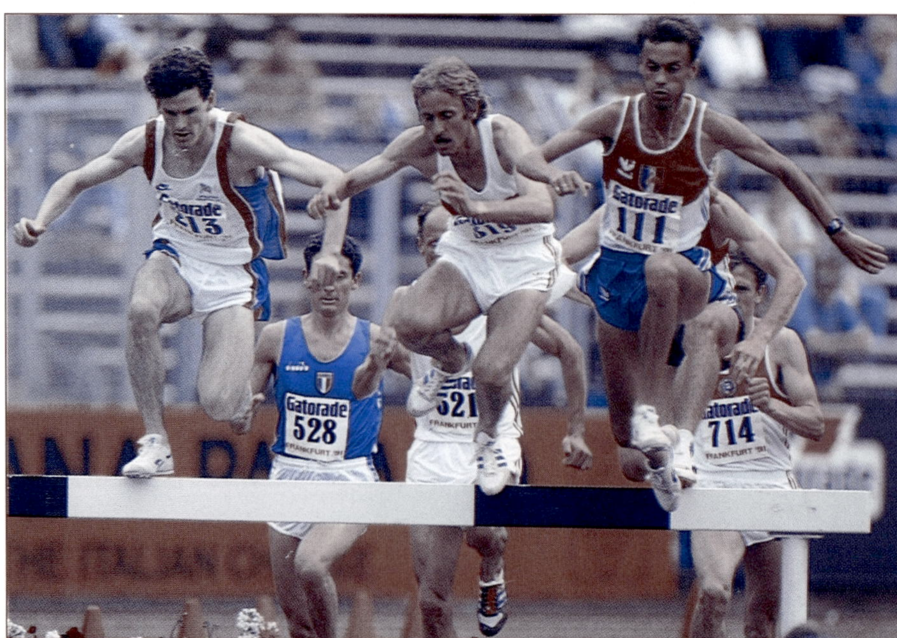

Running – finishing

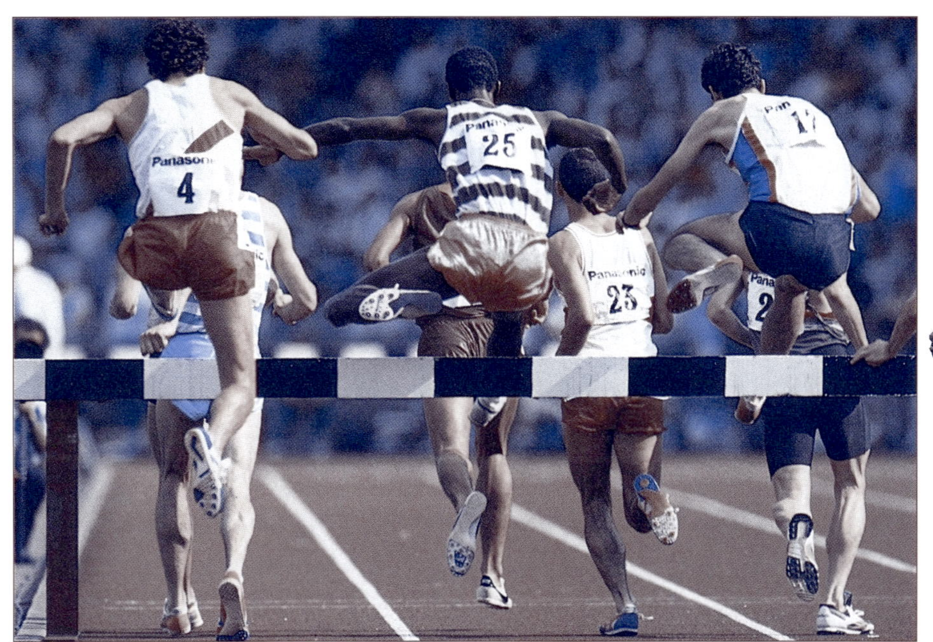

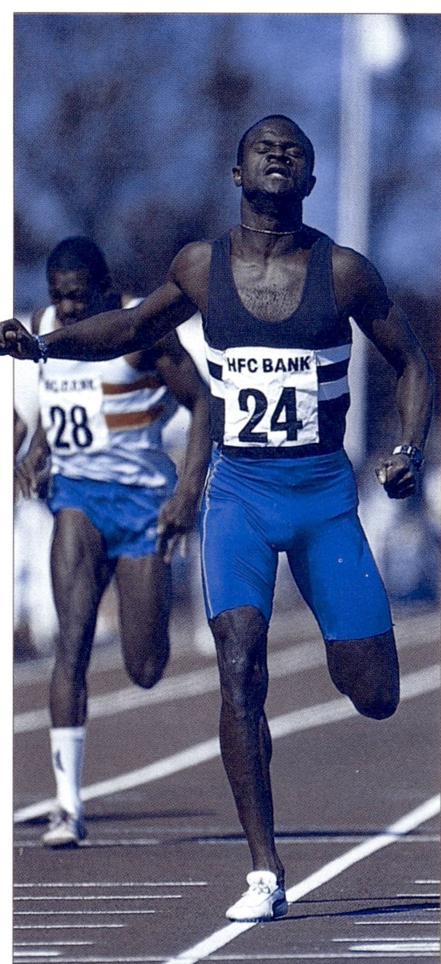

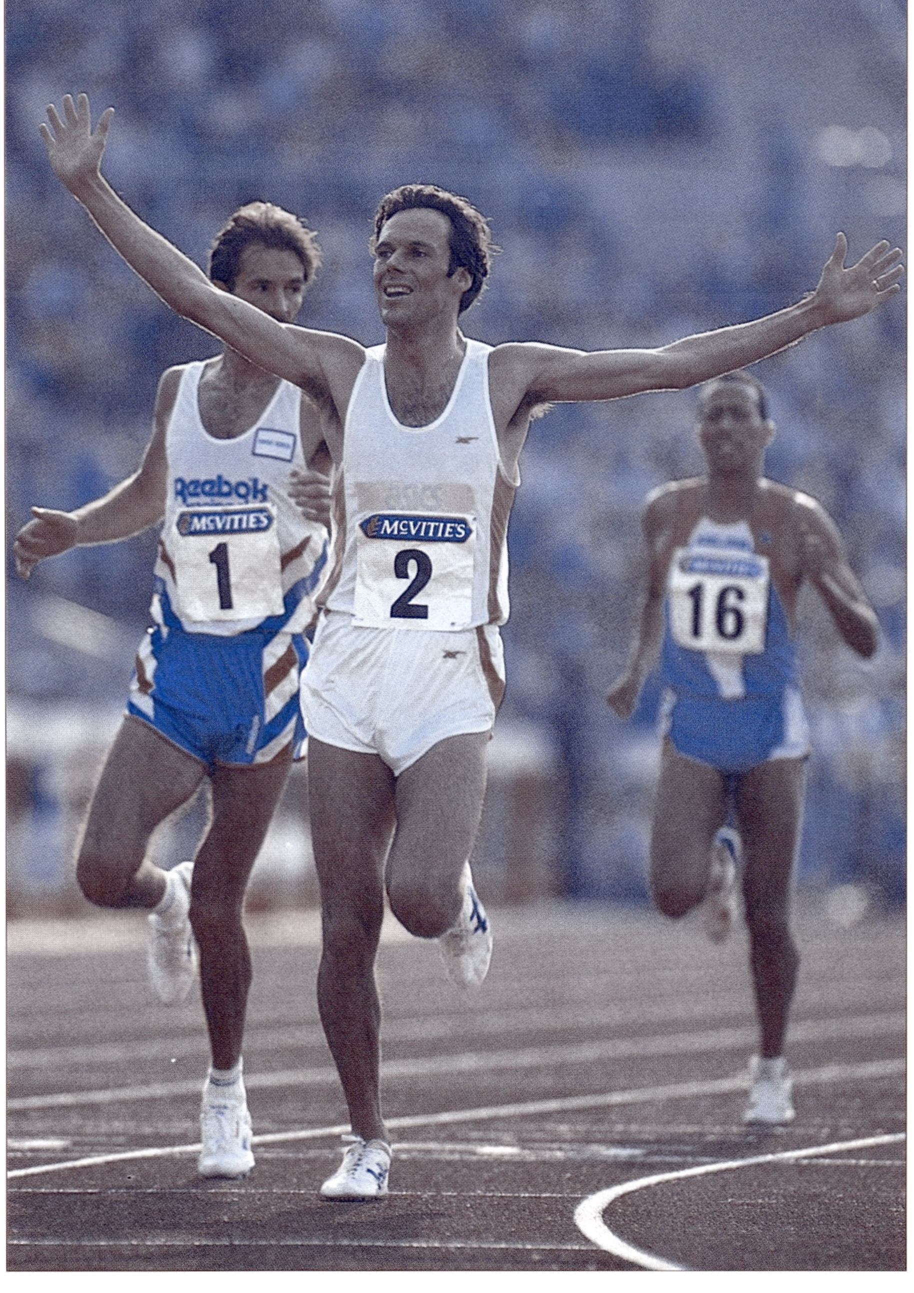

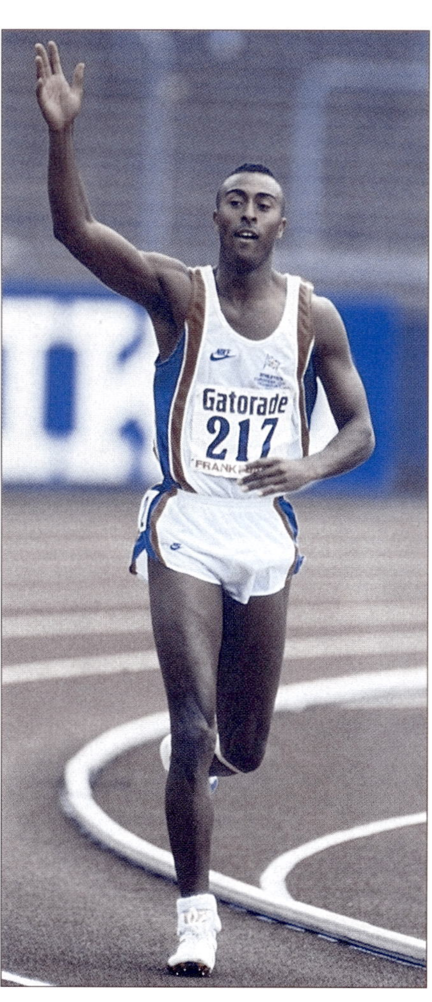

Running – marathon · cross country · speed walking

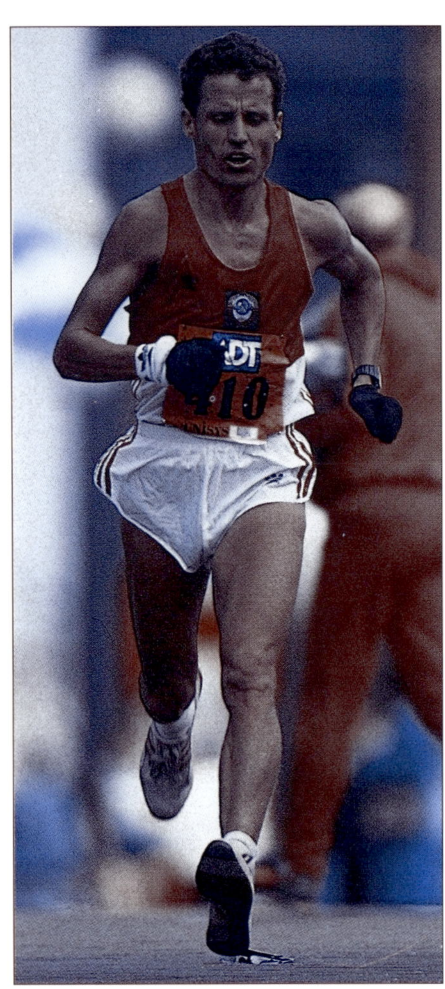

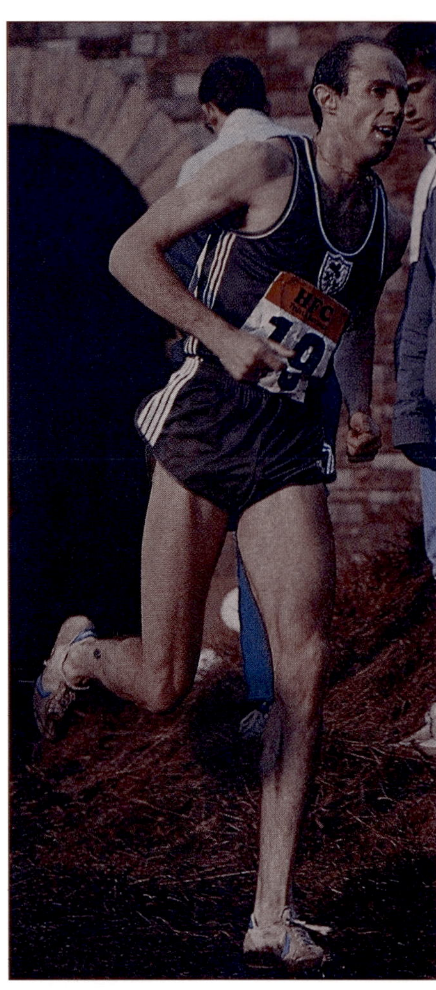

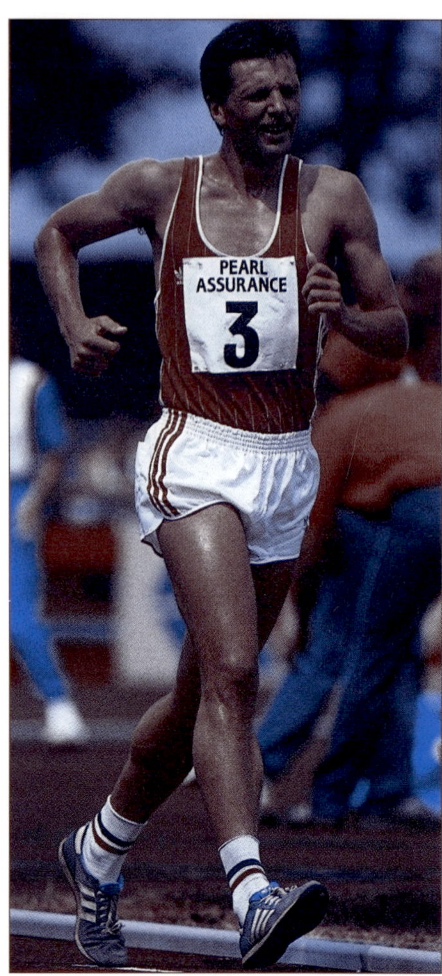

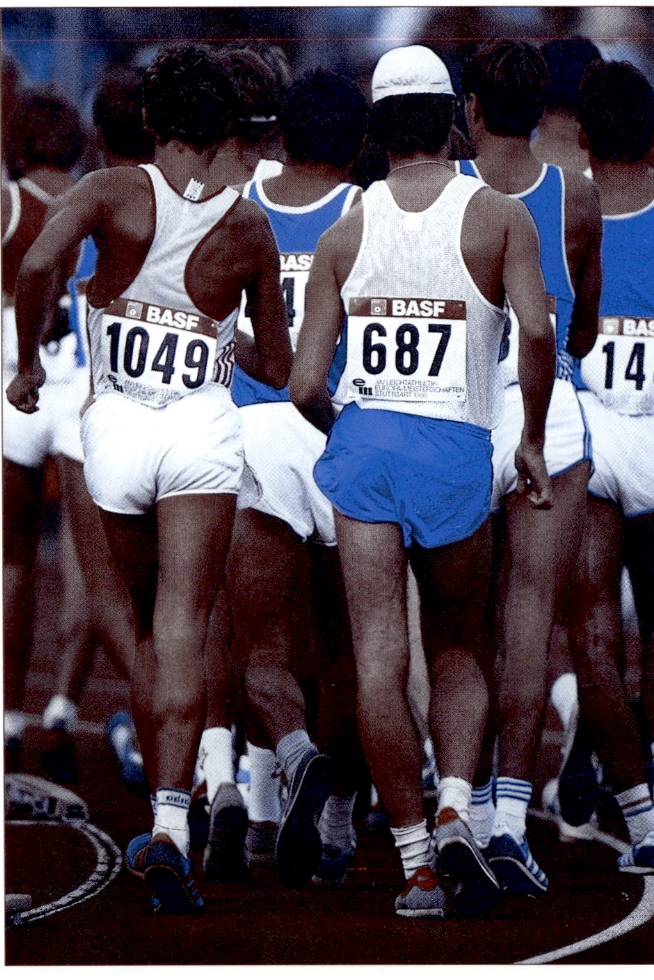

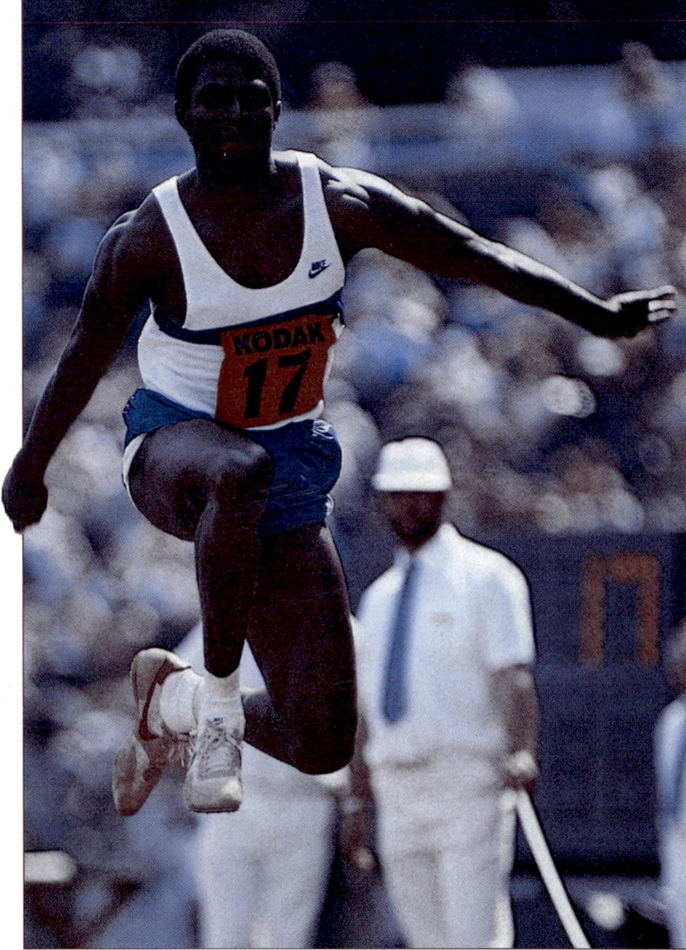

Long jump

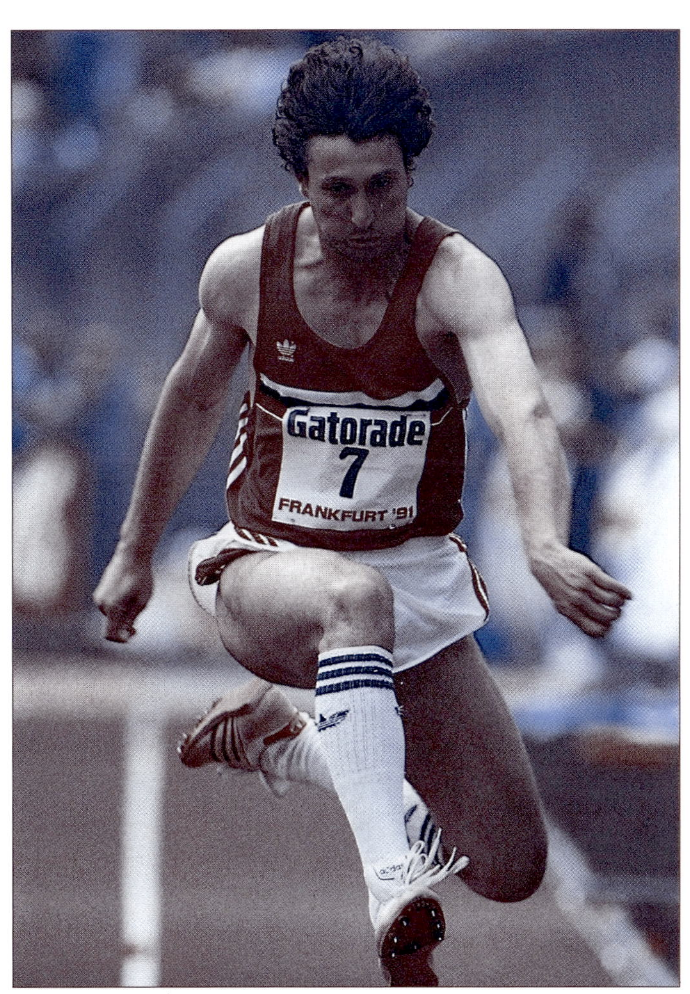

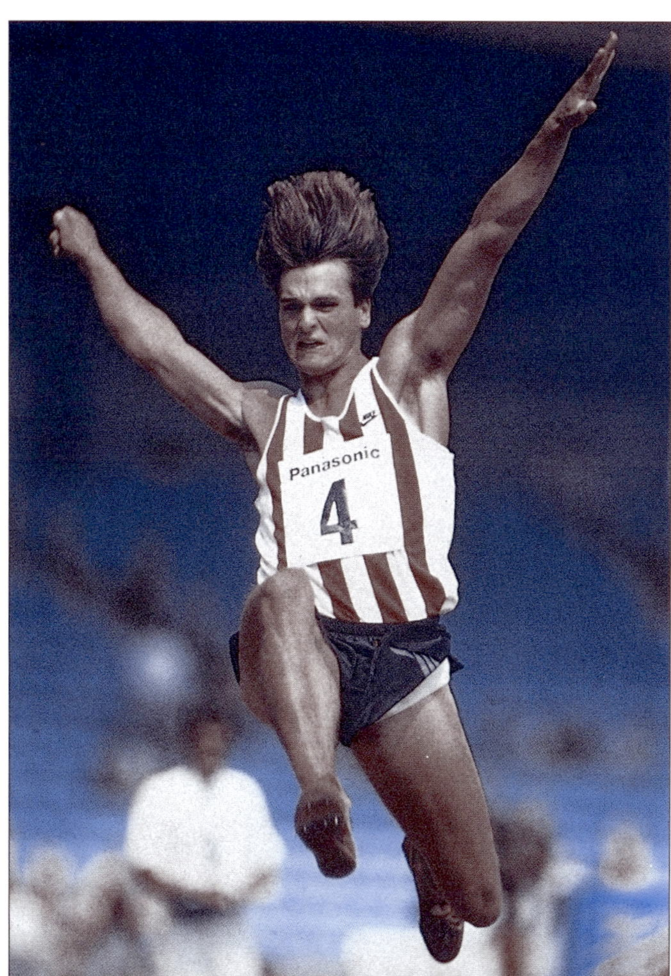

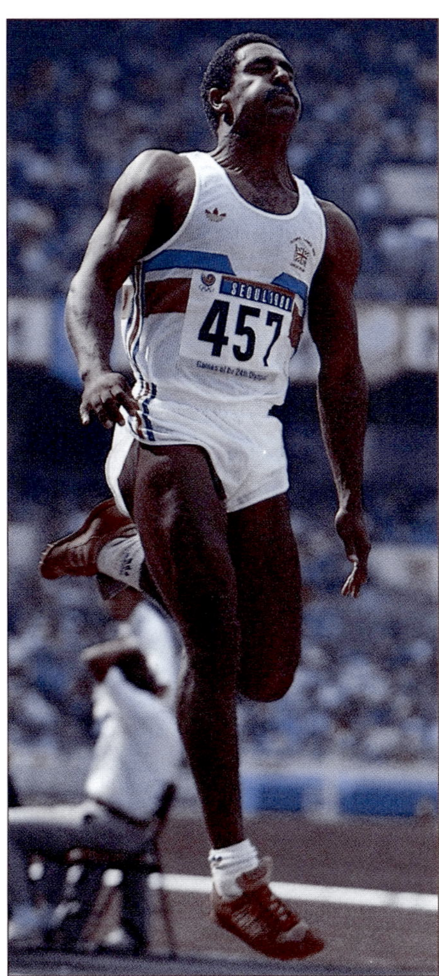

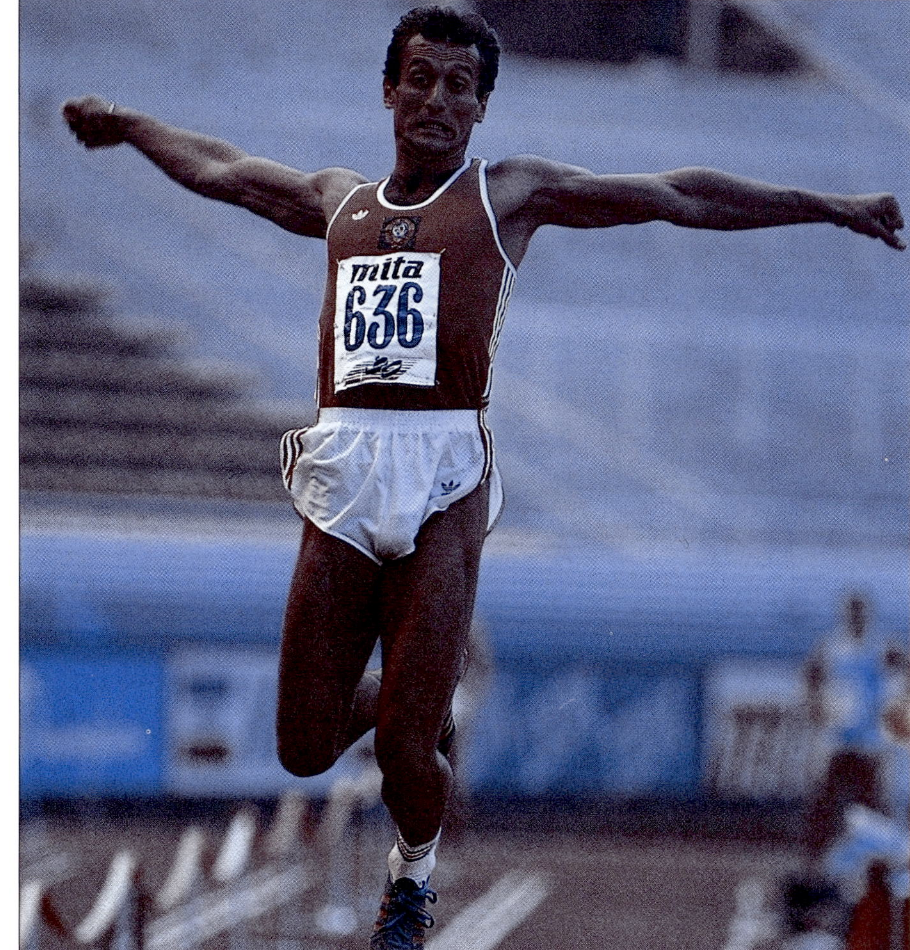

High jump

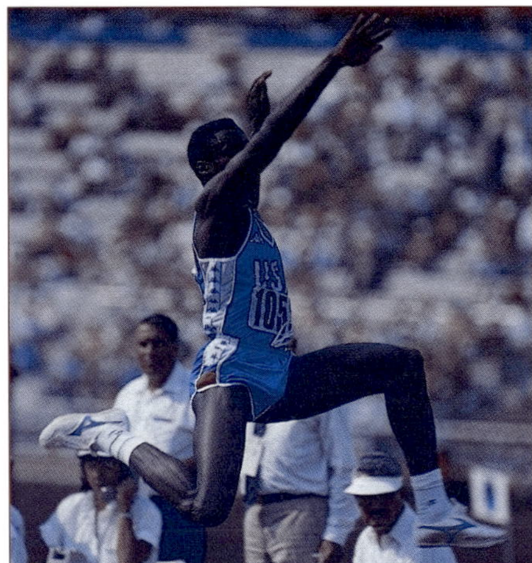

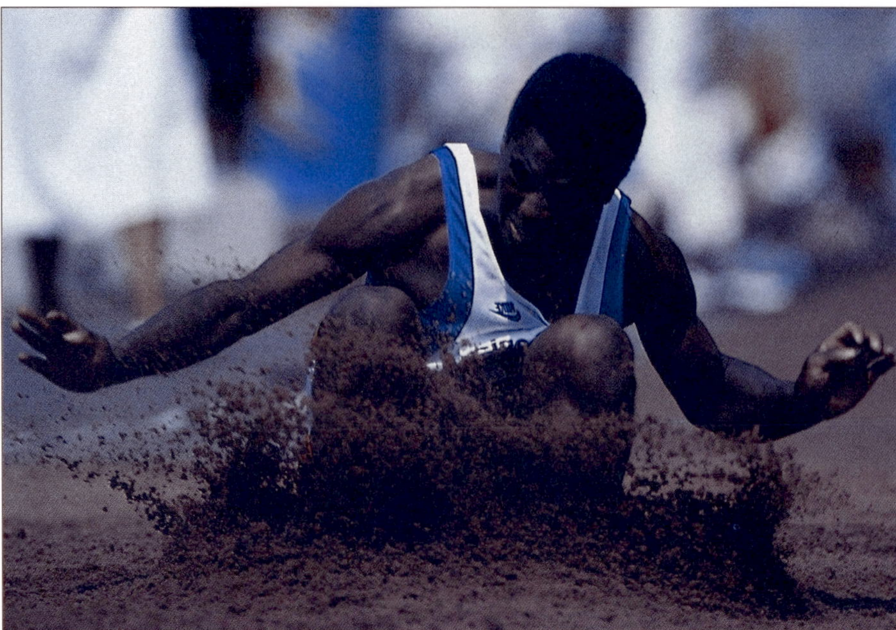

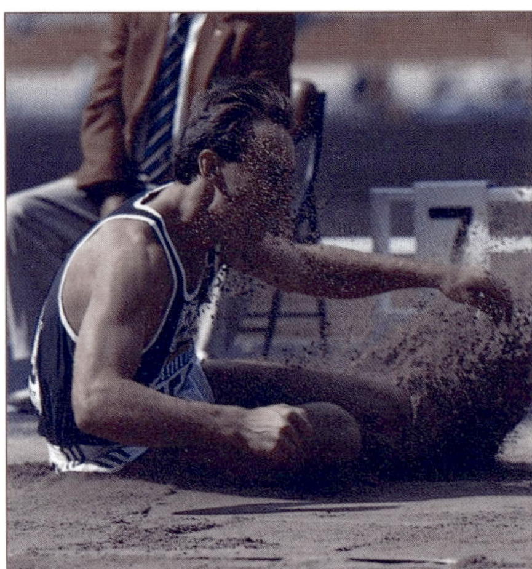

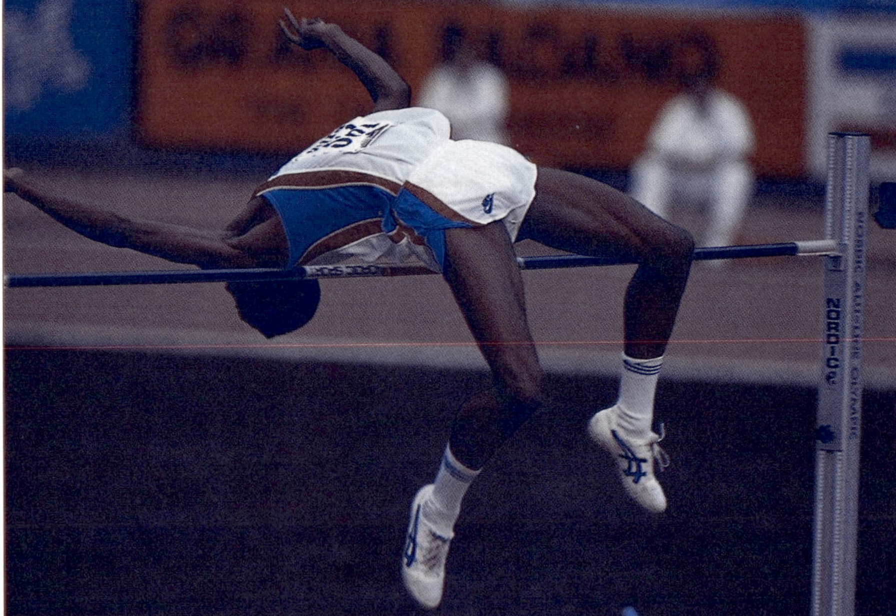

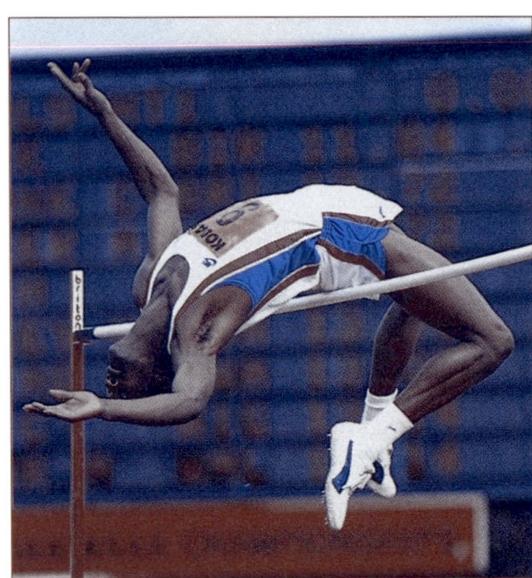

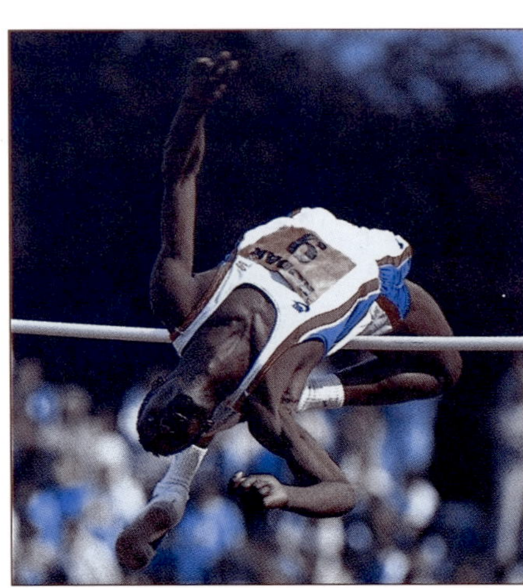

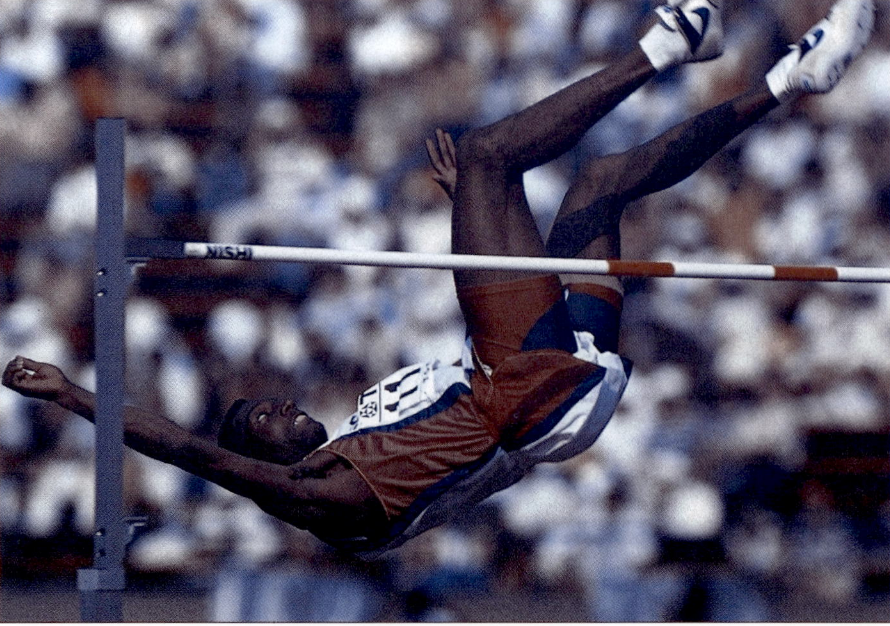

Pole vault

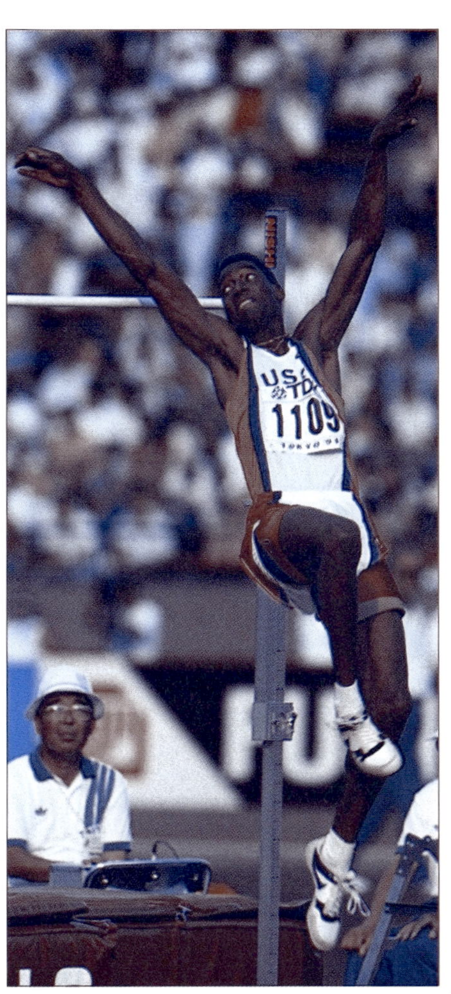

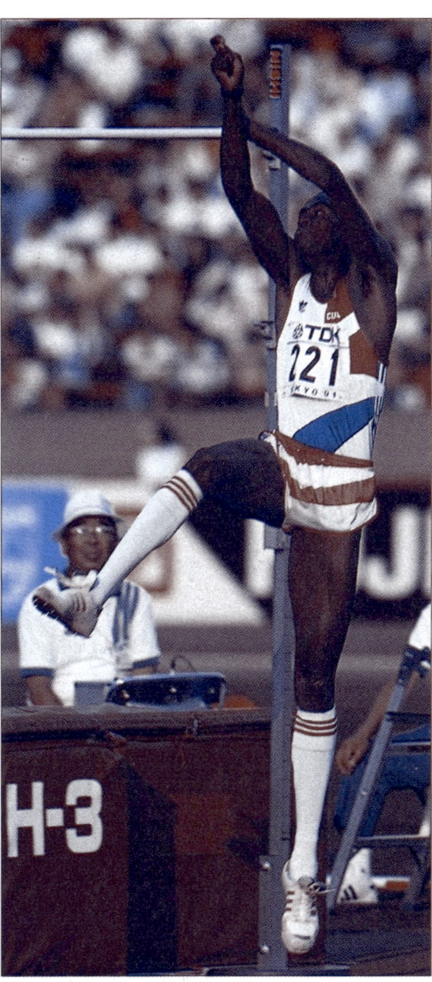

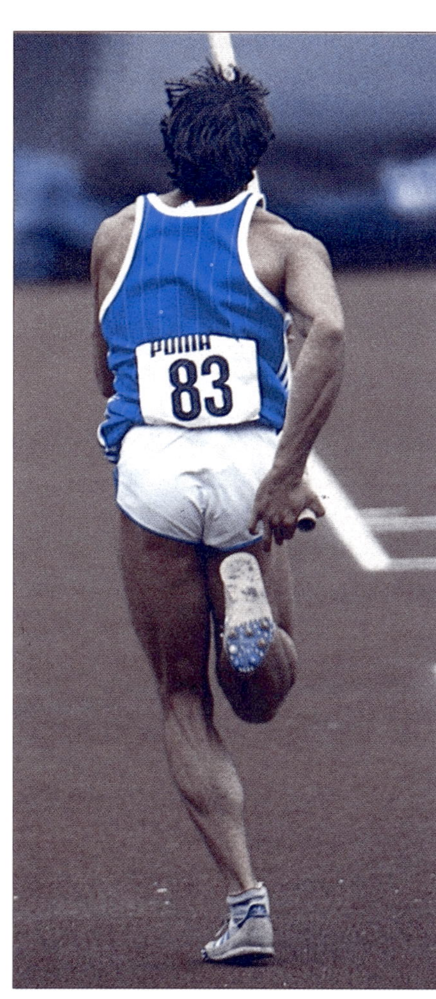

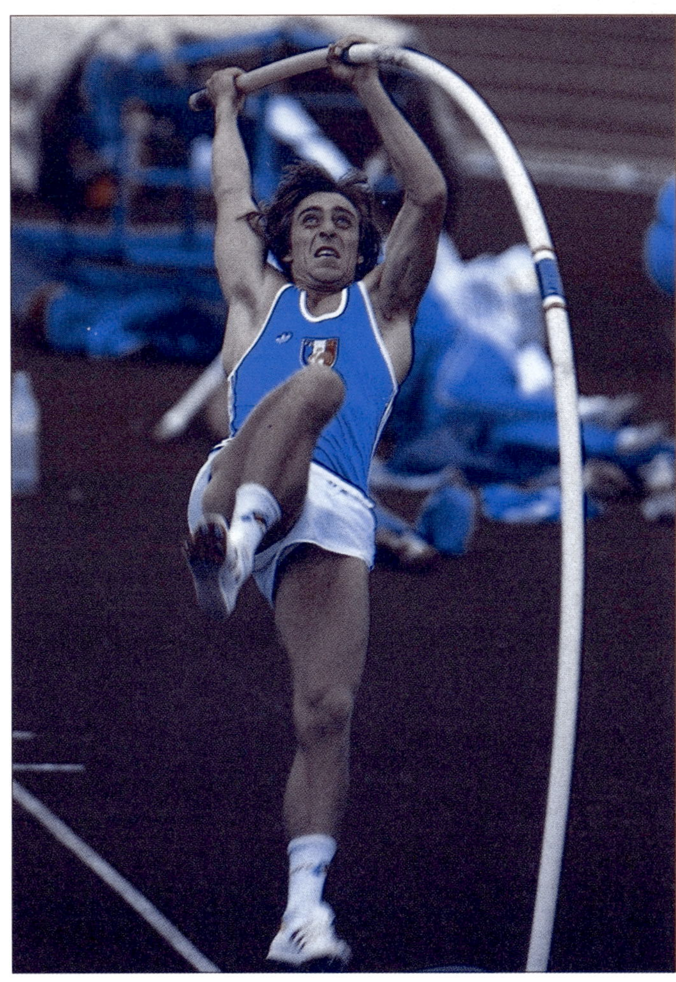

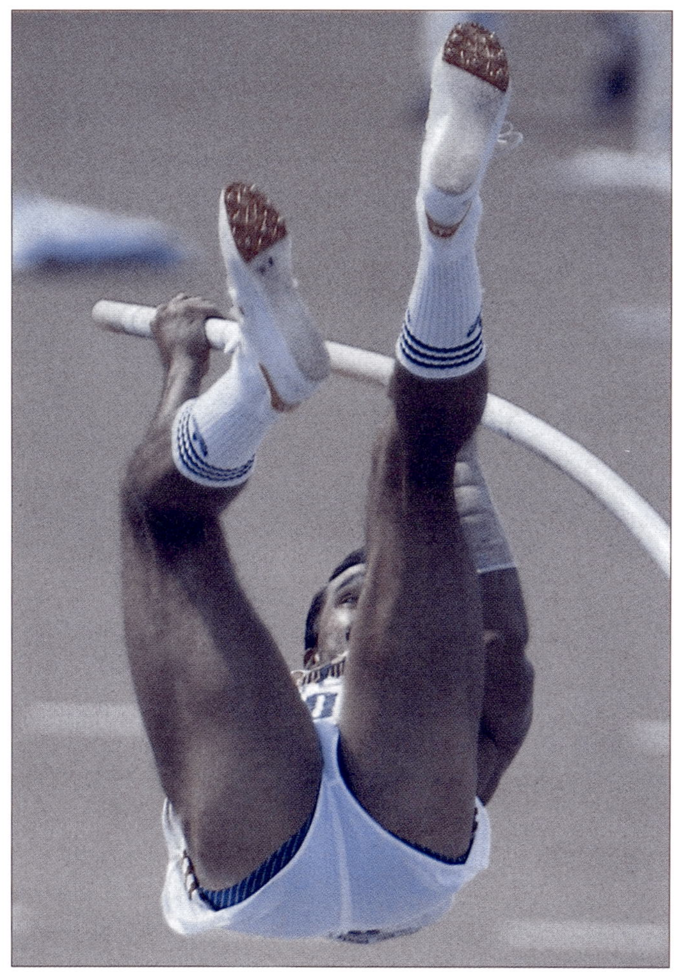

The javelin

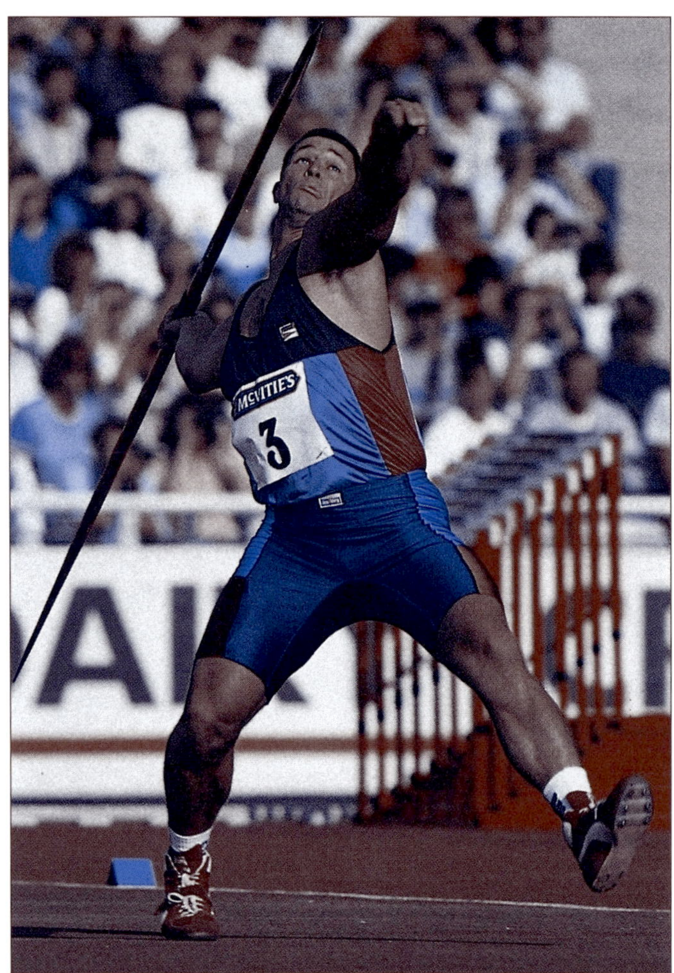

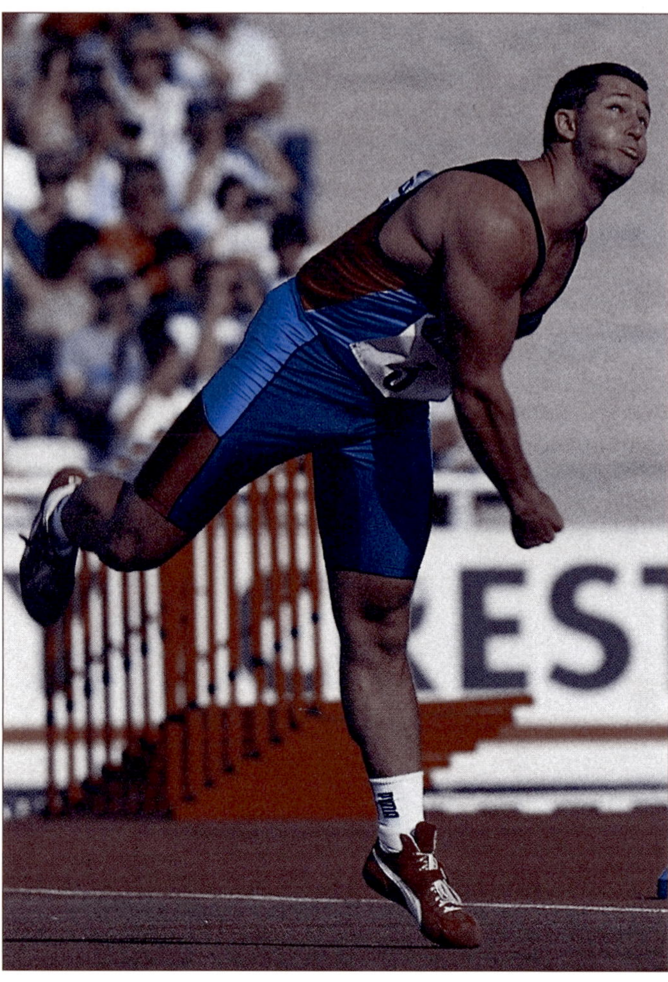

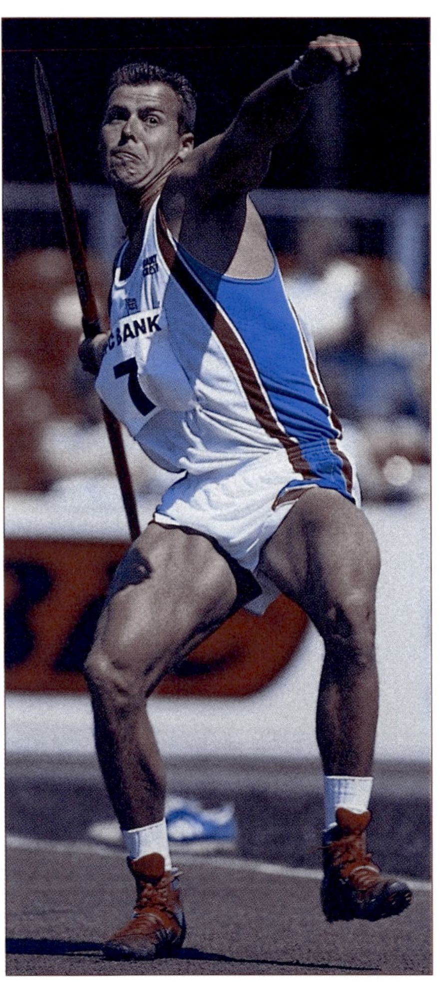

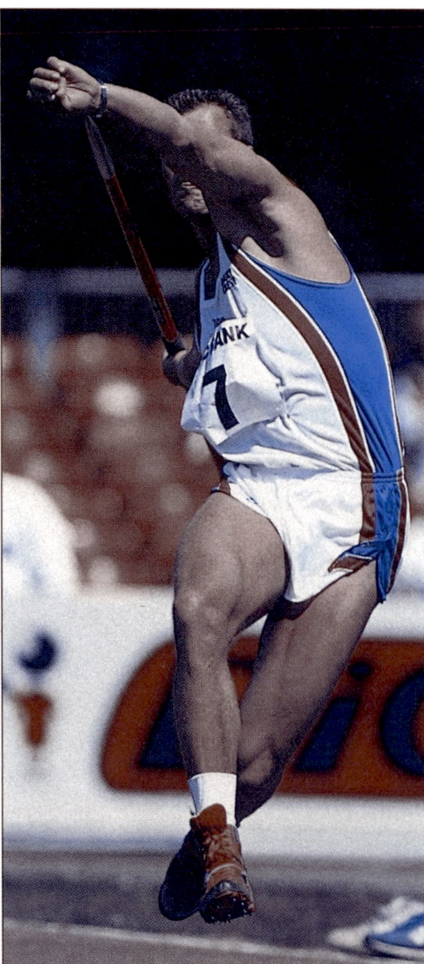

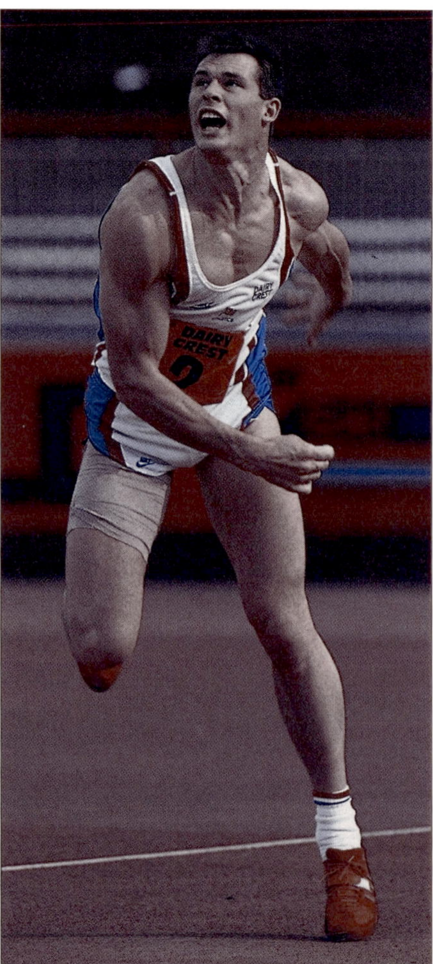

The discus · the shot put

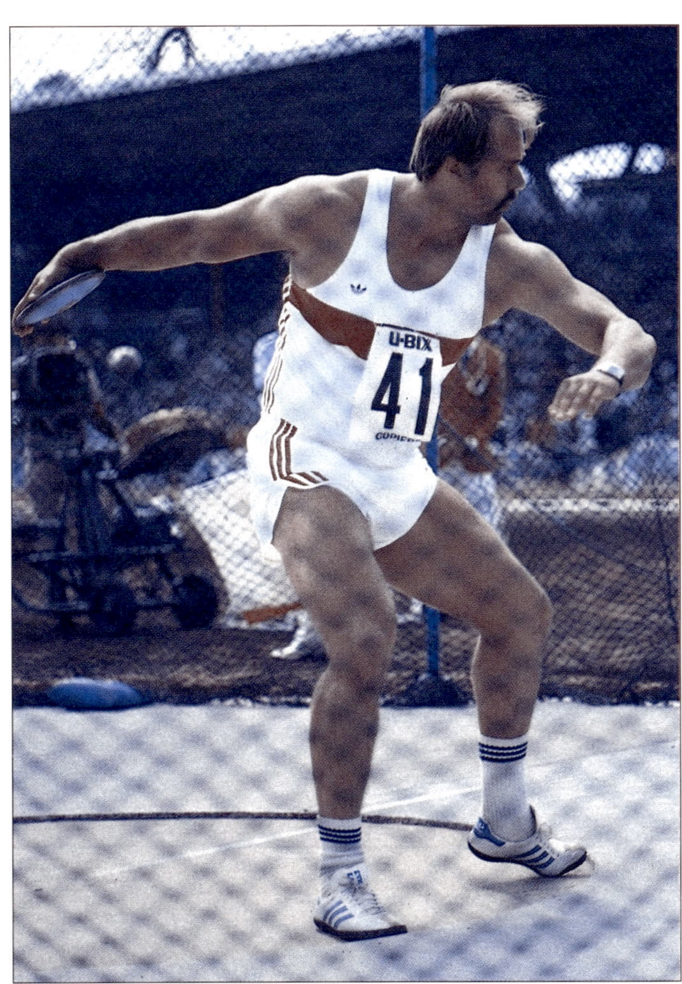

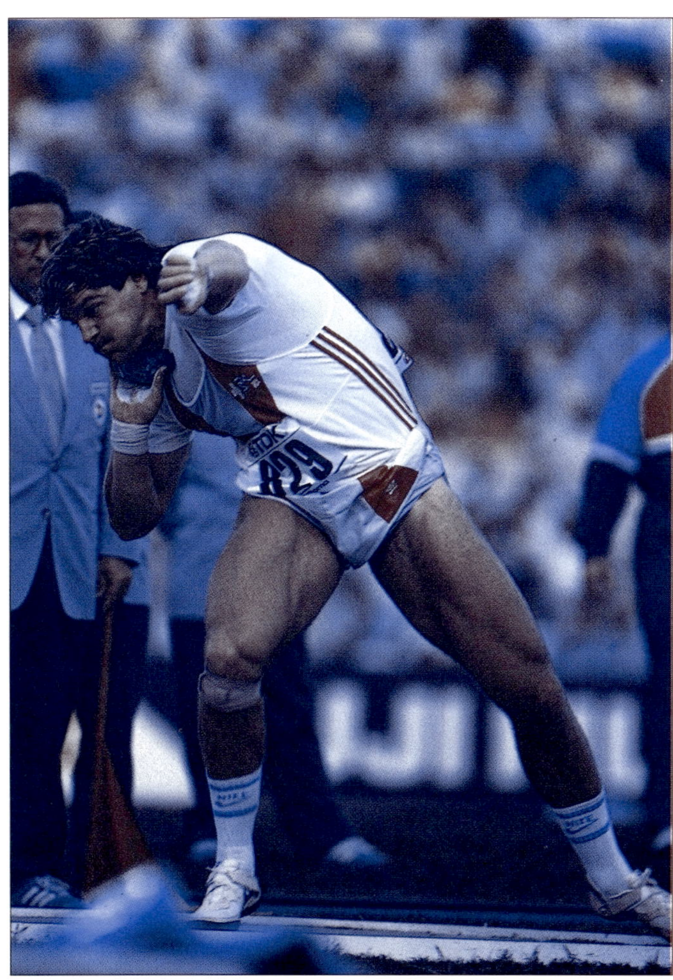

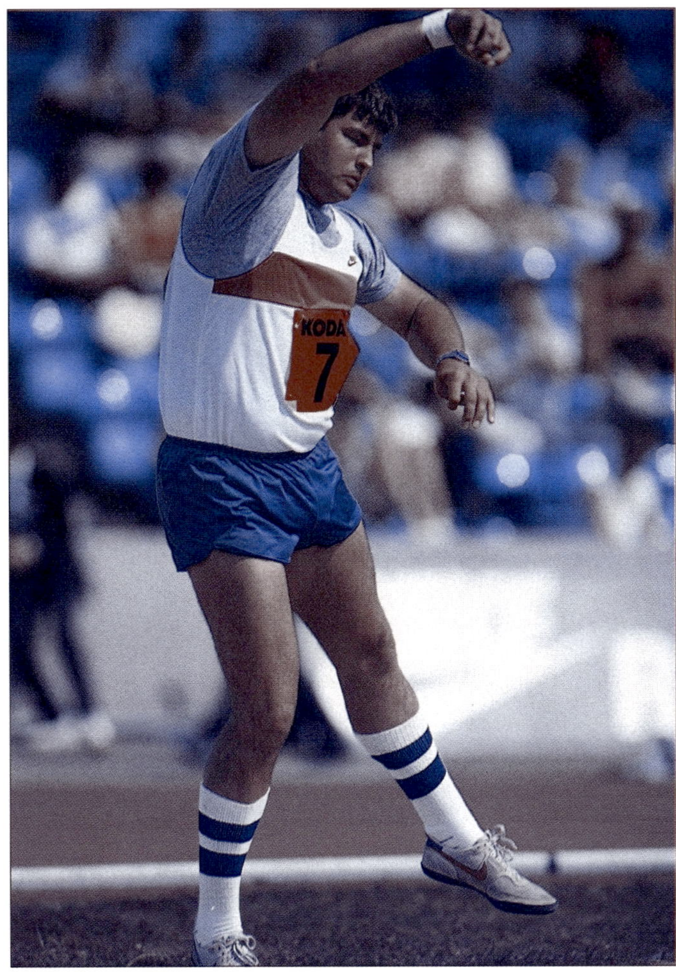

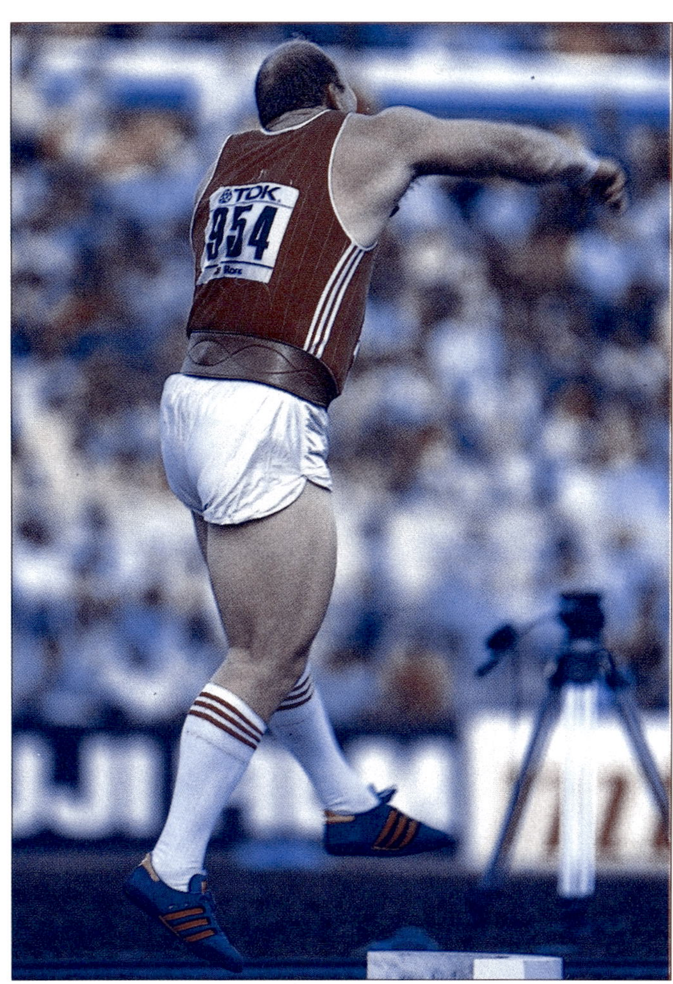

Hammer throwing · track officials

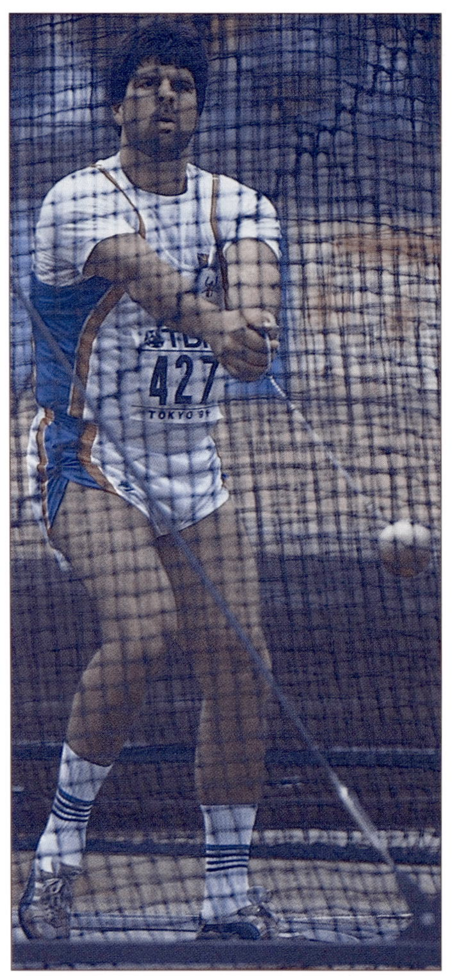

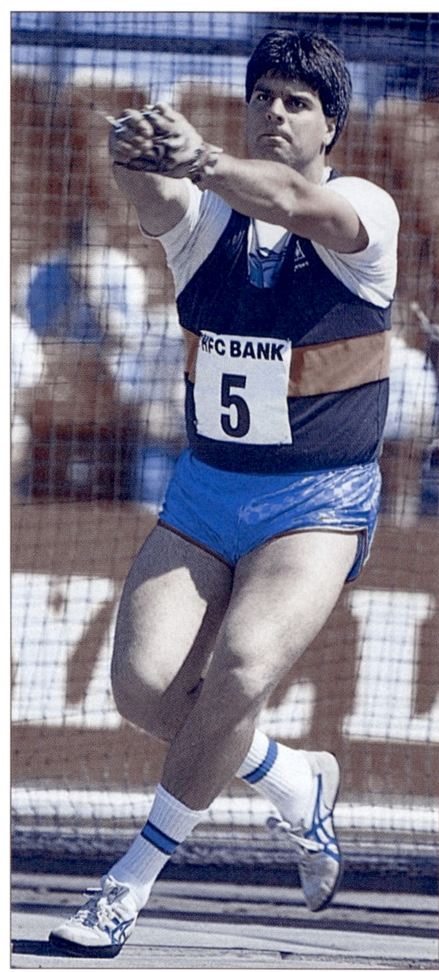

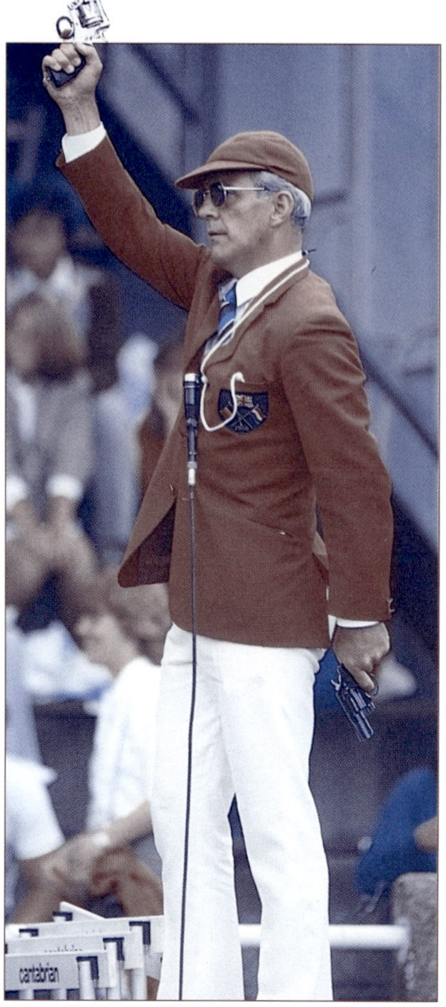

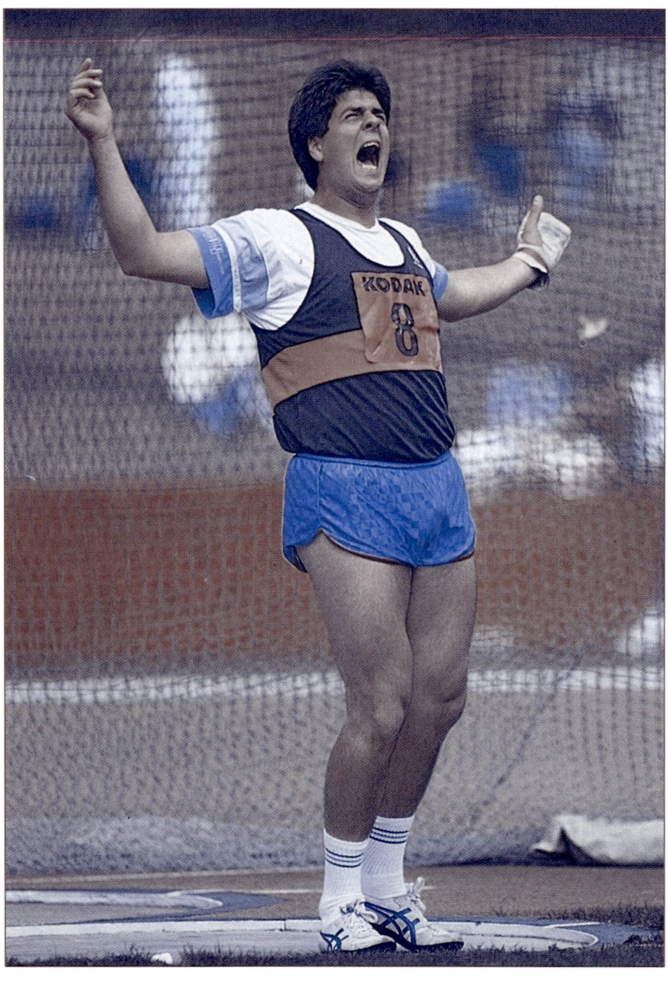

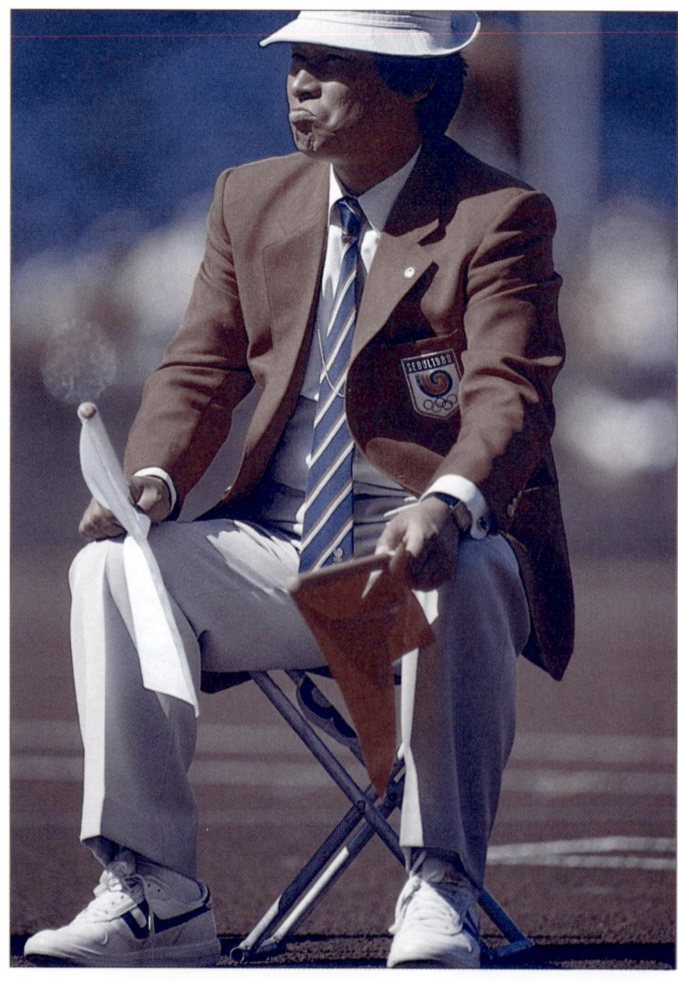

Running – starting

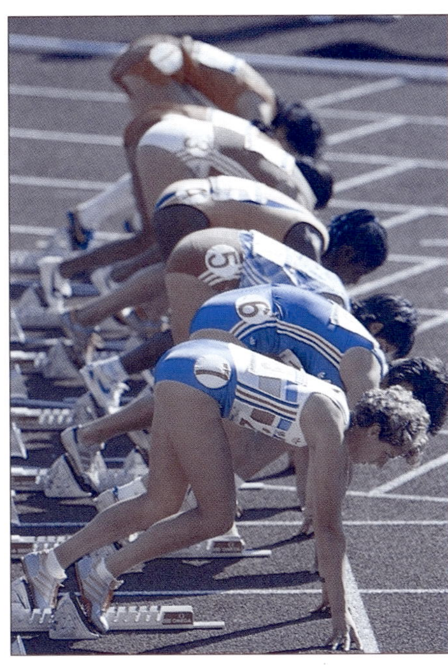

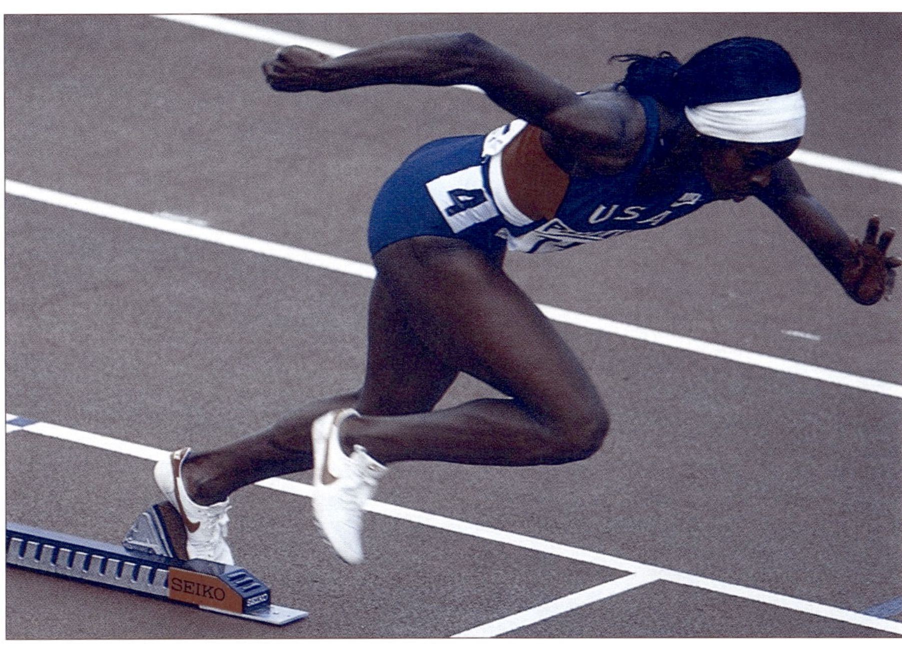

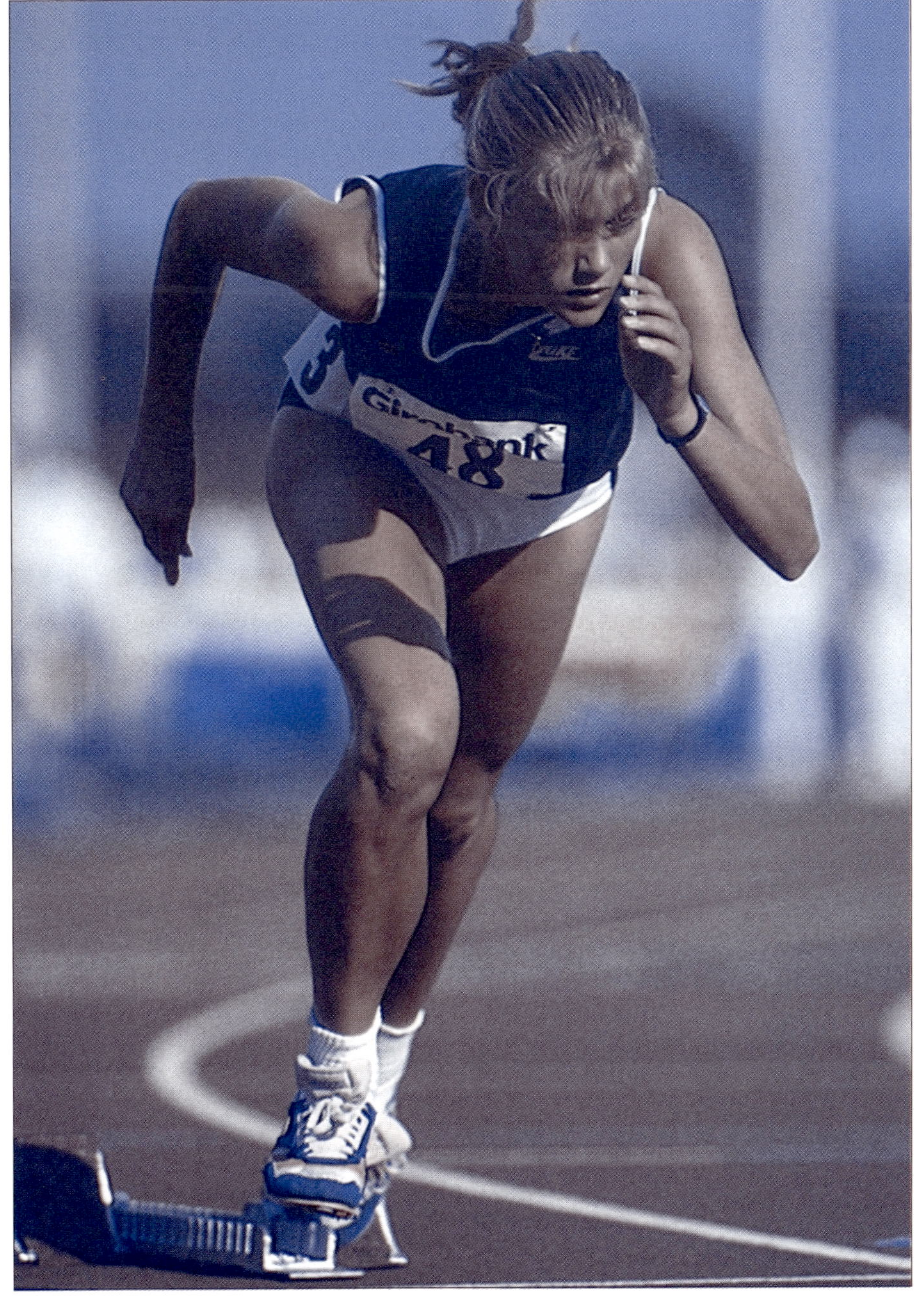

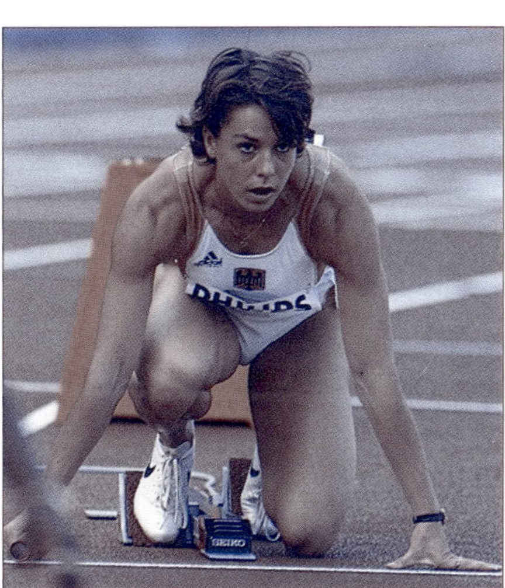

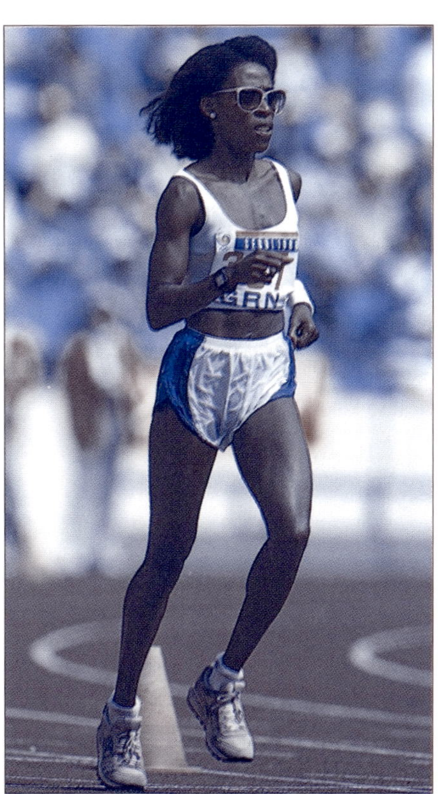

Running – relay · hurdles

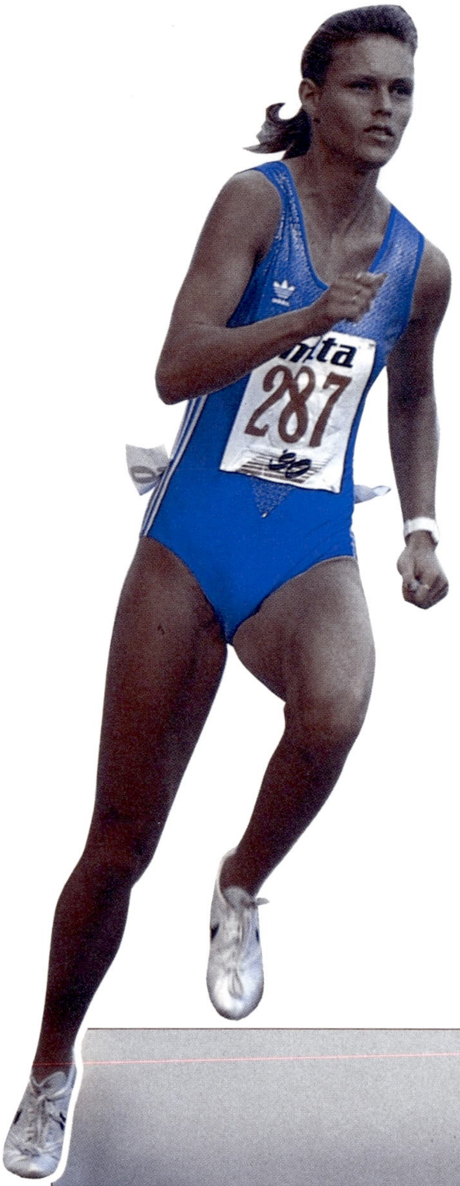

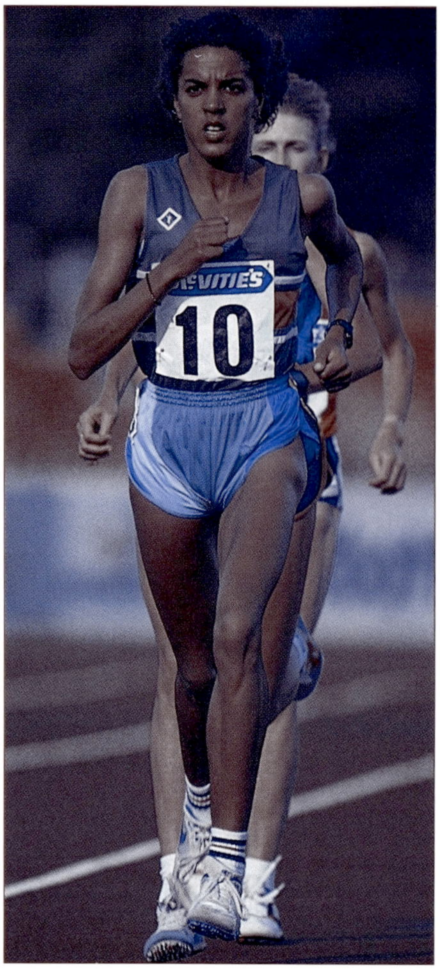

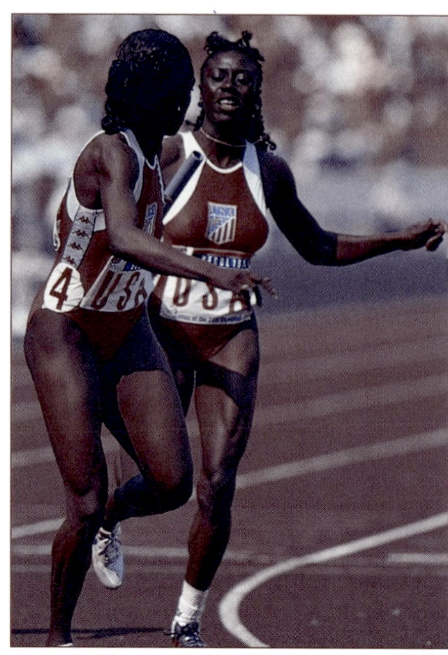

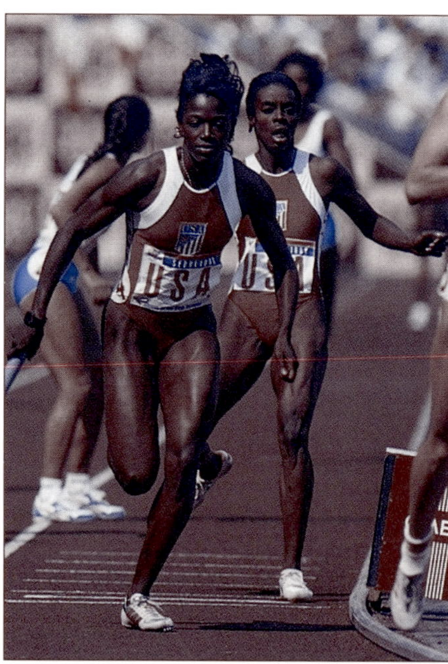

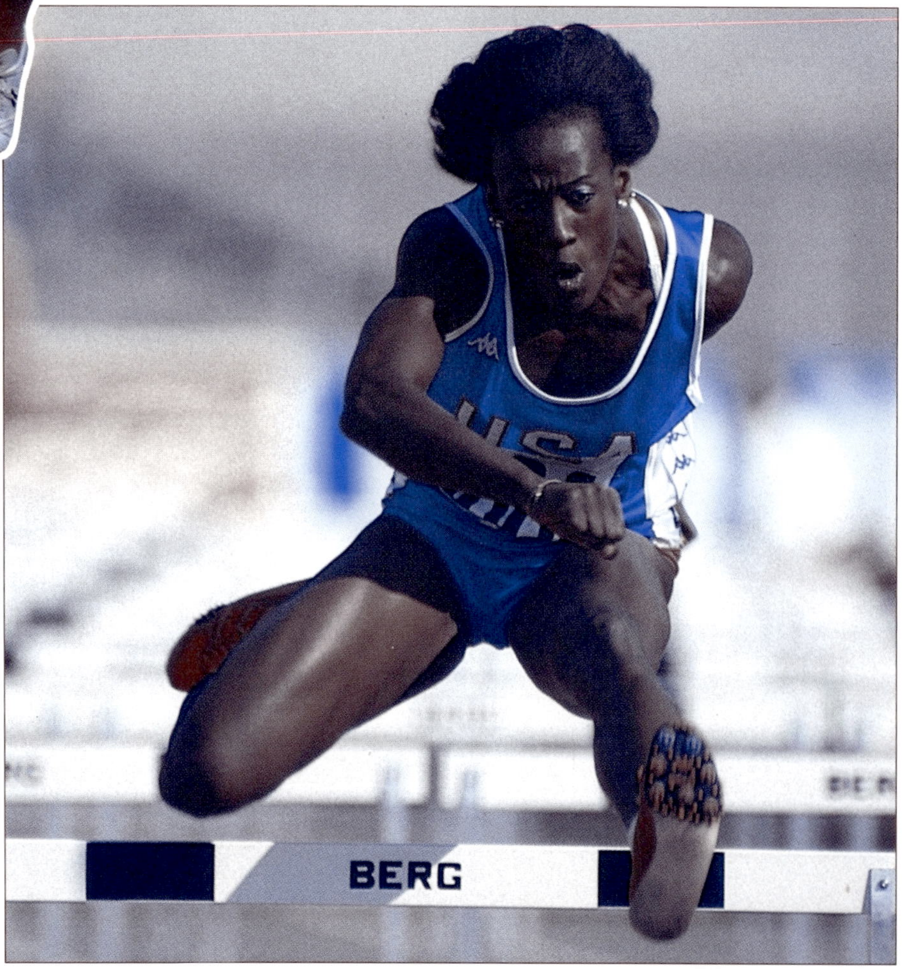

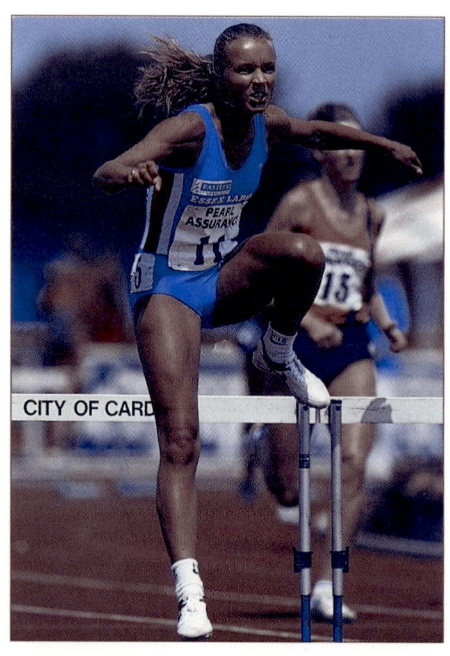

finishing · cross country · marathon · walking

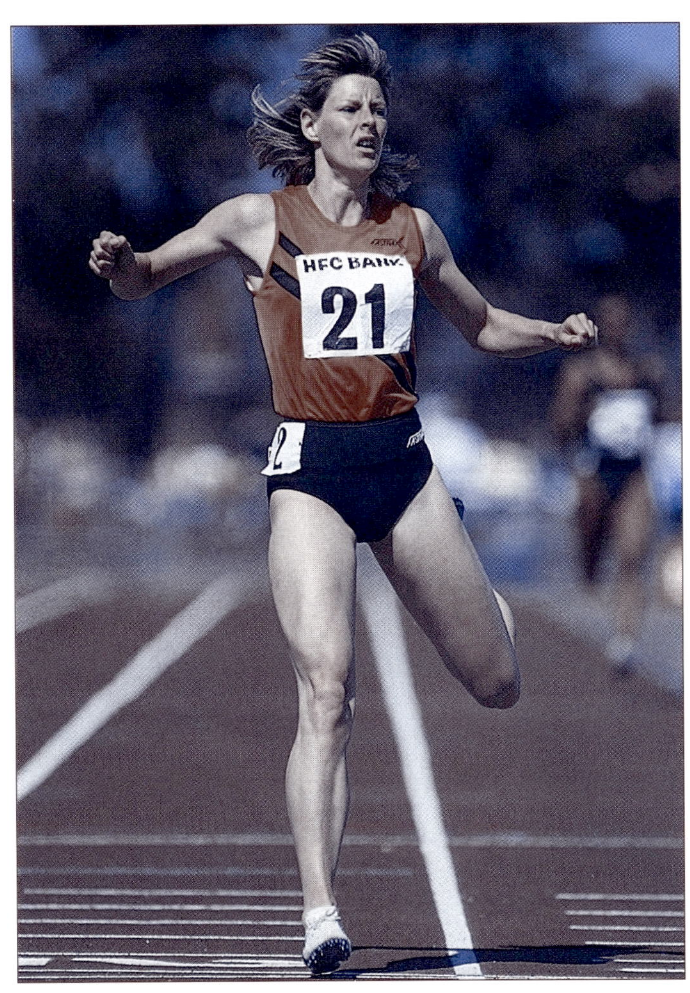

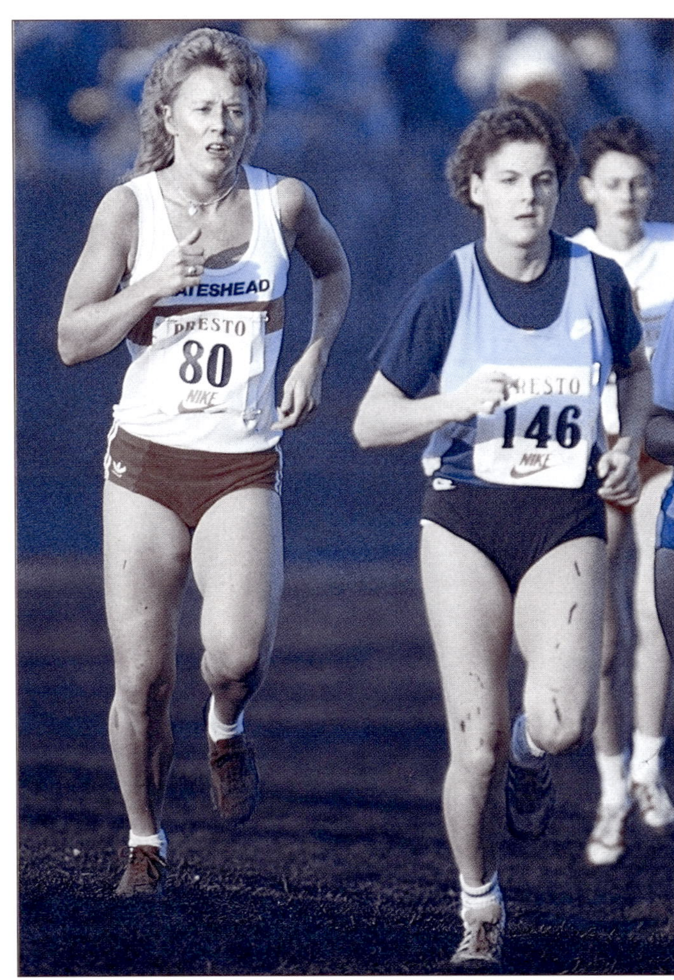

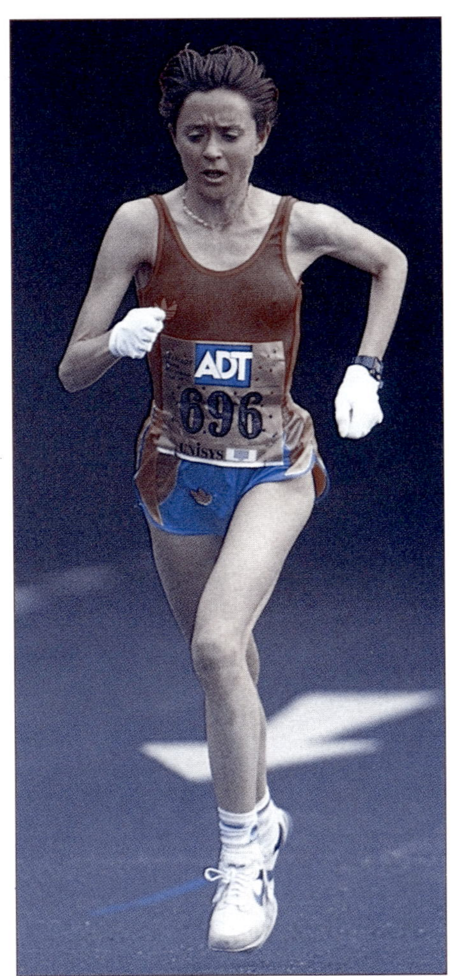

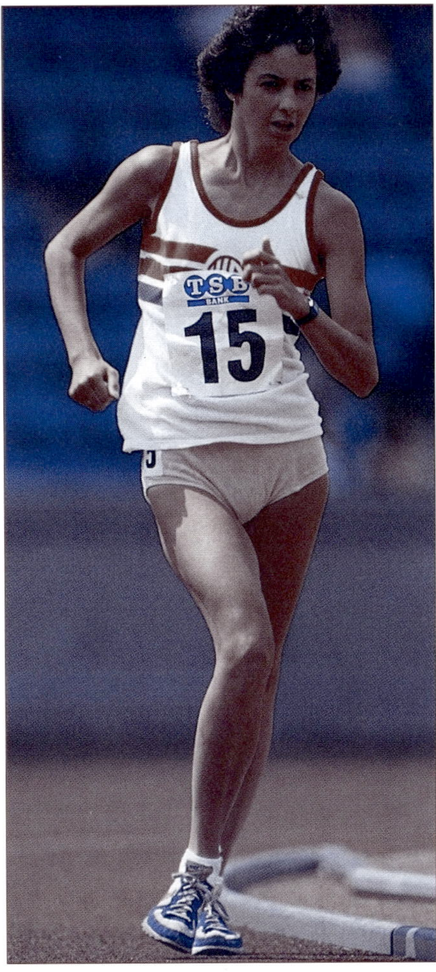

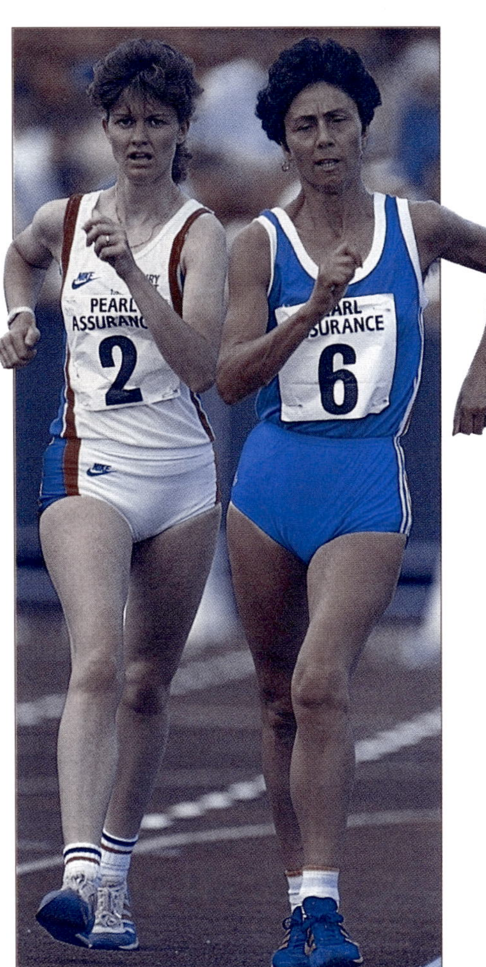

Long jump

KODAK
1
KODAK
16
KODAK
3

TSB
8

SEOUL1988
9
Games of the 24th Olympiad

HFC BANK
2

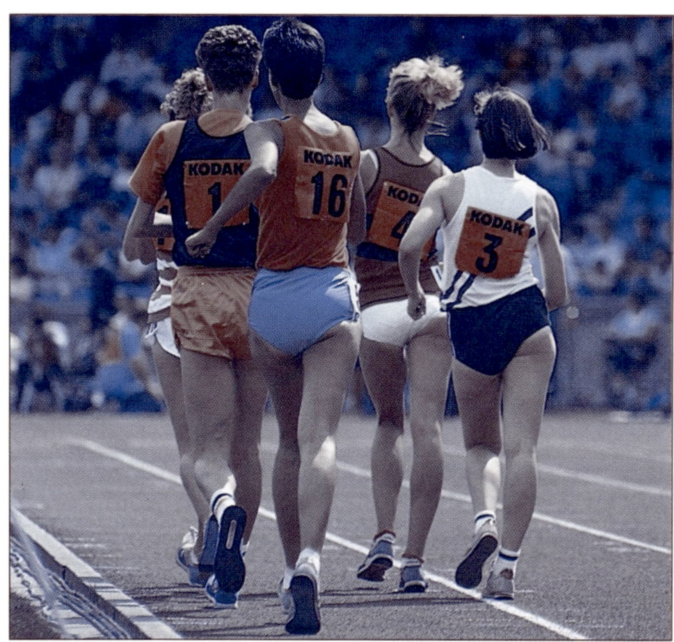

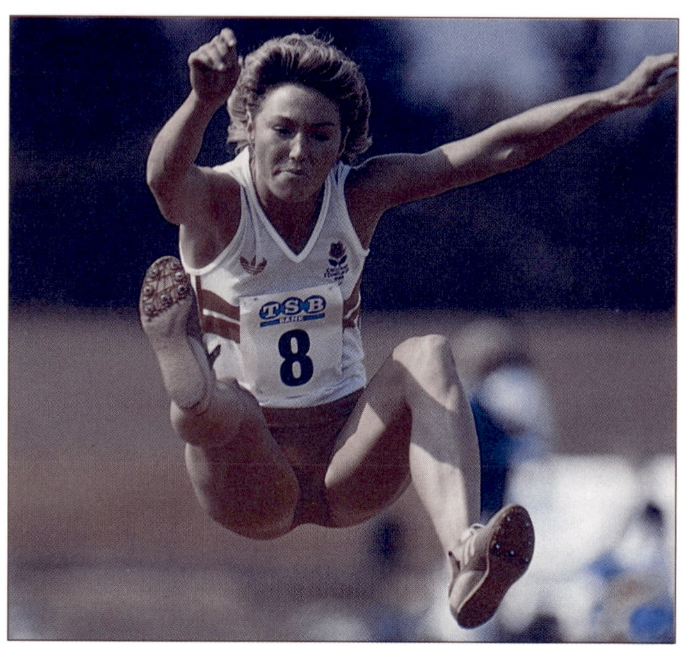

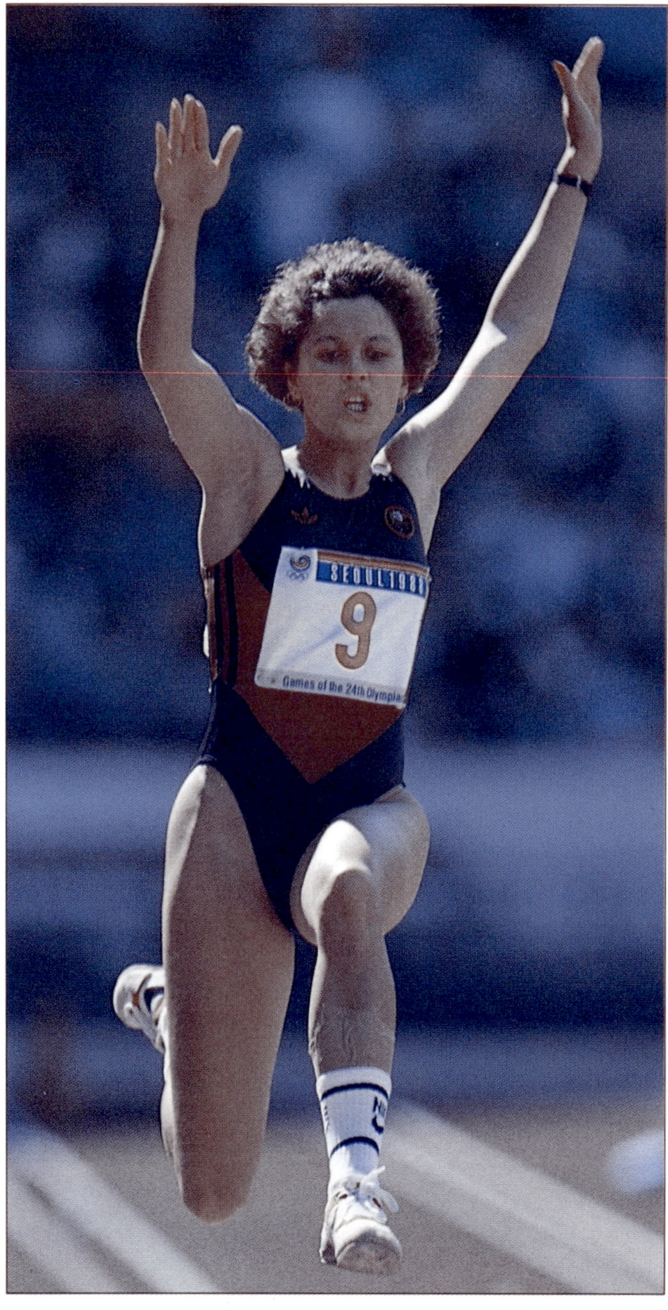

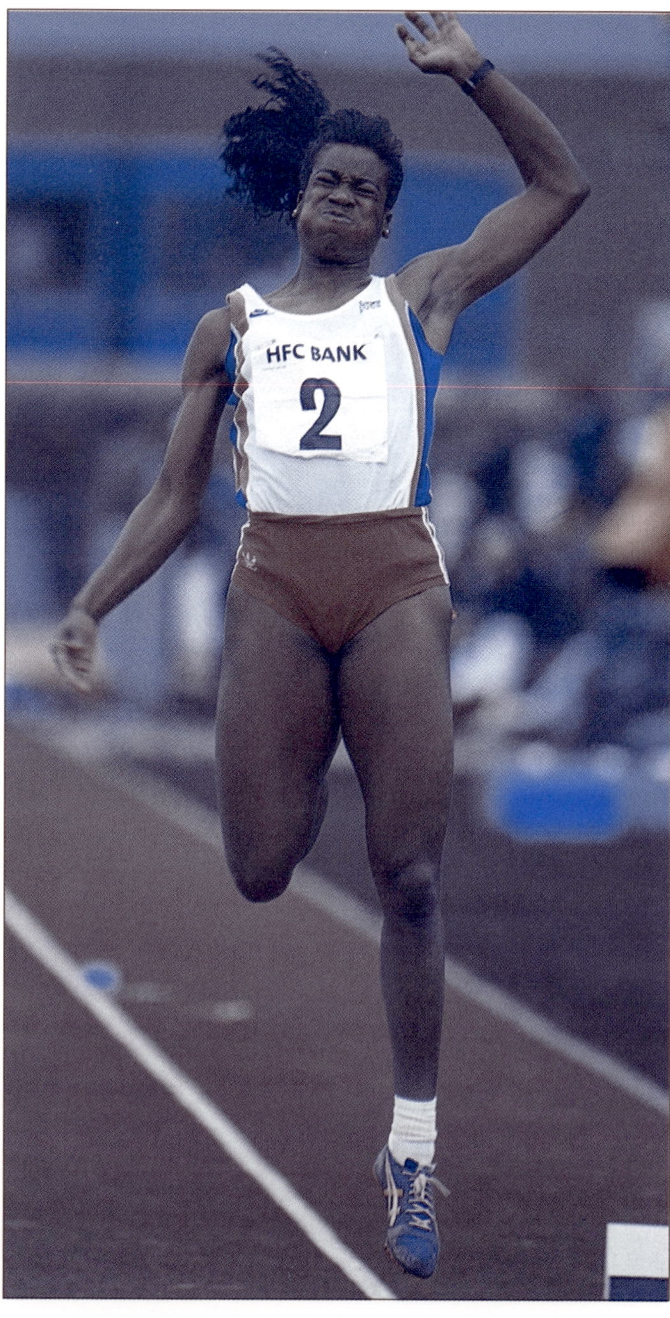

High jump

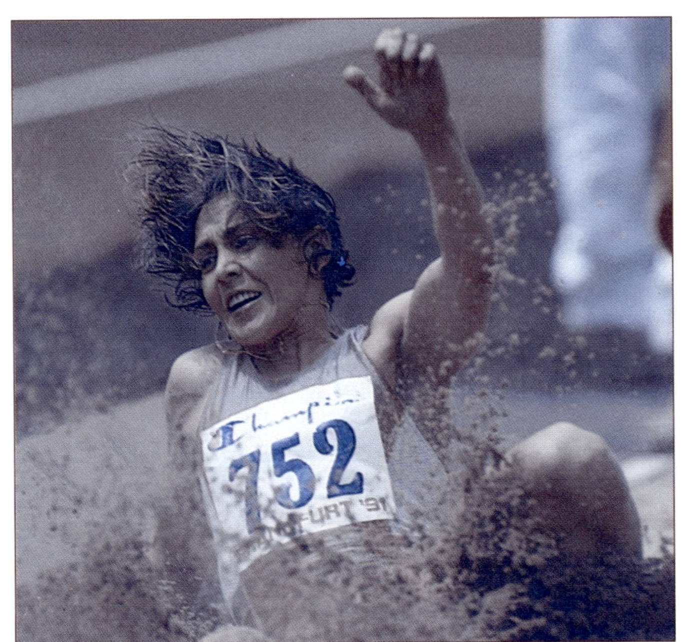

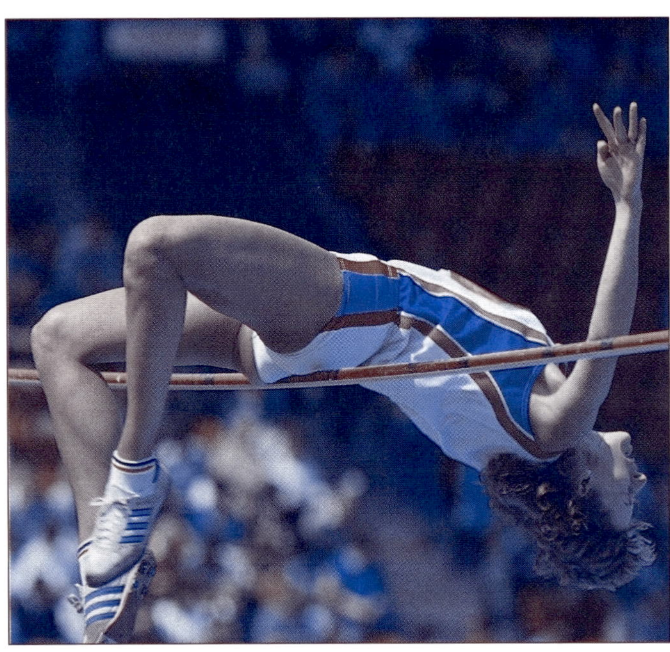

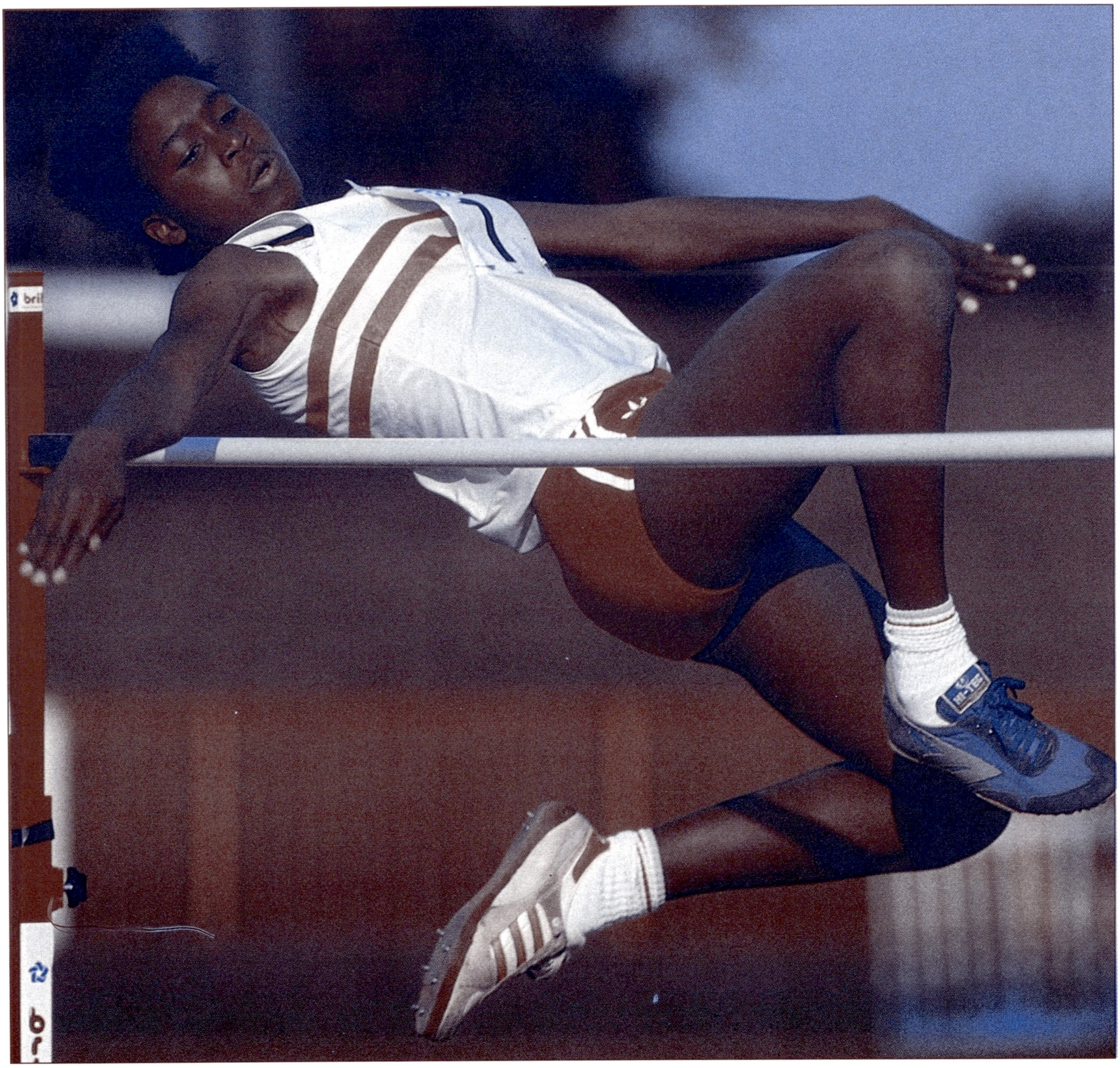

The javelin

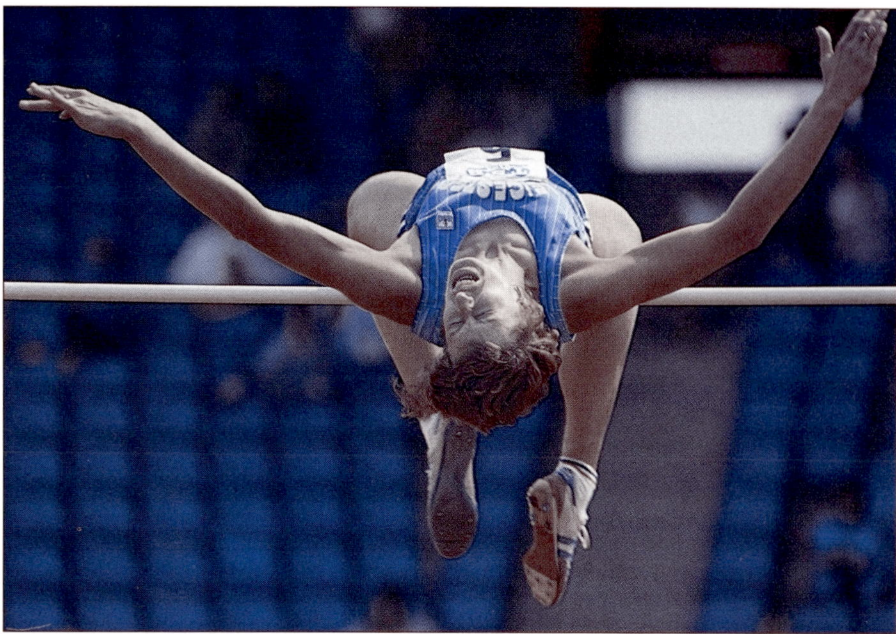

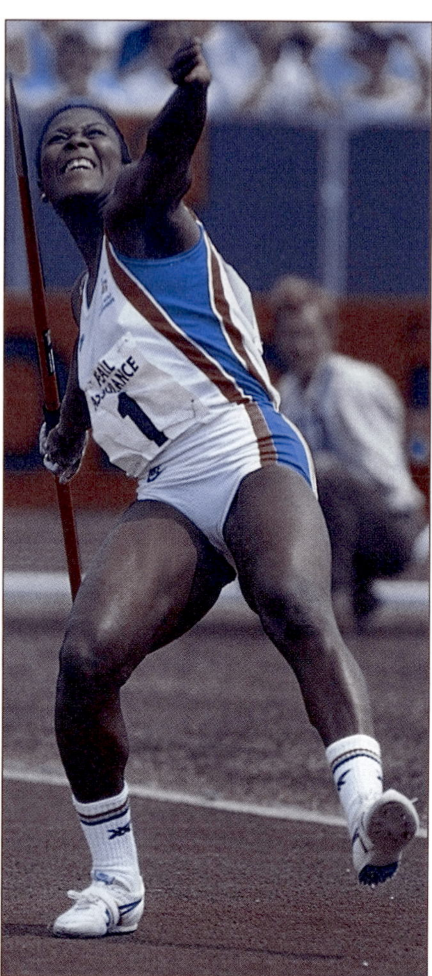

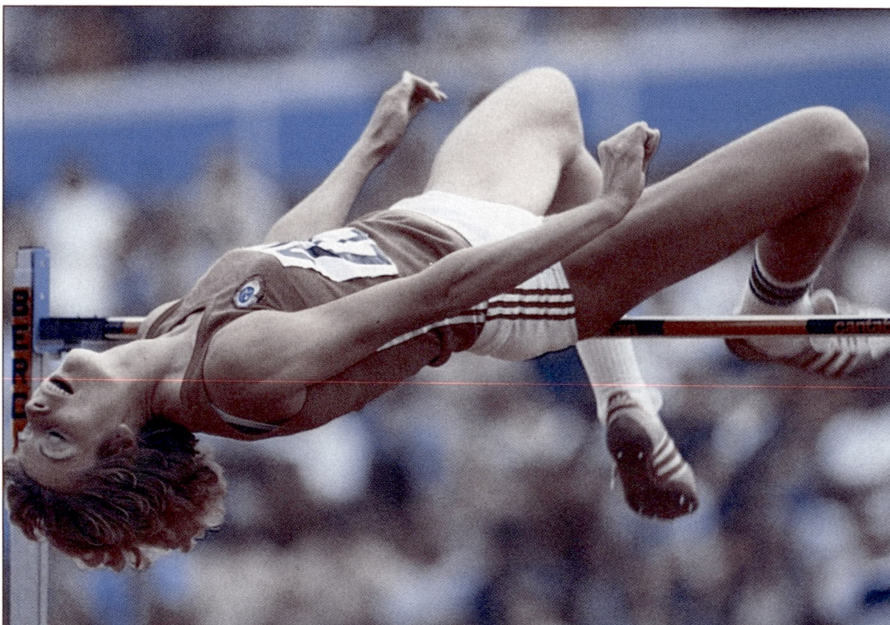

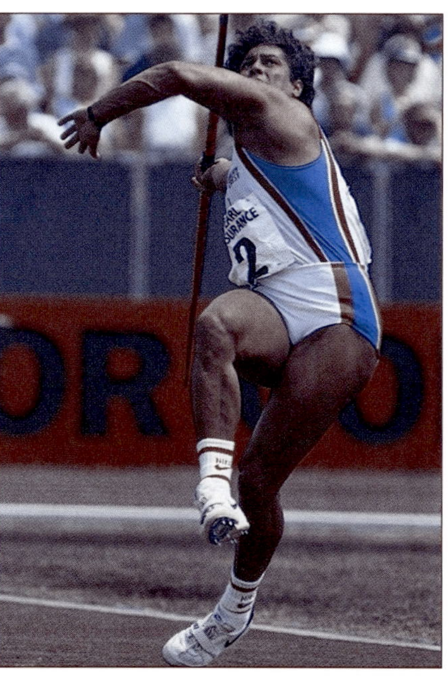

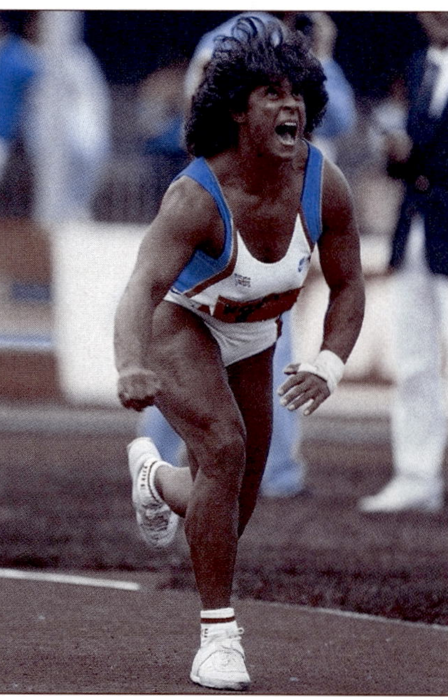

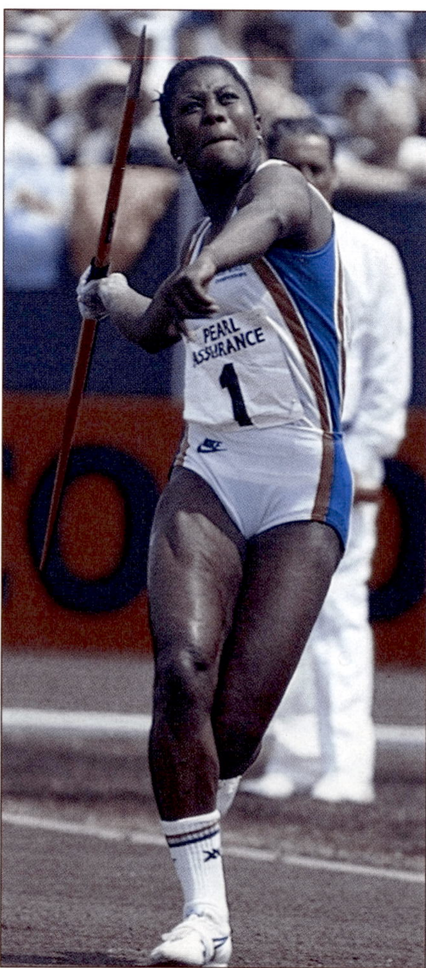

The discus · the shot put

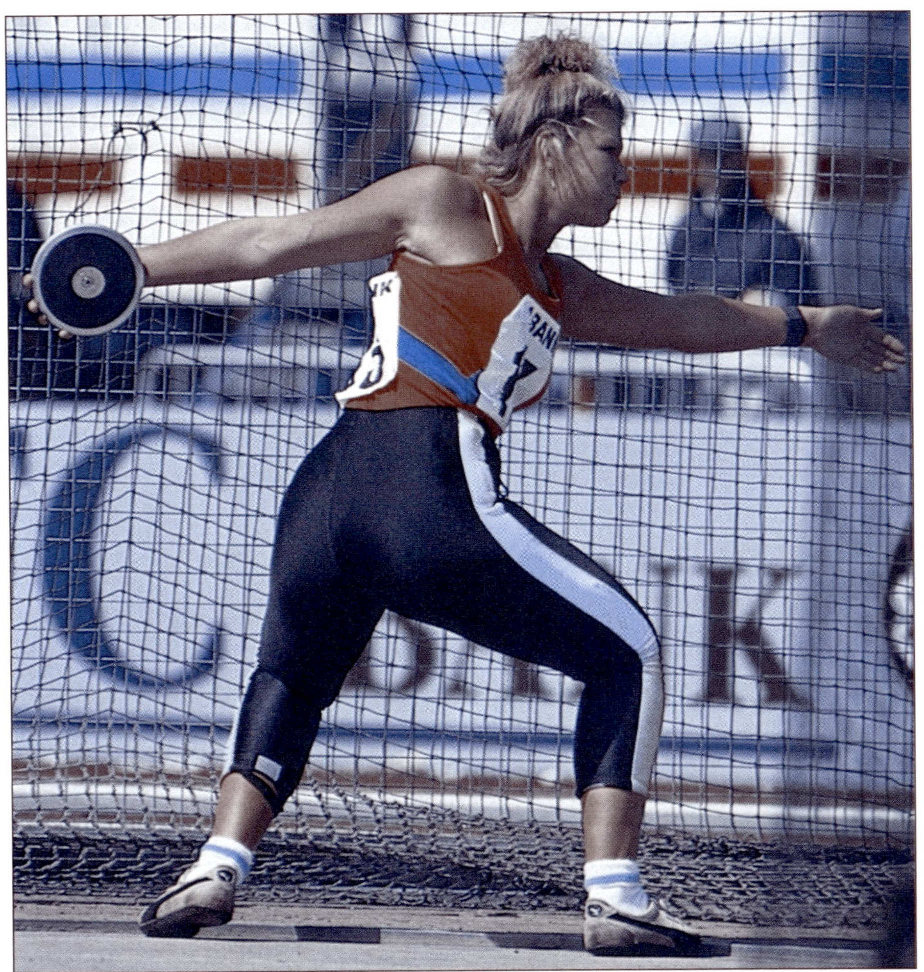

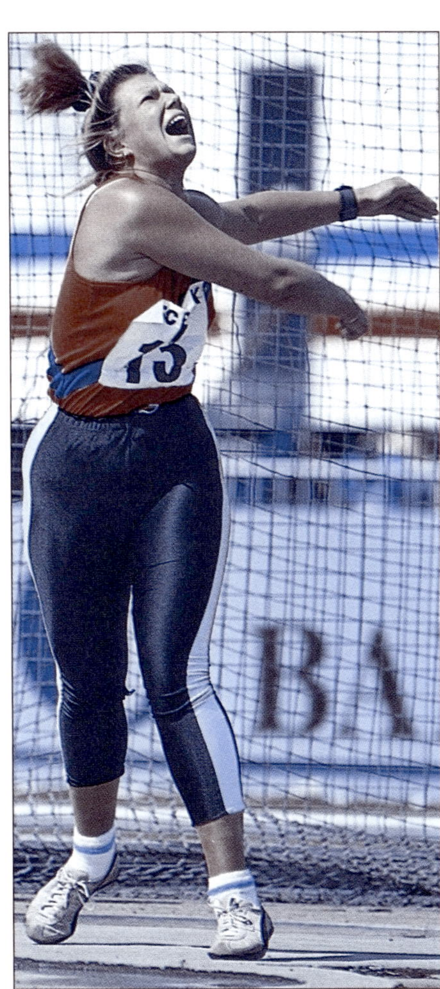

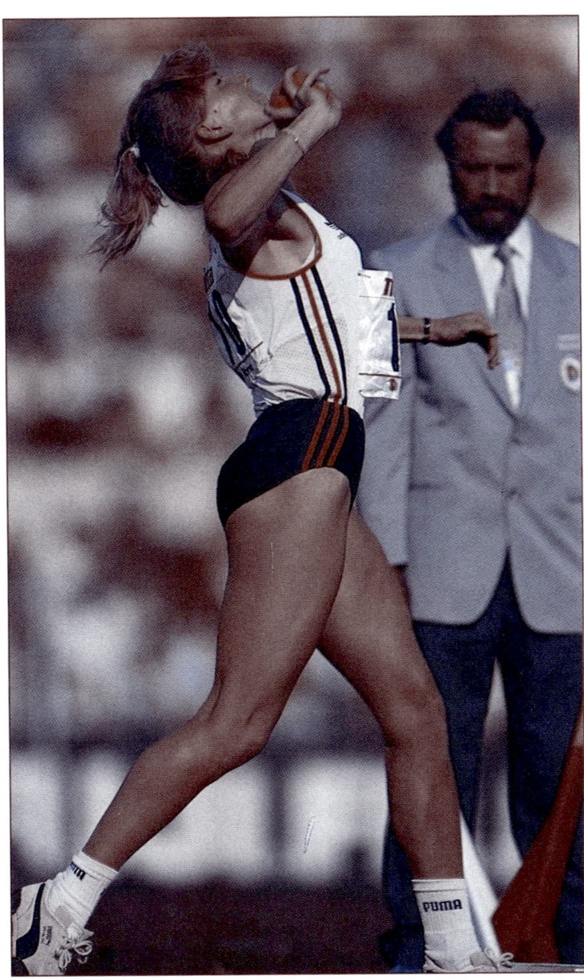

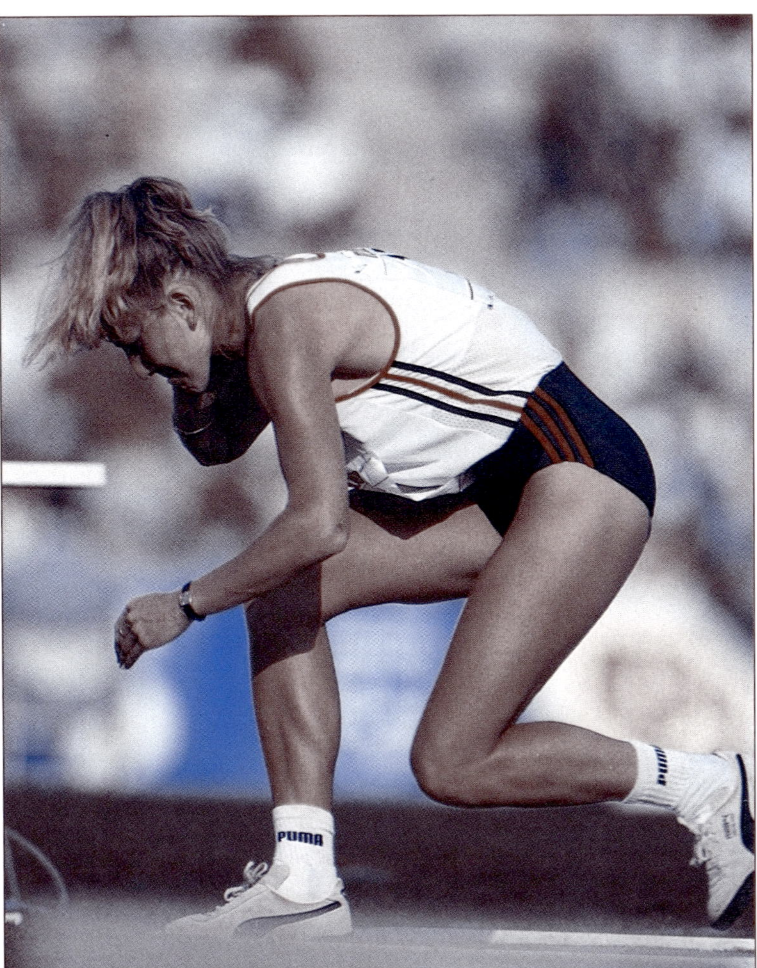

Horse

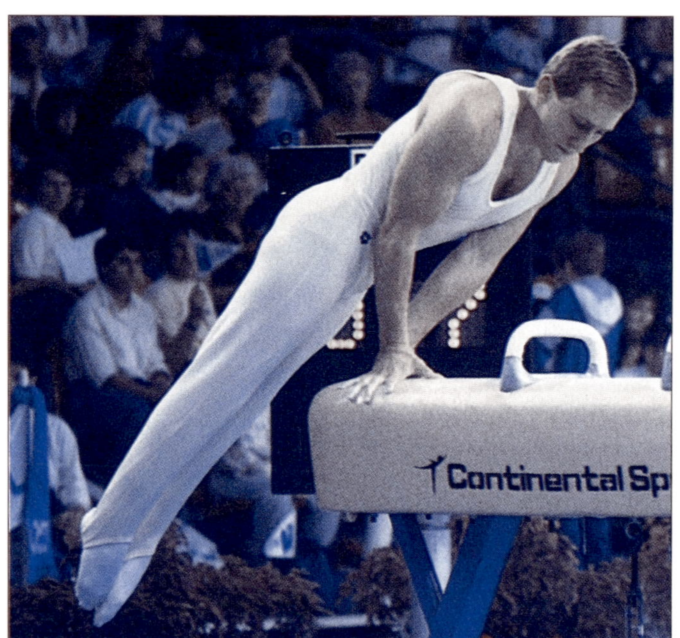

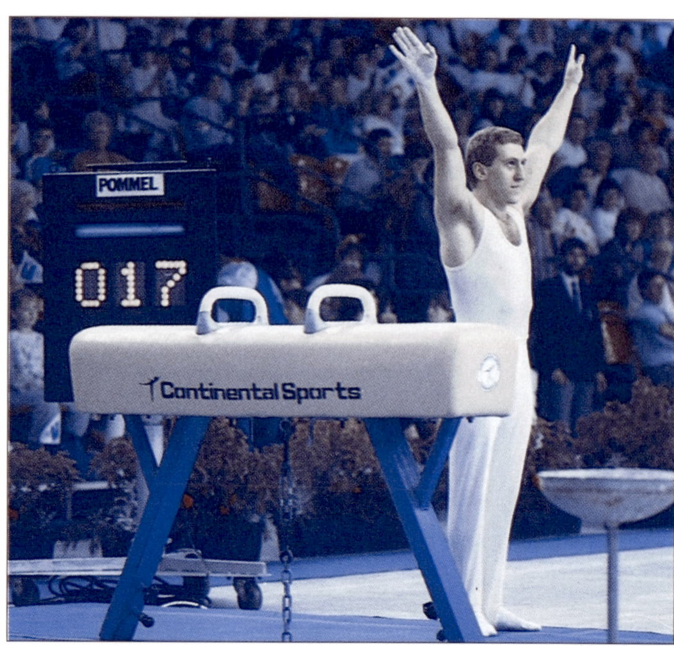

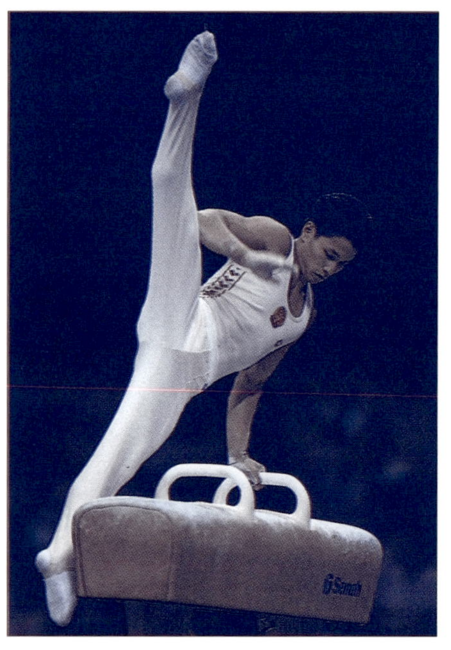

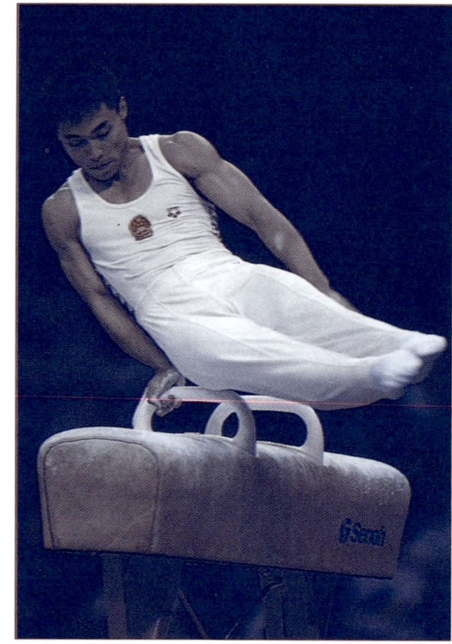

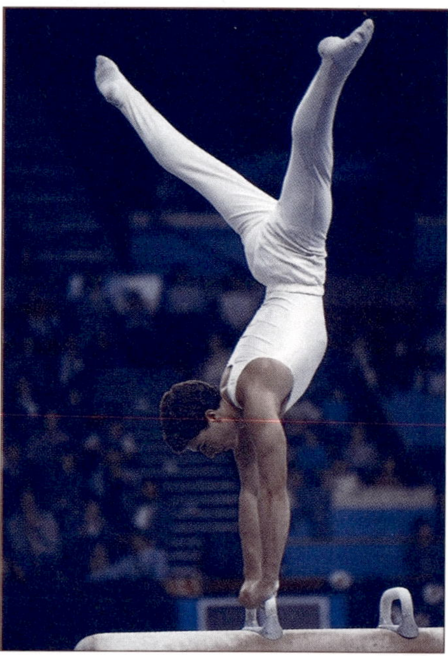

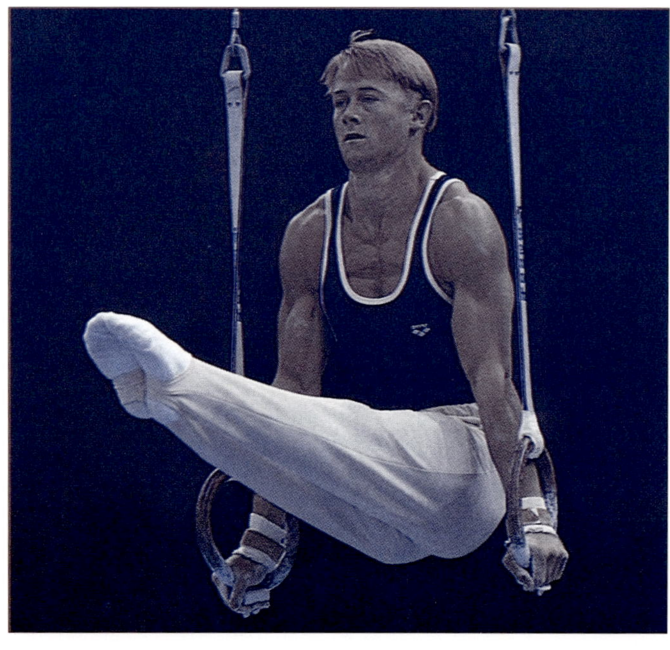

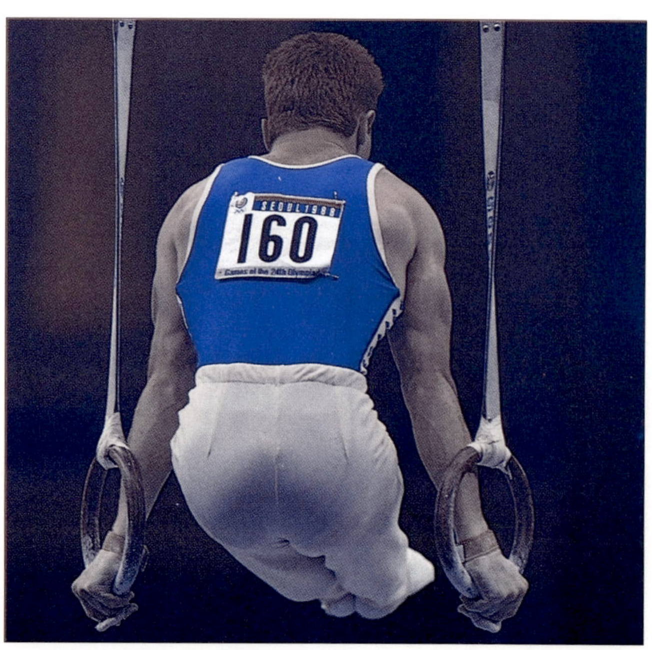

Rings

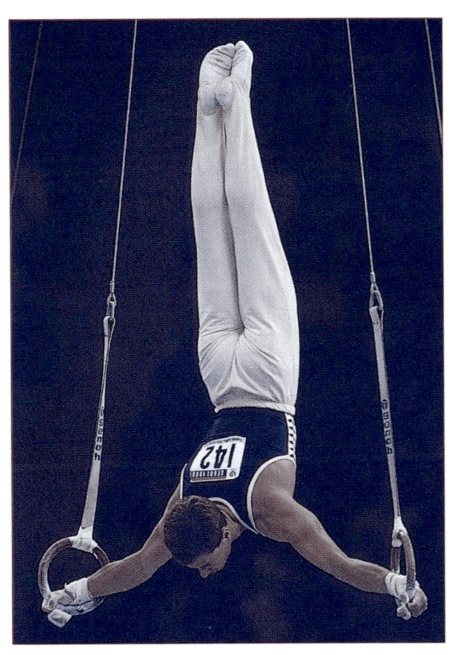

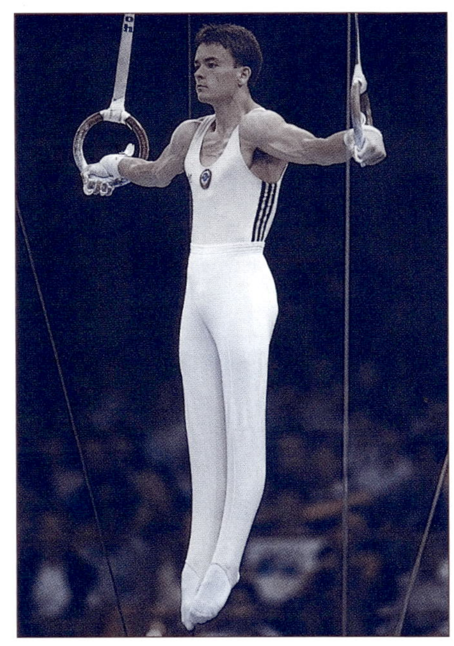

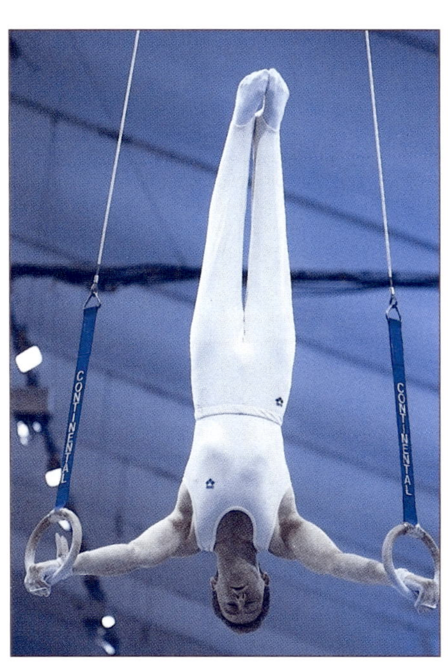

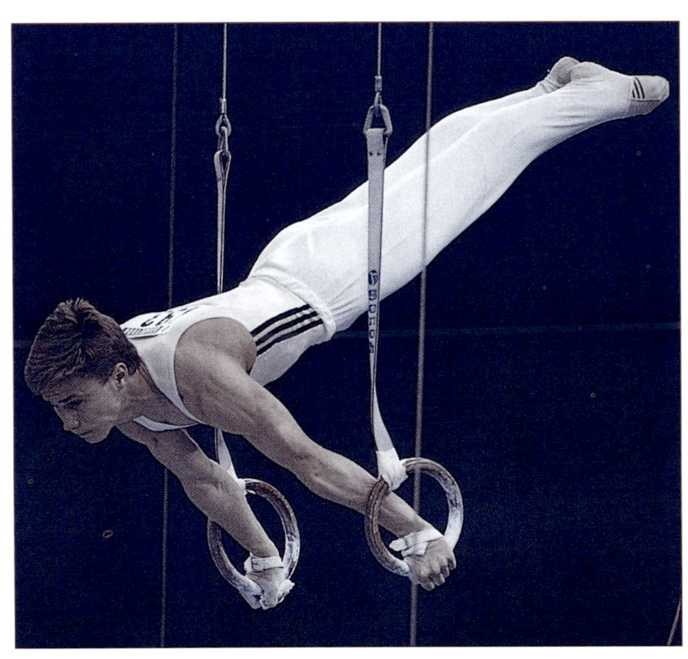

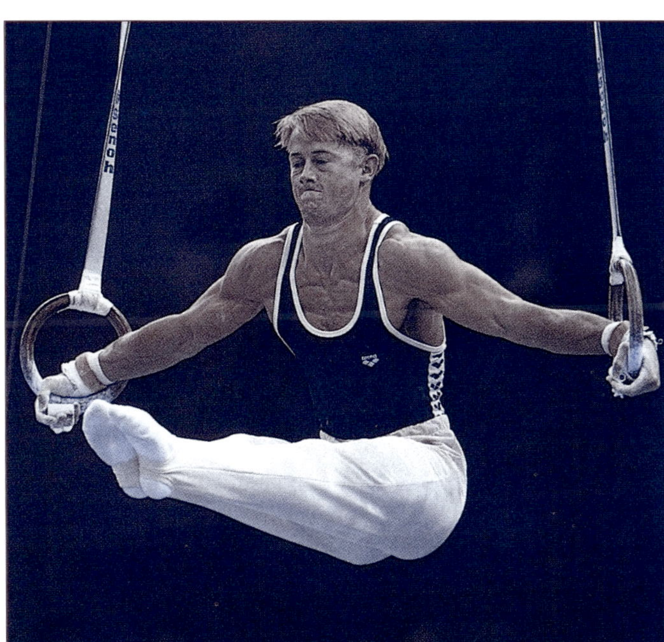

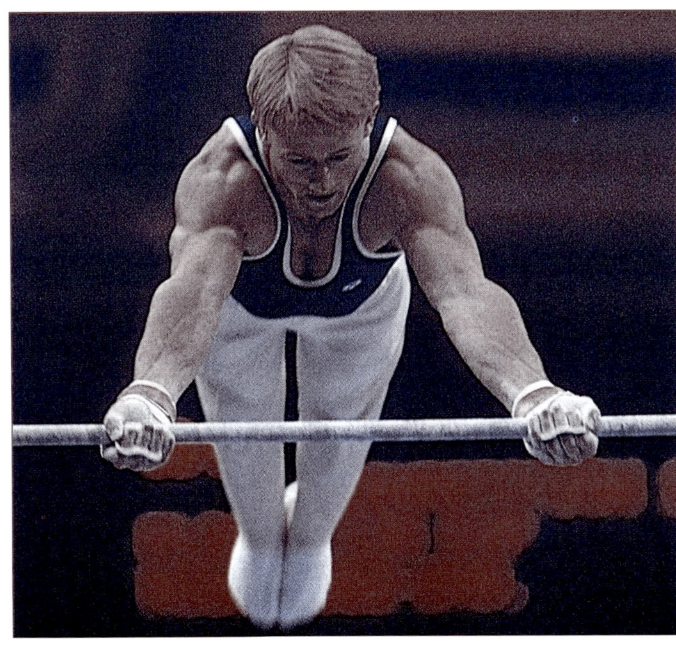

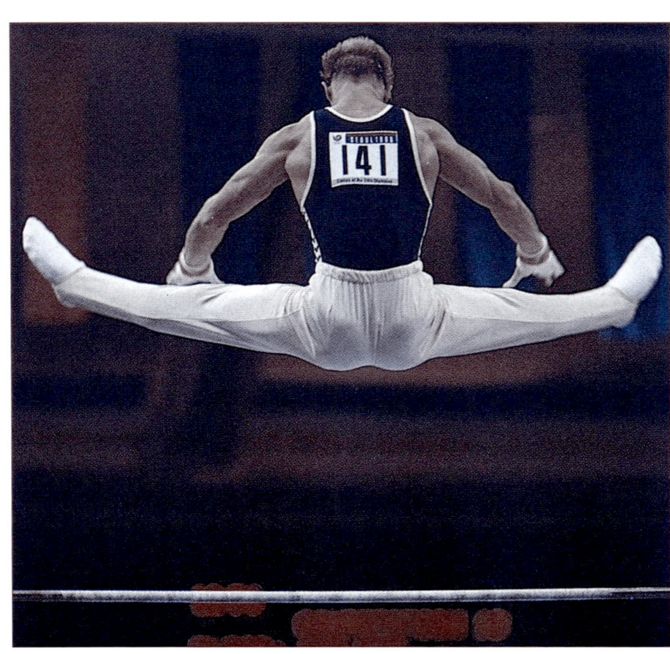

Parallel bars

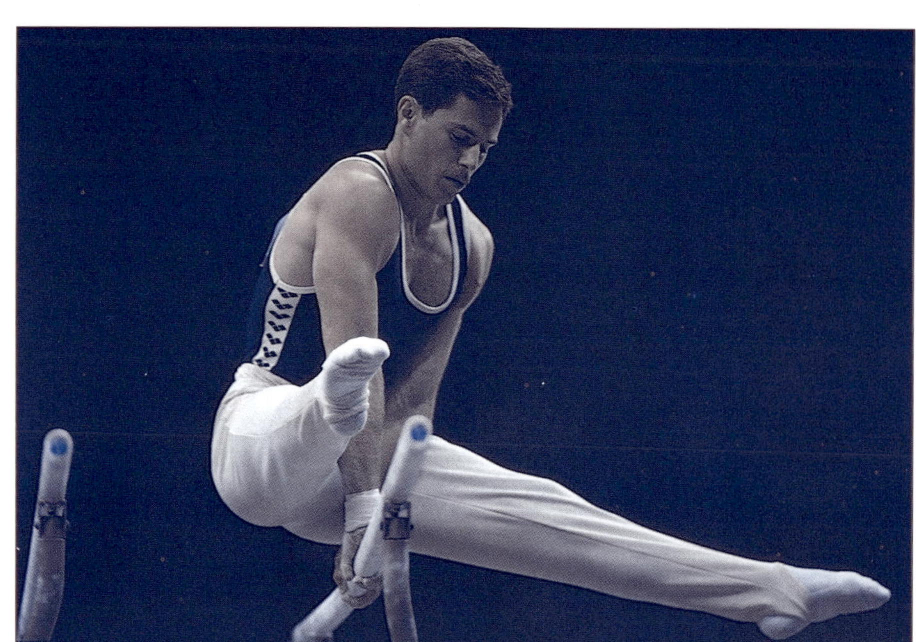

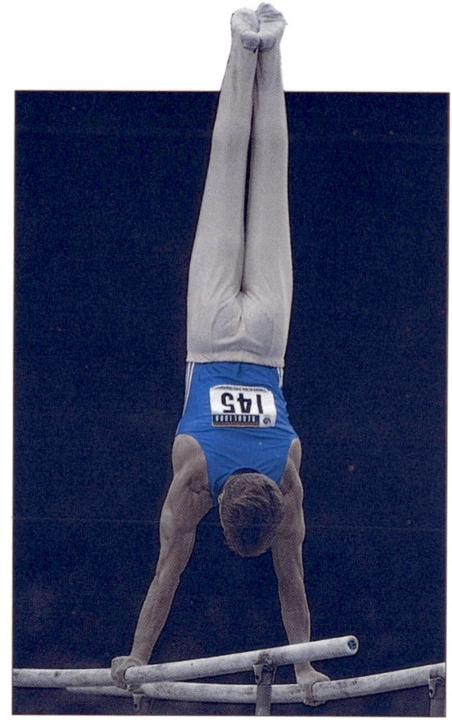

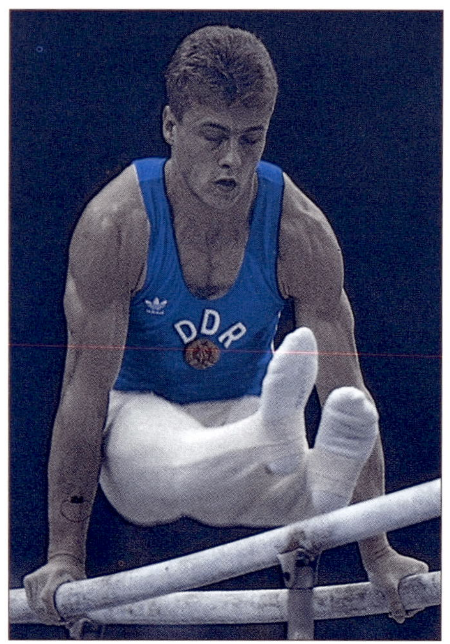

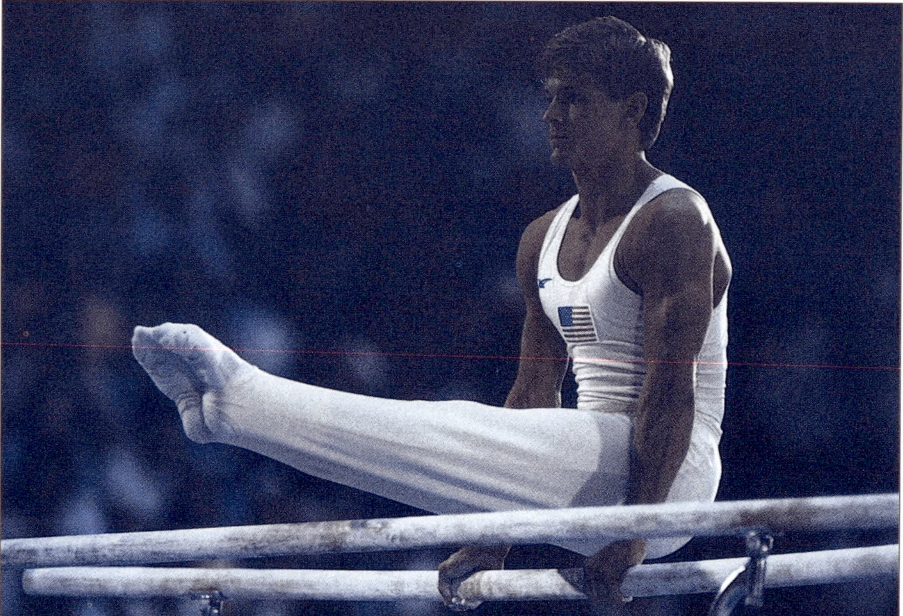

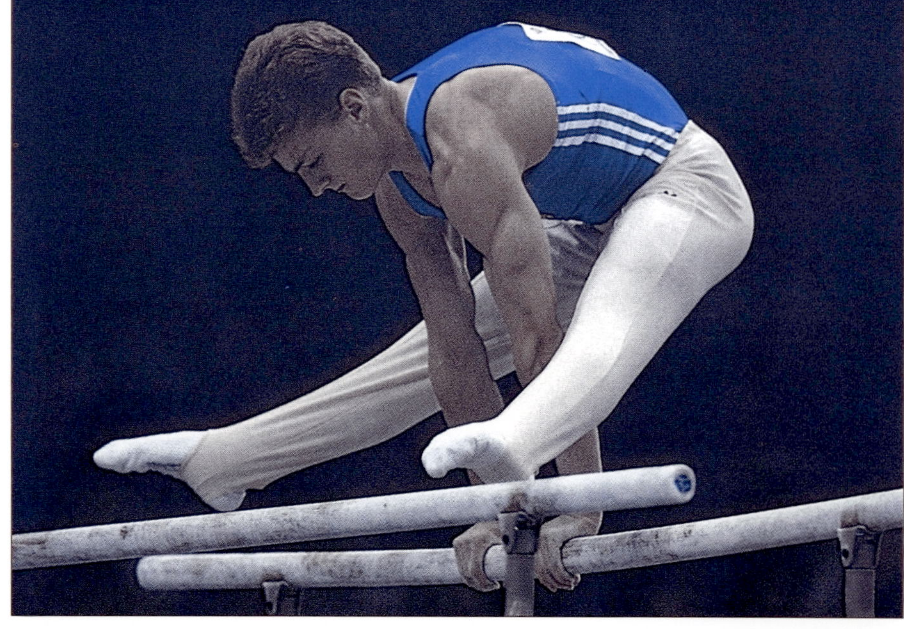

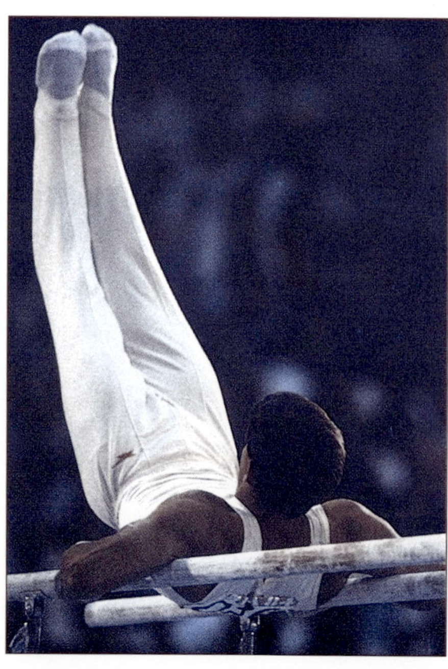

Floor exercises

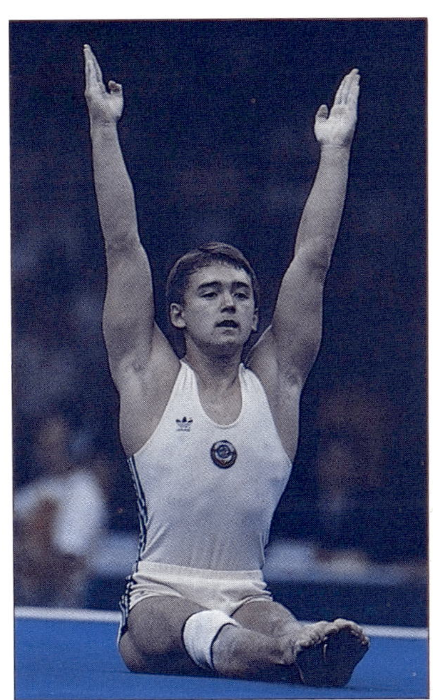

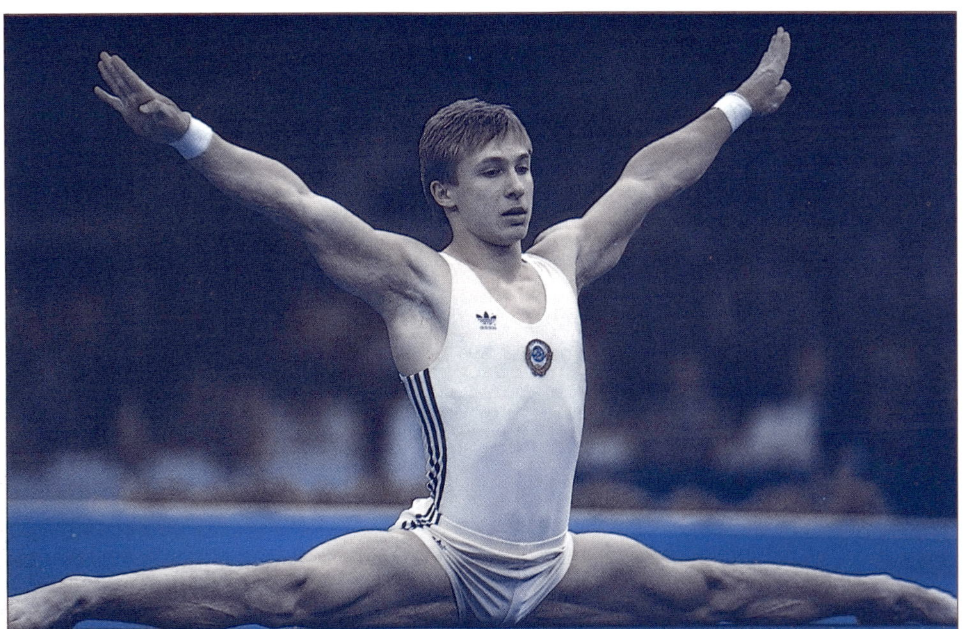

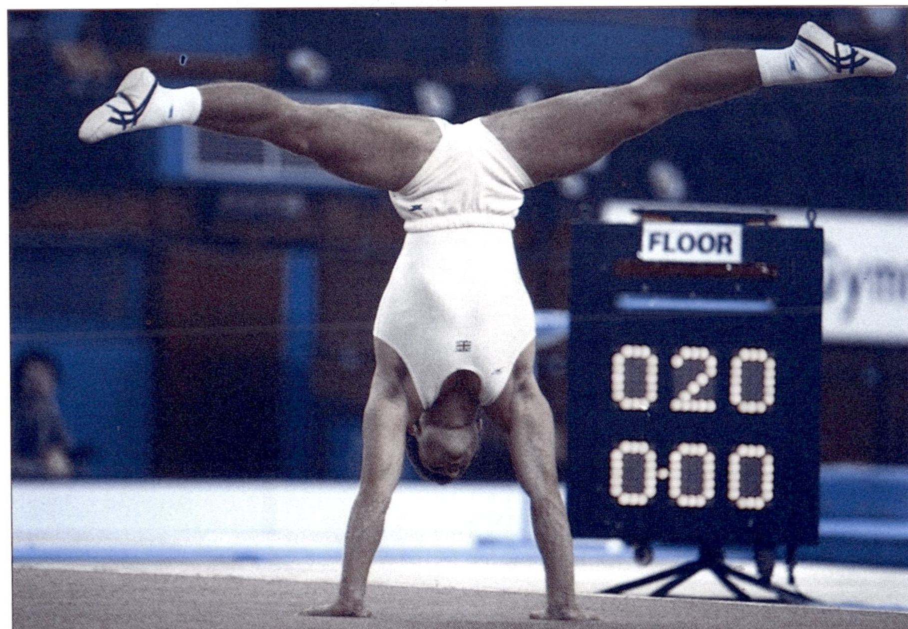

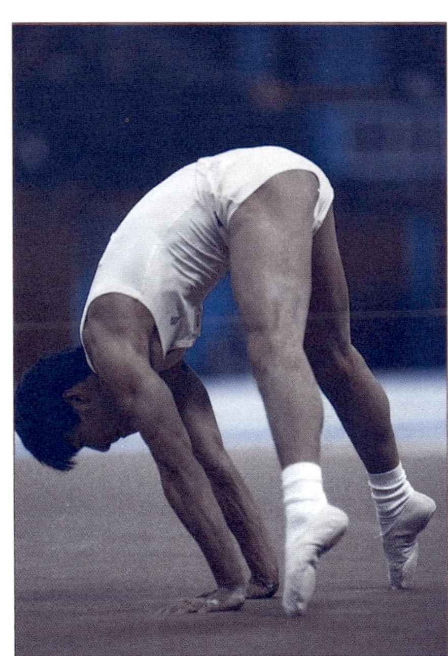

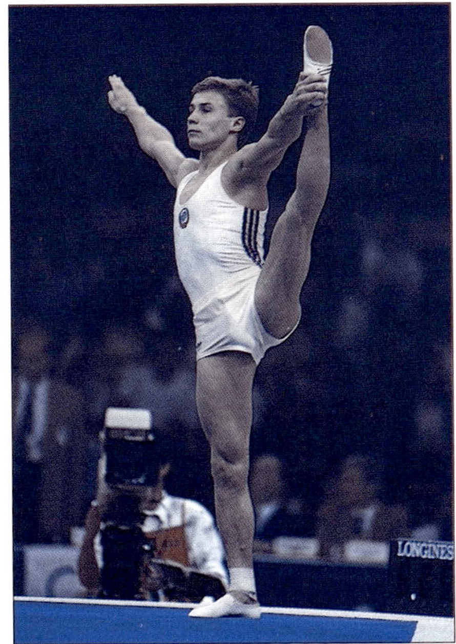

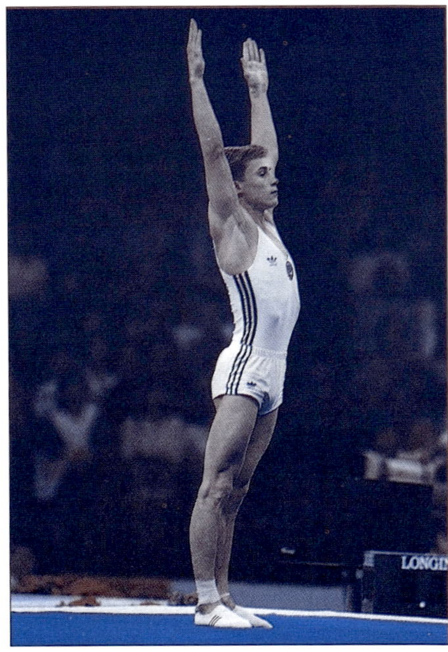

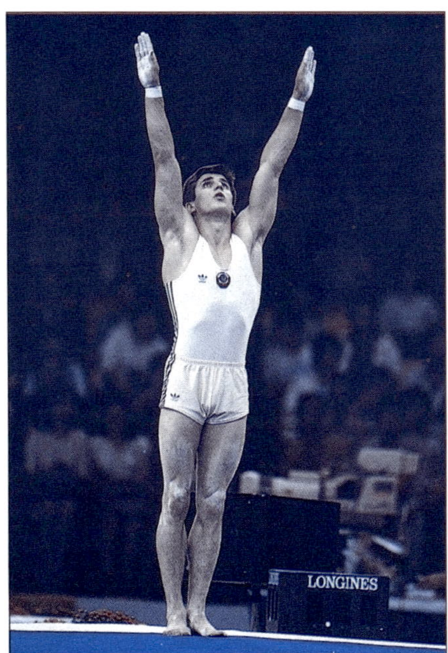

Asymmetric bars

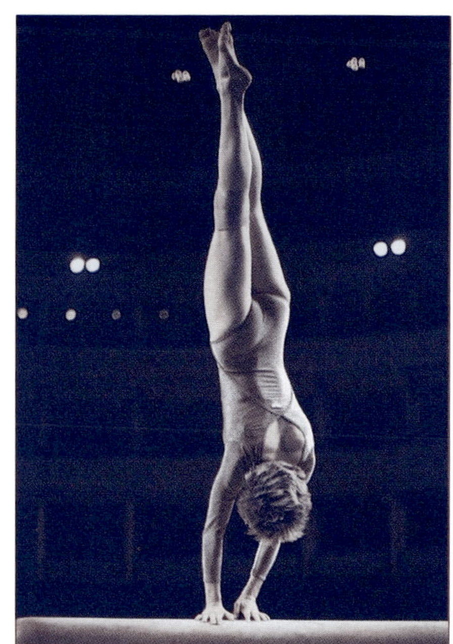

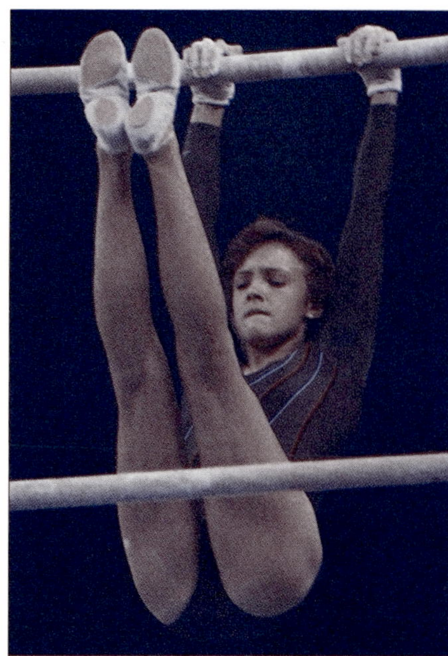

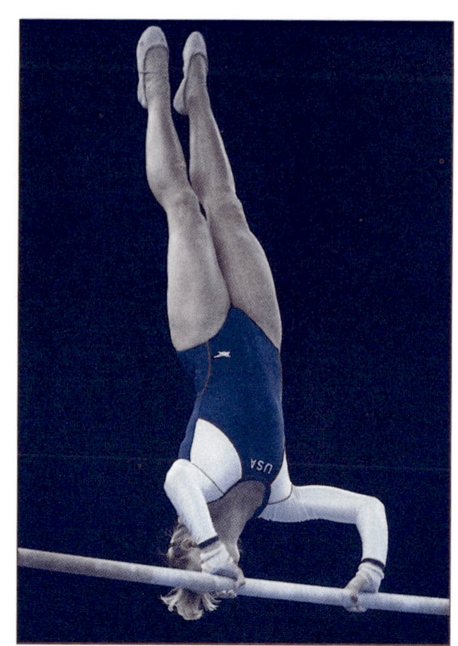

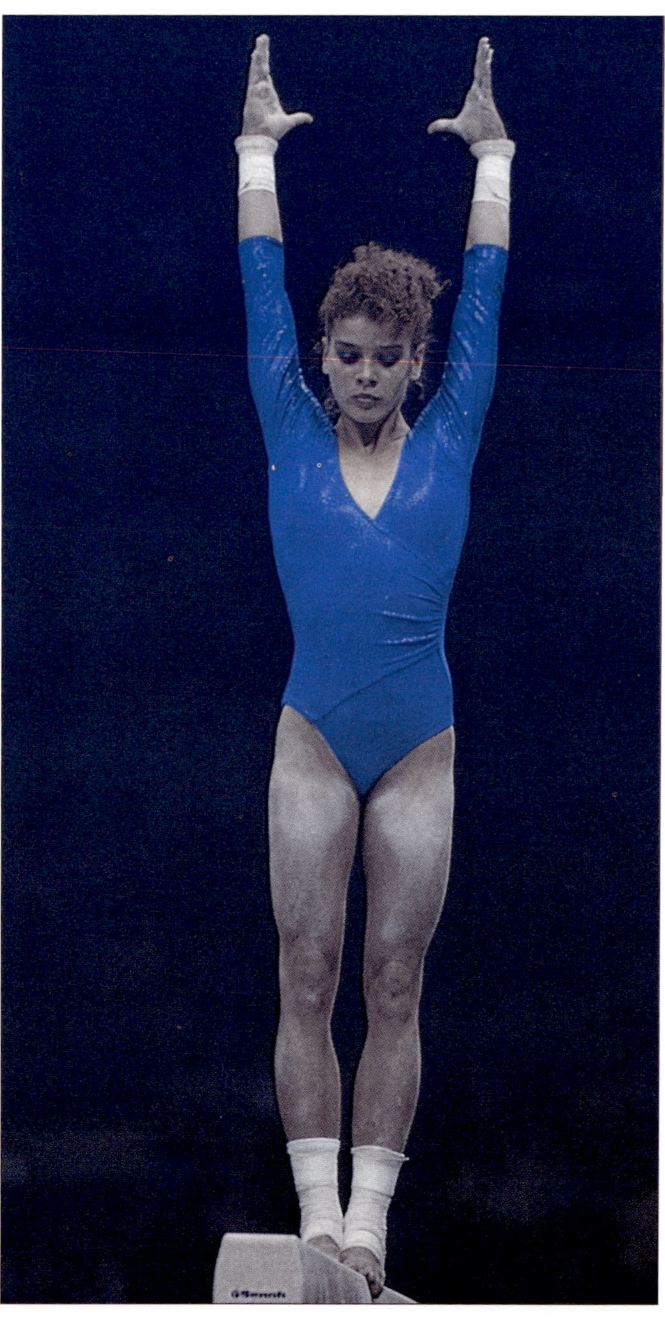

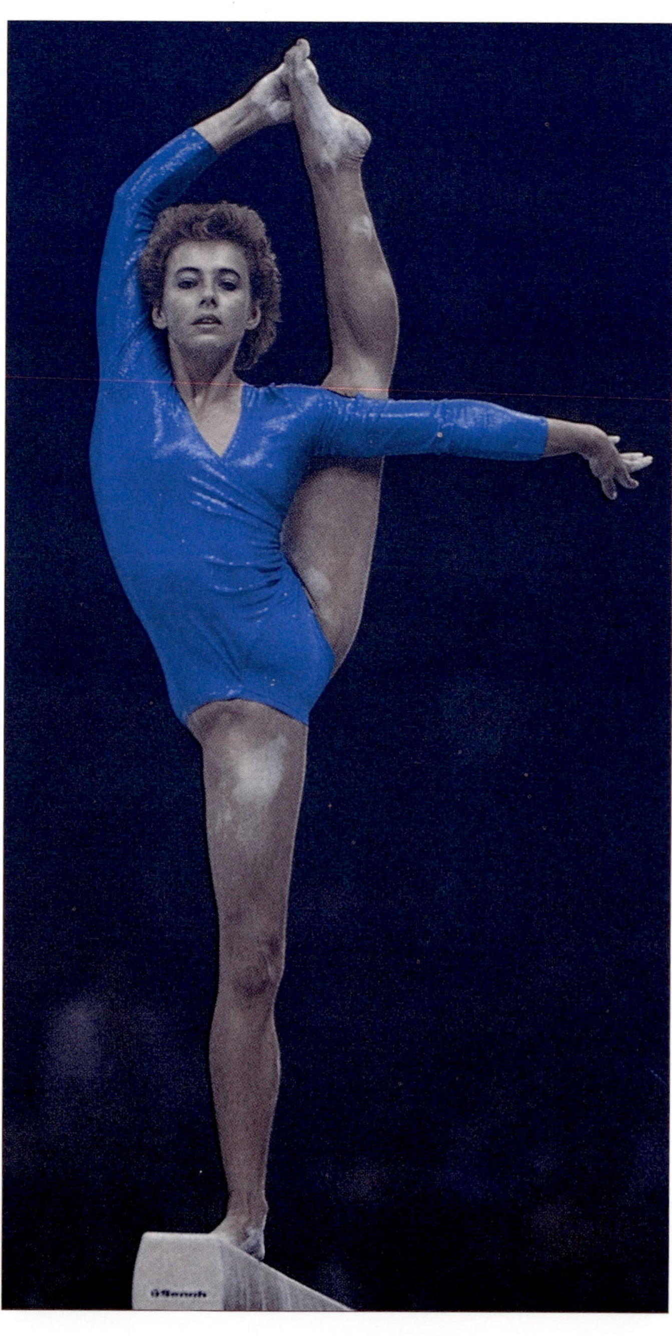

Beam

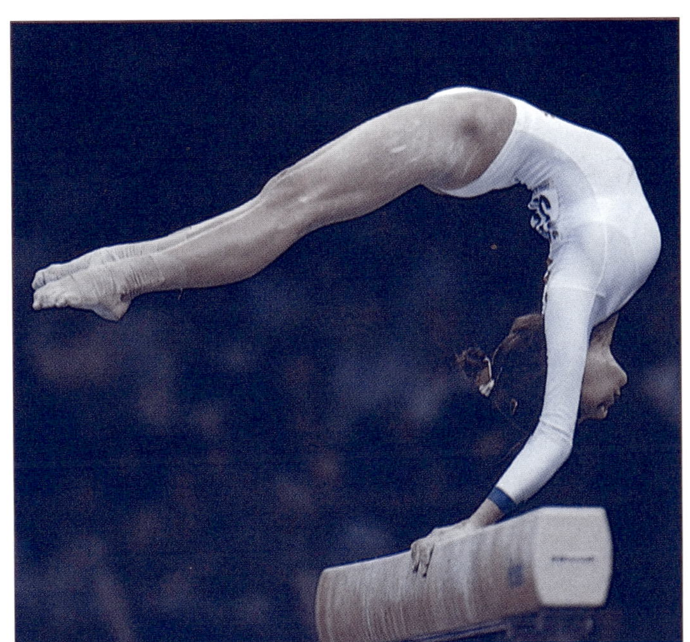

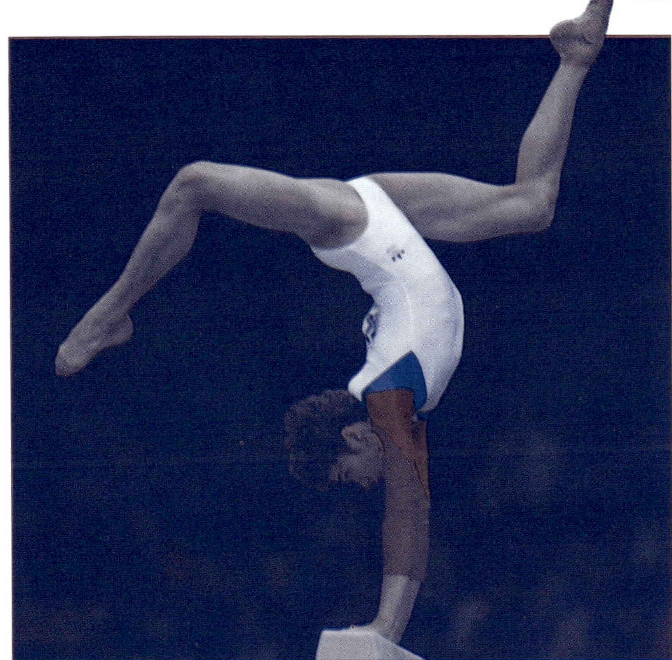

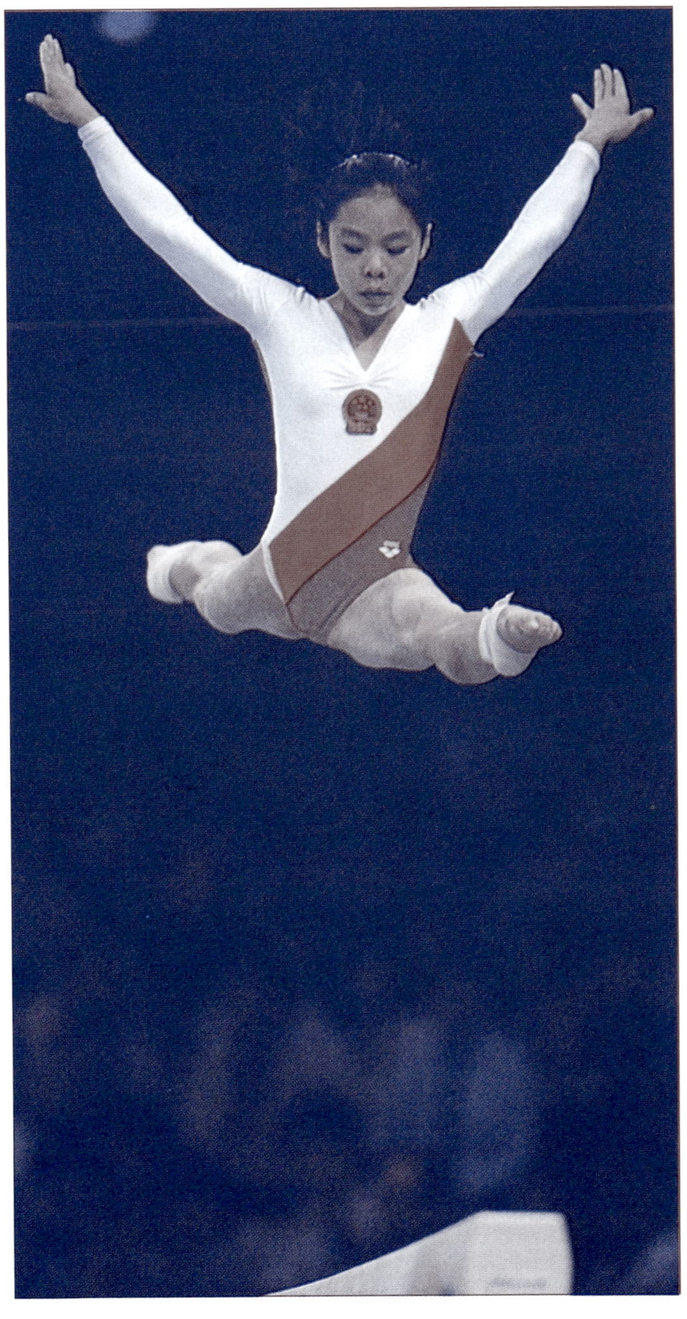

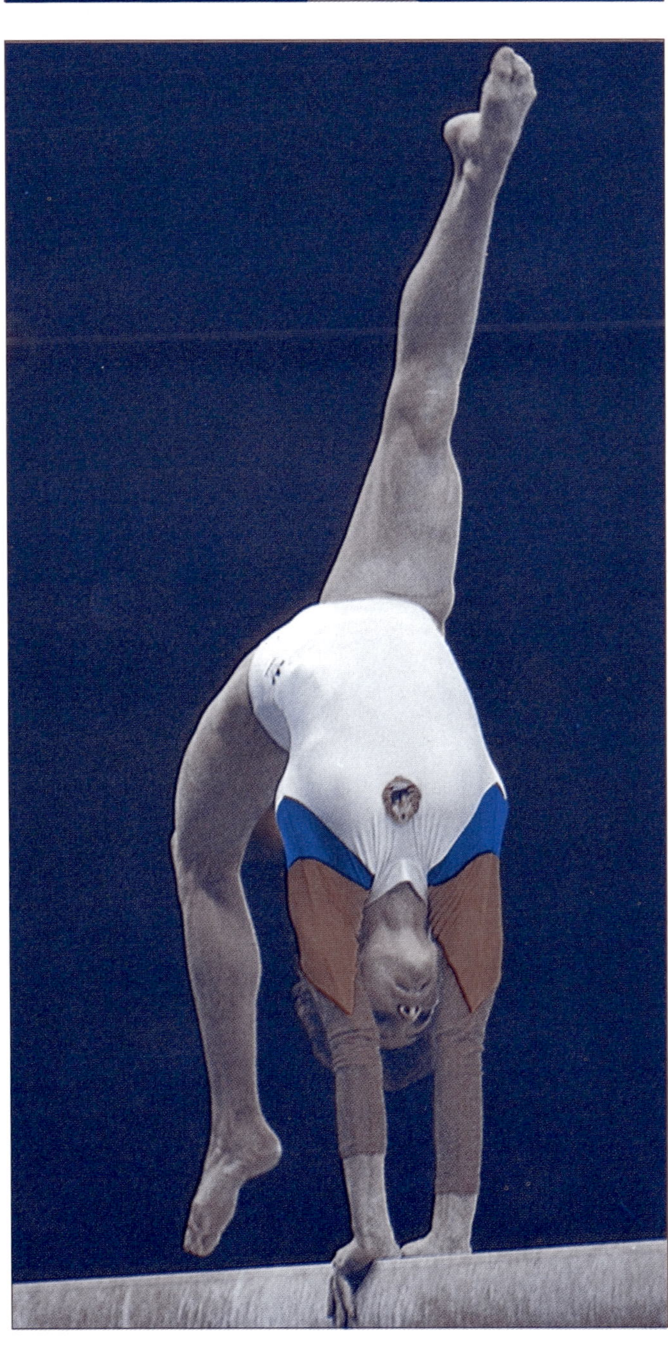

Beam

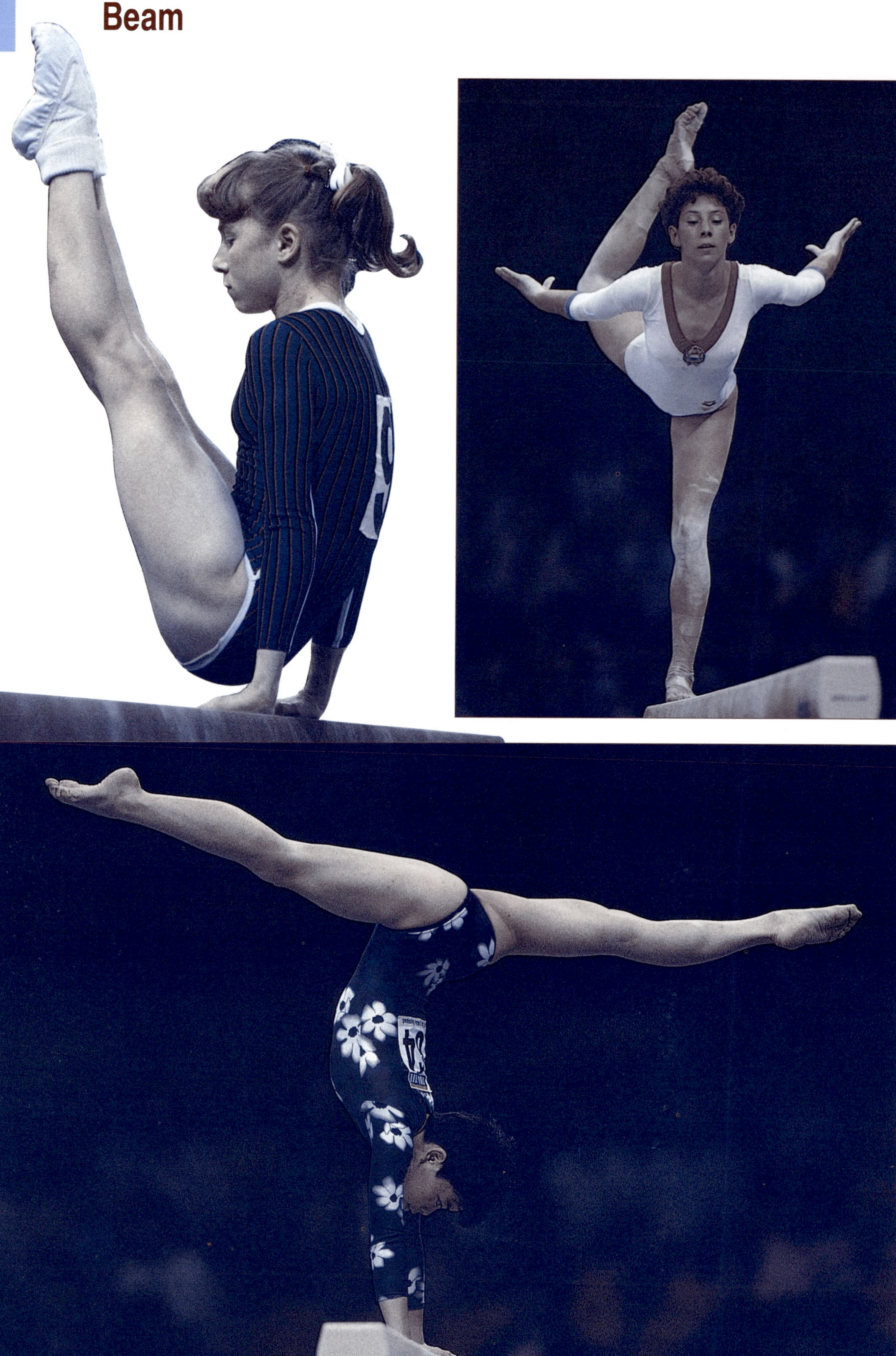

Floor exercises

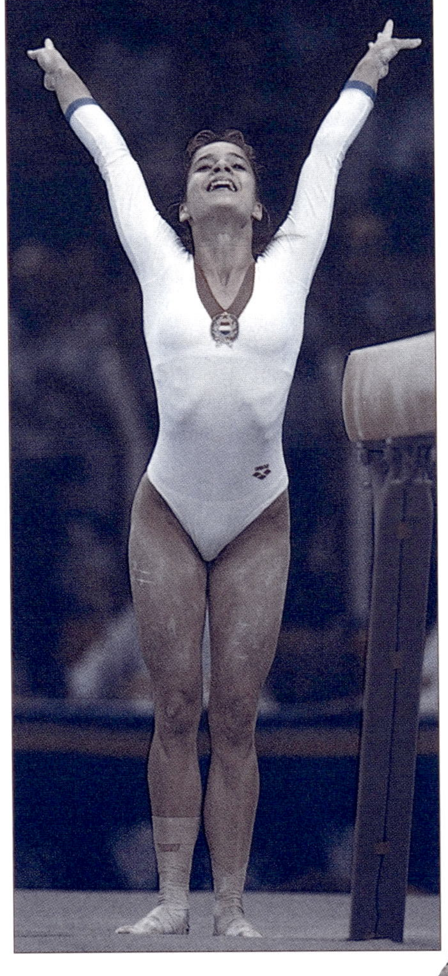

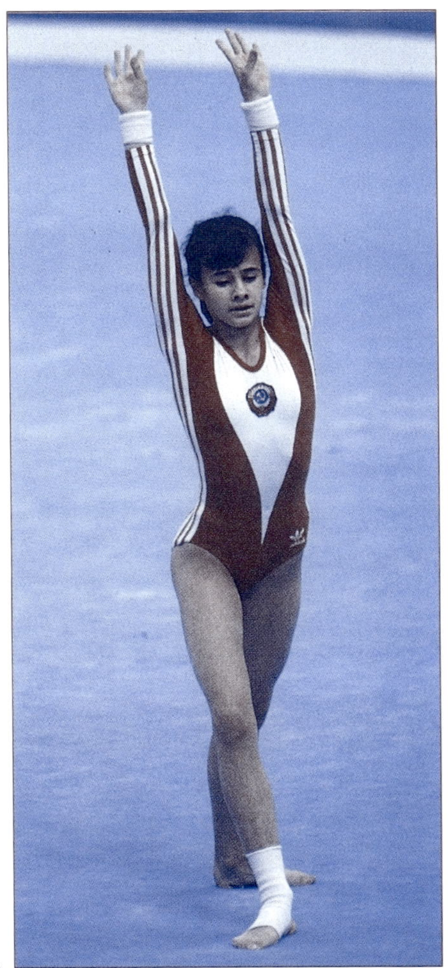

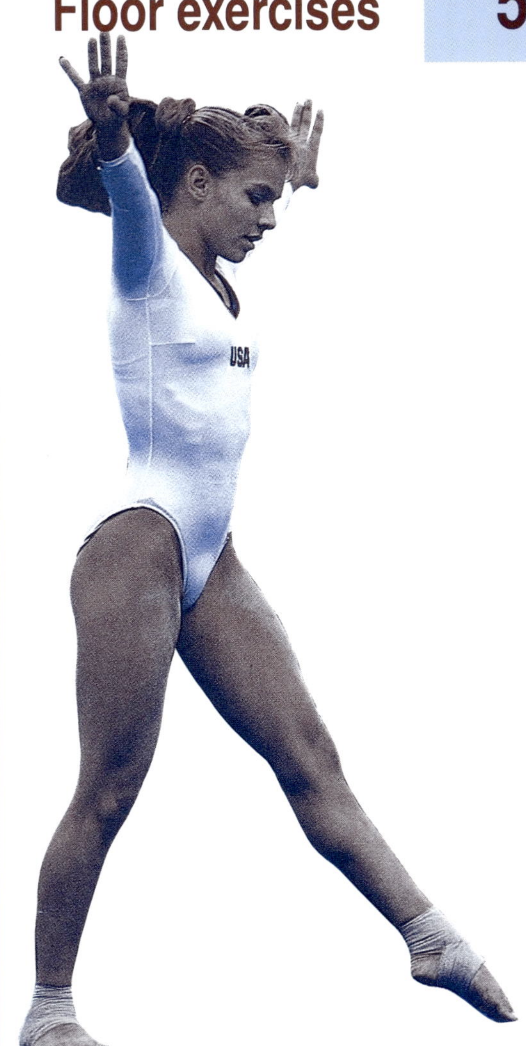

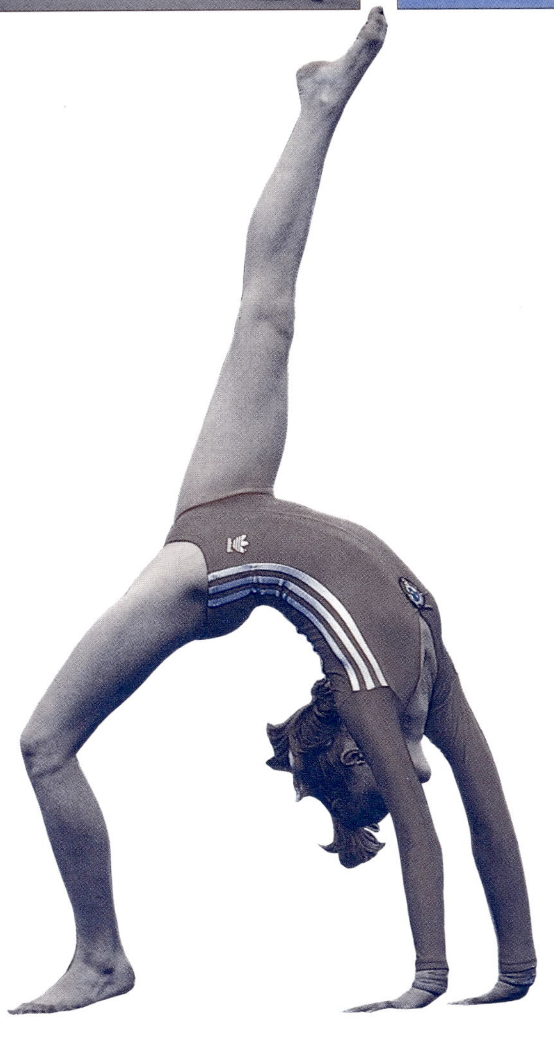

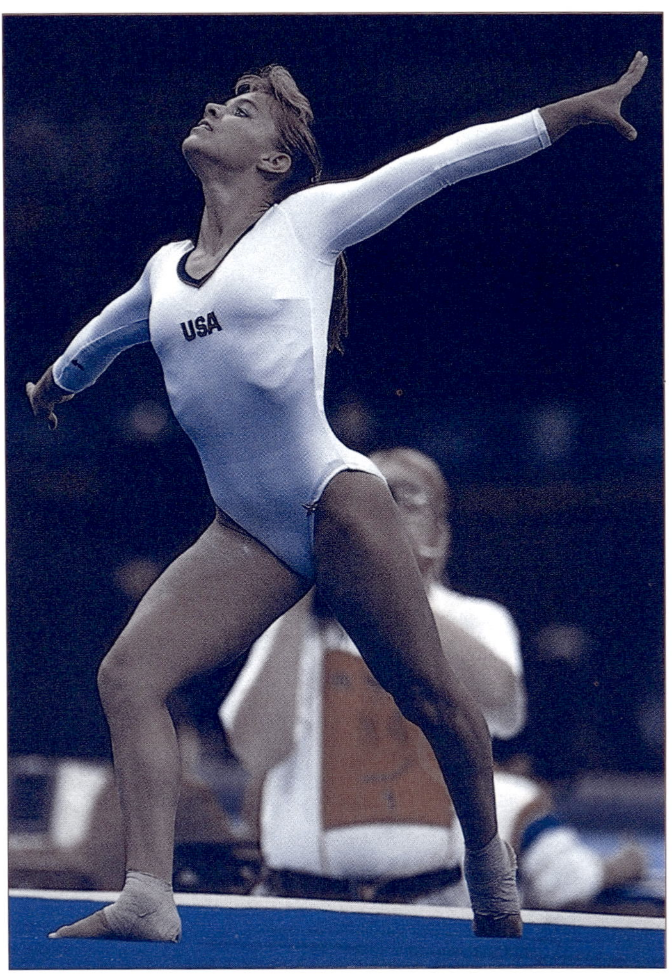

Floor exercises

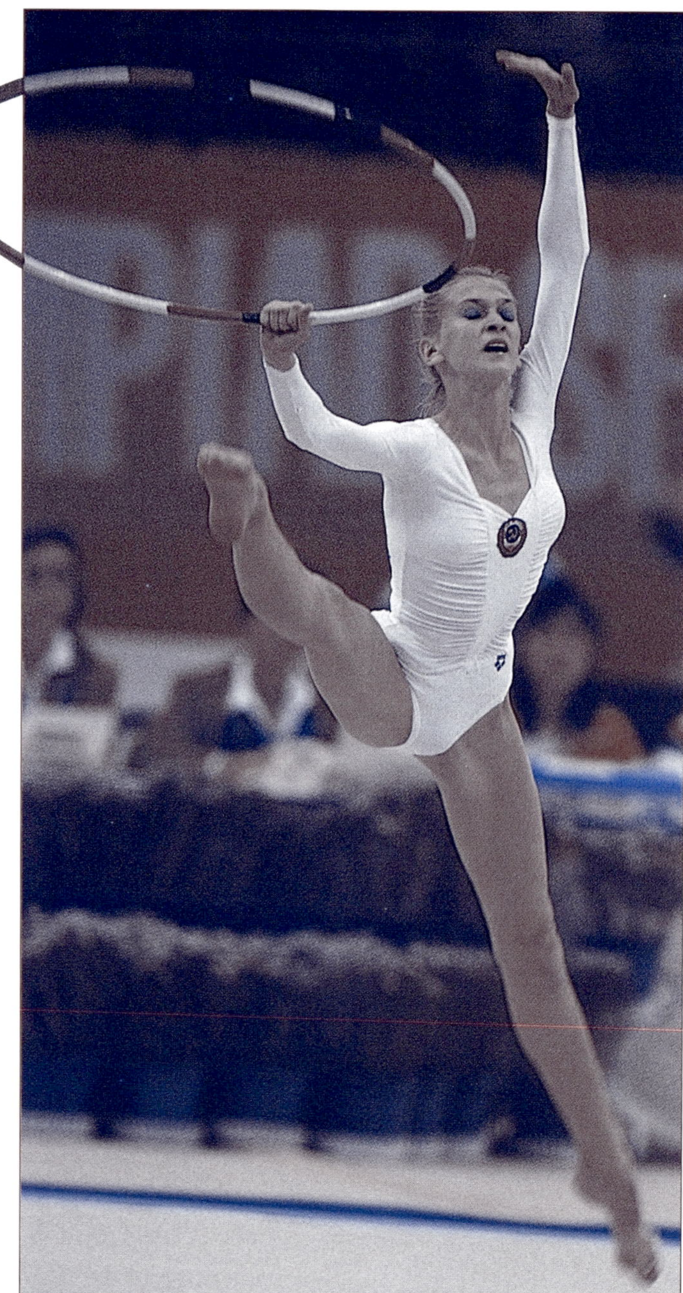

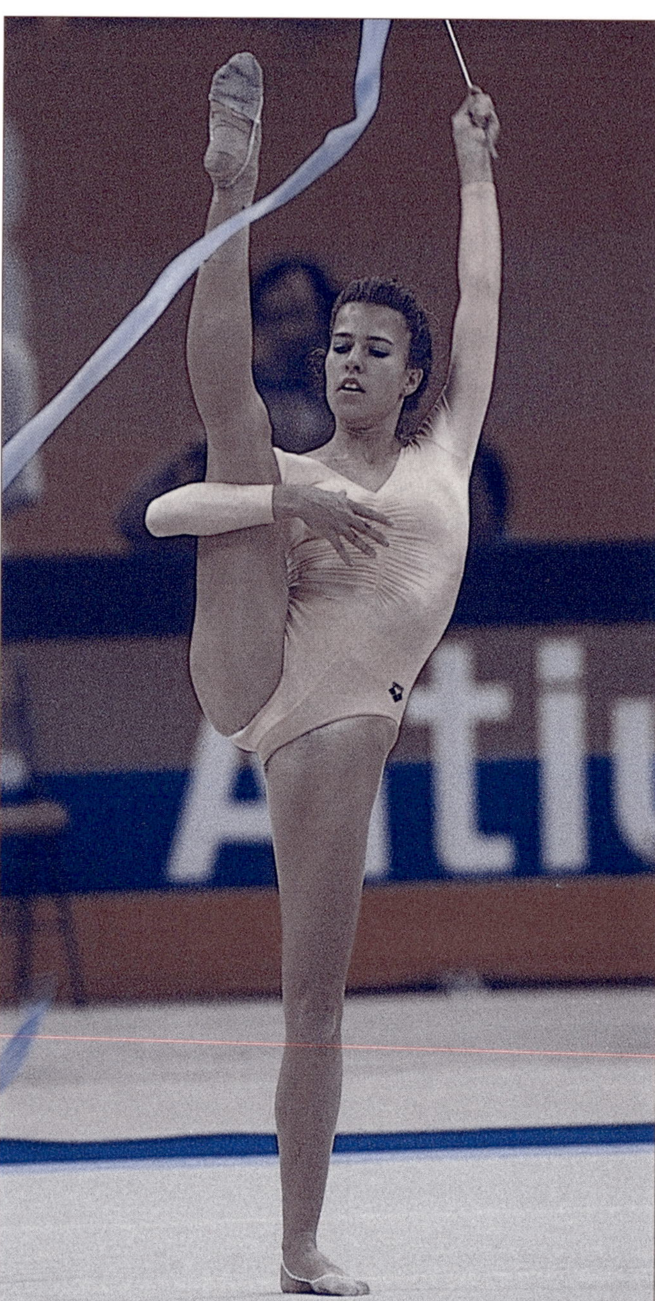

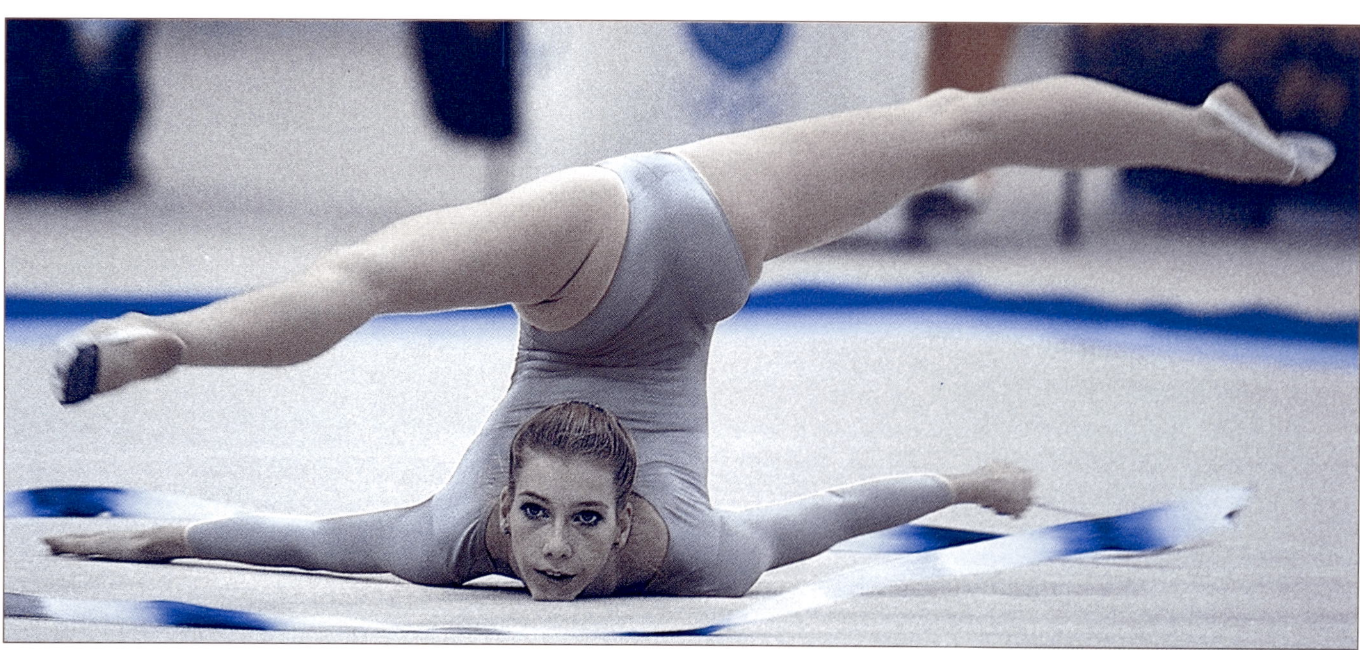

Trampolining

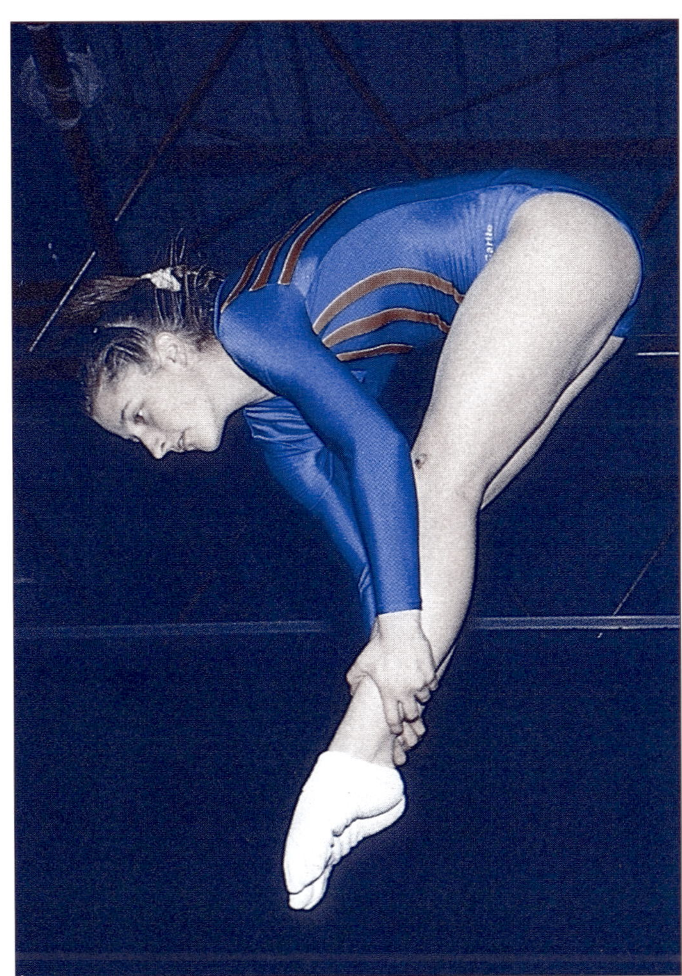

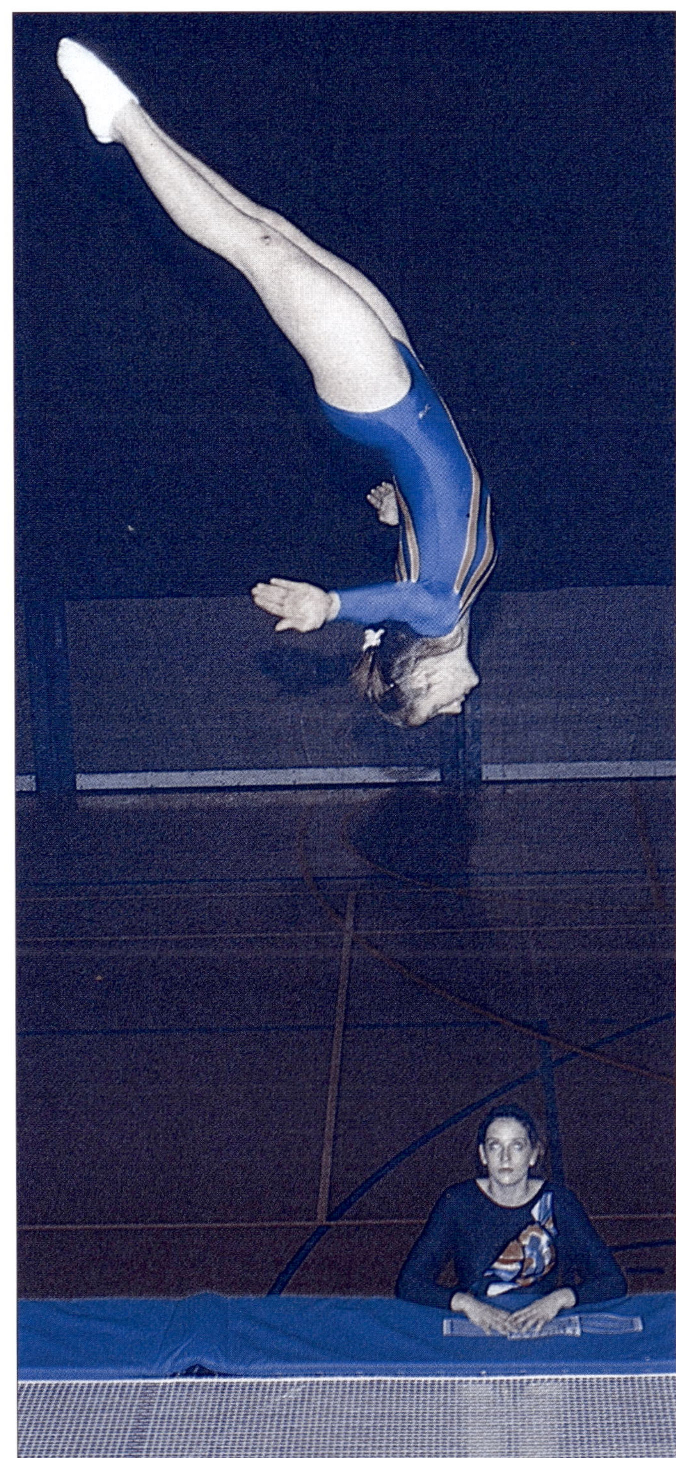

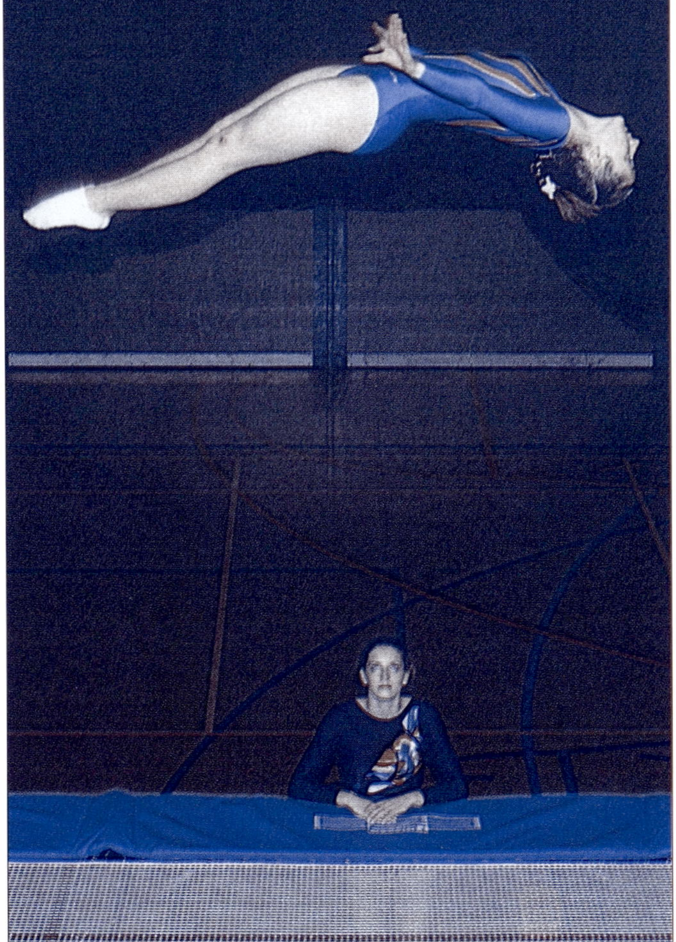

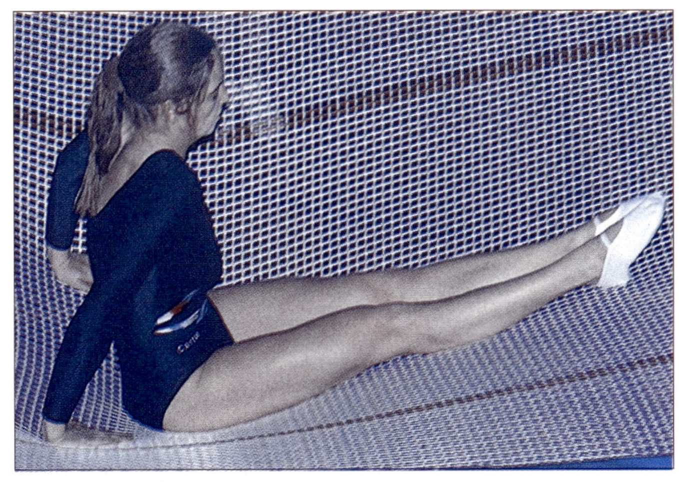

Fencing – male

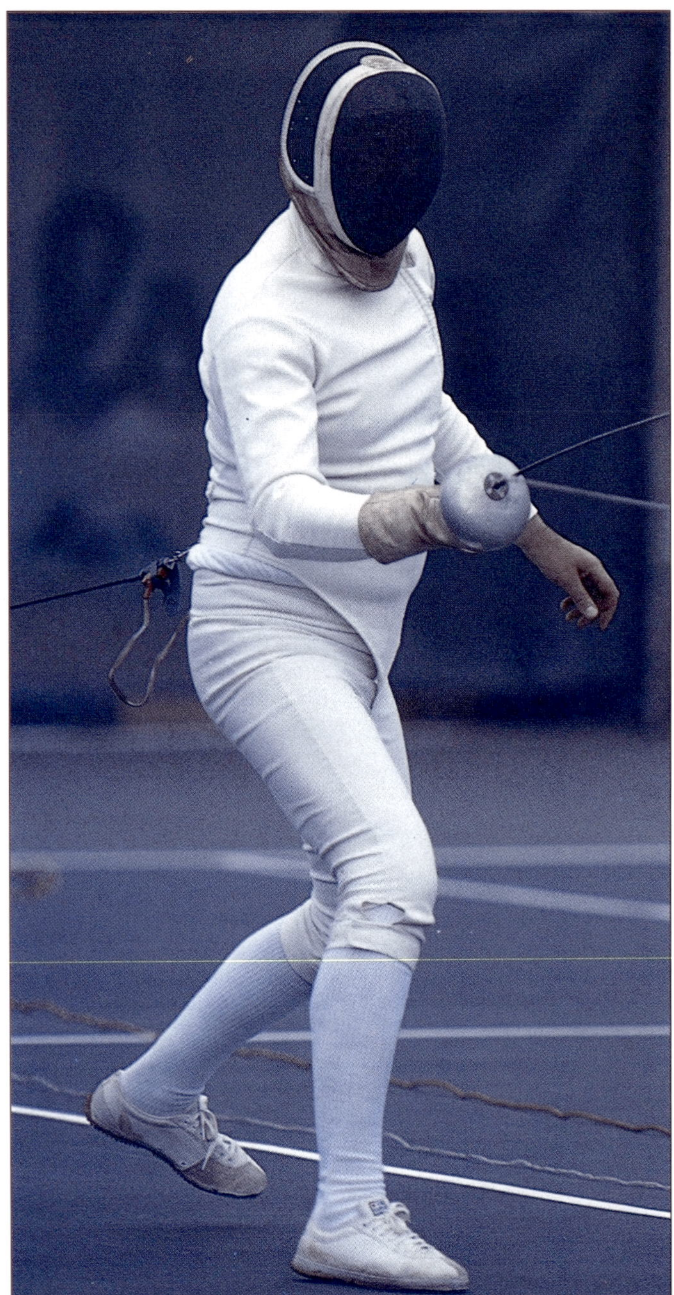

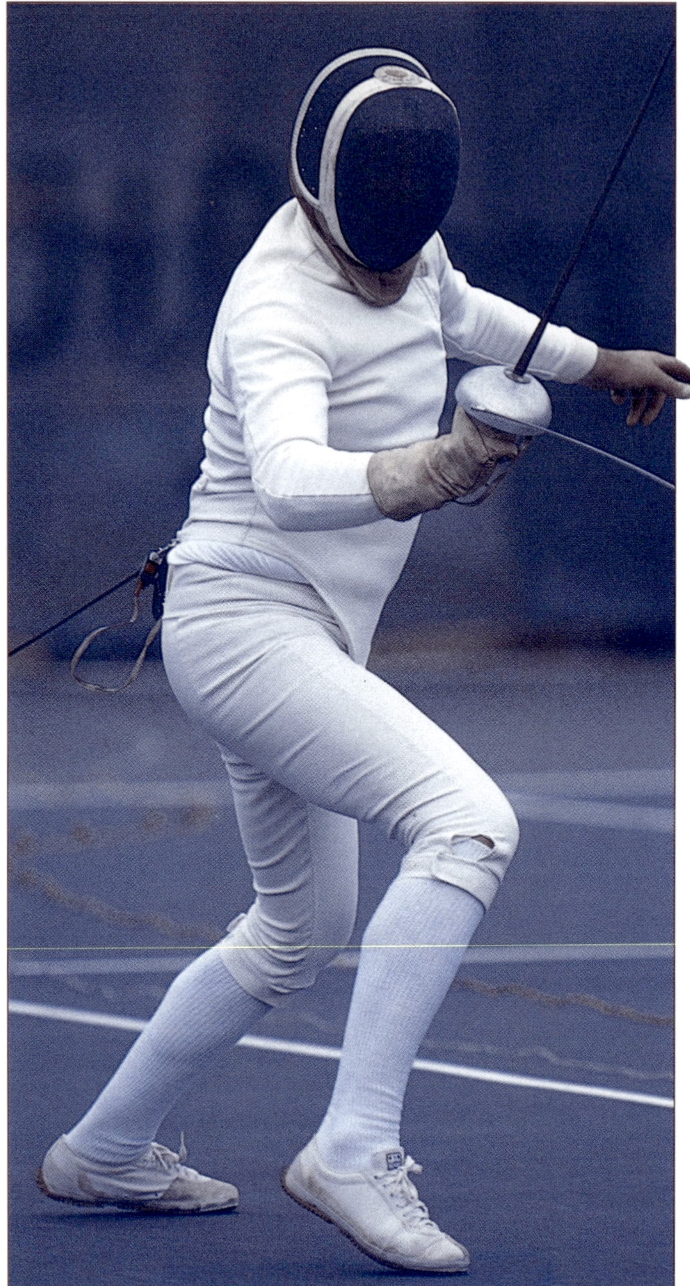

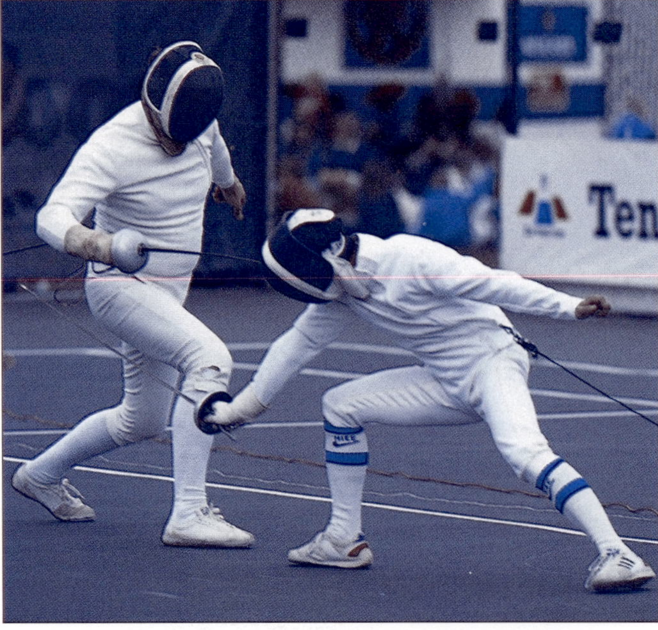

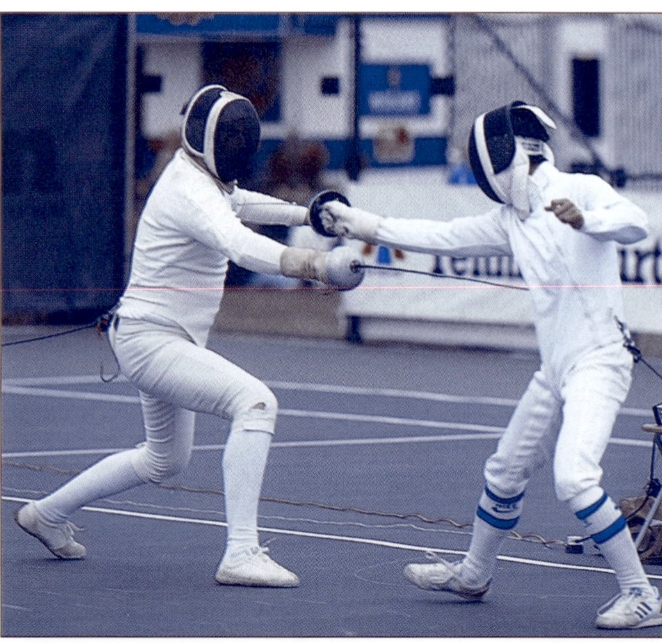

Fencing – male/female

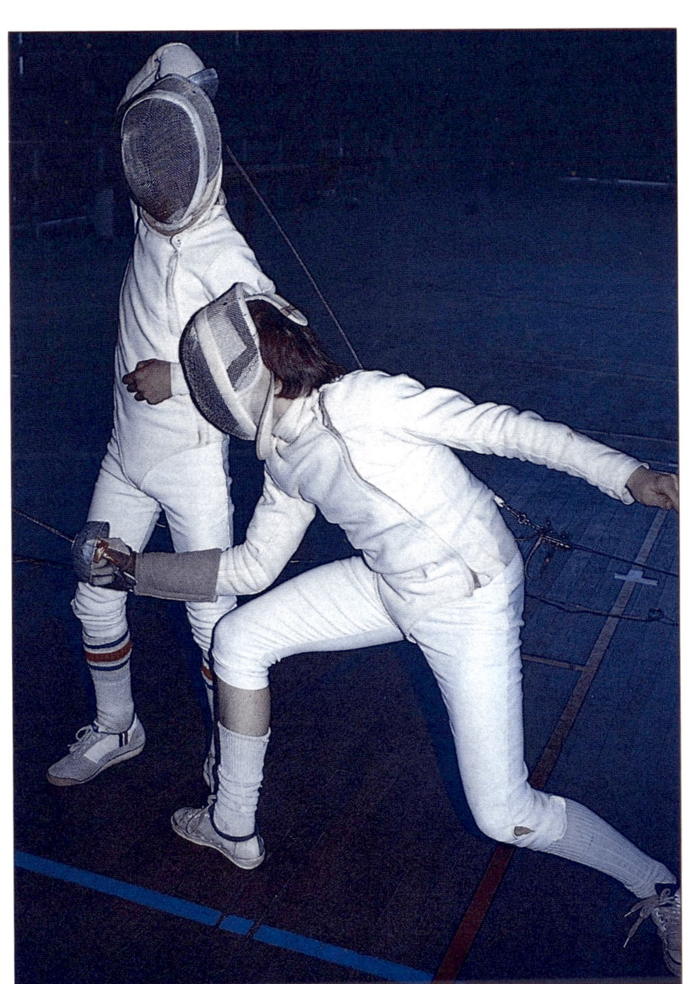

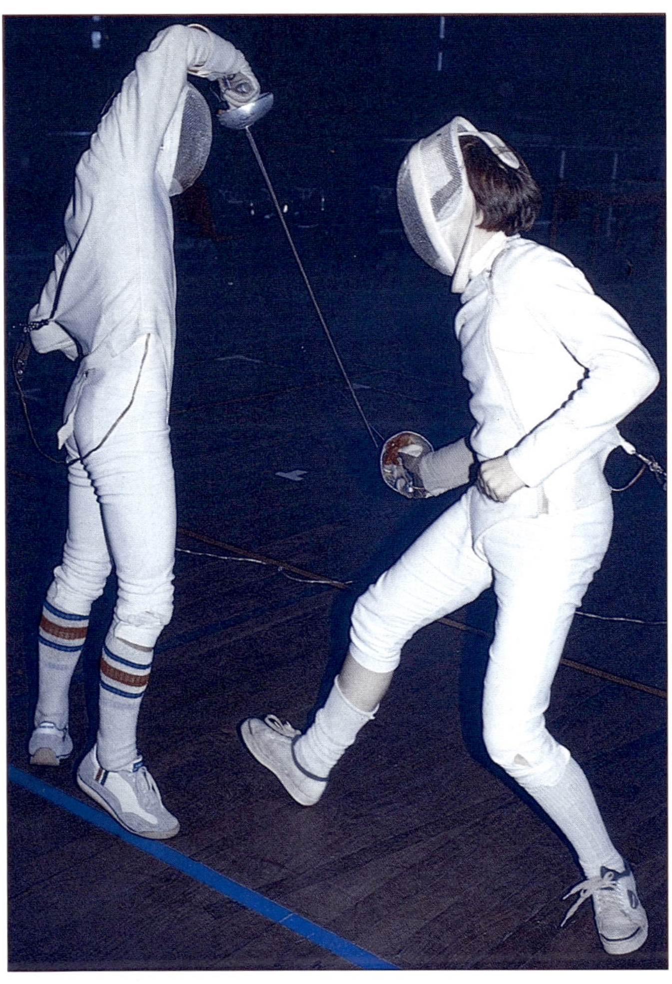

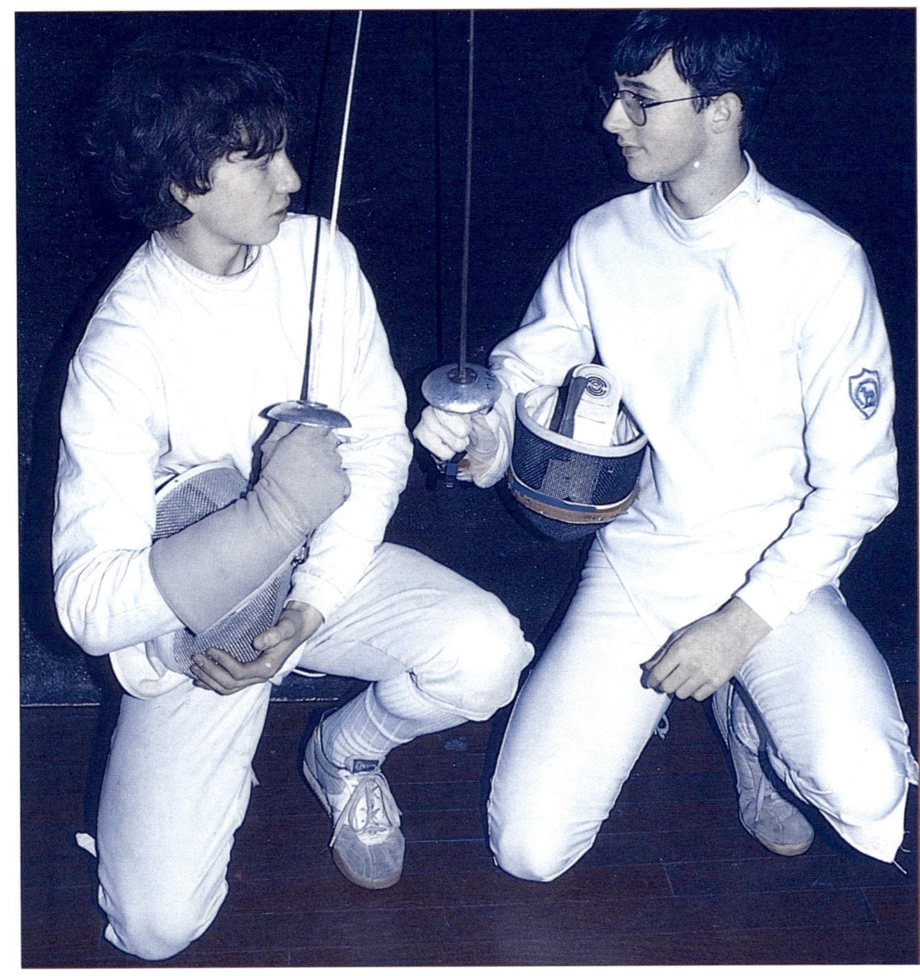

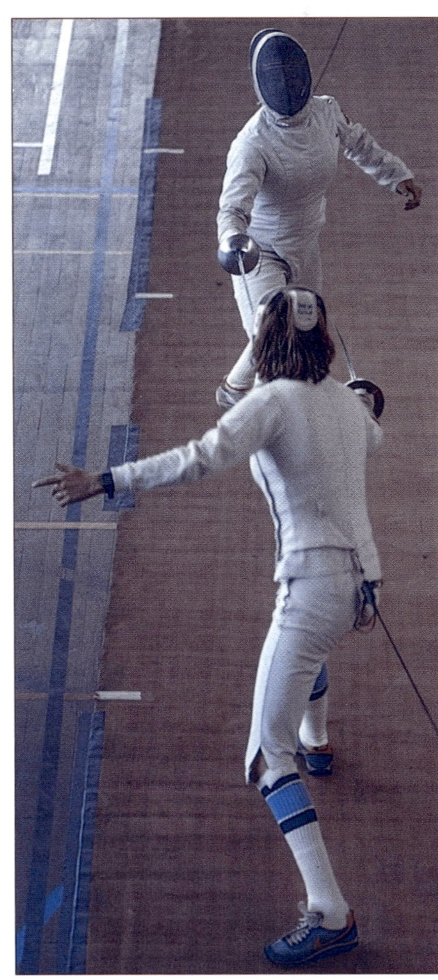

Judo

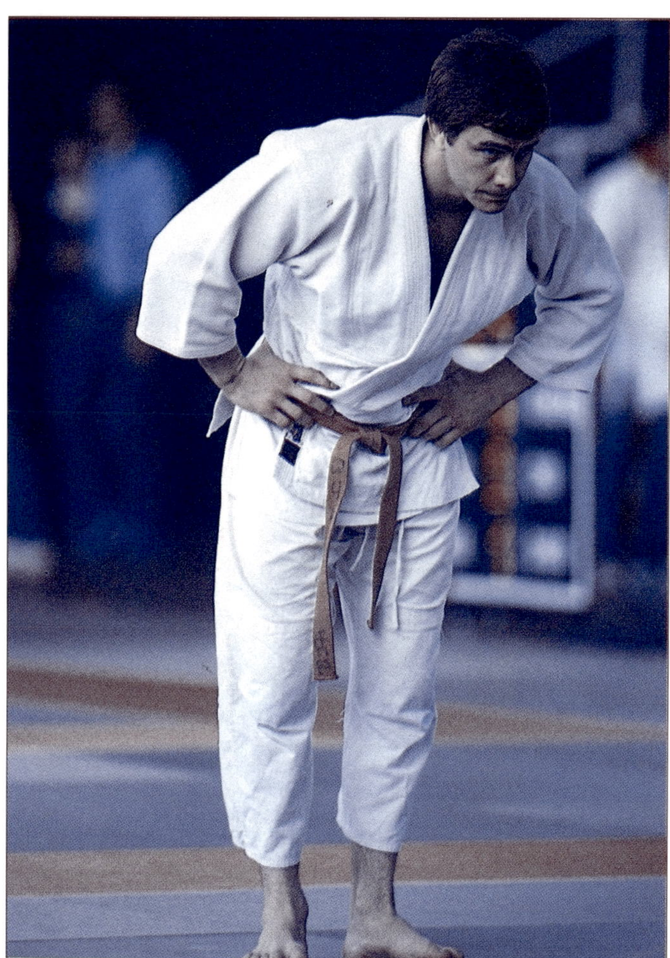

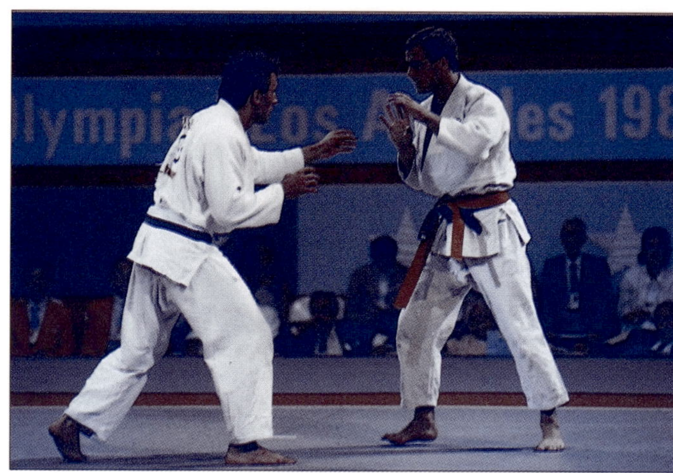

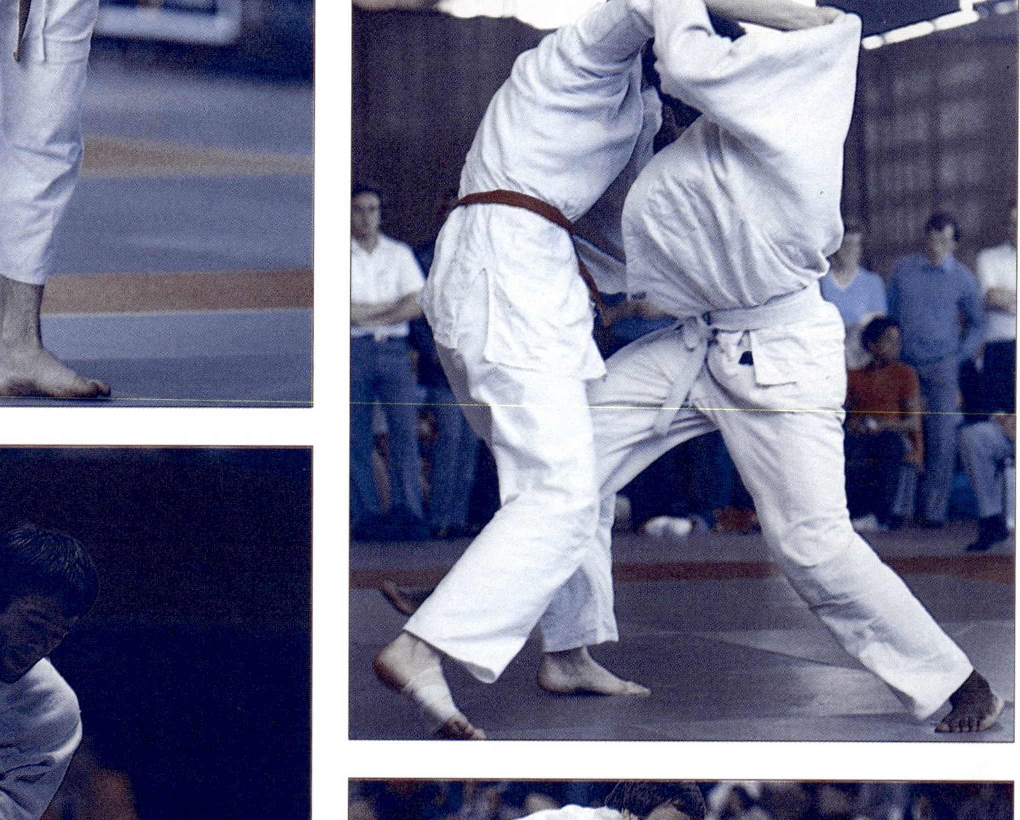

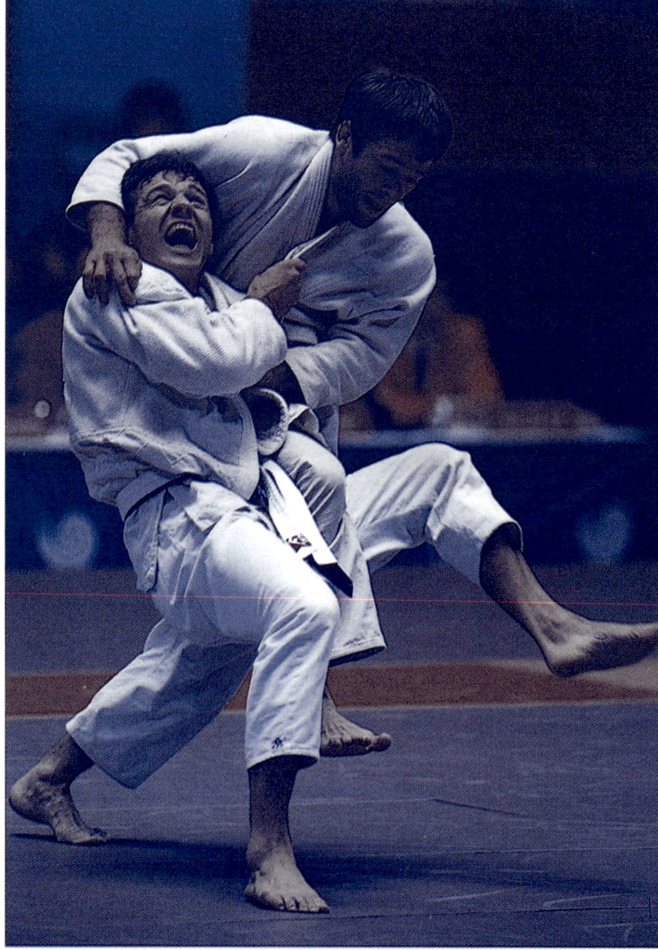

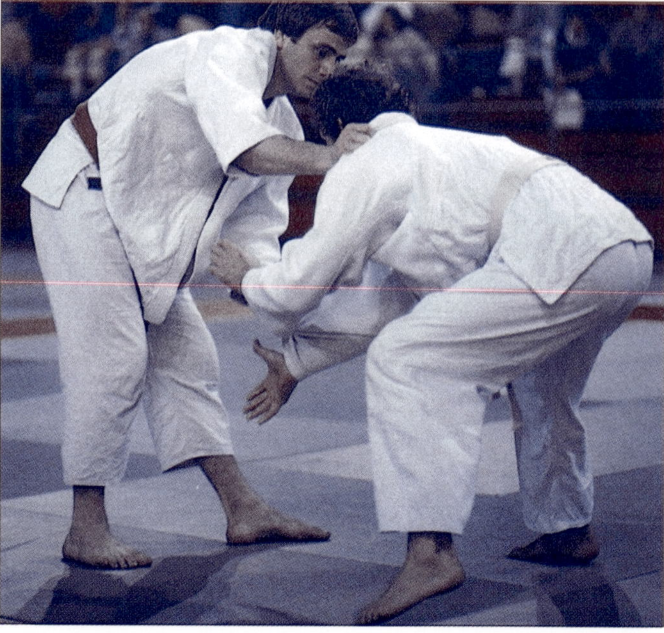

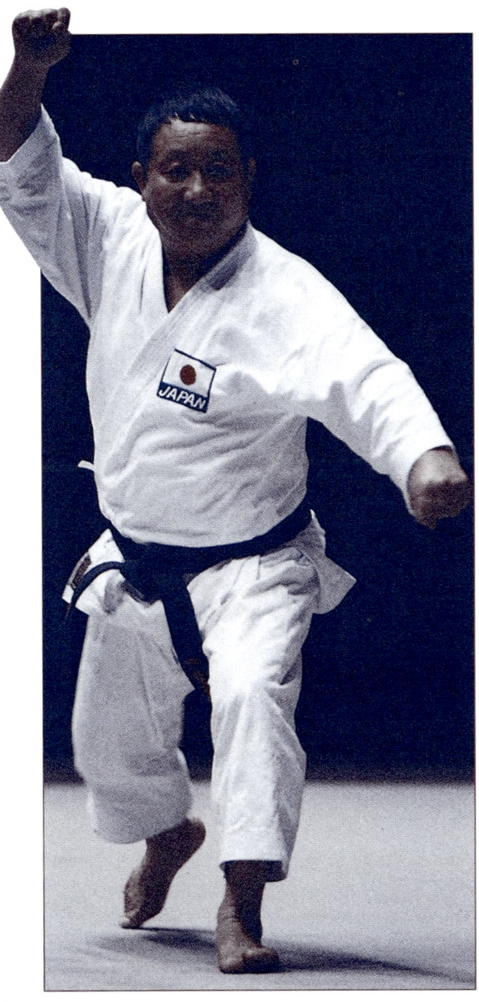
JAPAN

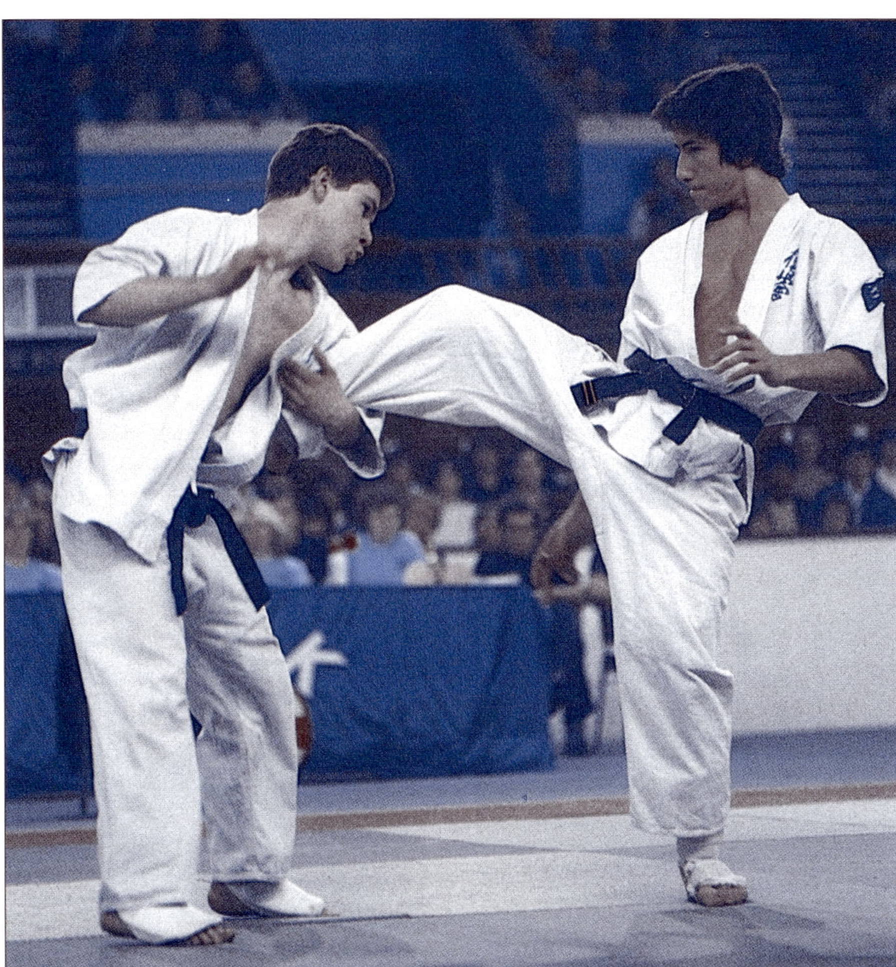

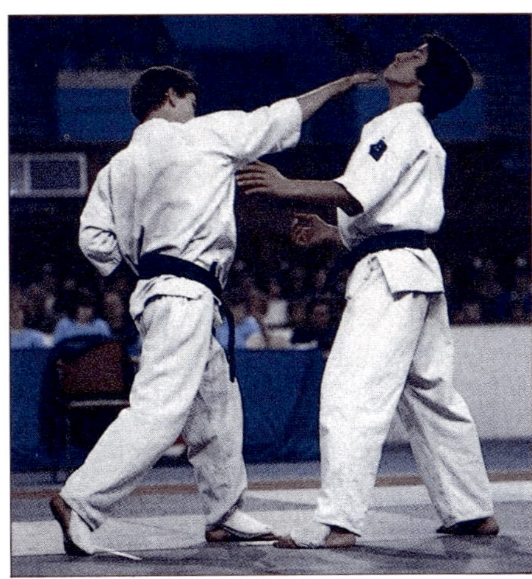

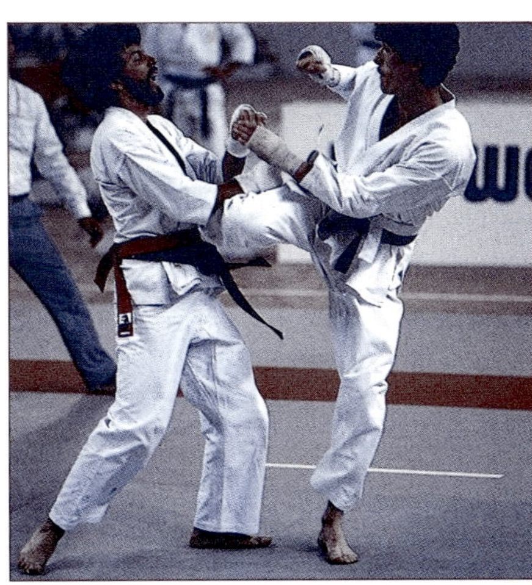

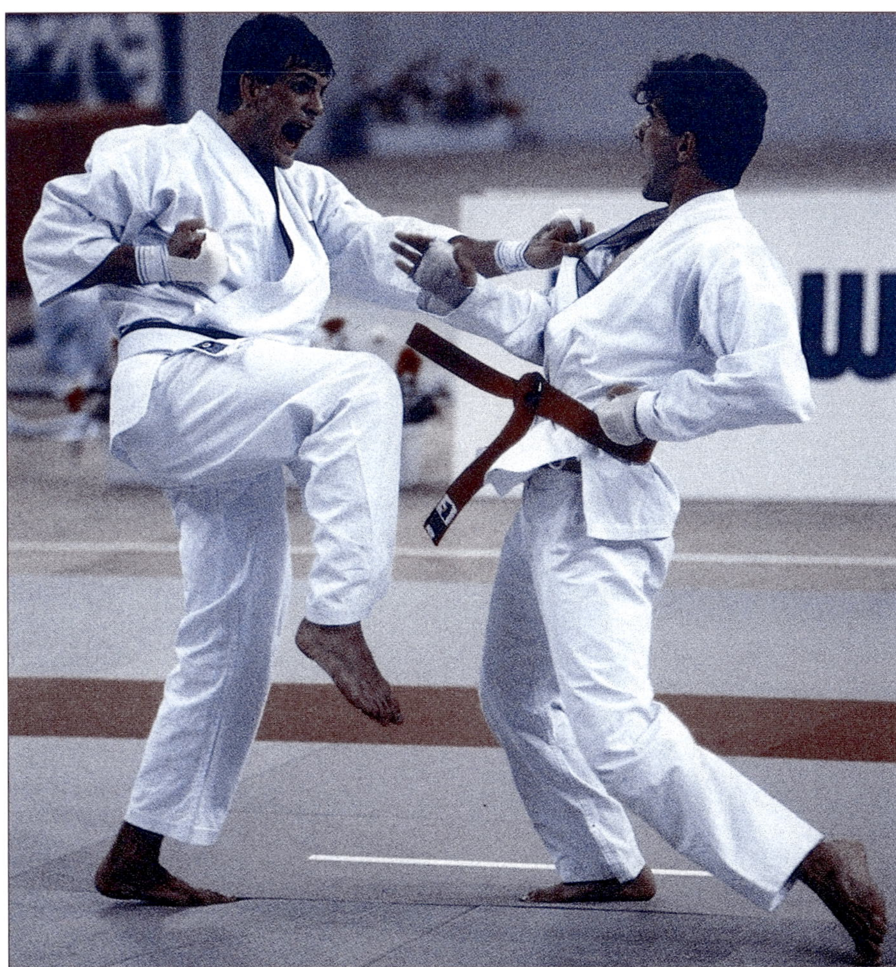

Wrestling

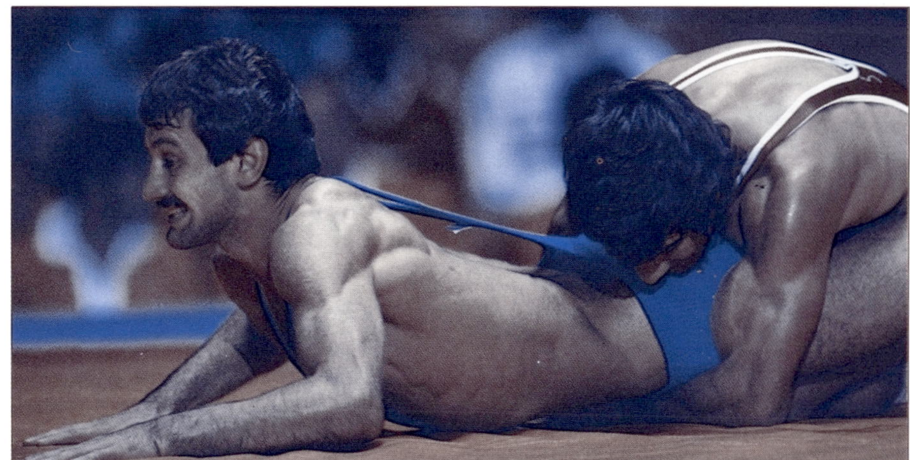

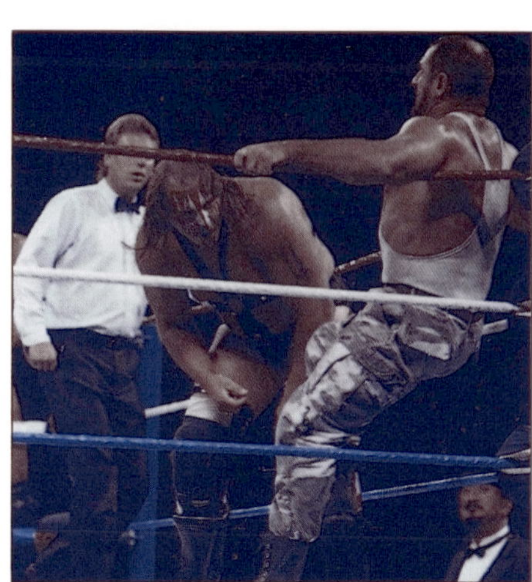

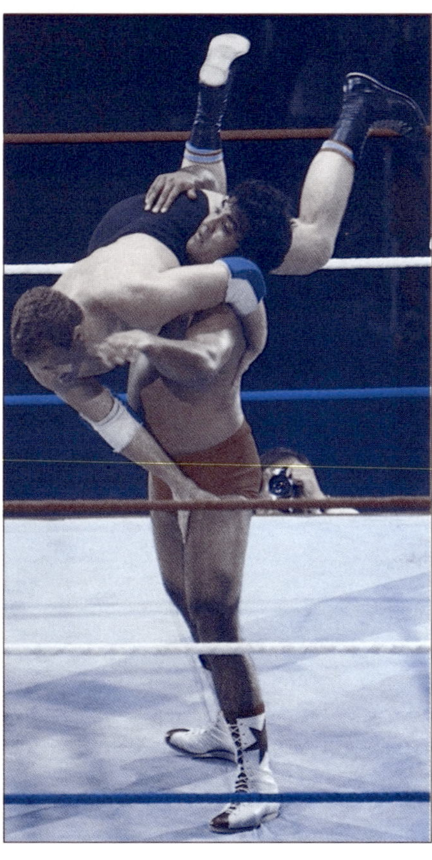

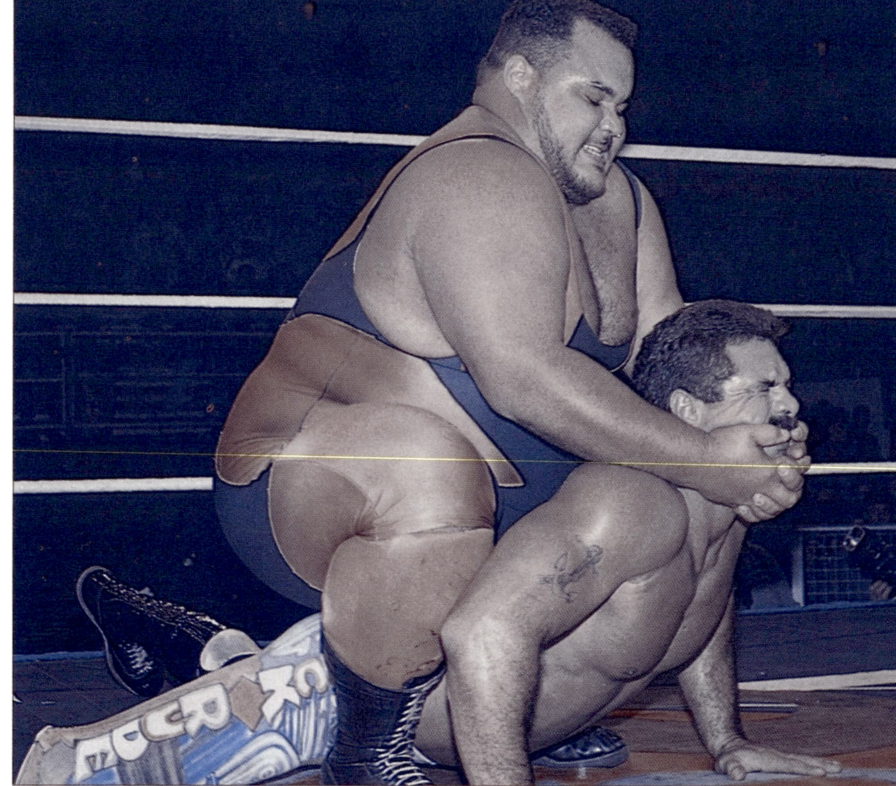

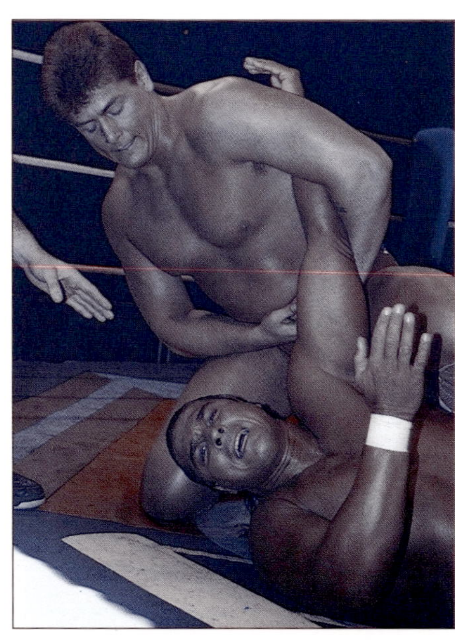

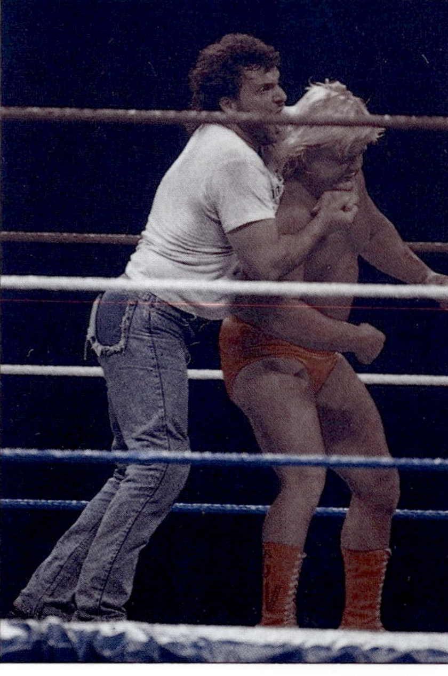

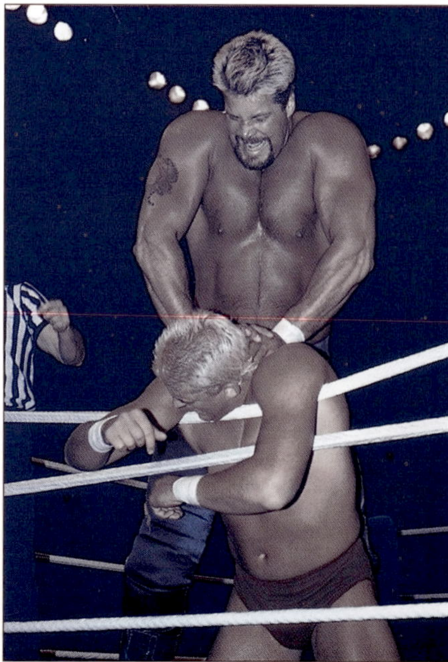

Sumo and arm wrestling

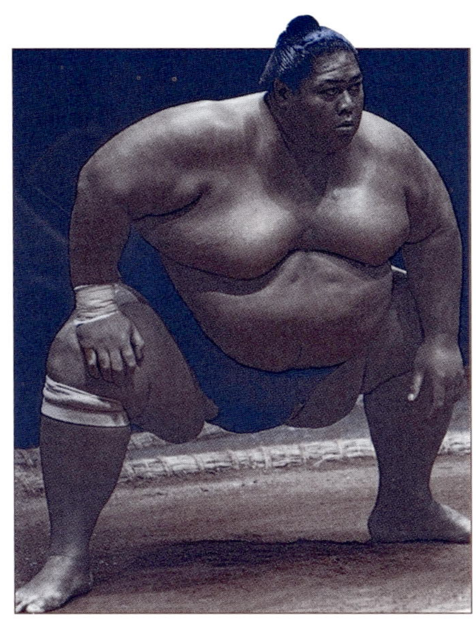

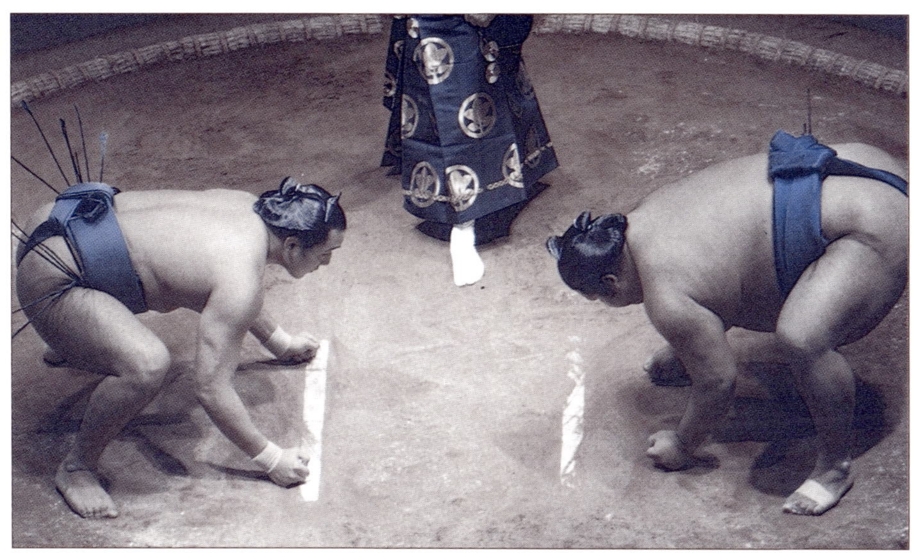

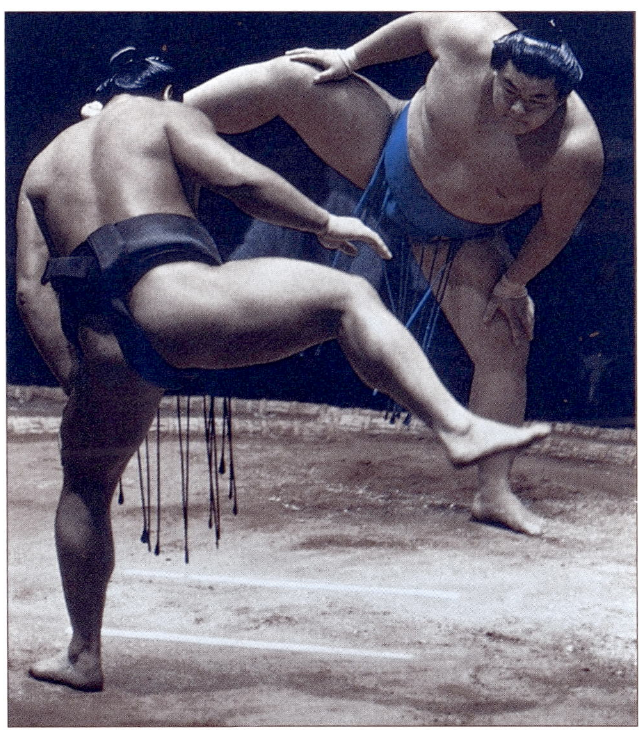

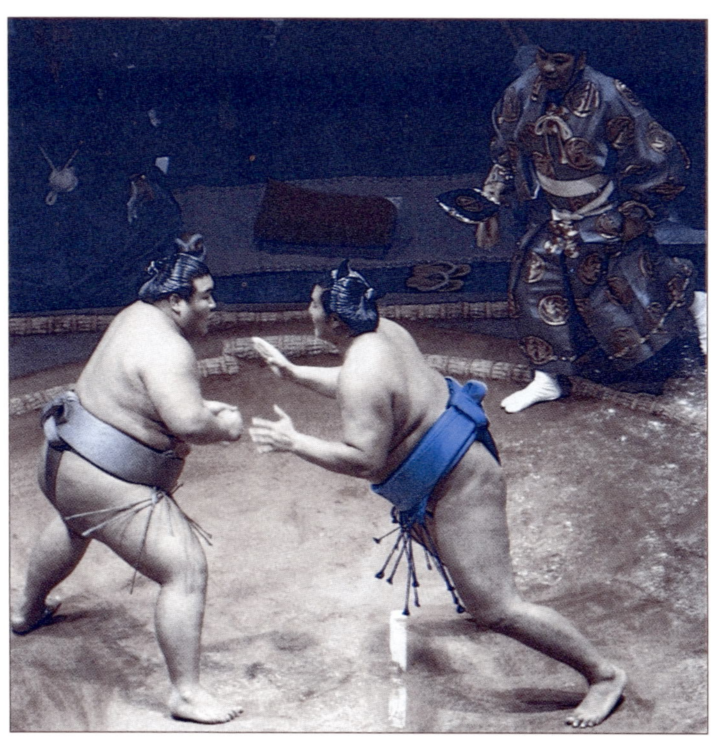

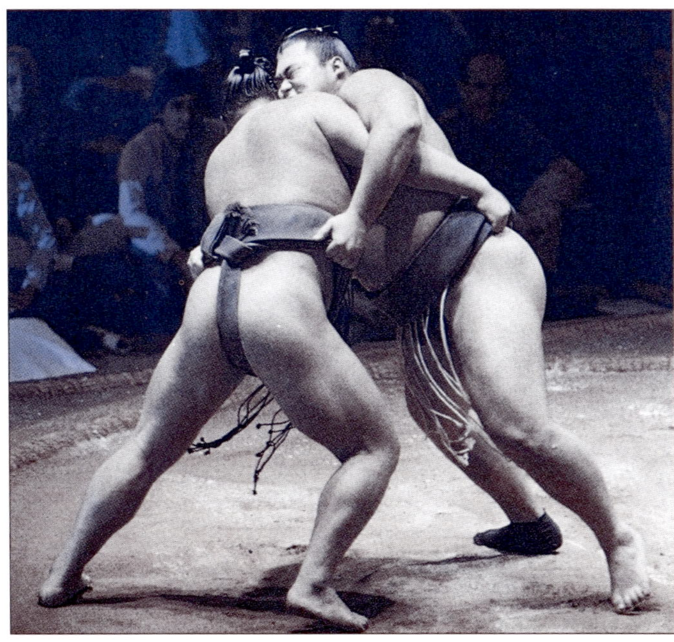

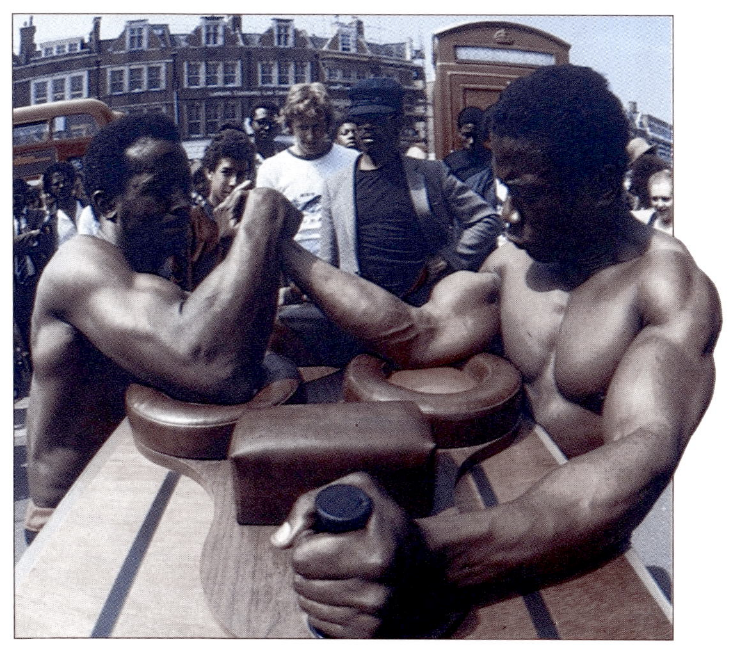

Boxing

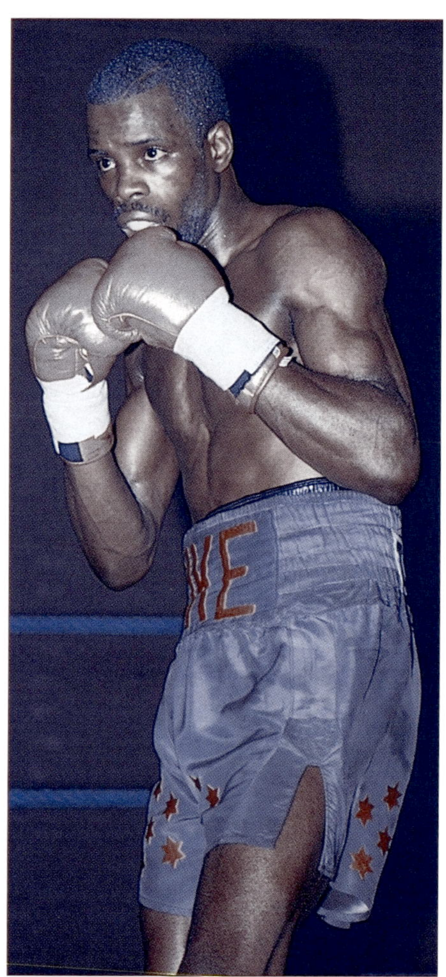

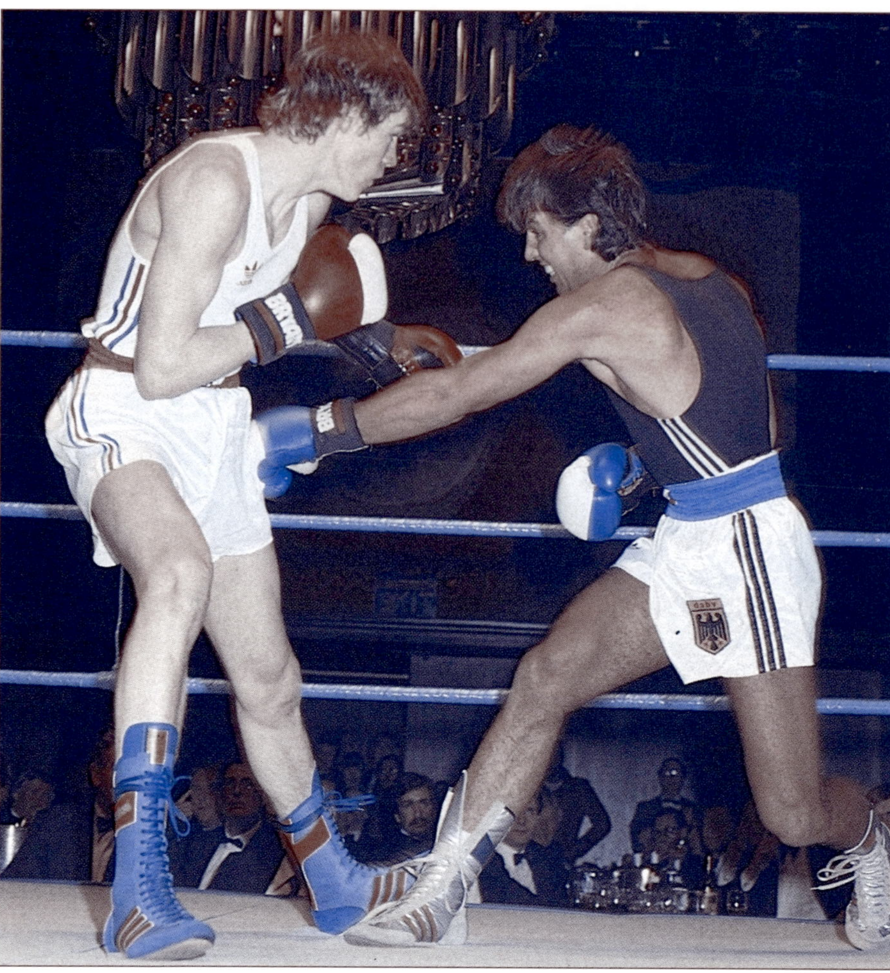

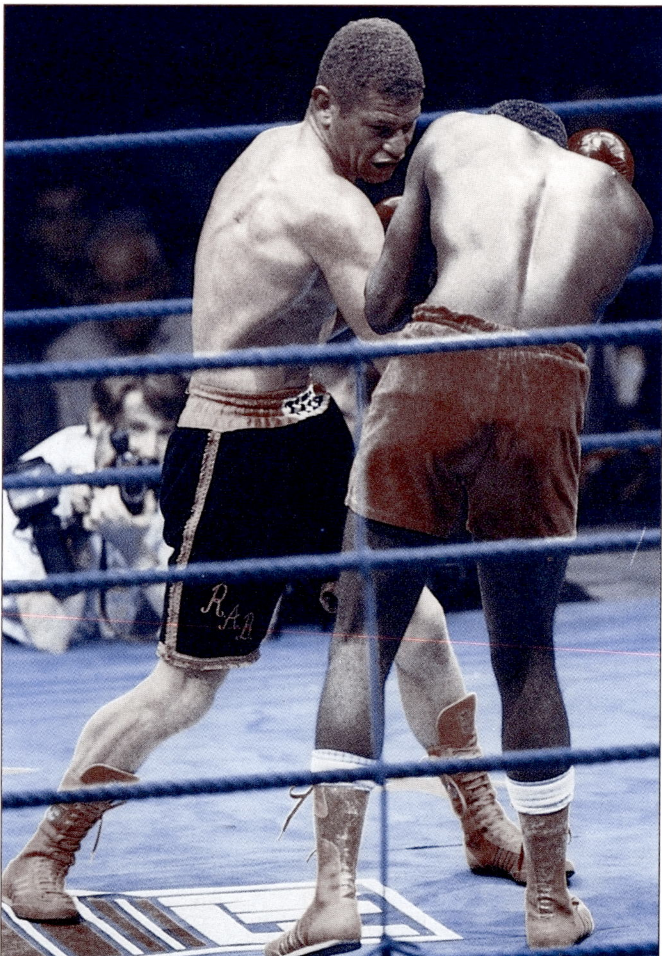

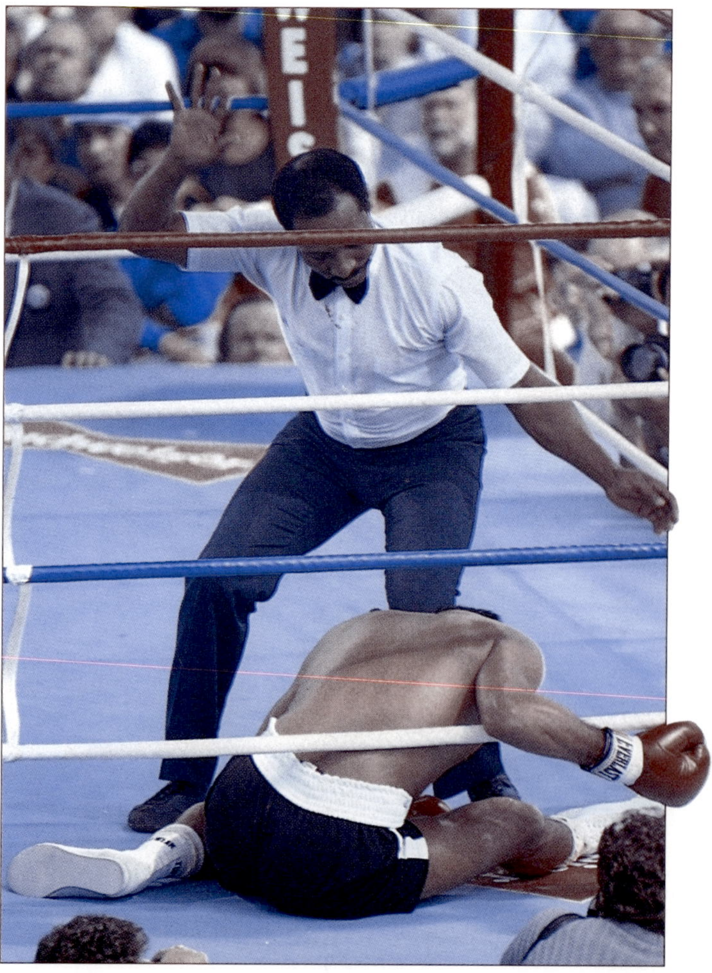

Weightlifting

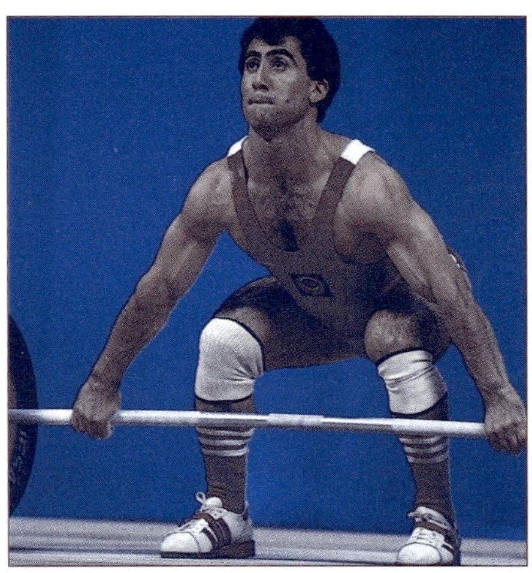

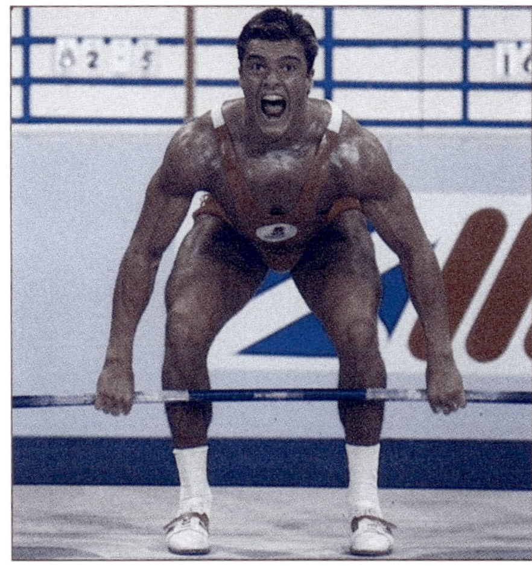

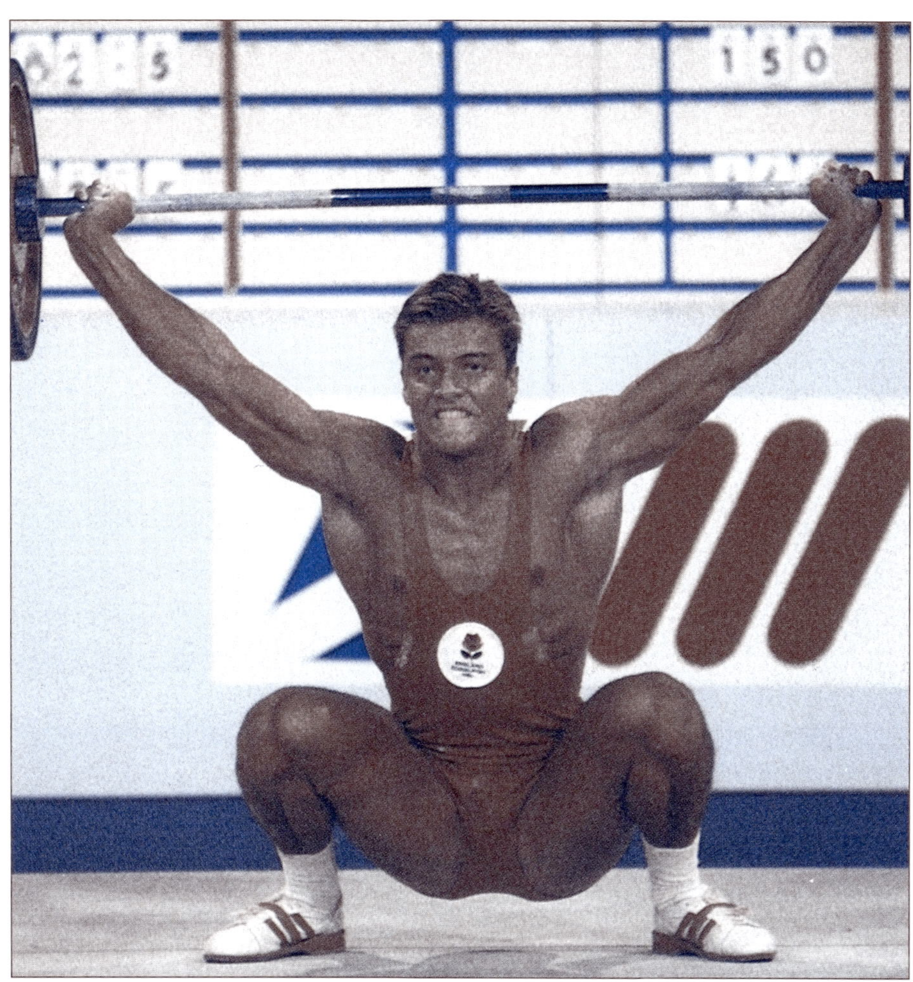

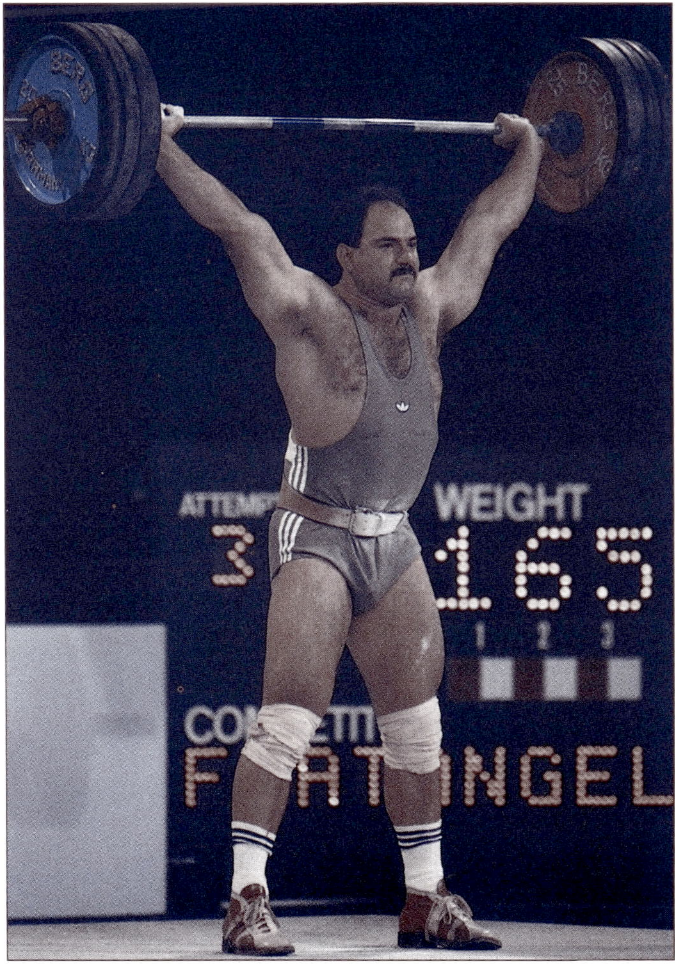

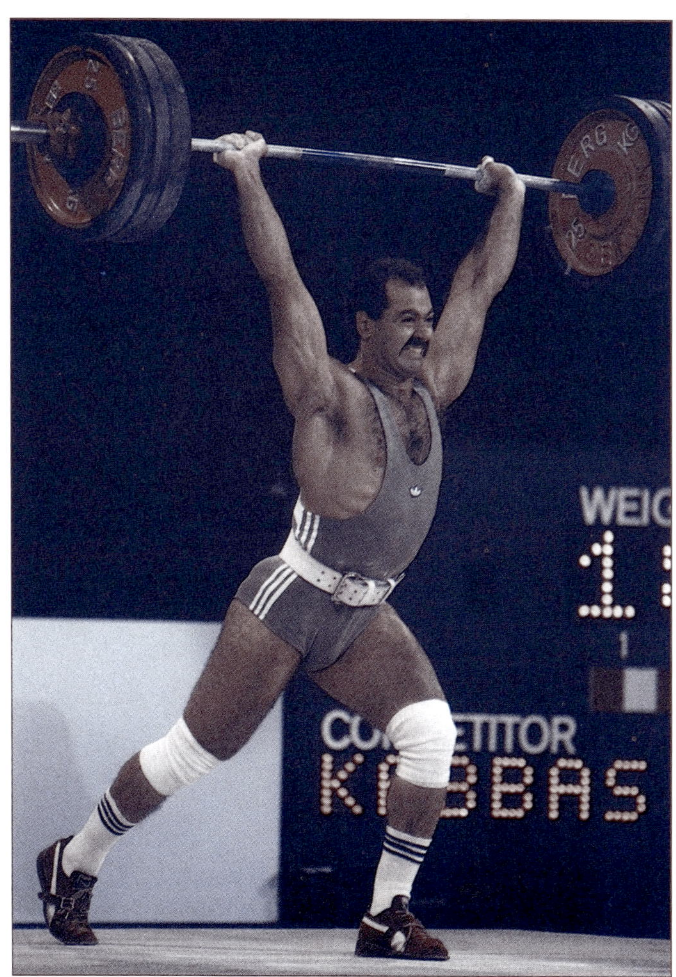

Shooting – clay pigeon

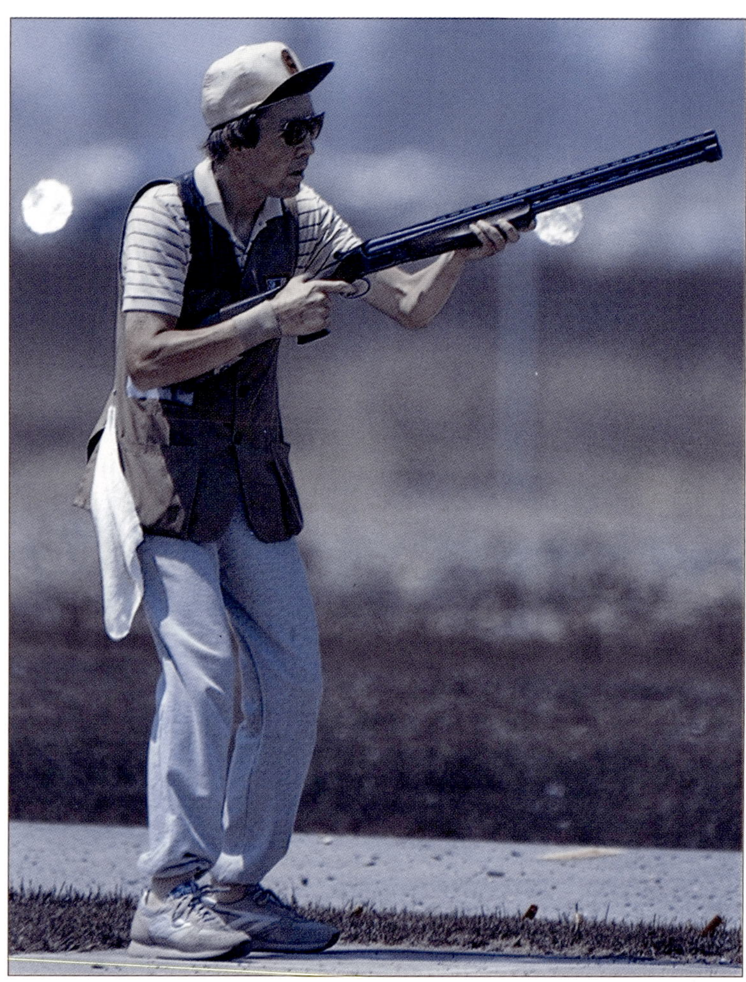

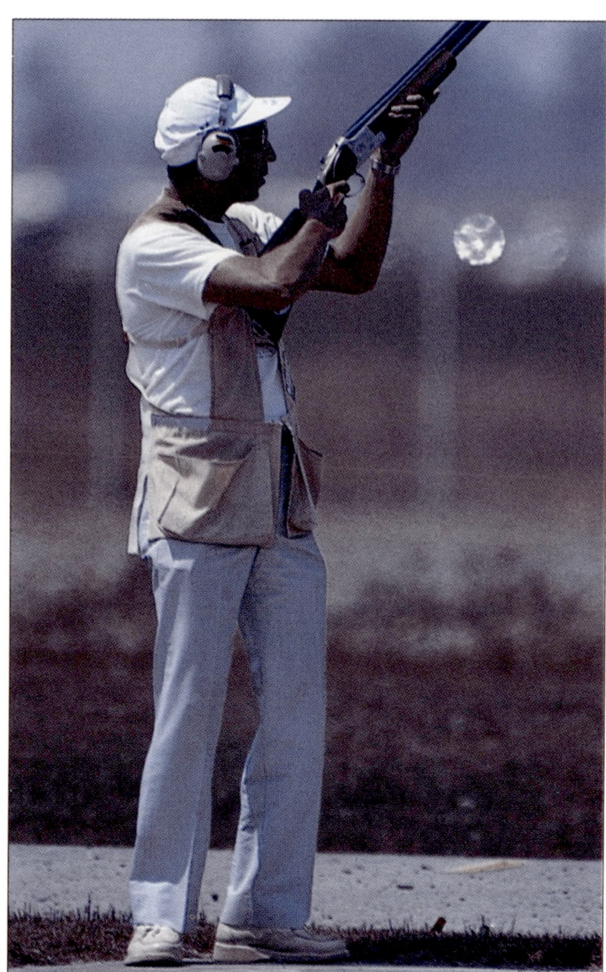

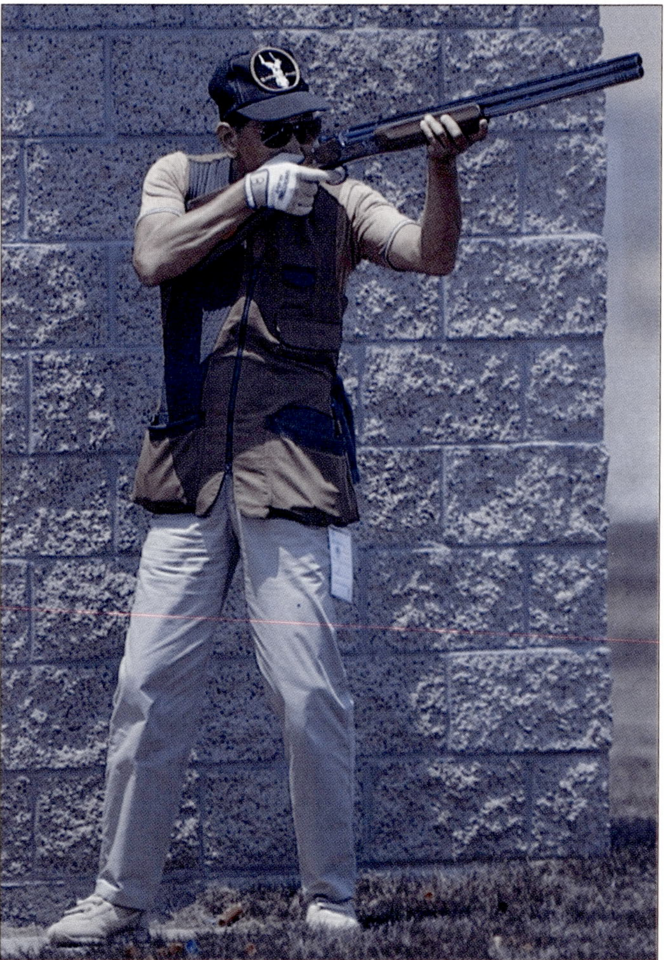

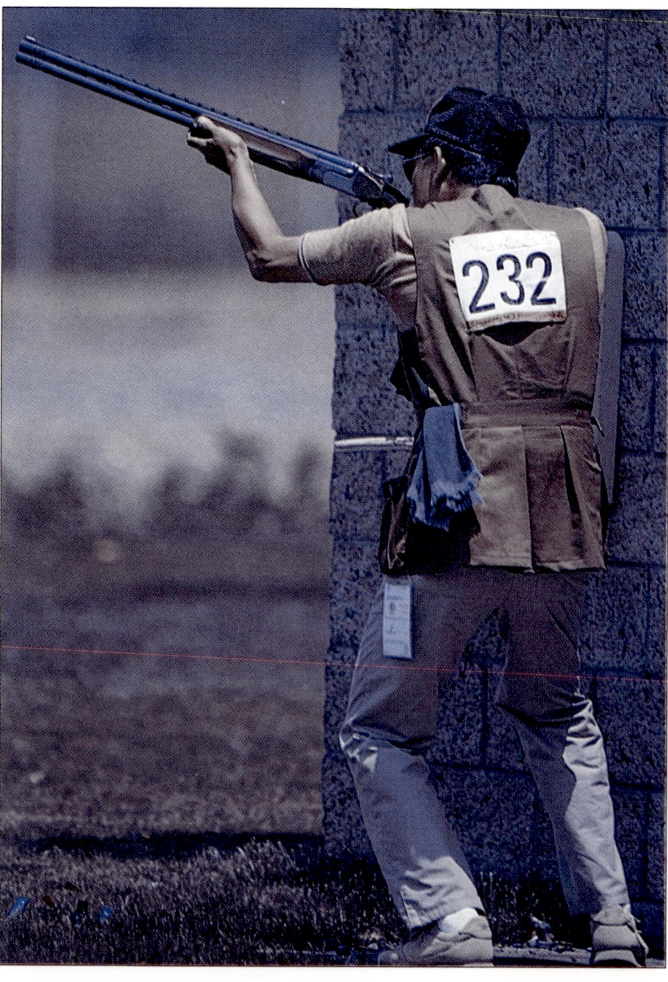

Shooting – clay pigeon

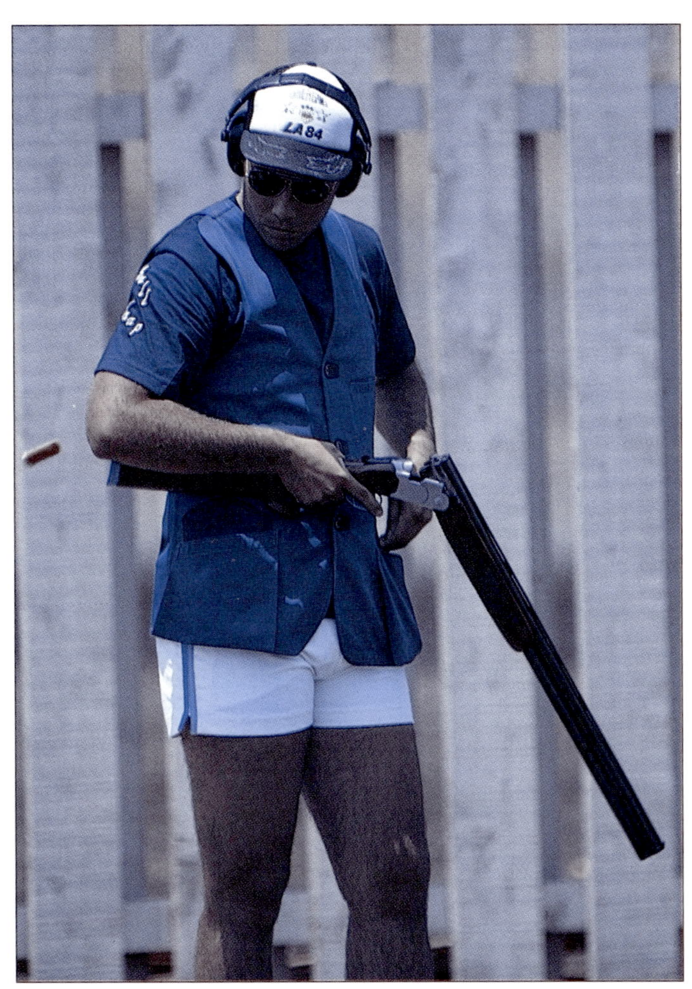

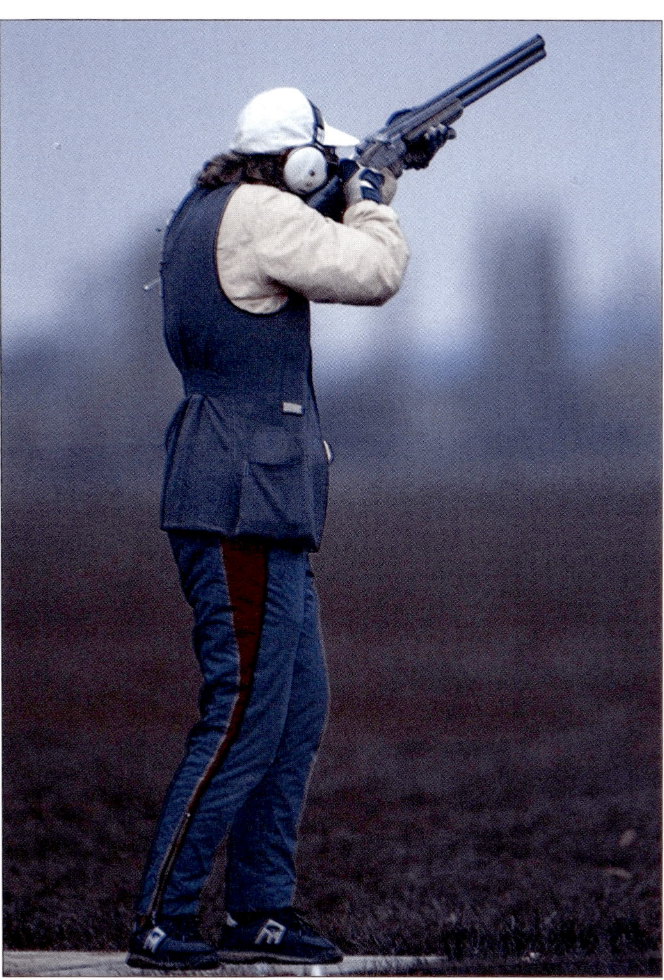

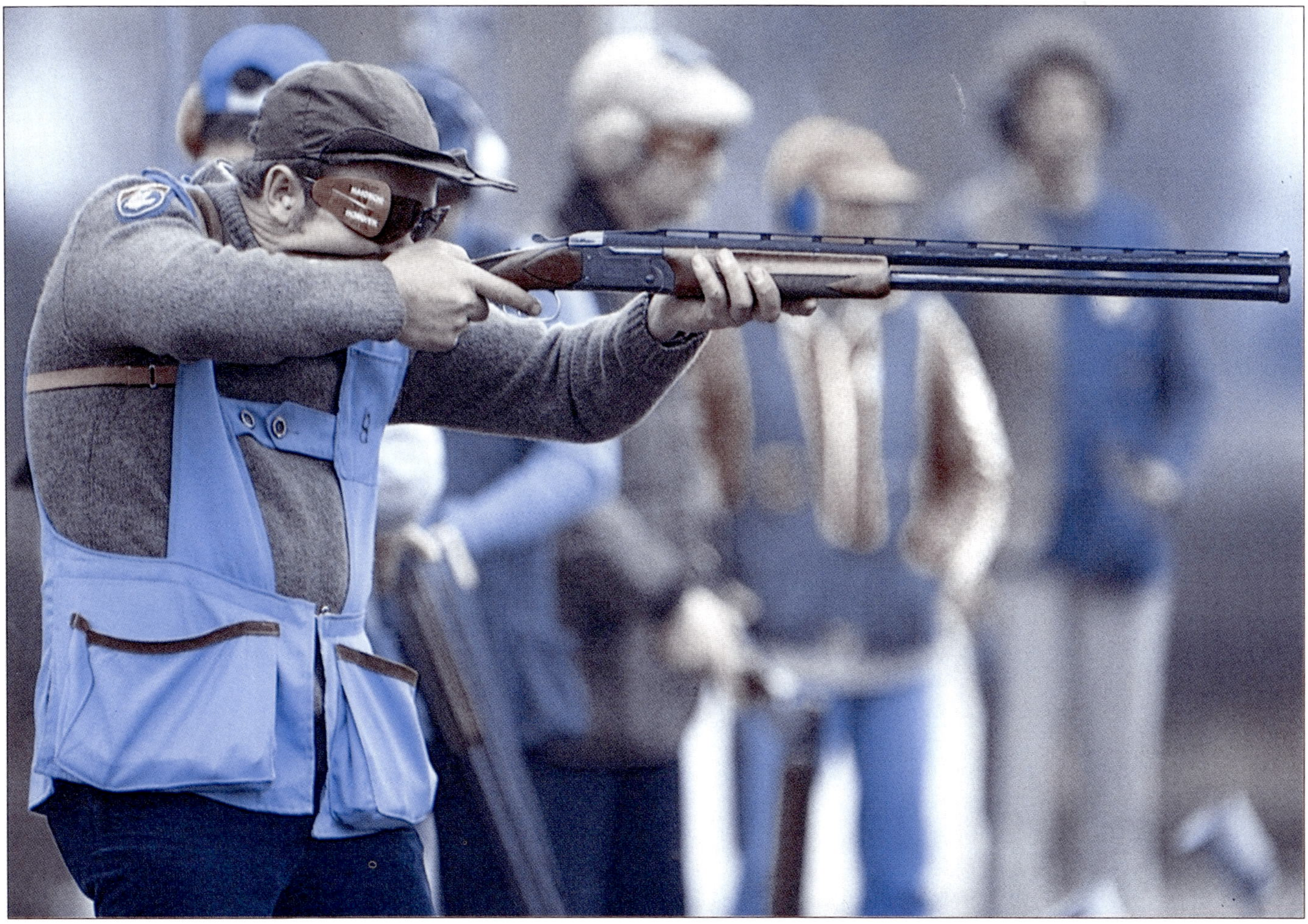

Shooting – game

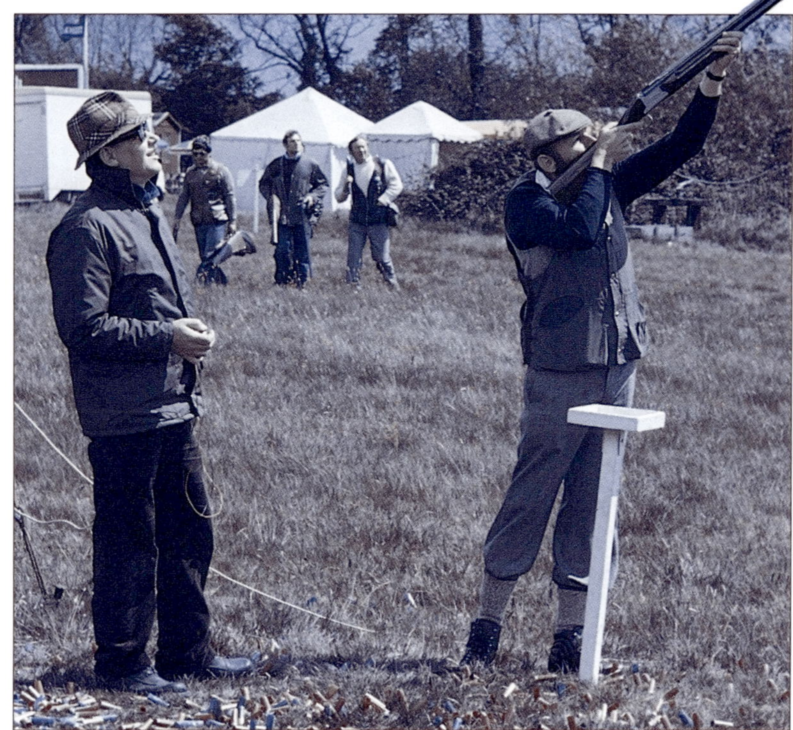

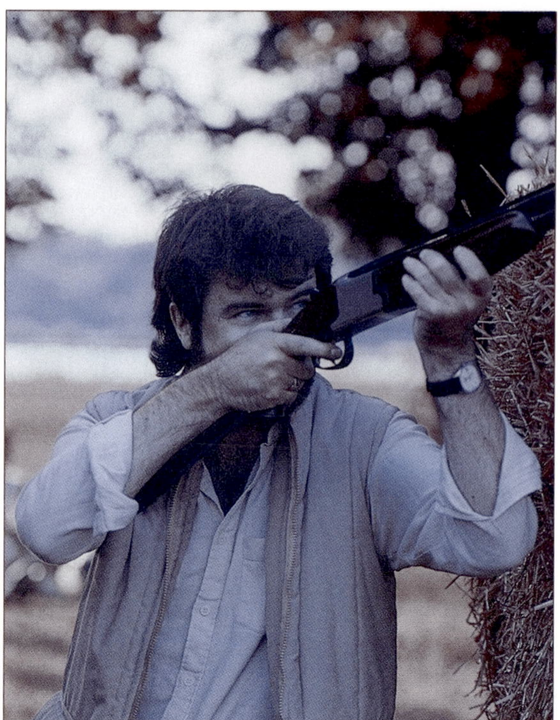

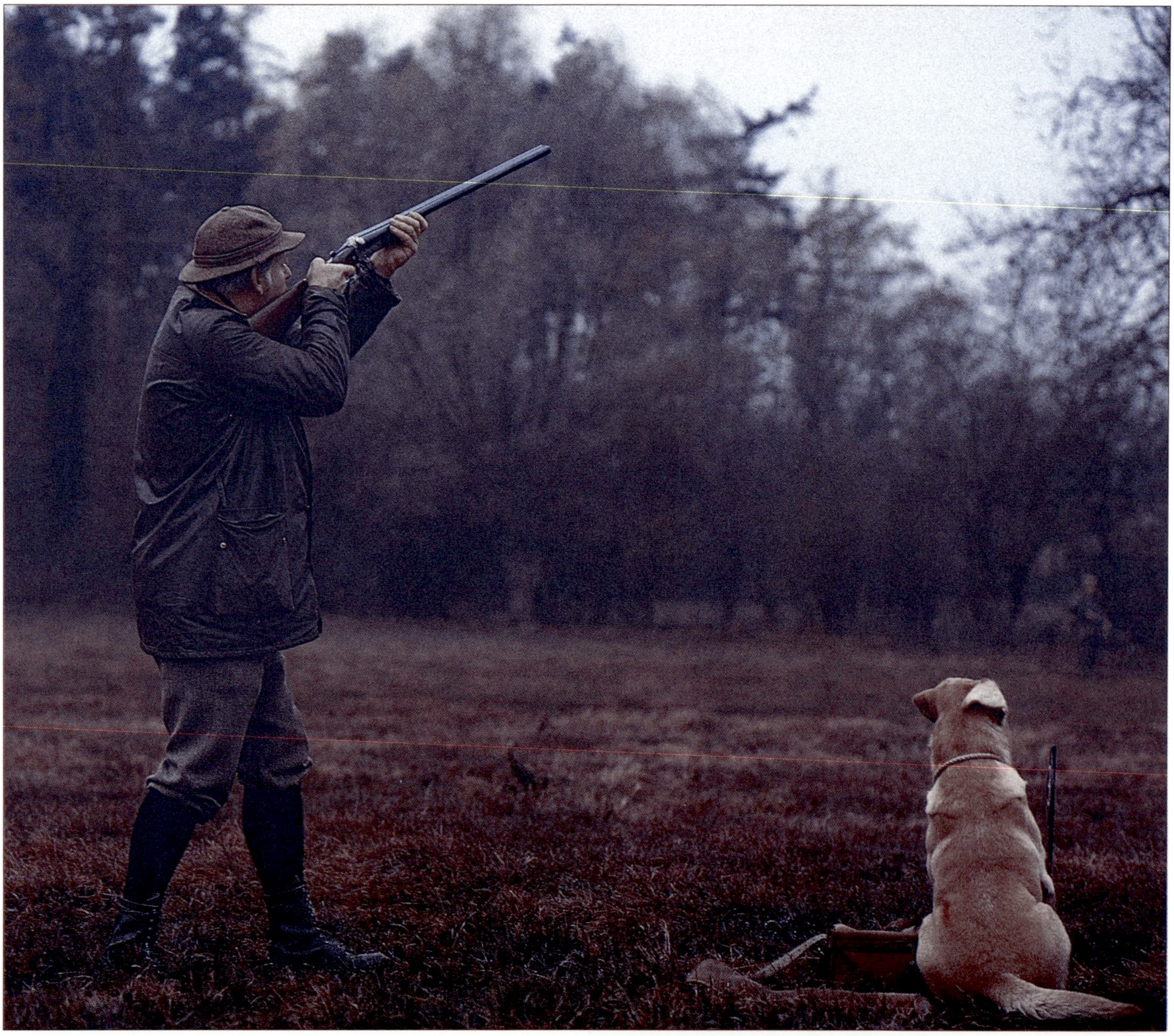

Shooting – small bore rifle

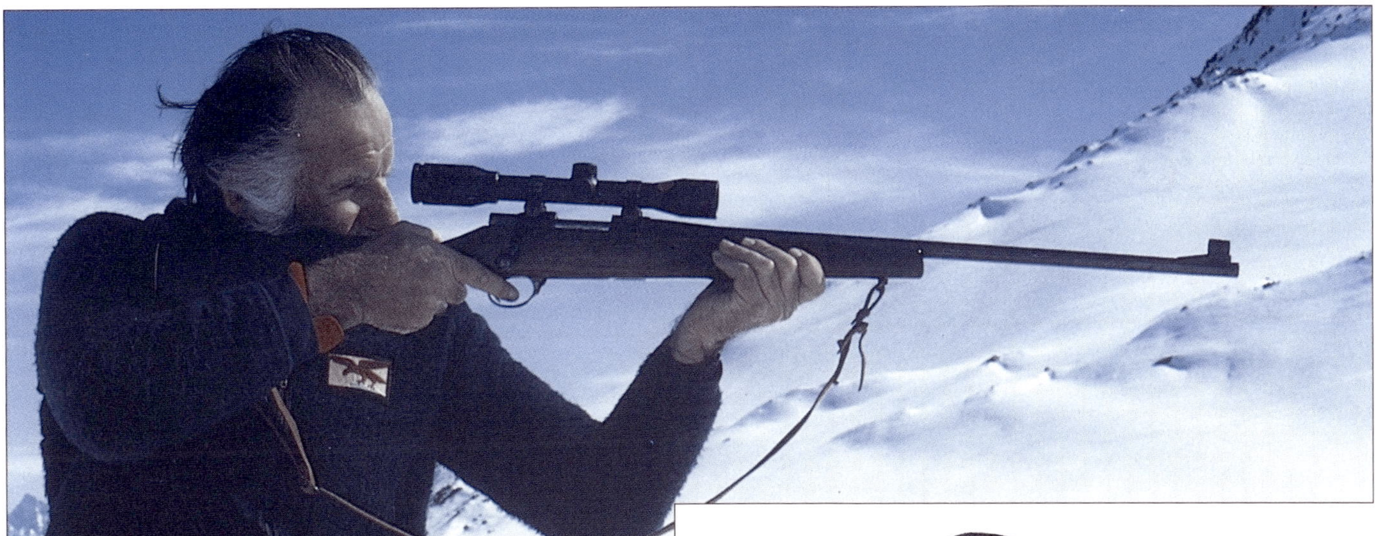

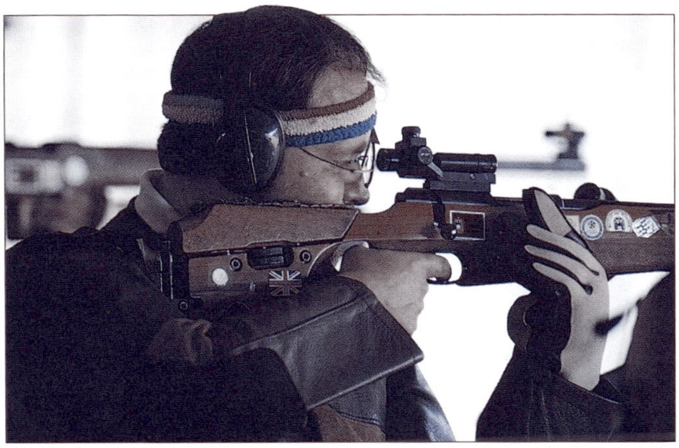

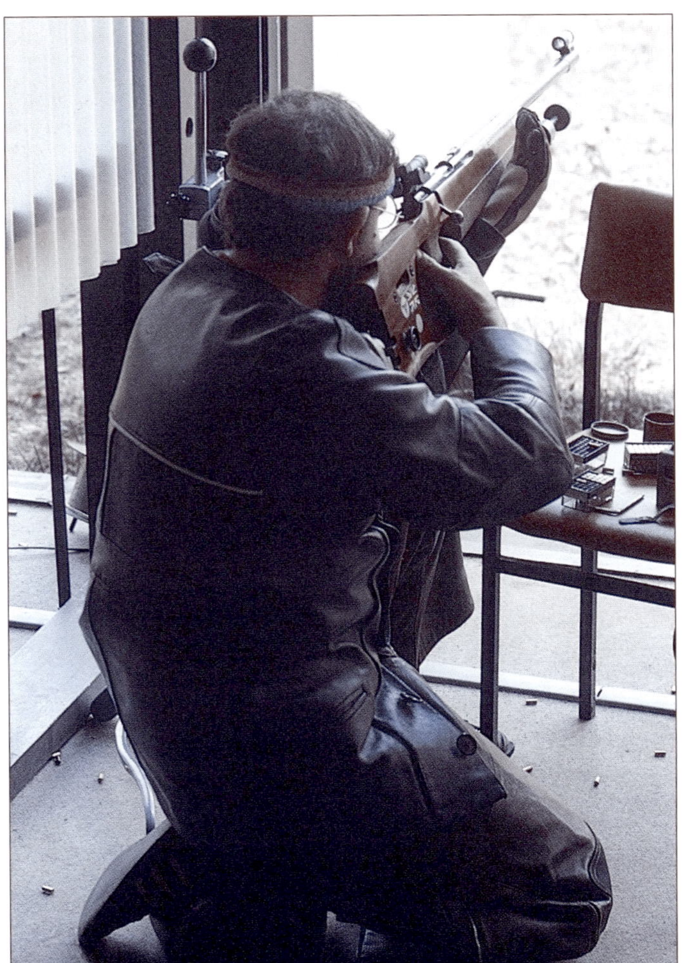

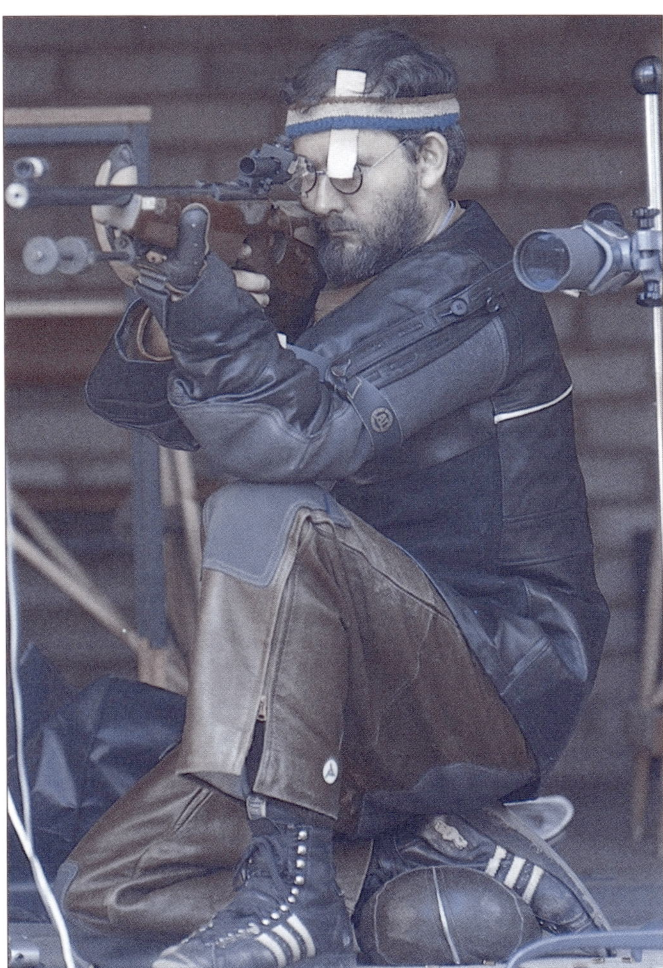

Archery

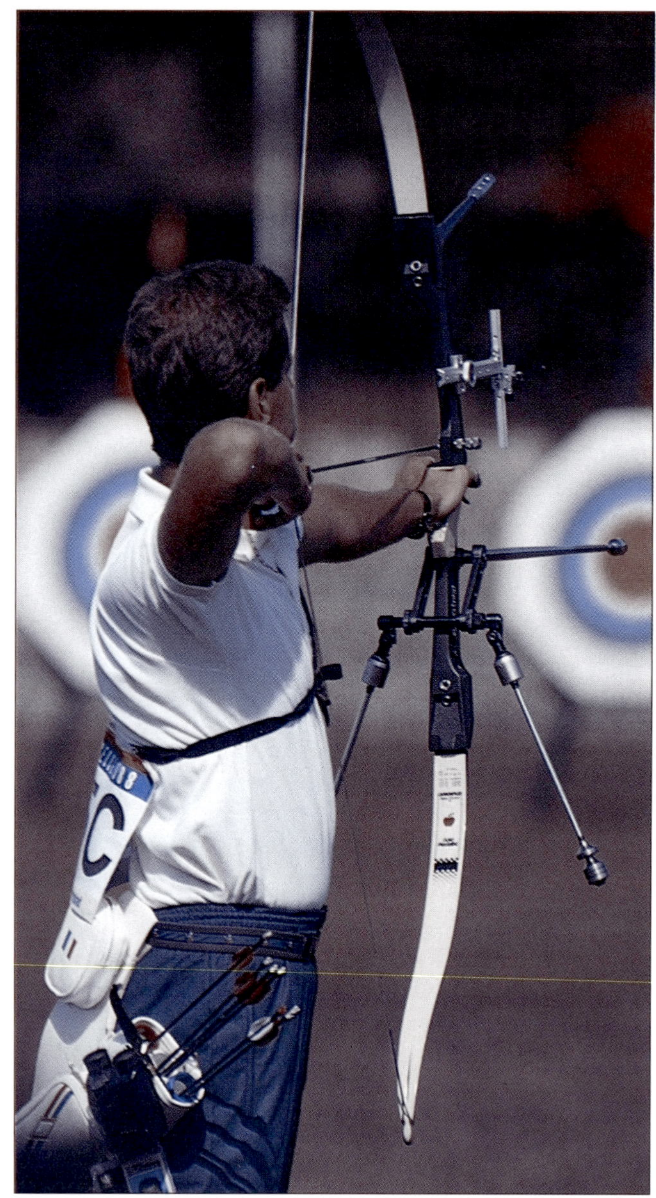

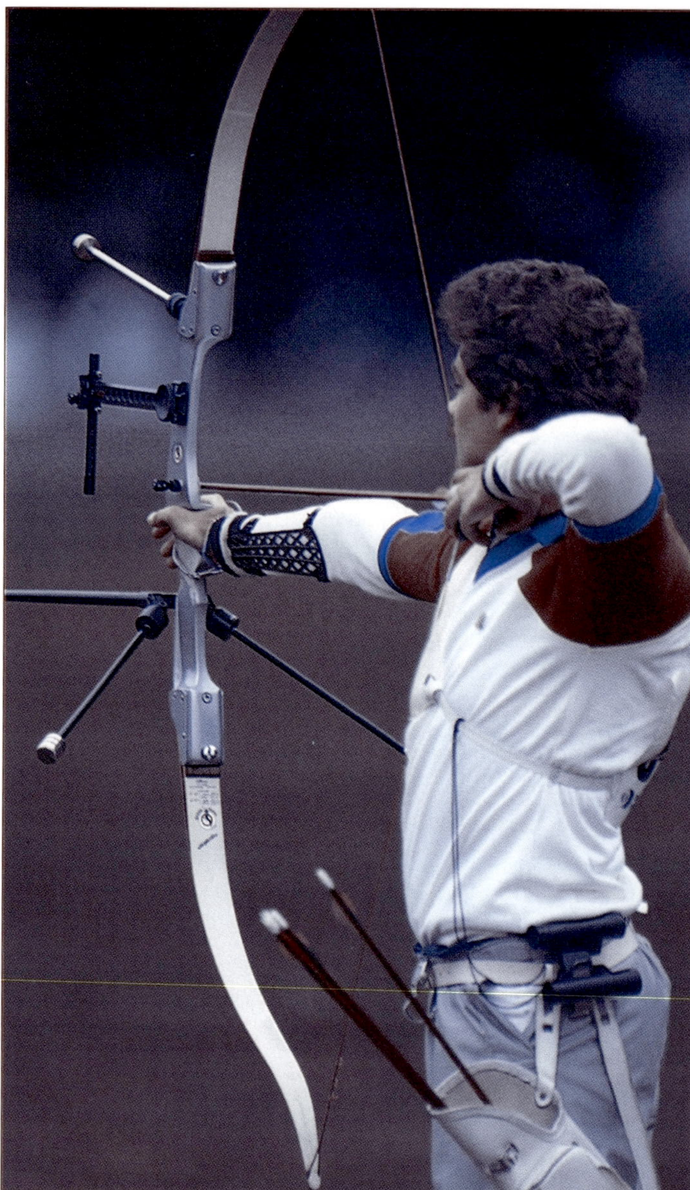

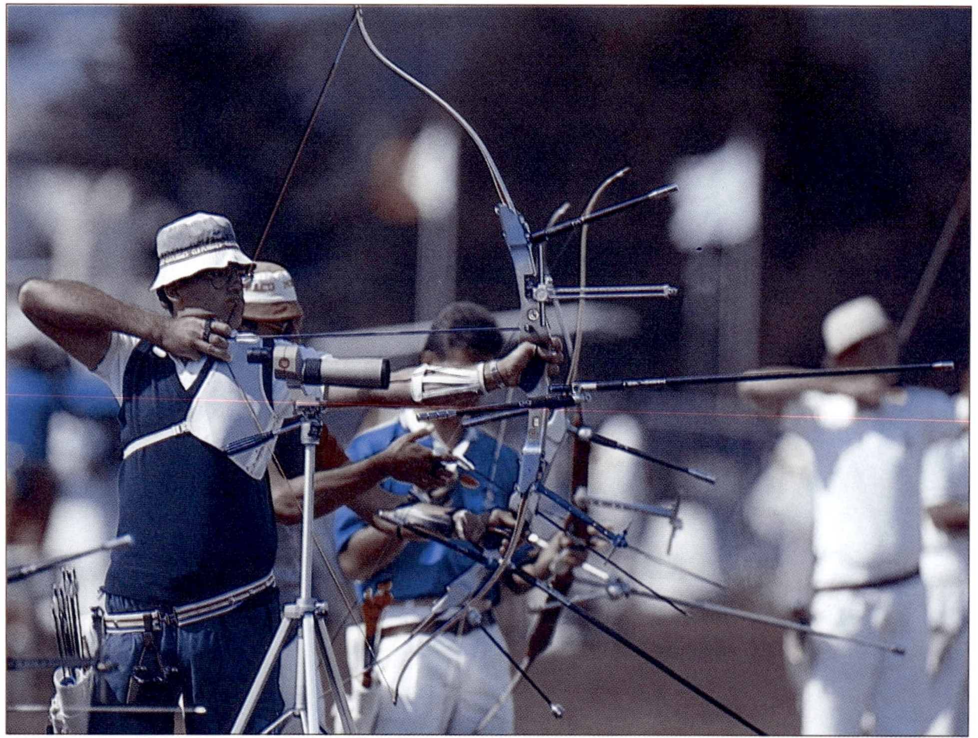

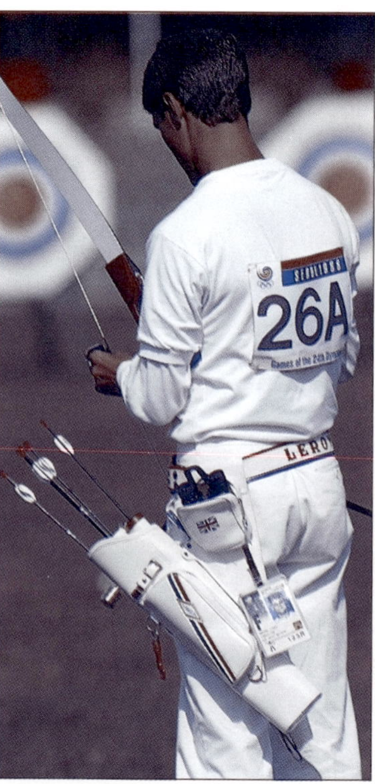

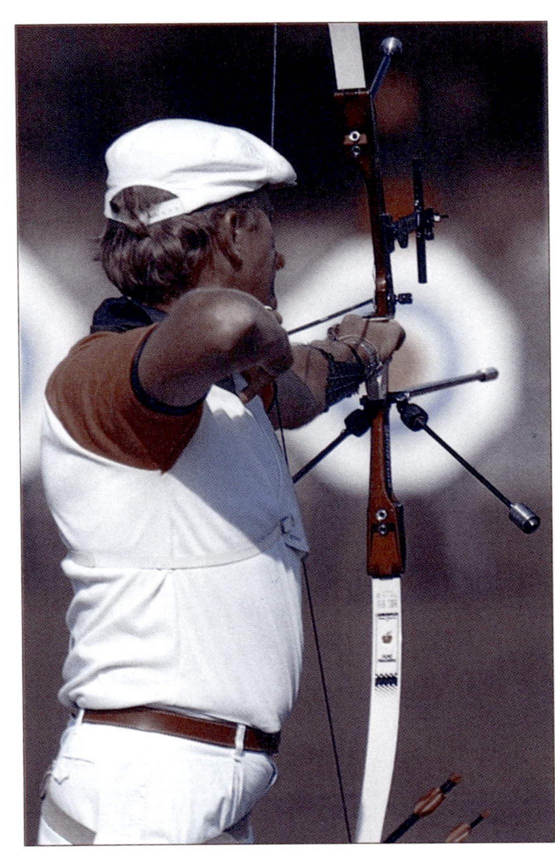

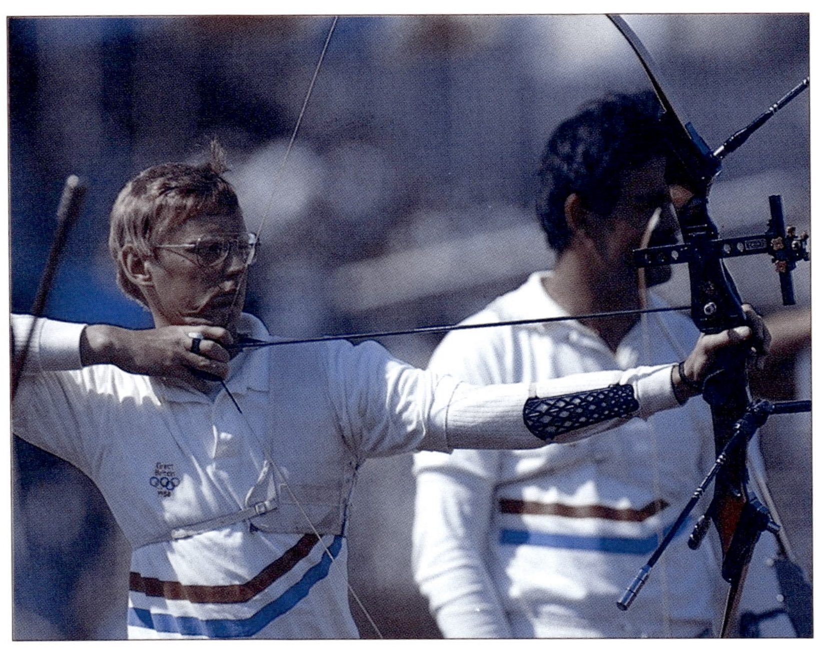

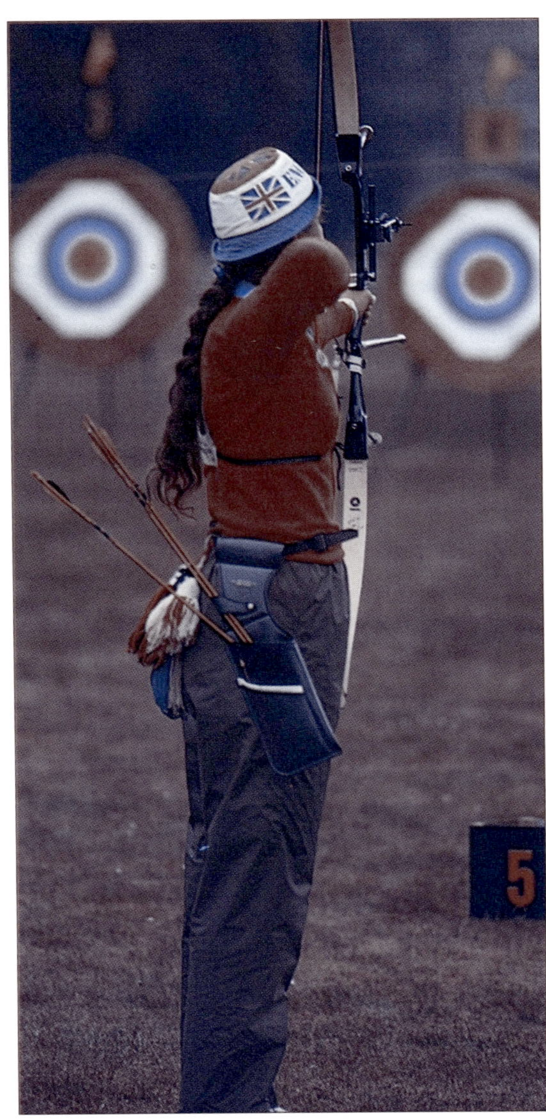
5

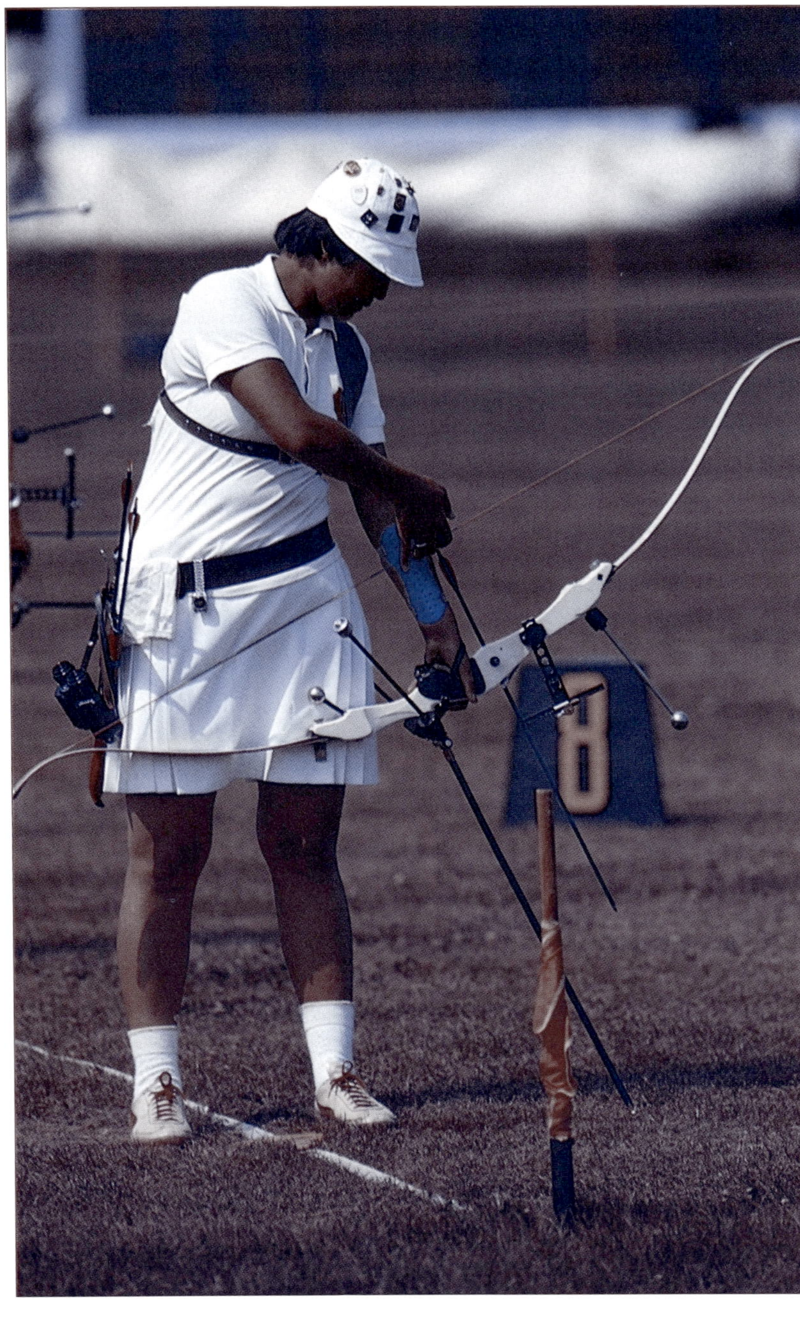
8

Diving – male

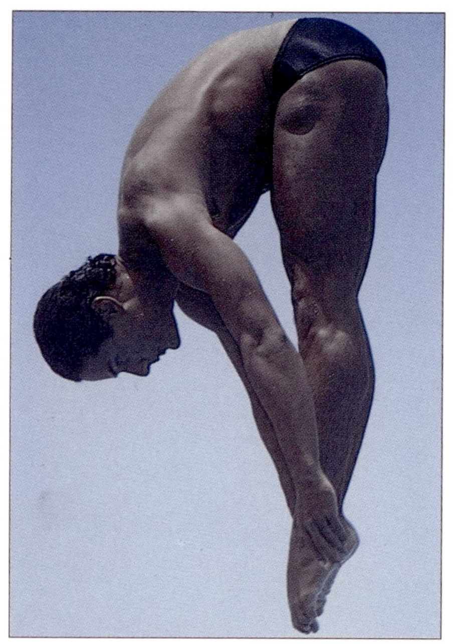
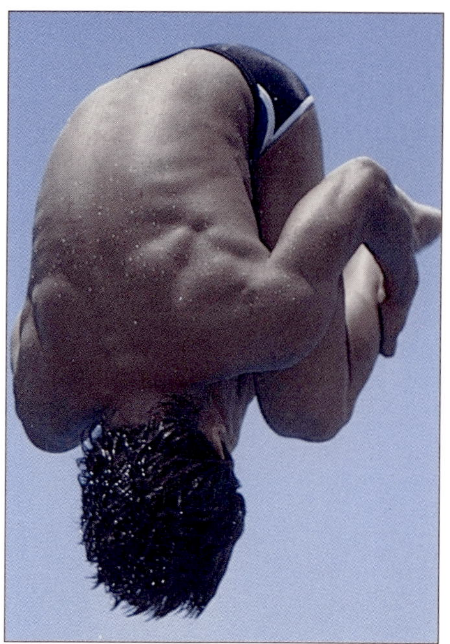
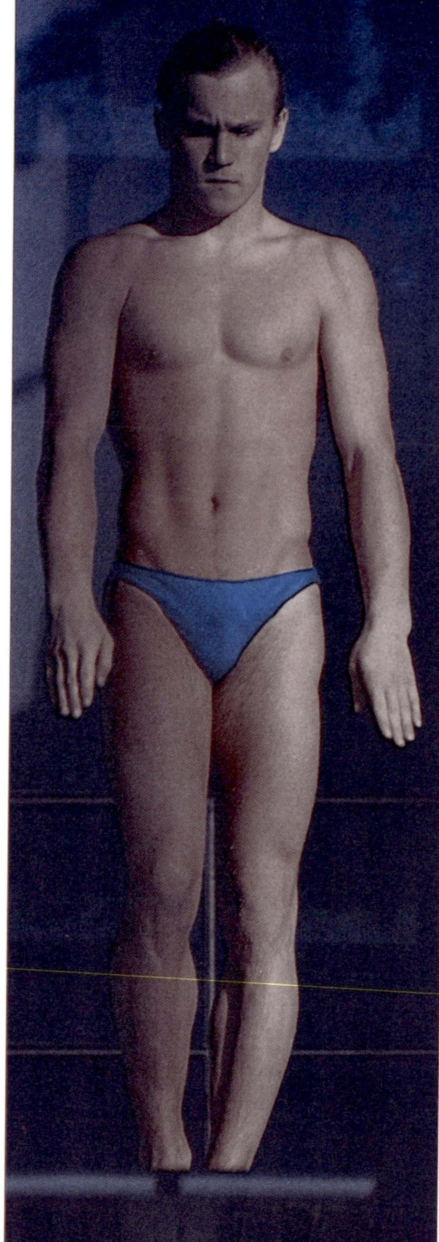
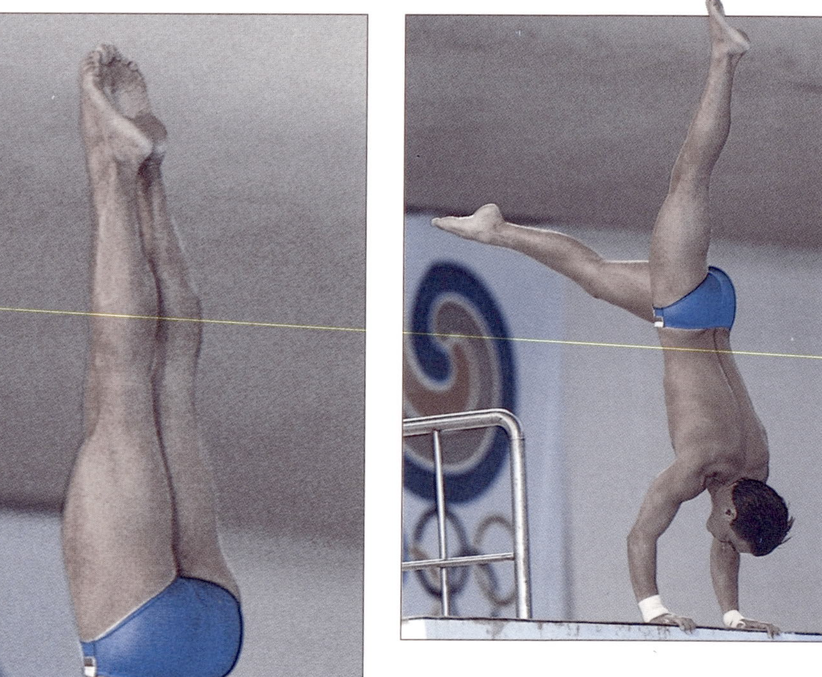
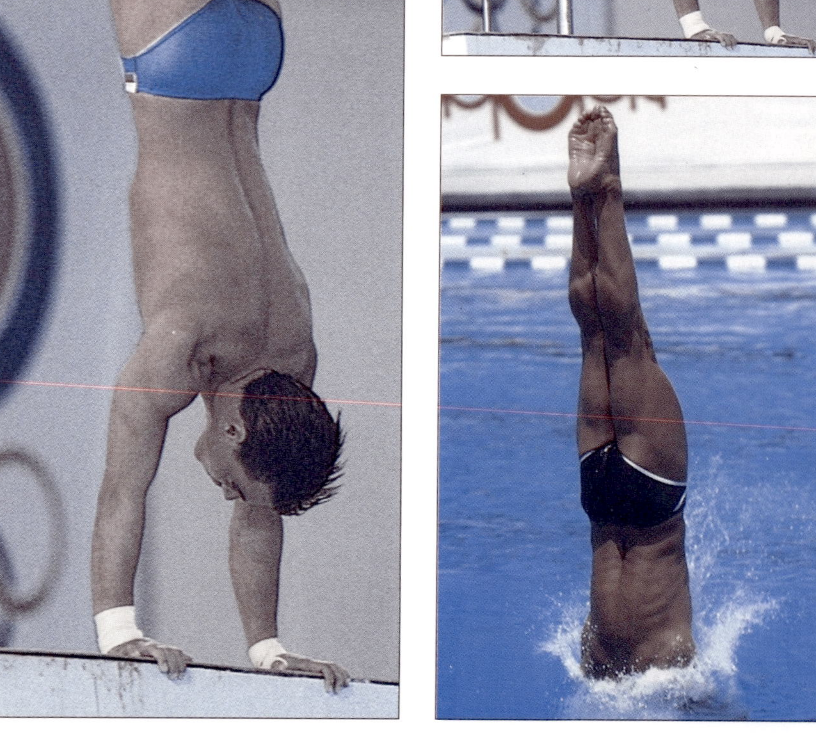
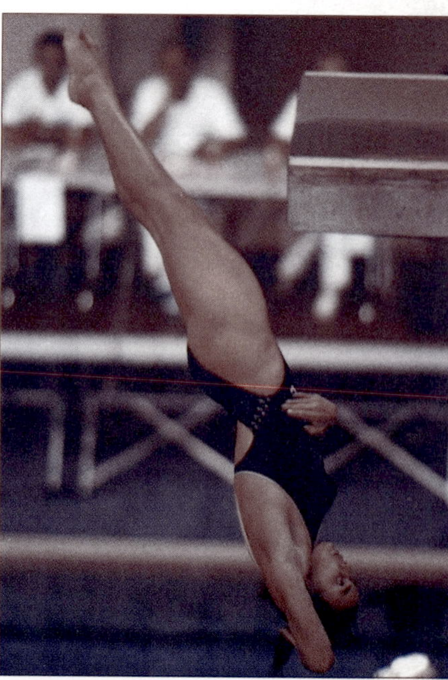

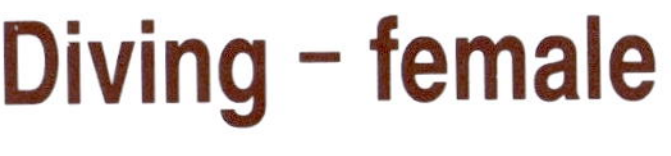

Diving – female

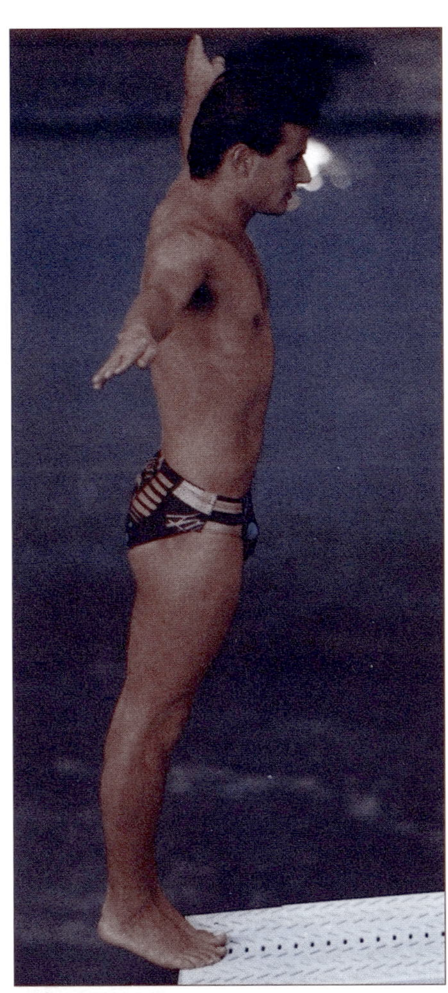

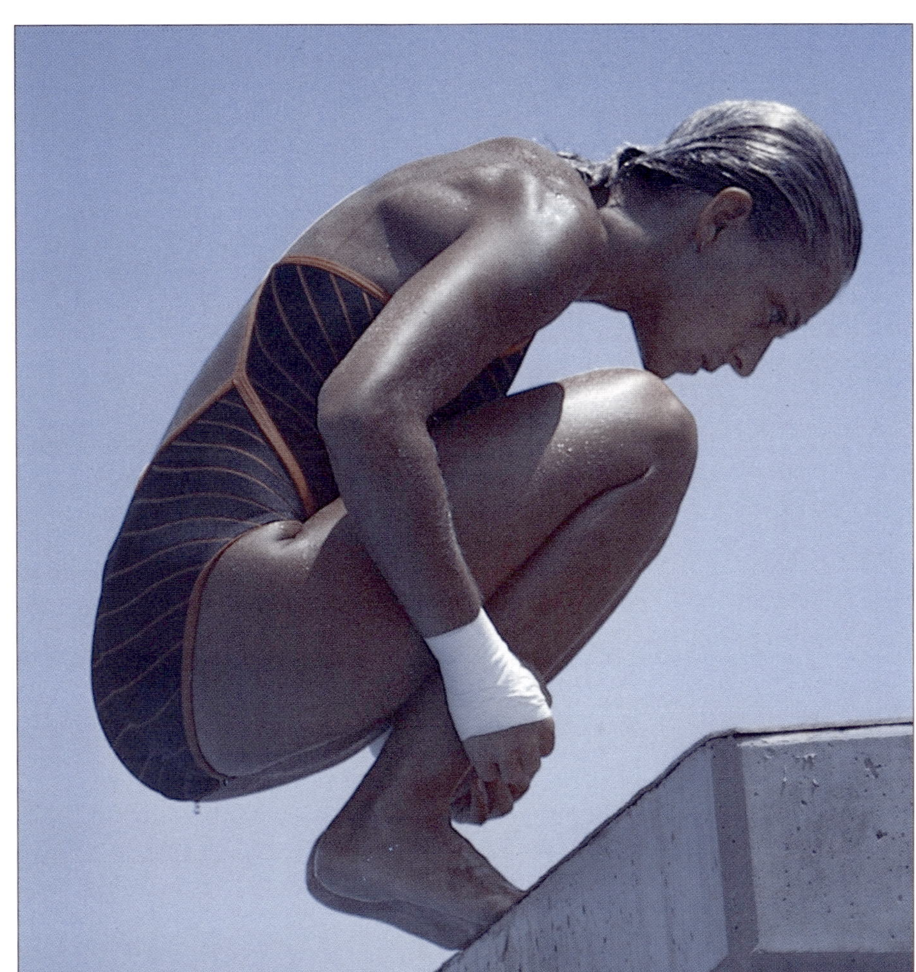

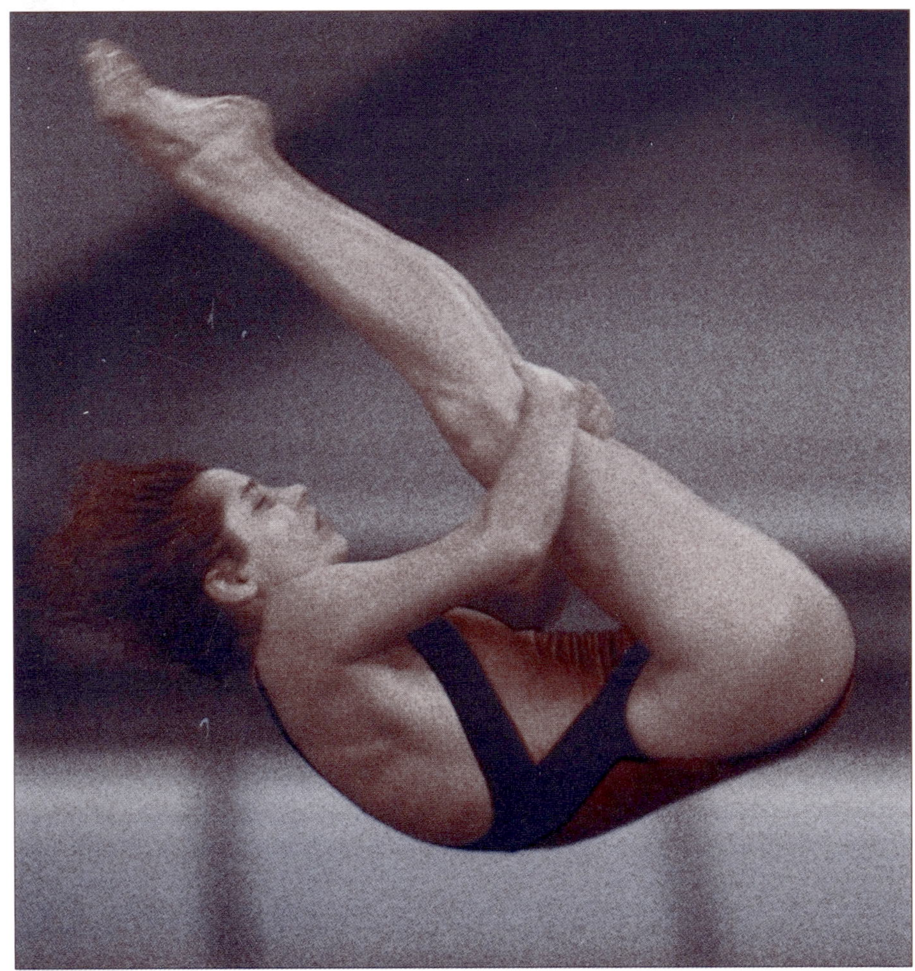

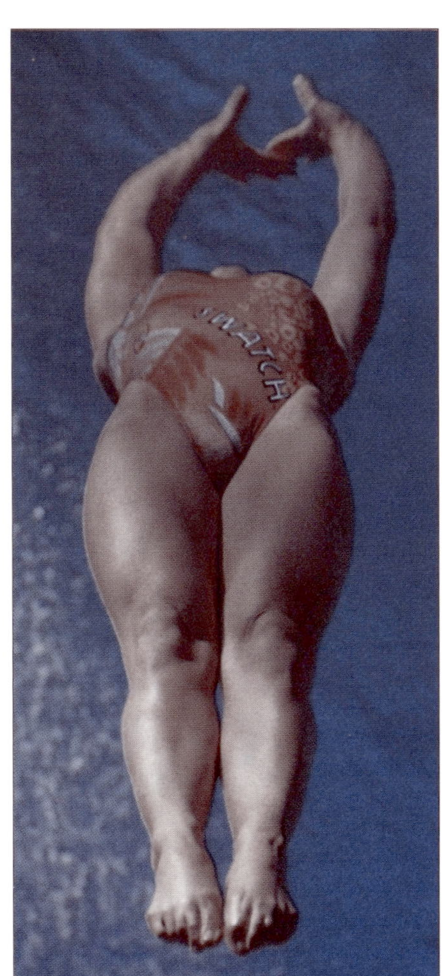

Swimming – male

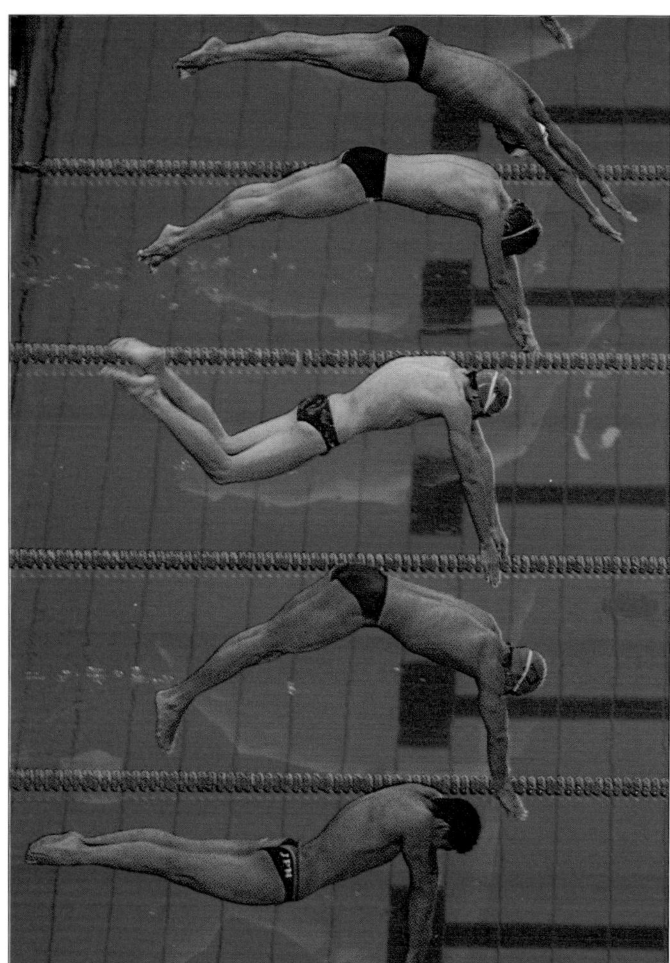

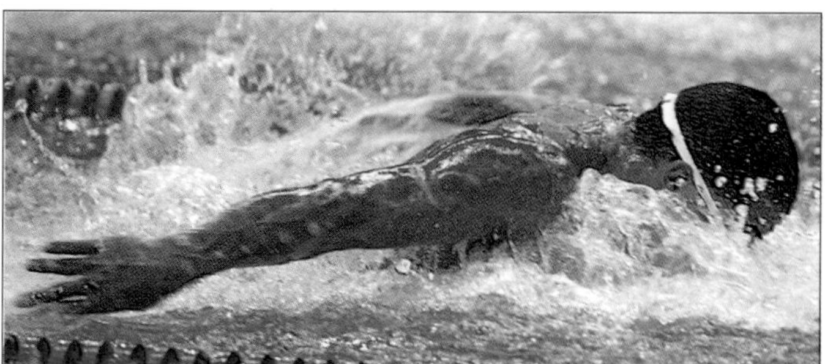

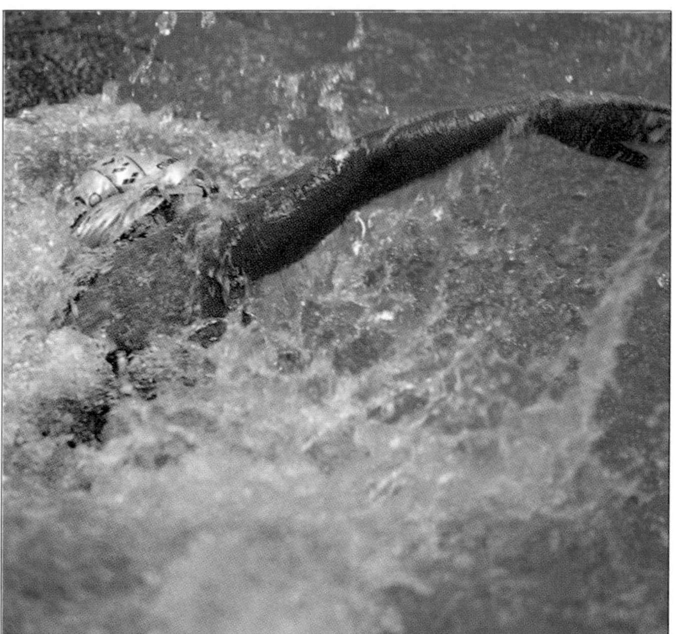

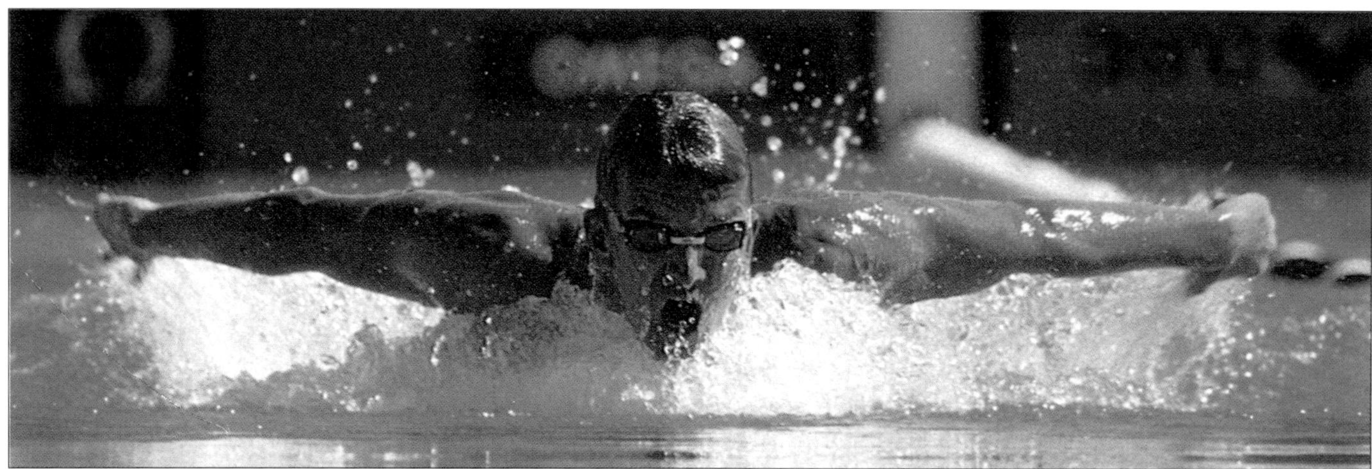

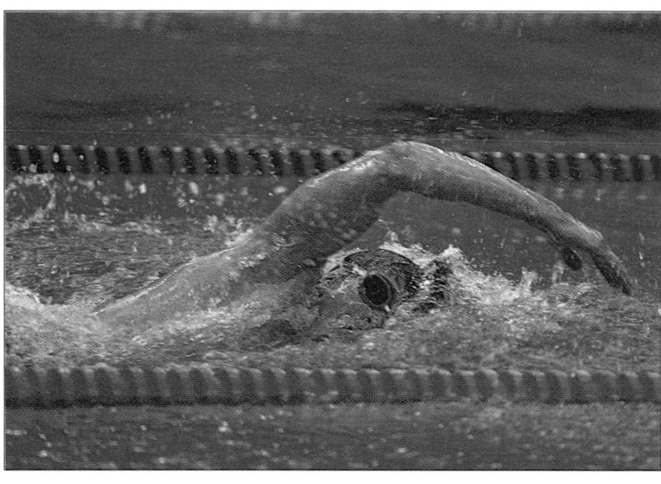

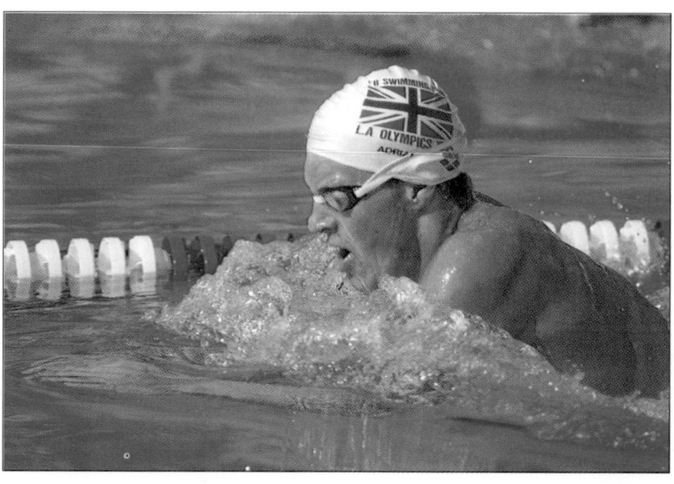

Swimming – female

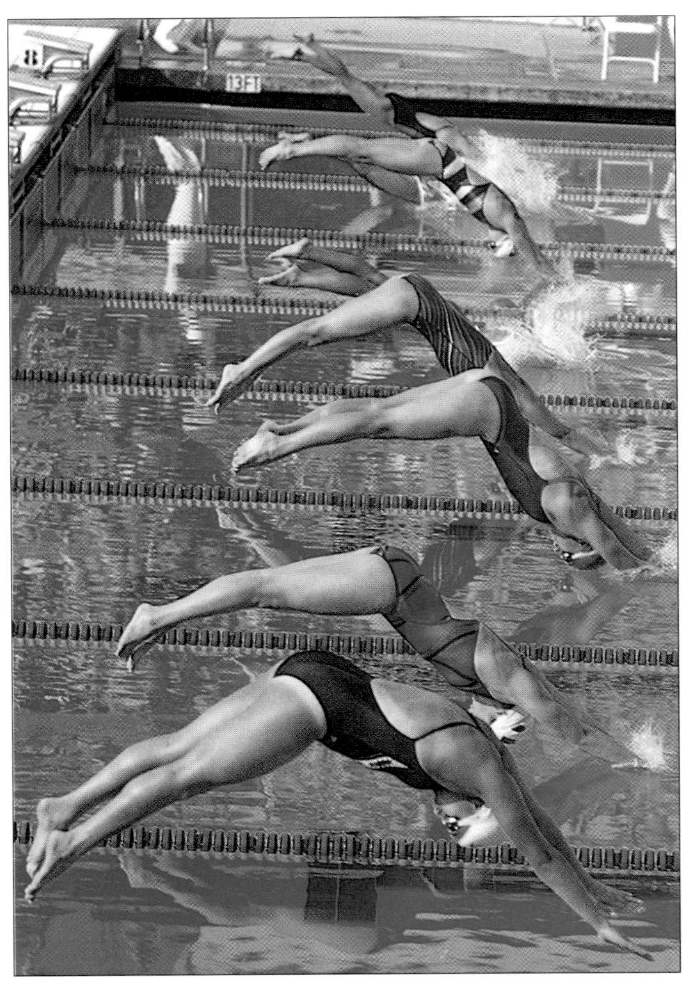

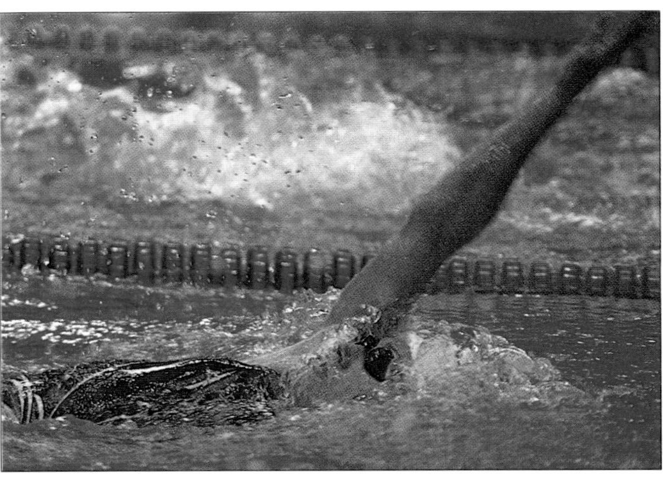

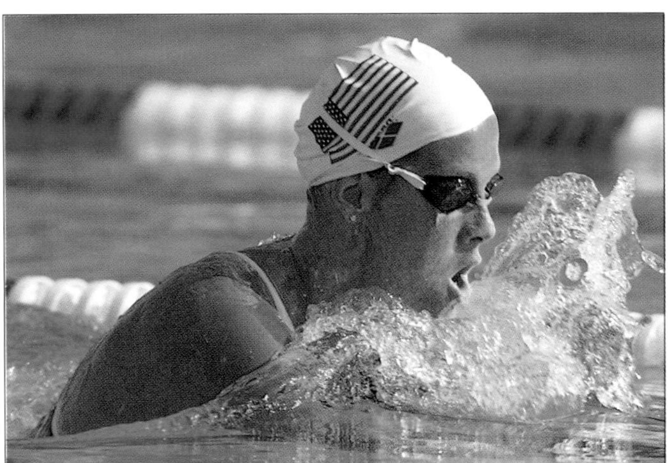

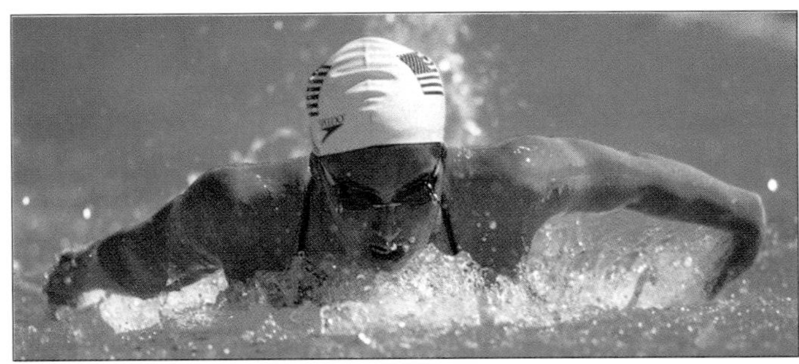

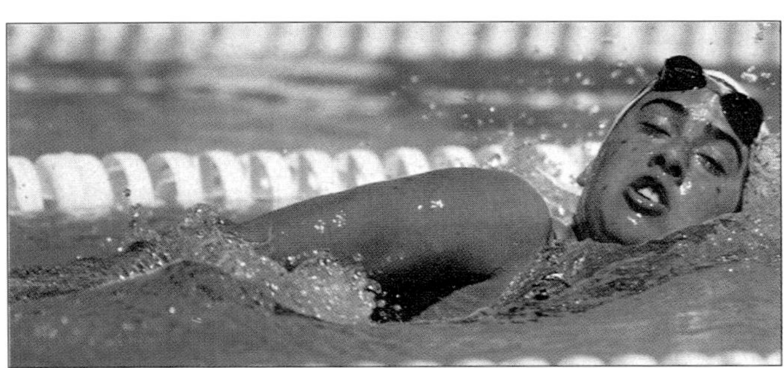

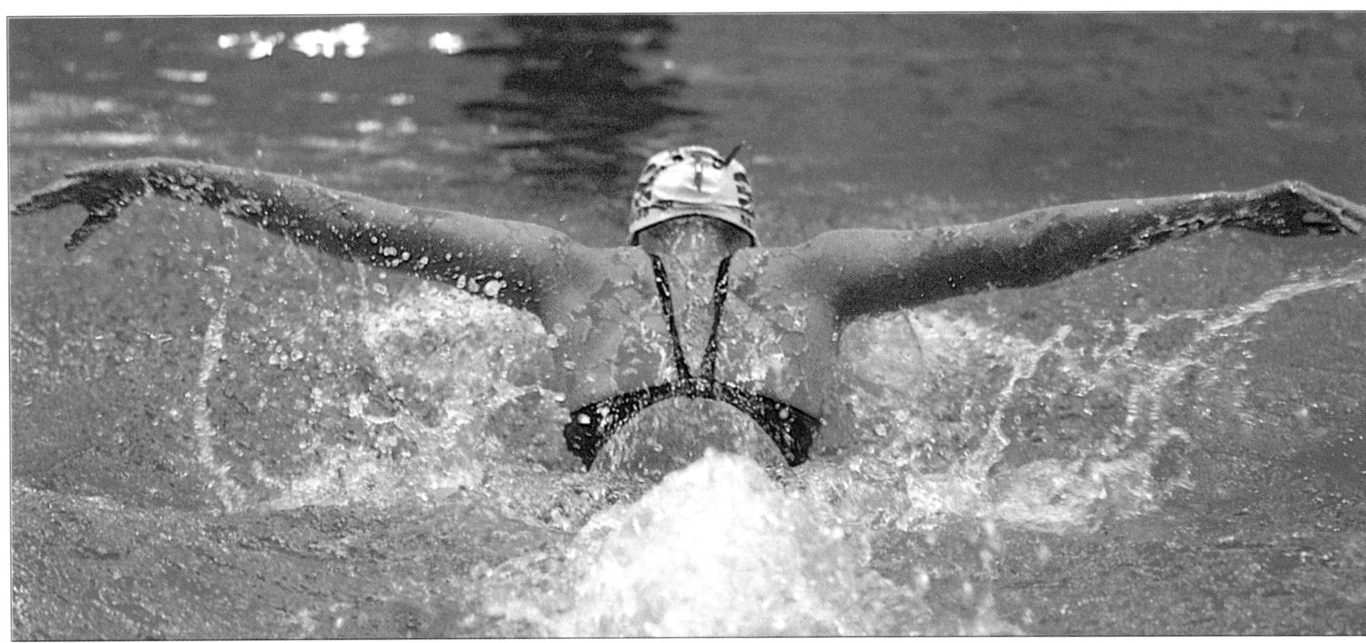

Synchronized swimming

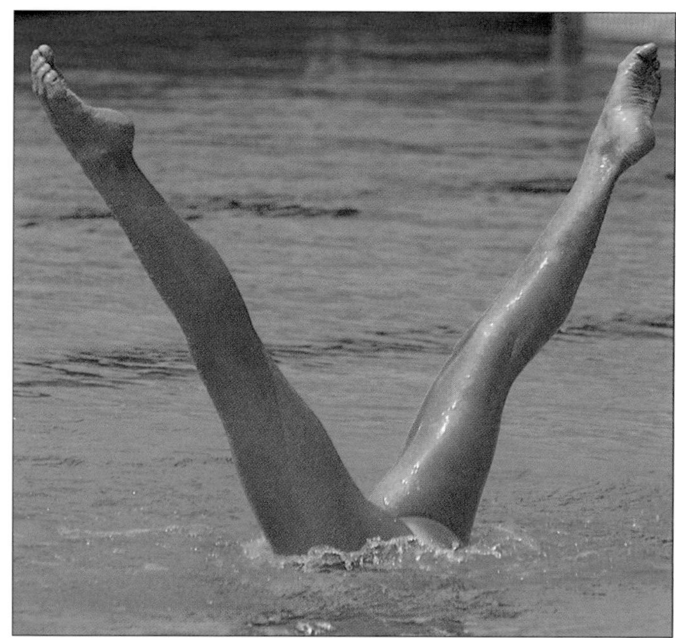

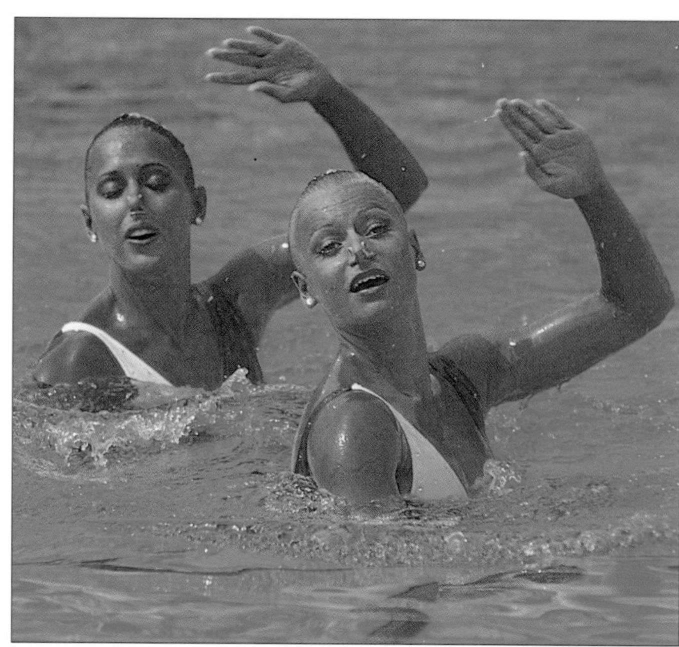

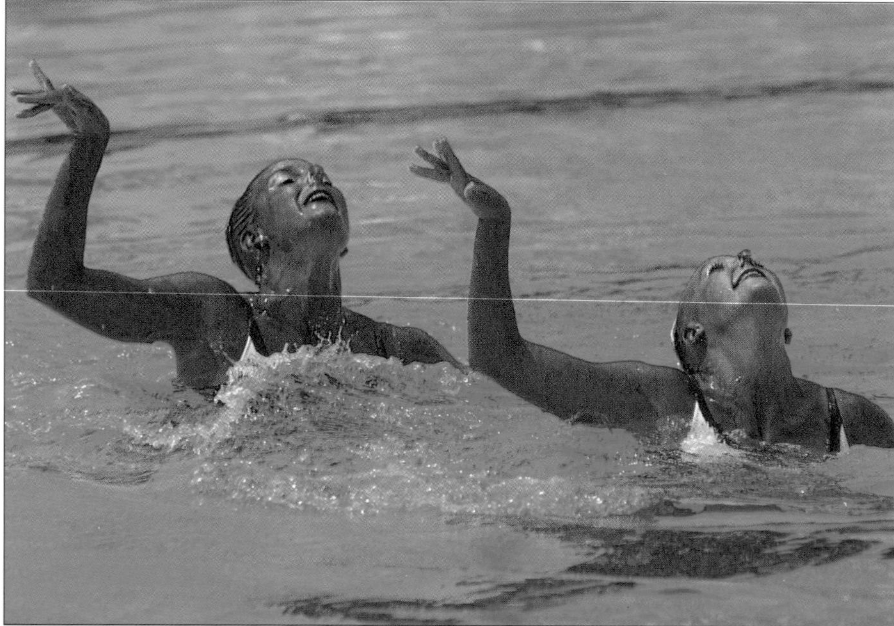

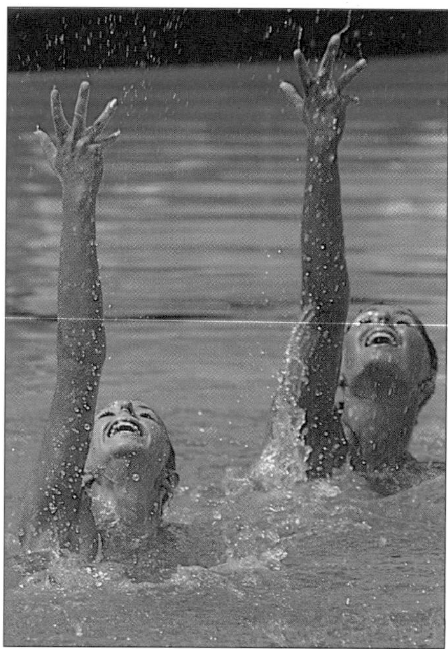

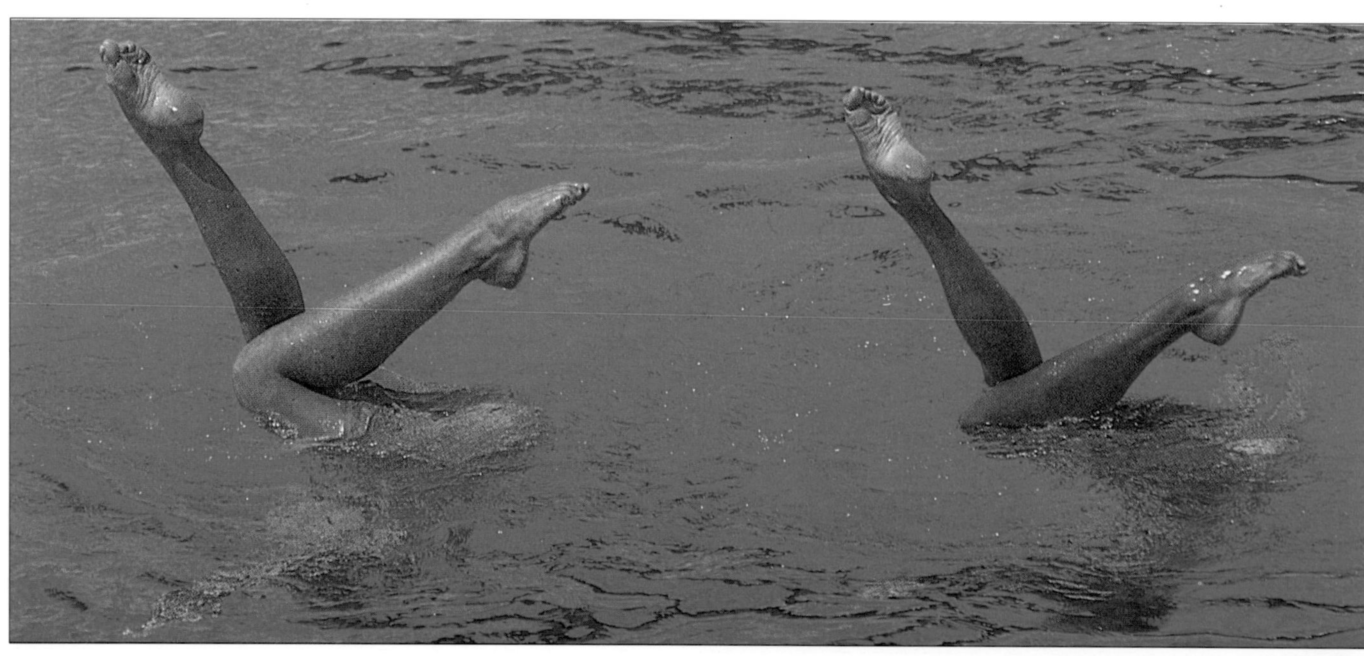

Synchronized swimming

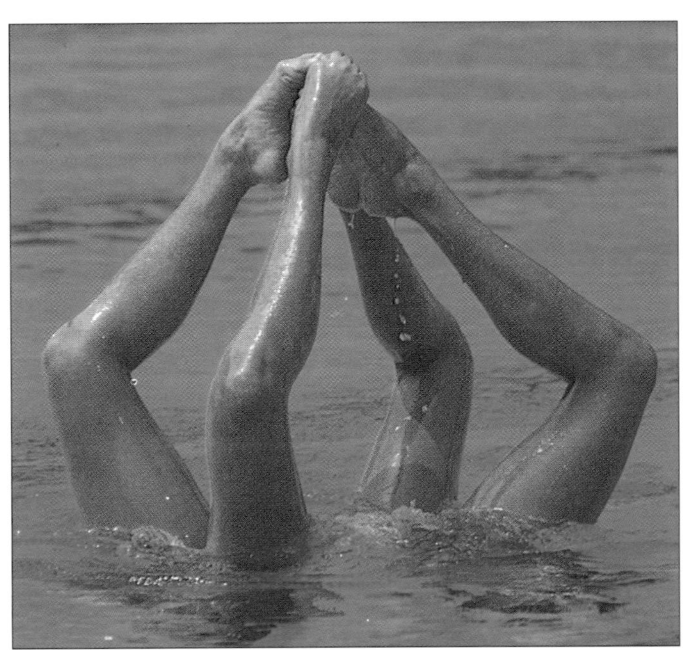

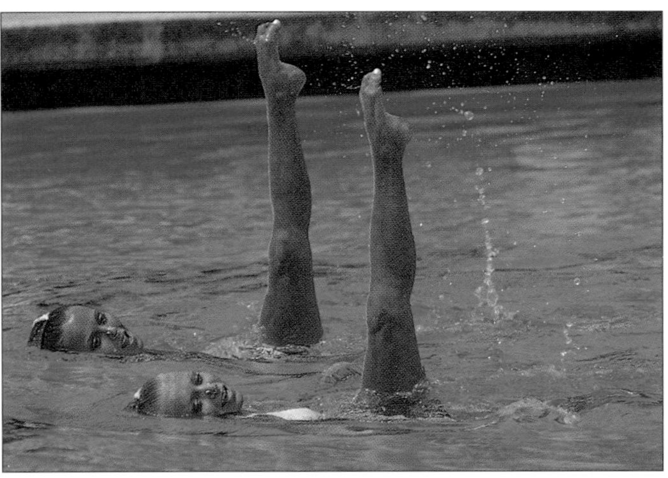

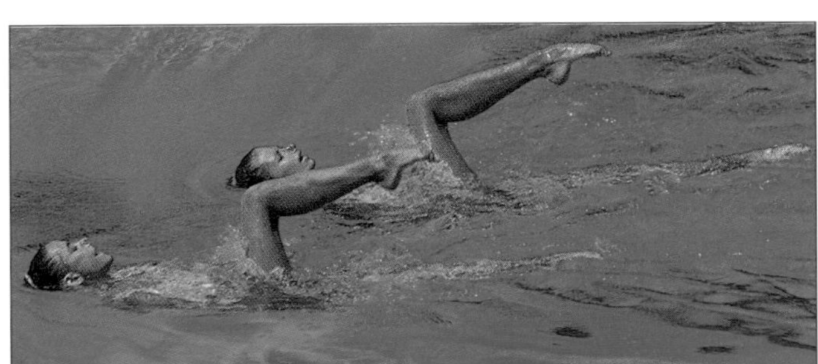

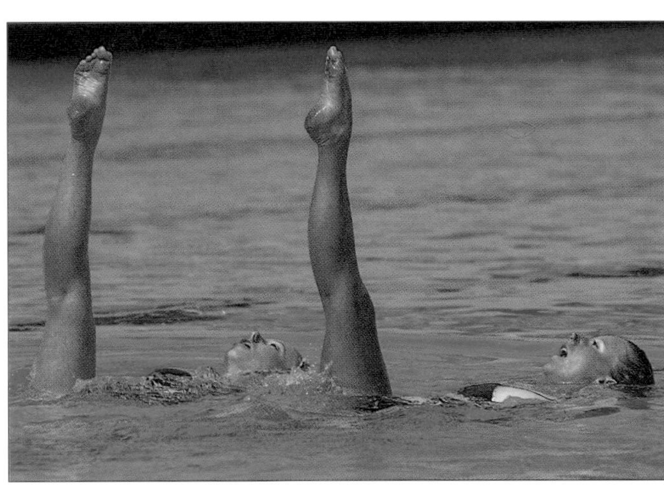

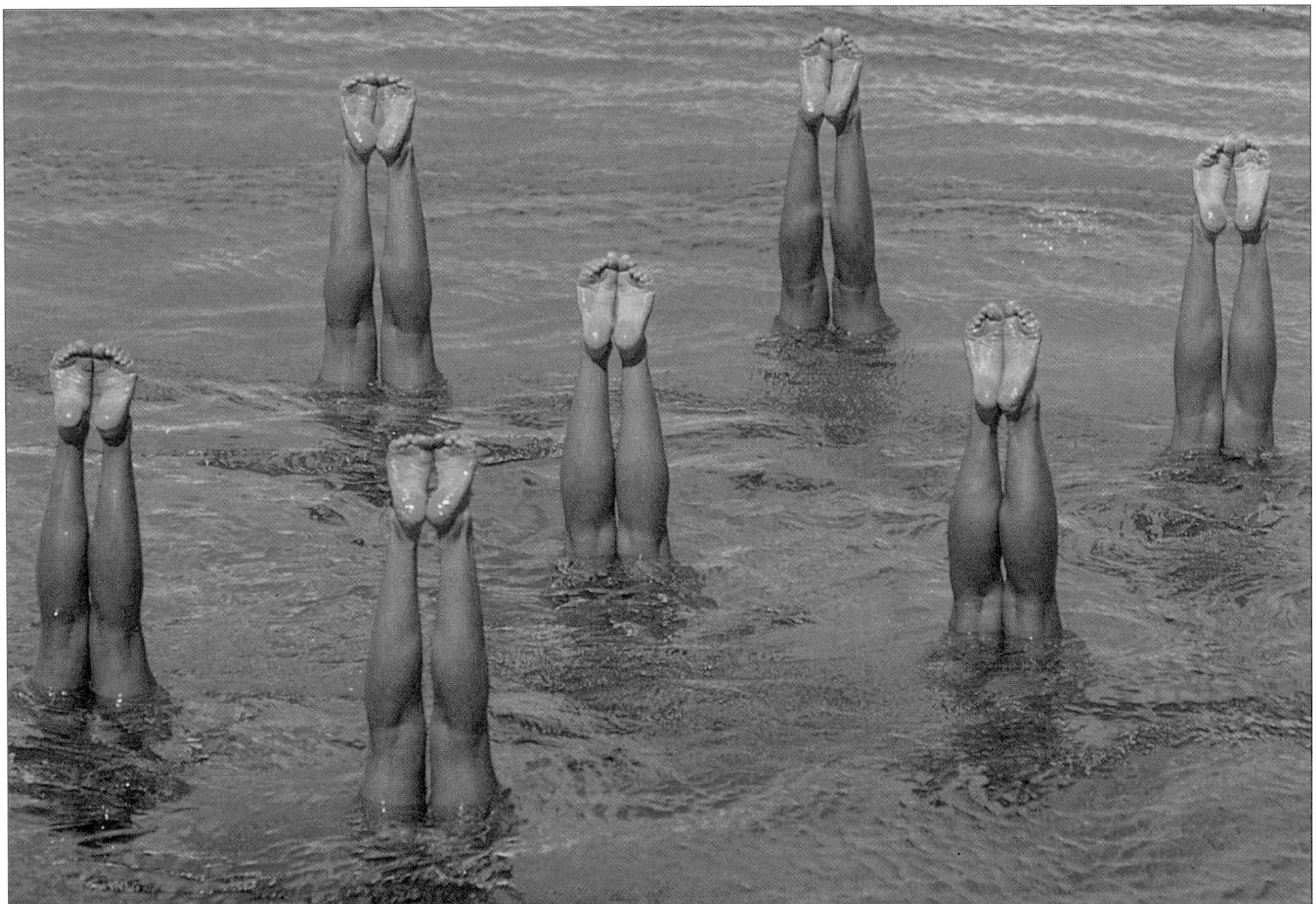

Surfing

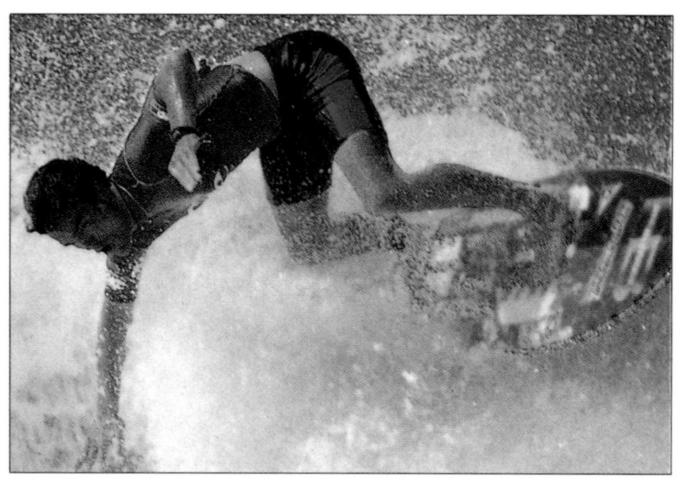

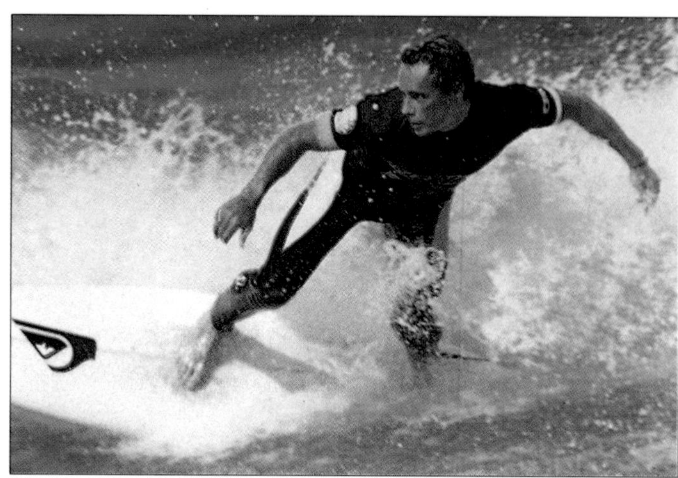

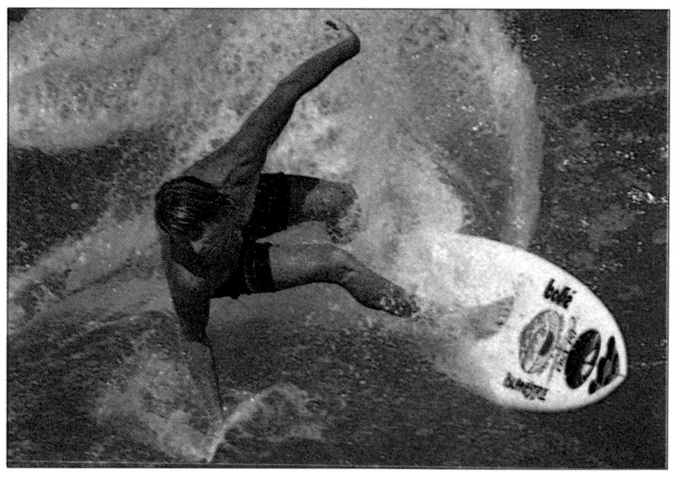

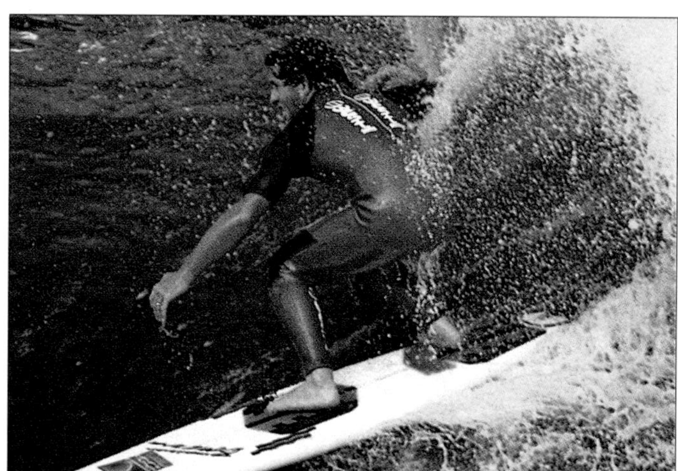

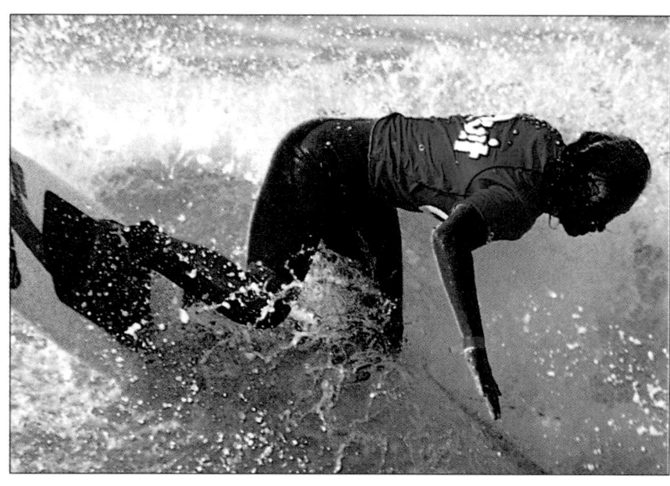

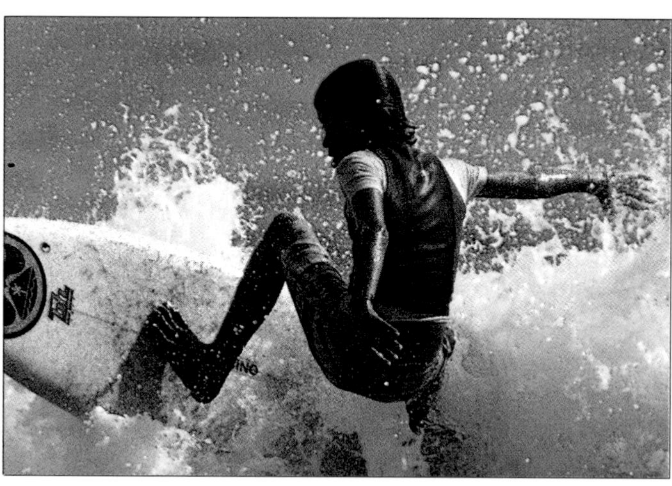

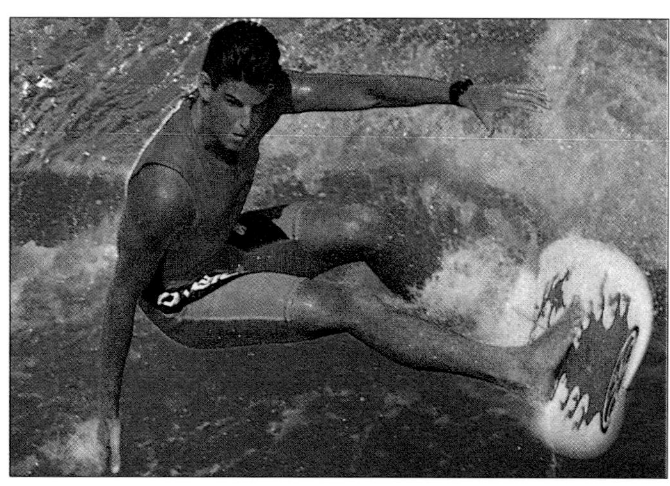

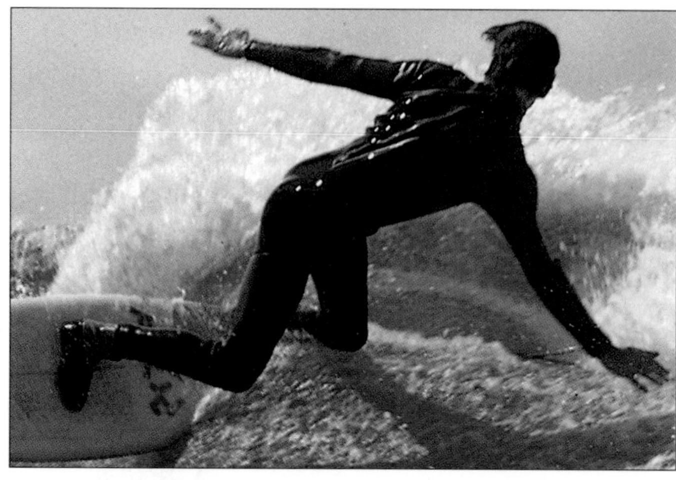

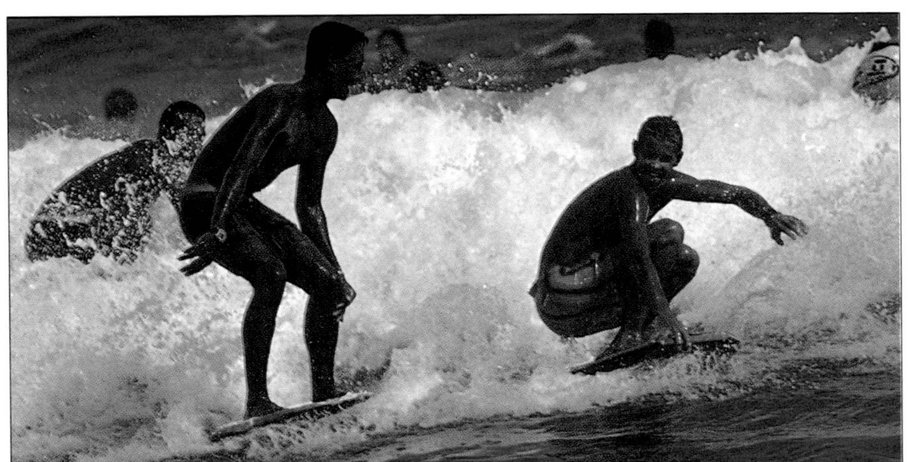
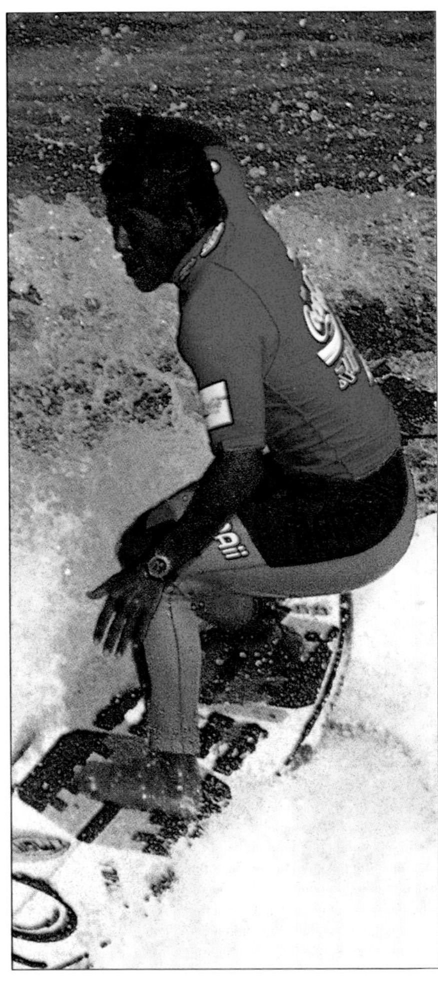
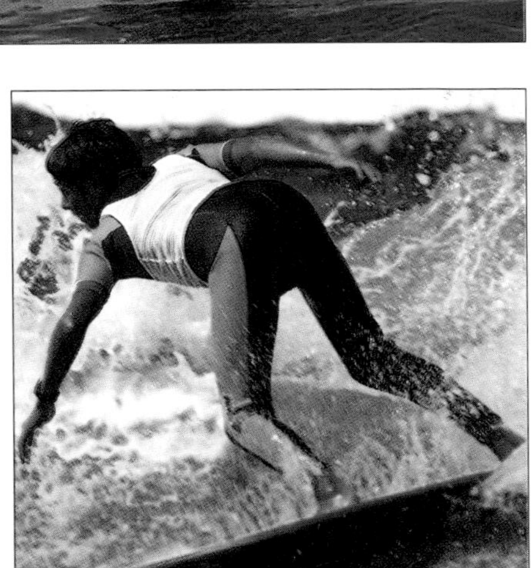
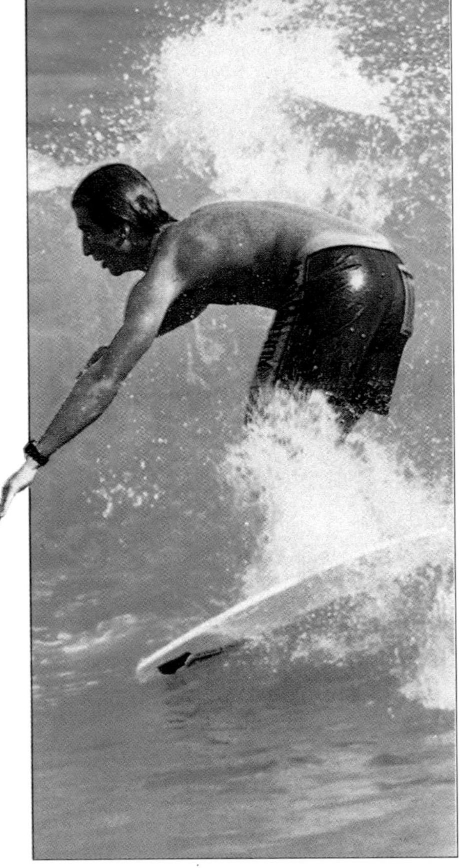
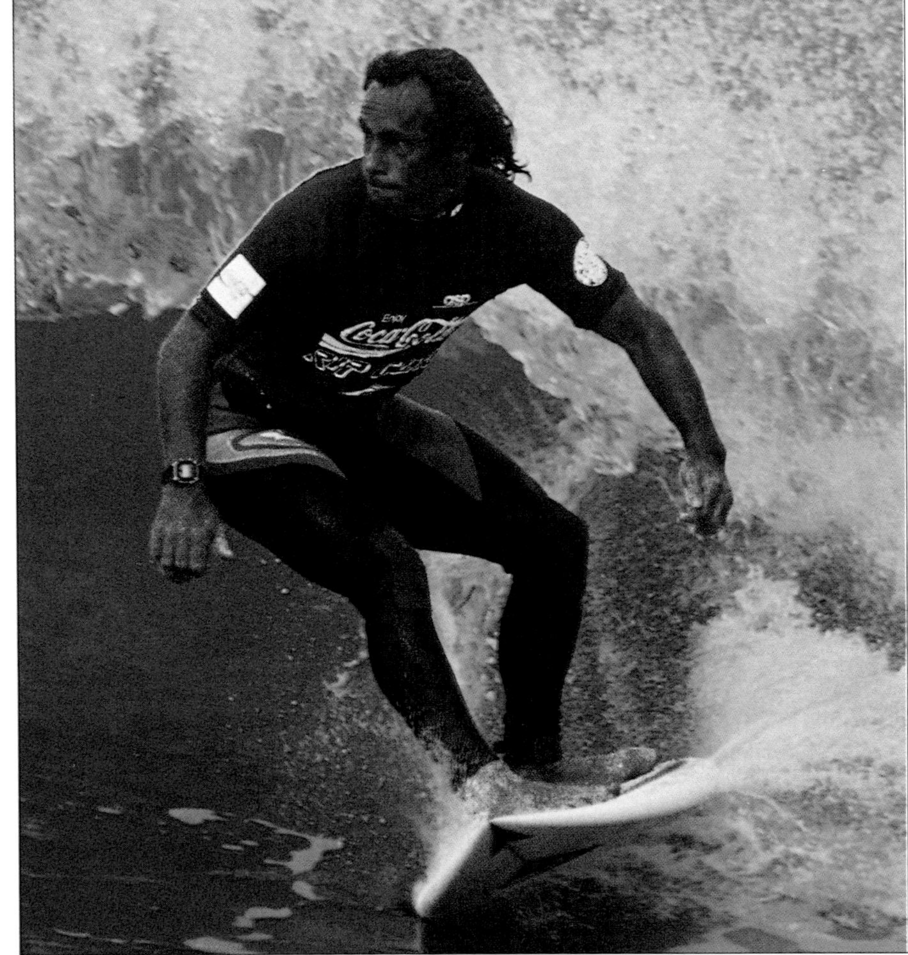
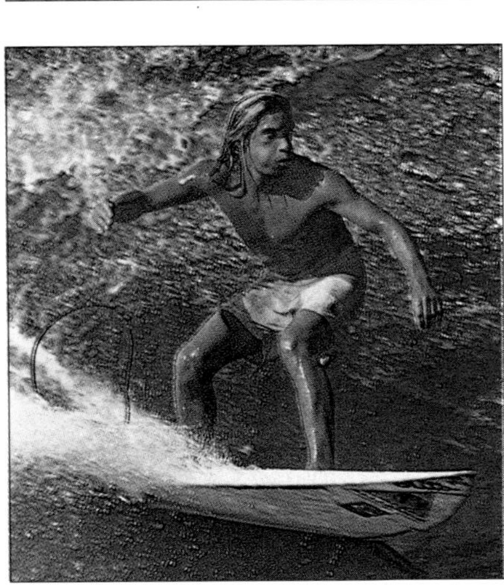

Windsurfing

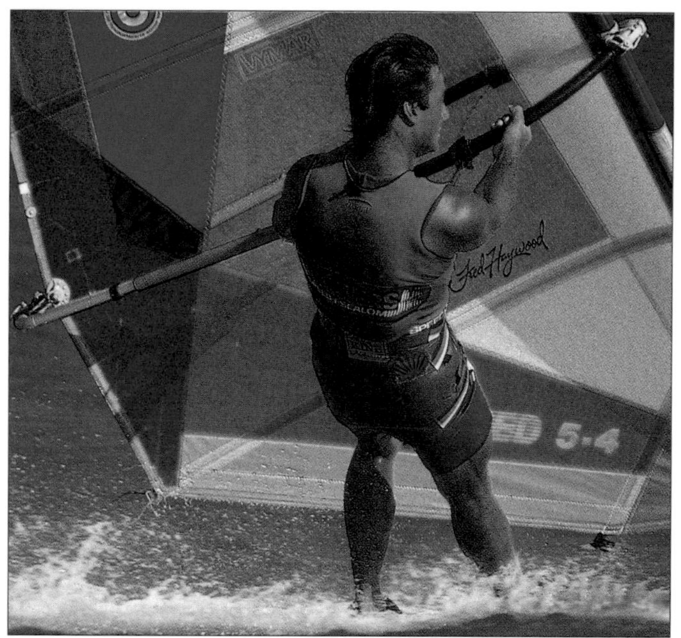

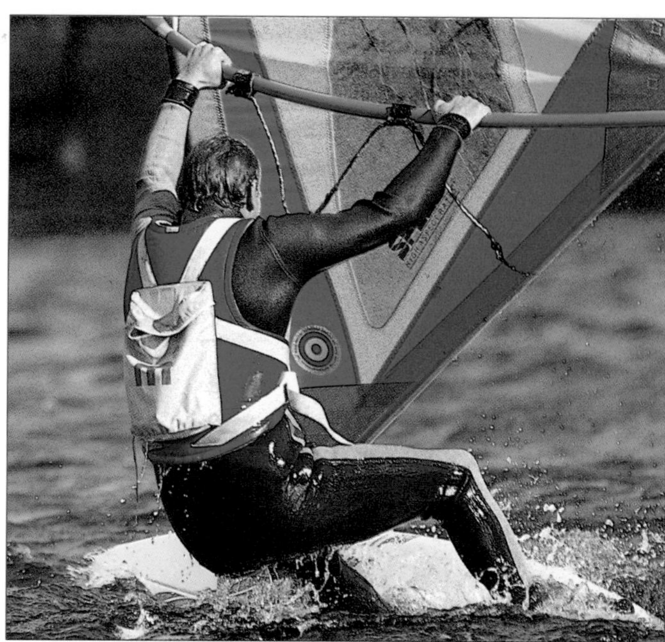

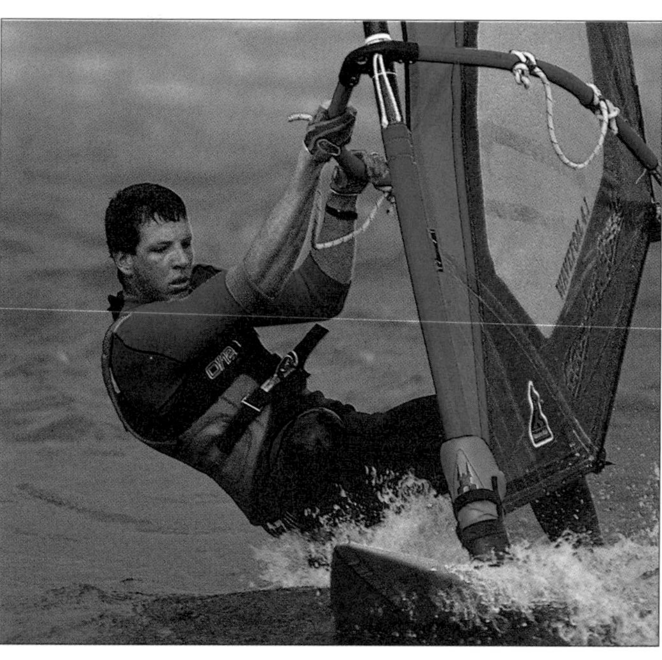

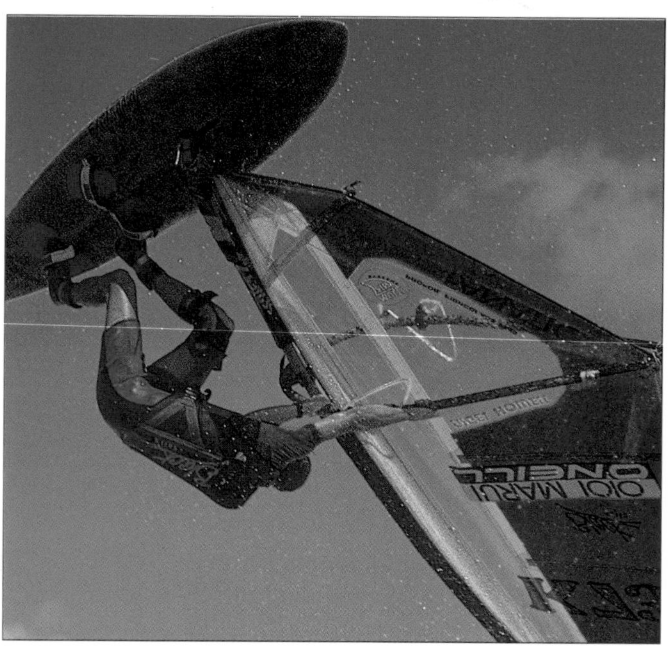

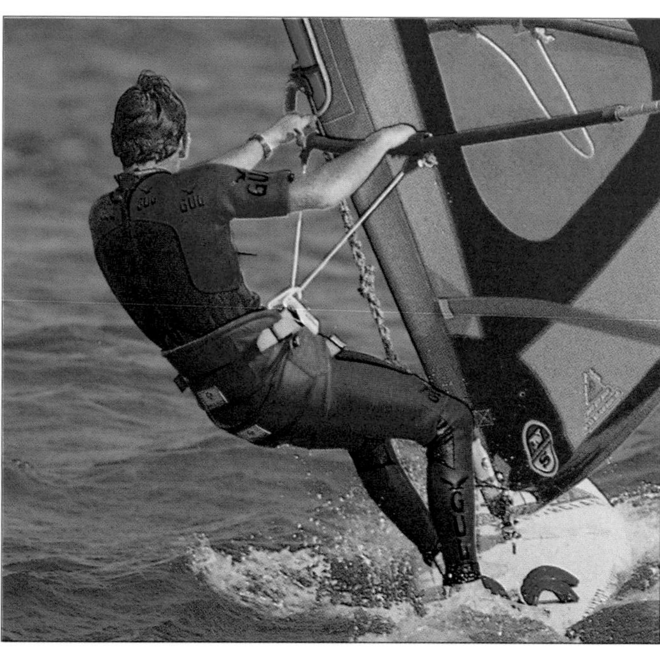

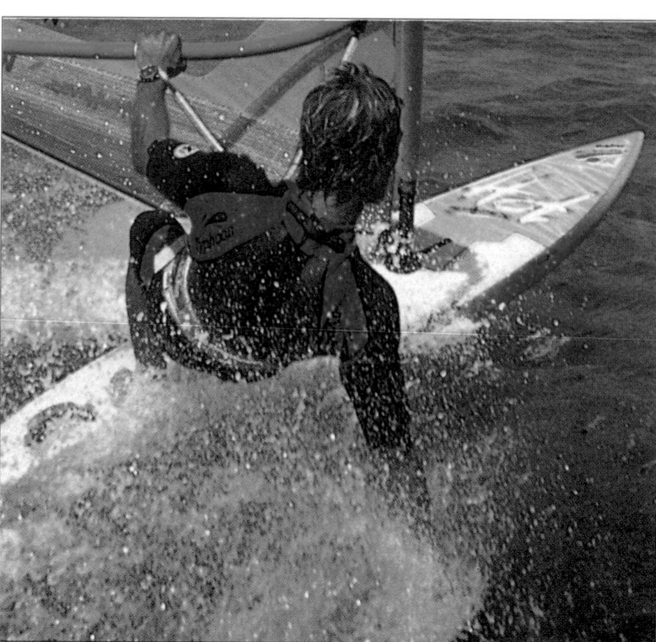

Windsurfing

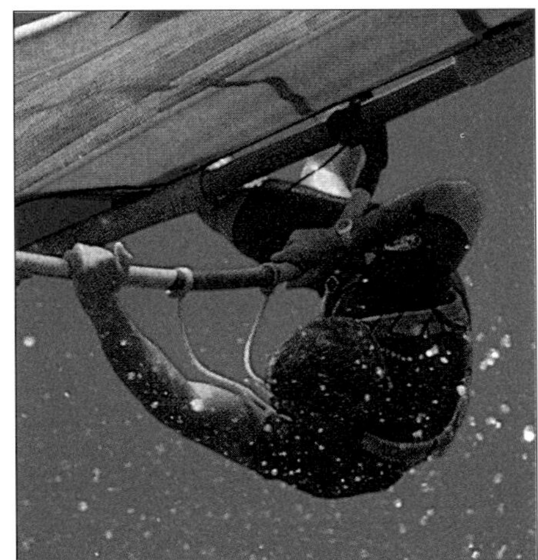

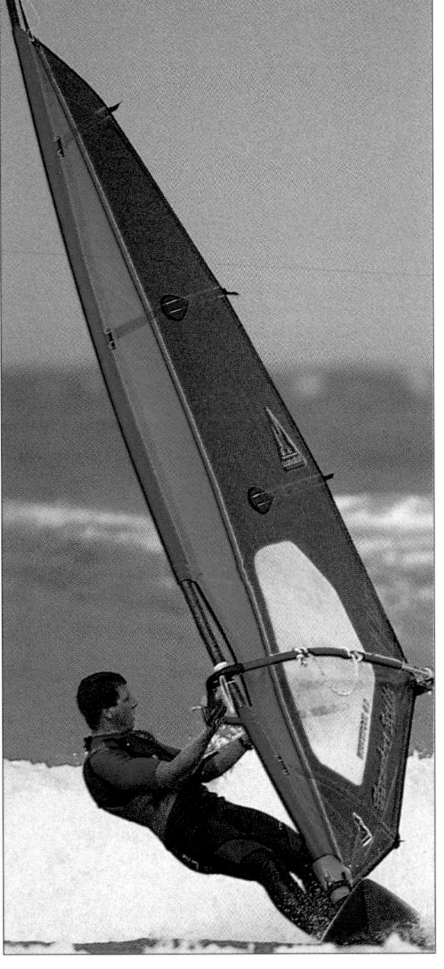

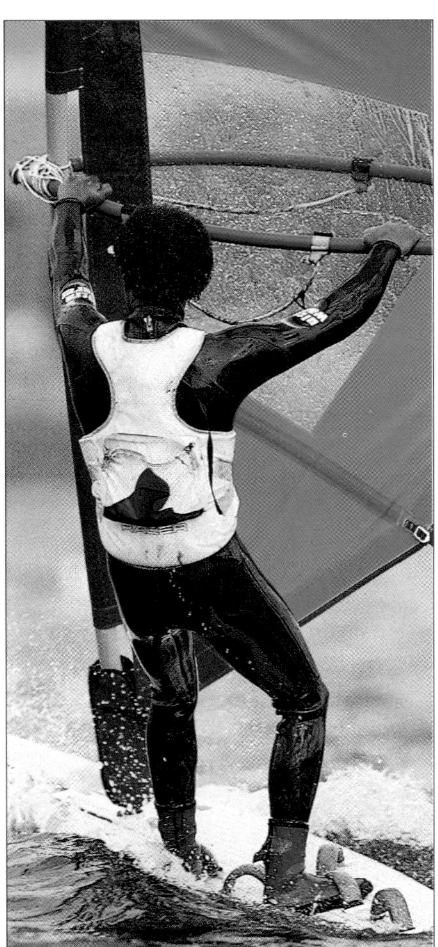

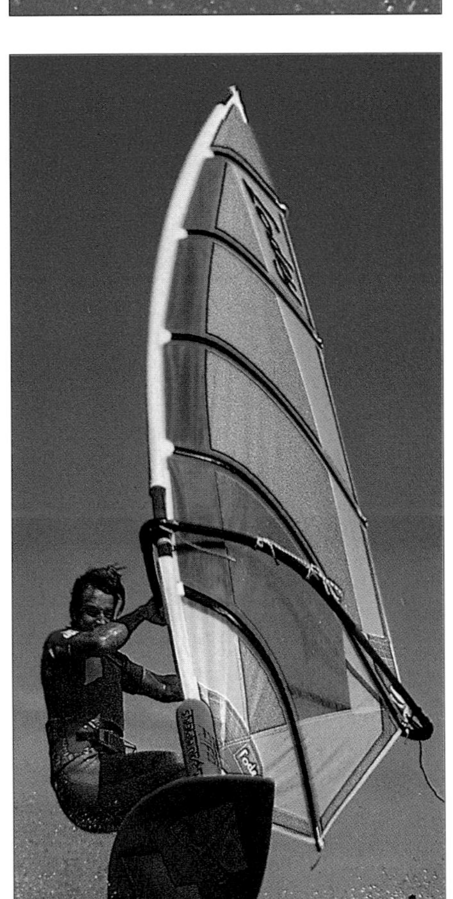

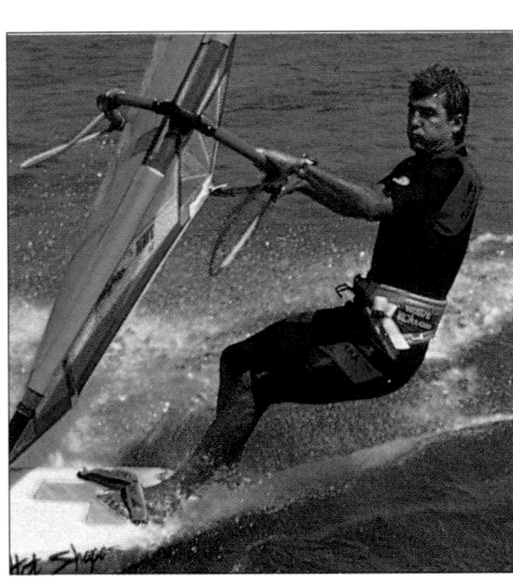

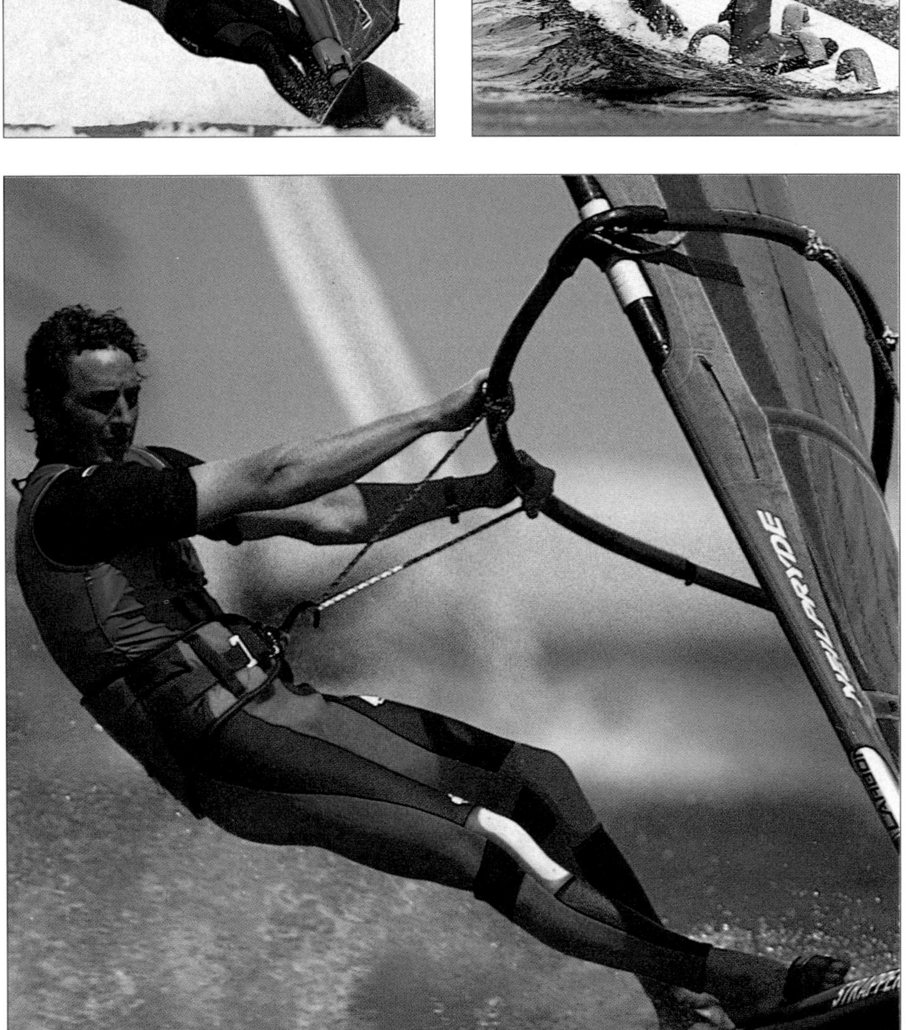

Water skiing – male

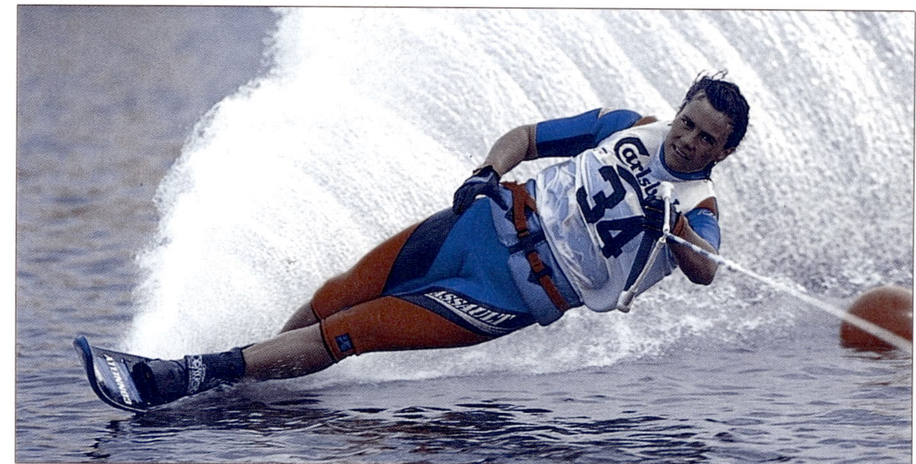
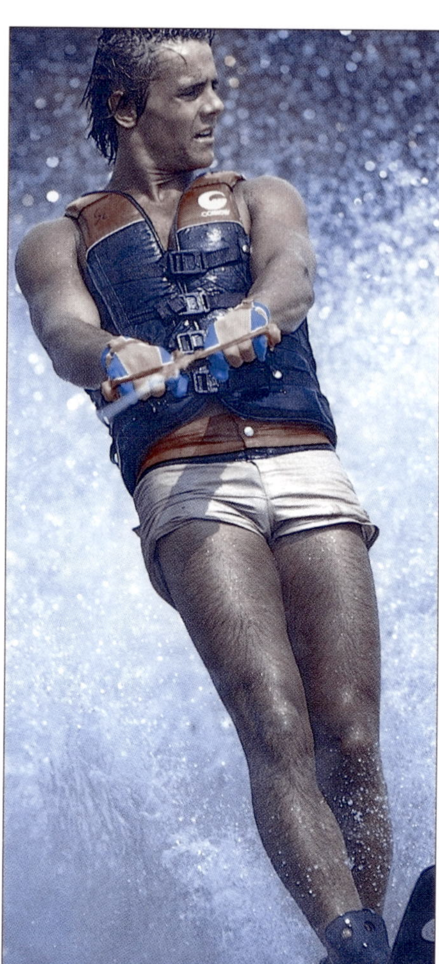
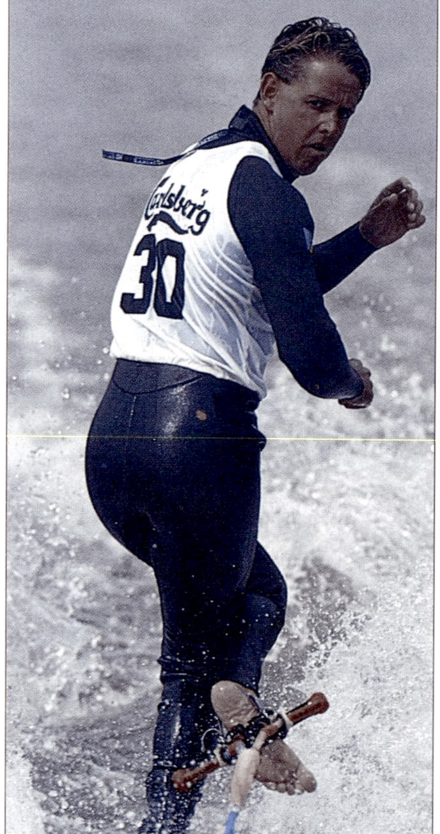
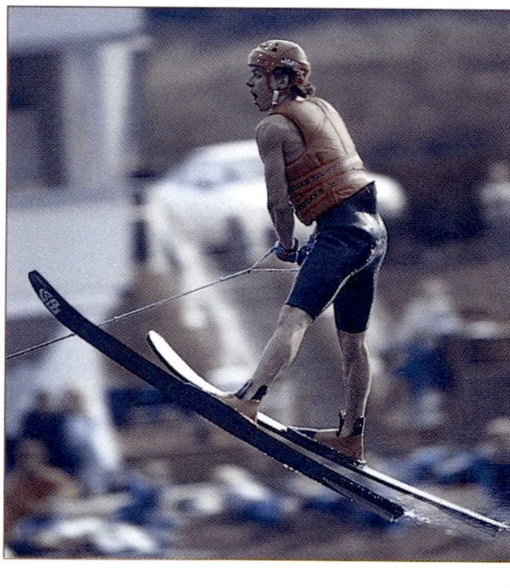
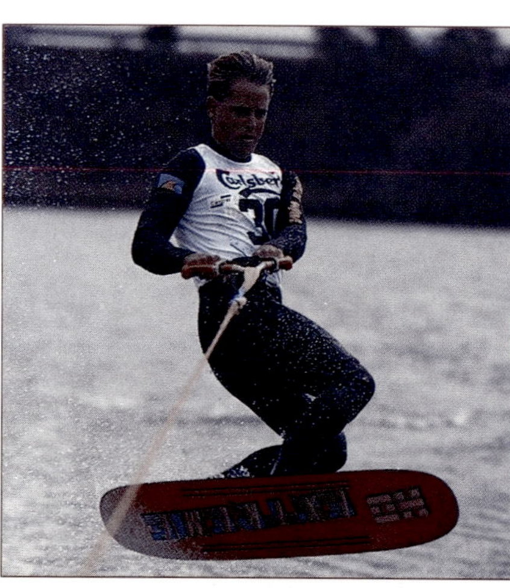
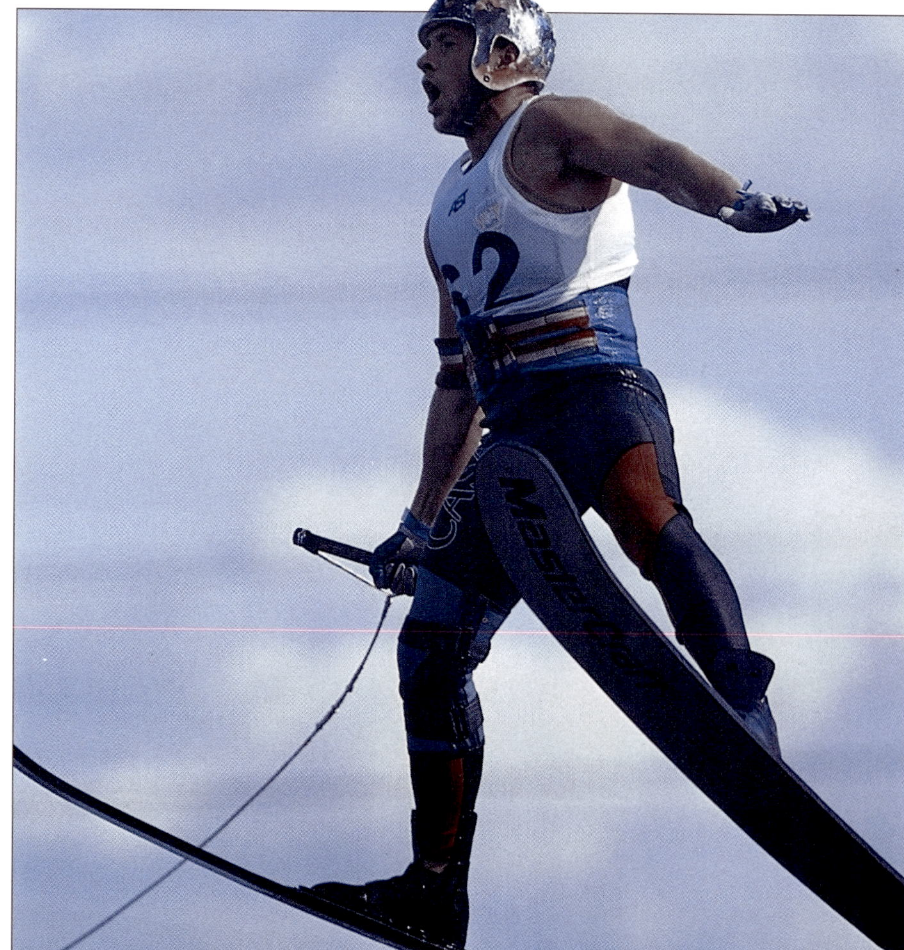

Water skiing – female

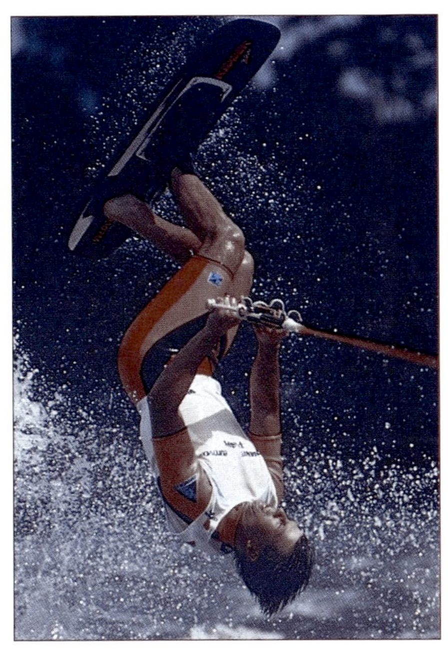
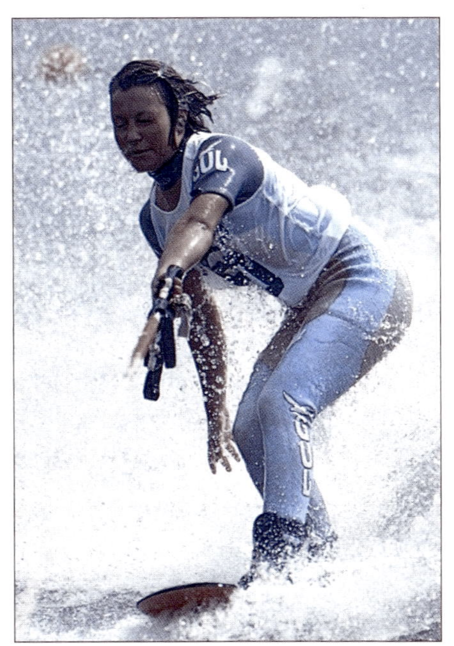
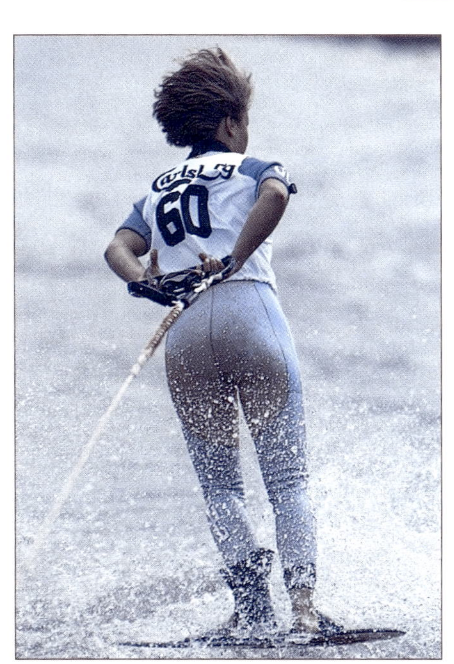

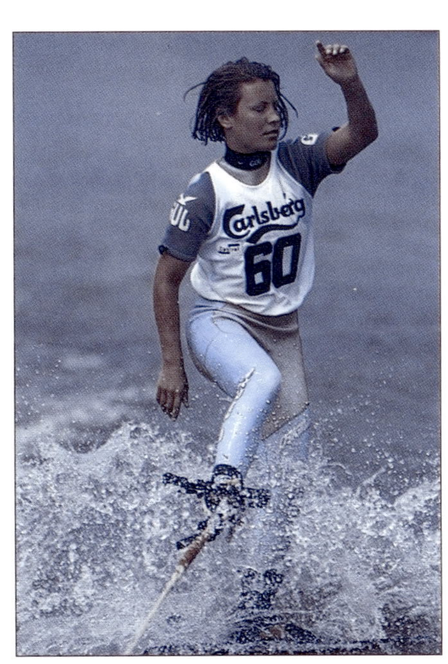

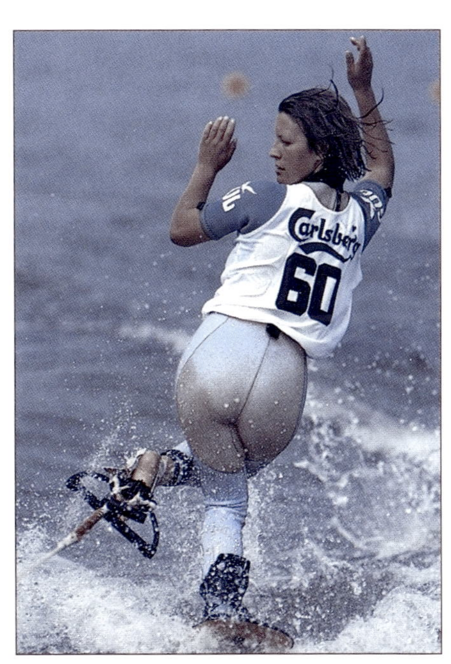

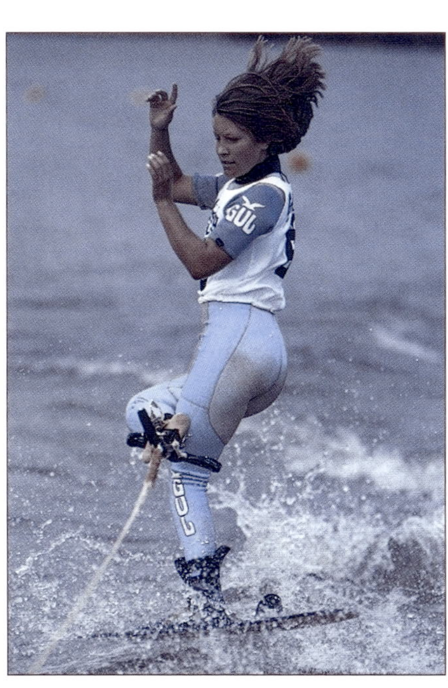
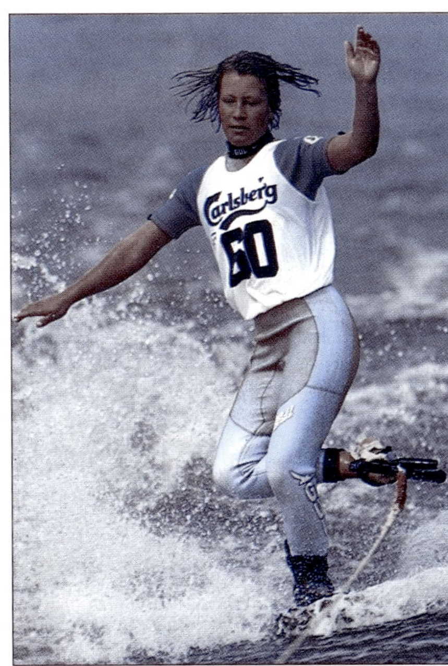

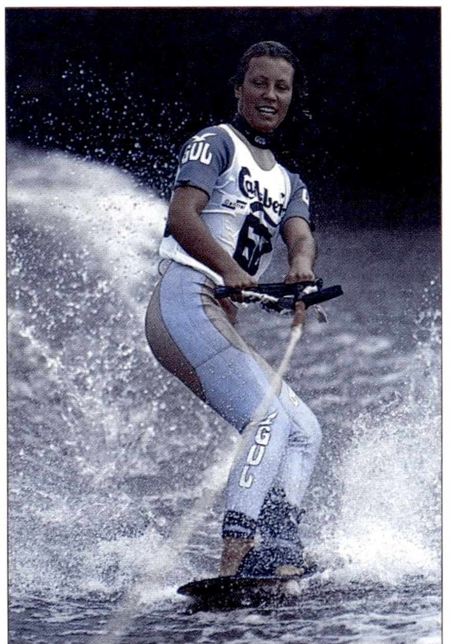
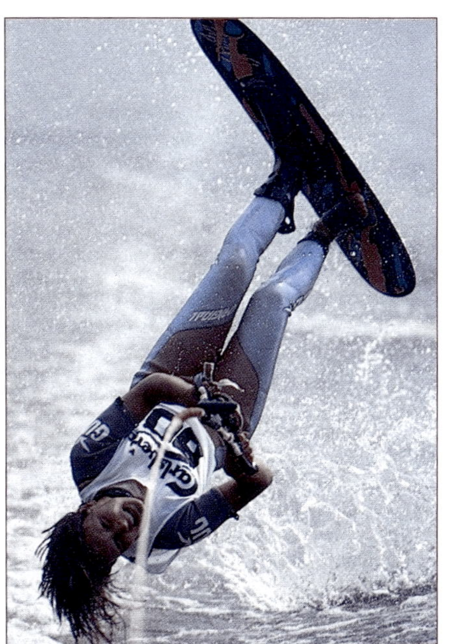

9.07 Canoeing

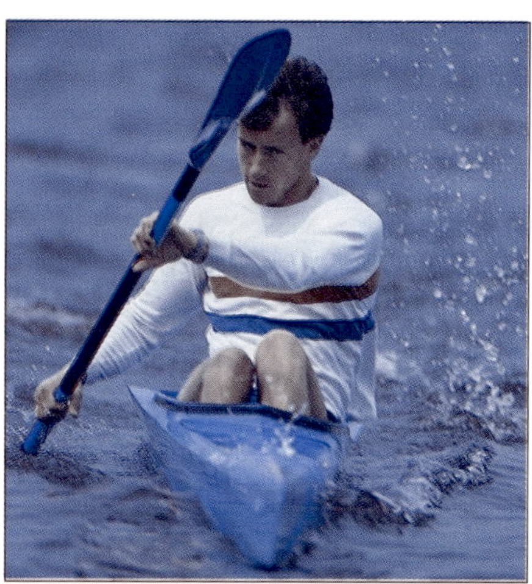

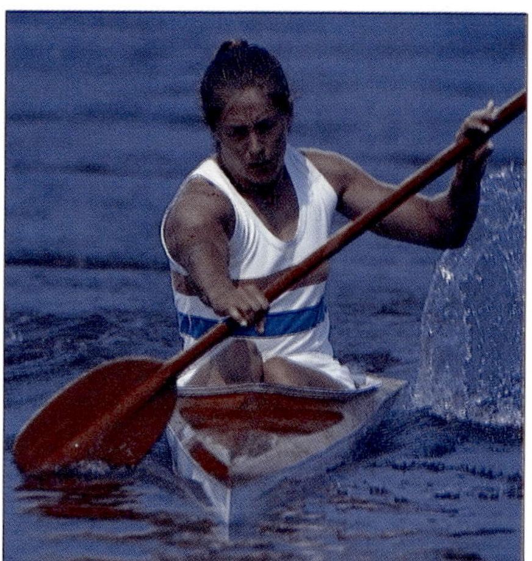

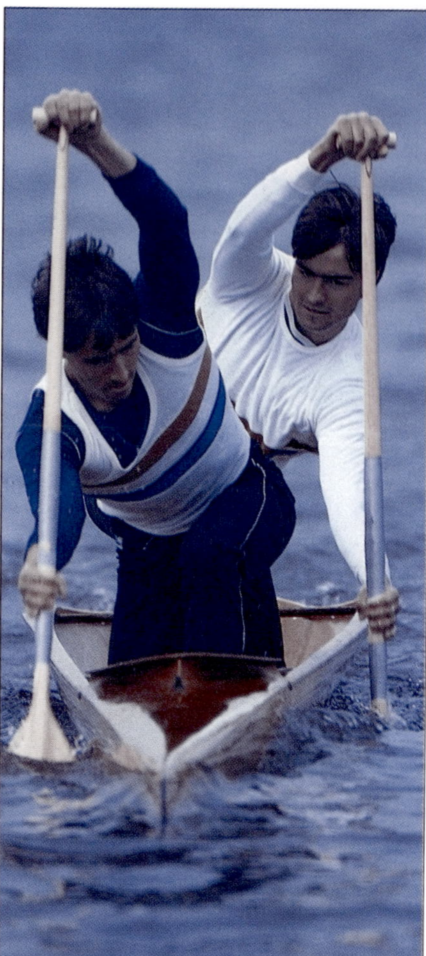

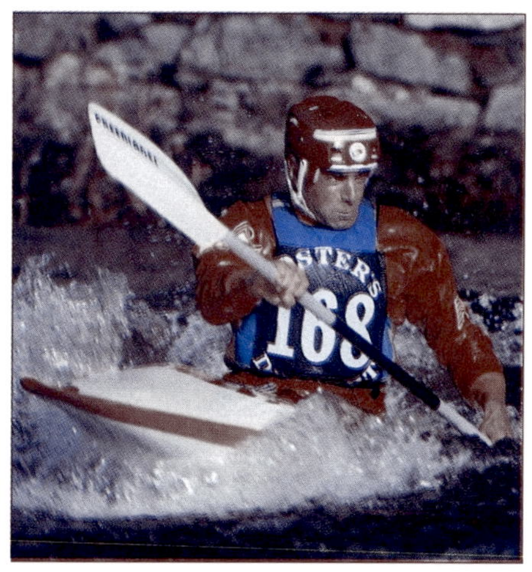

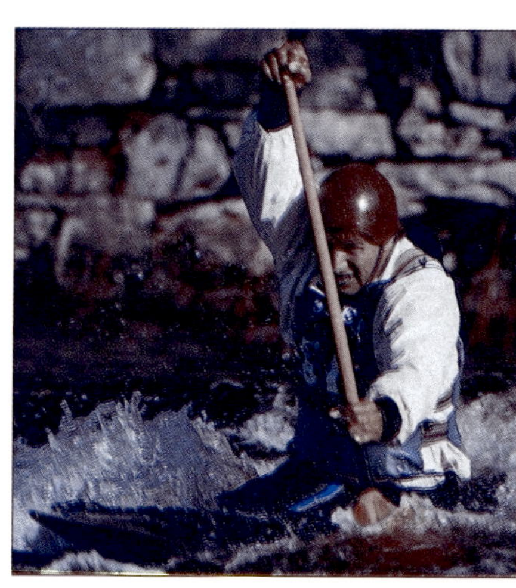

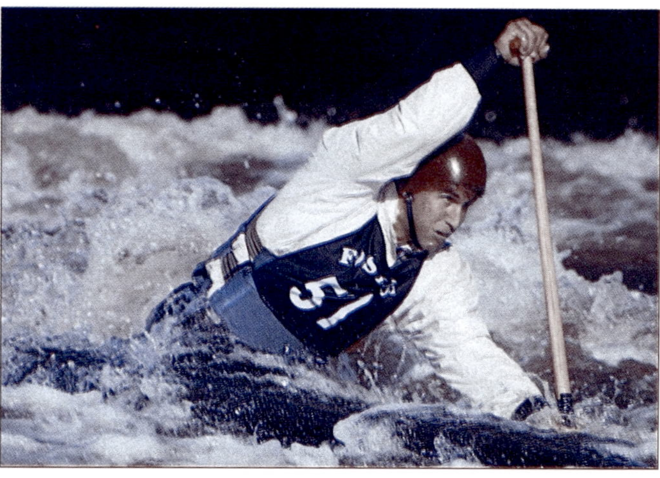

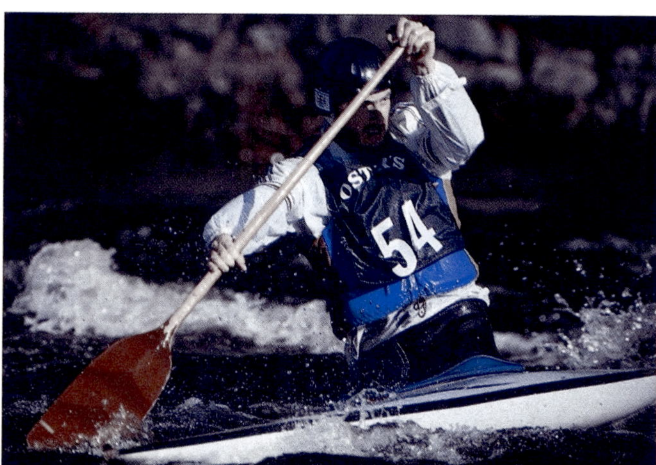

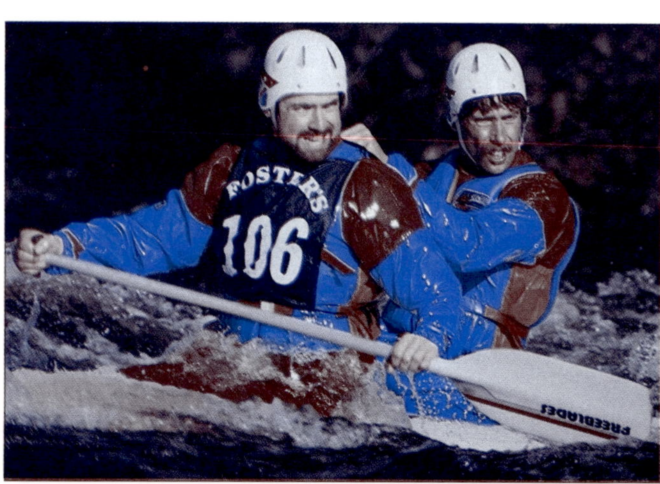

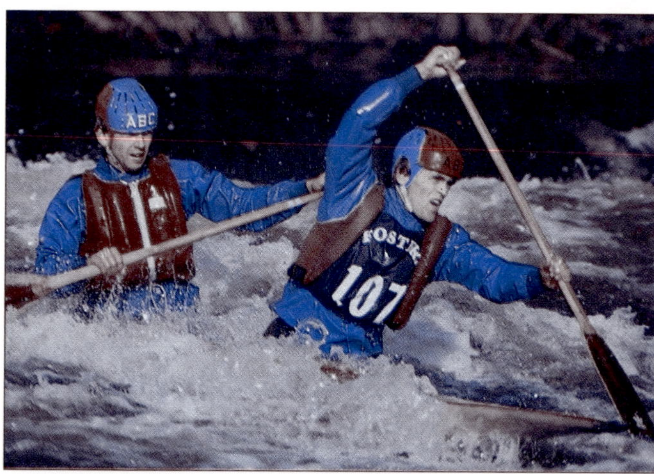

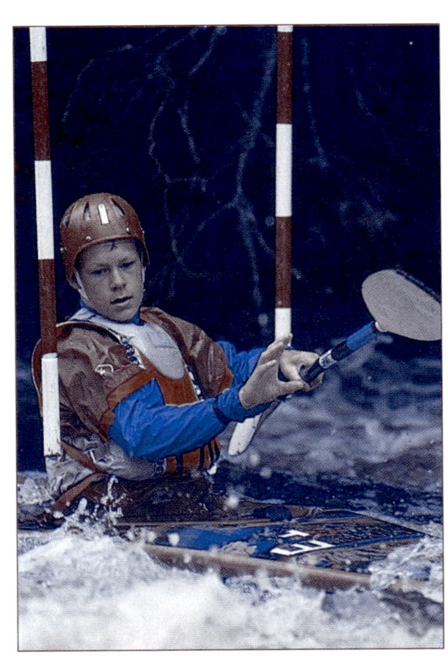

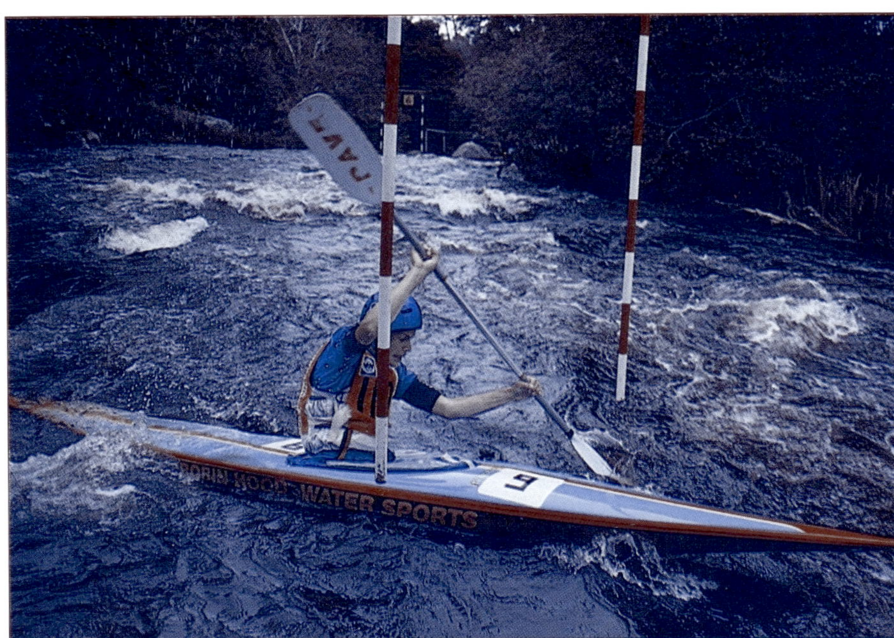
WATER SPORTS

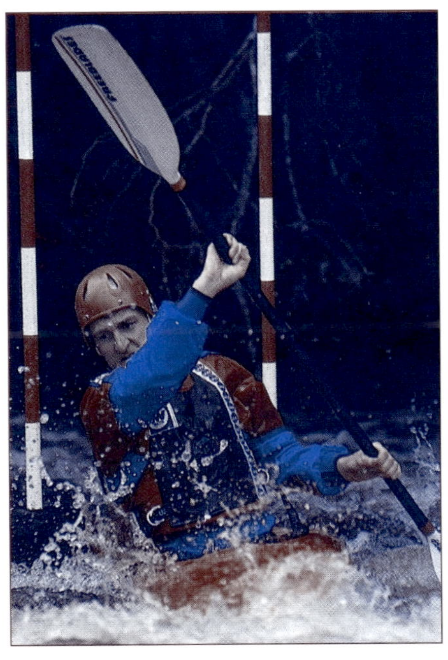

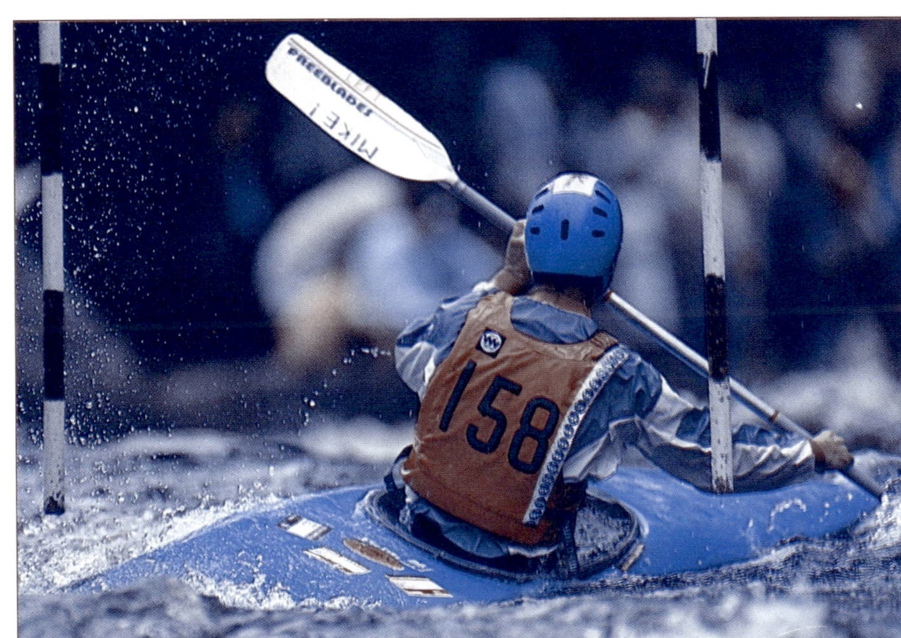
FREEBLADES
MIKE T
158

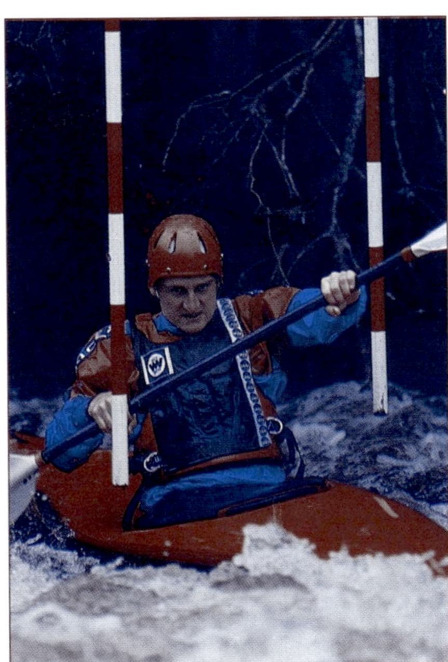

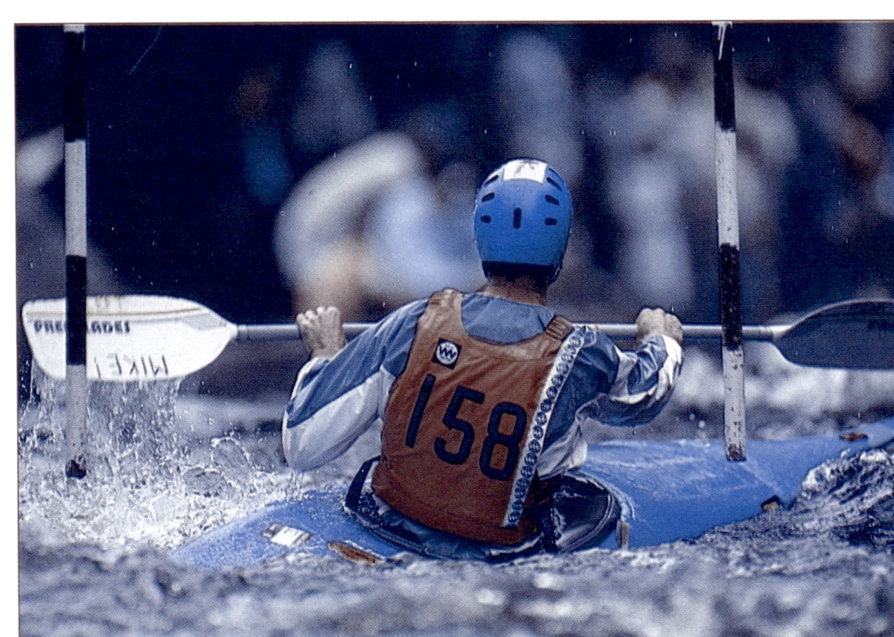
MIKE T
158

Rowing – male

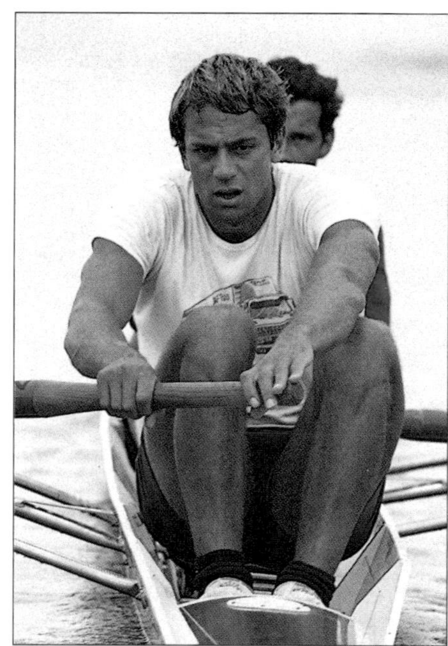

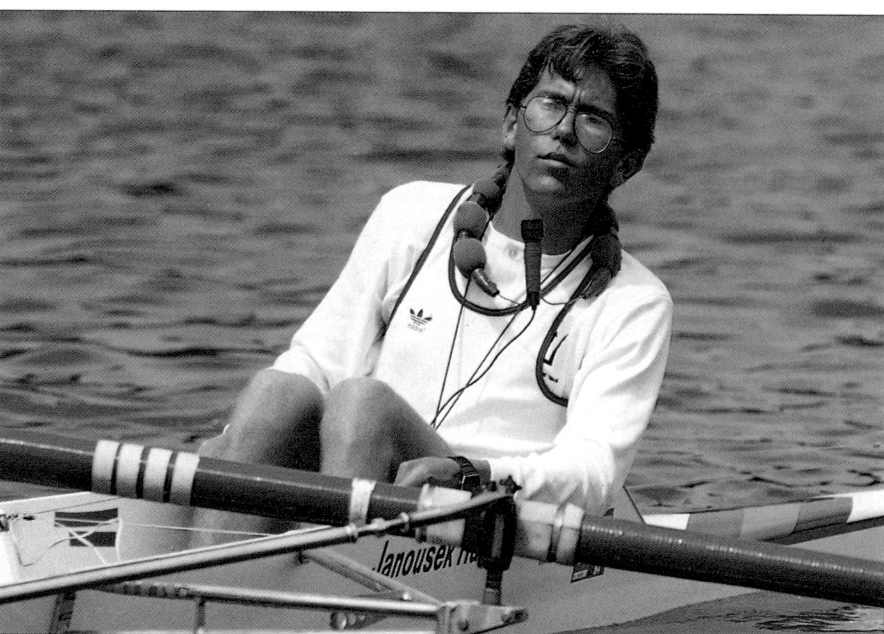

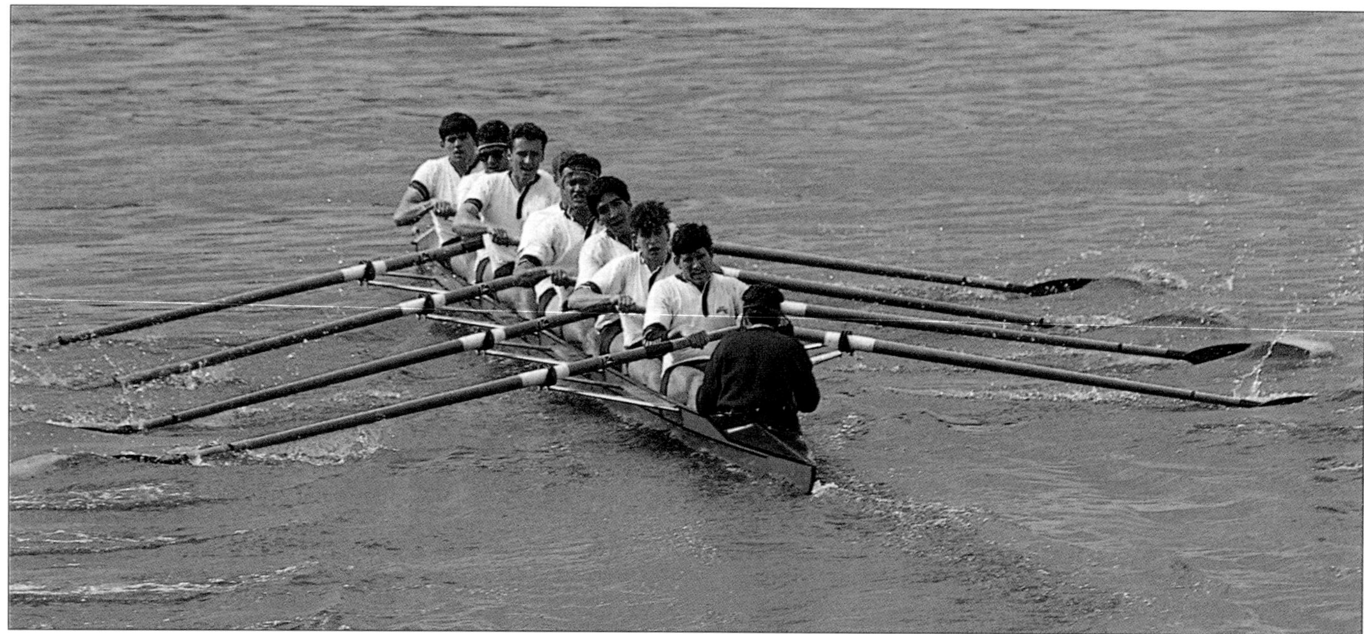

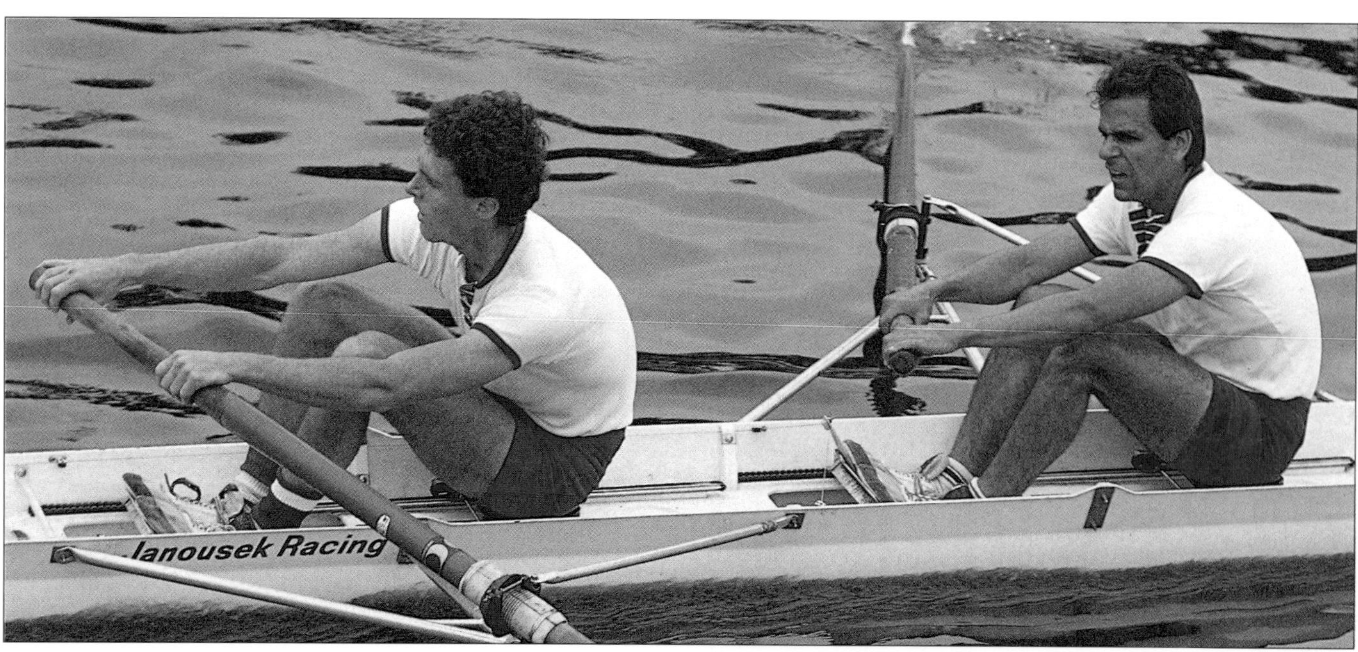

Rowing – male/female

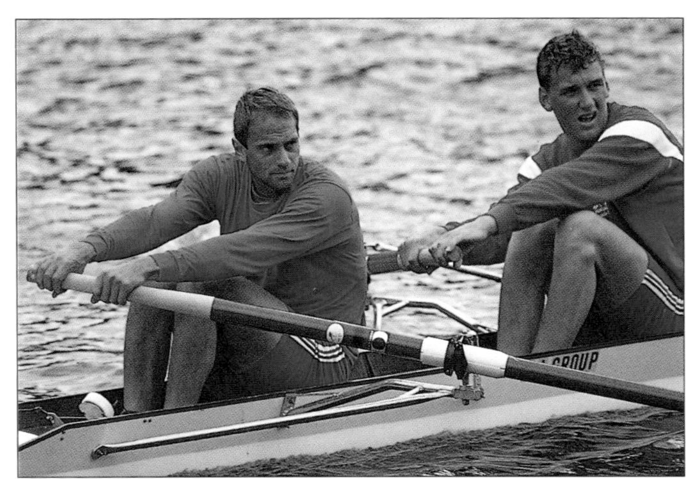

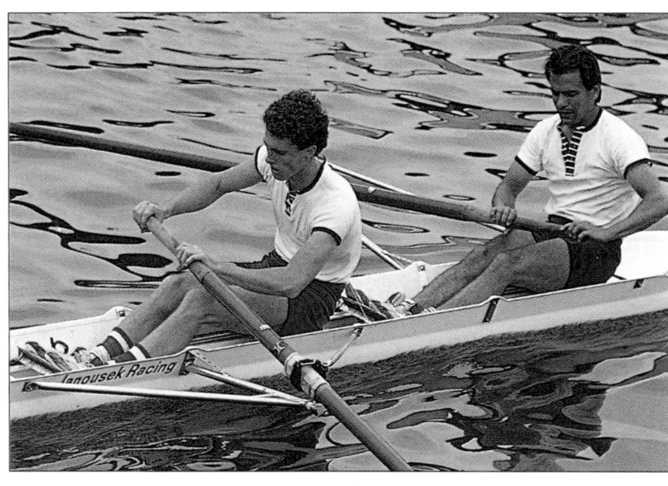

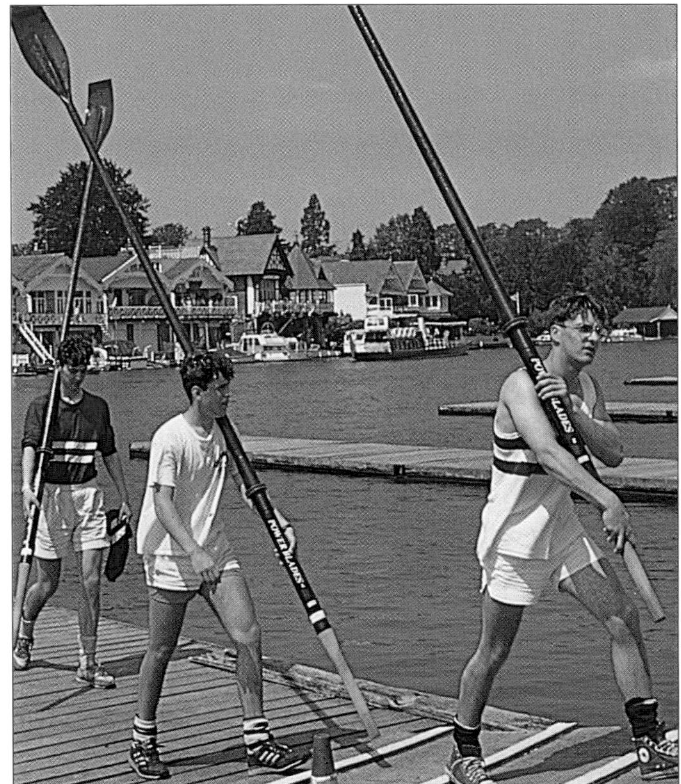

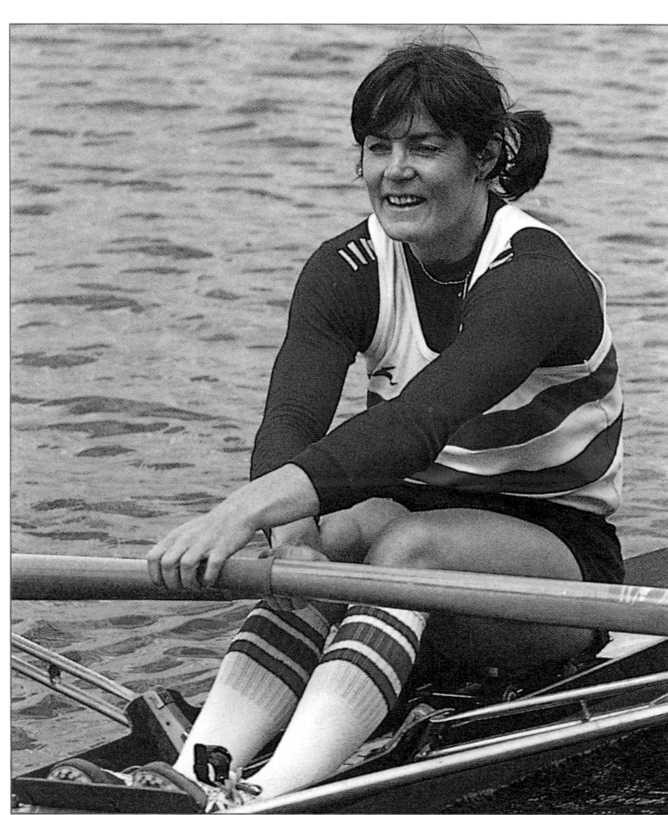

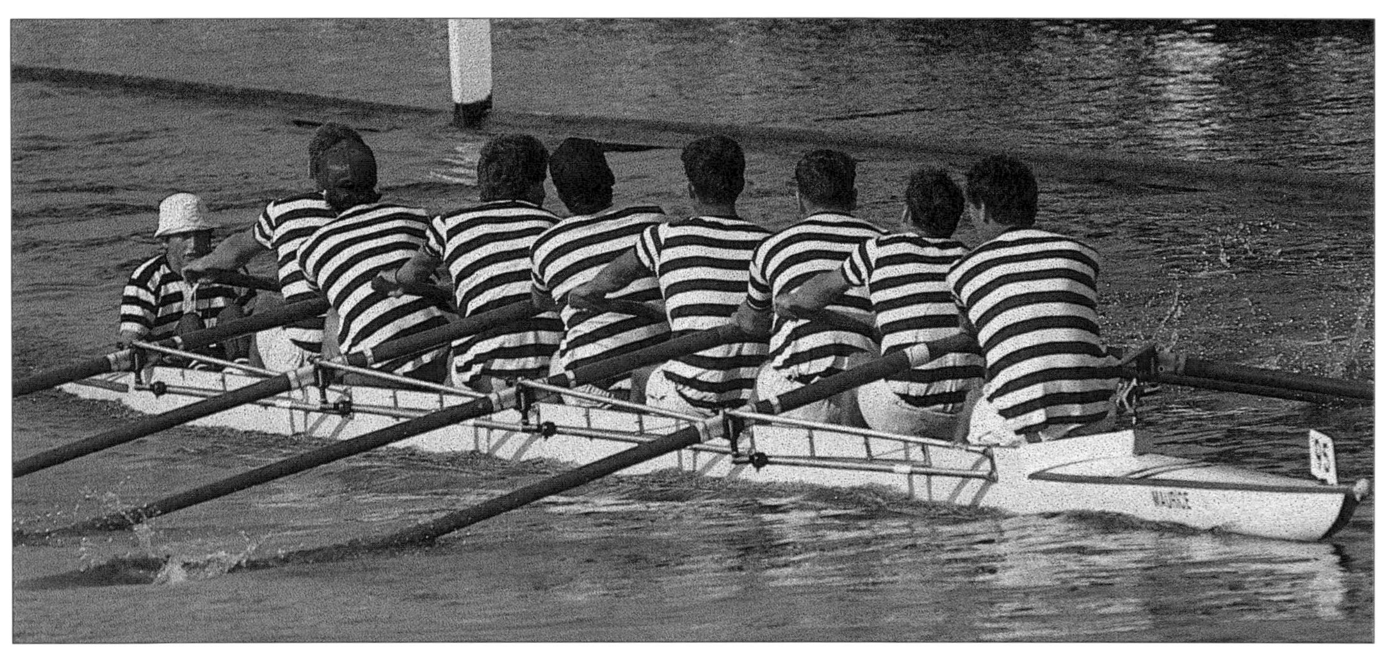

Sailing

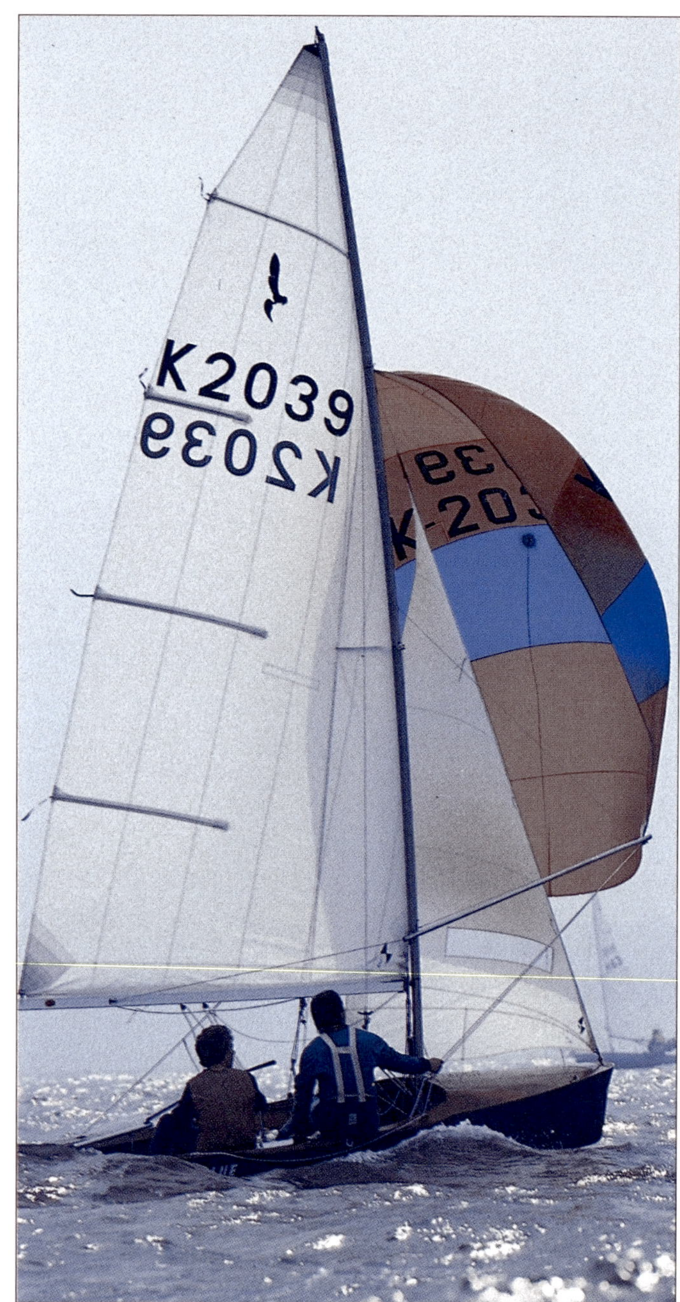

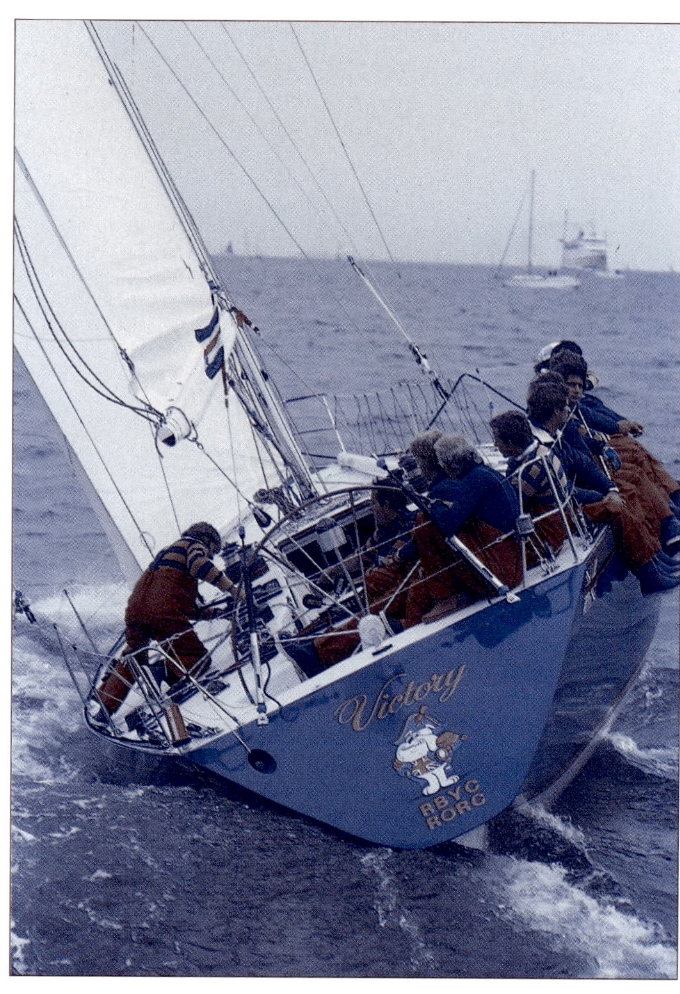

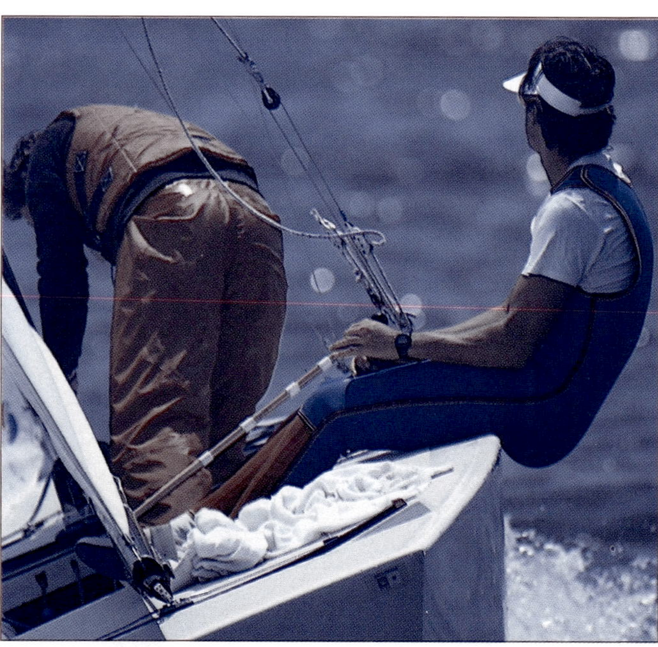

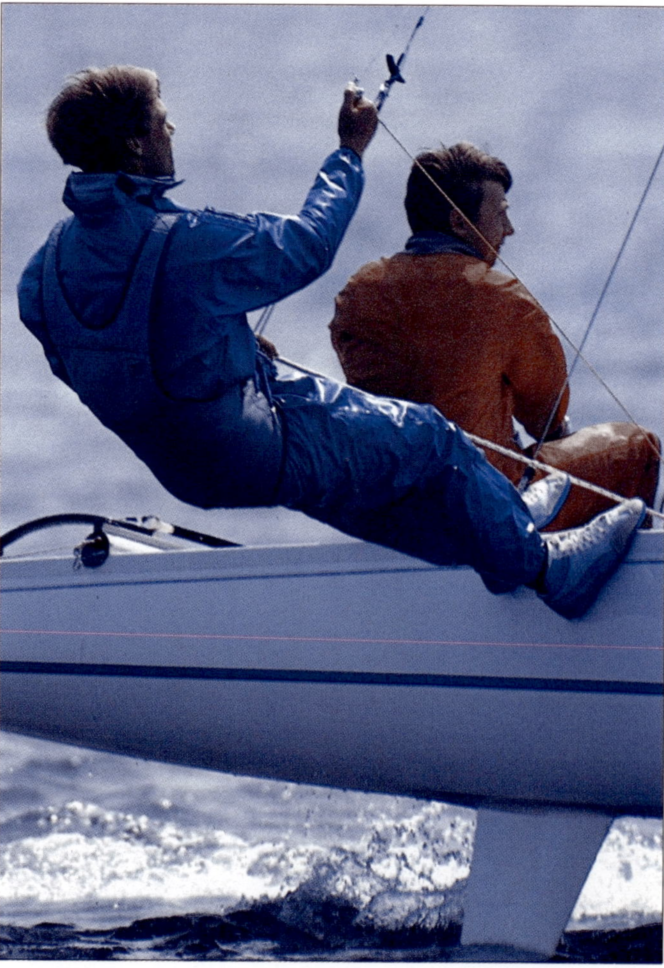

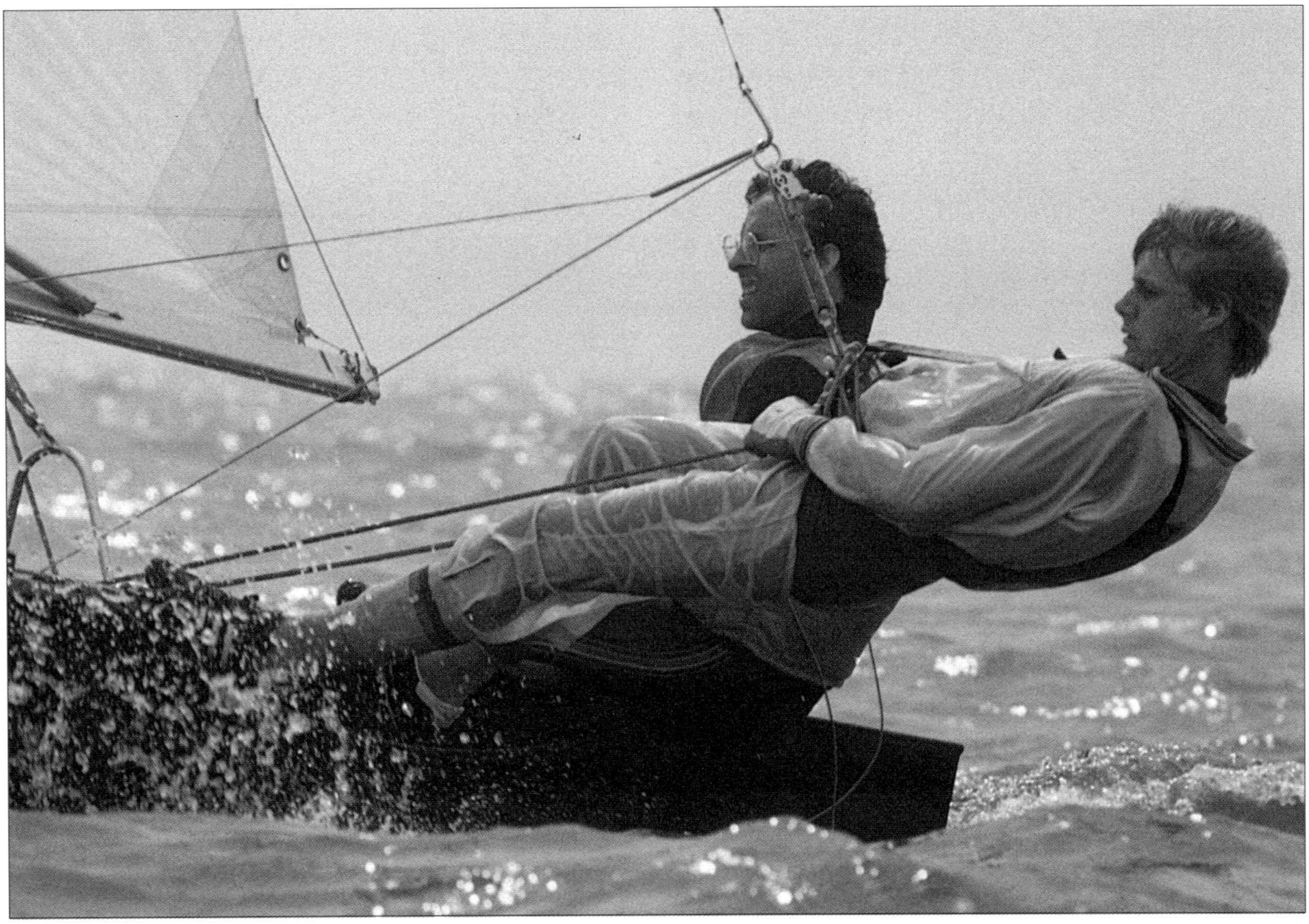

Sailing

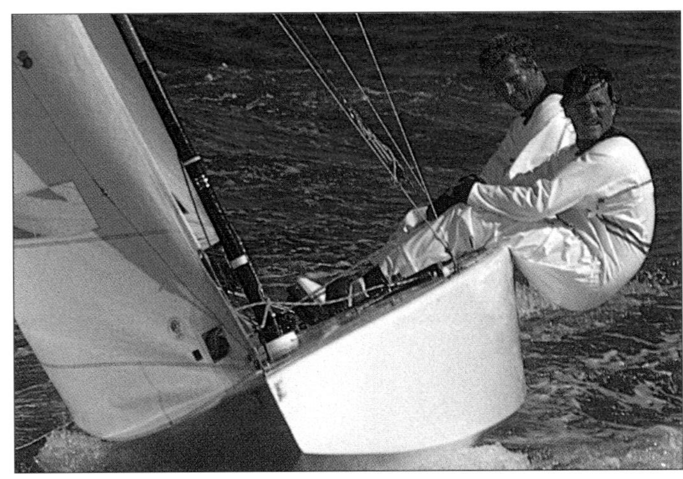

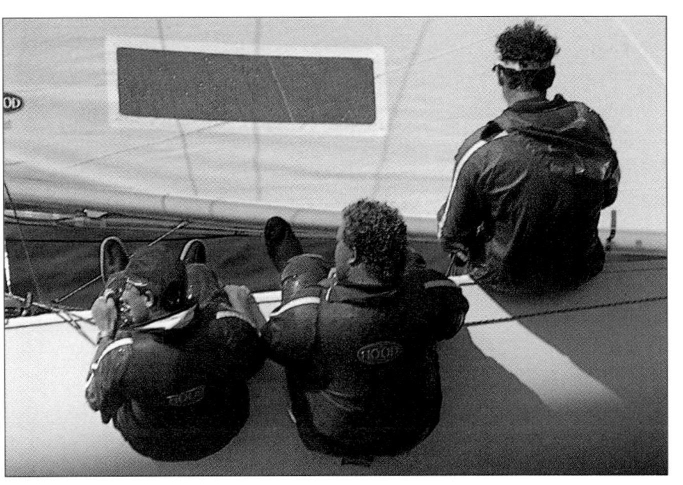

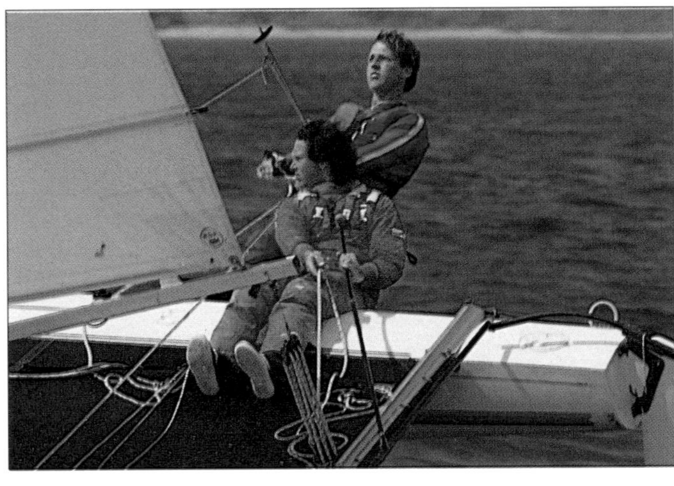

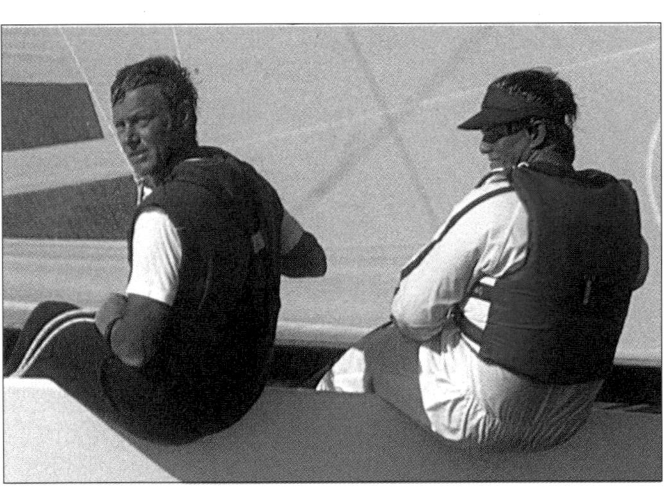

Fishing – fresh water

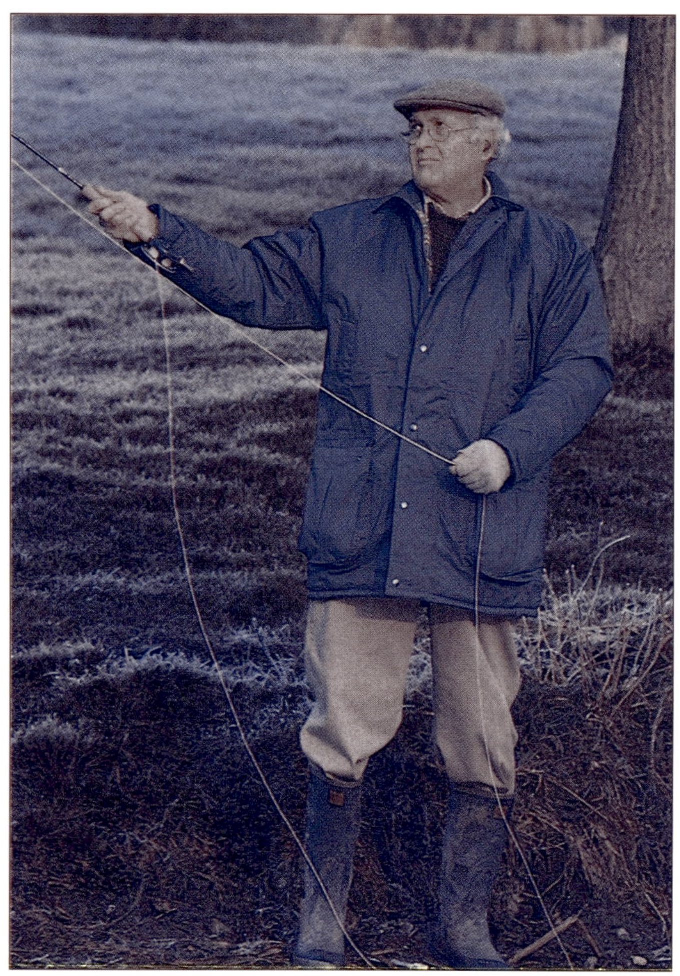

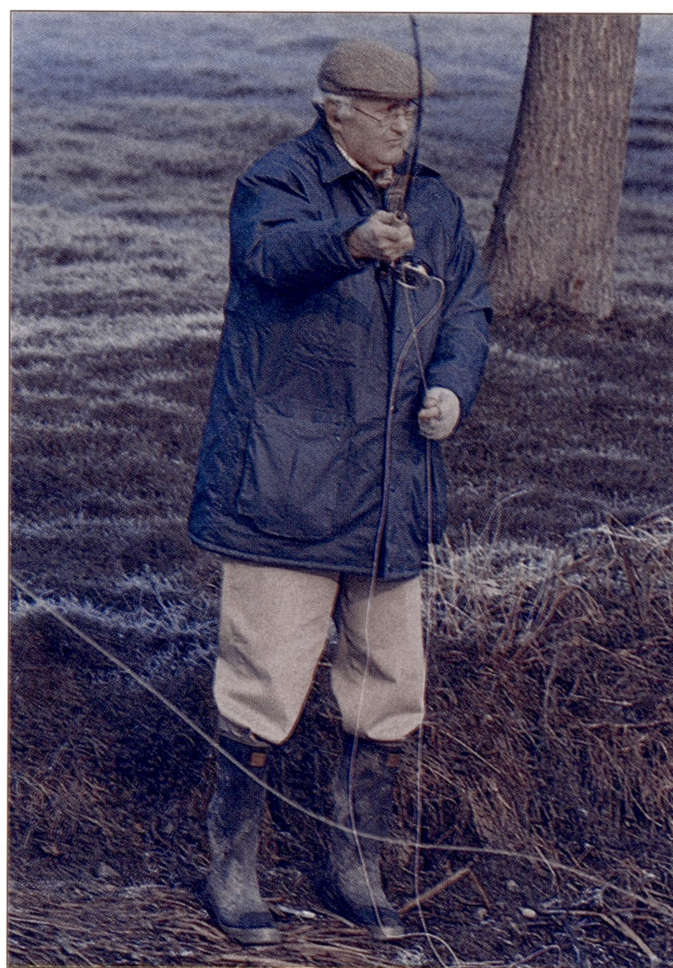

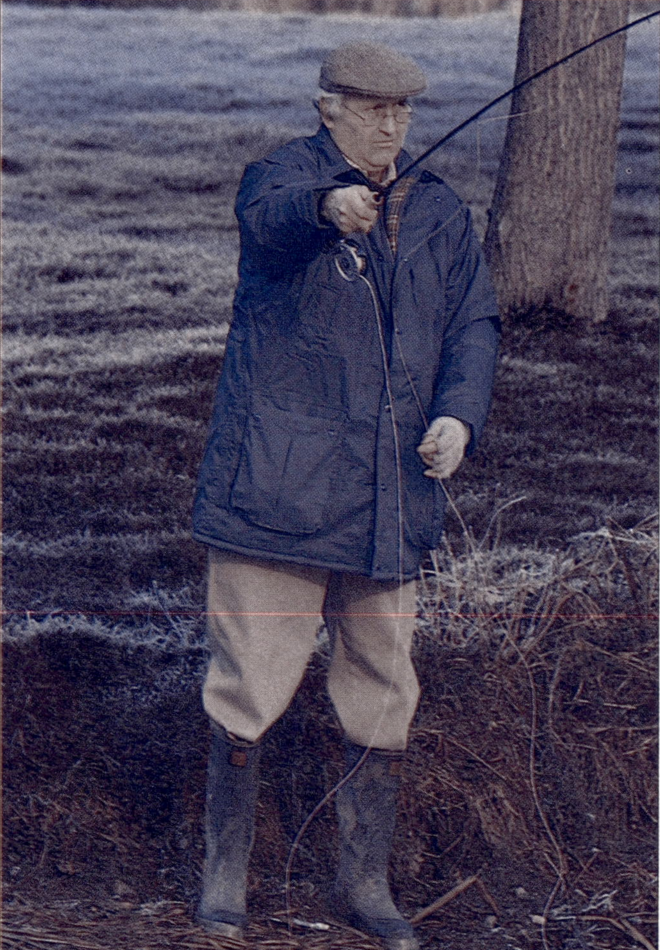

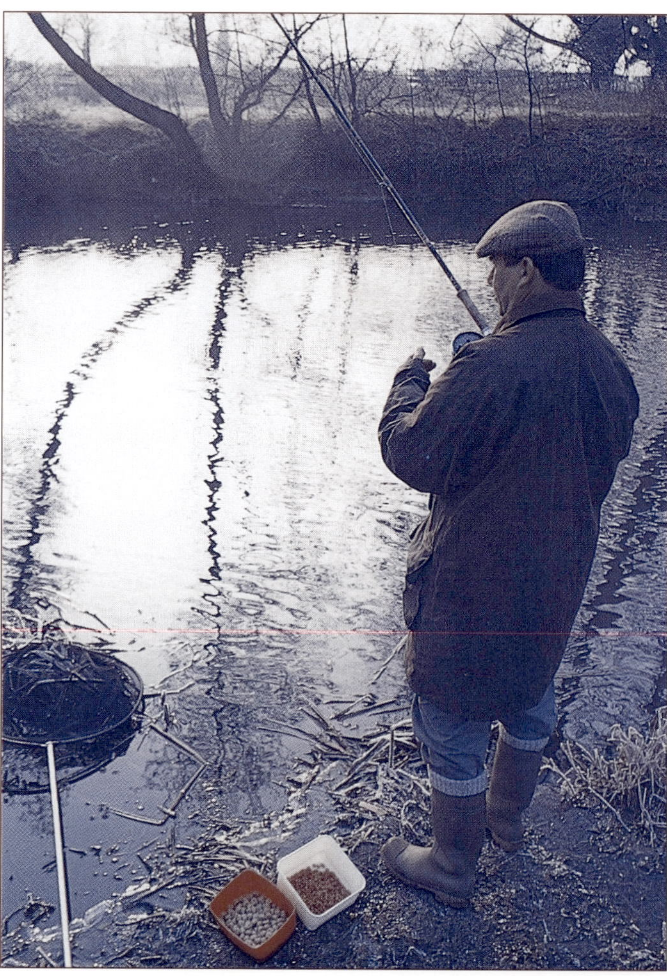

Fishing – fresh water

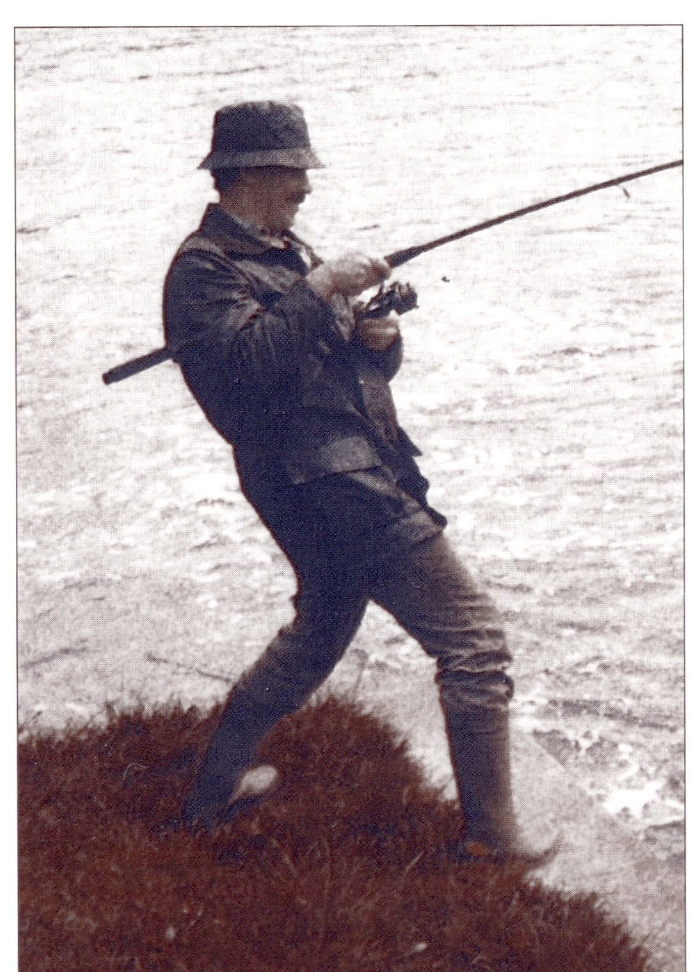

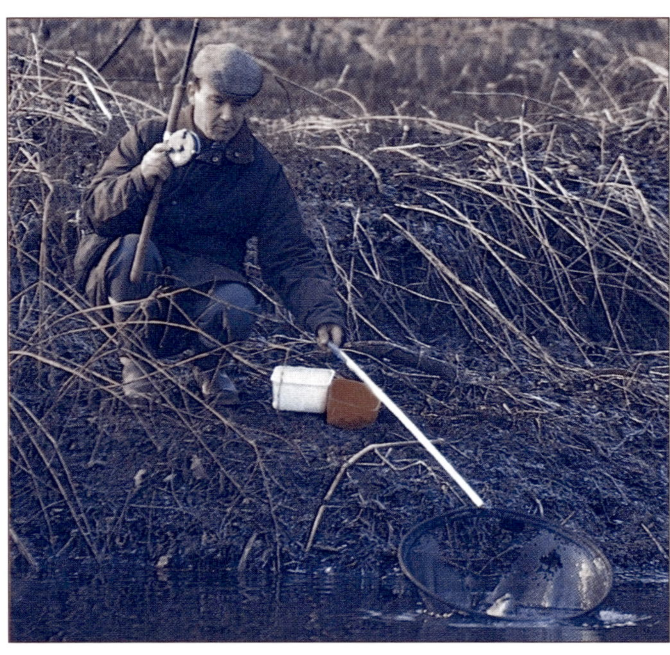

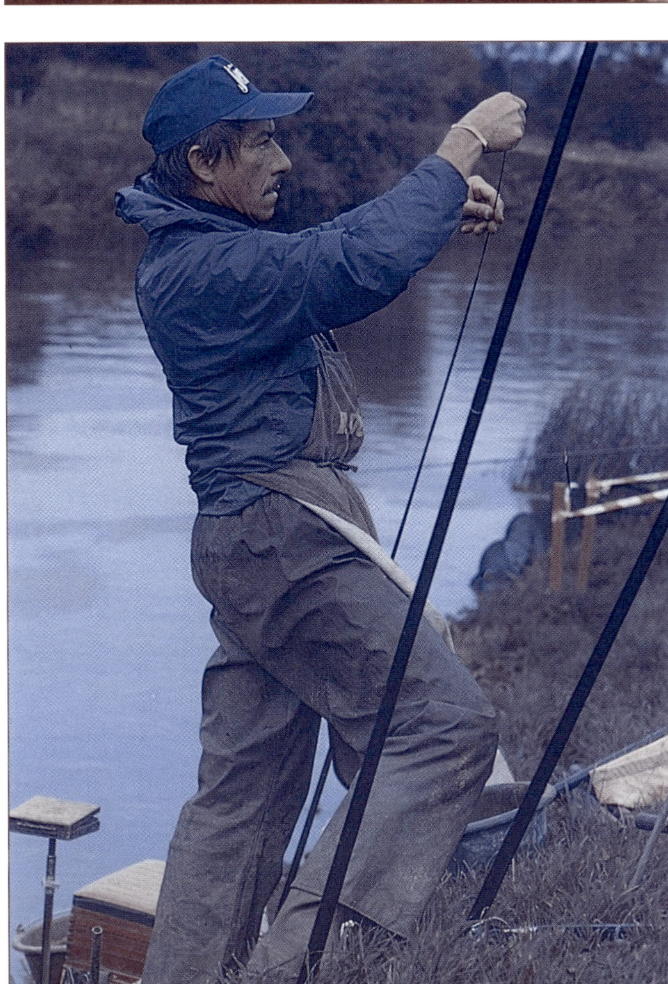

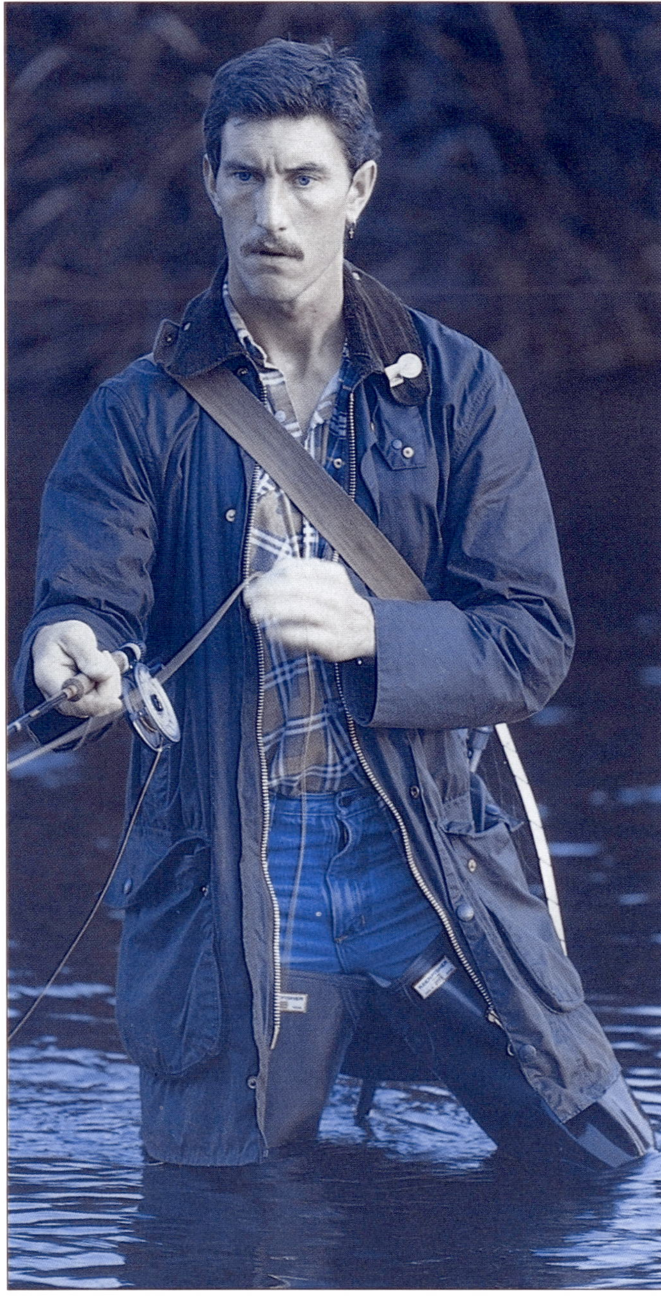

Fishing — fresh water

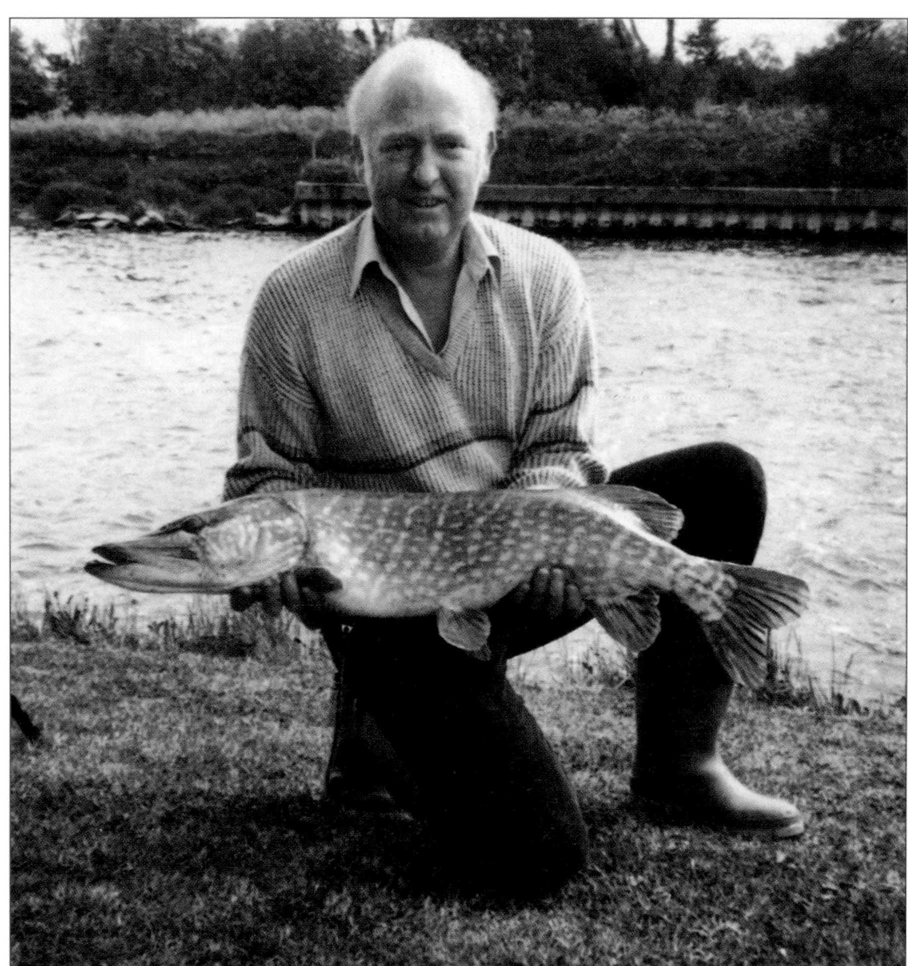

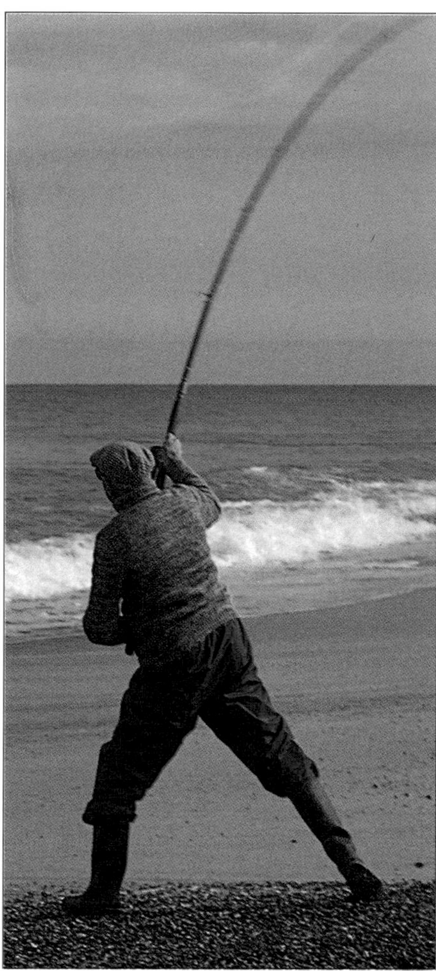

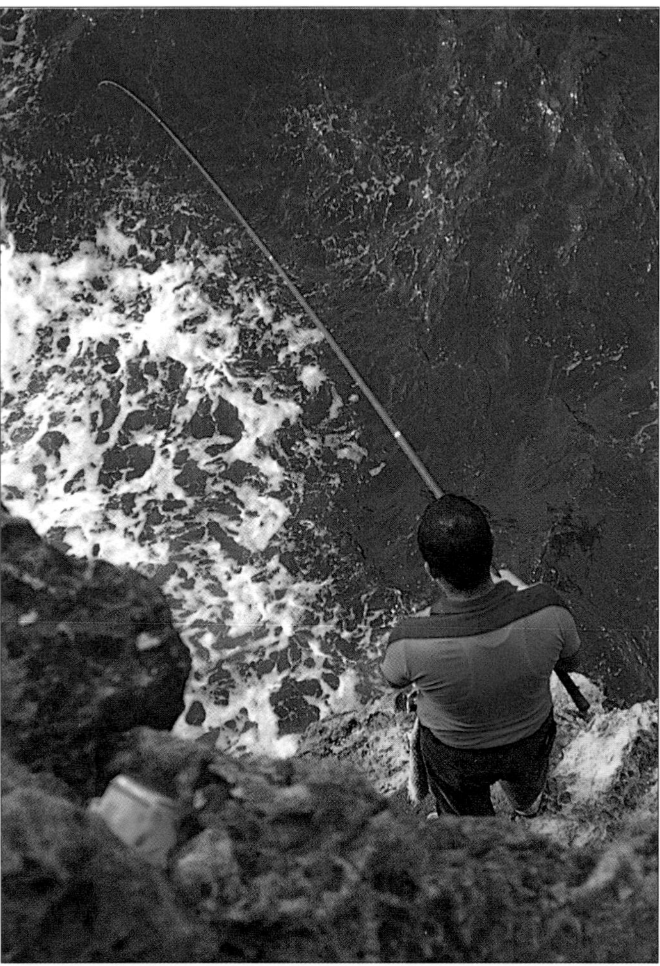

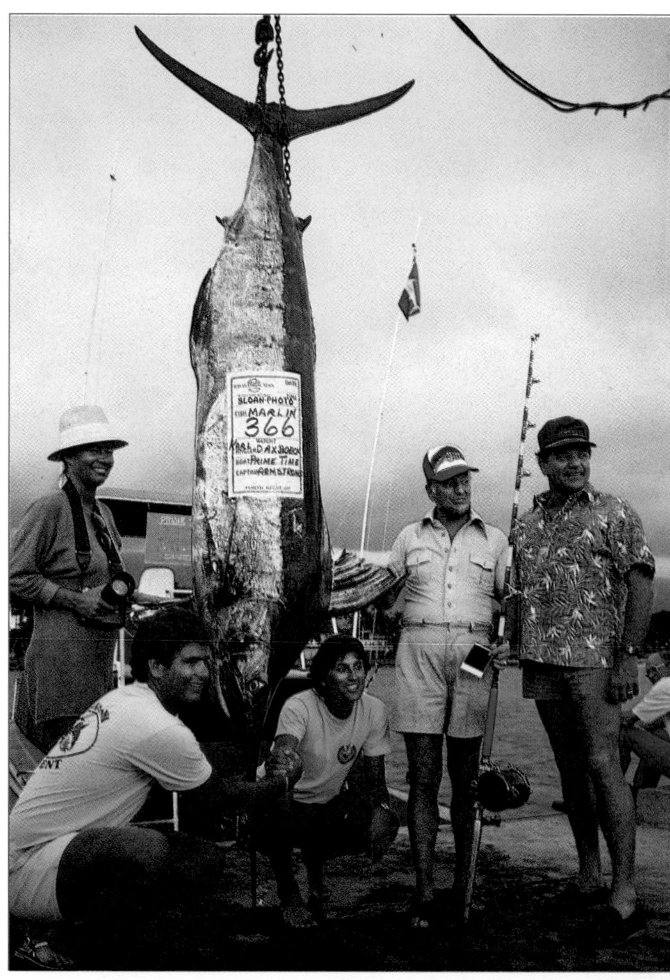

Fishing – sea

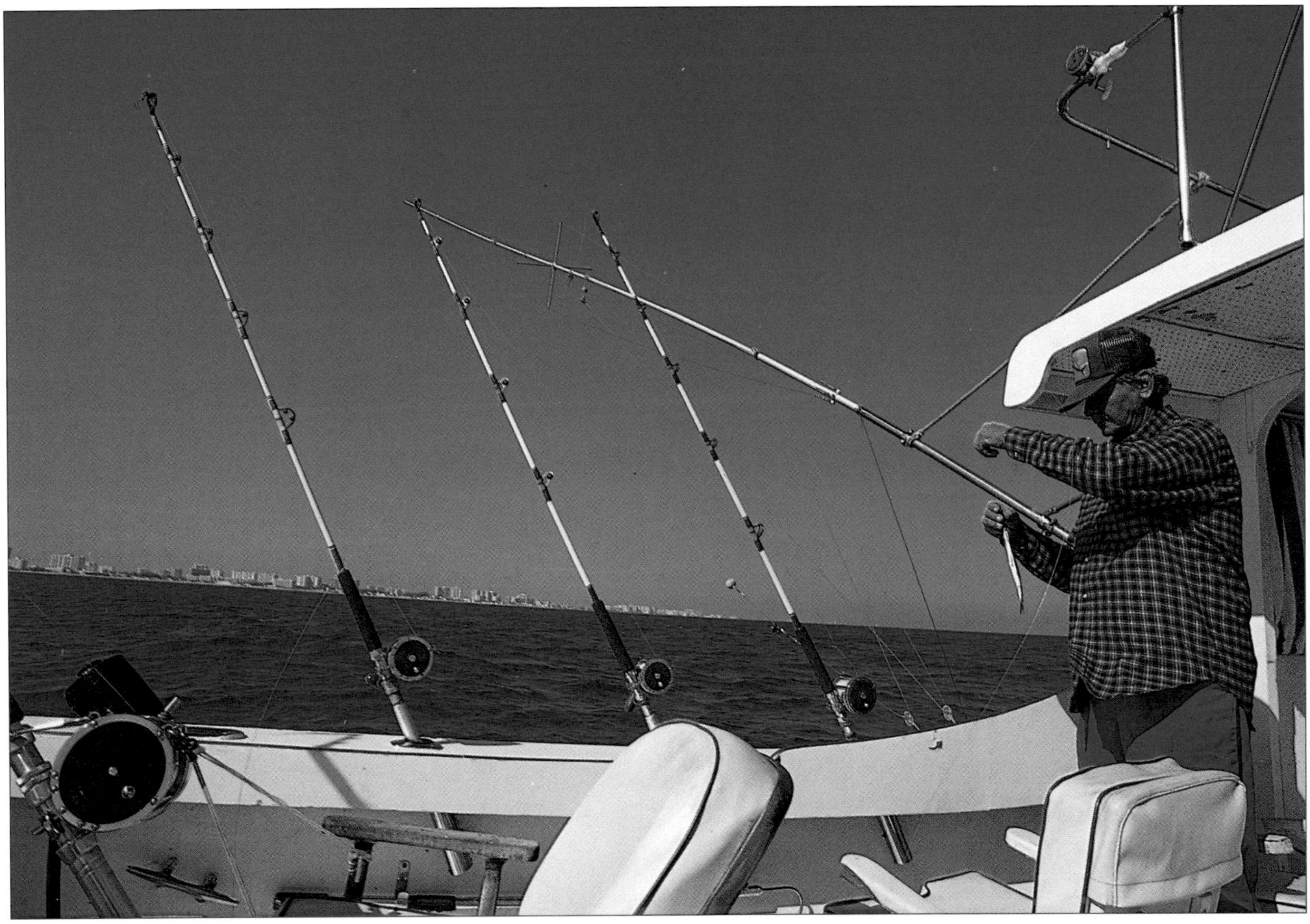

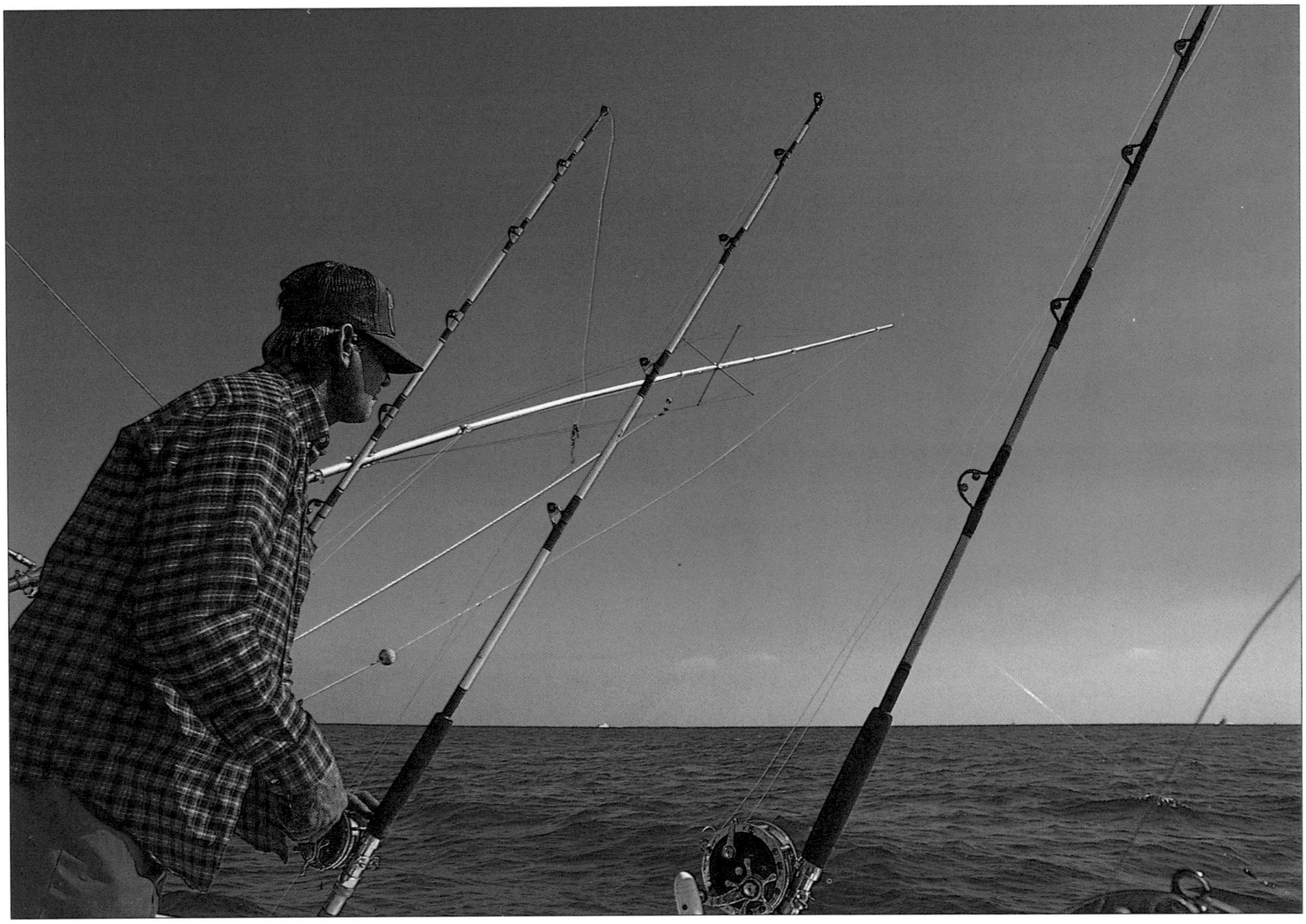

Skiing – male · downhill · slalom · cross country

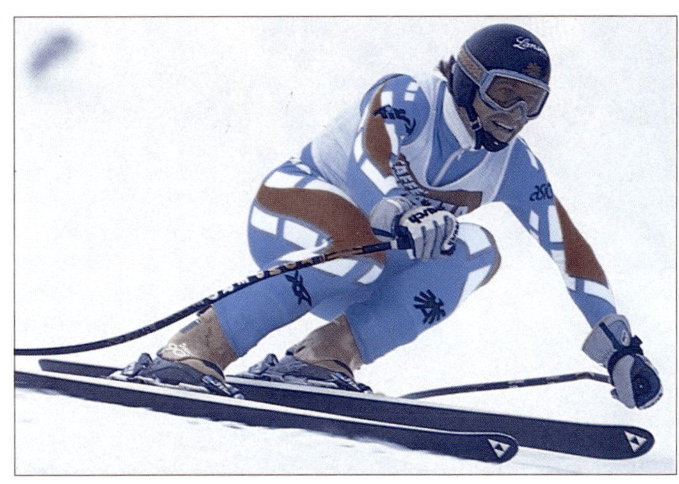

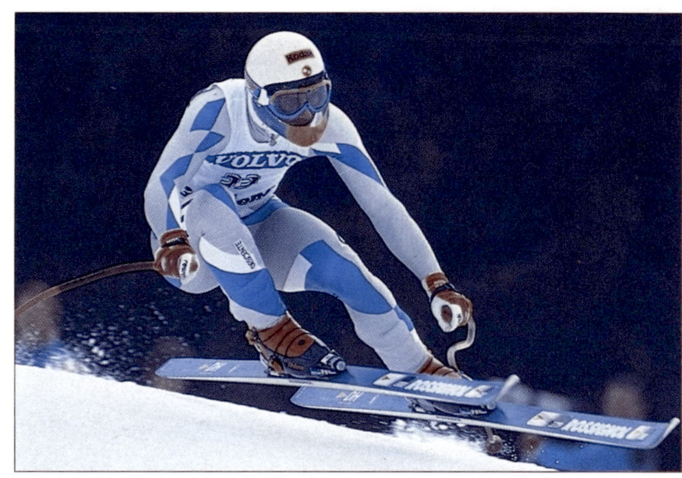

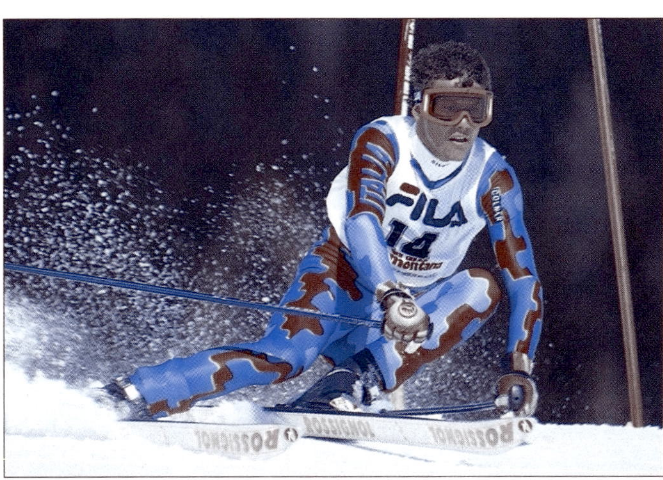

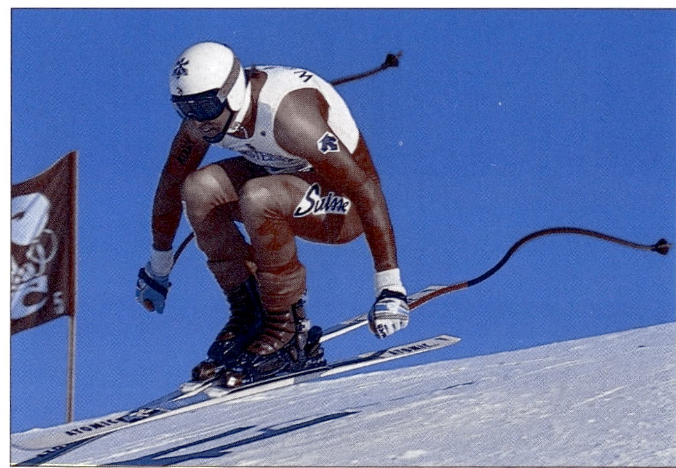

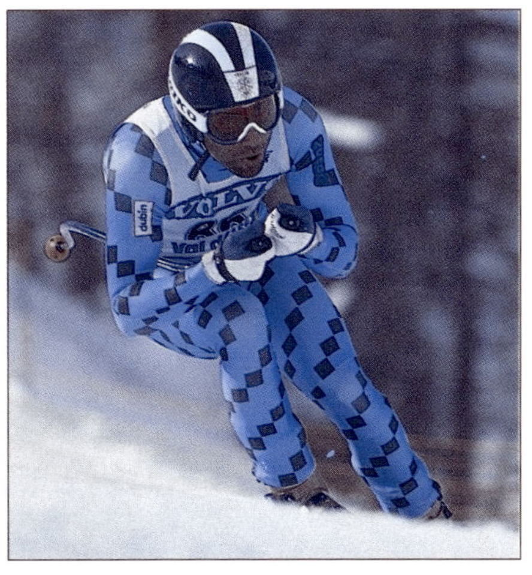

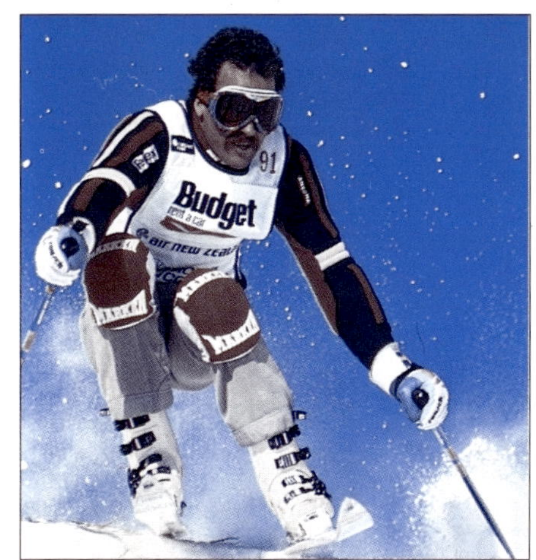

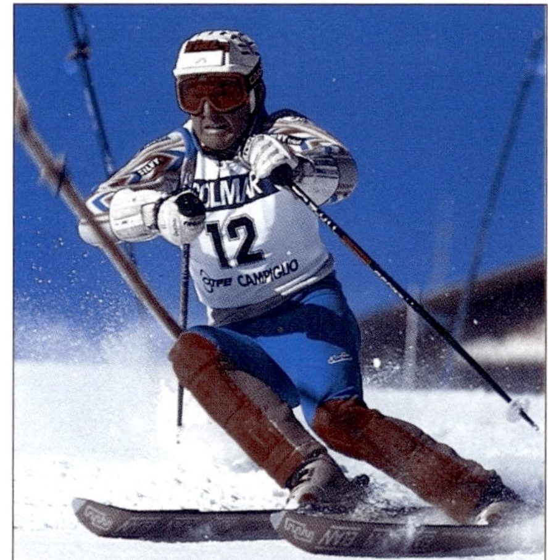

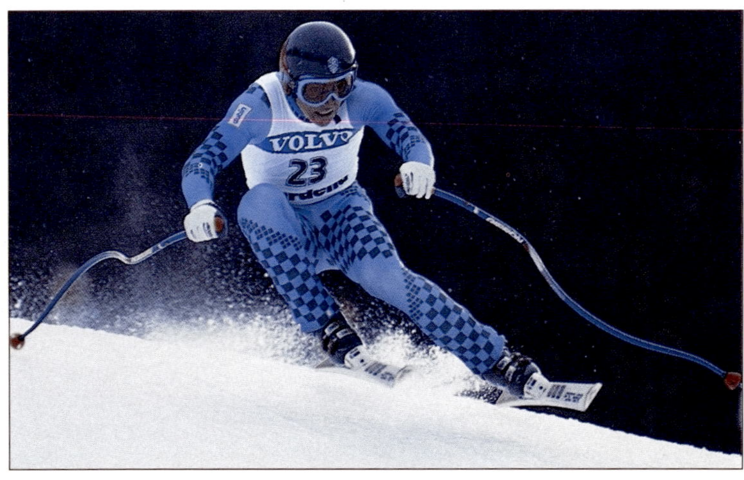

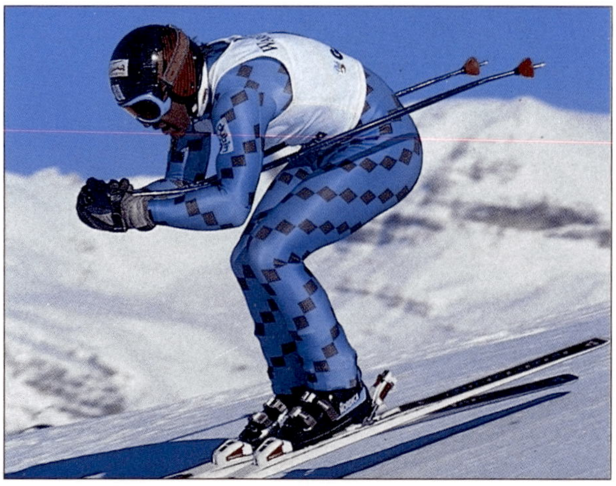

Skiing – male · cross country · biathlon

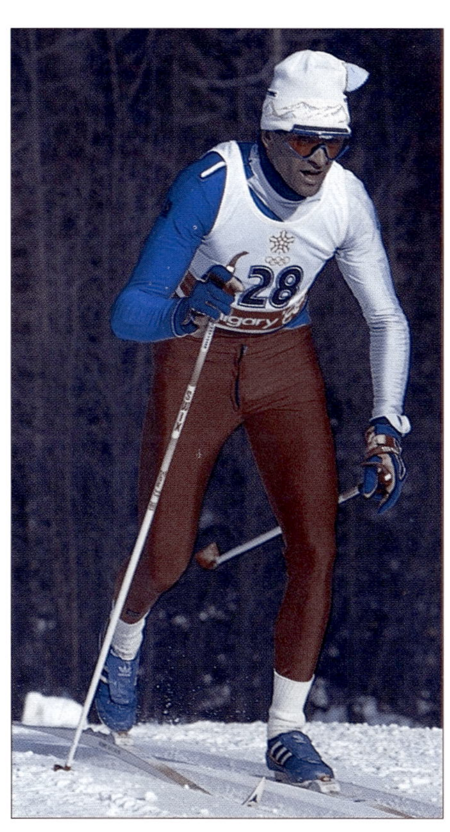

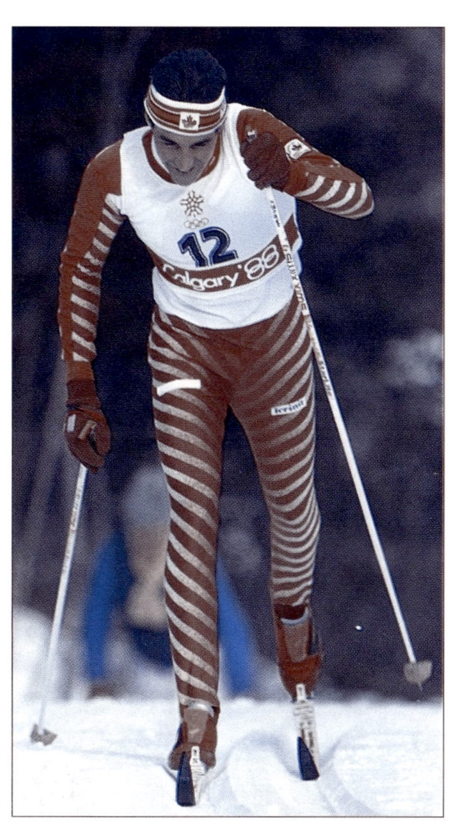

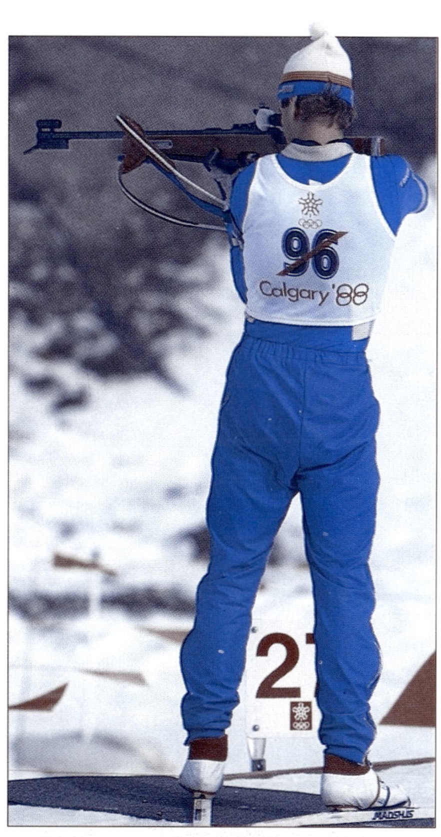

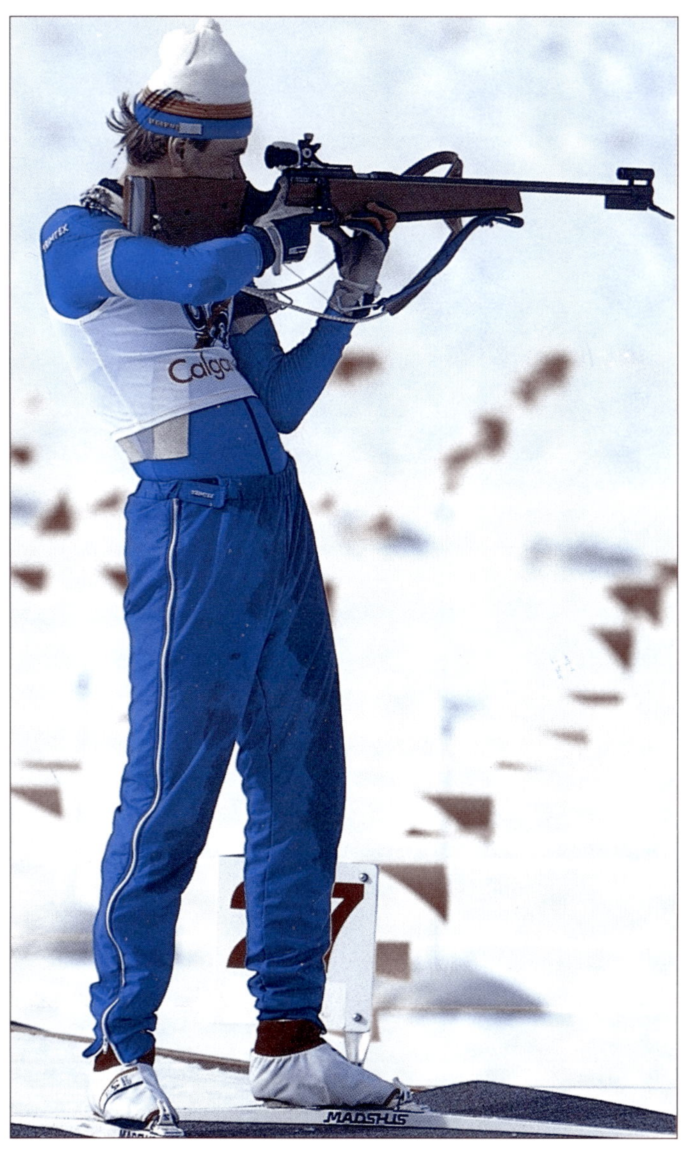

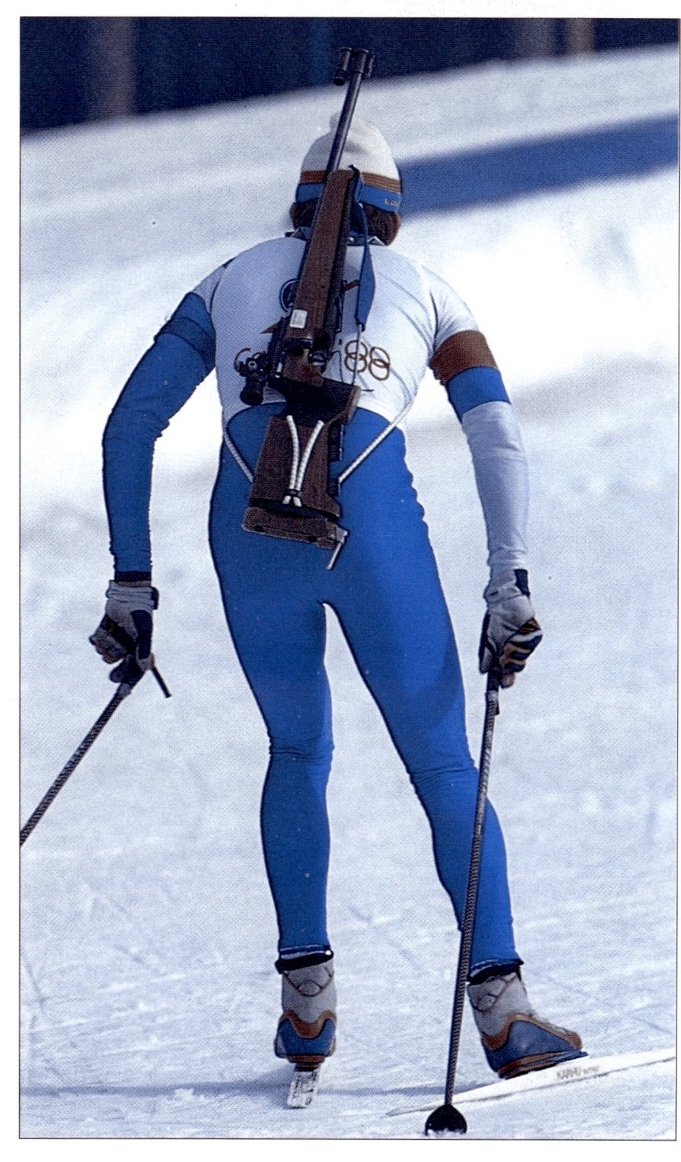

Skiing – male · ski-jumping

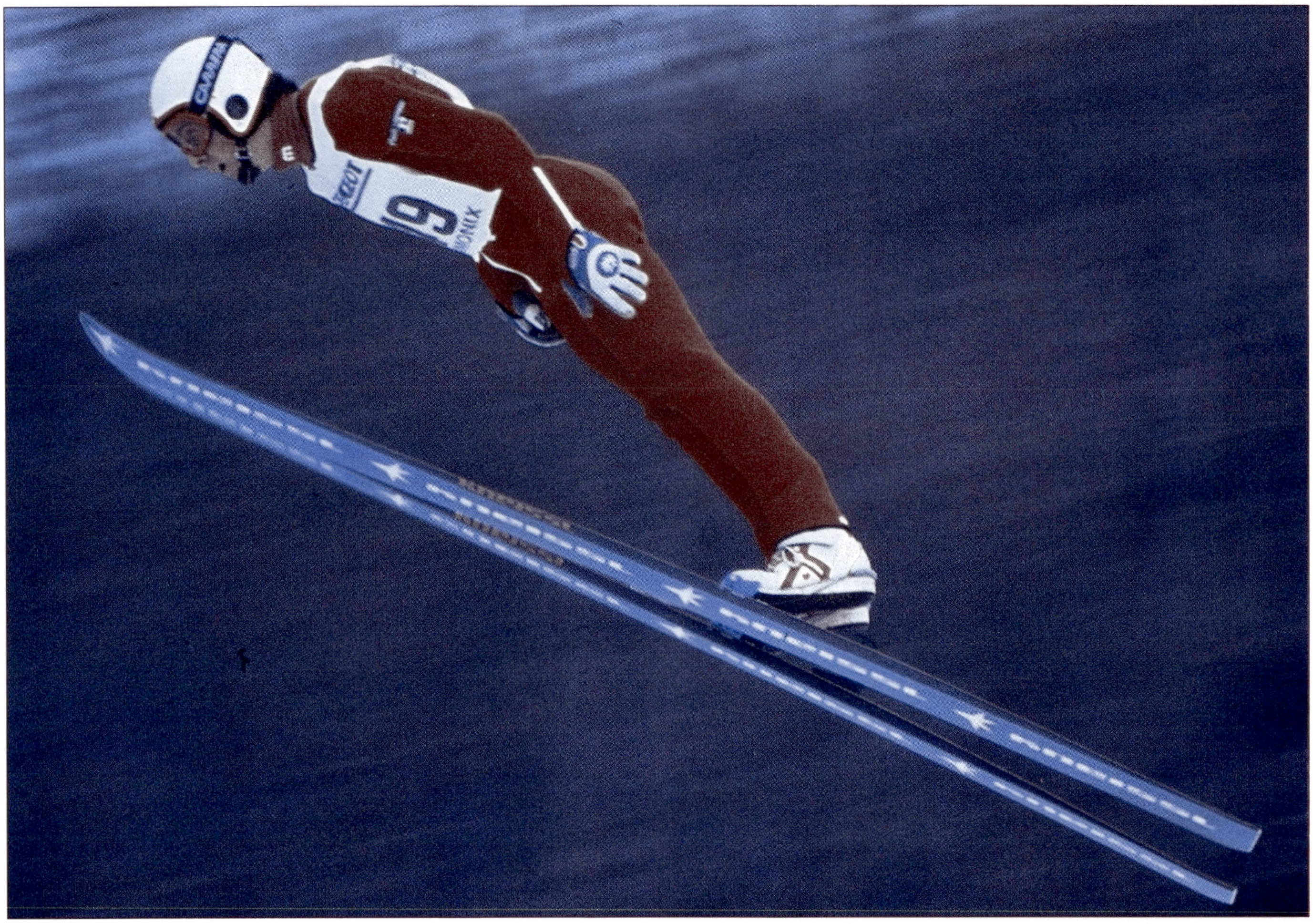

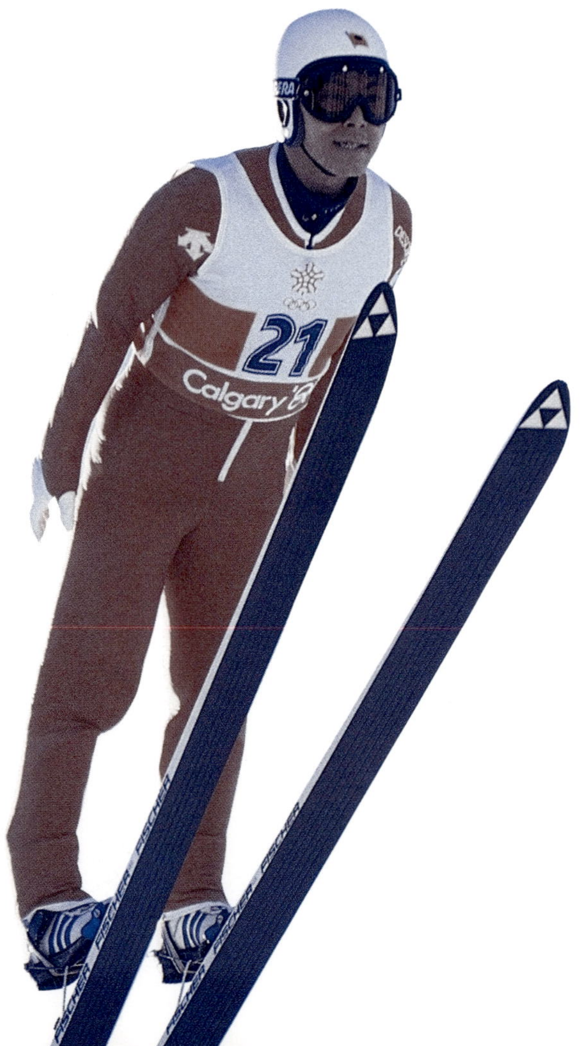

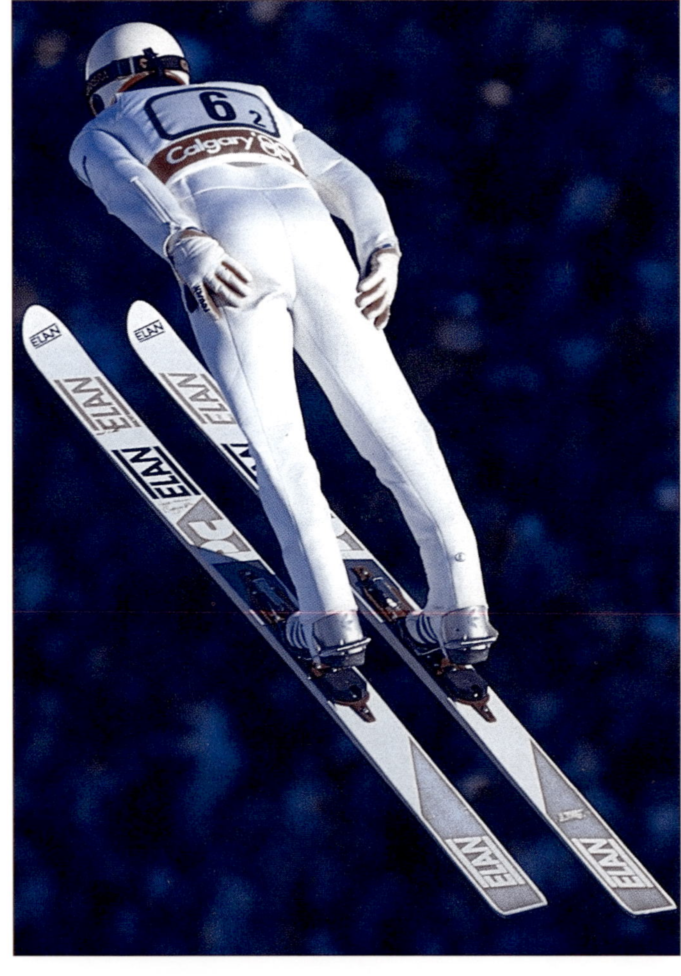

Skiing — female · downhill · slalom · cross country

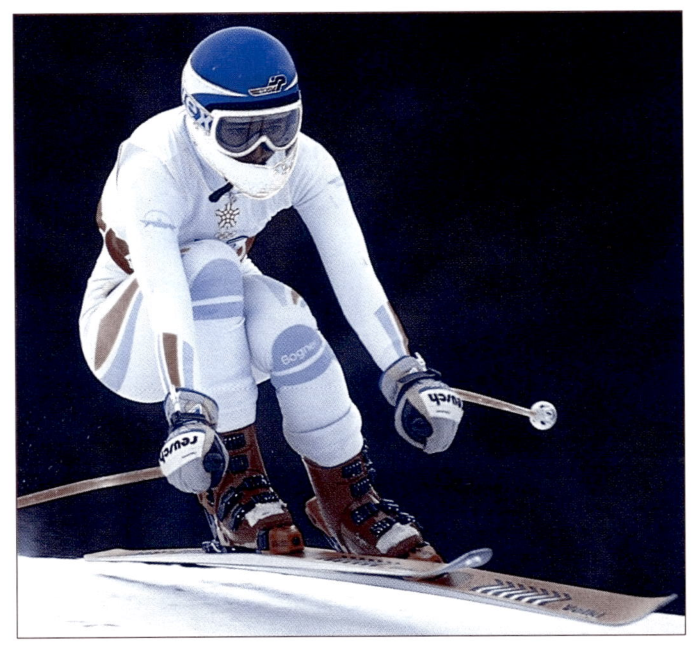

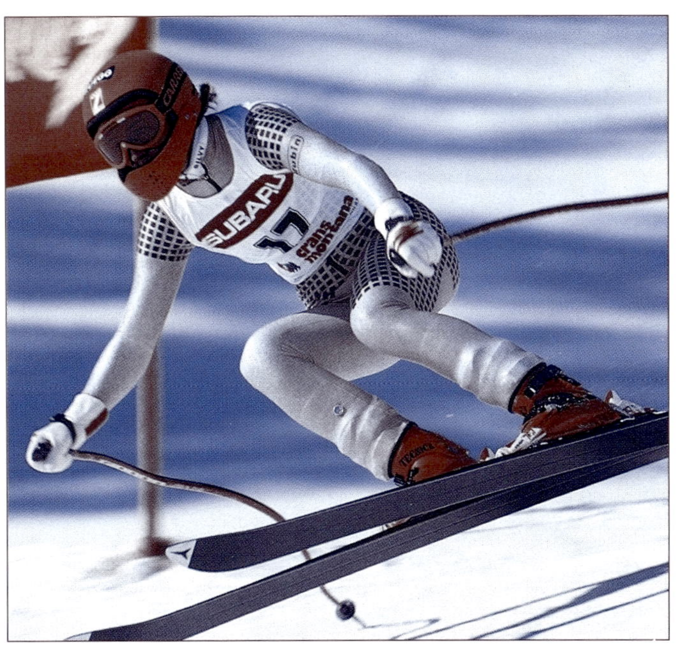

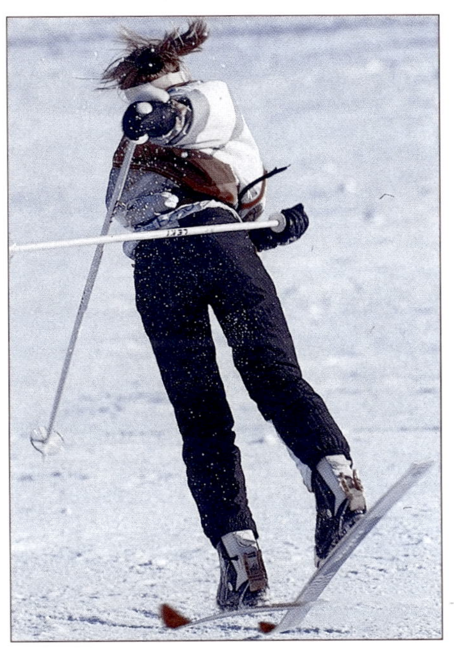

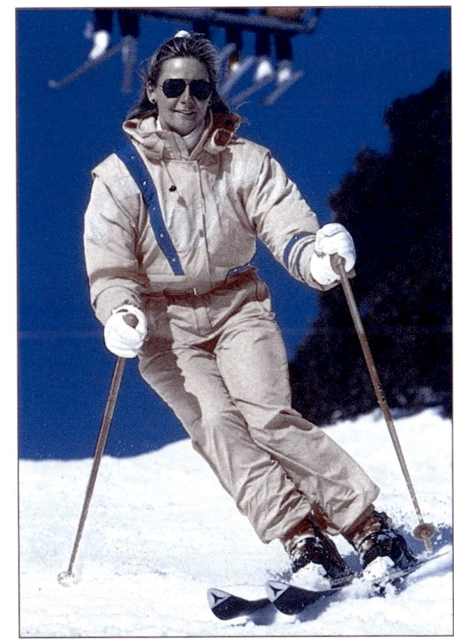

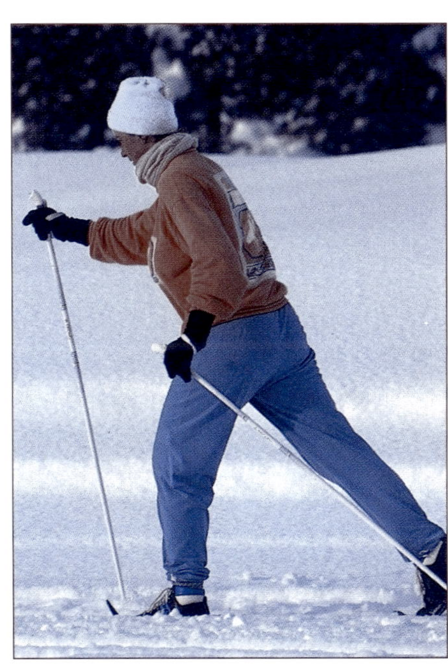

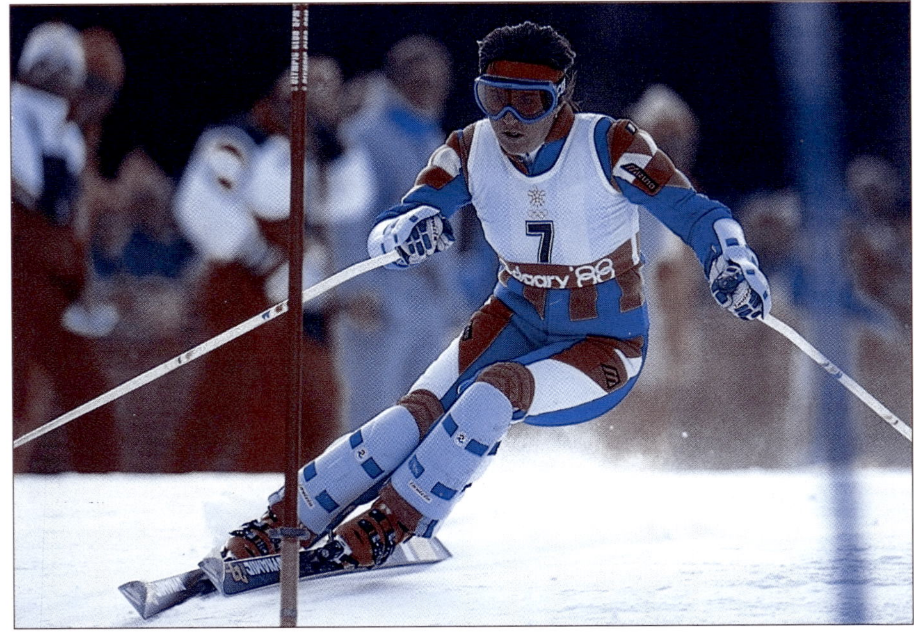

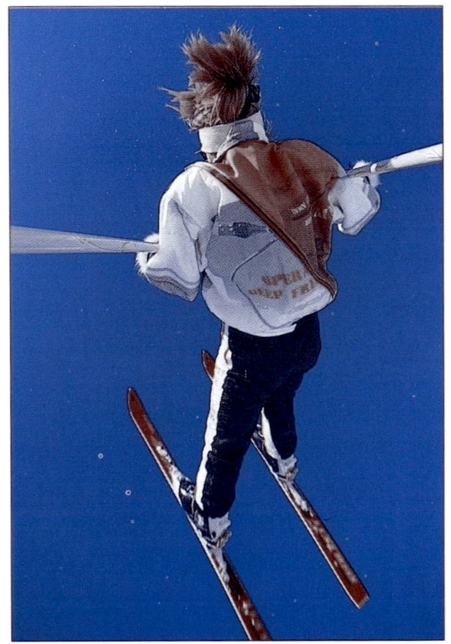

Snowboarding

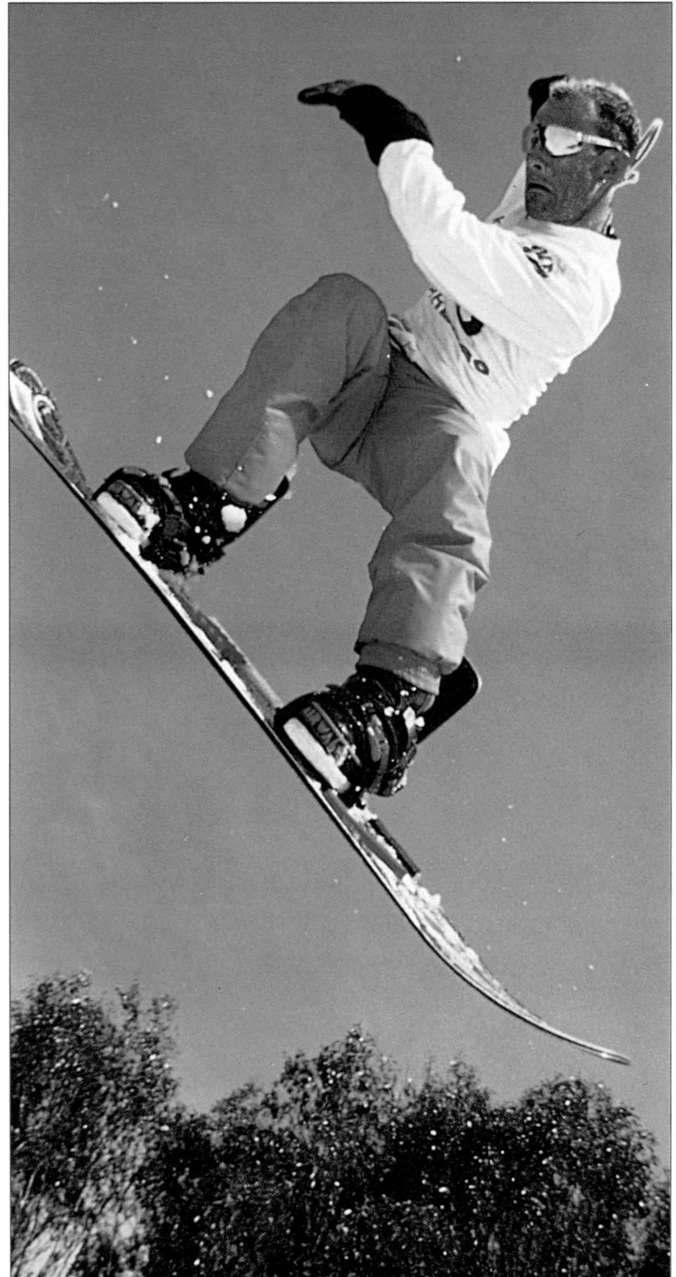

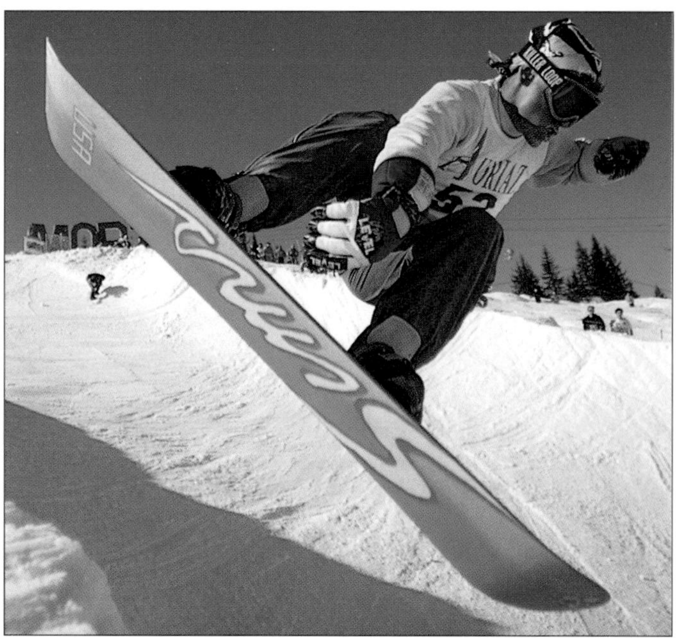

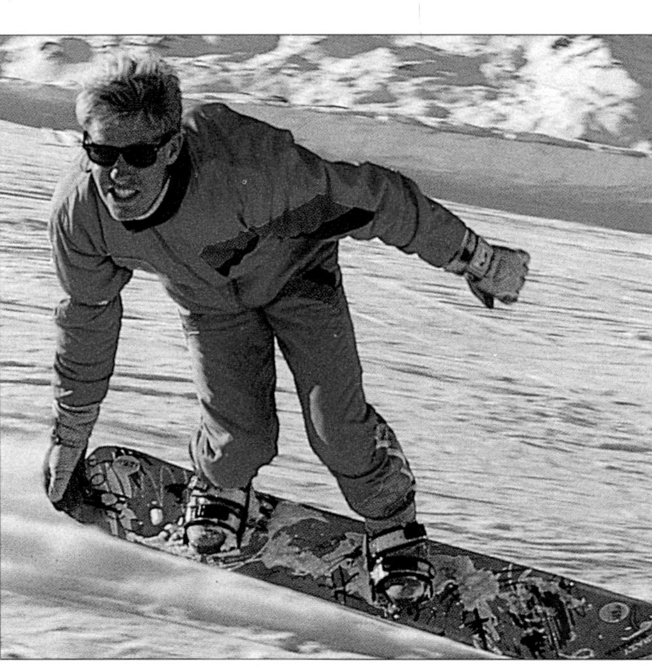

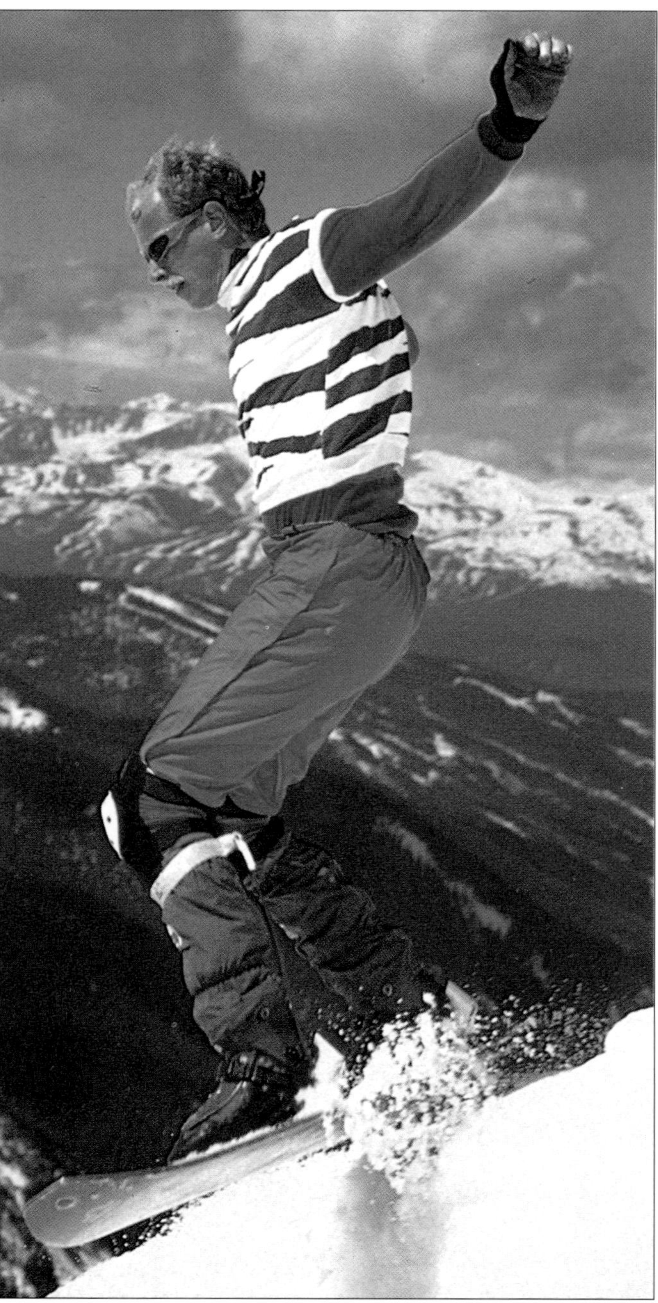

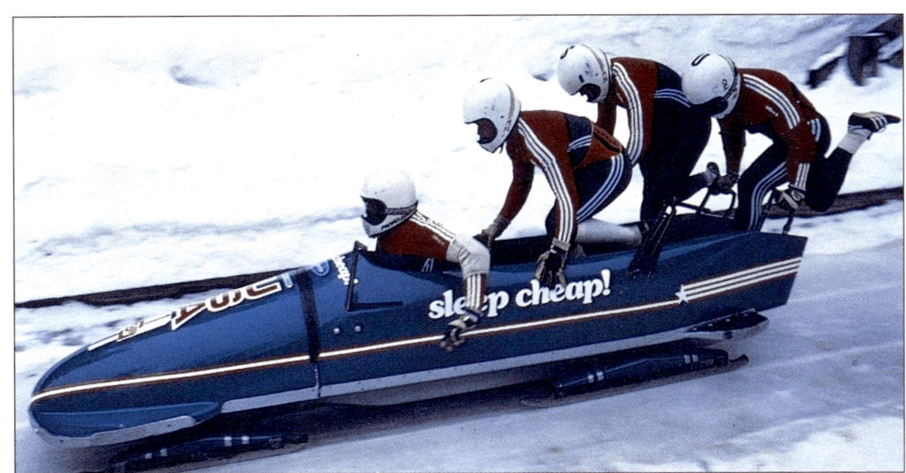
sleep cheap!

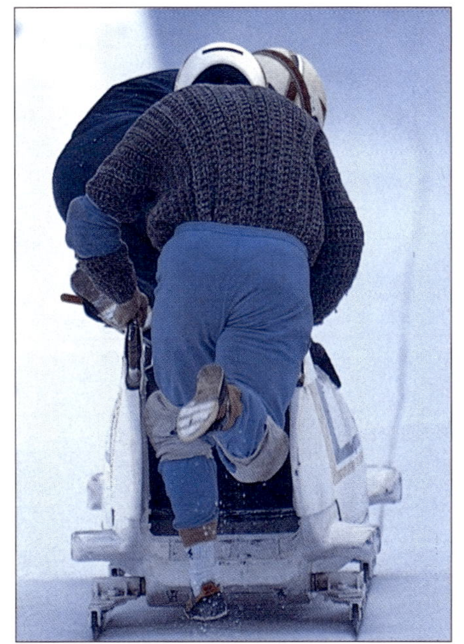

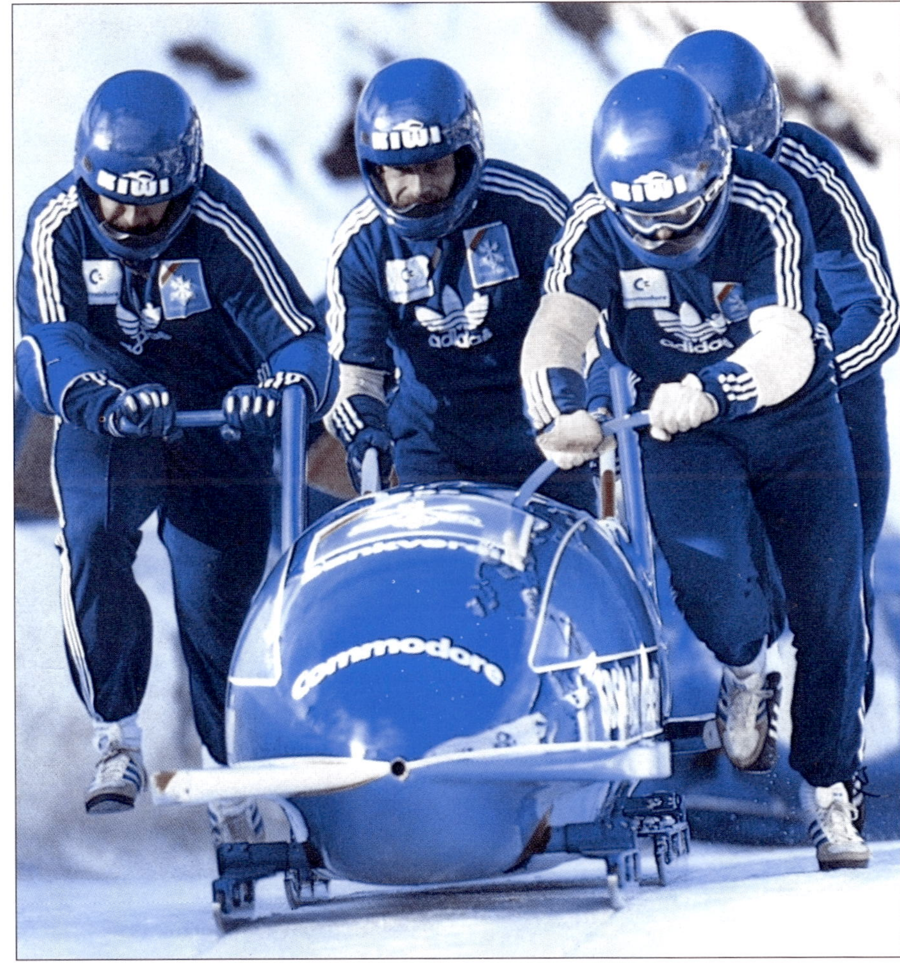
KIWI
adidas
Commodore

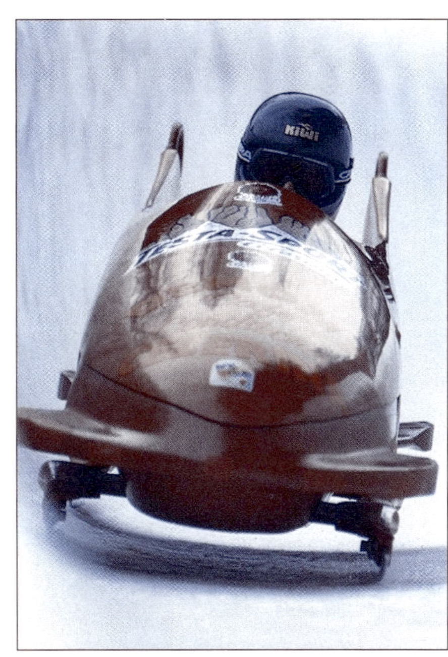
KIWI

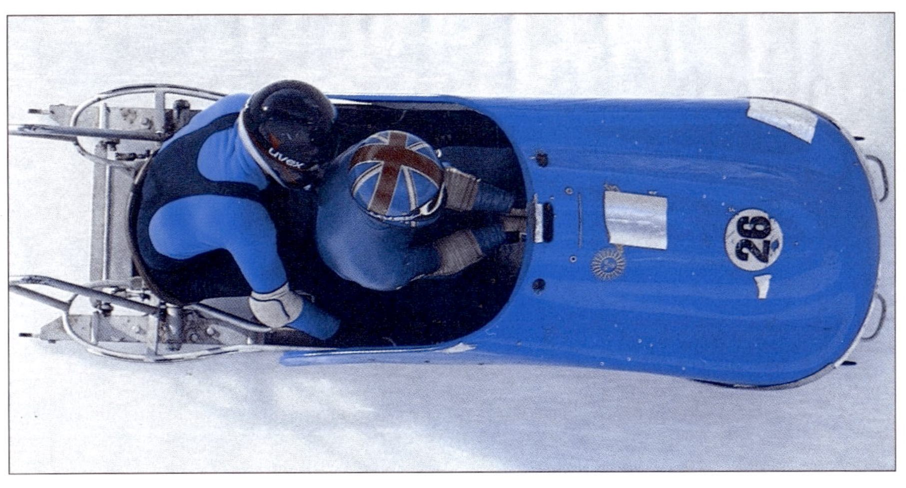
uvex
26

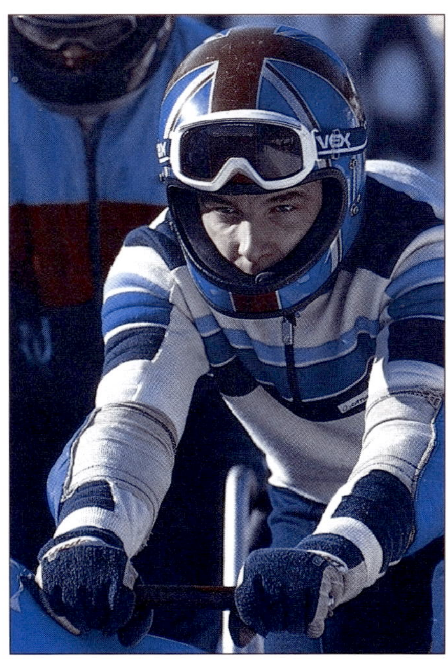
uvex

Luge · tobogganing

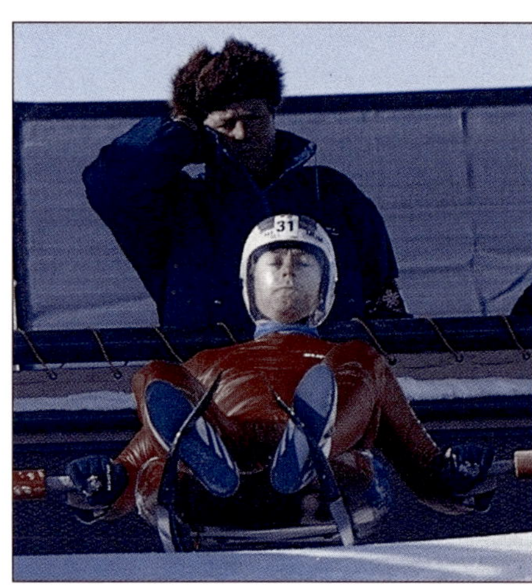

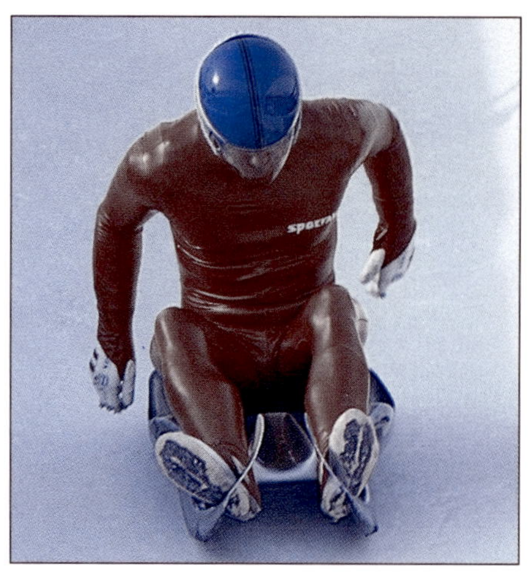

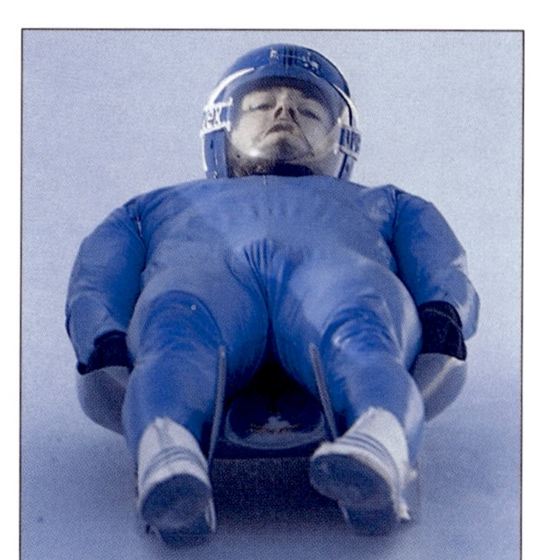

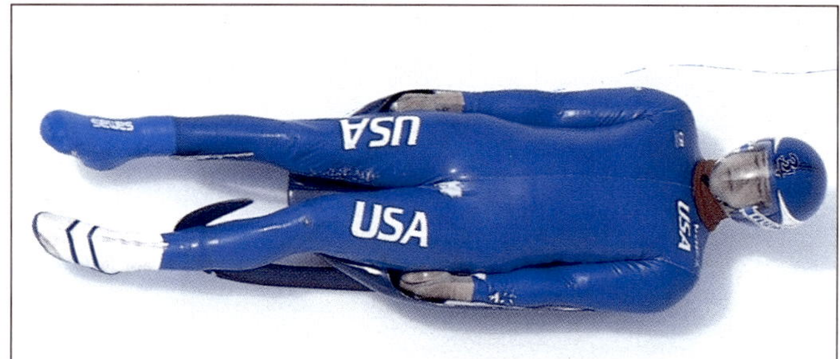

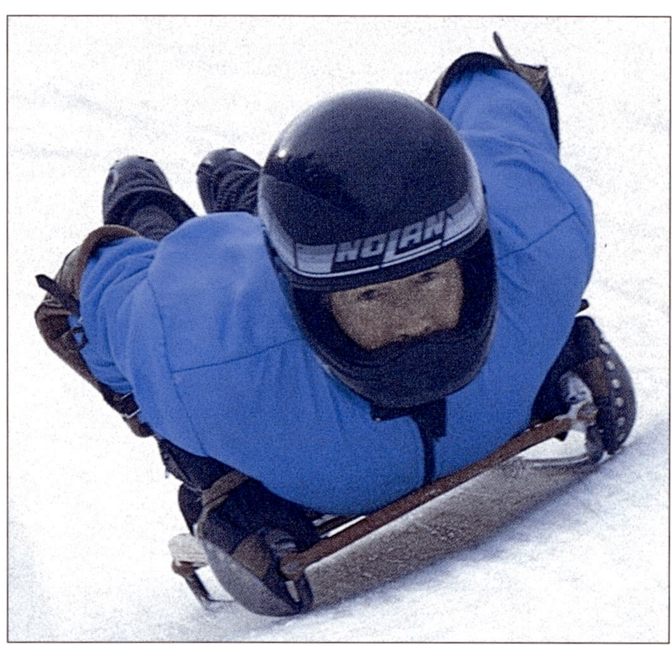

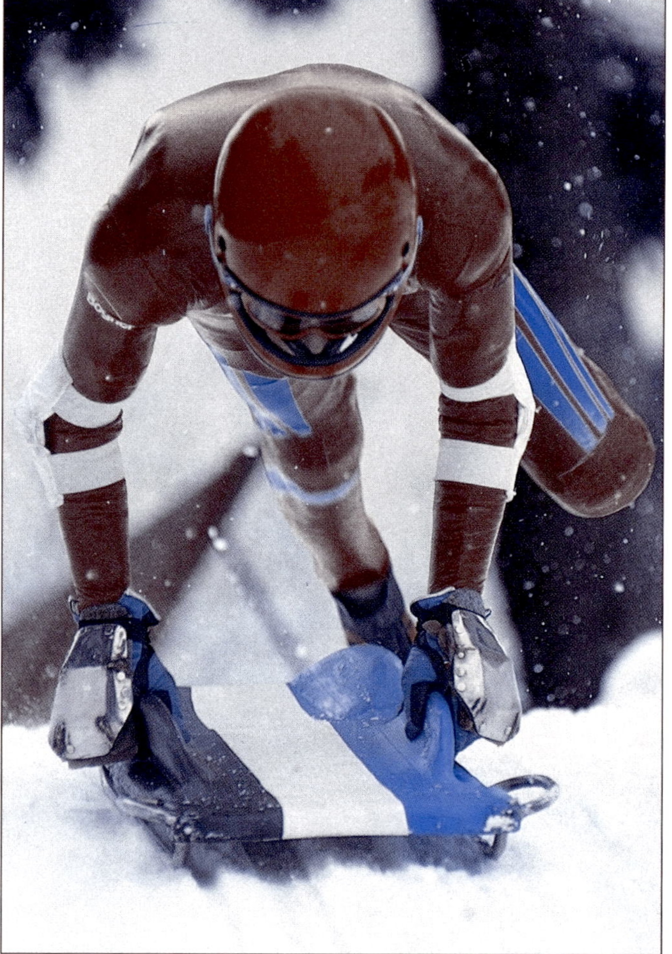

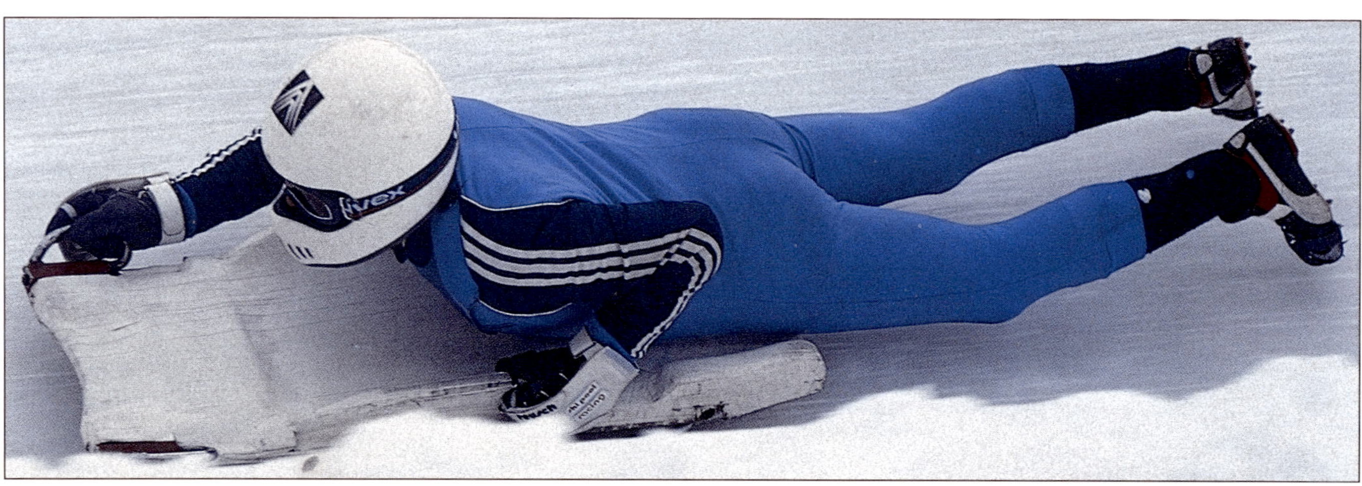

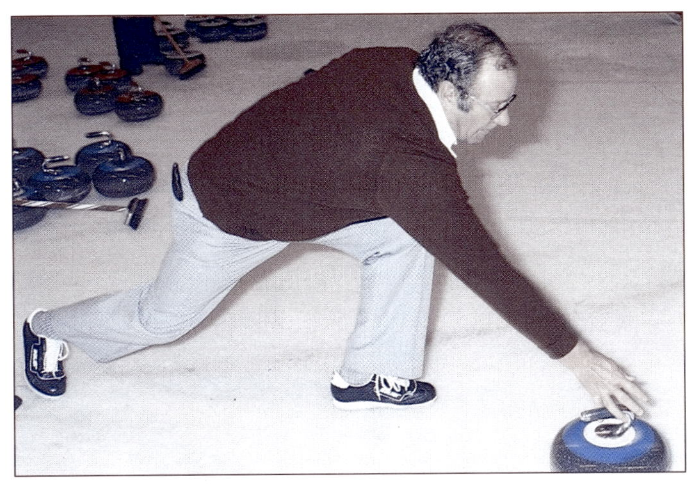

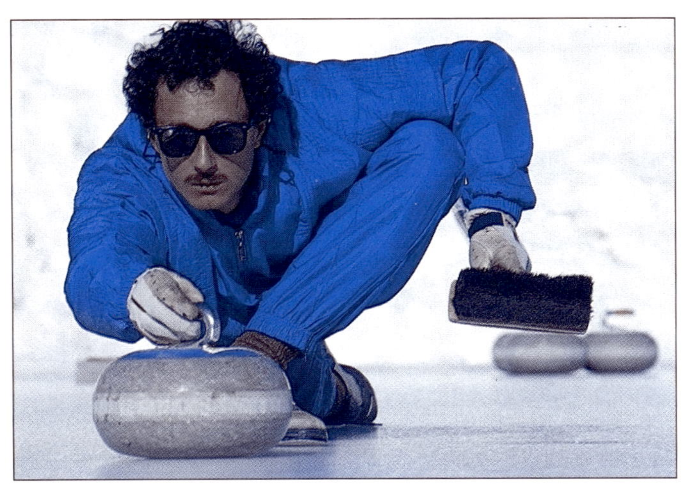

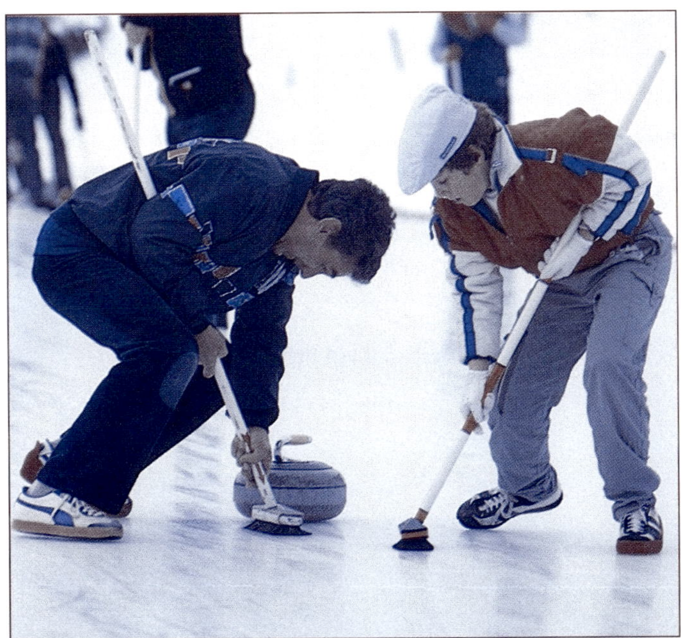

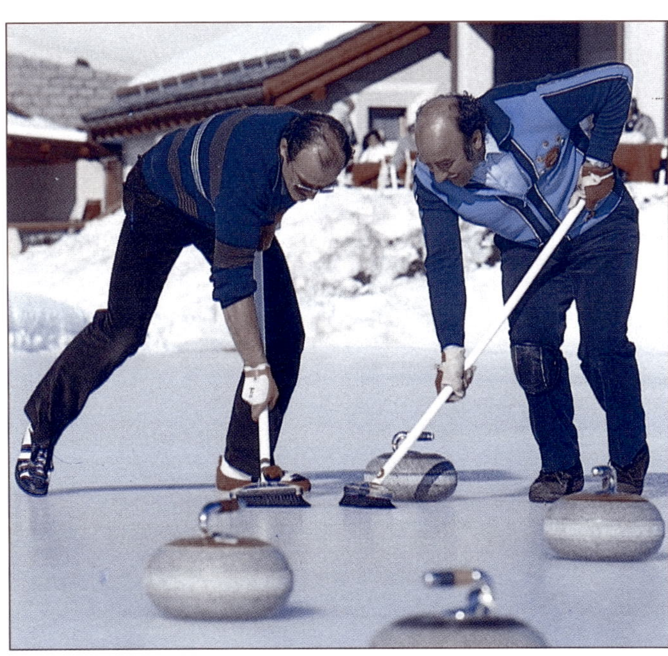

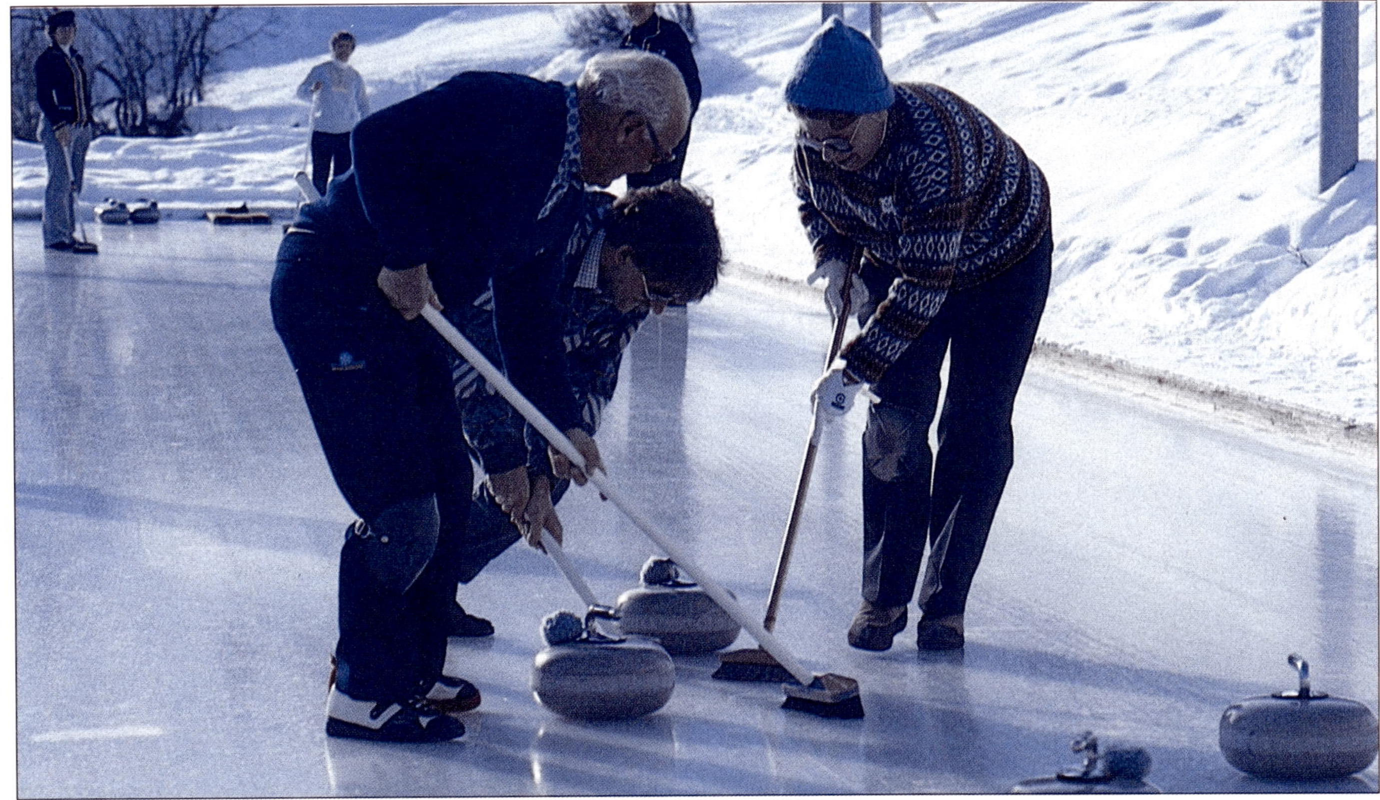

Skating – male · speed · figure

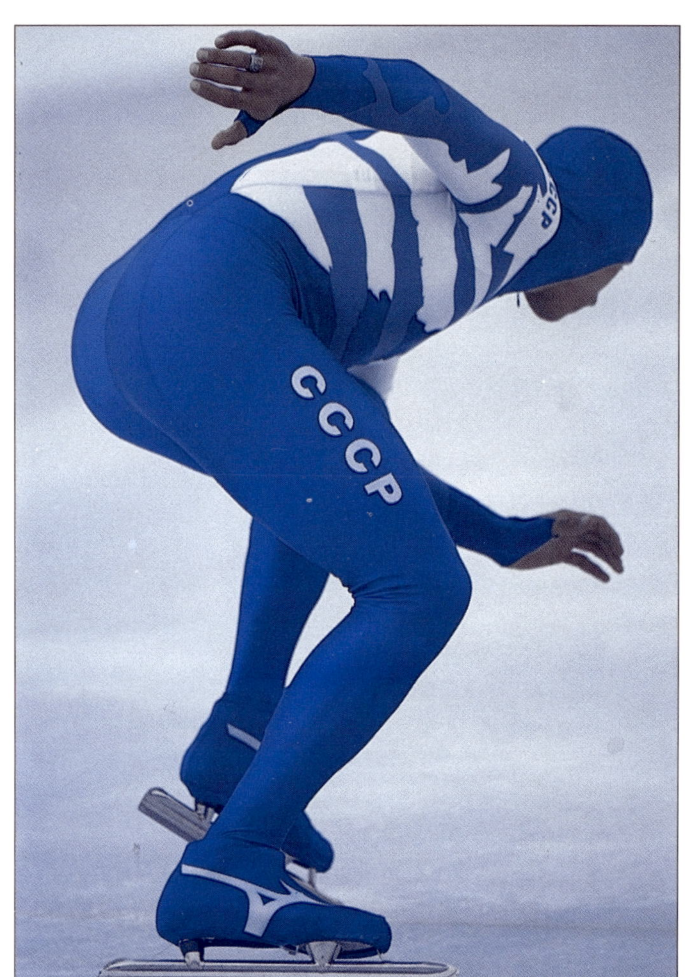

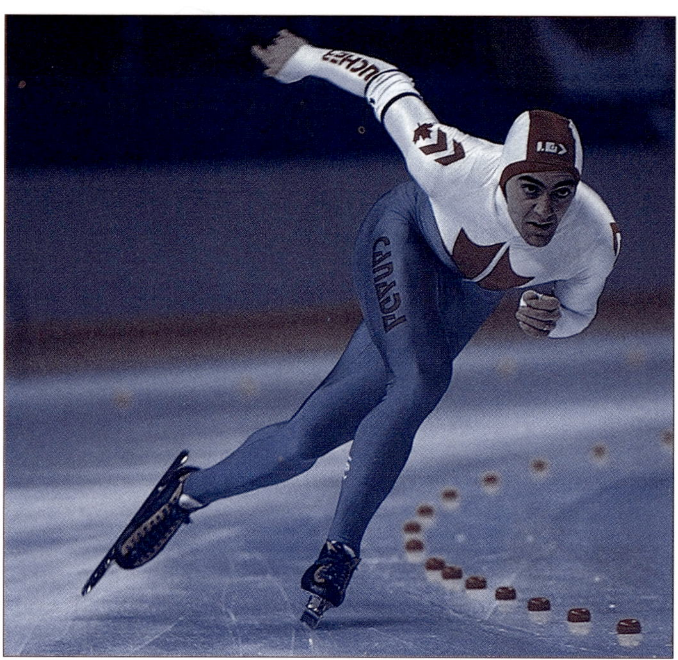

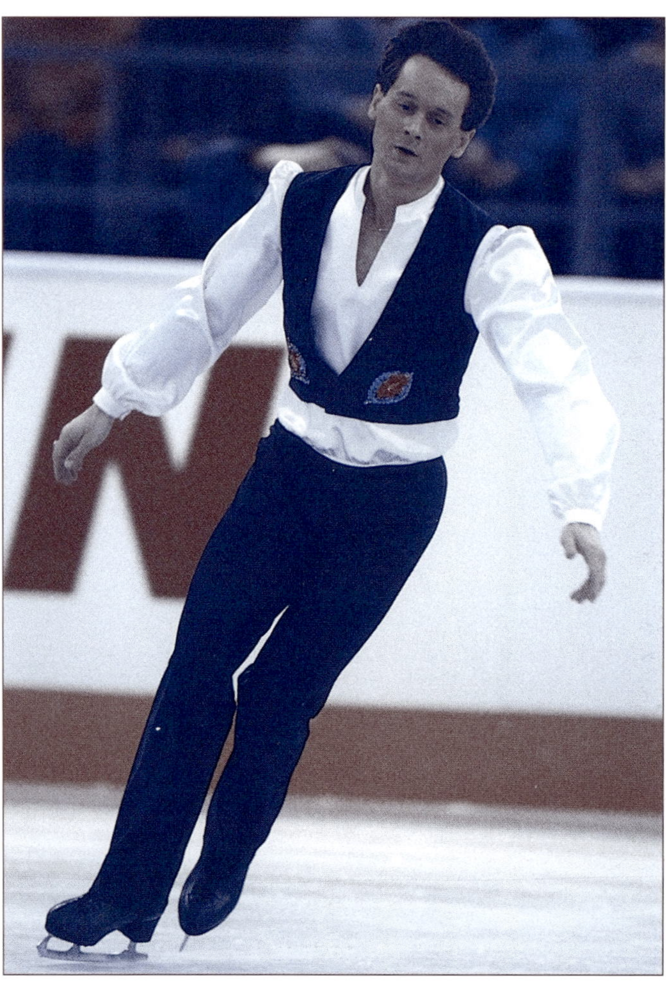

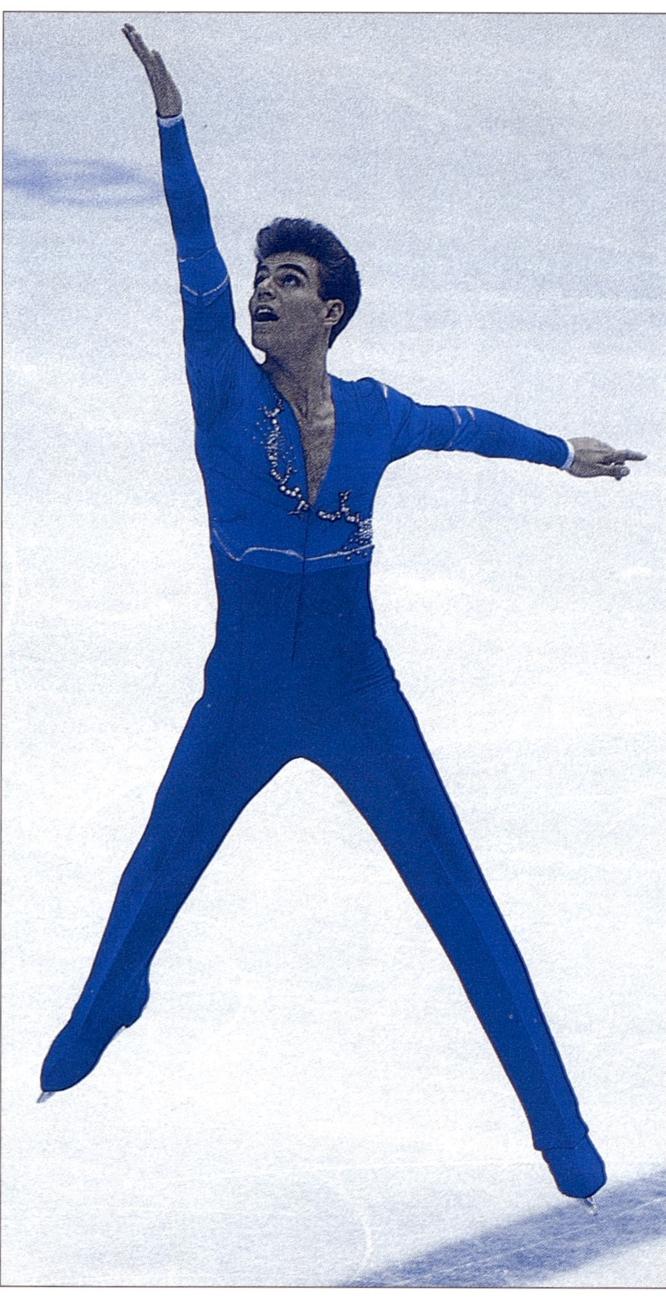

Skating – male · figure

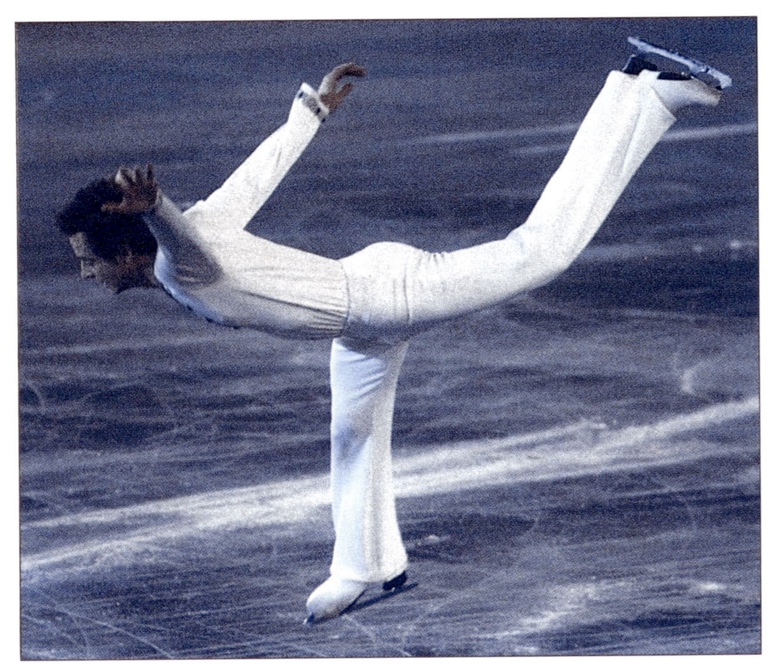

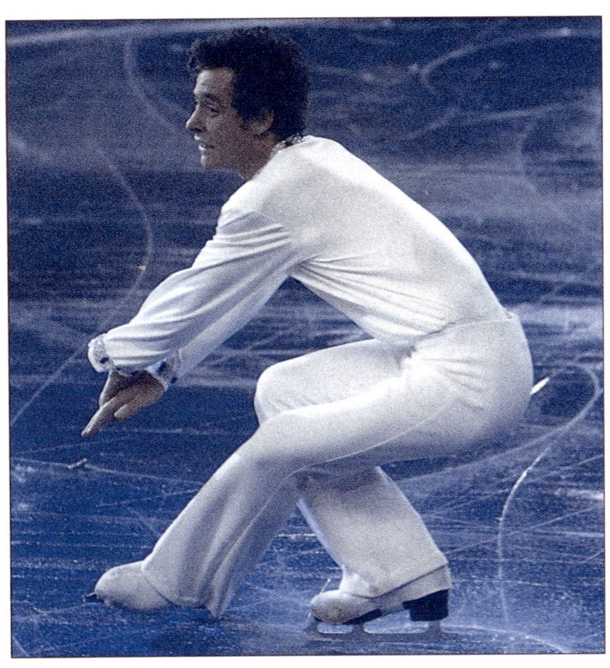

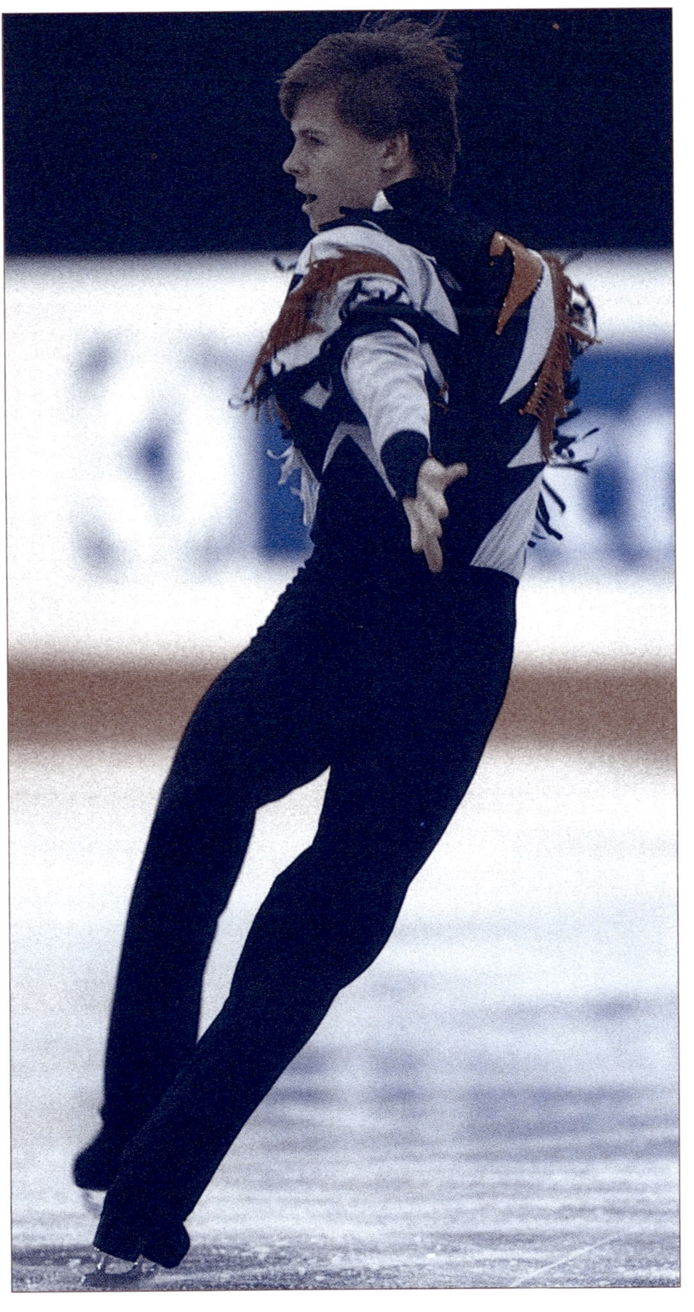

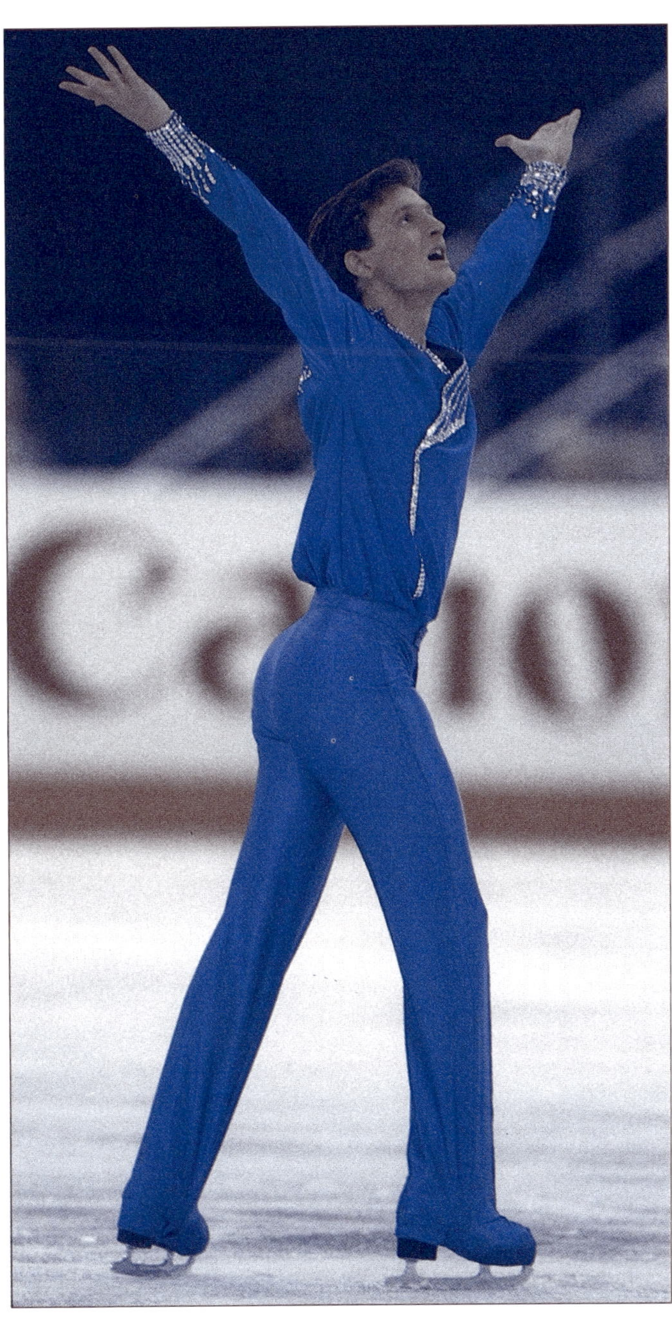

Skating – female

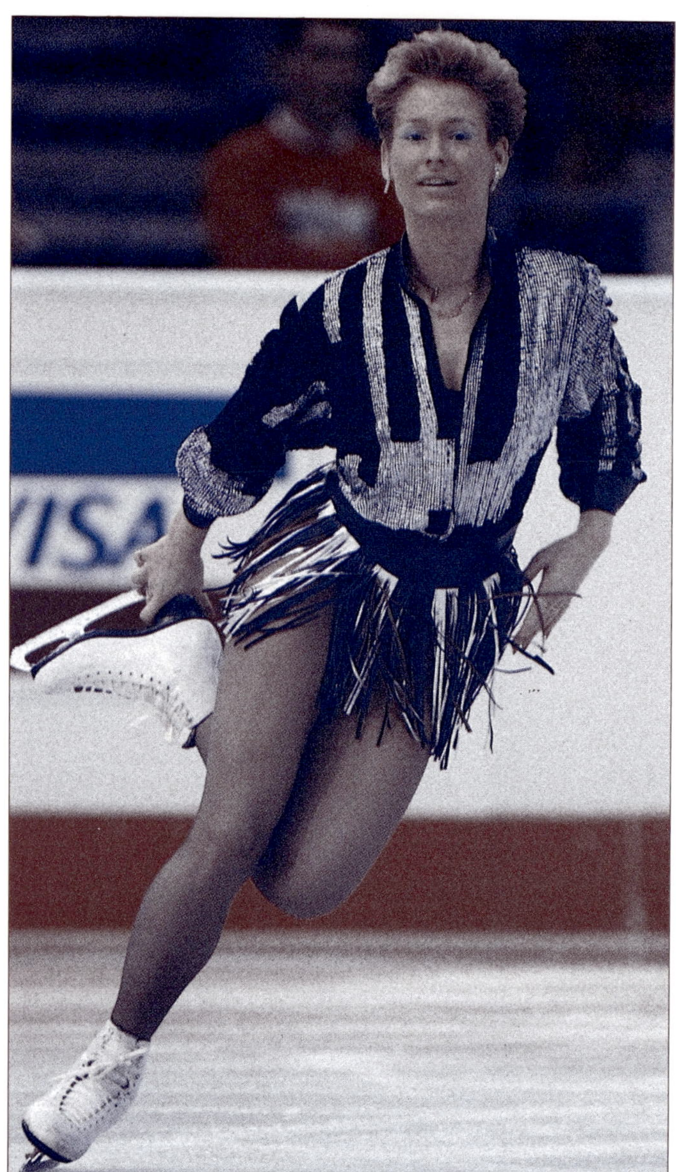

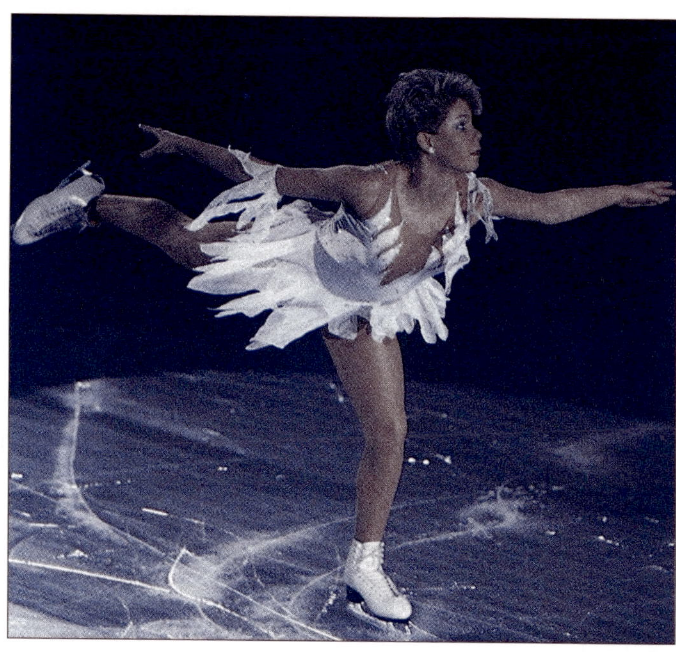

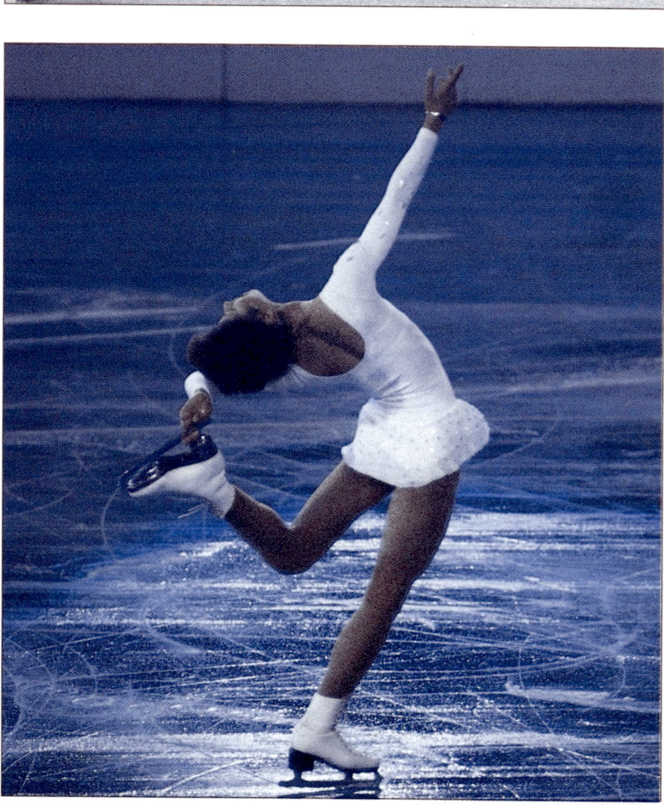

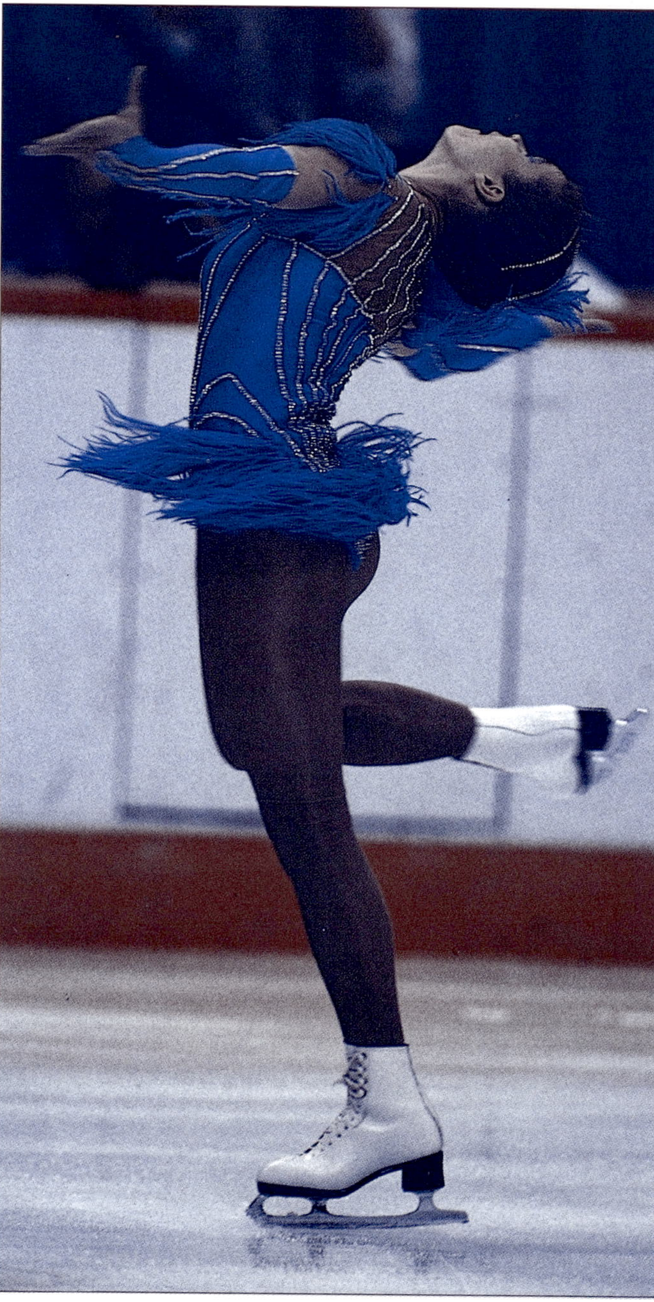

Skating – female

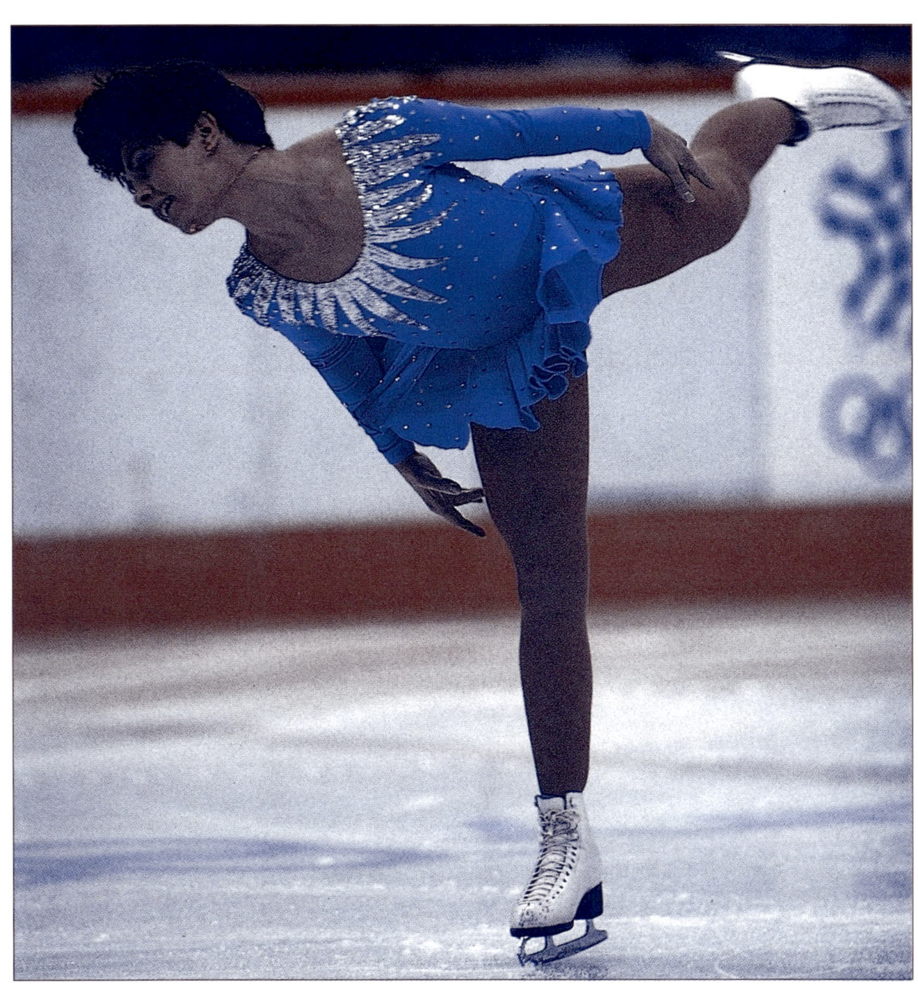

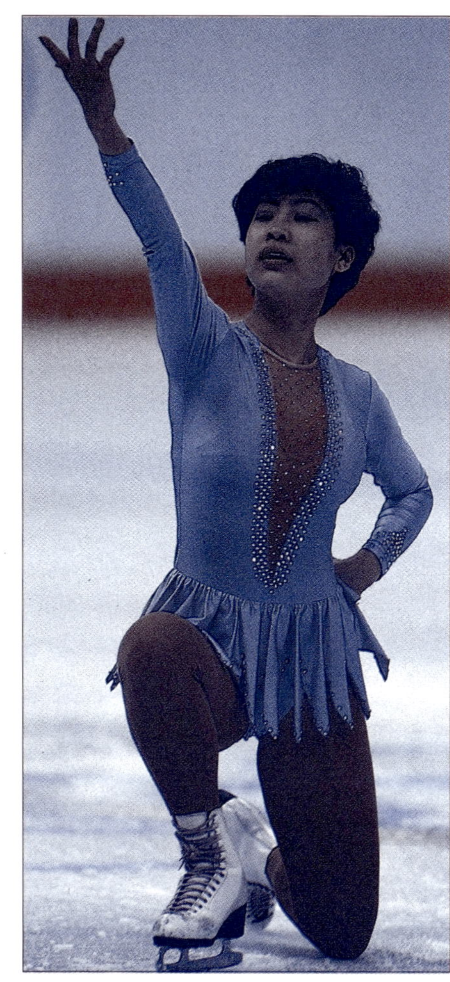

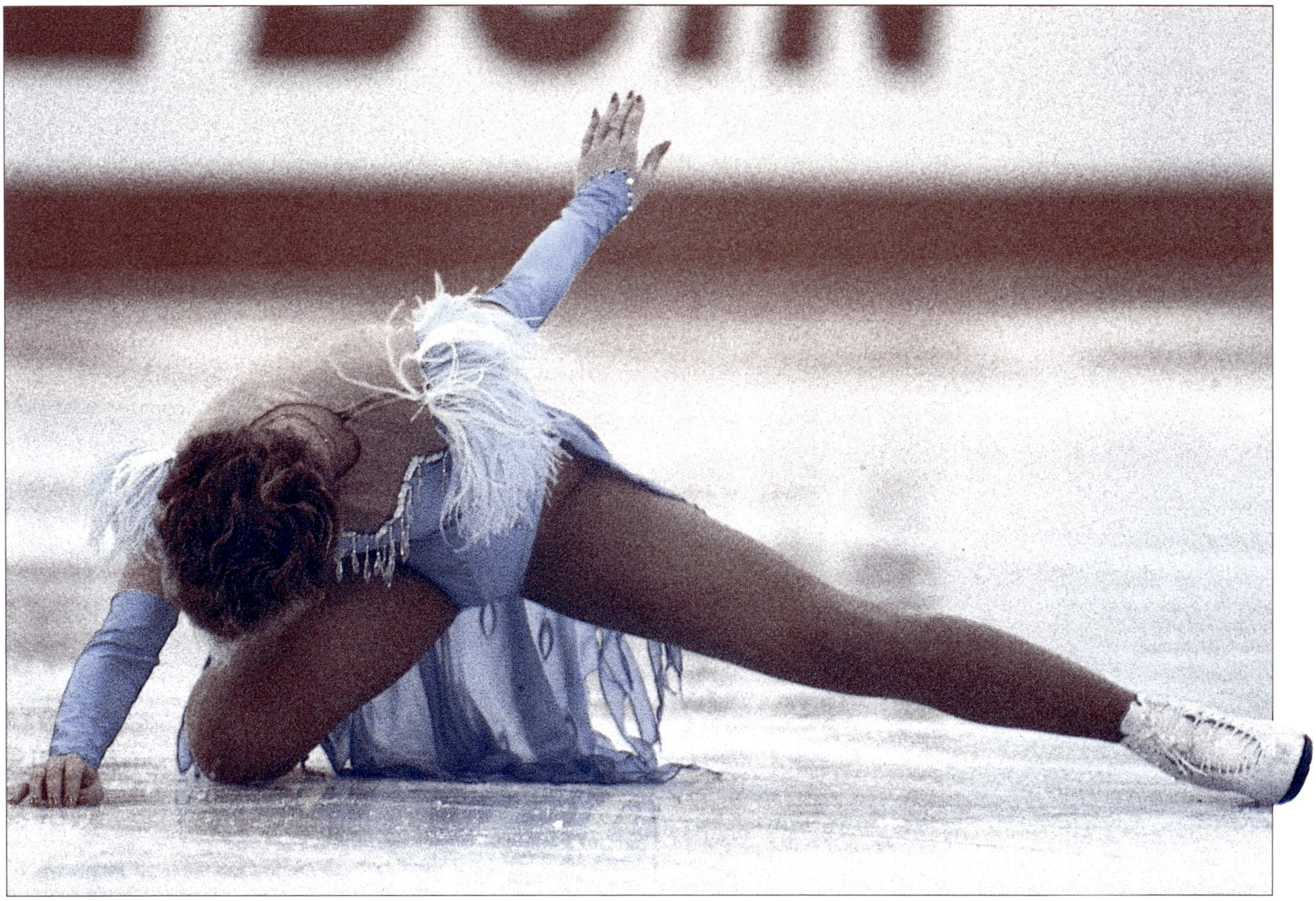

Skating – pairs · dance

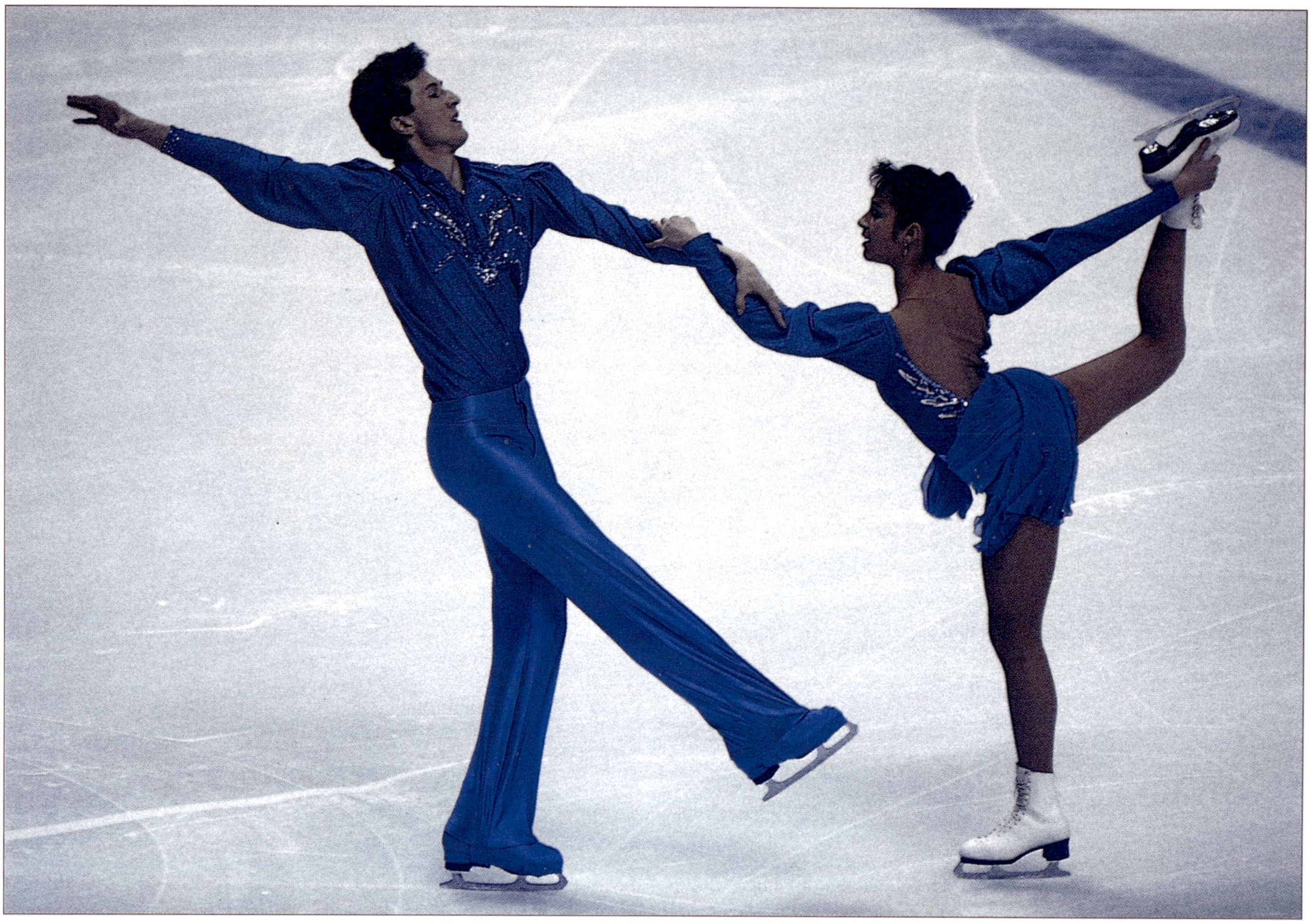

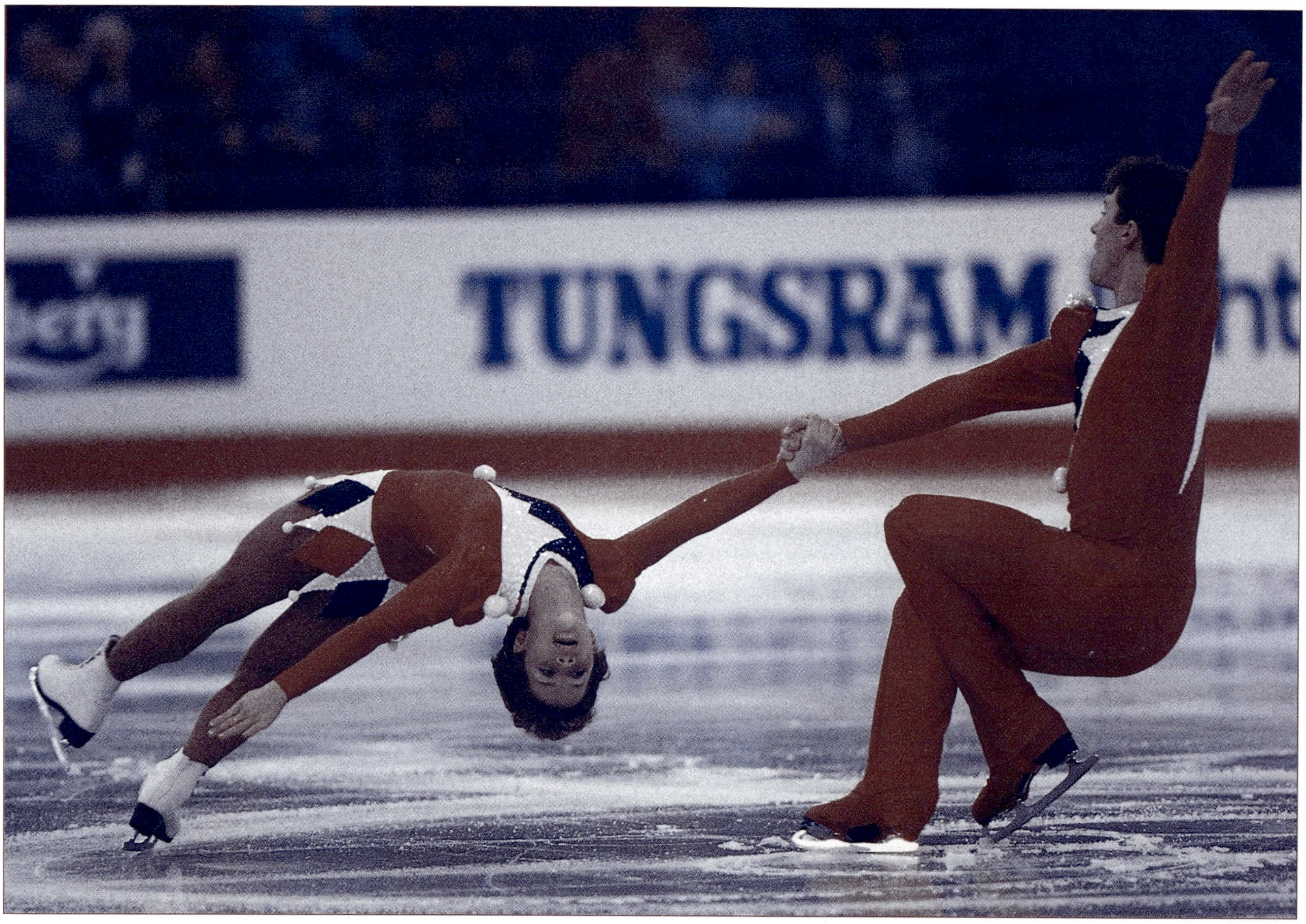

Skating – pairs · dance

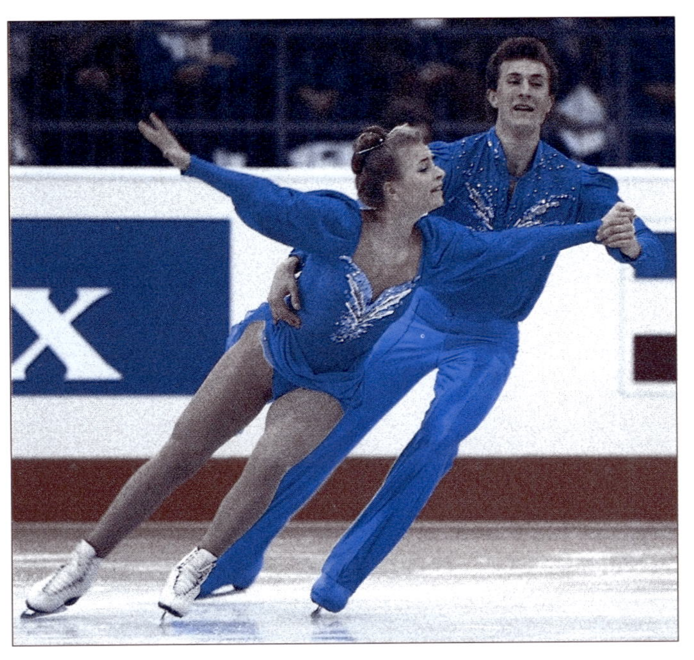
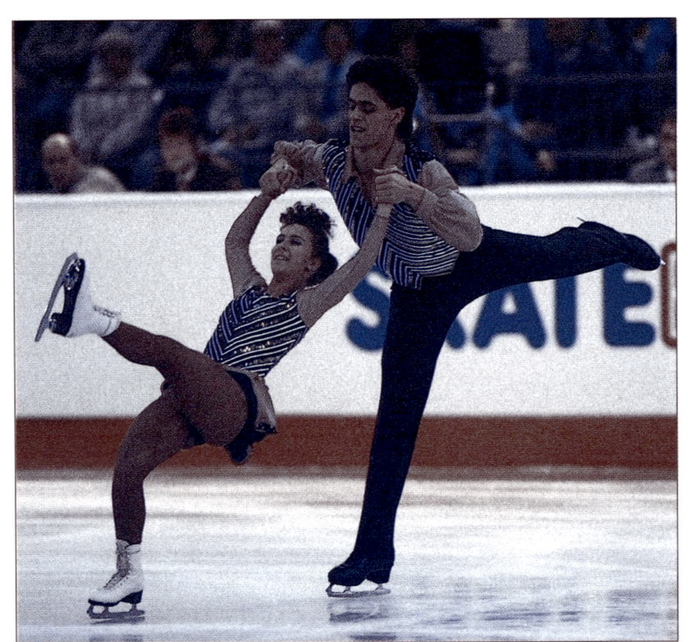
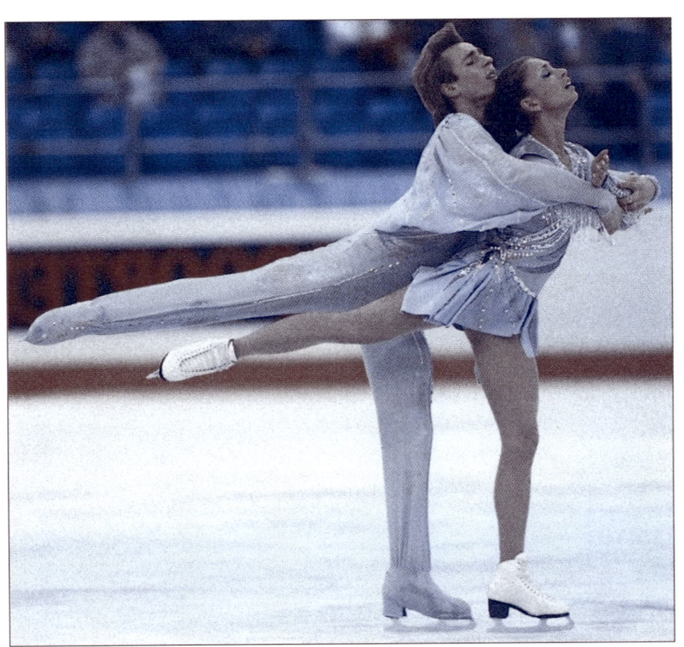
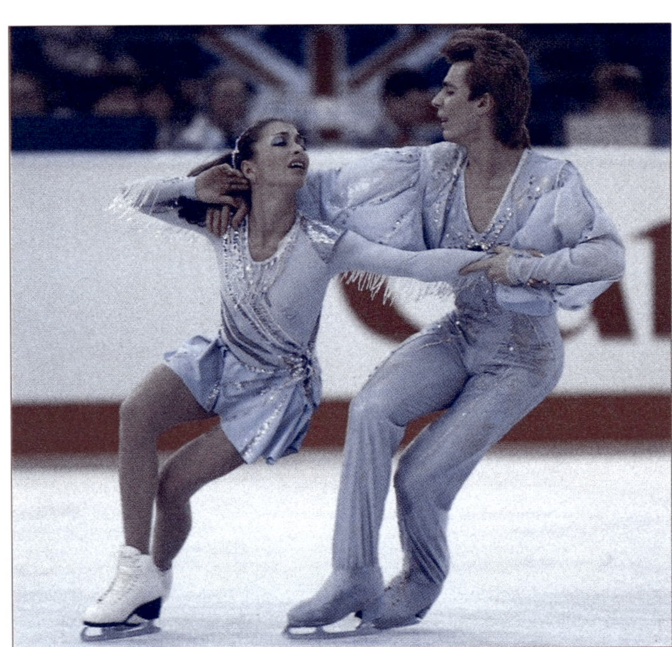
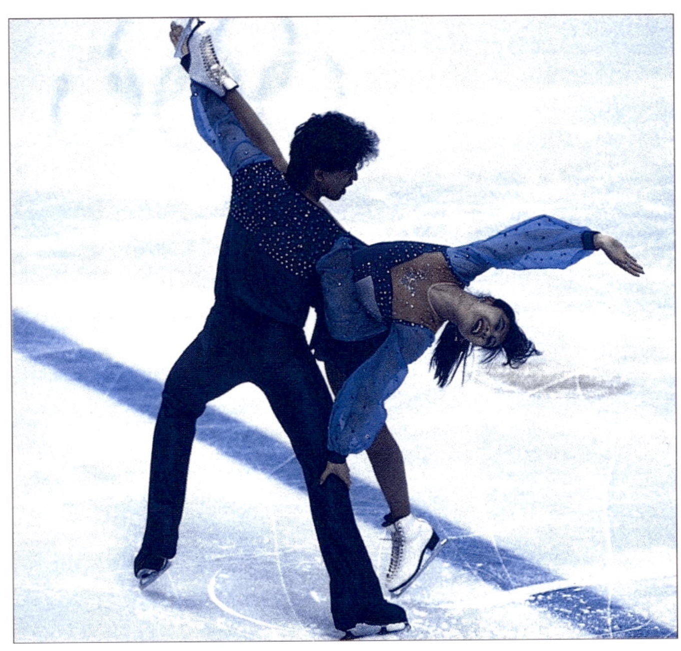
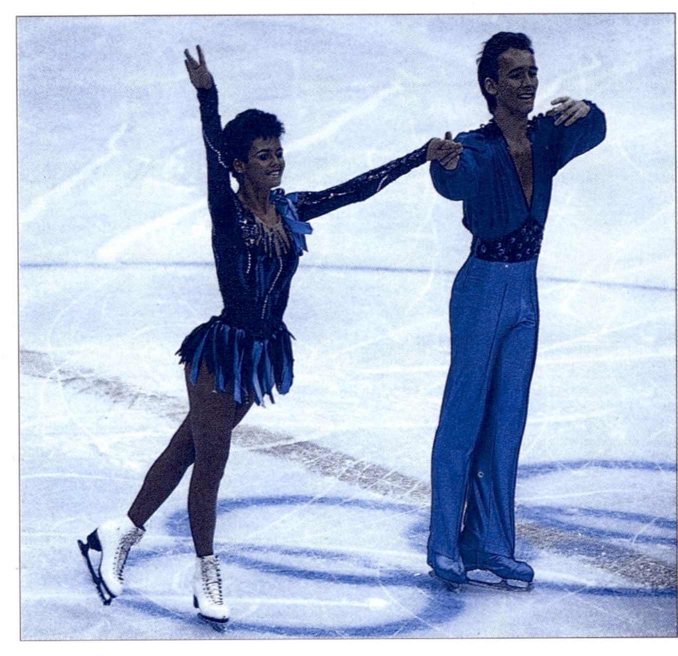

Ice hockey

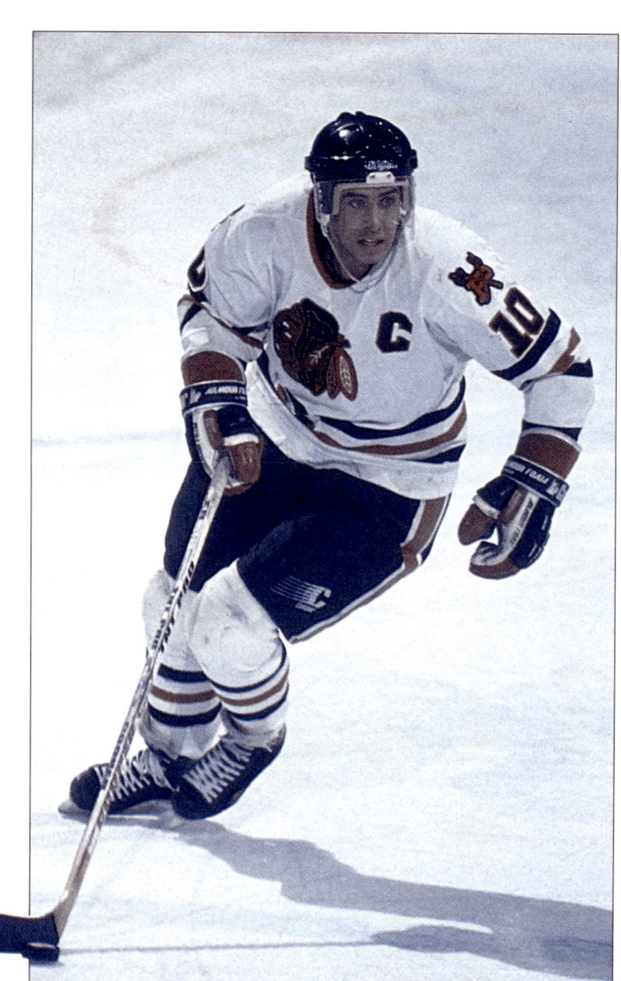

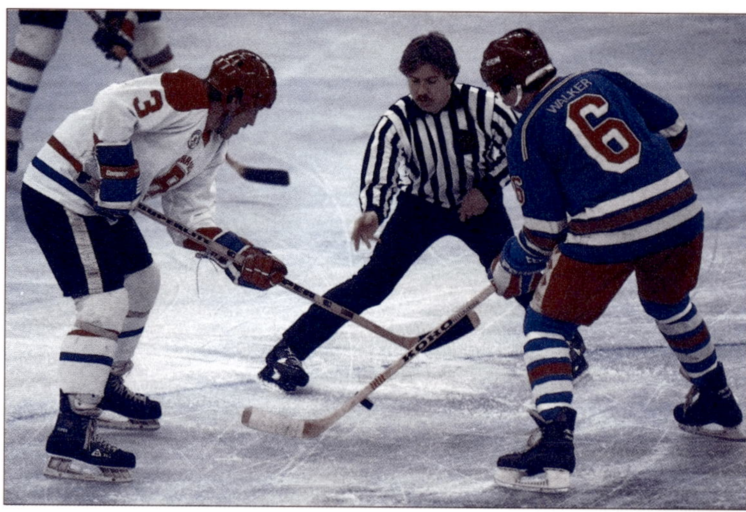

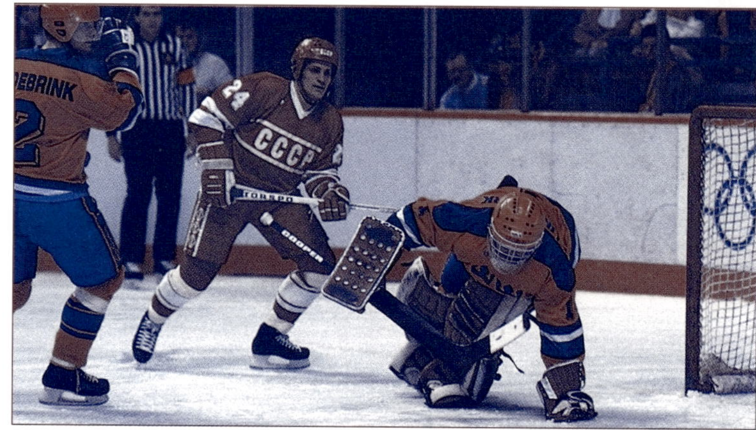

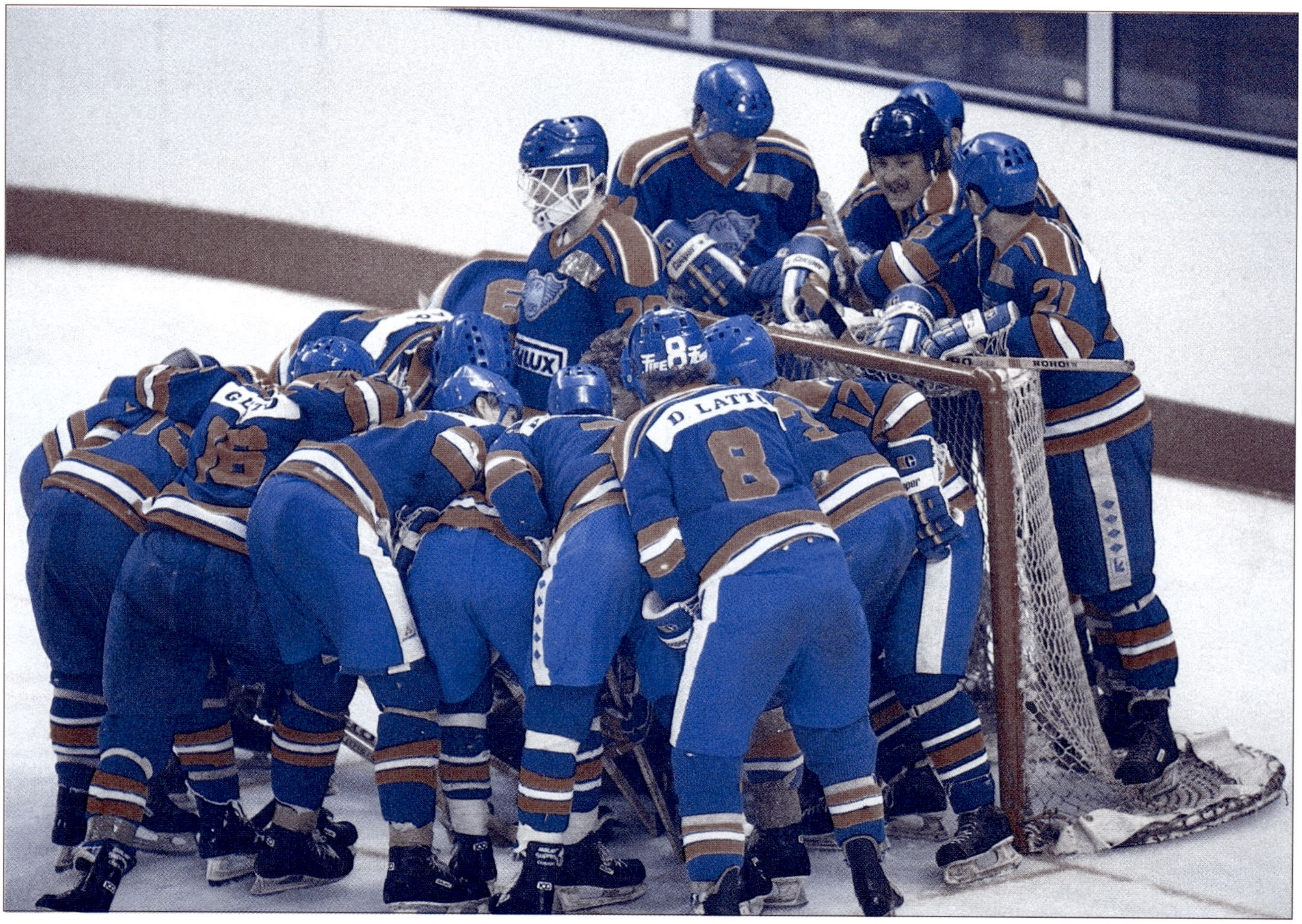

Ice hockey

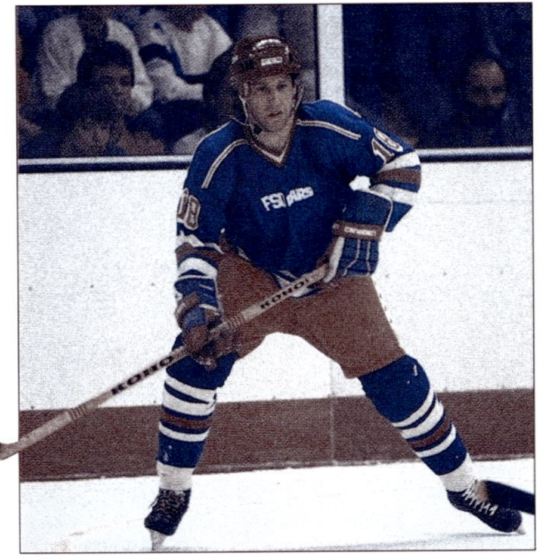

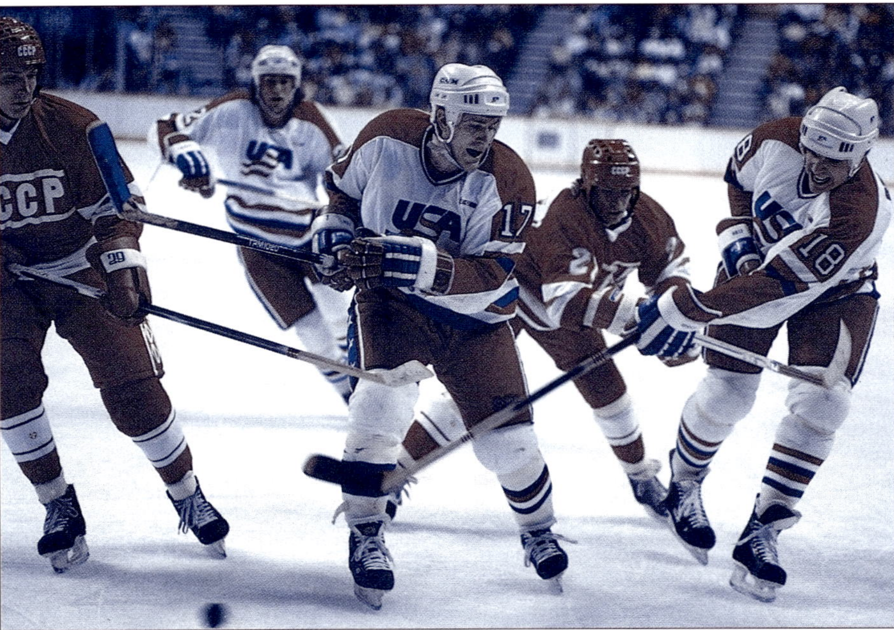

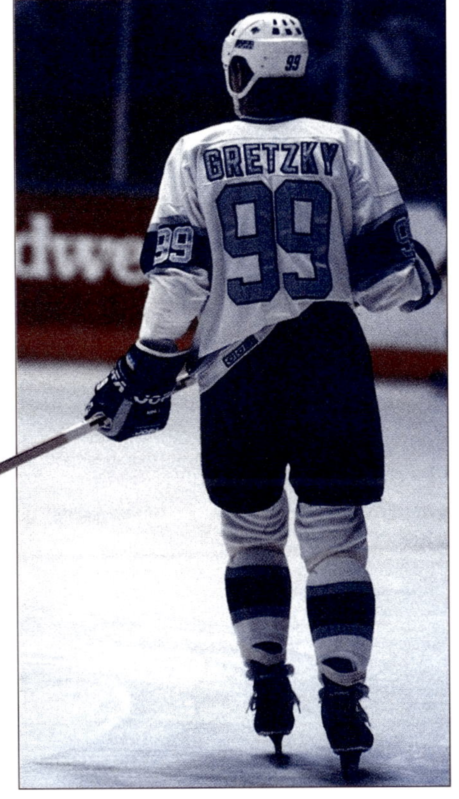

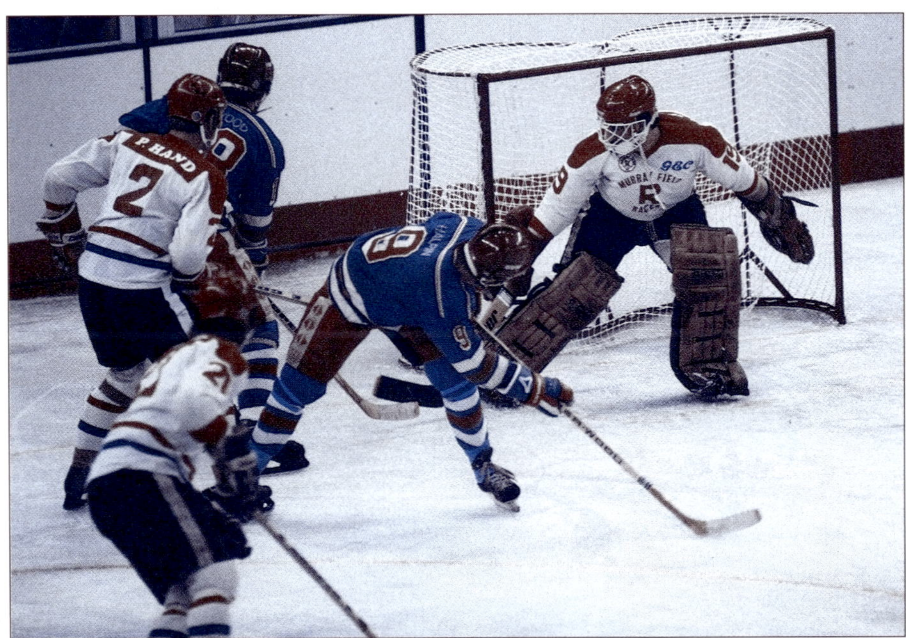

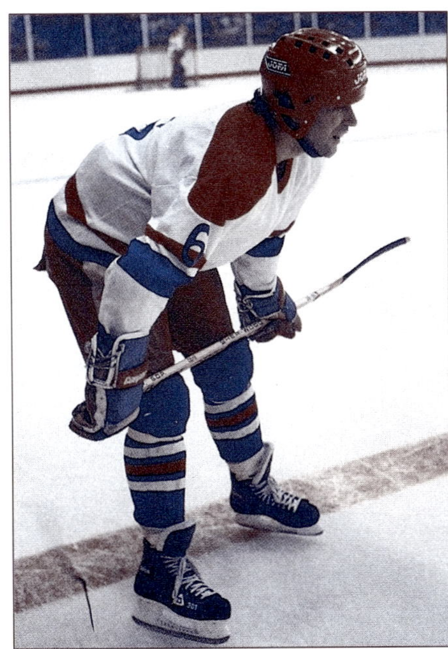

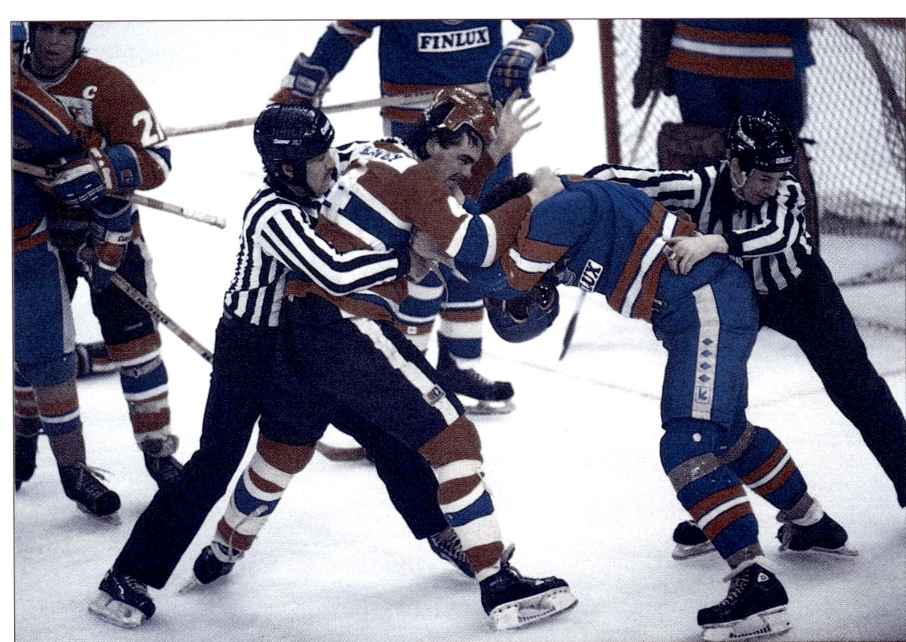

Rock climbing – male

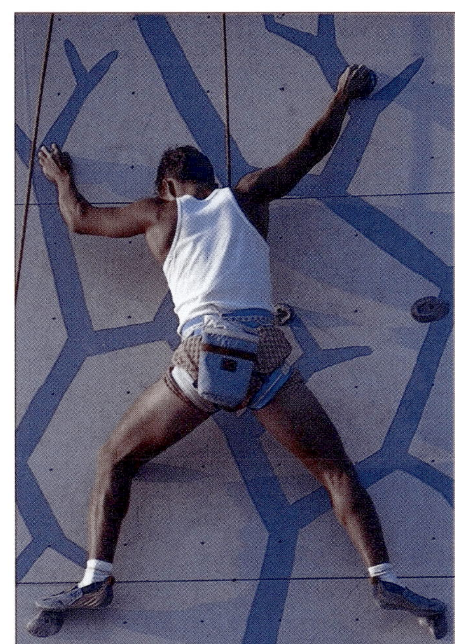

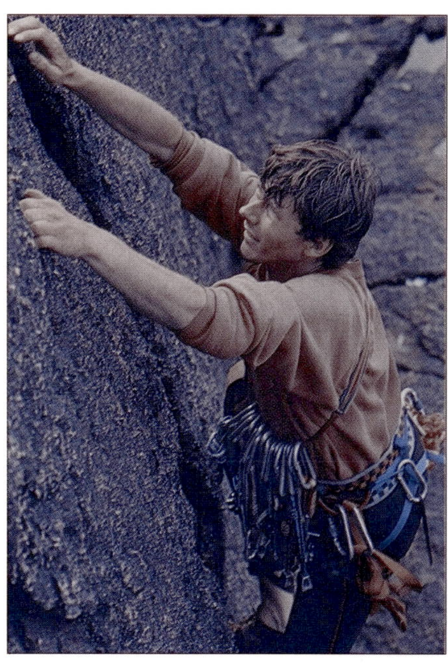

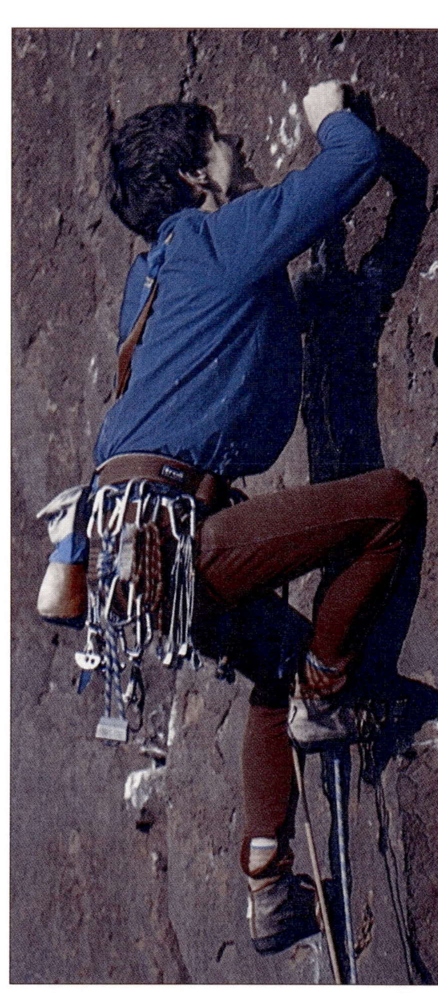

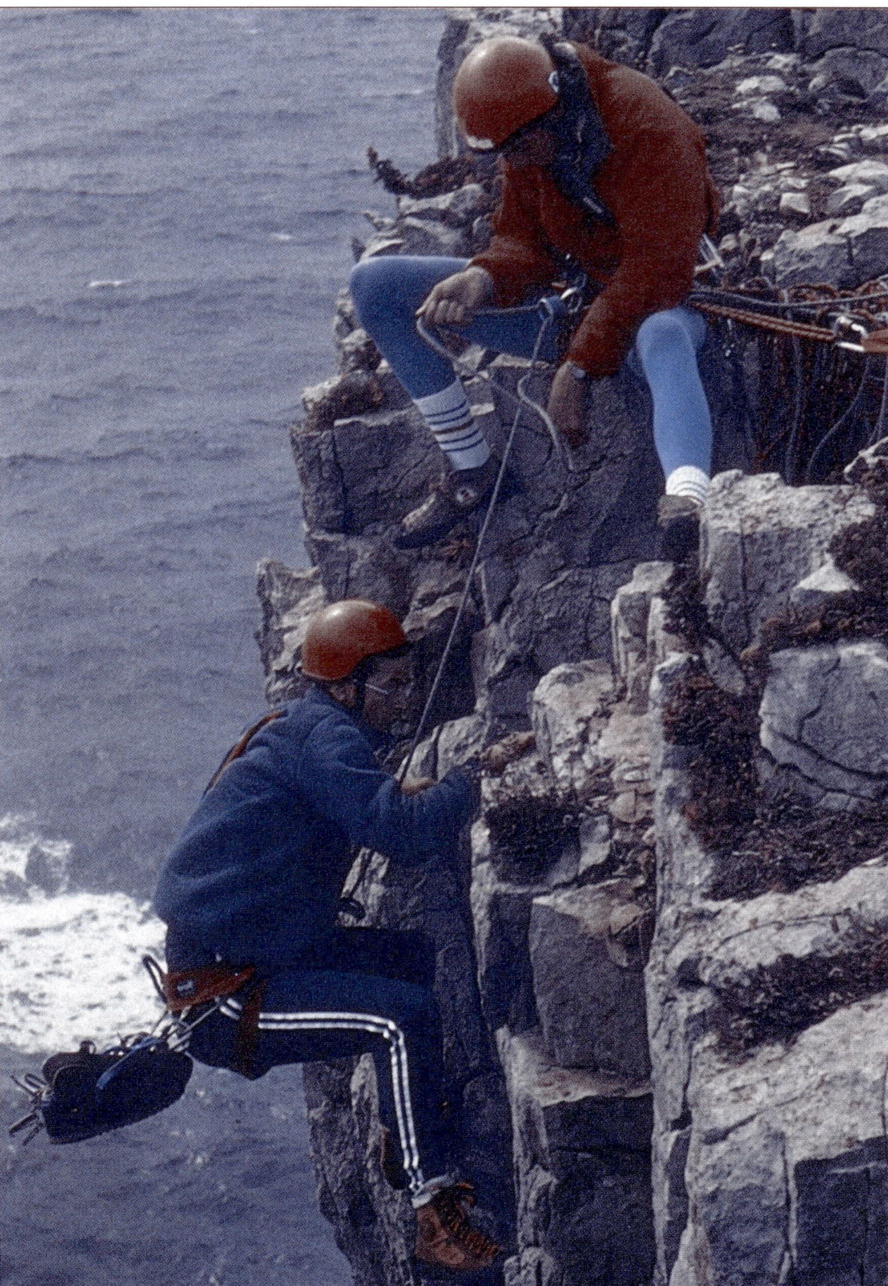

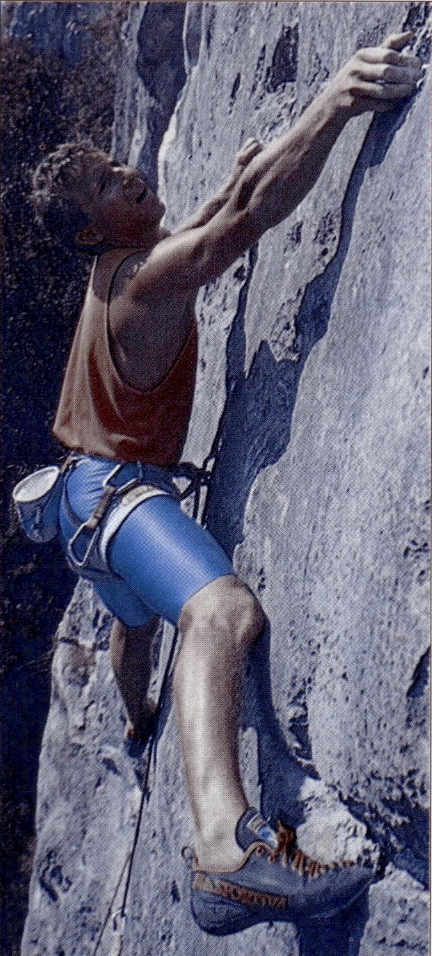

Rock climbing – male/female

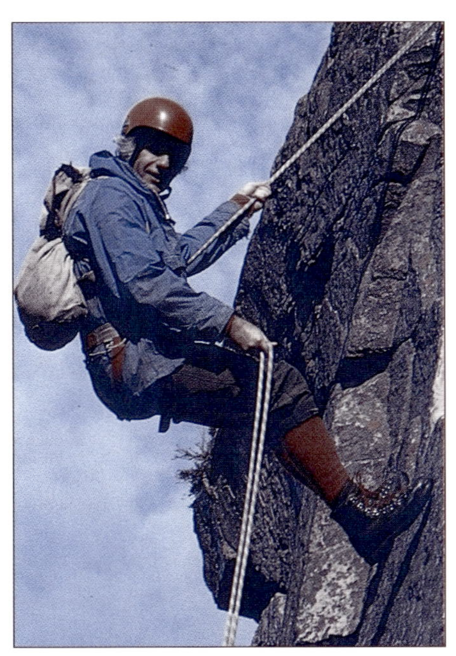

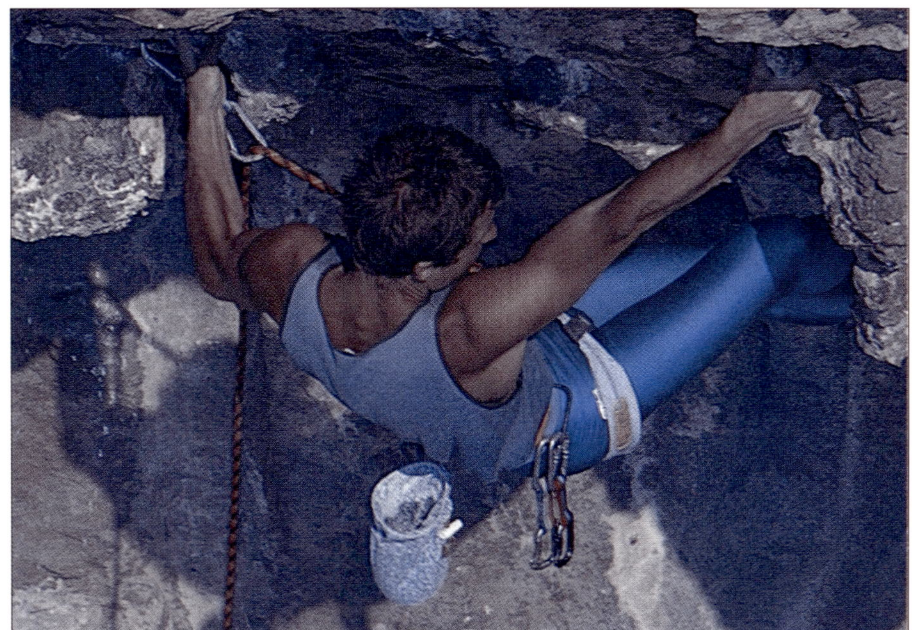

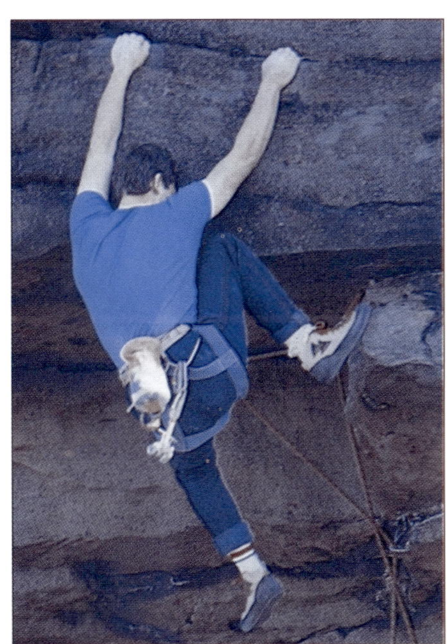

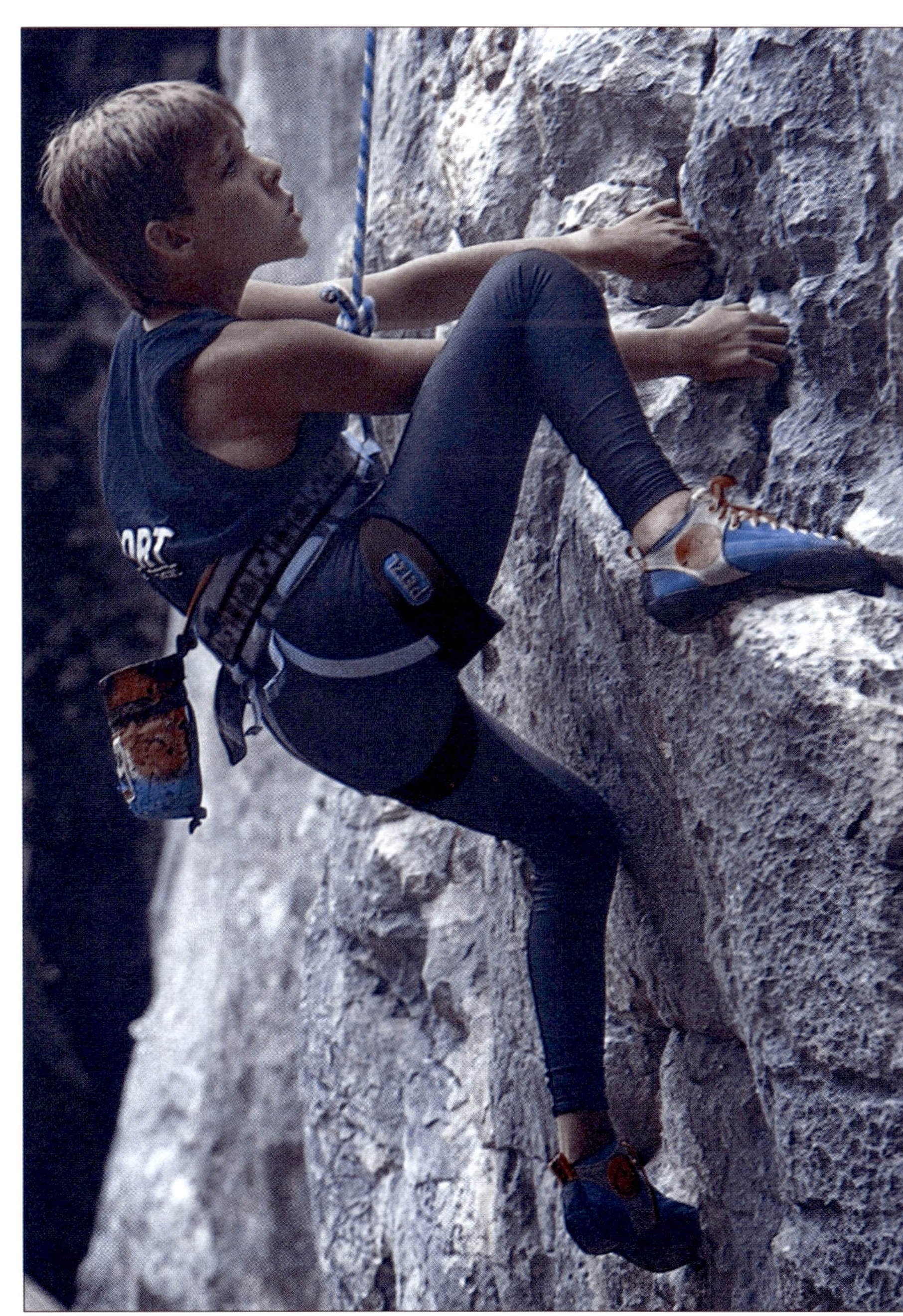

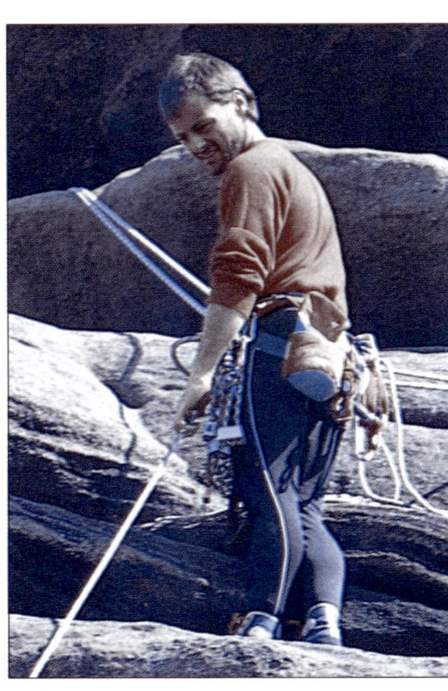

Hang gliding

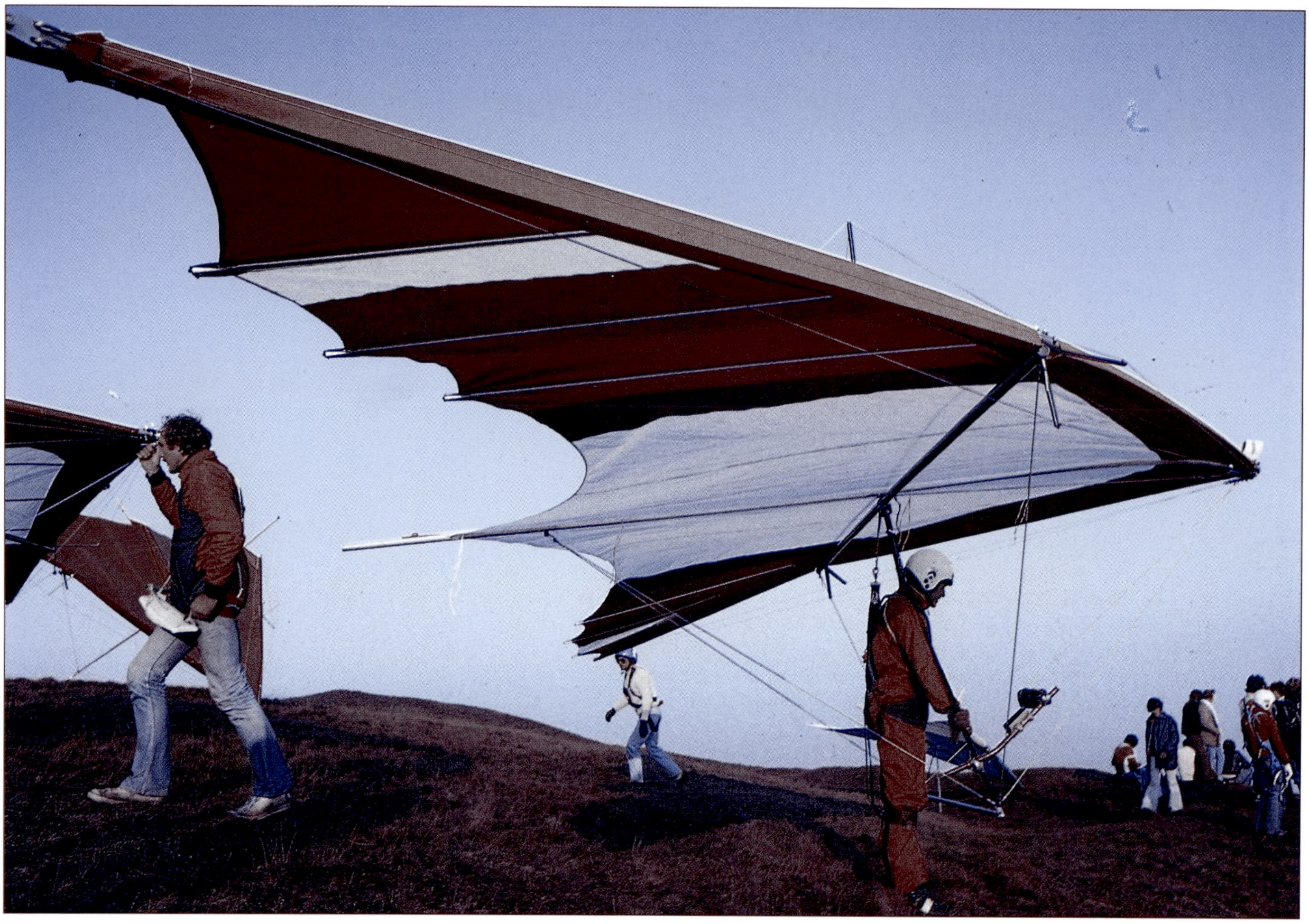

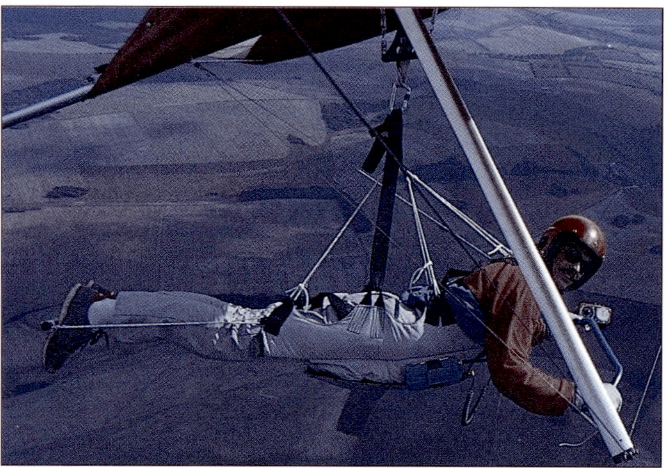

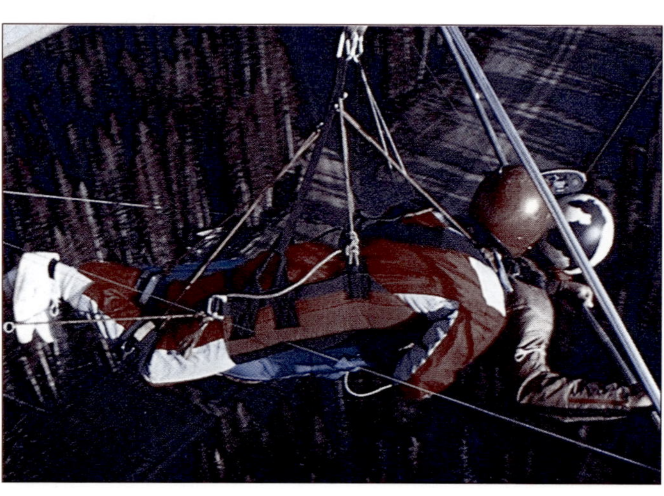

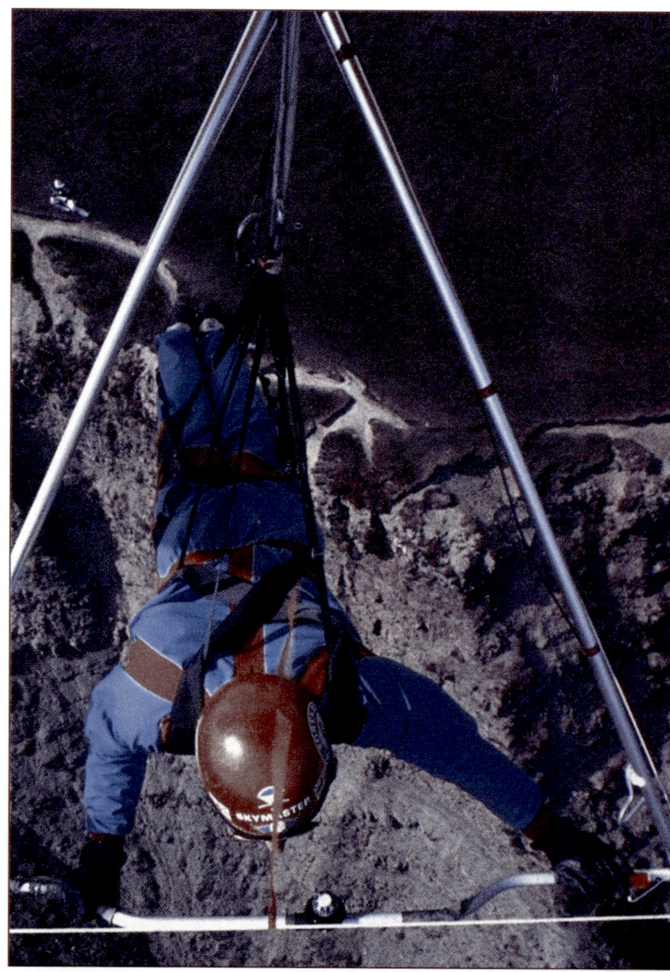

Parachuting

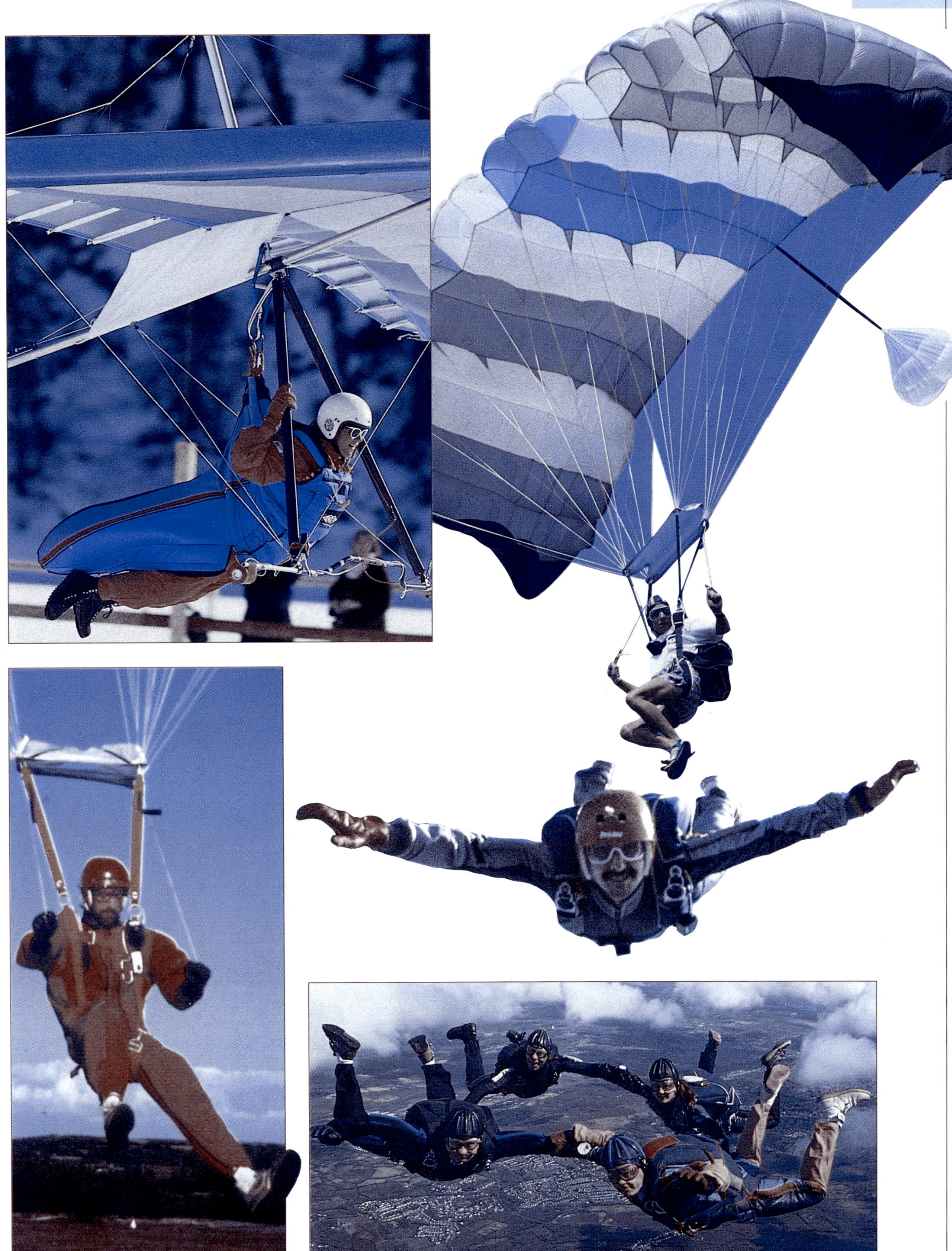

Cycling – BMX · cross country

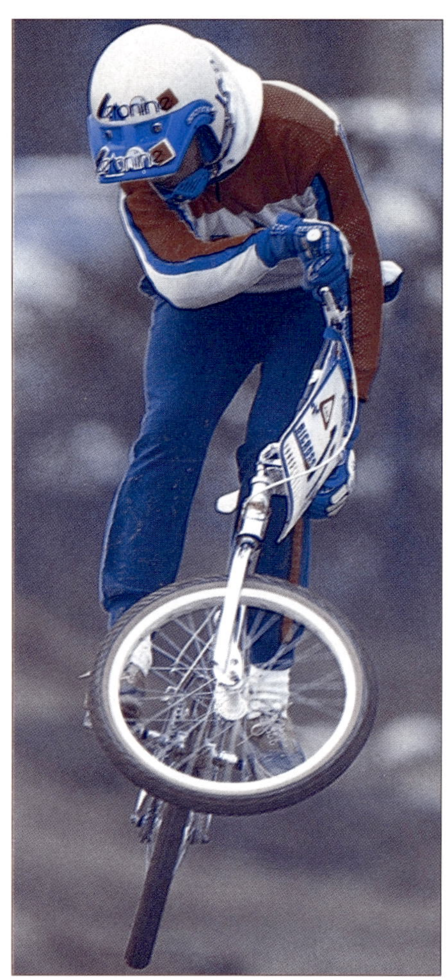

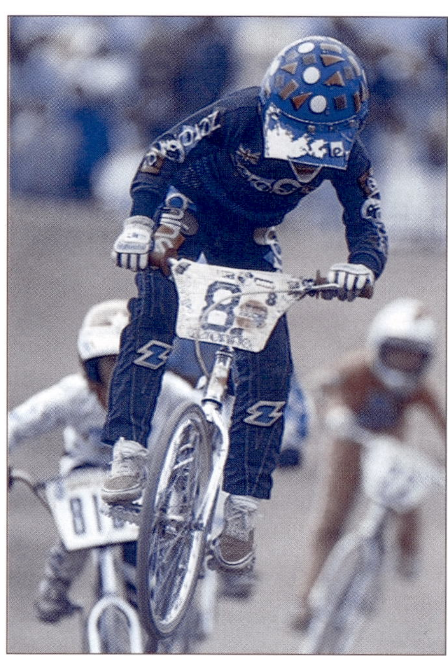

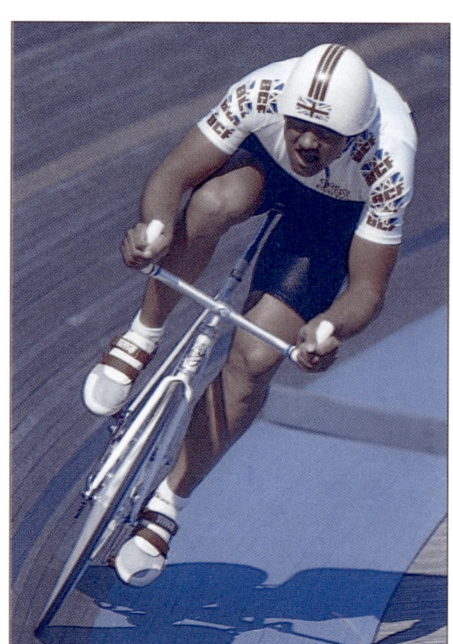

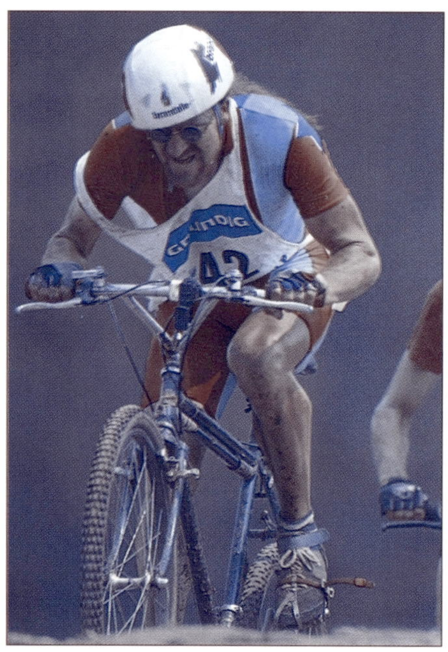

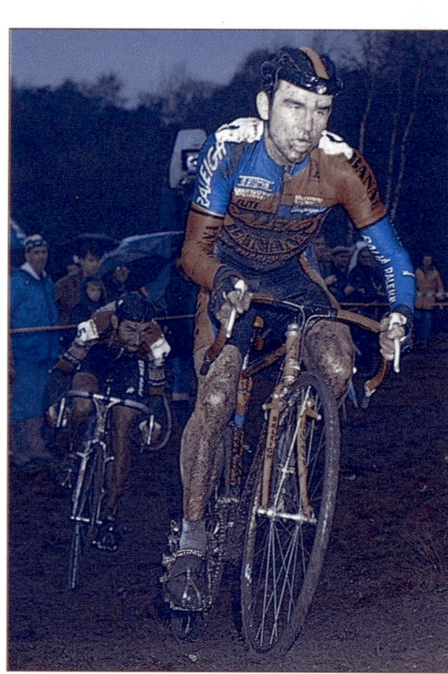

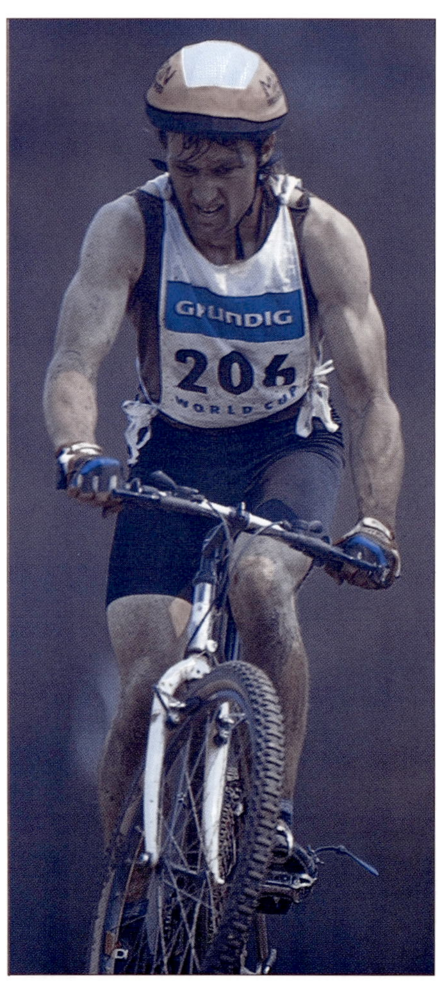

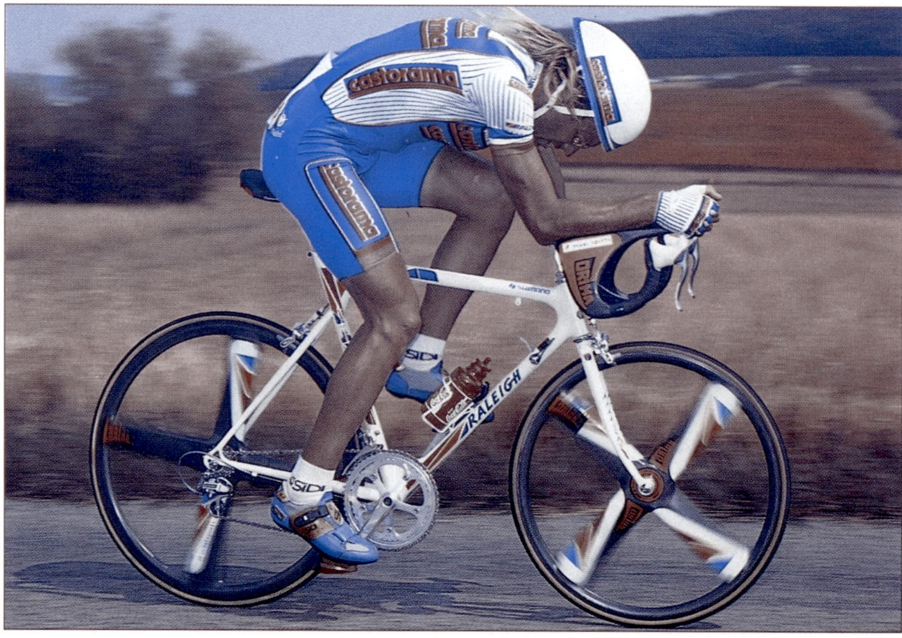

Cycling — track · road

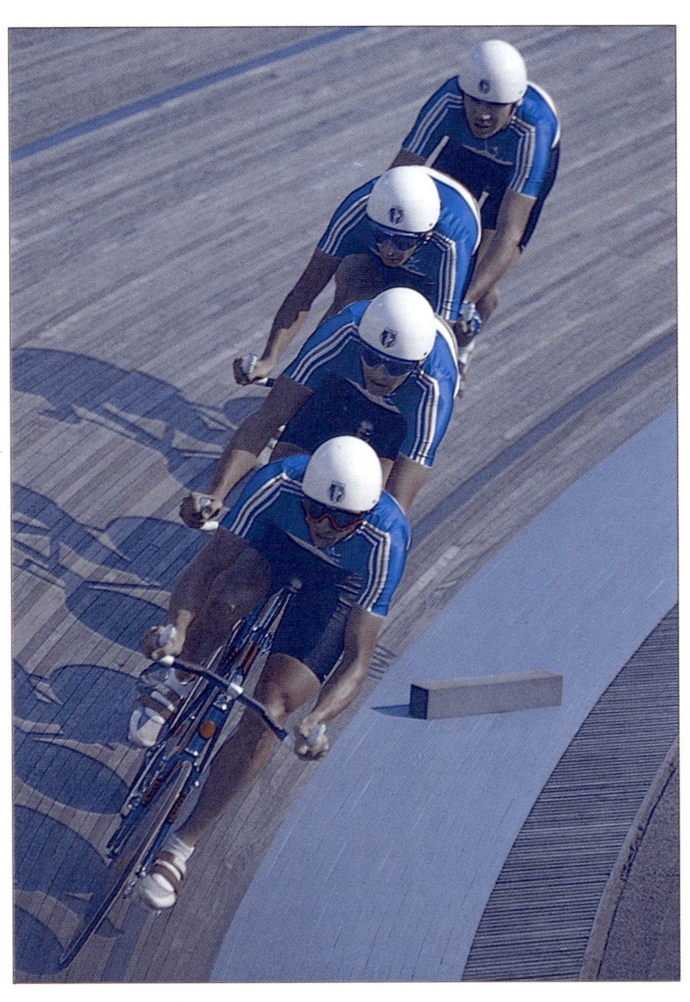

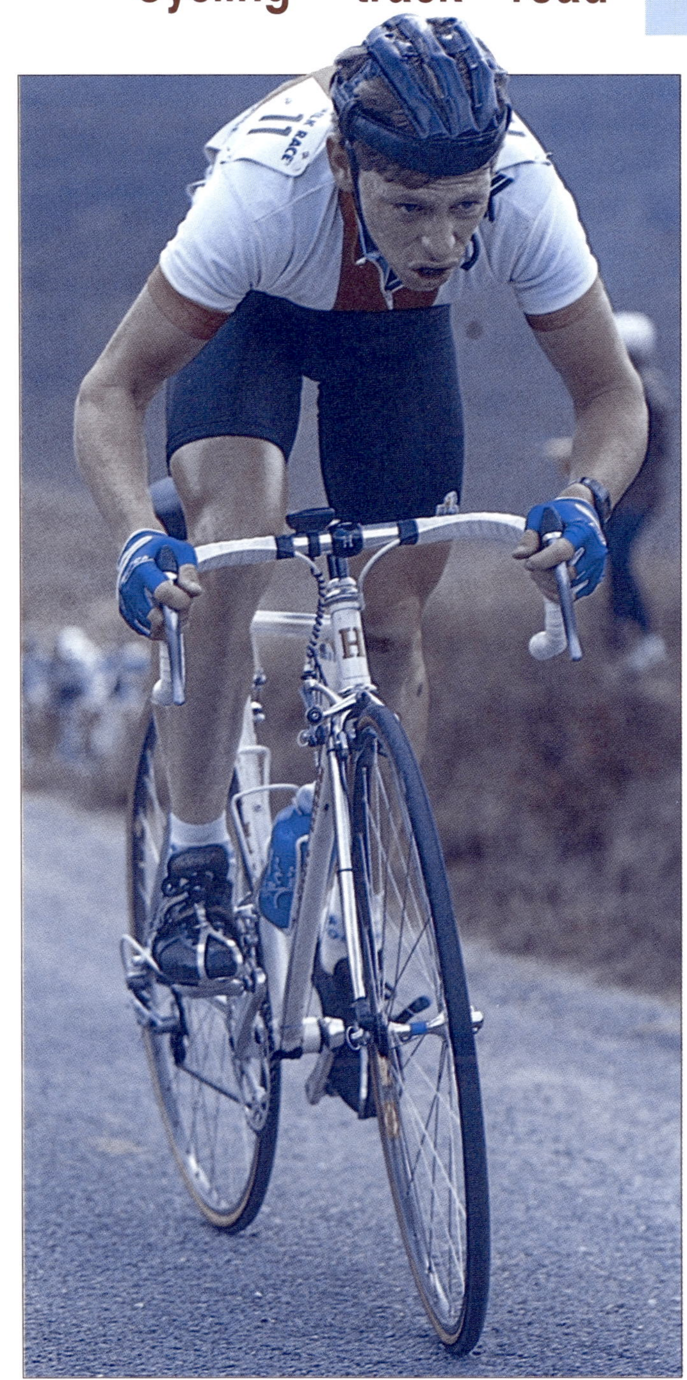

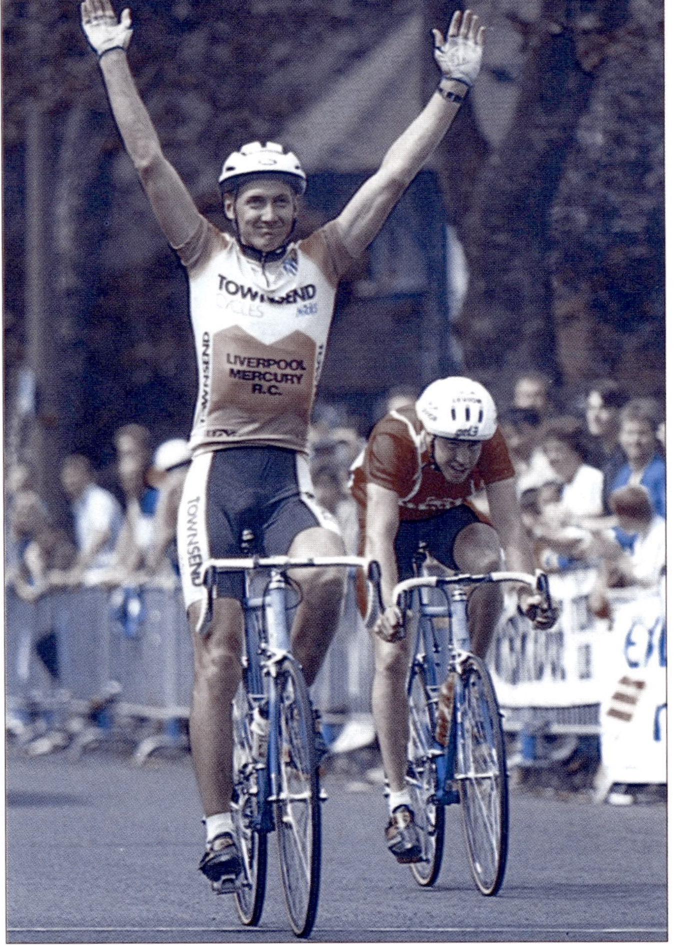

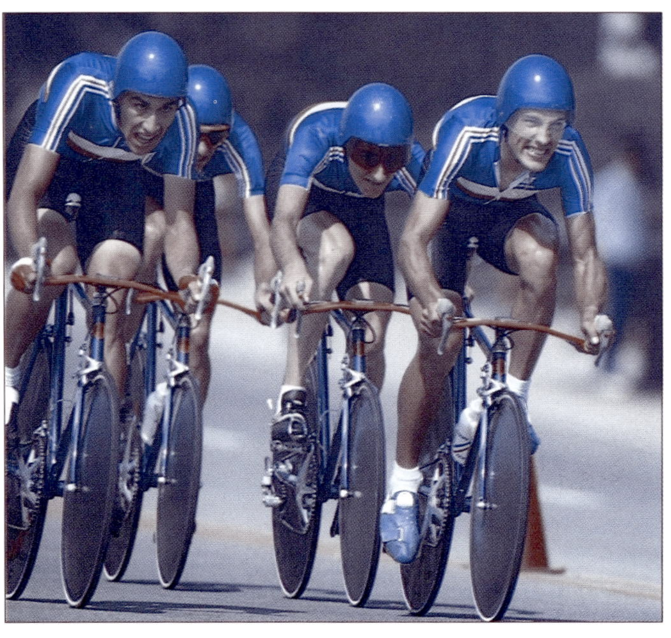

Dressage

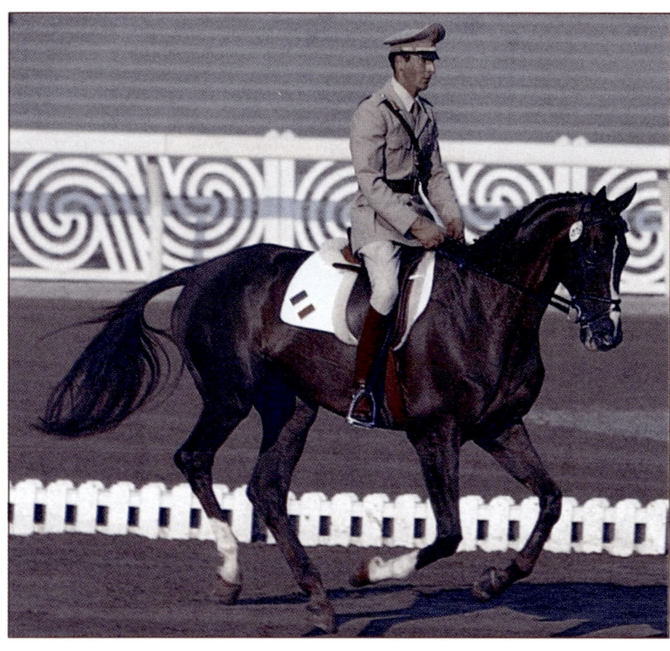

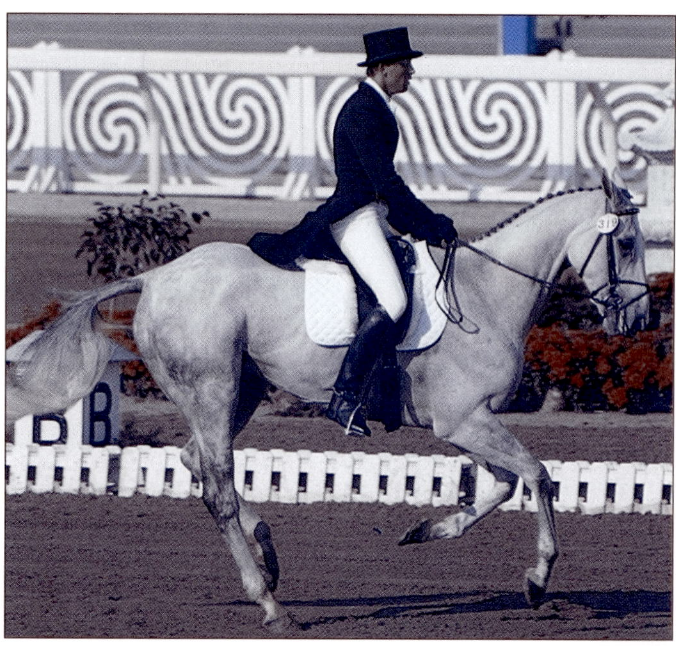

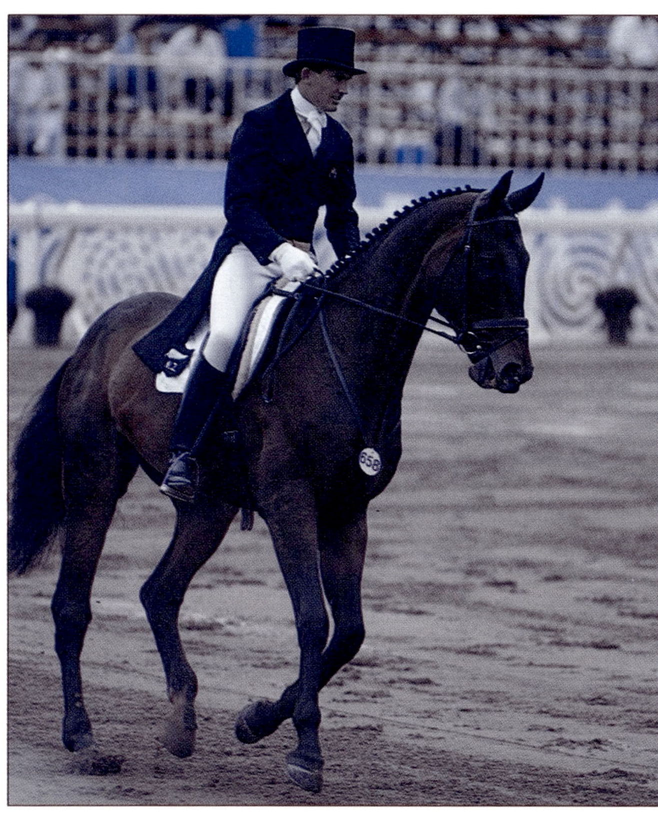

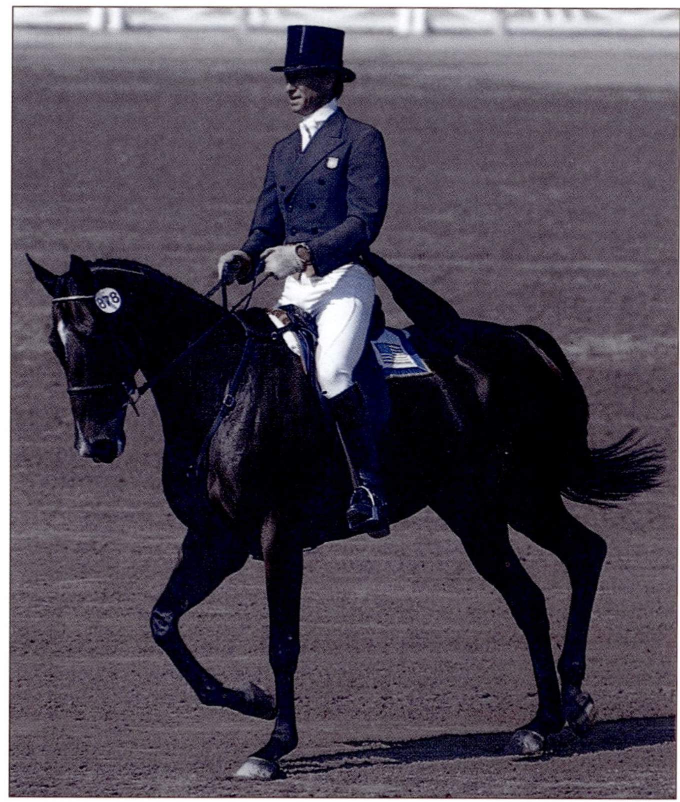

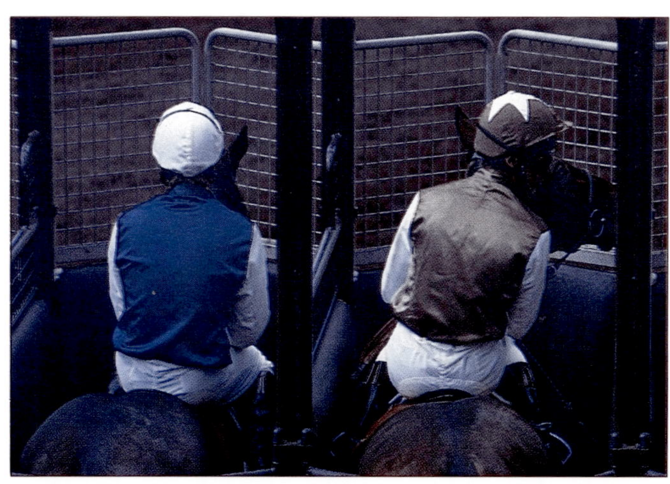

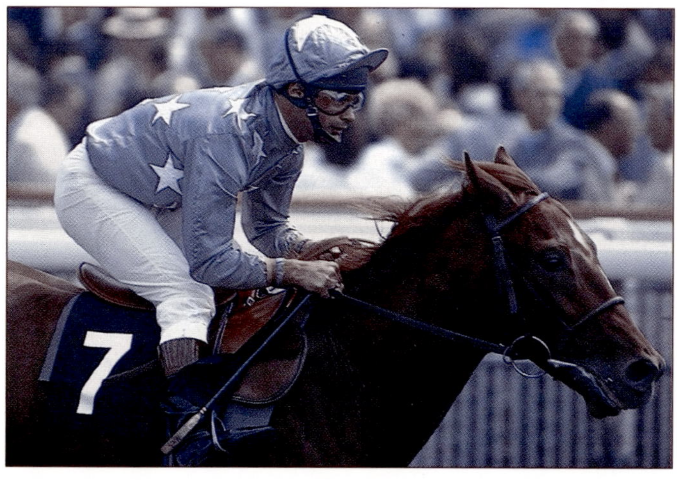

Flat racing · hurdles

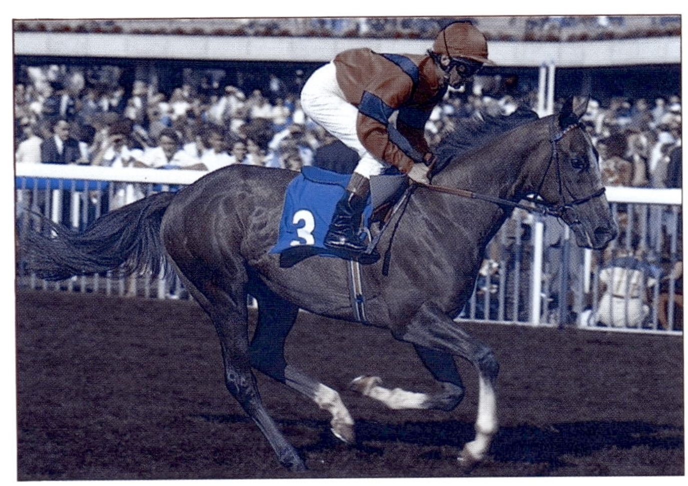

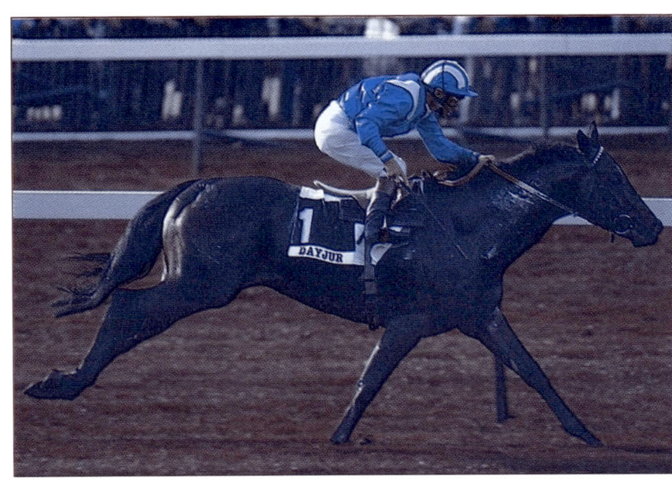

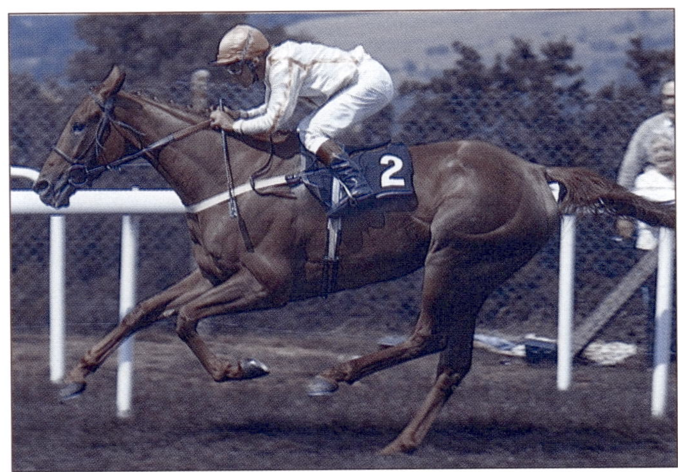

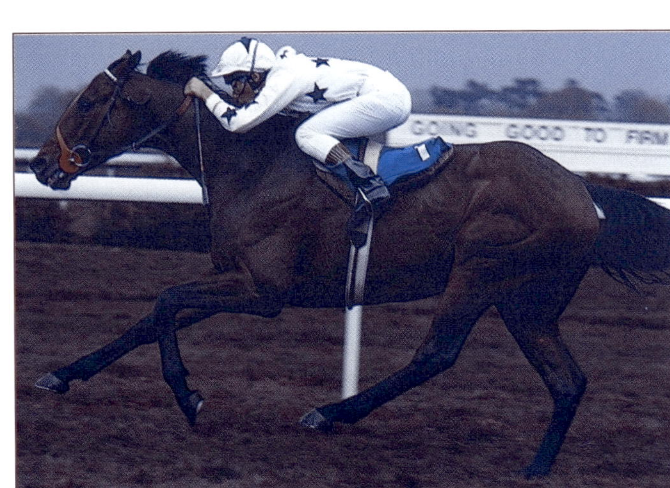

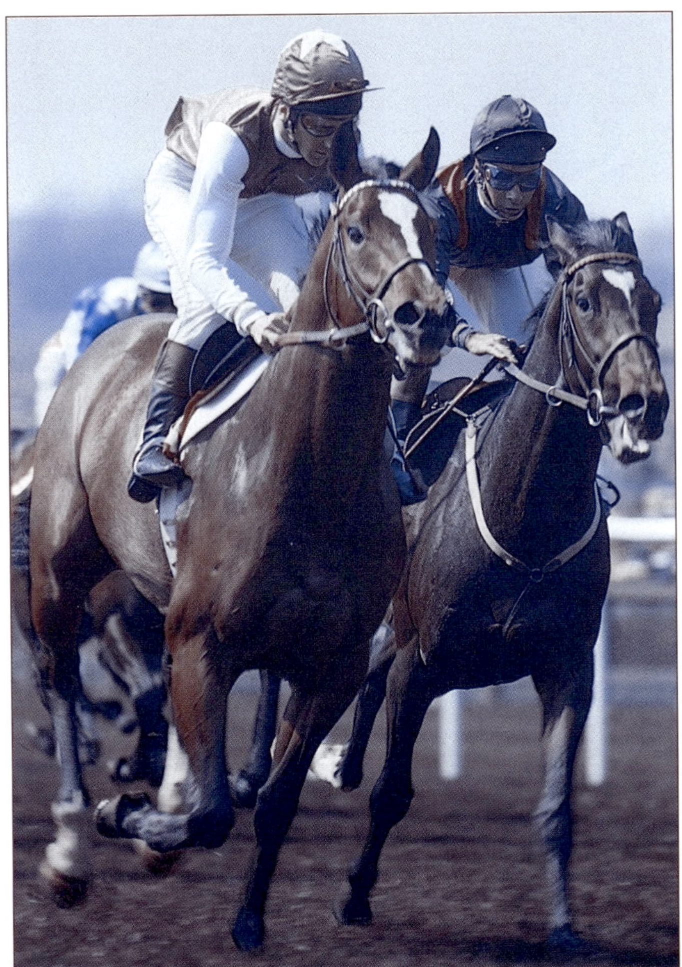

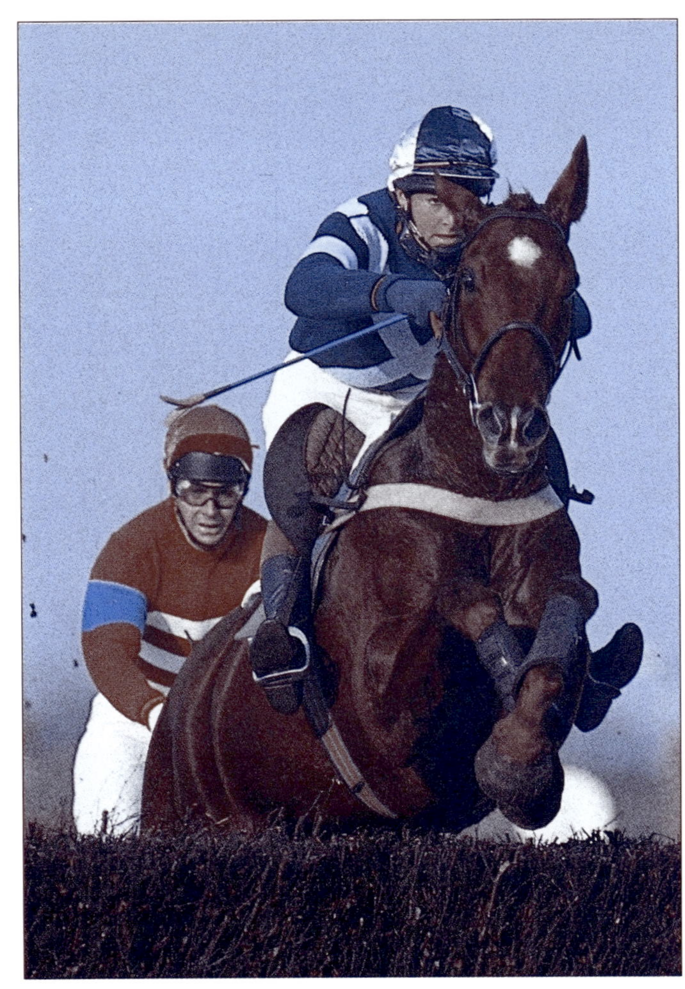

Horse racing – hurdles

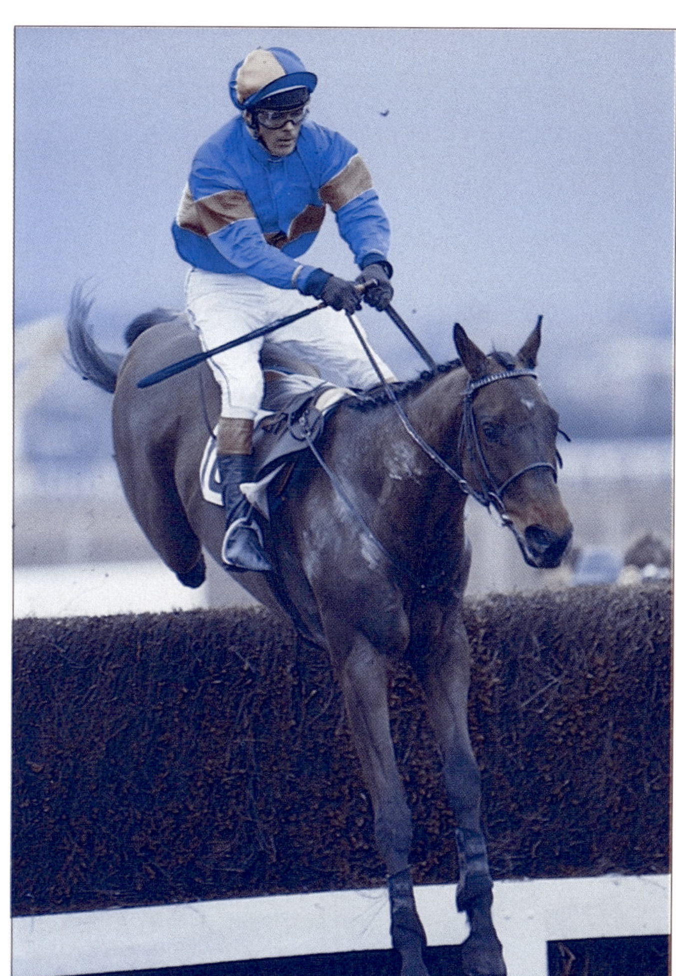

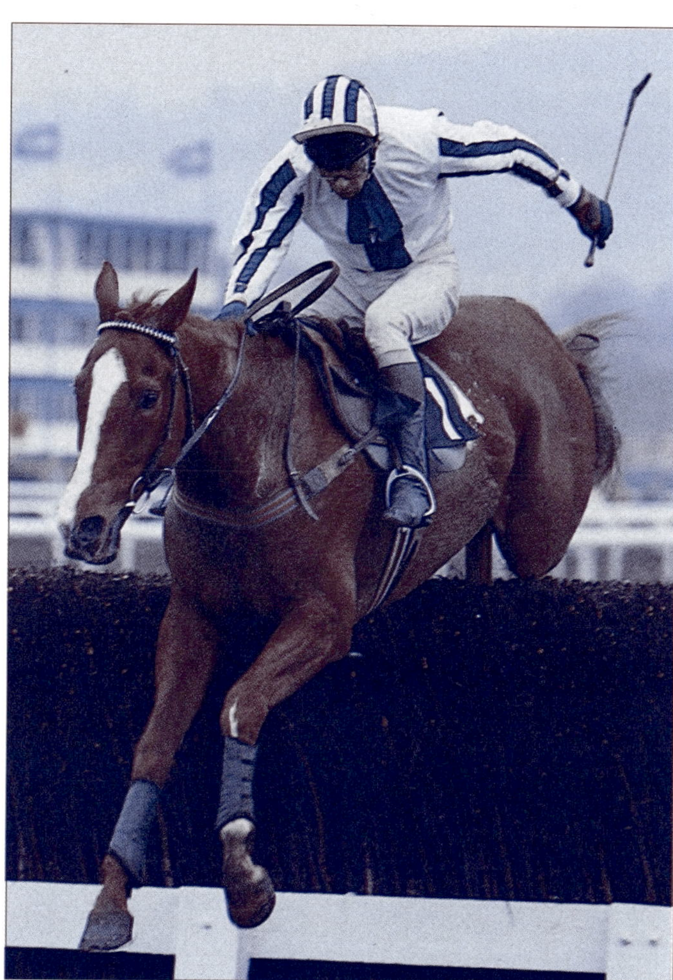

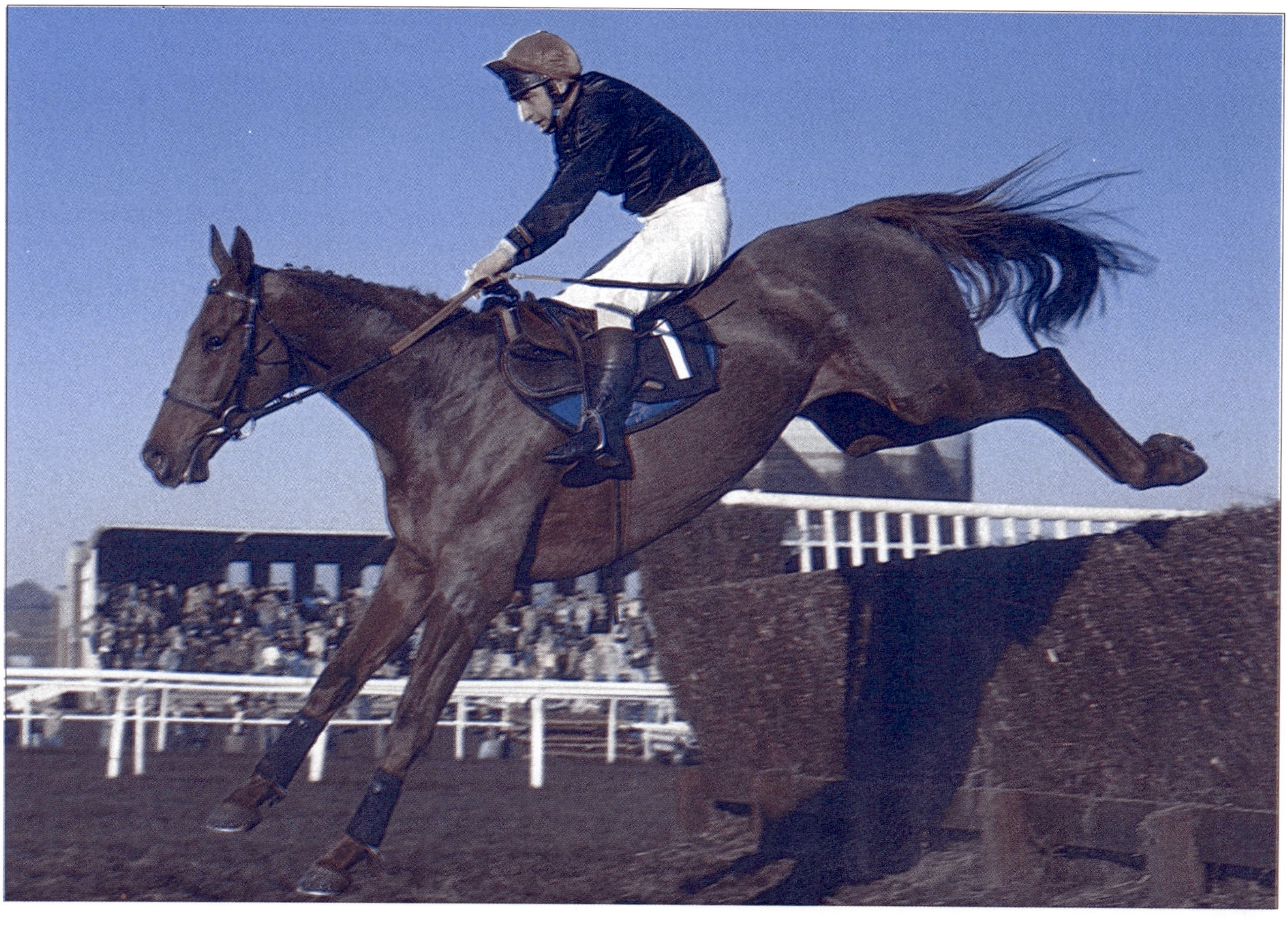

Cross country

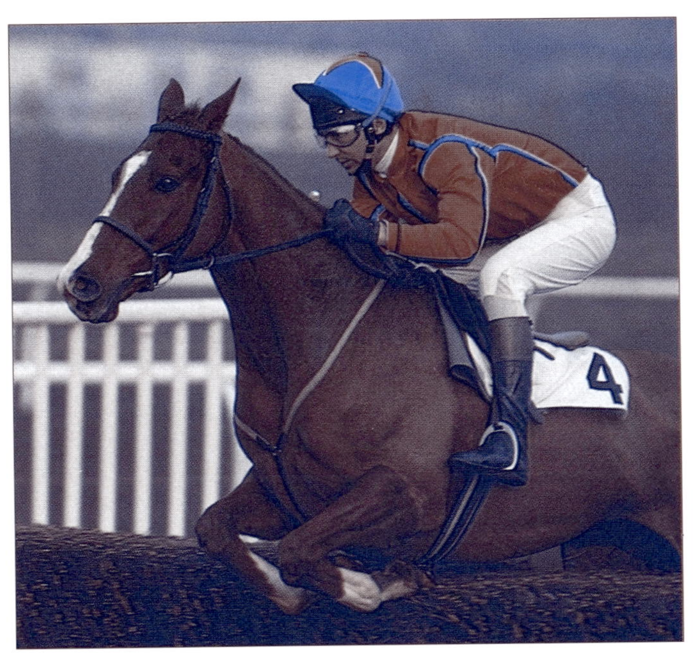

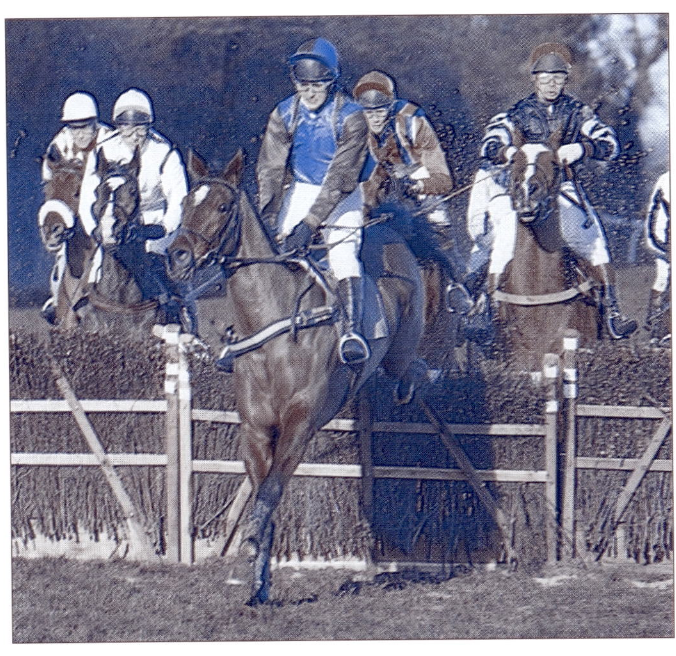

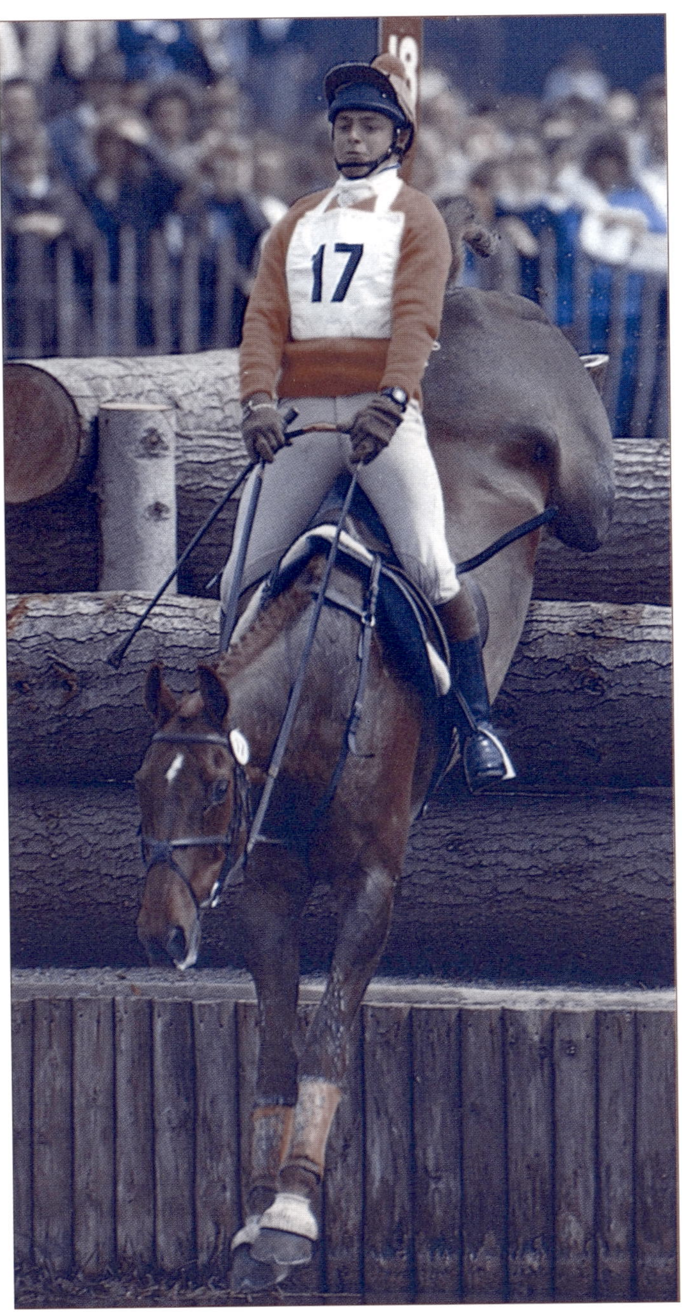

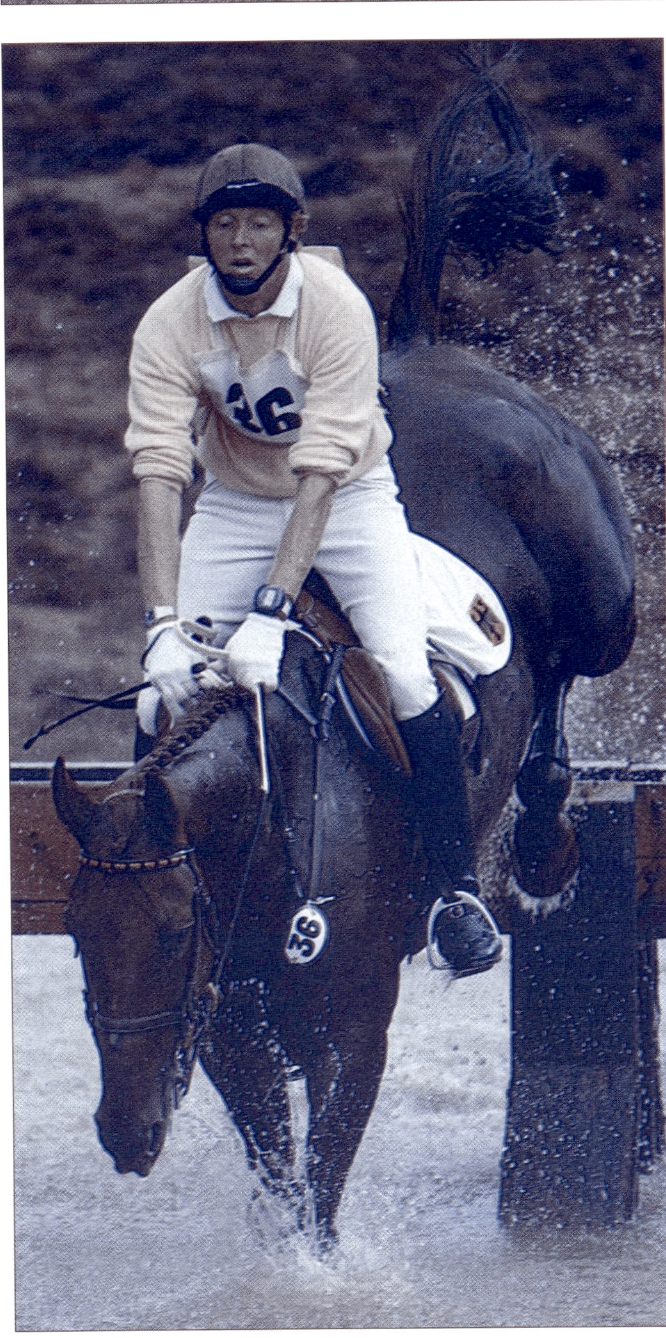

Show jumping

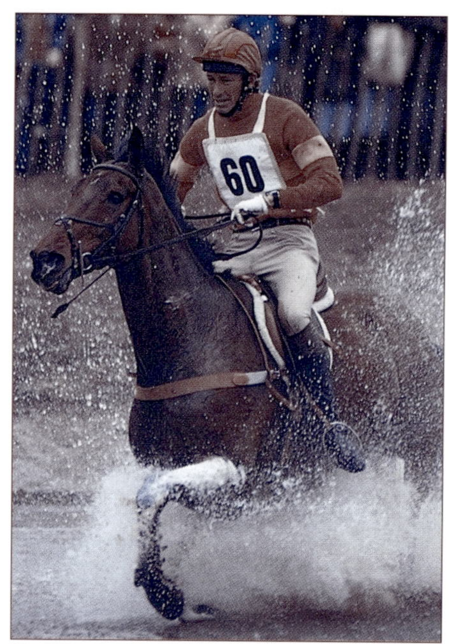

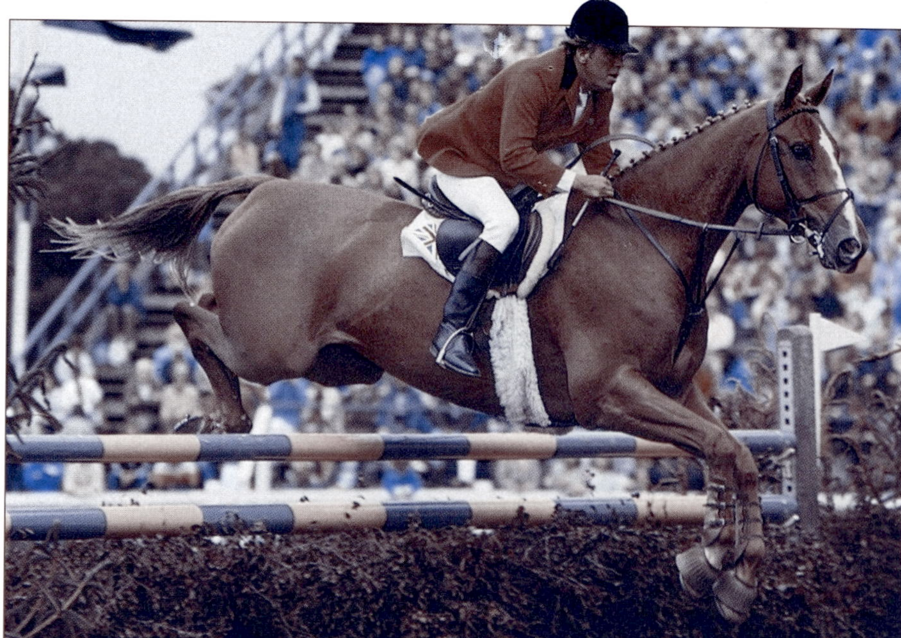

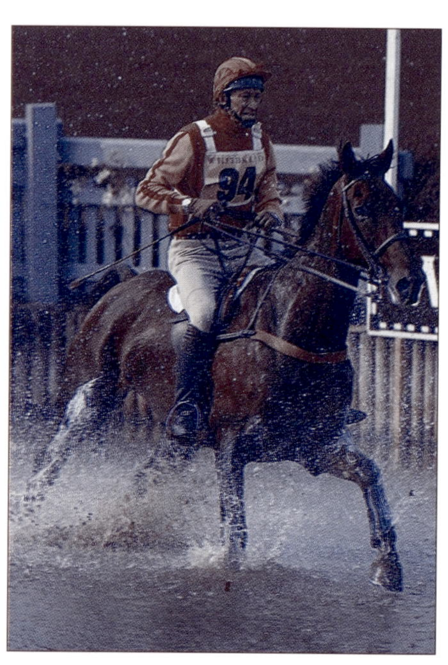

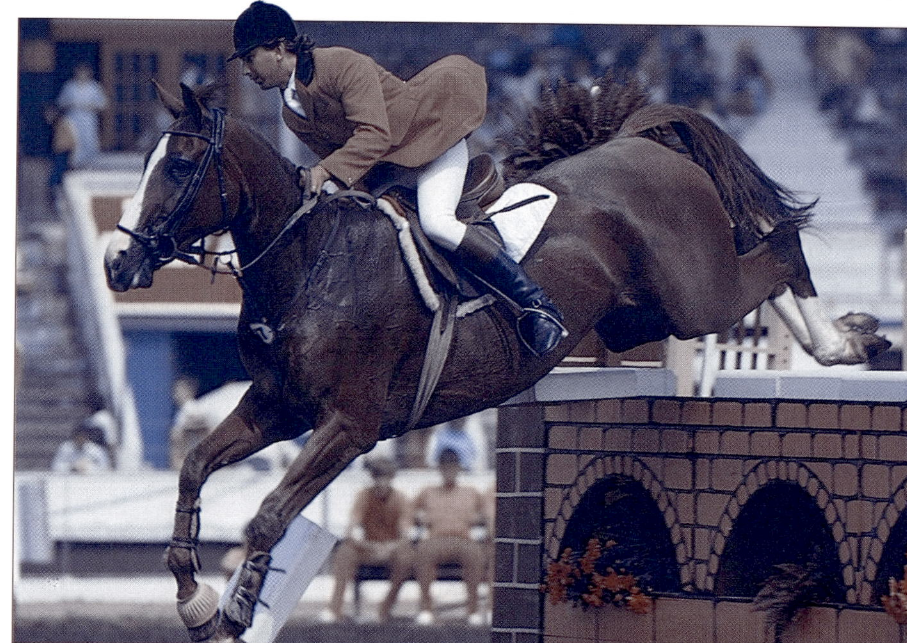

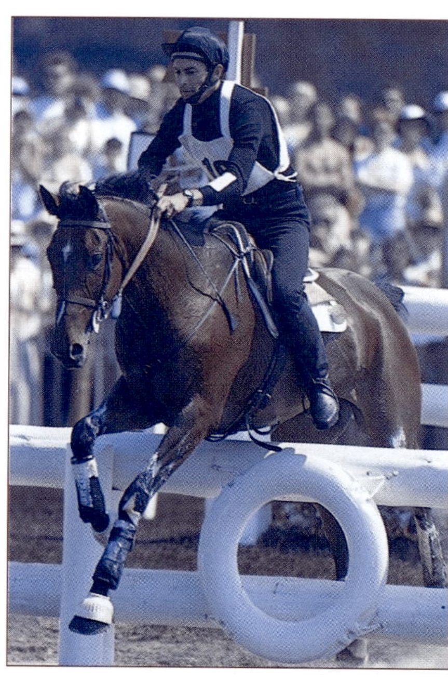

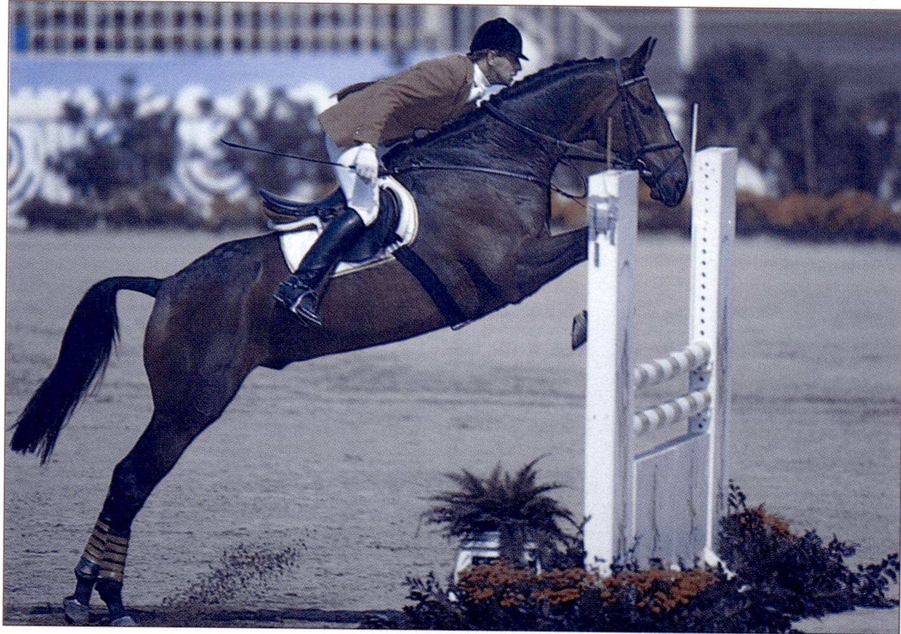

Show jumping

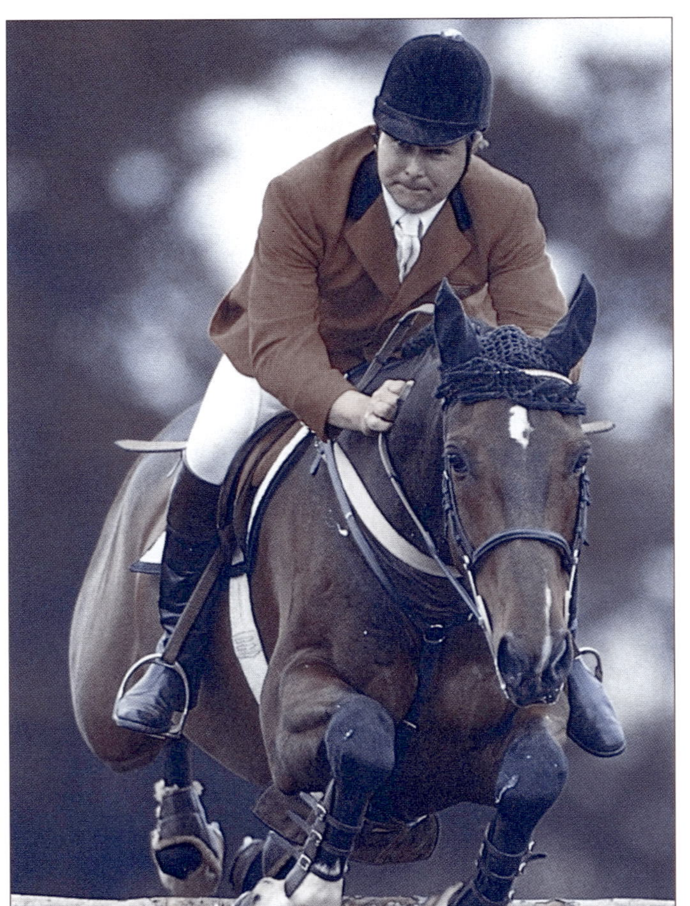

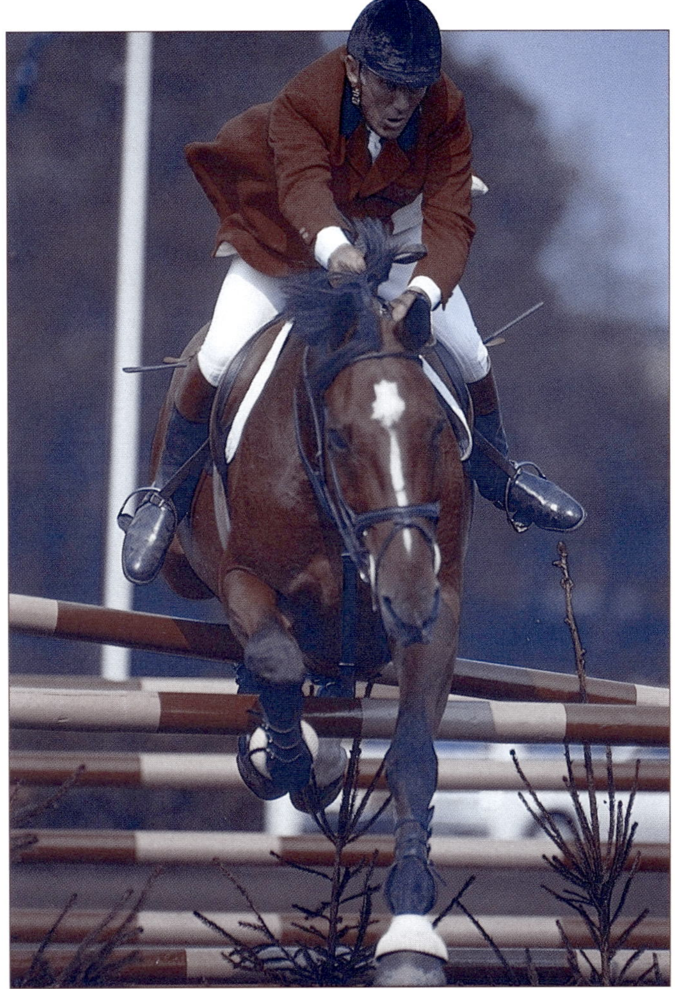

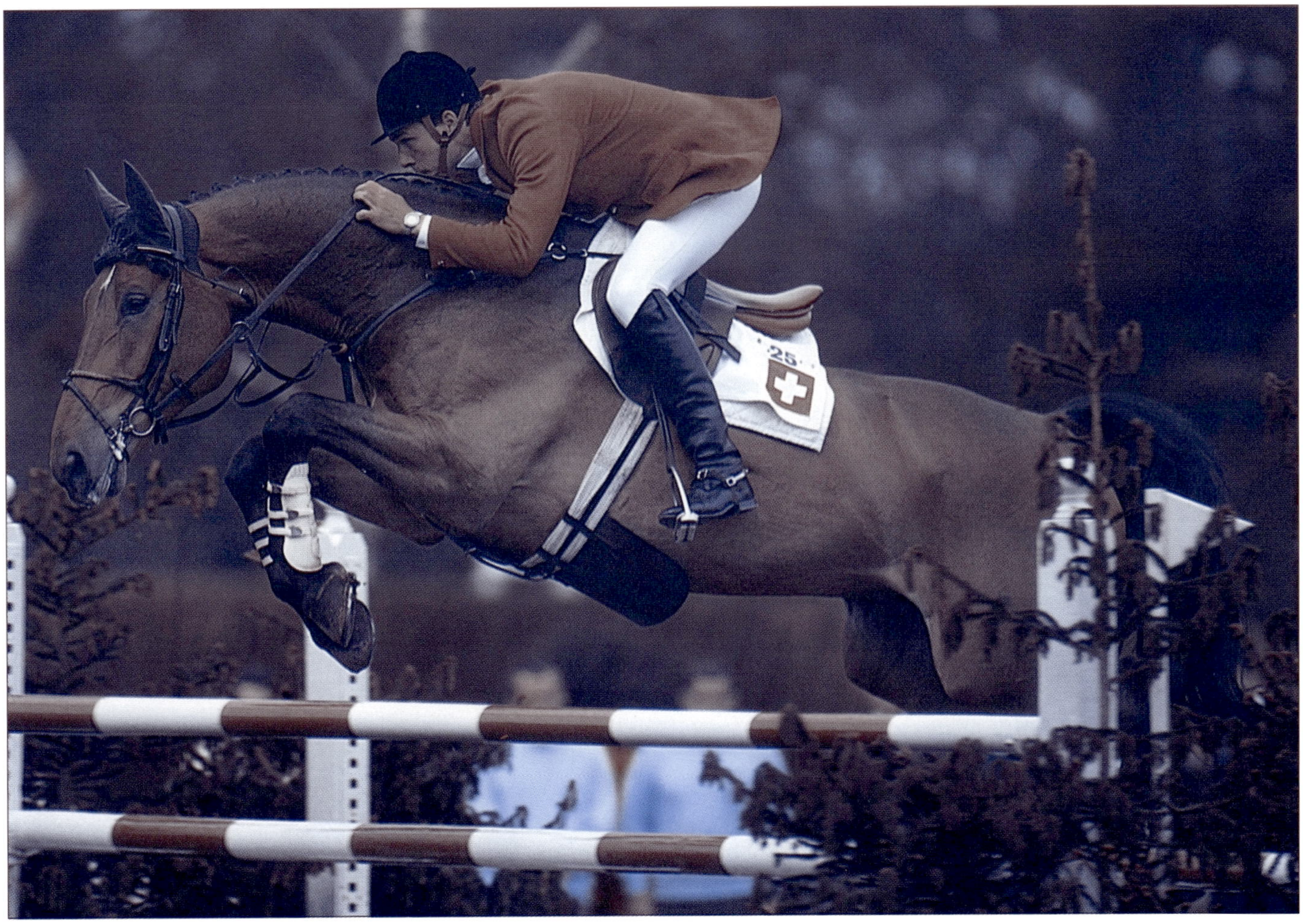

Carriage driving

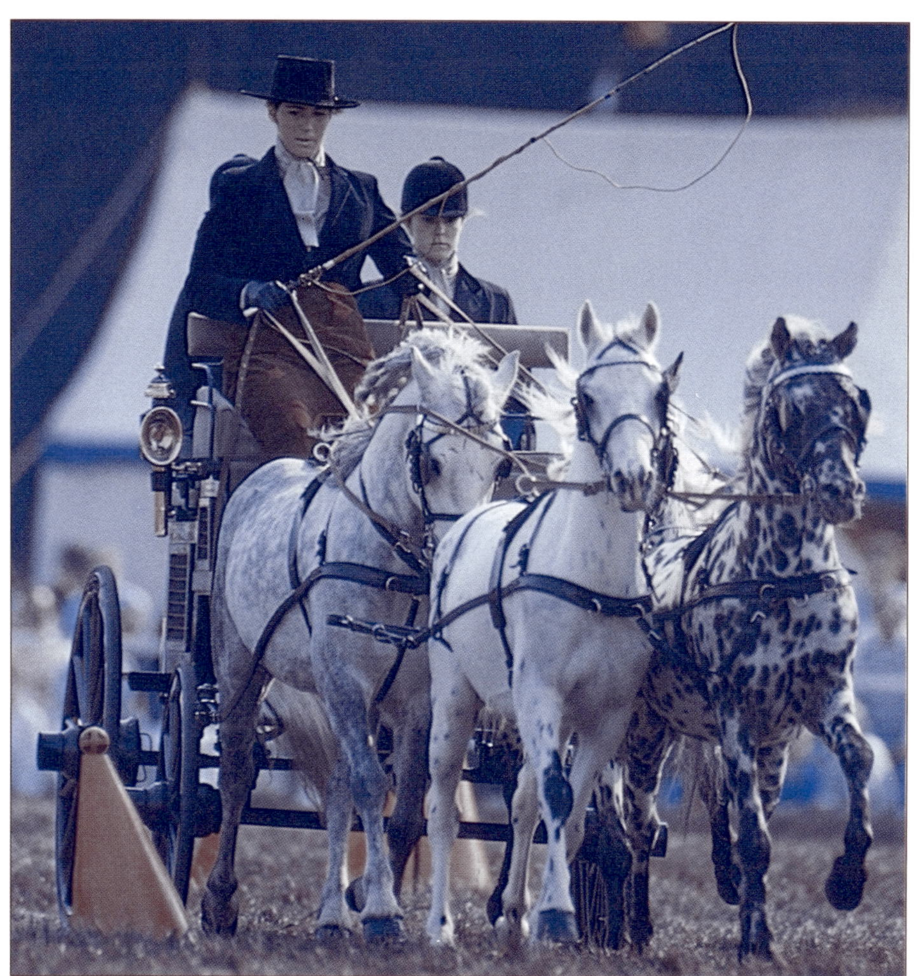

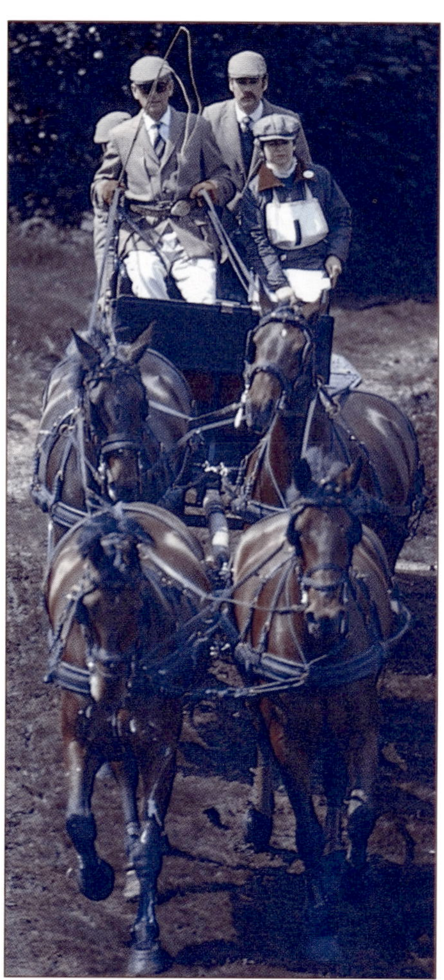

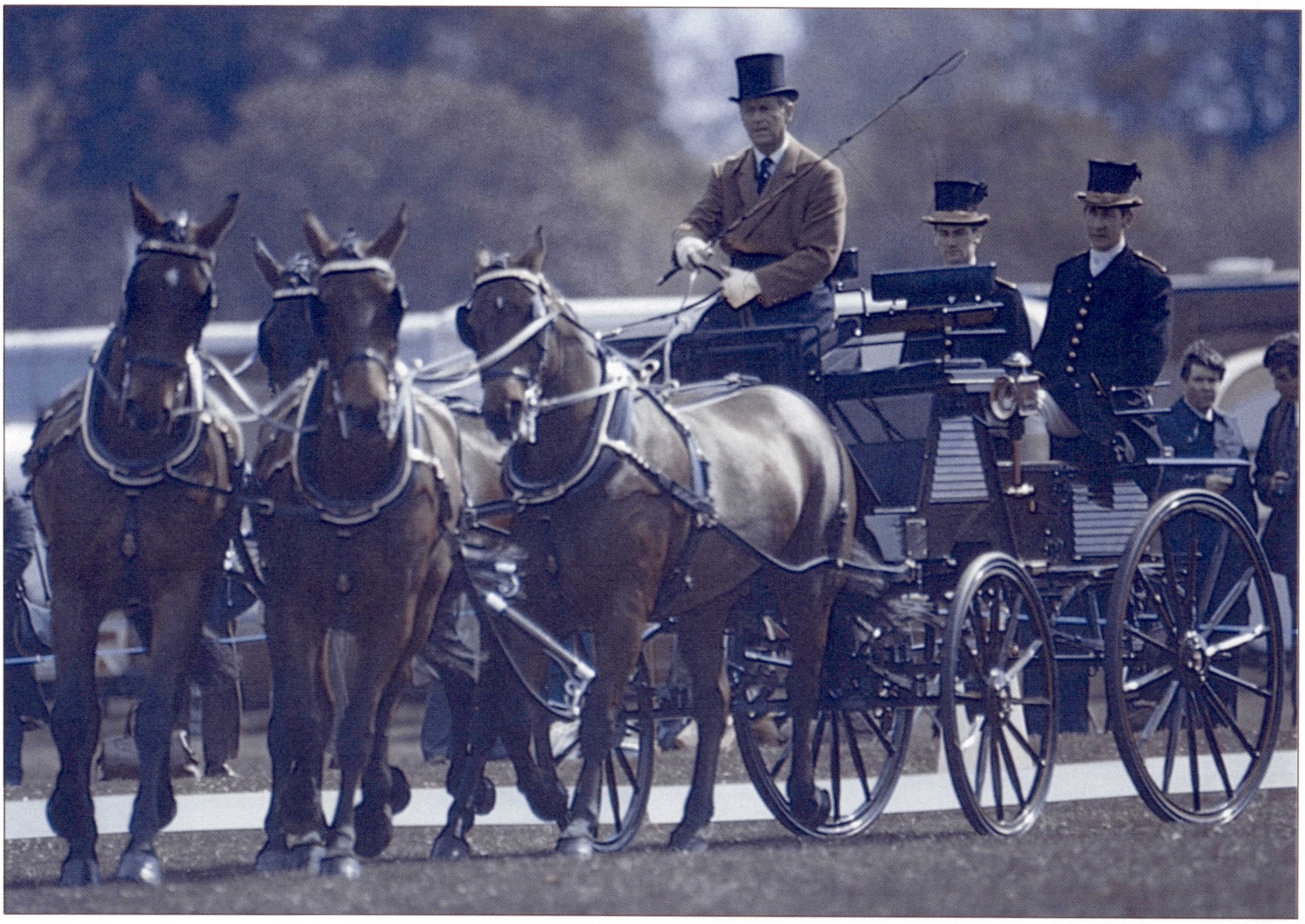

Carriage driving

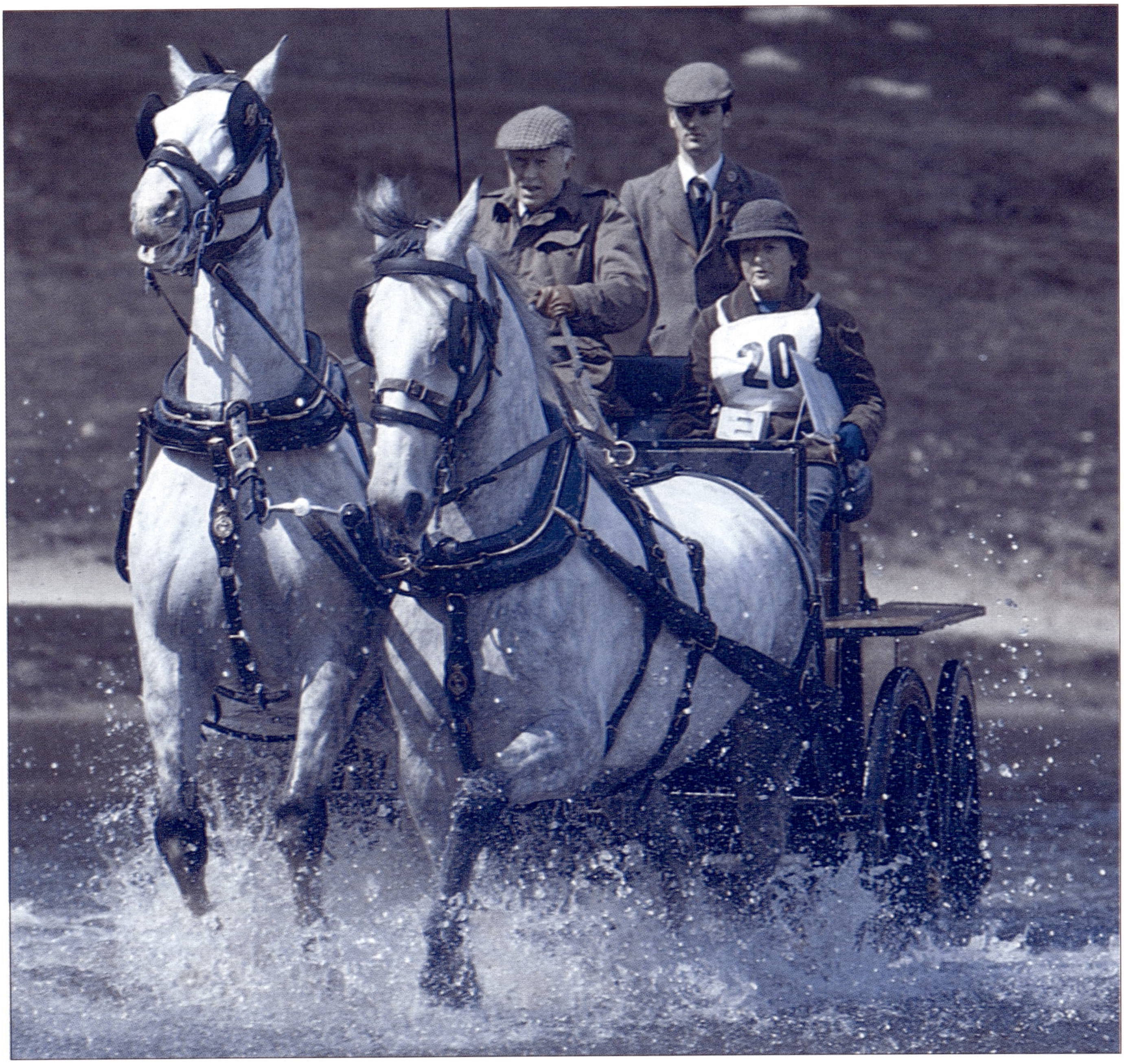

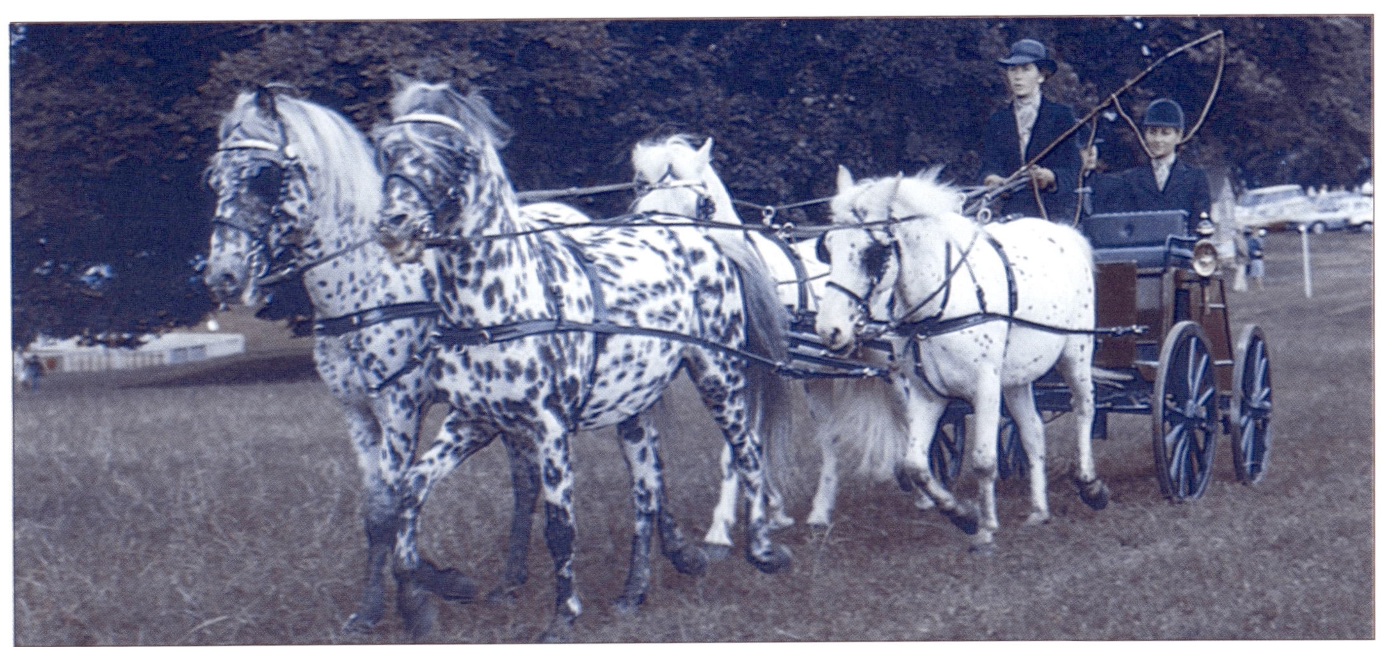

Carriage driving

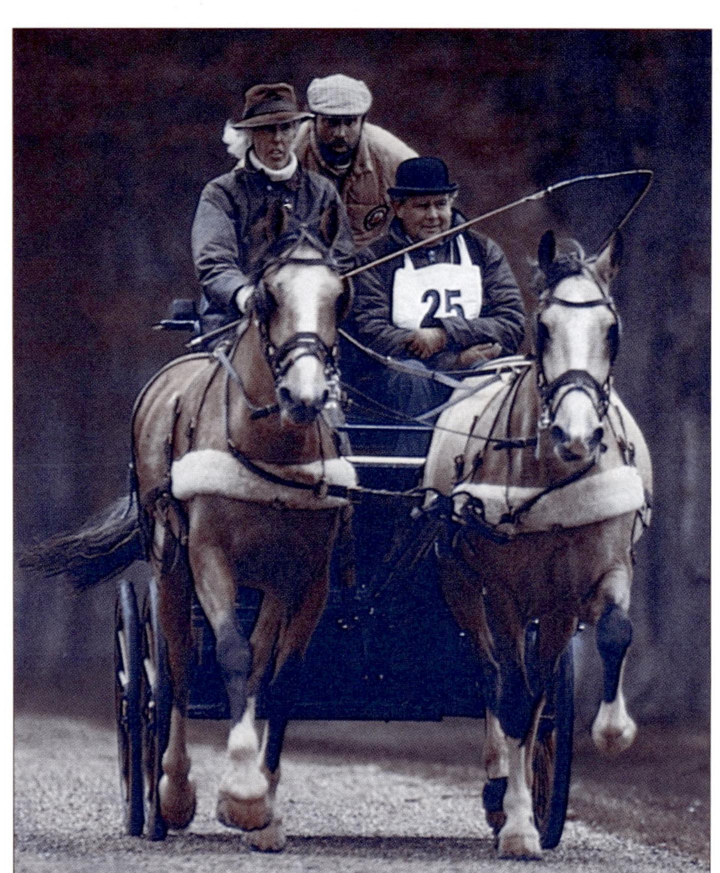

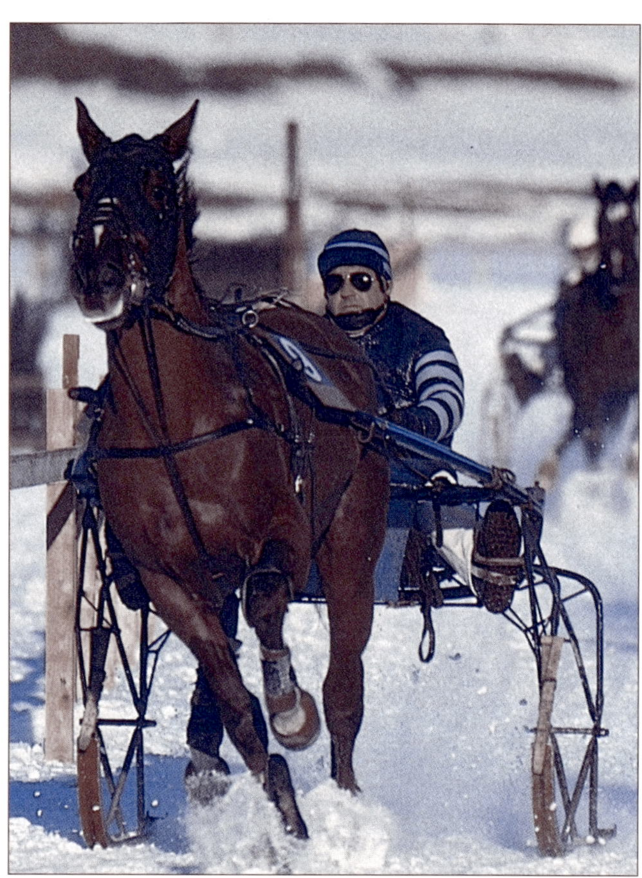

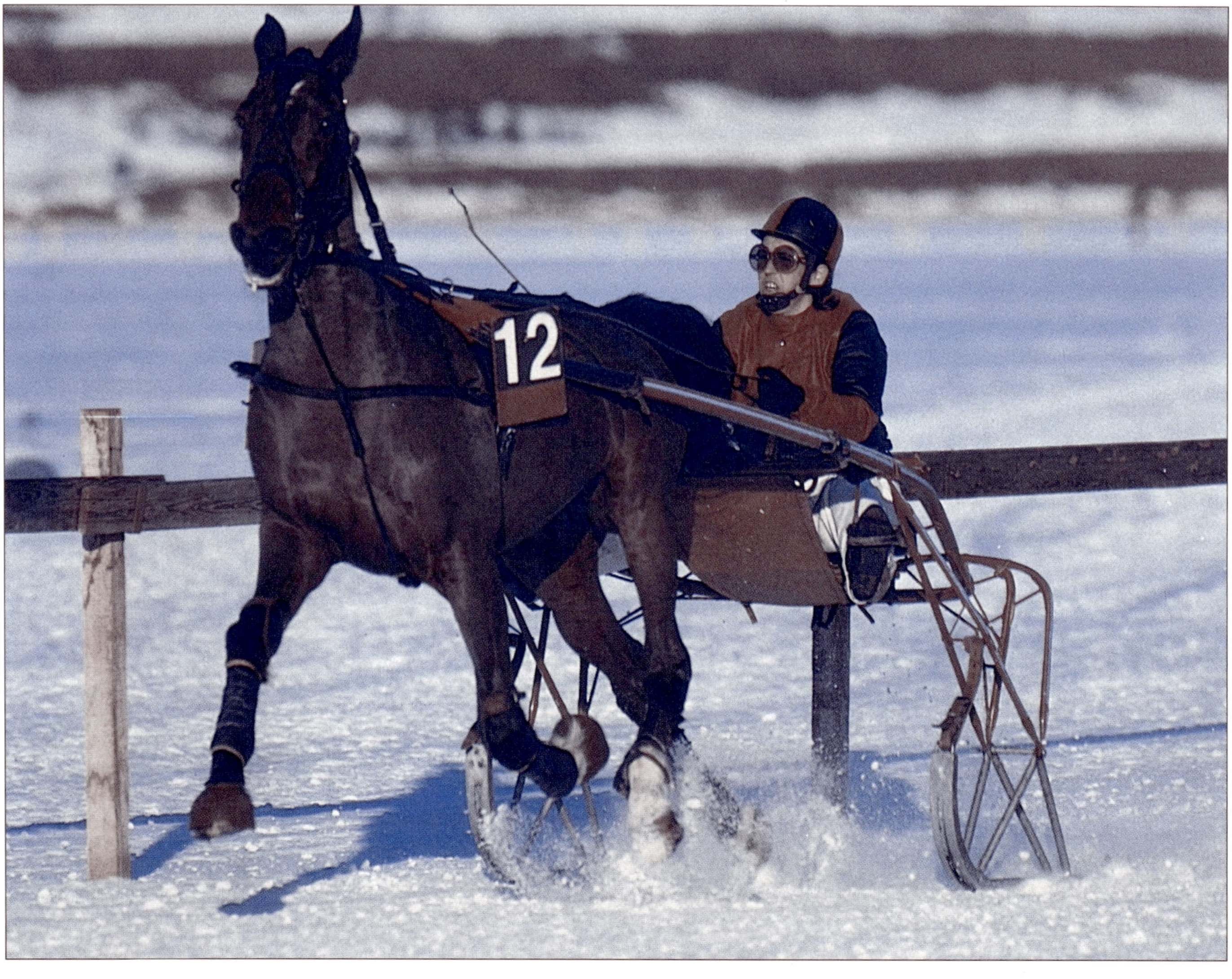

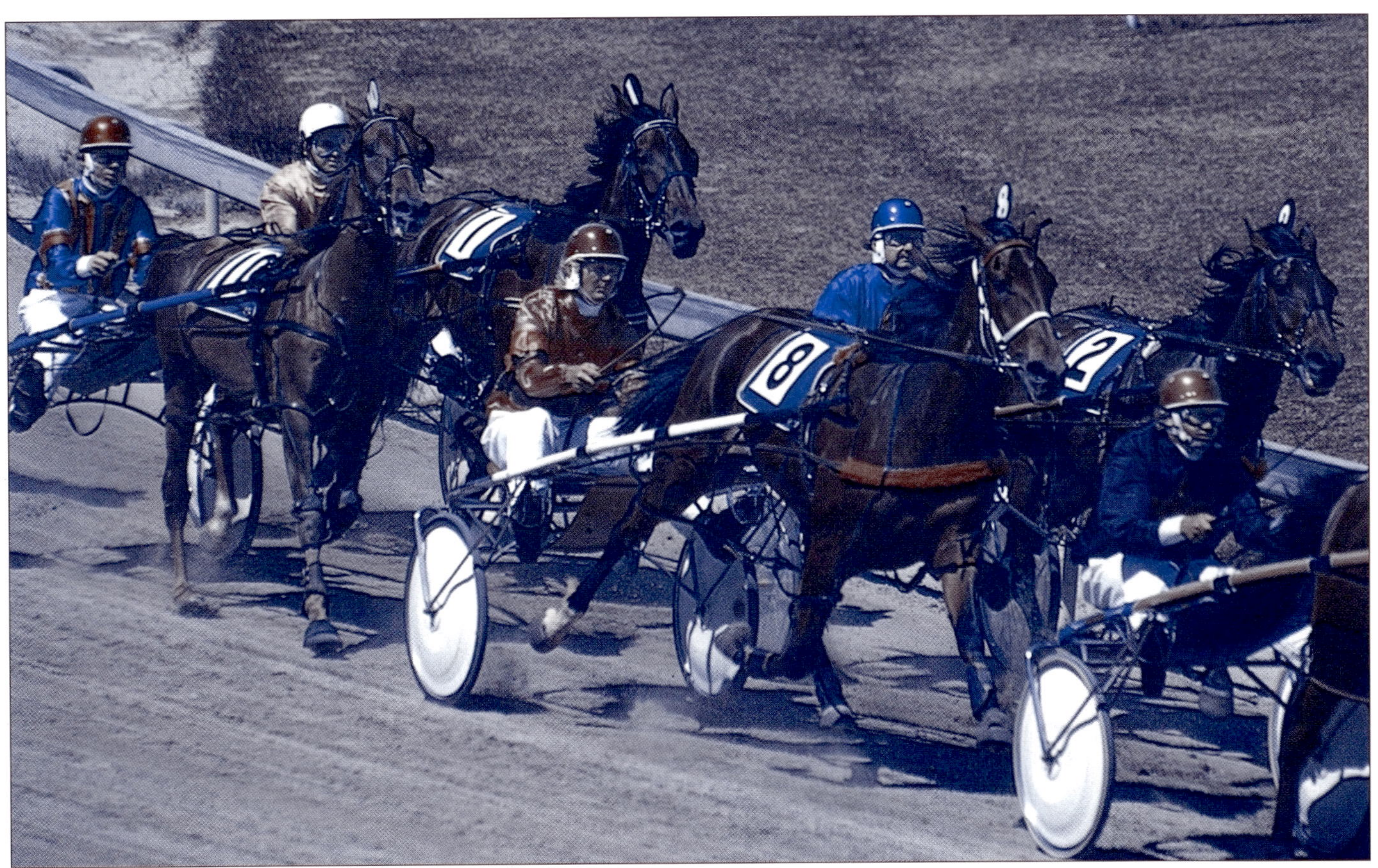
8
2

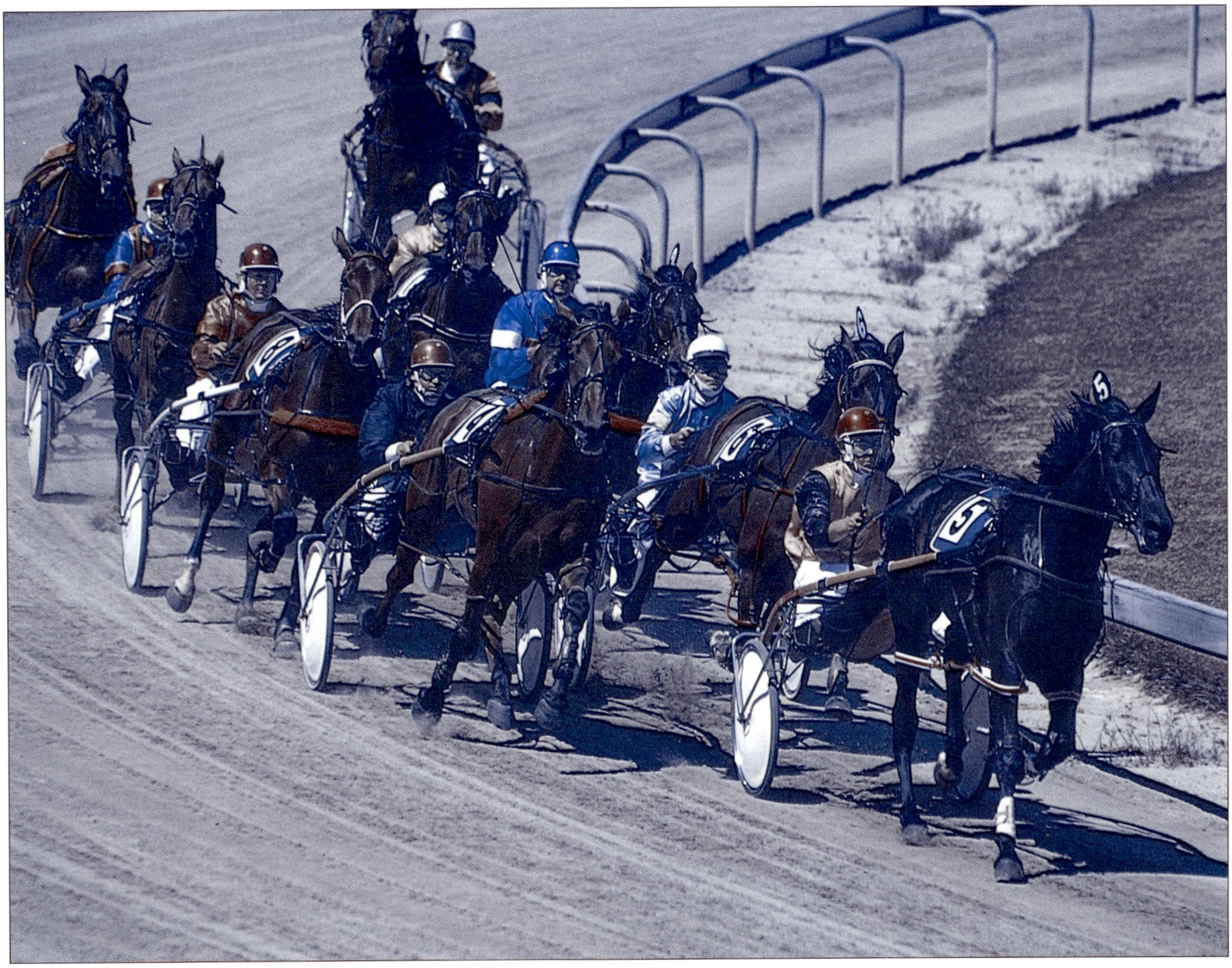

Polo

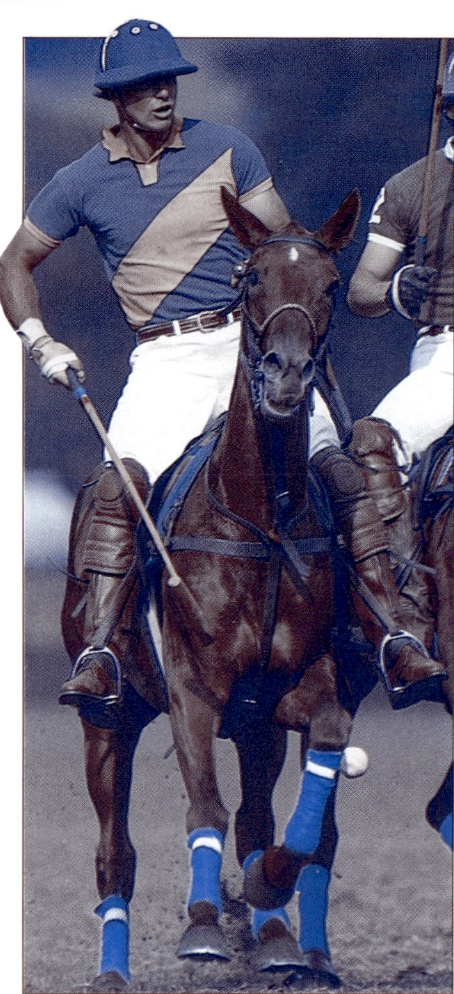

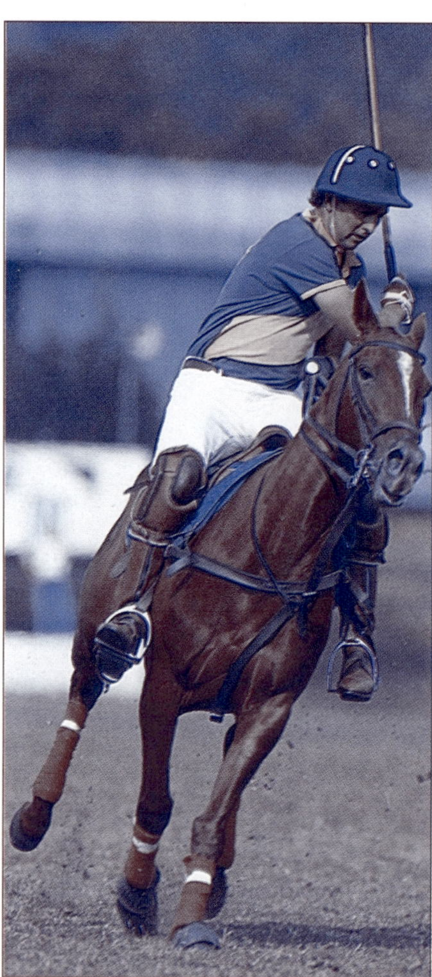

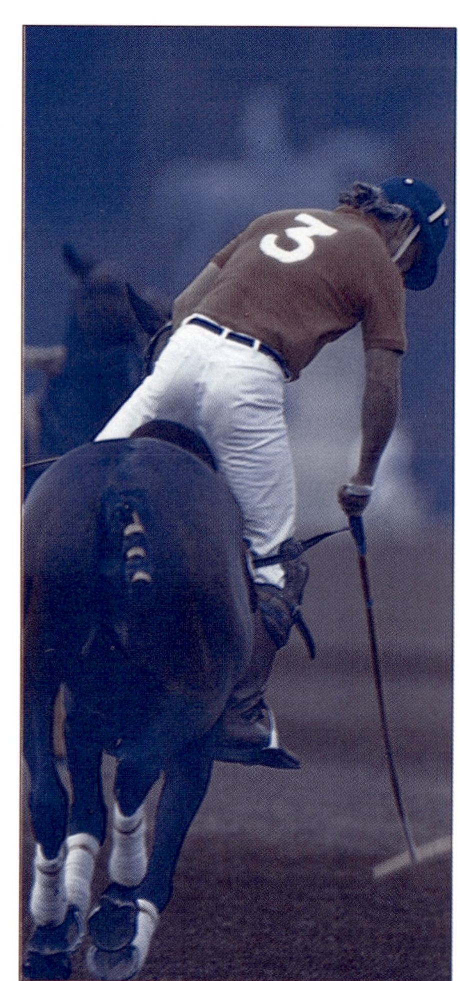

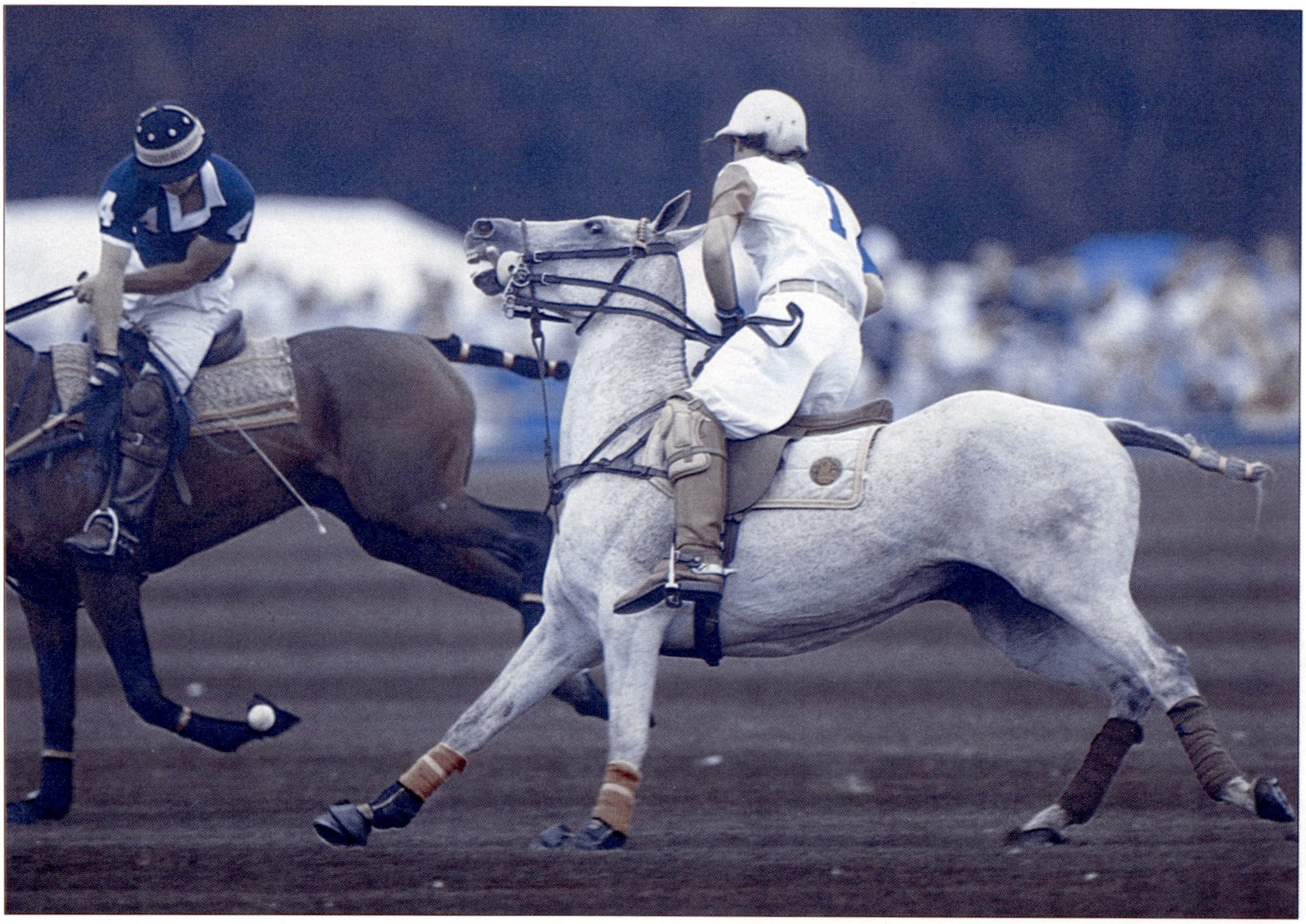

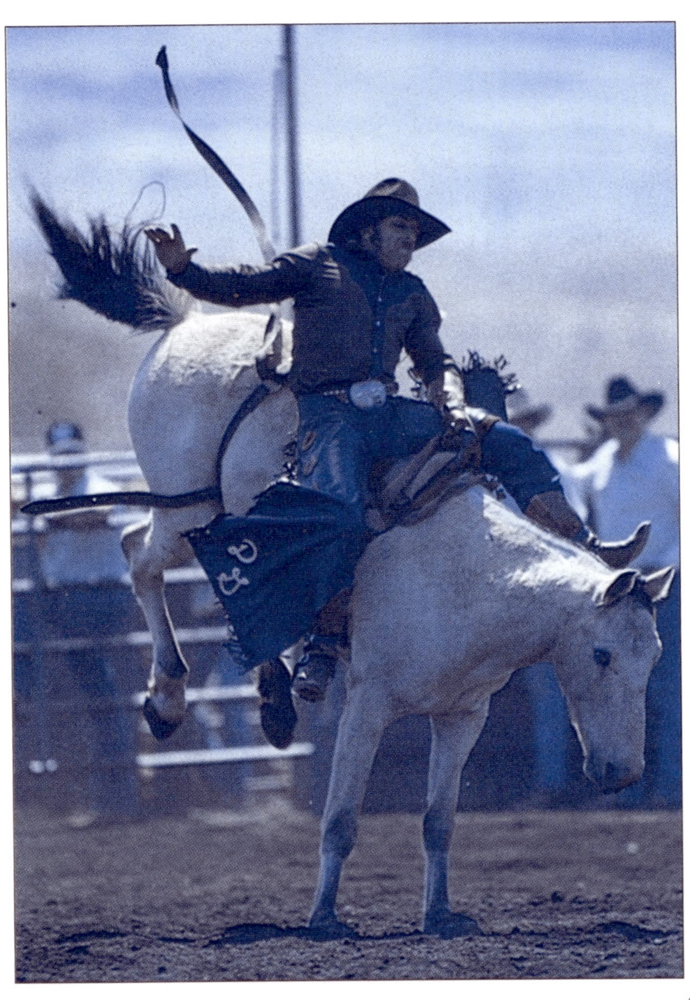

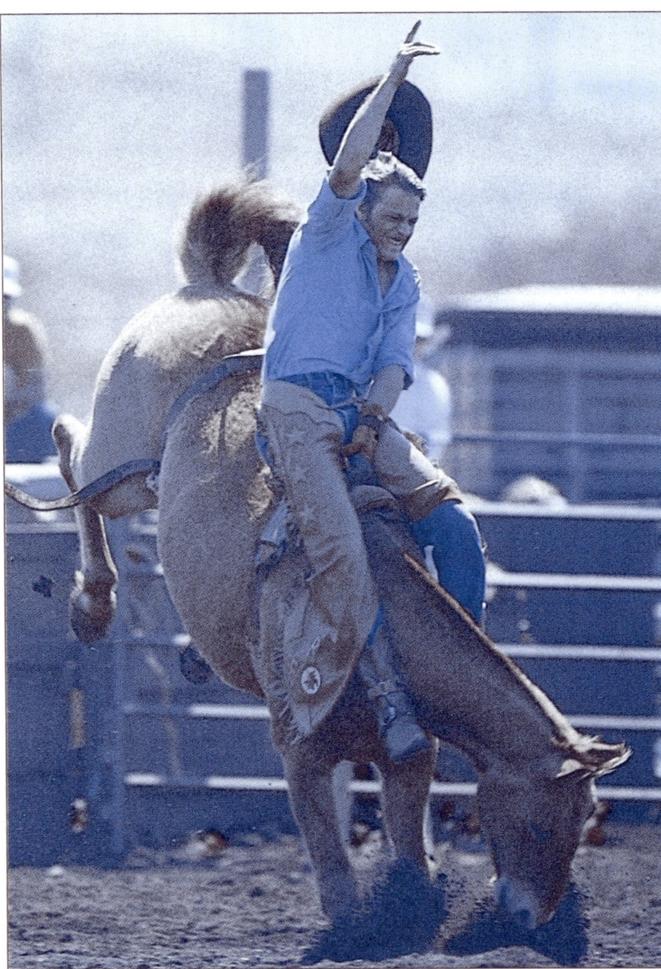

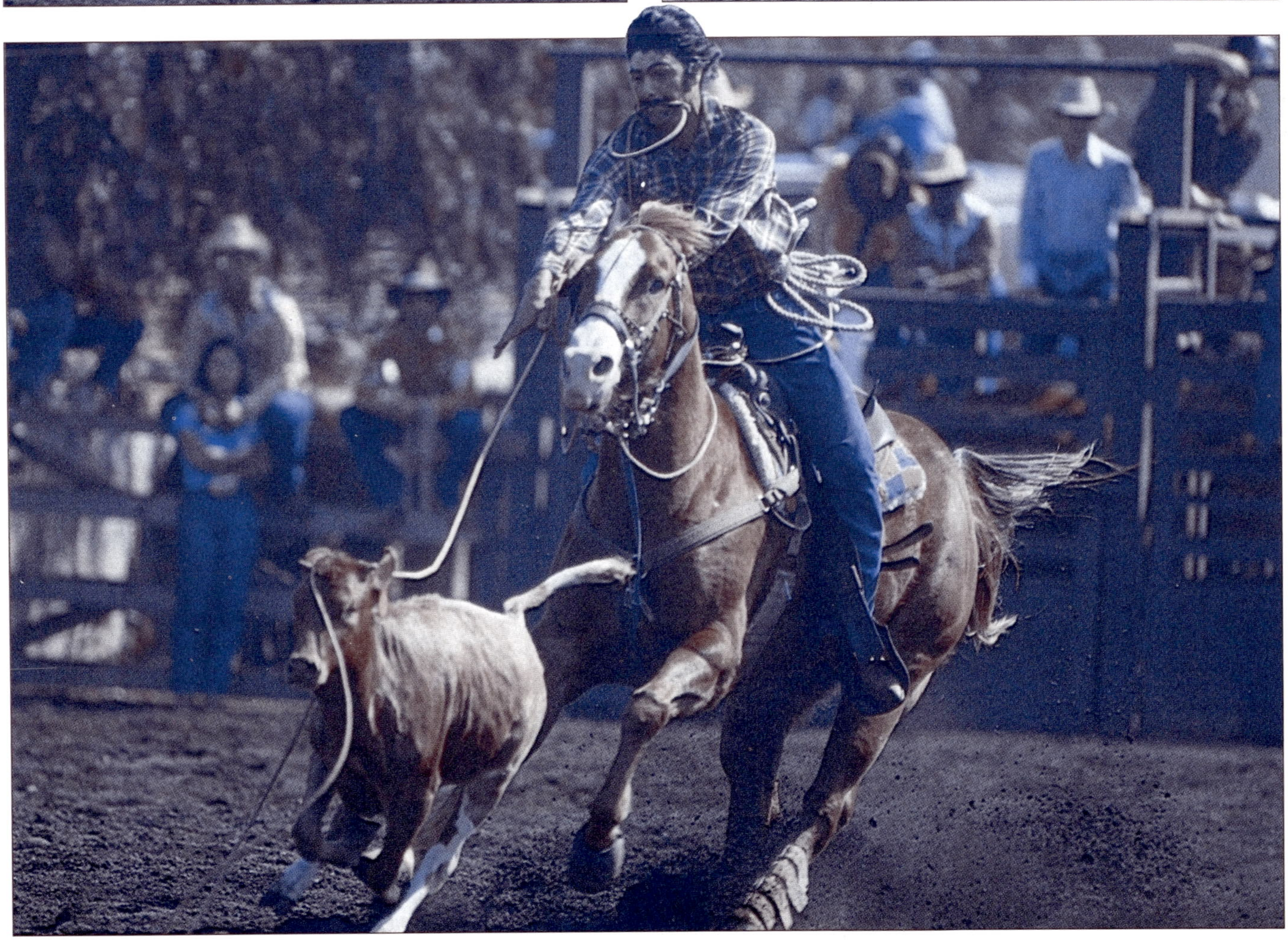